# COMPLETE PHOTOGRAPHIC
# BIRDS
## of Southern Africa

**Ian Sinclair**

**Peter Ryan**

Dedicated to the memory of the late William McDowell, a giant
in Irish Ornithology. And to Daryn and Kiera.

IAN SINCLAIR

To my parents for tolerating my youthful eccentricities and to
Molly and Coleen, for sharing me with my camera.

PETER RYAN

Published by Struik Nature
(an imprint of Random House Struik
(Pty) Ltd)
Reg. No. 1966/003153/07
80 McKenzie Street, Cape Town, 8001
PO Box 1144, Cape Town, 8000
South Africa

www.randomstruik.co.za

Log on to our photographic website
www.imagesofafrica.co.za
for an African experience.

First published in 2009

10 9 8 7 6 5 4 3 2 1

**Publisher:** Pippa Parker
**Managing editor:** Helen de Villiers
**Editor:** Emily Bowles
**Designer:** Louise Topping
**Proofreader:** Tessa Kennedy
**Picture researcher:** Colette Stott
**Distribution maps:** Tom Parker
**Illustrator:** Sally MacLarty

Reproduction by Hirt & Carter Cape (Pty) Ltd

Printed and bound by Paarl Print,
Oosterland Street, Paarl, South Africa

ISBN 978 1 77007 388 3

Also available in Afrikaans as
*Volledige Fotografiese Veldgids: Voëls
van Suider-Afrika*
ISBN 978 1 77007 589 4

Front cover: Livingstone's Turaco (PCHAD) Back cover: Black Crake (MDA) (top left), Woodland
Kingfisher (MDA) (top centre), Three-banded Plover (MDA) (top right) Spine: Narina Trogon (AF)
Title page: African Penguin (PR) Contents page: Cape Sugarbird (PR) Page 4: Green-backed Heron (CVR)

# CONTENTS

# SPONSOR'S FOREWORD

The *Complete Photographic Field Guide: Birds of Southern Africa* is in many respects a ground-breaking publication. It is the most comprehensive collection of southern African bird photographs yet published. Aided by advances in digital technology, the authors and publisher were spoiled for choice, with literally hundreds of thousands of images from which to choose.

At SASOL, a major fuel and petrochemicals producer on the African continent, we recognise the value of our bird life and vigorously pursue ways to minimise our environmental footprint and conserve the region's natural heritage. We embrace environmental sustainability as a core business imperative. It is integral to our sustainable development philosophy that we actively seek to balance our financial, social and environmental performance.

We are pleased to support this publication aimed at engendering an appreciation for our natural heritage, and, in particular, our magnificent bird life.

The *Complete Photographic Field Guide: Birds of Southern Africa* is another demonstration of our commitment to conserving the diversity of our bird population and will enable enthusiasts and beginners alike to appreciate the abundance and beauty of birds in our country and throughout southern Africa. Enjoy it.

**Pat Davies**
Chief Executive
SASOL Limited

sasol
*reaching new frontiers*

# AUTHORS' ACKNOWLEDGEMENTS

Our sincere thanks go to the many photographers who contributed images to this project. Even if none of your pictures was selected, we greatly appreciate the opportunity to sift through the large numbers of images submitted – this book would not exist without your generosity. It is invidious to single out specific contributors, but the following deserve special mention: Mark Anderson, Hugh Chittenden, Albert Froneman, John Graham, Trevor Hardaker, Warwick Tarboton and Chris van Rooyen. John and Trevor also provided much useful advice and information, and John kindly checked through a draft of the book. We also thank our birding colleagues over the years, especially those who also joined the digital revolution in bird photography. The Monday picture club pushed us to take better images – thanks to John Graham, Trevor Hardaker and Barrie Rose. The Directorate, Antarctica and Islands of the Department of Environment Affairs and Tourism provided the opportunity to visit the Antarctic and sub-Antarctic through research projects at the Percy FitzPatrick Institute, whereas Alan Foggett of Starlight Cruises gave the chance to cruise in more tropical waters. Off the Cape, we've shared many a memorable day at sea with Harry Dilley on the *Zest*.

As ever, the team at Random House Struik, led by Pippa Parker and Helen de Villiers, managed this project with professionalism, patience and good humour. We are especially grateful to Louise Topping, who designed and redesigned plates until she was doubtless heartily sick of them – we hope this experience hasn't put her off birds for life! Colette Stott managed the vast number of images that flooded across her desk without ever losing her cheerful smile, and Tom Parker worked diligently to draft the status bars and the revised distribution maps. Emily Bowles edited the text efficiently, and Tessa Kennedy proofread it with attention to the finest detail. The Afrikaans edition was kindly translated by Jan Moodie.

Finally, we thank SASOL for their generous sponsorship of this project. Their ongoing support of field guides has resulted in southern Africa having arguably the best resources for amateur naturalists, enhancing environmental awareness, and ultimately promoting a sustainable future for the region.

# INTRODUCTION

Southern Africa has a rich avian heritage that has attracted considerable interest in birds and their identification. This is reflected in the wide range of bird books available. Modern field guides to birds of the region first appeared in the early 1980s. Their compact design, with range maps and concise accounts appearing opposite plates of the species, revolutionised field identification of birds. Among the earliest of these was Ian Sinclair's *Field Guide: Birds of Southern Africa*, first published in 1984. It has been popular ever since, and remains the only comprehensive photographic field guide to the region's birds.

Historically, birders have preferred illustrated guides to photographic ones, on the grounds that an artist can illustrate more of the distinguishing features of a species. However, photography has come a long way in the last 25 years. The advent of auto-focus, image-stabilised lenses and digital photography has allowed the average birder to take high-quality photographs of birds going about their daily business (not just delivering food to their nests). And where one photo may not be able to convey all the key features of a species, two or three pictures can often do the trick. With this in mind we set out to gather together the best available photographs of southern African birds, and to use them to update Sinclair's classic field guide.

We believe the results speak for themselves, both in terms of quality and variety. When the original guide was published, there were no photographs available for 55 species. Today we have images – generally of a high standard – for all but four species: Mottled and Scarce swifts, Green Tinkerbird and Red-capped Crombec. We hope that the book will spur on amateur and professional photographers alike to target those species where there are no images, or where the images are rather weak, so that future editions can be even more valuable aids to bird identification in the region.

## Scope of the book

The book covers all birds recorded in the southern African subregion, defined as the region south of the Zambezi and Kunene rivers. This includes Namibia, Botswana, Zimbabwe, southern Mozambique, Swaziland, Lesotho and South Africa. Traditionally the region extends 200 nautical miles to sea, but we have included the African sector of the Southern Ocean, Antarctica, and the islands in the region (Tristan da Cunha archipelago, and Gough, Bouvet, the Prince Edward and the Crozet islands), places where many of southern Africa's non-breeding seabirds breed. Anyone fortunate enough to travel to these isolated wilderness areas, which include South Africa's only overseas possession, the Prince Edward Islands, as well as the South African weather station on Gough Island, will find this information invaluable. Also, with the increased attention being paid to seabirds, especially off the Cape, the list of species not recorded in southern Africa that are present in the adjacent Southern Ocean has gradually dwindled. Only eight species of seabird that breed in the African sector of the Southern Ocean are as yet unrecorded from southern Africa's territorial waters: Emperor, Adélie and Chinstrap penguins, Snow Petrel, Common and South Georgian diving-petrels, Crozet Shag and Kerguelen Tern.

We have included the few landbirds breeding on the islands (five at Tristan, two at Gough and one at the Prince Edward and Crozet islands), but have excluded vagrants that have not been recorded from southern Africa. Although the list of vagrants recorded on Tristan makes tantalising reading for twitchers working southern Africa's west coast, their inclusion would add too many marginal species to the book. For interest, the species confirmed to occur are listed here. Most come from South America on the prevailing westerlies. The following are vagrants to Tristan and Gough islands that have not yet been recorded in southern Africa: Speckled Teal *Anas flavirostris*, Cocoi Heron *Ardea cocoi*, Solitary Sandpiper *Tringa solitaria*, Spotted Sandpiper *Actitis macularia*, Sharp-tailed Sandpiper *Calidris acuminata*, Upland Sandpiper *Bartramia longcauda*, Rufous-chested Dotterel *Charadrius modestus*, Red-gartered Coot *Fulica armillata*, Paint-billed Crake *Neocrex erythrops*, Common Nighthawk

*Chordeiles minor* and Eastern Kingbird *Tyrannus tyrannus*. The list of putative vagrants is even longer, with 'a small blue bird' being, perhaps, the most intriguing record.

The space allocated to each species, and the number of photographs of each, is not constant, but is determined by the range of variation within a species. Those with only a single plumage are afforded less space than those that vary with age, sex and/or season. To a lesser extent we have also been constrained by the paucity of certain types of image. This applies mainly to photographs of birds in flight, although juvenile plumages are also less well represented than we would like in many cases. Again, here is scope for photographers to contribute to future editions.

## Southern Africa

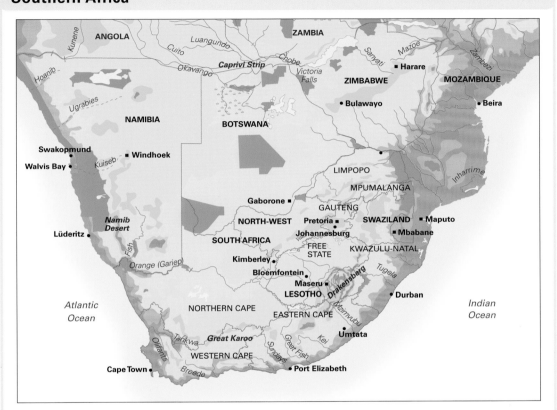

## Southern Ocean Islands

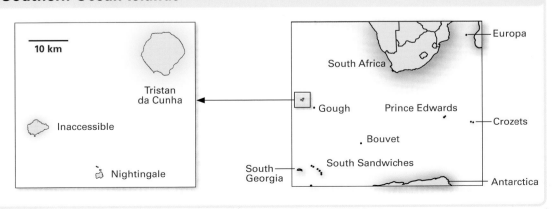

# Southern Africa and its avifauna

To date, more than 950 bird species have been recorded from southern Africa. This guide recognises 958 species, but a few species are 'lumped' in other works. Compared to the 7th edition of *Roberts' Birds of Southern Africa*, we have split Yellow-billed from Black Kite, Barrow's Korhaan from White-bellied Bustard, Cinnamon-bellied from Rufous-bellied Tit, and Damara from Black-headed Canary. Together with species recorded in the adjacent Southern Ocean, the guide covers 975 species. More than 100 species are confined to southern Africa – a remarkably high proportion for a relatively small region of a large continent. The main reason for this high level of endemism is the south-west arid zone, which is largely restricted to southern

Africa, and is isolated from other arid zones in north and north-east Africa. However, numerous endemics are also associated with the fynbos of the Western and Eastern Cape, the grasslands of the eastern plateau of South Africa and Lesotho, and the eastern highlands of Zimbabwe. Whereas endemics tend to be most abundant in the south and west, total diversity increases in the north and east of the region.

Most birds tend to occur in specific habitats, and in terrestrial systems these often broadly follow the distributions of the main plant communities or biomes. Southern Africa supports a diversity of biomes, illustrated in the map below. These biomes tend to follow rainfall patterns, with the hyper-arid Namib Desert

## Biomes of southern Africa

| | | |
|---|---|---|
| Namib Desert | Afromontane forest | Arid savanna |
| Fynbos | Karoo | Grassland |
| Lowland forest | Moist savanna | |

A Sociable Weaver nest in the arid Nama Karoo. The west supports relatively few species, but many of them are found nowhere else.

A seasonal wetland in the savanna biome. The east is home to a greater number of species, but most of them have ranges that extend further north in Africa.

along the Namibian coast gradually merging into Karoo habitats, and thence into arid savannas in the north, and grassland further south. Moving farther east, the arid savannas merge into more mesic savannas and ultimately into woodland. Forests are confined to areas of relatively high rainfall, with Afromontane forest occurring sporadically along the eastern mountain chain from the Cape Peninsula to the eastern highlands of Zimbabwe and Mount Gorongoza, Mozambique, increasing with elevation further north. Thicket and coastal forest occur along the coastal lowlands from the Eastern Cape into Mozambique, and locally up the Zambezi River to northern Botswana and into Namibia's Caprivi Strip. In the extreme southwest, the floristically diverse fynbos is largely confined to the winter-rainfall region of the Western and Eastern Cape.

## The order of birds in the book

Despite overwhelming evidence that the 'traditional' Wetmore sequence (with penguins and other seabirds following ostriches, etc.) does not reflect the actual relationships among birds, there has been resistance to accepting the 'Sibley sequence' followed in *Roberts' Birds of Southern Africa*, 7th ed, which is informed by genetic studies. Also, although great strides have been made in untangling the evolutionary relations among birds, there is still some way to go before we have a reasonably stable structure. This is especially true regarding relationships among

bird orders. Even since *Roberts' Birds of Southern Africa*, 7th ed. was published in 2005, there have been new discoveries regarding relationships among some African passerine groups. For example, hyliotas were part of an early radiation of African passerines, not allied to the warblers; and wattle-eyes and batises should be placed in their own family, separate from the bush-shrikes.

These discoveries led to a dilemma – in what sequence should the birds be presented in this book? Given different views on the subject, we have remained true to the sequence used by the SASOL field guides, which largely follow the traditional sequence familiar to most birders in the region. Within this broad framework, some species have been shuffled to appear with species that look similar, even if they are not closely related, simply to aid comparison and, ultimately, identification (e.g. penduline tits are placed with eremomelas among the warblers, and Boulder Chat with the babblers). No sequence will please everyone, so we have been as pragmatic as possible. In some cases, species have been moved from their traditional homes simply for convenience of plate layout (e.g. African Pitta and Spotted Creeper). Extralimital Southern Ocean seabirds (including the Lesser Sheathbill) are included in the main sequence with related species found in southern Africa, whereas the endemic landbirds from Tristan and Gough islands are grouped together at the end of the book.

# How to use the book

The group index on the inside cover should aid rapid navigation to the right section of the book. Once you have reached the right section, correct identification depends on using the photographs in conjunction with the information in the texts, maps and seasonality bars. The book is laid out in traditional field-guide format, with concise species accounts opposite the images of the birds.

## FLYCATCHERS

Insectivorous passerines that catch at least some prey by hawking. Bills slender, short and broad, often with rictal bristles to aid catching aerial prey. Sexes alike in most species. Juvs spotted buff above and mottled below in muscicapids; like dull females in crested flycatchers. Monogamous and territorial.

**1 African Dusky Flycatcher** *Muscicapa adusta*

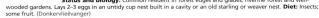

**12 cm; 10–14 g** A small, compact flycatcher. Appears short-winged and dumpy compared with Spotted Flycatcher; crown plain; typically in more forested habitats. Smaller and shorter-tailed than Ashy Flycatcher; upperparts grey-brown (not blue-grey). Breast and flanks have ill-defined streaking. Juv. has buff-spotted upperparts; breast mottled dark brown. **Voice:** High-pitched, descending 'tseeeuu'; also a sharper 'ti-ti-ti-trrrrr' or 'tsirit'; alarm call is a series of sharp clicks. **Status and biology:** Common resident in forest edges and glades, riverine forest and well-wooded gardens. Lays 2–3 eggs in an untidy cup nest built in a cavity or an old starling or weaver nest. **Diet:** Insects; some fruit. (Donkervlieëvanger)

**2 Spotted Flycatcher** *Muscicapa striata*

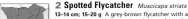

**13–14 cm; 15–20 g** A grey-brown flycatcher with a dark-streaked crown and indistinctly streaked breast. Larger and longer-winged than African Dusky Flycatcher, with a more boldly-streaked

Group introductions (as in 'Flycatchers' above) provide information on the identification of the group in general, as well as biology that is common to members in that group.

Individual species accounts highlight key identification features, describe the species' calls (**Voice**), and record various aspects of the bird's status, preferred habitat and biology. Rarity and/or vagrancy are noted at the start of the identification text in cases where a species is unlikely to be encountered. This refers to the region as a whole, so that common Southern Ocean species are not identified as vagrants even if they are vagrants to southern Africa. Thereafter, the accounts briefly describe the main plumages, and highlight the most important characters for separating the species in question from similar species. Adult plumages are described first (male then female), followed by juvenile and immature plumages, if these are distinct. For species with seasonal plumage differences, breeding plumage is usually described first, except where breeding plumage is very short-lived (e.g. some herons and cormorants) or where non-breeding plumage is the norm in southern Africa (e.g. Palearctic migrant waders and terns).

**Status and biology** reports the abundance of each species in the region (a rough estimate, not linked to conspicuousness of the birds), its movements and population size (where known), global conservation status, habitat preferences and basic breeding biology (clutch size and a brief description of the nest and nest site) and diet. Breeding biology is given only for species that breed in the region. Category labels for abundance are, in descending order: 'abundant', 'common', 'fairly common', 'uncommon', 'scarce', 'rare' and 'vagrant'. 'Locally common' is used for species with restricted distributions (either in terms of specific habitat requirements or absolute range size). **Diet** is given, followed by the Afrikaans common name.

# Abbreviations used in this book

| | | | | |
|---|---|---|---|---|
| ♂ | male | br. | breeding |
| ♀ | female | non-br. | non-breeding |
| ad. | adult | N | north/northern |
| sub-ad. | sub-adult | E | east/eastern |
| imm. | immature | S | south/southern |
| juv. | juvenile | W | west/western |
| trans. | transitional | | |

Data for both the maps and the status bars were taken largely from the *Atlas of Southern African Birds* (BirdLife South Africa, 1997), and the 7th edition of *Roberts' Birds of Southern Africa* (John Voelcker Bird Book Fund, 2005). Anyone wanting more information on the region's birds should consult these works.

## Seasonality bars

Seasonality of occurrence and breeding are shown in the calendar bars; they indicate the months when species are present in the region, with pale shading showing presence in reduced numbers (e.g. in some migratory shorebirds many juveniles overwinter). The bars also show the timing of breeding throughout the region, with 'B' indicating months of peak laying and 'b' other months when laying has been recorded. Unfortunately, this cannot reflect regional differences in laying dates. In most species, breeding is aligned to rainfall, and so occurs earliest in the southwest, winter rainfall area, and latest in the northwest, where summer rainfall tends to fall later than it does in the eastern half of the region.

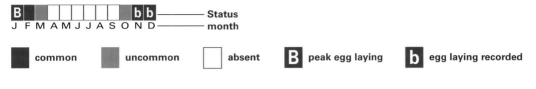

## Distribution maps

Distribution is shown on the accompanying range maps. The maps summarise where each species occurs, based loosely on the *Atlas* (Bird Life South Africa, 1997) maps. Where the *Atlas* records indicate marked differences in the frequency of occurrence of species across the range, in this book two tones are used, with the darker tone indicating where a species is more commonly encountered. Different colours are used to distinguish resident birds from visitors: green for residents, red for summer visitors and blue for winter visitors. Species that generally migrate are treated as seasonal visitors even if some individuals remain year-round.

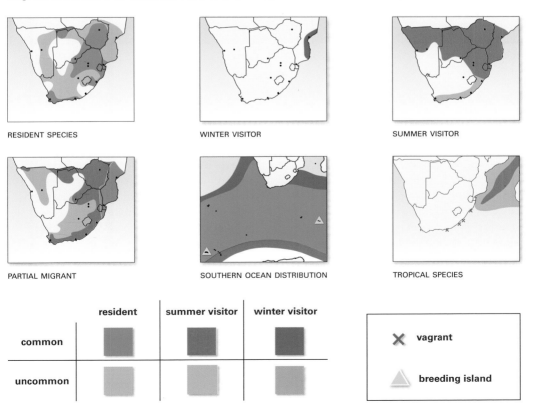

IST/PA

Digital cameras have revolutionised bird photography.

## Photographing birds

Just a few decades ago, it was common knowledge that you couldn't go birding and photograph birds at the same time. This is not necessarily the case any longer; bird photography has moved from a specialised activity into the birding mainstream thanks to the advent of digital photography. Many birders now derive enormous pleasure from photographing the birds they see while out birding. The freedom to take large numbers of images at very little cost (other than the time spent going through them afterwards) has all sorts of benefits, from aiding the identification of difficult species in the field (e.g. prions and diving-petrels at sea) to documenting fine plumage details and moult patterns and reading ring numbers.

It is beyond the scope of this book to provide detailed advice on photographing birds. However, two rules of thumb apply: invest in the best equipment you can afford,

and don't be afraid to take lots of pictures. Serendipity plays a large role in capturing good images of birds, especially action shots. Of course, patience and a good knowledge of your subject helps too, but some of the most striking images are taken simply by our being in the right place at the right time – and remembering to press the shutter release!

One word of warning: please put the bird's well-being ahead of your desire to get the perfect shot. Even with modern telephoto lenses, good images rely to a large extent on getting closer to a bird than is usually the case for normal birding. Make sure that your actions don't impact adversely on the bird or its habitat. Be especially cautious if photographing near a nest. Many sought-after species are unfortunately rare and threatened, and it is unconscionable for your actions to put birds under even more pressure.

# GLOSSARY

**Accidental** A vagrant or stray species not normally found within the region.

**Altricial** A chick's initially being dependent on its parents for food and heat (i.e. hatches naked and with eyes closed).

**Aposematic** Bright, striking coloration, typically associated with poisonous or distasteful organisms.

**Arboreal** Tree-dwelling.

**Breeding endemic** A species that breeds only in a particular region, but undertakes movements or migrations during the non-breeding seasons such that a measureable proportion of the population leaves the region.

**Colonial** Associating in close proximity while roosting, feeding or nesting.

**Commensal** Living with or near another species, without being interdependent.

**Crepuscular** Active at dawn and dusk.

**Cryptic** Pertaining to camouflage coloration.

**Culminicorn** The plate along the top of the upper mandible of a petrel or albatross.

**Diurnal** Active during daylight hours.

**Eclipse plumage** Dull plumage attained by male ducks and sunbirds during a transitional moult, after the breeding season and before they acquire brighter plumage.

**Endemic** A species whose breeding and non-breeding ranges are confined to a particular region.

**Feral** A species that has escaped from captivity and now lives and breeds in the wild.

**Flight feathers** The longest feathers on the wings and tail.

**Flush** Put to flight.

**Form** A colour variant within a species; the colour variation may or may not be linked to sub-specific status.

**Frons** Forehead.

**Fulvous** Reddish-yellow or tawny.

**Gorget** A band of distinctive colour on the throat.

**Immature** A bird that has moulted from juvenile plumage, but has not attained adult plumage; can also include juvenile plumage.

**Irruption** A rapid expansion of a species' normal range.

**Jizz** A general impression of size, shape and behaviour.

**Juvenile** A young bird in its first fully feathered plumage.

**Leucistic** Describes a white (or whitish) form of a particular species, with no melanin in some or all of its feathers.

**Melanistic** Describes a dark form of a particular species, the colour resulting from high levels of a pigment, melanin. In southern Africa, most frequently encountered among raptors, especially hawks.

**Migrant** A species that undertakes (usually) long-distance flights between its breeding and non-breeding areas.

**Mirrors** The white spots on the primaries of gulls.

**Montane** Pertaining to mountains.

**Nearctic** Temperate and arctic N America and Greeland.

**Near-endemic** A species whose range is largely restricted to a region, but extends slightly outside the region's borders. (In southern Africa, this category includes mostly species whose ranges extend into the arid regions of south-western Angola.)

**Nocturnal** Active at night.

**Non-passerine** All birds that are not part of the order Passeriformes.

**Nuchal** Describes the back or nape of the neck.

**Overwintering** A bird that remains in the subregion instead of migrating to its breeding grounds.

**Palearctic** North Africa, Greenland, Europe, Asia north of the Himalayas and southern China.

**Passerine** The largest order of birds (Passeriformes), comprising mostly small, perching songbirds, but also some larger species such as crows and ravens.

**Pelagic** Ocean dwelling.

**Precocial** A chick's being able to walk and feed itself within a few hours of hatching.

**Race** A geographical population of a species; a subspecies.

**Range** A bird's distribution.

**Raptor** A bird of prey.

**Rectrices** Tail feathers.

**Remiges** Flight feathers of the wing.

**Resident** A species not prone to migration, remaining in the same area all year.

**Rufous** Reddish-brown.

**Semi-altricial** A chick's being confined to its nest and depending on its parents for food, but hatching with a layer of down and, usually, open eyes.

**Speculum** A patch of distinctive colour on the wing.

**Sub-adult** A bird intermediate in age and plumage between immature and adult.

**Subterminal** A band or other mark close to (but not at) the tip of the feather.

**Supercilium** A plumage pattern above a bird's eye.

**Syndactyl** Having toes 3 and 4 fused at the base (e.g. kingfishers, hornbills).

**Territory** The area a bird establishes and then defends against others for breeding, feeding, or both.

**Vagrant** Rare and accidental to the region.

**Zygodactyl** Having toes 2 and 3 pointing forward, 1 and 4 backwards (e.g. woodpeckers, parrots and cuckoos).

# Illustrated glossary

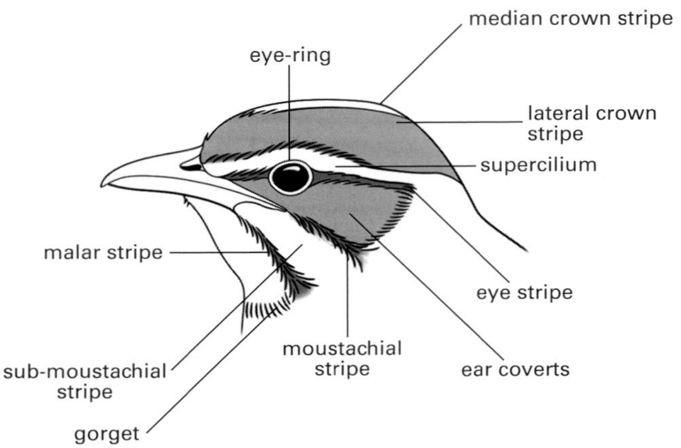

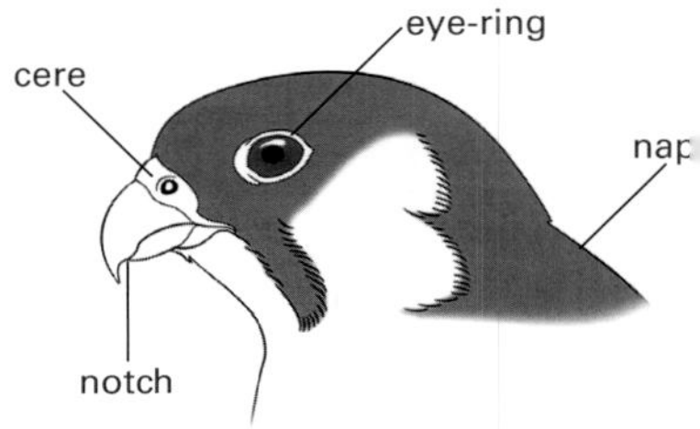

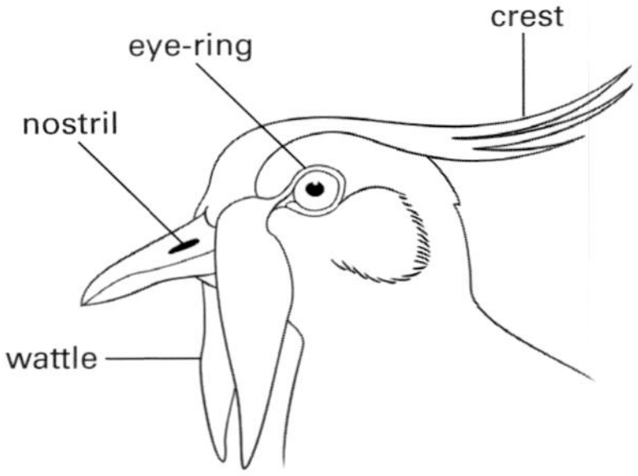

median crown stripe

eye-ring

lateral crown stripe

supercilium

malar stripe

eye stripe

sub-moustachial stripe

moustachial stripe

ear coverts

gorget

cere

eye-ring

nape

notch

crest

eye-ring

nostril

wattle

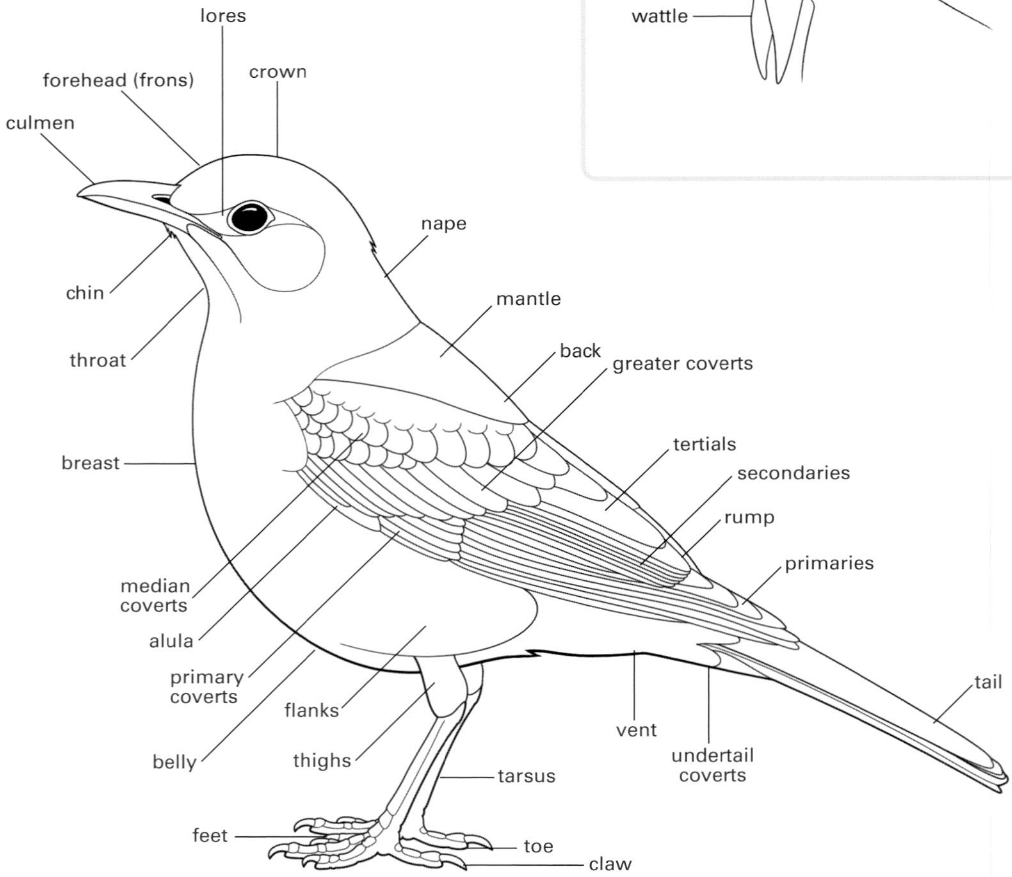

lores

forehead (frons)

crown

culmen

nape

mantle

chin

back

greater coverts

throat

tertials

secondaries

breast

rump

primaries

median coverts

alula

primary coverts

flanks

tail

belly

thighs

vent

undertail coverts

tarsus

feet

toe

claw

## Upperwing

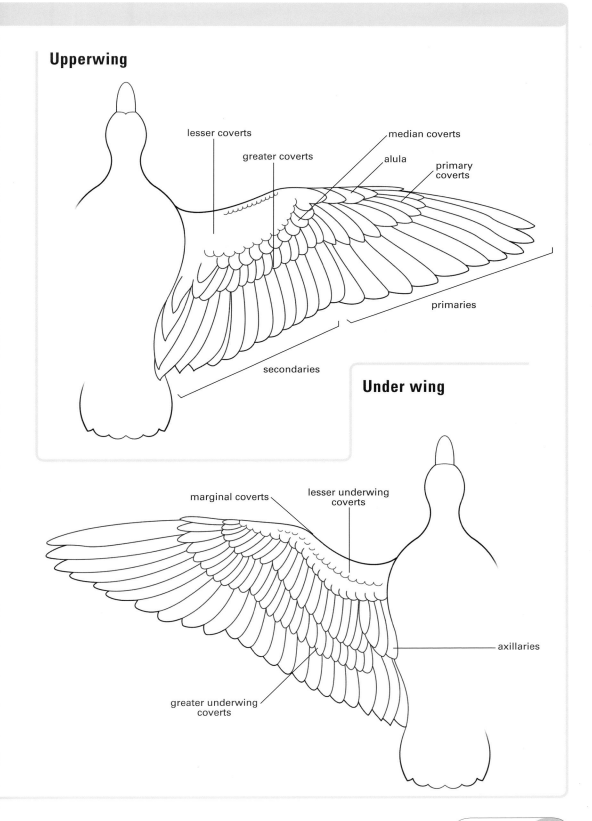

lesser coverts

greater coverts

median coverts

alula

primary coverts

primaries

secondaries

## Under wing

marginal coverts

lesser underwing coverts

axillaries

greater underwing coverts

# PENGUINS

Flightless seabirds, supremely adapted for pursuit diving. Wings reduced to small, rigid flippers ideal for 'flying' underwater. Sexes alike; juv. plumage distinct. Come ashore for 3–4 weeks to moult all feathers simultaneously, living off stored reserves. All are monogamous, and, apart from Emperor Penguin (p. 18), usually retain the same mate in successive years. In most species, both sexes incubate. Chicks semi-altricial, fed by both parents.

## 1 African Penguin *Spheniscus demersus*

b b B B B B B B b b b b b
J F M A M J J A S O N D

**60–70 cm; 2.2–3.5 kg** Ad. has distinctive black-and-white face and breast pattern. Sometimes has double breast band, as in Magellanic Penguin, but upper band is narrower; also lacks pink line extending to base of bill. Juv. lacks bold patterning, varying from greyish-blue to brown above; some juvs moult part or all of their heads to ad. plumage before their first complete moult (**1 juv. A**). **Voice:** Loud, donkey-like braying at colonies, especially at night. **Status and biology: VULNERABLE.** Br. endemic. Fairly common at sea, usually within 20 km of shore; vagrant >50 km offshore. 50 000 pairs breed at islands off the W and S coasts. Breeds all year; lays 2 eggs. **Diet:** Mainly pelagic fish (sardines, anchovies); juvs target slower-moving fish. (Brilpikkewyn)

## 2 Magellanic Penguin *Spheniscus magellanicus*

**70–76 cm; 3–5.2 kg** Rare vagrant. Slightly larger than African Penguin, with 2 breast bands; upper band broader. Juv. similar to juv. African Penguin, but often shows faint stripe on breast and flanks. **Voice:** Braying call, similar to African Penguin. **Status and biology:** Breeds in S America; 1 record in Cape Town harbour was probably ship-assisted, but has reached Tristan. **Diet:** Pelagic fish. (Magellaanse Pikkewyn)

## 3 Little Penguin *Eudyptula minor*

**40–45 cm; 0.8–1.6 kg** Rare vagrant. A diminutive penguin, resembling a tiny, recently fledged African Penguin, but has pale, creamy-grey (not dark grey) feet, plain face with no bare facial skin, and a much smaller, weaker bill. Eyes usually paler, and divide between blue-grey upperparts and white underparts better defined than African Penguin. **Voice:** Loud growls and groans at colonies at night. **Status and biology:** Breeds in sthn Australia and New Zealand; 1 record from Ichaboe Island, Namibia, April 2005. **Diet:** Small fish and squid. (Kleinpikkewyn)

## 4 Northern Rockhopper Penguin *Eudyptes moseleyi*

J F M A M J J A S O N D

**48–58 cm; 1.8–3.2 kg** A fairly small penguin with a short, stubby, red bill and yellow crest that starts just in front of eye (does not meet on forehead, as in Macaroni Penguin). Ad. head plumes much longer and more luxuriant than Southern Rockhopper; more extensive black on under-flipper. Juv. browner above, with a dull red bill; yellow crest reduced or absent, but has peaked crown feathers; only separable from Southern Rockhopper by flipper pattern. **Voice:** Deep, raucous 'kerr-aak, kerr-aak kerrak kerrak-kerrak-kerrak' at colonies. **Status and biology: ENDANGERED.** Regular vagrant to sthn Africa, mostly moulting juvs Nov–Mar. 250 000 pairs breed on Tristan, Gough, Amsterdam, St Paul (80% at Tristan and Gough, where numbers decreasing). Breeds in spring; lays 2 eggs, but only raises 1 chick, usually from larger, second-laid egg. **Diet:** Crustaceans, small fish and squid. (Noordelike Geelkuifpikkewyn)

## 5 Southern Rockhopper Penguin *Eudyptes chrysocome*

J F M A M J J A S O N D

**45–55 cm; 2–3 kg** Slightly smaller than Northern Rockhopper; ad. has shorter crest and less extensive dark tips to under-flipper. Local *E. c. filholi* has narrow pink line around base of bill; much thinner than Macaroni Penguin. Juv. only separable from Northern Rockhopper by flipper pattern. **Voice:** 'Kerr-ik kerrik kerik-kerik-kerik-kerik', distinctly higher-pitched than Northern Rockhopper. **Status and biology: VULNERABLE.** Rare vagrant to sthn Africa. 2 million pairs breed at sub-Antarctic islands; 110 000 pairs at Prince Edwards, but decreasing. Breeds in summer; lays 2 eggs, but only raises 1 chick, usually from larger, second-laid egg. **Diet:** Crustaceans, small fish and squid. (Suidelike Geelkuifpikkewyn)

## 6 Macaroni Penguin *Eudyptes chrysolophus*

J F M A M J J A S O N D

**68–75 cm; 3.1–5.5 kg** Larger than rockhopper penguins, with massive bill, broad pink gape and golden crest meeting across forehead (although not obvious at sea). Some birds on the Prince Edwards have white face with yellow wash around base of bill, resembling Royal Penguin, *E. schlegeli*, from Macquarie Island. Juv. duller, with little or no crest. **Voice:** Deep, exultant braying at colonies; occasional 'harr' at sea. **Status and biology: VULNERABLE.** Vagrant to S Africa, but abundant further S; 10 million pairs breed at sub-Antarctic islands; 375 000 pairs at the Prince Edwards. Mainly feed in Antarctic waters. Breeds in summer; lays 2 eggs. **Diet:** Crustaceans, small fish and squid. (Langkuifpikkewyn)

## 1 Emperor Penguin *Aptenodytes forsteri*

**100–130 cm; 20–30 kg** The largest penguin, mainly confined to Antarctic pack ice, although a few juvs stray N to the sub-Antarctic. Only likely to be confused with King Penguin, but much bigger, with proportionately shorter bill and flippers; neck patches less well defined and mainly golden (not orange); bill stripe smaller. Juv. paler; neck patches whitish. At sea, appears bulkier than King Penguin, with shorter neck; body rides higher in the water. **Voice:** Loud, trumpeted 'hra-ra-ra-ra' at colonies; usually silent at sea. **Status and biology:** Not recorded in sthn Africa; fairly common in areas with sea ice. 220 000 pairs breed in winter on fast ice around Antarctica. Males huddle together to incubate the single egg on their feet, losing 40% of mass during 3–4 month fast; feed chicks an oil-rich secretion until females return. **Diet:** Fish, squid and crustaceans; deepest diving bird, recorded to 564 m, with dives lasting up to 22 min. (Keiserpikkewyn)

## 2 King Penguin *Aptenodytes patagonicus*

**88–95 cm; 9–15 kg** A large, long-flippered penguin with distinctive orange neck patches and pinkish-orange plate on sides of bill. Smaller and more slender than Emperor Penguin, with neater, richer coloration. Juv. duller with creamy neck patch. **Voice:** Loud, trumpeted 'dhu-du-du-du' at colonies; occasional 'dhuu' at sea. **Status and biology:** Rare vagrant to S Africa; common further S; mainly forages in Antarctic waters. 2.2 million pairs breed at sub-Antarctic islands; 225 000 pairs at the Prince Edwards. Clumsy ashore; breeds year-round in dense colonies on flat ground with sheltered landing beaches. Lays 1 egg, incubated on feet by both sexes; few chicks hatched in late summer survive. **Diet:** Mainly myctophid fish, also some squid and crustaceans; dives recorded to 343 m and lasting for up to 9 min. (Koningpikkewyn)

## 3 Gentoo Penguin *Pygoscelis papua*

**75–80 cm; 4.2–7.2 kg** A fairly large, elegant, long-tailed penguin with distinctive white flecking above eye and narrow white eye-ring. Feet and bill orange. Flippers long with pale orange wash on underside. Juv. has paler throat and smaller white 'ear' patches. **Voice:** Loud cawing at colonies. **Status and biology: NEAR-THREATENED.** Rare vagrant to S Africa; fairly common in Antarctic and sub-Antarctic; usually remains close to islands. 300 000 pairs globally; 1 500 pairs at the Prince Edwards. Breeds in summer in Antarctic, winters further N. Lays 2 eggs. **Diet:** Mainly crustaceans. (Gentoo pikkewyn)

## 4 Adelie Penguin *Pygoscelis adeliae*

**70–72 cm; 3.8–6.6 kg** A medium-sized penguin with broad white eye-rings. Feathers on rear of crown can be raised into a short crest. Feathers extend over base of bill. Juv. has white throat, but face black (unlike Chinstrap Penguin). **Voice:** Trumpeting display call 'arr-ar-ar-ar-ar-raaa'; usually silent at sea. **Status and biology:** Not recorded in sthn Africa; typically remains near sea ice, but vagrants reach sub-Antarctic. 2.4 million pairs breed in summer at ice-free areas in Antarctica and surrounding islands, including Bouvet. Lays 2 eggs. **Diet:** Mainly crustaceans, especially Antarctic krill. (Adéliepikkewyn)

## 5 Chinstrap Penguin *Pygoscelis antarctica*

**68–74 cm; 3.5–5.2 kg** A medium-sized penguin with a distinctive, thin black line across its throat and face. Told from Adelie Penguin by white face with striking black eyes. Juv. has face speckled grey. **Voice:** Display call 'ah kawk kawk kawk'; usually silent at sea. **Status and biology:** Not recorded in sthn Africa; vagrants reach sub-Antarctic. Often rests on icebergs and sea ice. 7 million pairs breed in summer on Antarctic Peninsula and surrounding islands, including Bouvet. Lays 2 eggs. **Diet:** Mainly crustaceans, especially Antarctic krill. (Bandkeelpikkewyn)

# ALBATROSSES

Large, long-winged seabirds, adapted for dynamic soaring; able to cover vast distances with little energy expenditure. Sexes alike, but imm. and juv. plumages distinct. All are monogamous, usually retaining the same mate in successive years, and lay a single egg. Both sexes incubate and feed the semi-altricial chick. Three main groups occur in sthn Africa: great albatrosses, mollymawks and sooty albatrosses. Great albatrosses (*Diomedea*) have pink bills and mostly white underwings at all ages. Plumage whitens with age throughout life. Ads have white backs and could be confused with gannets (p. 52) and occasional Shy Albatrosses (p. 24) with white backs. All great albatrosses take so long to raise their single chick that they usually take a year off after a successful breeding attempt.

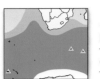

## 1 Wandering Albatross *Diomedea exulans*

J F M A M J J A S O N D

**110–135 cm; 7–11 kg** A huge, hump-backed albatross with a pink bill. Underwing white with black tip, trailing edge, and leading edge to carpal joint. Juv. chocolate-brown, with white face and underwings. As birds age, they become progressively whiter: body becomes mottled ('leopard' stage), then all-white, with fine vermiculations concentrated on back and breast, forming shadow breast band; then upperwing starts to whiten, initially from centre of wing over elbow (not from leading edge, as in Southern Royal Albatross, p. 22). Throughout these stages, birds have black tail tip (mostly white in royal albatrosses). Males whiten faster than females; after 20 years black only on flight feathers and a few covert tips. Old males differ from ad. Southern Royal Albatross by pinker bill with no dark cutting edge. Feathering doesn't extend far onto lower mandible (as is case in royal albatrosses), giving a steeper-looking forehead. Often has pink mark on side of neck (absent in royal albatrosses). Probably cannot be separated reliably from Tristan Albatross at sea. **Voice:** Grunts and whinnies in display, occasionally at sea. **Status and biology: VULNERABLE.** Regular in oceanic waters; occasionally visits trawlers, but seldom joins feeding mêlée. 12 000 pairs breed at sub-Antarctic islands; 3 000 at the Prince Edwards. Lays in summer; takes 11 months to raise a chick; rarely breeds in year following a successful attempt. **Diet:** Mainly squid and carrion. (Grootalbatros)

## 2 Tristan Albatross *Diomedea dabbenena*

**100–110 cm; 6–7 kg** Slightly smaller than Wandering Albatross, with a shorter bill; plumage takes longer to whiten, not attaining fully white plumage of old male Wandering Albatrosses. Birds at sea probably not identifiable with certainty. Typical ad. males have mostly dark upperwing with pale patch on elbow, but some have more extensive white upperwings. Most ad. females retain some brown feathers on crown, back, breast and flanks, but old females resemble ad. males. **Voice:** Similar to Wandering Albatross. **Status and biology: CRITICAL.** Mainly remains in S Atlantic; known to occur off the W coast of sthn Africa, but abundance uncertain. 2 200 pairs, almost all on Gough Island. Br. biology similar to Wandering Albatross, but suffers high chick mortality to mice. **Diet:** Mainly squid and carrion. (Tristangrootalbatros)

## 1 Northern Royal Albatross *Diomedea sanfordi*

J F M A M J J A S O N D

**107–122 cm; 6–8 kg** Same size and shape as Wandering Albatross (p. 20), but head looks sleek due to shallower forehead; bill yellow-pink with a black cutting edge visible at close range. Lacks pink mark on neck typical of Wandering Albatross complex. Best identified by crisp black upperwing contrasting with white body and tail. Underwing is like Wandering Albatross's, but has broader black carpal patch. Juv. has some black in outer tail and slight scalloping on back, but has much less black in tail than a Wandering Albatross with dark upperwings. Black carpal patch narrower than ad. **Voice:** Silent at sea. **Status and biology: ENDANGERED.** Rare visitor to S Africa, mainly along the shelf edge; attends fishing vessels more than Wandering Albatross. 5 200 pairs globally, all breeding at islands off New Zealand. **Diet:** Mainly squid. (Swartvlerkkoningalbatros)

## 2 Southern Royal Albatross *Diomedea epomophora*

J F M A M J J A S O N D

**115–122 cm; 7–11 kg** Similar to Northern Royal Albatross, but upperwing whitens with age from leading edge; carpal bar usually narrower. Juv. is similar to juv. Northern Royal Albatross; may retain mainly black upperwing and some black in outer tail and on scapulars for 10–12 years. White tail separates it from Wandering Albatross (p. 20), except for very old birds. Upperwing generally more finely marked than equivalent Wandering Albatross, and lacks pink mark on neck. **Voice:** Silent at sea. **Status and biology: VULNERABLE.** Rare visitor to S Africa; more common in oceanic waters than Northern Royal Albatross. 8 500 pairs globally, all breeding at islands off New Zealand. **Diet:** Mainly squid. (Witvlerkkoningalbatros)

# MOLLYMAWKS

Medium to small, dark-backed albatrosses; *Thalassarche* confined to the S Ocean. Generally more common than great albatrosses. Each species has diagnostic bill and underwing patterns, although bill colour changes with age and underwing whitens with age in some species. Identification of juvs and imms in the shy albatross complex is not well-understood; probably only ads and sub-ads can be separated reliably at sea.

## 1 Shy Albatross *Thalassarche cauta*

J F M A M J J A S O N D

**90–100 cm; 3–5 kg** Largest mollymawk, with extensive white on underwing; upperwing and mantle paler than other mollymawks; very rarely has white back. Underwing has narrow black border; black 'thumb-print' on leading edge near body diagnostic for the Shy-complex (including vagrant Salvin's and Chatham albatrosses). Ad. has pale grey cheeks and white crown; bill pale olive-grey with yellow tip. Imm. has grey-washed head, often with incomplete grey breast band; bill is grey with black tip. Fresh juv. **(1 A)** has smooth grey wash on head and neck, recalling Salvin's Albatross. Sometimes treated as 2 species: Shy Albatross (*T. c. cauta* that breeds off Tasmania) averages slightly smaller than White-capped Albatross (*T. c. steadi* from the New Zealand sub-Antarctic islands) and most ads have a paler, yellowy culminicorn (top of bill). 95% occurring off sthn Africa are *T. c. steadi*; almost all records in sthn Africa of *T. c. cauta* are juvs or imms. **Voice:** Loud, raucous 'waak' when squabbling over food. **Status and biology: NEAR-THREATENED.** Common non-br. visitor to fishing grounds along shelf edge; generally occurs closer to land than other albatrosses; uncommon in oceanic waters. 120 000 pairs (90% *T. c. steadi*) breed at islands off New Zealand and Tasmania; 1 pair recently found breeding on Prince Edward Island. **Diet:** Squid, fish, crustaceans and fishery wastes. (Bloubekalbatros)

## 2 Salvin's Albatross *Thalassarche salvini*

**90–100 cm; 3.2–5 kg** Rare vagrant. Forms part of the Shy Albatross complex; underwing similar. Ad. has grey wash to neck and face, contrasting with pale crown; bill grey-sided with paler, yellowish band along upper and lower mandible, and dark spot on lower mandible tip. Imm. is virtually identical to Shy Albatross, but black primary tips are slightly more extensive and head averages darker grey. **Voice:** Silent at sea. **Status and biology: VULNERABLE.** Occasionally recorded off W Cape. 40 000 pairs breed off New Zealand; 4 pairs on Crozets. **Diet:** Squid and fishery wastes. (Salvinalbatros)

## 3 Chatham Albatross *Thalassarche eremita*

**90–100 cm; 3–4.8 kg** Rare vagrant. Forms part of the Shy Albatross complex; underwing similar. Ad. has unmistakable yellow bill with dark tip to lower mandible, and dark, uniform grey head. Juv. similar to juv. Salvin's Albatross, but averages even darker on head and neck and has a pinkish bill with a dark tip. **Voice:** Silent at sea. **Status and biology: CRITICAL.** Only 4 records, all off W Cape in winter. 4 000 pairs breed on Pyramid Rock, Chatham Islands, New Zealand. **Diet:** Squid and fishery wastes. (Chathamalbatros)

### 1 Black-browed Albatross *Thalassarche melanophrys*

J F M A M J J A S O N D

**80–95 cm; 3–4.6 kg** Medium-sized mollymawk. Ad. has orange bill with a reddish tip, and a small black eyebrow. Underwing darkest of ad. mollymawks, with a broad black leading edge and narrower trailing edge. Juv. underwing dark grey with paler centre, lightening with age. Juv. bill dark horn-grey with black tip, gradually becoming yellow with darker tip. Amount of grey on head and neck is variable, usually forming incomplete collar. **Voice:** Grunts and squawks when squabbling over food. **Status and biology: ENDANGERED.** Common year-round, but ads mostly Apr–Sep. Most abundant at shelf edge, but also in oceanic waters; usually close inshore only during storms. 700 000 pairs breed in summer at sub-Antarctic islands; most birds in sthn Africa come from S Georgia, where numbers decreasing. **Diet:** Squid, fish, crustaceans and fishery wastes. (Swartrugalbatros)

### 2 Grey-headed Albatross *Thalassarche chrysostoma*

J F M A M J J A S O N D

**75–88 cm; 3–4.2 kg** Similar to Black-browed Albatross, showing comparable progression of underwing with age. Ad. has grey head, paler grey neck and black bill with yellow stripe along upper and lower mandibles. Juv. has darker grey head, merging into mantle; cheeks almost white in some individuals. Juv. bill all-dark (not black-tipped); soon develops yellow tinge to tip of upper mandible. **Voice:** Rattling display call at colonies; squawks when squabbling over food. **Status and biology: VULNERABLE.** Rare visitor to sthn Africa, mostly juv. birds, Jun–Sep; joins other albatrosses feeding at trawlers. Ads largely remain S of Subtropical Convergence. 125 000 pairs breed at sub-Antarctic islands; 11 000 at the Prince Edwards. Breeds in summer; rarely breeds in year following a successful attempt. **Diet:** Mainly squid. (Gryskopalbatros)

### 3 Laysan Albatross *Phoebastria immutabilis*

**80 cm; 2–3.5 kg** Rare vagrant. Small, slender albatross, superficially similar to imm. Black-browed Albatross, but with dark-washed cheek, brown lower back extending onto rump, and distinctive underwing pattern with black streaks on underwing coverts; pinkish feet project beyond tail in flight. Juv. as ad.; bill slightly greyer. **Voice:** Silent at sea. **Status and biology:** Breeds in N Pacific; 2 records from SW Indian Ocean, possibly of same bird. **Diet:** Squid and fish. (Swartwangalbatros)

### 1 Atlantic Yellow-nosed Albatross *Thalassarche chlororhyncho*

J F M A M J J A S O N D

**72–80 cm; 1.8–2.8 kg** A small, slender albatross with a relatively long bill. Underwing has crisp black margin, with leading edge roughly twice as broad as trailing edge. Ad. has black bill with yellow stripe along upper mandible, becoming reddish towards tip. Differs from Indian Yellow-nosed Albatross by having grey wash on head and nape (slightly paler on forecrown); at close range, base of yellow stripe on upper mandible is broad and rounded (not pointed). Juv. bill all-black; head white; hard to separate from juv. Indian Yellow-nosed Albatross, but some show grey wash on mantle. In the hand, shape of plates at base of bill differs. **Voice:** High-pitched reeling call in flight and on ground at colonies; throaty 'waah' and 'weeeeh' notes when squabbling over food. **Status and biology: ENDANGERED.** Fairly common year-round in small numbers; often the most abundant albatross off Namibia. 30 000 pairs breed in summer in loose colonies on level ground at Tristan and Gough. **Diet:** Fish, squid and crustaceans. (Atlantiese Geelneusalbatros)

### 2 Indian Yellow-nosed Albatross *Thalassarche carteri*

J F M A M J J A S O N D

**75–80 cm; 2.1–2.9 kg** Slightly larger than Atlantic Yellow-nosed Albatross; head appears smaller. Ad. has only a faint grey wash on the cheek; at close range, base of yellow bill stripe is pointed (not rounded). Juv. similar to juv. Atlantic Yellow-nosed Albatross, but entire head and neck white. **Voice:** Similar to Atlantic Yellow-nosed Albatross. **Status and biology: ENDANGERED.** Fairly common year-round; ventures further N in winter. Most common albatross off KZN. 36 000 pairs breed in summer in dense, cliff-side colonies at sthn Indian Ocean islands; 7 500 pairs at Prince Edward Island but none on Marion Island. **Diet:** Fish, squid and crustaceans. (Indiese Geelneusalbatros)

### 3 Buller's Albatross *Thalassarche bulleri*

**76–81 cm; 2.2–3.3 kg** Rare vagrant. A fairly small mollymawk with neat underwing at all ages; pattern similar to that of yellow-nosed albatrosses, but margins fractionally narrower. Head and neck washed grey, with pale forecrown. Ad's bill has broad yellow stripe along upper mandible and narrow stripe on lower mandible. Ad. most likely confused with ad. Atlantic Yellow-nosed Albatross or Grey-headed Albatross (p. 26). Juv. has dark horn-coloured bill with black tip and smooth grey wash on head and neck; could be confused with juv. Shy Albatross (p. 24). **Voice:** Silent at sea. **Status and biology: VULNERABLE.** Only 4 records from S Africa; 30 000 pairs breed at islands off New Zealand. **Diet:** Fish and squid. (Witkroonalbatros)

# SOOTY ALBATROSSES

Small albatrosses with sooty brown plumage, white eye-rings and long, wedge-shaped tails. Wings exceptionally long and narrow; appear more slender than giant-petrels (p. 30) or juv. gannets (p. 52).

## 1 Sooty Albatross *Phoebetria fusca*

**84–90 cm; 2–3 kg** Ad. readily identified by its dark brown plumage, with pale shafts to primary and tail feathers. At close range, yellow stripe is visible on lower mandible (all-black in juvs). Juv. and imm. have conspicuous buff collar and mottling on back, but this does not extend to rump as in Light-mantled Sooty Albatross. **Voice:** Wailing 'peeoooo' call in flight and from cliffs at colonies; silent at sea. **Status and biology: ENDANGERED.** Rare visitor to oceanic waters off sthn Africa; fairly common further S. 15 000 pairs breed at sub-Antarctic islands; 7 000 at Tristan/Gough and 2 200 at the Prince Edwards. Breeds in summer; rarely breeds in year following a successful attempt. **Diet:** Mainly squid; also small birds. (Bruinalbatros)

## 2 Light-mantled Sooty Albatross *Phoebetria palpebrata*

**80–90 cm; 2.6–3.6 kg** Similar to Sooty Albatross, but with much paler neck collar, shading into paler, greyish back that contrasts with upperwings. At close range, white eye-ring is shorter and broader, and bill has a lilac stripe. On land, head appears peaked (rounded in Sooty Albatross). Juv. only slightly paler above than juv. Sooty Albatross. Imm. has mottled body, but pale plumage extends lower on back and appears colder grey-brown. **Voice:** Similar to Sooty Albatross. **Status and biology: NEAR-THREATENED.** Rare vagrant to sthn Africa; fairly common S of the Antarctic Convergence; regular to Subtropical Convergence. 22 000 pairs globally; 350 at the Prince Edwards. Br. biology and diet as for Sooty Albatross. (Swartkopalbatros)

# PETRELS

Small to large seabirds. Most are long-winged, adapted for dynamic soaring, but some have smaller wings for swimming underwater. Nostrils tube-shaped, joined on top of bill. Sexes alike in plumage; males slightly larger. All are monogamous, usually retaining the same mate in successive years, and lay a single white egg. Both sexes incubate and feed the semi-altricial chick. There are several major groups. Giant-petrels are the largest species: huge, lumbering petrels weighing more than small albatrosses, with massive, pale bills. They are the only petrels with age-related plumage differences; all flight feathers are moulted annually, often resulting in large gaps in the primaries.

## 3 Southern Giant-Petrel *Macronectes giganteus*

J F M A M J J A S O N D

**86–100 cm; 2.5–5.8 kg** Ad. typically has paler head and breast, contrasting with dark body, but definitive identification requires seeing greenish bill tip. Juv. is dark brown, becoming lighter with age; greenish bill tip not well defined. Rare white morph (**3 A**) has odd dark feathers; some leucistic birds are pure white. **Voice:** Whinnies and neighs in displays and conflicts. **Status and biology: NEAR-THREATENED.** Fairly common in coastal waters, scavenges at fishing boats and around seal colonies; follows ships in oceanic waters. 30 000 pairs breed at sub-Antarctic islands; 2 750 pairs at the Prince Edwards and 250 at Gough. Breeds in loose colonies in open sites; lays 6 weeks later than Northern Giant-Petrel, but occasional hybrids occur. **Diet:** Carrion, birds, fish, squid and crustaceans. Larger males compete at carcasses; females forage at sea. (Reusenellie)

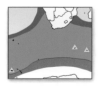

## 4 Northern Giant-Petrel *Macronectes halli*

J F M A M J J A S O N D

**81–98 cm; 2.8–5.8 kg** Very similar to Southern Giant-Petrel, but has a reddish tip to the bill, which appears dark-tipped at a distance. Ad. has more uniformly pale grey plumage. Lacks white morph. Juv. is dark brown, becoming paler with age; reddish bill tip is less marked than in ad. **Voice:** Like Southern Giant-Petrel. **Status and biology: NEAR-THREATENED.** Fairly common in coastal waters; scavenges at fishing boats; visits seal colonies more frequently than Southern Giant-Petrel. 12 000 pairs breed at sub-Antarctic islands; 650 at the Prince Edwards. Breeds singly against protection of rocks. **Diet:** Similar to Southern Giant-Petrel. (Grootnellie)

# SMALL FULMARINE PETRELS

A group of mostly high-latitude petrels related to giant-petrels. All have distinctive plumages with no age or sex differences, posing few identification pitfalls. Breed on cliffs or among rocks.

## 1 Pintado Petrel *Daption capense*

**35–40 cm; 350–550 g** A small, black-and-white petrel with distinctive chequering on the back, rump and upperwing. Tail tipped black. Very rare leucistic birds may appear all-white, or have only faint greyish markings. **Voice:** High-pitched 'cheecheecheechee' when feeding. **Status and biology:** Common non-br. visitor to coastal waters May–Nov. with stragglers to Jan. Inveterate ship follower. At least 200 000 pairs breed in summer on sub-Antarctic and Antarctic islands, including Bouvet and Crozets. **Diet:** Mainly crustaceans; gather in large flocks to scavenge small scraps at fishing boats. (Seeduifstormvoël)

## 2 Antarctic Petrel *Thalassoica antarctica*

**40–45 cm; 550–780 g** Larger than Pintado Petrel; brown above, with white subterminal band across wings and narrow brown tip to tail. **Voice:** Silent at sea. **Status and biology:** Common in Antarctic waters, often in large flocks; occasionally reaches the Prince Edwards in winter; rare vagrant to sthn Africa. Often roosts on icebergs and floes. 250 000 pairs breed at ice-free mountains in Antarctica and adjacent islands. Largest colony at Swarthamaren, Dronning Maud Land, S of Africa. **Diet:** Mainly crustaceans. (Antarktiese Stormvoël)

## 3 Southern Fulmar *Fulmarus glacialoides*

**45–51 cm; 670–1 000 g** A pale grey petrel with white underparts and white panels in the darker grey outer wing. At close range, dark-tipped, pink bill with blue nostrils is diagnostic. Flight is light and buoyant. **Voice:** High-pitched cackle when squabbling over food. **Status and biology:** Rare visitor to sthn Africa, mostly Jun–Oct. Scavenges at trawlers, often among flocks of Pintado Petrels. At least 200 000 pairs breed in Antarctica and adjacent islands, including Bouvet. **Diet:** Mainly crustaceans; also fish and squid, including fishery wastes. (Silwerstormvoël)

## 4 Snow Petrel *Pagodroma nivea*

**30–40 cm; 200–380 g** Unmistakable snow-white petrel with black bill, eyes and feet. Only possible confusion is with very rare leucistic Pintado Petrel. Largely confined to areas with sea ice. As a result, it flaps more than other petrels because dynamic soaring requires wave troughs, which are damped by sea ice. Two races differ in size, probably as a result of historical segregation during past ice ages, but now co-occur and interbreed. **Voice:** Loud screeches at colonies; usually silent at sea. **Status and biology:** Not recorded from sthn Africa. At least 65 000 pairs breed at ice-free mountains in Antarctica and adjacent islands. **Diet:** Mainly crustaceans. (Witstormvoël)

## 5 Blue Petrel *Halobaena caerulea*

**28–30 cm; 160–240 g** A small, blue-grey petrel with white underparts. Superficially similar to prions, but larger, with diagnostic white-tipped tail. Differs from prions in its white frons and black crown and nape, lacking a pale supercilium. At a distance, has darker and better defined grey breast patches, and body is more elongate, tapering from shoulders to relatively long tail. Flight action is more petrel-like: fast and direct, rising higher above water than prions. Juv. paler on head; finely scaled white above. **Voice:** Dove-like cooing at br. islands; silent at sea. **Status and biology:** Rare visitor to sthn Africa, occasionally irrupting in large numbers, but usually remains S of 45°S. 1 million pairs breed at sub-Antarctic islands in summer, but return to colonies sporadically year-round; 150 000 pairs breed at the Prince Edwards. **Diet:** Mainly crustaceans, but scavenges anything floating, including insects and bits of plastic. (Bloustormvoël)

# PRIONS

Small, blue-grey petrels with dark 'M' marks across the upperwing, and white underparts. Flight rather fluttery and erratic. Easily separated from other petrels, but species identification is very tricky; depends on subtle differences in head and tail patterns, best achieved with photographs. Many individuals in the Broad-billed-Salvin's-Antarctic complex cannot be identified at sea. All breed in burrows.

## 1 Broad-billed Prion *Pachyptila vittata*

**27–30 cm; 160–220 g**  The largest prion, with the broadest and darkest bill, but bill size overlaps narrowly with that of Salvin's Prion. Appears large-headed with a steep forehead; whitish supercilium and dark grey face less well developed than Salvin's Prion; more likely to occur in Atlantic Ocean. Grey breast patches well developed. Blackish 'moustache' from gape typically curves up to join dark ear coverts; also shows a more extensive, darker grey carpal patch, but these features are hard to observe in the field. **Voice:** Deep, cooing calls at colonies; silent at sea. **Status and biology:** Apparently a rare visitor to sthn Africa. Breeds in early summer at Tristan and Gough (6 million pairs) and around New Zealand (1.5 million pairs). **Diet:** Mainly copepods and other small crustaceans, filtered using baleen-like lamellae on sides of bill (hence common name of whale-bird). (Breëbekwalvisvoël)

## 2 Salvin's Prion *Pachyptila salvini*

**26–29 cm; 120–200 g**  Intermediate in size and coloration between Broad-billed and Antarctic prions, with narrow overlap in measurements. Bill bluer than Broad-billed Prion, and facial pattern more pronounced; moustache usually shorter. Appears larger-headed than Antarctic Prion, typically with a distinctly broader and deeper bill. Most likely to occur in Indian Ocean. **Voice:** Similar to Broad-billed Prion. **Status and biology:** Rare visitor to sthn Africa. 5 million pairs breed in summer at the Prince Edwards and Crozets. **Diet:** Mainly small crustaceans. (Marionwalvisvoël)

## 3 Antarctic Prion *Pachyptila desolata*

J F M A M J J A S O N D

**25–28 cm; 120–180 g**  By far the most abundant prion in sthn African waters. Bill is relatively narrow and distinctly bluish. Tends to have smaller breast smudges than larger Salvin's and Broad-billed prions; facial pattern better defined than most Broad-billed Prions. Easily confused with Slender-billed Prion (see that species). **Voice:** Similar to Broad-billed Prion. **Status and biology:** Common non-br. visitor, occurring in large flocks. Subject to occasional 'wrecks' when large numbers of dead and dying birds come ashore. 20 million pairs breed in summer at sub-Antarctic islands and Antarctica, most on S Georgia. **Diet:** Mainly small crustaceans. (Antarktiese Walvisvoël)

## 4 Slender-billed Prion *Pachyptila belcheri*

J F M A M J J A S O N D

**25–27 cm; 120–170 g**  Resembles Antarctic Prion, but with paler head, smaller, paler grey breast patches and a long, slender bill that is visible at close range. Head appears more rounded, recalling Fairy Prion, with a long, white supercilium that broadens behind eye, white lores, and narrow, blue-grey (not dark grey) cheeks. Black tail tip is reduced, with outer 2–3 tail feathers blue-grey (only outer tail feather grey in Antarctic Prion). **Voice:** Silent at sea. **Status and biology:** Rare visitor to shelf waters, but large numbers irrupt in some years from normal range in Antarctic waters. 3 million pairs breed in summer at sub-Antarctic islands, mainly Kerguelen and the Falklands. **Diet:** Crustaceans, fish and small squid; picks larger prey items rather than filtering prey. (Dunbekwalvisvoël)

## 5 Fairy Prion *Pachyptila turtur*

**24–26 cm; 110–170 g**  The smallest prion; relatively easy to identify by its broad black tail tip, usually rather plain face and short, dumpy bill. Some birds show a stronger supercilium, recalling Slender-billed Prion, but short bill and extensive black tail tip diagnostic. **Voice:** Soft, cooing calls at colonies; silent at sea. **Status and biology:** Vagrant to S Africa; most records of beached birds. Typically remains S of 40°S. 2 million pairs breed in summer at sub-Antarctic islands, Tasmania and off New Zealand, including 2 000 pairs at the Prince Edwards. Regularly visits br. cliffs during day. **Diet:** Mainly small crustaceans. (Swartstertwalvisvoël)

# GADFLY PETRELS

Medium-sized petrels characterised by erratic, towering and very rapid flight action. Bills dark; shorter and deeper than shearwaters and *Procellaria* petrels. Wings usually angled. No age or sex differences in plumage. All-dark species could be confused with smaller Jouanin's and Bulwer's petrels (p. 44). Seldom occur close to shore unless there are strong onshore winds. All breed in burrows.

## 1 Soft-plumaged Petrel *Pterodroma mollis*

J F M A M J J A S O N D

**32–37 cm; 220–350 g**  A small gadfly petrel with a variable dark breast band and white throat. White underparts contrast with dark underwings. Upperparts grey, with faint, darker 'M' across upperwings. Rare dark morph **(1 A)** lacks silvery highlights of Kerguelen Petrel (p. 38), has more slender neck, longer, more pointed wings, and is often mottled on belly. Flight rapid and erratic, with deep wing beats. **Voice:** Ghostly 'oooo' in flight at colonies, loud shrieks from ground; silent at sea. **Status and biology:** Uncommon in shelf waters; common offshore year-round. 2 million pairs breed in summer at sub-Antarctic islands, most on Tristan/Gough (paler nominate race); 15 000 on the Prince Edwards (darker *P. m. dubia*). **Diet:** Mainly squid. (Donsveerstormvoël)

## 2 White-headed Petrel *Pterodroma lessonii*

J F M A M J J A S O N D

**40–45 cm; 500–800 g**  A large, chunky gadfly petrel with a diagnostic whitish head and tail. Dark eyes accentuated by blackish feathering around eyes, contrasting with pale head. Larger and more bulky than Soft-plumaged Petrel; lacks dark cap and breast patches. **Voice:** Silent at sea. **Status and biology:** Rare visitor to sthn Africa from oceanic waters. 250 000 pairs breed in summer at sub-Antarctic islands. **Diet:** Mainly squid. (Witkopstormvoël)

## 3 Barau's Petrel *Pterodroma baraui*

**38–40 cm; 400 g**  The only gadfly petrel in the region with mostly white underwings. Most likely to be confused with Soft-plumaged Petrel, but is larger with a darker cap and smaller grey breast patches. From a distance could potentially be confused with Cory's Shearwater (p. 40), but flight action differs; bill short and black. **Voice:** Silent at sea. **Status and biology:** ENDANGERED. Vagrant to tropical E coast, with a record off the Cape. Some 4 000 pairs breed on Reunion. **Diet:** Squid and fish. (Baraustormvoël)

## 4 Atlantic Petrel *Pterodroma incerta*

J F M A M J J A S O N D

**42–45 cm; 450–700 g**  A large, brown gadfly petrel with a conspicuous white lower breast and belly. Much larger than Soft-plumaged Petrel, with chocolate brown (not grey) plumage and no dark 'M' on upperwing. In worn plumage, neck and mantle can appear mottled brown. Given a poor view, could be confused with a pale morph jaeger. **Voice:** Loud 'kee-kee-kee' at colonies; silent at sea. **Status and biology:** ENDANGERED. Vagrant to sthn Africa. 1.8 million pairs breed in winter on Gough and Tristan (rare). Main threat is chick predation by introduced rodents. **Diet:** Mainly squid. (Atlantiese Stormvoël)

## 5 Great-winged Petrel *Pterodroma macroptera*

J F M A M J J A S O N D

**38–42 cm; 460–700 g**  A dark brown petrel with a short, stubby, black bill. Wings long and slender, held angled at wrist. Wing and bill shape, dark (not silvery) underwing and short neck differentiate it from Sooty Shearwater (p. 40). Smaller than White-chinned Petrel (p. 38), with black (not whitish) bill and gadfly jizz. Soars high above water in typical gadfly action, but flight tends to be more relaxed than other gadfly petrels. **Voice:** Whistles in flight at colonies; ground call is a high-pitched 'ki-ki-ki-ki'; silent at sea. **Status and biology:** Common non-br. visitor. In calm weather roosts on the water in small flocks. 250 000 pairs of the nominate race breed in winter at sub-Antarctic islands; up to 100 000 on Gough; 20 000 at the Prince Edwards. **Diet:** Mainly squid, but scavenges at fishing boats if few other birds present. (Langvlerkstormvoël)

## 1 Kerguelen Petrel *Lugensa brevirostris*

**33–36 cm; 220–400 g** A small, compact petrel recalling a *Peterodroma* petrel, but not closely related. It appears large-headed with a thick 'bull-neck'; eyes large, often appearing hooded. Smaller and greyer than Great-winged Petrel (p. 36), with shorter, more rounded wings that show silvery highlights, especially on leading edge, and often extending onto breast. Flight rapid and erratic with rapid, stiff, shallow wing beats. Towers up to 50 m above sea, often hanging motionless or fluttering kestrel-like. **Voice:** Wheezy, high-pitched calls at colonies; silent at sea. **Status and biology:** Vagrant to sthn Africa; irrupts in large numbers in some years, but usually remains S of 45°S. 200 000 pairs breed in summer on sub-Antarctic islands; 100 000 at Gough and 20 000 at the Prince Edwards. **Diet:** Squid, crustaceans and carrion. (Kerguelense Stormvoël)

# *PROCELLARIA* PETRELS

**Large petrels, superficially recalling large shearwaters, but flight is more languid, with less stiff wings held slightly bent at wrist. No age or sex differences in plumage. All breed in burrows.**

## 2 White-chinned Petrel *Procellaria aequinoctialis*

J F M A M J J A S O N D

**51–58 cm; 1–1.6 kg** Probably the most frequently encountered petrel in sthn Africa. A large, blackish-brown petrel with a whitish bill. At close range, black 'saddle' to bill is visible. White throat is variable in extent: conspicuous in some individuals, but reduced or ë absent in others. Quite often has odd white patches on head, belly or wings (2 A). **Voice:** High-pitched screams at colonies; often calls 'titititititi' when sitting at sea. **Status and biology:** VULNERABLE. Common year-round, but probably decreasing due to longline fishing. Most abundant in shelf waters, where it scavenges at fishing boats. Often follows ships. 2 million pairs breed in summer at sub-Antarctic islands; 15 000 pairs at the Prince Edwards. **Diet:** Squid, crustaceans, fish and fishery wastes. (Bassiaan)

## 3 Spectacled Petrel *Procellaria conspicillata*

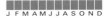
J F M A M J J A S O N D

**50–56 cm; 1–1.3 kg** Similar to White-chinned Petrel, but with a diagnostic white spectacle and dusky bill tip. Size of spectacle varies; incomplete in some birds, but usually shows some white on forehead. When spectacle is narrow, it is not connected to white throat. Beware odd White-chinned Petrels with large white throats or white head markings, often on the crown or nape. **Voice:** Deep croaks and groans at colonies; silent at sea. **Status and biology:** VULNERABLE. Rare visitor to sthn African waters year-round, but more common in summer; attends trawlers. 10 000 pairs breed in summer at Inaccessible Island, Tristan. **Diet:** Similar to White-chinned Petrel. (Brillbassiaan)

## 4 Grey Petrel *Procellaria cinerea*

J F M A M J J A S O N D

**48–50 cm; 950–1 200 g** A pale, silvery-grey petrel with white underparts, dark underwings and a yellowish bill. Grey-brown of head extends far down cheeks, with only narrow, white throat. Told from pale shearwaters by dark grey (not white) underwing. **Voice:** Rattling and moaning calls at colonies; silent at sea. **Status and biology:** NEAR-THREATENED. Rare visitor to sthn African waters; seldom strays N of 40°S. 100 000 pairs breed in winter at sub-Antarctic islands; 10 000 at Gough and 6 000 at the Prince Edwards. **Diet:** Squid, crustaceans and fish; sometimes scavenges from fishing boats. (Pediunker)

# SHEARWATERS

Small to medium-sized petrels. Most species are adapted for diving, using wings and feet underwater. Flight usually low over the water, with fairly straight, stiff wings. Despite relatively small wings, several species undertake trans-equatorial migrations. No age or sex differences in plumage. Usually breed in burrows.

## 1 Sooty Shearwater *Puffinus griseus*

J F M A M J J A S O N D

**40–46 cm; 700–950 g**  A brown shearwater with diagnostic pale, silvery underwing centres (intensity varies with light conditions). Bill long, slender and dark. Narrow, pointed wings are held straight, with little bend at wrist. Flight intersperses rapid bursts of flapping with short glides, but becomes petrel-like in strong winds. **Voice:** Silent at sea. **Status and biology: NEAR-THREATENED.** Common in coastal waters year-round, but most abundant May–Sep. 5 million pairs breed in summer at sub-Antarctic islands, mostly off New Zealand. Most of population migrates to N hemisphere in winter. **Diet:** Small fish, crustaceans and fishery wastes. (Malbaartjie)

## 2 Flesh-footed Shearwater *Puffinus carneipes*

J F M A M J J A S O N D

**45–50 cm; 550–680 g**  A dark brown shearwater with a dark-tipped, flesh-coloured bill and flesh-coloured legs and feet. Appears larger than Sooty Shearwater; lacks silvery underwing, but has pale primary bases; flight is more petrel-like, with wings more bent at wrist. Smaller than White-chinned Petrel (p. 38), and pale bill is much more slender. Rounded tail and pale bill, legs and feet distinguish it from Wedge-tailed Shearwater. **Voice:** Silent at sea. **Status and biology:** Uncommon to locally common visitor year-round, mainly off E coast. 220 000 pairs breed in summer at S temperate islands in Indian Ocean, Australia and New Zealand. **Diet:** Fish, squid and fishery wastes. (Bruinpylstormvoël)

## 3 Wedge-tailed Shearwater *Puffinus pacificus*

J F M A M J J A S O N D

**40–45 cm; 300–450 g**  A slender shearwater with a long, graduated tail that appears pointed in flight. Mostly dark-morph birds recorded from African waters: dark brown all over, with dark bill, legs and feet (unlike Flesh-footed Shearwater). Pale morph is brown above and white below, with clear-cut cap. Superficially resembles Great Shearwater (p. 42), but lacks pale rump and nape; white underwing is mottled brown (not uniform white). Flight is light and buoyant on broad wings, held bowed forward and down. **Voice:** Ghostly wailing at colonies; silent at sea. **Status and biology:** Rare visitor to tropical E coast; occasional birds come ashore and call at night on islands in Algoa Bay. 100 000 pairs breed at tropical and subtropical islands. **Diet:** Mainly fish and squid; often feeds in association with game fish and other predators. (Keilstertpylstormvoël)

## 4 Cory's Shearwater *Calonectris diomedea*

J F M A M J J A S O N D

**42–50 cm; 480–750 g**  Ash-brown above and white below with a rather large, yellow bill. Upperparts paler than Great Shearwater (p. 42), but often shows pale crescent at base of tail. Flight is slow and languid on broad wings; stays close to water, not banking and shearing as much as other shearwaters. Atlantic race *C. d. borealis* has more robust bill, more extensive dark cap and fully dark primaries on underwing (but this is tricky to see and dependent on light conditions). **Voice:** Silent at sea. **Status and biology:** Common Palearctic migrant. 1.5 million pairs breed at islands in N Atlantic (*C. d. borealis*) and Mediterranean ('Scopoli's Shearwater', *C. d. diomedea*). **Diet:** Mainly fish; often forages in association with dolphins and game fish, taking some prey in the air. (Geelbekpylstormvoël)

## 5 Streaked Shearwater *Calonectris leucomelas*

**45–48 cm; 450–580 g**  Rare vagrant. Similar to Cory's Shearwater, but with white face and streaked crown, nape and cheeks. Underwing coverts finely streaked, appearing darker than coverts of Cory's Shearwater, especially on primary coverts. **Voice:** Silent at sea. **Status and biology:** 3 records from W Cape and KZN, Aug–Oct. Breeds at islands in NW Pacific; migrates S to SE Asia, New Guinea and Australasia. **Diet:** Mainly fish and squid. (Gestreepte Pylstormvoël)

## 1 Great Shearwater  *Puffinus gravis*

**45–51 cm; 800–1 100 g**  A dark-capped shearwater with a diagnostic dark belly patch, pale nuchal collar and broad white rump. Darker above than Cory's Shearwater (p. 40), with dark bill. Underwing is mostly white, with indistinct lines across coverts. Flight action more dynamic than Cory's Shearwater, with more rapid wing beats and straighter wings. **Voice:** Staccato wailing at colonies; usually silent at sea. **Status and biology:** Common mainly on passage; 5 million pairs breed at Tristan and Gough islands, with a small colony in the Falklands. **Diet:** Mainly fish, including fishery wastes. (Grootpylstormvoël)

## 2 Manx Shearwater  *Puffinus puffinus*

**30–38 cm; 250–520 g**  The largest black-and-white shearwater in the region, with a relatively long, slender bill and pointed wings. Black upperparts contrast sharply with white underparts; often has white bands extending up onto sides of rump; undertail coverts white. Black cap extends below eye. Flight action comprises glides interspersed with rapid beats of stiff, straight wings, similar to Sooty Shearwater (p. 40), not rapid, fluttery flight of Little Shearwater. **Voice:** Silent at sea. **Status and biology:** Uncommon Palearctic migrant to shelf waters, mostly Oct–Apr, although in oceanic waters on migration. Often found among Sooty Shearwater flocks. 300 000 pairs breed at islands in temperate N Atlantic. **Diet:** Mainly fish. (Swartbekpylstormvoël)

## 3 Balearic Shearwater  *Puffinus mauretanicus*

**32–38 cm; 480–550 g**  Rare vagrant. Formerly considered a race of Manx Shearwater; slightly larger, with brown (not black) upperparts, and lacking sharp contrast on face. Typically has dark axillaries and dusky underparts and underwings, although this is variable. Some individuals are almost all-dark, resembling a small Sooty Shearwater (p. 40). **Voice:** Silent at sea. **Status and biology:** CRITICAL. 4 records from coastal waters off W coast. 2 500 pairs breed at the Balearic Islands, Spain. **Diet:** Small fish and squid. (Baleariese Pylstormvoël)

## 4 Tropical Shearwater  *Puffinus bailloni*

**28–32 cm; 140–200 g**  A small shearwater; intermediate in bill size, wing shape and flight action between Little and Manx shearwaters. Dark brown above, appearing black in some lights. Most birds have diagnostic dark undertail coverts (white in Manx and Little shearwaters), but some juvs have white undertail. **Voice:** Silent at sea. **Status and biology:** Uncommon in tropical and subtropical waters off E coast. 100 000 pairs breed at tropical islands in Pacific and Indian oceans; 100 pairs at Europa Island, Mozambique Channel; much larger populations in Seychelles. **Diet:** Mainly small fish. (Tropiese Kleinpylstormvoël)

## 5 Little Shearwater  *Puffinus assimilis*

**25–30 cm; 210–290 g**  A tiny, black-and-white shearwater. Appreciably smaller than Manx Shearwater, with short, rounded wings and narrow black trailing edge to underwing (similar in width to leading edge, not twice as wide, as in Manx Shearwater). Distinctive flight action alternates rapid wing beats with short glides. White-faced *P. a. tunneyi* **(5 A)** (Australia and central Indian Ocean) is more common off the E coast; dark-faced, silvery-grey *P. a. elegans* **(5 B)** (sub-Antarctic islands), more common off the W and S coasts, is sometimes treated as a separate species, Antarctic Little Shearwater. **Voice:** High-pitched, trilling 'whit-it-it-it-it' at colonies; silent at sea. **Status and biology:** Rare visitor to coastal waters in S, mostly May–Sep; regular in oceanic waters. 200 000 pairs of *P. a. elegans* (20 000 pairs at Tristan and Gough); 40 000 pairs of *P. a. tunneyi*. **Diet:** Fish, squid and crustaceans. (Kleinpylstormvoël)

# BULWERIA PETRELS

Fairly small, dark brown petrels with long wings and tails. No age or sex differences in plumage. Breed in caves and rock crevices.

### 1 Bulwer's Petrel *Bulweria bulwerii*

J F M A M J J A S O N D

26–28 cm; 80–120 g Vagrant. A small, dark brown petrel with a diagnostic, long, wedge-shaped tail that is usually held closed and appears pointed. Superficially like a large *Oceanodroma* storm-petrel, with deeper, stubby bill and paler grey-brown bar across upperwing coverts. Flight is buoyant and graceful, gliding low over the water. **Voice:** Silent at sea. **Status and biology:** Rare Palearctic migrant to the W coast; may be more regular in oceanic waters among large flocks of Leach's Storm-Petrels. 100 000 pairs breed at islands in the N Atlantic and Pacific; small numbers off Mauritius. (Bleekvlerkkeilstert)

### 2 Jouanin's Petrel *Bulweria fallax*

30–32 cm; 150–180 g Rare vagrant. Larger than Bulwer's Petrel with different flight action; pale bar on upperwing coverts reduced or absent. Usually seen in calm, tropical oceans, where it flies low over the water with long glides interspersed with rapid, deep wing beats. In windy conditions, arcs and wheels high over the waves with dynamic, gadfly-like flight. Long, pointed tail could cause confusion with noddies, but lacks pale crown, and bill is short and stubby. Most likely confused with Great-winged Petrel (p. 36), but is smaller, with longer neck and tail; wings more slender. **Voice:** Silent at sea. **Status and biology:** NEAR-THREATENED. 5 sightings in Mozambique Channel. Thousands of pairs breed at Socotra, off the Horn of Africa. **Diet:** Small fish and squid. (Donkervlerkkeilstert)

# STORM-PETRELS

Small pelagic seabirds with relatively large, broad wings and fluttering flight. Nostrils tube-shaped, joined on top of bill. Their 3 toes are webbed. Feed by surface-seizing or -pattering; rarely dive. No age or sex differences in plumage. Monogamous; all lay a single white egg in a burrow or rock crevice. Both sexes incubate and feed the semi-altricial chick.

### 3 Leach's Storm-Petrel *Oceanodroma leucorhoa*

b b
J F M A M J J A S O N D

19–22 cm; 40–50 g Larger than Wilson's and European storm-petrels (p. 46), with a long, forked tail and narrow, V-shaped white rump. Best identified by its long wings and languid flight action: glides low over waves with wings held forward and bent at wrist, flapping infrequently. Wing beats deep, causing erratic changes in direction. White rump usually divided by dusky central line. **Voice:** Rhythmical chattering and trilling at night at colonies; silent at sea. **Status and biology:** Fairly common, singly or in small groups, in oceanic waters beyond continental shelf, mostly Oct–Apr. In calm weather, roosts on water, often with Great-winged Petrels; seldom follows ships. 8 million pairs breed in N Atlantic and N Pacific; 25 pairs at guano islands off W Cape, S Africa. **Diet:** Small crustaceans, fish and squid. (Swaelstertstormswael)

### 4 Matsudaira's Storm-Petrel *Oceanodroma matsudairae*

25 cm; 60–65 g Rare vagrant. A large storm-petrel with long, broad wings. Flight action similar to Leach's Storm-Petrel, but has brown rump, more prominent pale bar across upperwing coverts and diagnostic white shafts to the outer 6 primary bases. Could be confused with Bulwer's Petrel, but tail forked (not wedge-shaped). **Voice:** Silent at sea. **Status and biology:** Breeds at NW Pacific islands; 2 records from E coast, S to Cape Point, May–Jul. **Diet:** Small crustaceans, fish and squid. (Oosterse Stormswael)

### 1 Wilson's Storm-Petrel *Oceanites oceanicus*

**15–19 cm; 30–40 g** A small, dark petrel with a broad, white rump that wraps around onto the flanks. Legs long; toes project beyond tail in flight; often dangle below bird when it is feeding by dancing over water, but can be retracted into belly plumage. Yellow toe webs are hard to see. Slightly larger than European Storm-Petrel, with square (not rounded) tail and broader, more rounded wings. Flight is swallow-like and direct, with frequent glides, but varies with wind strength. Can show paler bar on underwing, but not as well marked as the white underwing stripe of European Storm-Petrel. **Voice:** Silent at sea. **Status and biology:** Common visitor to shelf waters; less abundant in oceanic waters. Often follows ships. 6 million pairs breed at sub-Antarctic islands and Antarctica. **Diet:** Crustaceans, small fish, squid and fishery wastes. (Gewone Stormswael)

### 2 European Storm-Petrel *Hydrobates pelagicus*

**14–18 cm; 23–31 g** Slightly smaller and darker than Wilson's Storm-Petrel, with a short, rounded tail and diagnostic white underwing bar; pale bar on upperwing coverts less pronounced and flight action typically more rapid and fluttery. Legs short; toes don't project beyond tail tip. **Voice:** Wheezy, nasal calls at colonies; silent at sea. **Status and biology:** Common Palearctic migrant, mostly over continental shelf. Often occurs in large flocks at trawlers; patters over water when feeding. 500 000 pairs breed in NE Atlantic. **Diet:** Similar to Wilson's Storm-Petrel. (Europese Stormswael)

### 3 Black-bellied Storm-Petrel *Fregetta tropica*

**19–21 cm; 50–60 g** A bulky storm-petrel with a broad white rump, underwings and belly, usually with a broad black line down the centre linking black breast and vent. From the side, black belly stripe can be hard to see. Back tinged brown, matching upperwing coverts, lacking grey-scaling of White-bellied Storm-Petrel. Both species have a characteristic flight action, gliding over the waves, seldom flapping, regularly kicking up a line of spray with one foot or the breast (**3 A**). **Voice:** High-pitched, whistled 'peeeee' at colonies; silent at sea. **Status and biology:** Fairly common passage migrant, although not all birds leave sub-Antarctic for warm temperate waters in winter. 150 000 pairs breed in summer at sub-Antarctic islands; 5 000 at the Prince Edwards. **Diet:** Small crustaceans, fish, squid and fishery wastes. Attends trawlers; sometimes follows ships. (Swartpensstormswael)

### 4 White-bellied Storm-Petrel *Fregetta grallaria*

**19–21 cm; 45–65 g** Similar to Black-bellied Storm-Petrel, but belly is all-white, extending onto vent. Back paler and greyer due to grey-edged feathers. Legs slightly shorter; toes seldom project beyond tail tip in flight. Identification complicated by white-bellied *F. t. melanoleuca* race of Black-bellied Storm-Petrel on Gough Island. **Voice:** Similar to B. bellied Storm-Petrel. **Status and biology:** Very rare over continental shelf; scarce in oceanic waters; seldom follows ships. 100 000 pairs breed at S temperate islands, most at Tristan. **Diet:** Small crustraceans, fish and squid. (Witpensstormswael)

### 1 Grey-backed Storm-Petrel *Garrodia nereis*

**15–18 cm; 26–34 g** A tiny storm-petrel with a black head and breast merging into a blue-grey back, rump and upperwing coverts. Belly and underwing coverts white. Lacks white rump of White-bellied Storm-Petrel (p. 46). Easily overlooked as it ghosts away from ships, matching the lead-grey sea. **Voice:** Soft, cricket-like call at colonies; silent at sea. **Status and biology:** Rare vagrant to sthn Africa (1 record April 2007); typically remains S of 40°S, usually fairly close to br. islands. 50 000 pairs breed at sub-Antarctic islands; 5 000 at Gough and 1 000 at Prince Edward Island. **Diet:** Mainly larvae of goose barnacles. (Grysrugstormswael)

### 2 White-faced Storm-Petrel *Pelagodroma marina*

**19–21 cm; 45–60 g** A pale, long-legged storm-petrel with diagnostic white underparts and a prominent white eye-stripe. Upperwing coverts pale brown; rump pale grey. Flight is erratic, with jerky wing beats; long toes extend beyond tail tip. When feeding it hovers and bounds over the water, pushing off with its feet. **Voice:** Mournful cooing at colonies; silent at sea. **Status and biology:** Vagrant to sthn Africa, mainly Apr–May. 1 million pairs breed in summer at temperate islands in NE Atlantic, S Atlantic and Australasia; 20 000 at Tristan and Gough. **Diet:** Small crustaceans and fish. (Witwangstormswael)

## DIVING-PETRELS

Small, dumpy petrels with short wings and tails. Wings reduced for flight underwater; have to flap very rapidly to stay airborne, buzzing low over the water. No age or sex differences in plumage. Could possibly be confused with Little Shearwater (p. 42) given a poor view. All breed in burrows.

### 3 Common Diving-Petrel *Pelecanoides urinatrix*

**20–25 cm; 100–160 g** A chunky diving-petrel with rather dark grey head and breast and dusky underwings. Hard to separate from South Georgian Diving-Petrel where their ranges overlap, but white trailing edge to secondaries reduced or absent. **Voice:** Querulous 'wooee-wip' at colonies; silent at sea. **Status and biology:** Not recorded from sthn Africa; generally remains close to br. sites year-round. 7 million pairs breed in summer at sub-Antarctic islands, SE Australia and New Zealand; 35 000 at Tristan and Gough; 10 000 at the Prince Edwards. **Diet:** Small crustaceans. (Gewone Duikstormvoël)

### 4 South Georgian Diving-Petrel *Pelecanoides georgicus*

**18–22 cm; 90–150 g** Slightly smaller than Common Diving-Petrel. Hard to identify at sea; typical birds have more obvious white line on scapulars, white trailing edge to secondaries and greater coverts (usually dark in Common Diving-Petrel), and clean white underparts (dusky breast and underwing in Common). Often shows a clean, rather contrasting face, with darker ear coverts. In the hand, has smaller bill and a black line along rear of leg. **Voice:** Squeaky calls at colonies; silent at sea. **Status and biology:** Not recorded from sthn Africa. 6 million pairs breed in summer at sub-Antarctic islands; 5 000 at the Prince Edwards. Forages further from br. islands. **Diet:** Small crustaceans. (Kleinduikstormvoël)

# TROPICBIRDS

Medium-sized, tropical pelagic seabirds that feed by plunge diving. Wings fairly short; wing beats stiff. Bills robust with serrate edges. The 4 toes are webbed, but feet reduced. Sexes alike, but juv. plumage distinct; ads have elongate central tail streamers. Monogamous; all lay one egg in a sheltered crevice or under vegetation. Both sexes incubate and feed the semi-altricial chick.

## 1 Red-tailed Tropicbird *Phaethon rubricauda*

J F M A M J J A S O N D

**60–70 cm (plus 35 cm streamer); 600–800 g** The palest tropicbird; ad. mostly white (tinged pink when breeding), with red bill and red tail streamers. Compared to other ad. tropicbirds, has thin (not broad) black primary tips on outer primaries and small black tips on scapulars. Juv. is more finely barred above than White-tailed Tropicbird, with less black in outer wing; bill is blackish. **Voice:** Deep 'kraak', similar to Caspian Tern (p. 188). **Status and biology:** Regular in Mozambique Channel, uncommon further S to W Cape; vagrant inland. Occasionally visits cliff sites for days or weeks. 3 000–4 000 pairs breed at Europa Island, Mozambique Channel. **Diet:** Fish and squid, including flying fish and flying squid. (Rooipylstert)

## 2 White-tailed Tropicbird *Phaethon lepturus*

J F M A M J J A S O N D

**45–50 cm (plus 40 cm streamer); 280–400 g** The smallest tropicbird; ad. has diagnostic orange-yellow bill, neat black facemask and extremely long, wispy, white or golden tail streamers (shafts black). In flight, has 2 black patches on each wing (outer primaries and median coverts). Juv. smaller than other juv. tropicbirds, with barred upperparts and black wing tips; bill yellow, with dark tip. Barring is sparser than juv. Red-tailed Tropicbird's, and black eye patch does not form nuchal collar as in juv. Red-billed Tropicbird. **Voice:** Loud 'kek kek kek' at colonies; silent at sea. **Status and biology:** Regular in Mozambique Channel; uncommon further S and off W coast. Breeds at tropical islands worldwide, including 2 200 pairs at Ascension Island, Atlantic Ocean, and 500–1 000 pairs at Europa Island, Mozambique Channel. **Diet:** Fish and squid. (Witpylstert)

## 3 Red-billed Tropicbird *Phaethon aethereus*

**60–65 cm (plus 40 cm streamer); 650–700 g** Rare vagrant. Ad. has large red bill and white tail streamers. Differs from Red-tailed Tropicbird by its finely barred back, which appears grey at a distance, and by its long, white (not red) tail streamers. Juv. heavily barred above, with black eye patch extending to nape to form nuchal collar; bill yellow with a dark tip. **Voice:** Occasional piercing screams at sea. **Status and biology:** Vagrant to oceanic waters off W and S coasts, probably from S Atlantic population of 1 200 pairs (mainly on Ascension Island). **Diet:** Fish and squid. (Rooibekpylstert)

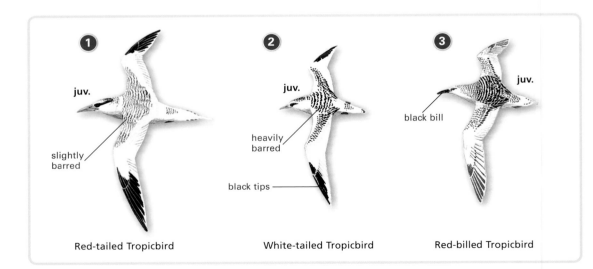

juv.

slightly barred

Red-tailed Tropicbird

juv.

heavily barred

black tips

White-tailed Tropicbird

juv.

black bill

Red-billed Tropicbird

# GANNETS AND BOOBIES

Large seabirds that feed by plunge diving. Bills dagger-like; nostrils concealed behind bill plates. 4 toes webbed. Sexes alike; juv. plumage distinct. Monogamous; often retain the same mate in successive years. Both sexes incubate and feed the altricial chicks.

## 1 Cape Gannet *Morus capensis*

b | | | | | | | | | b b B B b b
J F M A M J J A S O N D

**84–95 cm; 2.3–3.1 kg** Ad. white with yellow wash on head, and black tail and flight feathers; some have 1–4 white outer tail feathers (**1 A**). Juv. is brown with white spots, whitening gradually, typically starting with head. Juv. could be confused with Brown Booby, but is larger and lacks clear-cut brown bib and white belly. **Voice:** Noisy 'warrra-warrra-warrra' at colonies and when feeding at sea. **Status and biology: VULNERABLE.** Br. endemic. Largely confined to continental shelf; often feeds at trawlers. 120 000 pairs breed in dense colonies in spring and summer at 6 islands off Cape and Namibia. Lays 1 egg (rarely 2). **Diet:** Mainly pelagic fish, but also fishery wastes. Large numbers follow sardine run up E coast to KZN in winter; others migrate up W coast to Gulf of Guinea. (Witmalgas)

## 2 Australian Gannet *Morus serrator*

**83–92 cm; 2–2.8 kg** Rare vagrant. Very similar to Cape Gannet, but has a darker, greyish eye, more golden wash to head and much shorter gular stripe (but none of these features is useful for identification at sea). All confirmed records are of birds at Cape Gannet colonies, where they are best located by their higher-pitched call. Ad. has 3 outer tail feathers white, but some Cape Gannets also show white outer tails. Juv. differs from juv. Cape Gannet only by its short gular stripe. **Voice:** Higher pitched than Cape Gannet's. **Status and biology:** Some 20 birds recorded, all at Cape Gannet colonies; has bred with Cape Gannet. **Diet:** Mainly small fish. (Australiese Malgas)

## 3 Red-footed Booby *Sula sula*

▬ ▬ ▬ ▬ ▬ ▬ ▬ ▬ ▬ ▬ ▬ ▬
J F M A M J J A S O N D

**66–77 cm; 820–950 g** A small, slender booby with a long, pointed tail. Ad. has bright red legs and a blue bill with a pink base; eye dark in most birds, but some golden. Brown morph is much smaller than juv. gannets, and has plain (not speckled) plumage. White morph (**3 A**) has yellow wash on head, but white tail and black carpal patches on underwing. Most common morph is white-tailed brown (**3 B**). Juv. is brown-streaked, with grey-brown bill and greyish-yellow feet. **Voice:** Usually silent at sea; occasional harsh 'karrk' alarm call. **Status and biology:** Regular in Mozambique Channel, uncommon further S, often after cyclones; 3 500 pairs breed at Europa Island, Mozambique Channel. Rare on W coast, presumably from Atlantic colonies (1 300 pairs breed at Fernando de Noronha). **Diet:** Flying fish and squid. (Rooipootmalgas)

## 4 Brown Booby *Sula leucogaster*

**64–74 cm; 900–1 300 g** Rare vagrant. Ad. dark brown with a white lower breast and belly, and a broad white underwing panel. Bill pale grey, washed blue-green; legs yellowish. Uniform upperparts and crisply defined white underparts distinguish it from juv. gannets. Juv. is duller brown above; has brown flecks on white belly, but lacks white speckling of juv. gannets. Differs from juv. Masked Booby by uniform brown upperparts and well-demarcated (not fuzzy) underpart pattern. **Voice:** Silent at sea. **Status and biology:** Vagrant to Namibia and E coast from br. islands in tropical S Atlantic and W Indian Ocean. Most records from E coast associated with tropical cyclones. **Diet:** Flying fish and squid. (Bruinmalgas)

## 5 Masked Booby *Sula dactylatra*

**80–90 cm; 1.8–2.4 kg** Rare vagrant. A large white booby with golden eyes and a small black facial mask. Lacks yellow head of ad. Cape Gannet and has broader black secondaries extending to body. Black (not white) tail and dark (not red) legs separate it from smaller, white-phase Red-footed Booby. Juv. has mottled brown head, back and rump; resembles Brown Booby, but has narrow white hind neck collar, less extensive brown on breast, and more white on underwing with a dark central bar (clearly defined, smaller white area in Brown Booby; juv. Red-footed Booby has all-dark underwings). **Voice:** High double honk; generally silent at sea. **Status and biology:** Not recorded from sthn Africa, but 1 at sea S of Cape Agulhas. Breeds at tropical islands from Red Sea to Tanzania. **Diet:** Mainly fish. (Brilmalgas)

# CORMORANTS AND SHAGS

Medium to large sea- and freshwater birds with long, slender necks and hook-tipped bills for grasping prey. Feed by pursuit diving, propelled by 4 webbed toes. Plumage partly wettable; have to return to land to roost. Flight rapid, direct. Sexes alike; males slightly larger. Have short-lived br. plumage. Juvs duller and paler. Monogamous; both sexes incubate and feed the altricial chicks.

## 1 Crozet Shag *Phalacrocorax melanogenis*

**70–75 cm; 1.8–2.2 kg** A striking, black-and-white cormorant confined to inshore waters around Marion, Prince Edward and the Crozet islands. Ad. black above, glossed purple on body and greenish on wings, contrasting with white underparts and wing bar; golden caruncles at base of bill, fleshy blue eye-ring, forecrown crest and pink feet all more prominent in br. plumage. Juv. much duller; lacks facial ornaments; eye-ring grey; grey-brown upperparts merge into white underparts. **Voice:** Nasal, crow-like honk. **Status and biology:** Uncommon resident; 1 200 pairs, decreasing at the Prince Edwards (320 pairs). Breeds in small colonies on rocky headlands and cliffs; lays 2–5 eggs. **Diet:** Fish, octopus and crustaceans. Feeds on bottom; seldom more than 1 km from shore. (Crozetduiker)

## 2 White-breasted Cormorant *Phalacrocorax lucidus*

b b b b b b b b b b b b
J F M A M J J A S O N D

**85–95 cm; 1.8–3.2 kg** Largest African cormorant. Ad. has white throat and breast, washed pink in marine populations; white thigh patches in br. plumage; yellow skin at base of bill; eyes turquoise. Juv. has white underparts and browner upperparts. **Voice:** Grunts and squeaks at colony; otherwise silent. **Status and biology:** Locally common resident at dams, lakes, large rivers, estuaries and shallow coastal waters; prefers sandy bottoms. Breeds colonially, laying 3–4 eggs in large stick nests in trees, bushes, reeds, cliffs or on the ground on islands; sometimes with herons, ibises, egrets, darters or other cormorants. **Diet:** Mainly fish. (Witborsduiker)

## 3 Bank Cormorant *Phalacrocorax neglectus*

b b b b b b b b b b b b
J F M A M J J A S O N D

**74–76 cm; 1.6–2.3 kg** Robust, all-dark marine cormorant confined to the Benguela coast (Cape Agulhas to central Namibia). Best told from Cape Cormorant by its angled head profile (steep forehead, flat crown) and heavier build; feeds singly. Br. ad. has white rump patch. Eyes turquoise, gradually turning brick red from the top with age. Juv. browner. Partial leucism quite regular (**3 A**). **Voice:** Wheezy 'wheee' at colony. **Status and biology: ENDANGERED.** Endemic. Only 3 000 pairs (9 000, 30 years ago). Breeds colonially on offshore rocks and islands; lays 1–3 eggs in nest built from fresh seaweed, plastered with guano. Occurs in coastal waters; seldom more than 20 km from colonies. **Diet:** Fish, crayfish, octopus and other marine invertebrates; forages on seabed up to 50 m deep. (Bankduiker)

## 4 Cape Cormorant *Phalacrocorax capensis*

B B b b b b b b B B B B
J F M A M J J A S O N D

**60–65 cm; 900–1 600 g** An all-dark marine cormorant; slightly smaller and more slender than rarer Bank Cormorant, with paler gular skin. Often occurs in large flocks; flies over the sea in long lines, hence the Afrikaans name 'Trekduiker'. Br. ad. glossy black with chrome yellow gular patch, turquoise eye and banded turquoise and black eye-ring; non-br. ad. duller. Juv. brown, with paler underparts; almost whitish in some birds; gular skin grey-brown. **Voice:** Nasal grunts and croaks, mainly at colony. **Status and biology: NEAR-THREATENED.** Br. endemic. Occurs in coastal waters and adjacent wetlands. Numbers have decreased over last 20 years; currently 100 000 pairs. Breeds colonially on cliffs and offshore islands; lays 1–4 eggs in nest built from vegetation, bones and feathers. **Diet:** Mainly pelagic fish; forages up to 50 km offshore; also on seabed up to 30 m deep. (Trekduiker)

## 1 Reed Cormorant *Phalacrocorax africanus*

**50–56 cm; 450–650 g**  A small, short-billed and long-tailed cormorant mainly found in freshwater habitats. Range overlaps narrowly with Crowned Cormorant at coastal wetlands, but it is slightly smaller with a longer, more graduated tail. Ad. glossy black with prominent forecrown crest in br. plumage; back feathers more contrasting than ad. Crowned Cormorant, with silver bases and broad black tips. Eyes red; facial skin orange; non-br. ad. duller. Juv. brown above, whitish below. **Voice:** Cackles and hisses at colony. **Status and biology:** Locally common resident at dams, lakes, rivers, estuaries and shallow coastal waters in Mozambique and N Namibia. Breeds colonially, laying 3–4 eggs in stick or reed nests in trees, bushes, reeds, cliffs or on the ground on islands; often with herons, ibises, egrets, darters or other cormorants. **Diet:** Small fish and frogs. (Rietduiker)

## 2 Crowned Cormorant *Phalacrocorax coronatus*

**54–58 cm; 680–850 g**  A small, short-billed and long-tailed marine cormorant confined to the S and W coasts (Tsitsikamma to N Namibia). Formerly treated as a race of Reed Cormorant, but is slightly larger, with a shorter, less graduated tail; ranges overlap narrowly in coastal wetlands; told apart with difficulty. Ad. glossy black with prominent forecrown crest; back feathers less contrasting than ad. Reed Cormorant, with narrower black tips; appears more uniform. Eyes red; facial skin orange. Non-br. ad. duller. Juv. brown with paler breast; lacks extensive white underparts of juv. Reed Cormorant. **Voice:** Cackles and hisses at colony. **Status and biology: NEAR-THREATENED**. Endemic; 3 000 pairs. Breeds colonially on cliffs and offshore islands, laying 2–4 eggs in nest built from vegetation, bones and feathers. Occurs in coastal waters, sometimes roosting in nearby wetlands. **Diet:** Fish, especially klipfish, and invertebrates; forages on seabed up to 20 m deep. (Kuifkopduiker)

# DARTERS

**Medium to large freshwater birds. Plumage fully wettable, allowing near neutral buoyancy at water surface, but foraging bouts short; have to return to land to prevent excessive heat loss. Feed by combination of stealth and pursuit diving, propelled by 4 webbed toes. Prey speared on dagger-like bills. Monogamous; both sexes incubate and feed the altricial chicks.**

## 3 African Darter *Anhinga rufa*

**80–92 cm; 1–1.7 kg**  Differs from cormorants by its long, very slender neck and head and long, pointed bill. When swimming, often only long neck and head are visible. Often glides in flight, with broad wings, deeply slotted outer primaries, and long, broad tail. Ad. has elongate, white-striped scapulars and wing coverts. Br. male has rufous foreneck, with white stripe down neck. Female and non-br. male have pale brown throat. Juv. has buffy neck and lacks streaking on back. **Voice:** Croaks when breeding; otherwise silent. **Status and biology:** Common resident of lakes, dams and slow-moving rivers; rarely coastal lagoons and estuaries. Breeds in colonies in trees or reeds, often with cormorants, herons and egrets. Lays 3–4 eggs in an untidy platform of sticks and reeds. **Diet:** Fish, frogs. (Slanghalsvoël)

# FRIGATEBIRDS

Large, tropical, pelagic seabirds with extremely long, angled wings and long, deeply forked tails. Males have naked red throat pouches that are inflated in display. Females larger than males. Feet tiny with 4 partially webbed toes. Feed by surface-seizing without landing or by stealing food from other birds. Soar to great heights. Plumage differs with age and sex. Monogamous; often retain the same mate in successive years. All lay 1 egg, usually in a stick platform built in a tree. Both sexes incubate and feed the semi-altricial chick. Breeding extremely protracted; typically raise at most 1 chick every 2 years.

### 1 Greater Frigatebird *Fregata minor*

J F M A M J J A S O N D

**86–104 cm; 1.1–1.5 kg** Underwing wholly dark at all stages, lacking white 'armpits' of Lesser Frigatebird. Ad. male black, with paler brown bar across upperwing coverts and reddish feet. Female has white breast and throat, grey chin and red eye-ring and feet. Juv. has whitish or tawny head and throat, dark breast band and white lower breast and forebelly. Imm. white from chin to belly, gradually darkening with age. **Voice:** Silent at sea. **Status and biology:** Regular in Mozambique Channel, vagrant further S; vagrant inland, usually after cyclones. Occasionally roosts ashore in trees. 1 000 pairs breed at Europa Island, Mozambique Channel. **Diet:** Fish and squid, especially flying fish and flying squid. (Grootfregatvoël)

### 2 Lesser Frigatebird *Fregata ariel*

J F M A M J J A S O N D

**70–82 cm; 700–900 g** Smaller and more angular than Greater Frigatebird, but hard to assess on lone birds. Ad. male black with diagnostic white 'armpits' extending from axillaries to sides of breast; lacks pale upperwing bars; feet dull red-black. Female has white breast extending as collar onto neck, red feet and red or blue eye-ring; differs from female Greater Frigatebird by black throat and white breast extending to armpits. Juv. has brownish head and mottled white breast. Imm. is variable, but typically has dark (brownish or black) throat, more extensive black on belly, and white breast extending to armpits. **Voice:** Silent at sea. **Status and biology:** Rare off E coast, seen mostly after summer cyclones. 1 000 pairs breed at Europa Island, Mozambique Channel. **Diet:** Fish and squid. (Kleinfregatvoël)

# PELICANS

Large to huge waterbirds with very long bills and a distensible pouch between their lower mandibles used to trap fish and other prey. Flight strong; often soar in thermals on broad wings with deeply slotted primaries. Swim with 4 webbed toes. Sexes alike in plumage, but males appreciably larger. Monogamous; both sexes incubate and feed the altricial chicks.

### 3 Great White Pelican *Pelecanus onocrotalus*

J F M A M J J A S O N D

**140–178 cm; 6–14 kg** A very large, white pelican with black flight feathers contrasting with white coverts in flight. Bill pouch yellow, with more of a sag in middle than Pink-backed Pelican's. Br. ad. has pink-tinged underparts, bare pink-orange face, short crest, yellow breast patch and red nail at tip of bill. Non-br. ads have yellow face. Juv. is finely mottled brown, whitening with age; lacks marked contrast between flight feathers and coverts. **Voice:** Usually silent; deep 'mooo' given at br. colonies. **Status and biology:** Locally common at lakes, estuaries and sheltered coastal bays (Namibia), usually within 200–300 km of colonies. Nests colonially on ground. 8 000 pairs breed at Walvis Bay, Dassen Island, Lake St Lucia and opportunistically at wetlands in Botswana and N Namibia. Lays 2 eggs, but older chick kills younger sibling should both eggs hatch. **Diet:** Fish, frogs, seabird chicks and offal. Often forages in flocks, working cooperatively to encircle prey. (Witpelikaan)

### 4 Pink-backed Pelican *Pelecanus rufescens*

J F M A M J J A S O N D

**125–140 cm; 4–7 kg** Smaller and greyer than Great White Pelican, with a pinkish back and a pinkish-yellow bill. Flight feathers are dark grey, but do not contrast strongly with coverts in flight. Br. birds have grey crest. Juv. mottled brown, becoming greyer with age; best distinguished from Great White Pelican by smaller size (and usually accompanied by ads). **Voice:** Usually silent; guttural calls at br. colonies. **Status and biology:** Locally common at lakes and estuaries. 200 pairs nest colonially in trees at wetlands in N KZN and N Botswana. Lays 2–3 eggs; does not exhibit obligate siblicide, but younger chicks often starve. **Diet:** Fish; typically fishes alone. (Kleinpelikaan)

# GREBES

Fairly small diving birds with rounded bodies and very short tails. Feed by pursuit diving, propelled by lobed toes. Legs well back on body; clumsy on land. Sexes alike, but many species have br. and non-br. plumage. Juvs have striped heads. Moults all flight feathers simultaneously. Monogamous; both sexes incubate and feed the precocial chicks, often carrying small chicks on their backs.

## 1 Great Crested Grebe *Podiceps cristatus*

bbbbbbbbbbbb
J F M A M J J A S O N D

**45–56 cm; 500–750 g** A large, long-necked grebe. Ad. has distinctive dark double crest and rufous-edged ruff ringing sides of head. Ruff of non-breeders is smaller and paler. Juv. has black-and-white striped head; lacks crests and head ruff. In flight, appears long and slender with neck extended and legs trailing; wings long and thin with conspicuous white secondaries and lesser coverts. **Voice:** Barking 'rah-rah-rah'; various growls and snarls. **Status and biology:** Locally common resident on large lakes and pans; rarely in estuaries and sheltered bays. Lays 2–5 eggs in a mound of vegetation anchored to emergent reeds or grasses. **Diet:** Mainly small fish; also tadpoles and freshwater invertebrates. (Kuifkopdobbertjie)

## 2 Black-necked Grebe *Podiceps nigricollis*

BBBBbbbbbbBB
J F M A M J J A S O N D

**28–33 cm; 300 g** Slightly larger than Little Grebe and appears more elegant thanks to its longer, more slender neck, more angular head and longer bill with an upturned tip. Eyes bright red. Br. ads have golden ear tufts, black head and throat, and chestnut flanks. Non-br. ads and imms have white cheeks, throat and flanks. On water, sits with back higher than, or level with, rump. Preening birds often roll over, flashing white belly. **Voice:** Seldom calls; mellow trill during display. **Status and biology:** Fairly common but localised resident and nomad at lakes, pans and occasionally in sheltered coastal bays. Often occurs in flocks. Breeds erratically, usually colonially, laying 2–6 eggs in a mound of vegetation. **Diet:** Fish and aquatic invertebrates. (Swartnekdobbertjie)

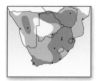

## 3 Little Grebe *Tachybaptus ruficollis*

BBBbbbbbBBBB
J F M A M J J A S O N D

**23–29 cm; 120–190 g** A small, compact grebe with a pale, fleshy gape flange. Bill short and relatively deep; head rounded. Br. ad. has rich chestnut sides to face and neck; non-br. ads duller. Juv. has black-and-white striped cheeks. On water, sits with rump higher than back. Faces away from sun and fluffs up rump feathers between dives; sleeks down feathers to expel air just before diving. **Voice:** Distinctive, whinnying trill frequently given. **Status and biology:** Common resident on lakes, dams and other freshwater bodies; rarely in estuaries and sheltered bays. Apparently flies at night to locate new wetlands. Lays 2–7 eggs in a floating nest constructed from aquatic vegetation. **Diet:** Fish, tadpoles and aquatic invertebrates. (Kleindobbertjie)

# HERONS, EGRETS AND BITTERNS

Tall, slender waterbirds with long legs and, usually, long necks. Bills dagger-like. Hunt mainly aquatic animals, typically by stealth, occasionally by active pursuit. Sexes alike, but often have distinct juv. plumages. Most breed in colonies; some bitterns solitary nesters. Monogamous; both sexes incubate and feed the semi-altricial chicks.

## 1 Goliath Heron *Ardea goliath*

| b | b | b | b | b | b | b | B | B | B | B | b |
|---|---|---|---|---|---|---|---|---|---|---|---|
| J | F | M | A | M | J | J | A | S | O | N | D |

**135–150 cm; 3–4.3 kg** The largest heron, with a massive, heavy bill. Rich chestnut head, neck and underparts recall much smaller Purple Heron, but has an unstriped head and blackish (not yellow) legs and bill. In flight, the huge, broad wings beat slowly and deeply. Juv. duller and less rufous, with foreneck, chest, belly and underwing coverts white, streaked with black. Recently fledged birds have buff margins to back feathers. **Voice:** Loud, low-pitched 'kwaaark'. **Status and biology:** Locally common resident and local nomad at lakes, dams, large rivers and estuaries, usually where there are extensive reeds or papyrus. Breeds singly or in small colonies, sometimes with other herons and egrets, laying 2–5 eggs on a platform of sticks and reeds either in a tree or reeds. **Diet:** Mainly fish, up to 1.5 kg; also other aquatic animals. (Reusereier)

## 2 Purple Heron *Ardea purpurea*

| B | b | b | b | b | b | b | B | B | b | b | b |
|---|---|---|---|---|---|---|---|---|---|---|---|
| J | F | M | A | M | J | J | A | S | O | N | D |

**78–86 cm; 550–1 200 g** A fairly large heron with a long, slender neck and bill. The black-striped rufous head and neck and dark grey wings are distinctive; much smaller than Goliath Heron, with black cap and paler bill and legs. Juv. duller and paler, with less well-marked head stripes and browner back. **Voice:** Hoarse 'kraaark'. **Status and biology:** Common resident and local nomad at wetlands, typically among sedges and reeds; seldom forages in the open. Breeds singly or in small colonies, laying 2–5 eggs on a platform of reed stems built in dense reeds. **Diet:** Fish, frogs, reptiles, birds and invertebrates. Sometimes takes chicks of birds nesting in reedbeds. (Rooireier)

## 3 Grey Heron *Ardea cinerea*

| b | b | b | b | b | b | B | B | B | B | B | b |
|---|---|---|---|---|---|---|---|---|---|---|---|
| J | F | M | A | M | J | J | A | S | O | N | D |

**90–100 cm; 1.1–2 kg** A large, greyish heron of aquatic habitats. Told in flight from Black-headed Heron by its uniform grey (not contrasting dark and pale) underwing. Ad. has mostly white head and neck, with black eye-stripe ending in a wispy plume. Foreneck streaked black, with broad black bands on either side of breast and belly, often showing as black shoulder patches. Bill yellow (orange-pink in pre-br. birds); legs yellow-brown (flushed red in pre-br. birds). Juv. duller with rather plain head; lacks black flanks; bill yellow-brown. Differs from juv. Black-headed Heron by its white (not black) ear coverts, pale flanks and yellow (not dark) upper legs. **Voice:** Harsh 'kraaunk' in flight. **Status and biology:** Common resident and local nomad at pans, dams, slow-flowing rivers, lagoons and estuaries. Breeds colonially (up to 100 pairs), often with other herons, egrets, cormorants and ibises. Lays 1–4 eggs on a platform of sticks or reeds, either in reeds or a tree. **Diet:** Mainly fish; also frogs, reptiles, birds, mammals and invertebrates. (Bloureier)

## 4 Black-headed Heron *Ardea melanocephala*

| B | B | b | b | b | b | b | b | b | B | B | B |
|---|---|---|---|---|---|---|---|---|---|---|---|
| J | F | M | A | M | J | J | A | S | O | N | D |

**86–94 cm; 1.2–1.9 kg** A large, greyish heron of terrestrial habitats. Slightly smaller than Grey Heron, with contrasting dark flight feathers and pale underwing coverts in flight. Black crown and hind neck contrast with white throat; underparts grey; bill and legs black. Juv. has slate-grey crown and hind neck and buff wash on foreneck; underparts paler. Differs from juv. Grey Heron by dark ear coverts, black legs and contrasting underwing pattern. **Voice:** Loud 'aaaaark'; various hoarse cackles and bill-clapping at nest. **Status and biology:** Common resident and local nomad in grassland, fields and scrubland; also marsh fringes, but seldom forages in water. Breeds colonially (up to 50 pairs), often with other herons, egrets, cormorants and ibises. Lays 2–4 eggs on a platform of sticks either in reeds or a tree. **Diet:** Small mammals, birds, reptiles and terrestrial invertebrates. (Swartkopreier)

## 1 Yellow-billed Egret  *Egretta intermedia*

**65–72 cm; 300–500 g** A medium-sized, white egret with a yellow bill and blackish legs and toes, with paler tibia. Neck shorter than Great Egret's; not held in such a pronounced 'S' shape; bill shorter and gape ends just below eye (behind eye in Great Egret). Larger and longer-necked than Cattle Egret with a longer bill. In br. plumage, has long plumes on back and chest, red bill and upper legs, and lime-green lores. **Voice:** Typical, heron-like 'waaaark'. **Status and biology:** Common resident and nomad at marshes and flooded grassland; rarely at estuaries. Breeds colonially (up to 70 pairs), usually with other egrets, herons, cormorants and ibises. Lays 2–3 eggs on a platform of sticks and reeds, either in reeds or in a tree. **Diet:** Small fish, frogs and invertebrates. (Geelbekwitreier)

## 2 Great Egret  *Egretta alba*

**85–95 cm; 800–1 400 g** The largest egret, structurally similar to larger herons, with a heavy bill. Legs and feet black. Br. ad. has elaborate plumes, black bill, lime-green lores and red eyes. Non-br. ad. has yellow bill and eyes; larger and heavier-billed than Yellow-billed Egret; gape extends behind the eye. Lacks yellow toes of much smaller Little Egret. **Voice:** Deep, heron-like 'waaaark'. **Status and biology:** Common resident and nomad at lakes, dams and estuaries. Breeds colonially (up to 200 pairs), usually with other egrets, herons, cormorants and ibises. Lays 2–5 eggs on a platform of sticks and reeds, either in reeds or in a tree. **Diet:** Mainly fish and frogs. (Grootwitreier)

## 3 Little Egret  *Egretta garzetta*

**55–65 cm; 450–600 g** A fairly small, slender egret with a black bill, black legs and contrasting yellow toes. Bill is more slender and slightly shorter than that of Western Reef Heron; lacks yellow lores extending onto the base of bill of smaller Snowy Egret, but beware age-related variation. Br. ad. has red eyes, orange face and elongate plumes on nape, mantle and foreneck. Non-br. ad. lacks plumes; eyes yellow, face grey-green. Juv. has greenish base to bill, duller yellow toes, and grey-green lower legs. **Voice:** Harsh 'waaark'. **Status and biology:** Common resident and local nomad at wetlands, estuaries and along the coast. Breeds colonially (up to 120 pairs), usually with other egrets, herons, cormorants and ibises. Lays 2–4 eggs on a platform of sticks and reeds, either in reeds or in a tree. **Diet:** Mainly small fish and frogs. Often actively pursues fish in shallow water; frequently uses other birds or animals to scare or herd fish. (Kleinwitreier)

## 4 Snowy Egret  *Egretta thula*

**56–60 cm; 350–450 g** Rare vagrant. Slightly smaller than Little Egret with a shorter bill and more extensive yellow lores extending onto the base of the bill. Br. ad. has brown eyes and orange-yellow lores and base of upper mandible. Non-br. ad. has duller bare parts. Juv. white; easily confused with juv. Little Egret. **Voice:** Harsh 'aarr'. **Status and biology:** Vagrant from N and S America; 1 record from sthn Africa: April 2002. **Diet:** Small fish, frogs and aquatic invertebrates. (Sneeuwitreier)

## 5 Little Blue Heron  *Egretta caerulea*

**64–70 cm; 300–400 g** Rare vagrant. A medium-sized heron with a black-tipped, pale grey bill; legs and feet greeny-grey. Ad. blue-grey with darker, purplish head and neck. Juv. white; easily confused with Little Egret, but has yellowish-green legs and distinctive 2-tone bill. Imm. has odd grey feathers, appearing mottled. **Voice:** Harsh 'thrrrr' when disturbed. **Status and biology:** Nearctic vagrant that winters in central and S America; several records from the W coast. Some individuals survive for several years. **Diet:** Aquatic invertebrates and small fish. (Kleinbloureier)

## 6 Western Reef Heron  *Egretta gularis*

**56–66 cm; 350–500 g** Rare vagrant. White morph **(6 A)** similar to Little Egret, but with a longer, heavier, yellow-brown bill and greeny-black legs with dull yellow lower tarsi merging into dull yellow toes. Dark morph **(6 B)** (not recorded from sthn Africa) is dark grey with a white throat and variable white patch on primary coverts, visible in flight. Imm. is greyish-brown or white, variably mottled with grey or grey-brown. **Voice:** Harsh 'gaaar'. **Status and biology:** Vagrant to coastal habitats from tropical coasts of W and E Africa; 1 record from Cape Point, April 2002. **Diet:** Mainly small fish and crabs. (Westelike Kusreier)

## 7 Cattle Egret  *Bubulcus ibis*

**48–54 cm; 280–450 g** A small, compact egret with a relatively short bill, neck and legs. Legs olive-yellow; bill yellow. Ad. has buff plumes on crown, mantle and breast, forming a shaggy bib; buff areas increase in br. season, but are never as extensive as Squacco Heron's (p. 66). Pre-br. birds have reddish bill and legs. Juv. has black legs immediately after fledging, but these soon pale. **Voice:** Heron-like 'aaaark' or 'pok-pok'. **Status and biology:** Common resident and nomad in a wide range of open habitats, including grassland, fields and coastline. Roosts in flocks, commuting up to 20 km to feeding areas. Breeds in colonies of up to 10 000 pairs, usually with other egrets, herons, cormorants and ibises. Lays 1–6 eggs on a platform of sticks and reeds either in reeds or in a tree. **Diet:** Insects, ticks, frogs and other vertebrates; uses large animals to flush prey, sometimes standing on animals and gleaning ectoparasites. (Veereier)

## 1 Black Heron *Egretta ardesiaca*

B B B b b b b b b b b B
J F M A M J J A S O N D

50–60 cm; 280–380 g  A small, slate-black egret, darker than Slaty Egret and ad. Little Blue Heron (p. 64) with black legs and orange-yellow toes (not dull yellow or greenish legs). Often uses its wings to form an 'umbrella' over head (1 A), shading water to attract small fish. Ad. has nape, back and breast plumes, which are pronounced in br. season. Juv. is slightly paler, lacking plumes. **Voice:** Deep 'kraak'. **Status and biology:** Locally common resident and nomad at lakes and marshes; occasionally estuaries. Breeds colonially (up to 20 pairs), usually with other herons, egrets, cormorants and ibises. Lays 2–4 eggs on a platform of sticks and reeds either in reeds or in a tree. **Diet:** Mainly small fish; also aquatic invertebrates. (Swartreier)

## 2 Slaty Egret *Egretta vinaceigula*

b B b b       A S O N D
J F M A M J J A S O N D

48–58 cm; 250–340 g  A dark grey egret with diagnostic rufous throat. Slightly smaller than Black Heron with greenish-yellow (not black) legs and feet; does not use its wings to shade water when feeding. Eyes yellow (black in pre-br. birds). Juv. paler; lacks head and breast plumes; legs greenish-grey. **Voice:** Heron-like squawks and alarm 'krrr krrr krrr'. **Status and biology: VULNERABLE.** Locally common resident and local nomad at marshes and vegetated lake shores. Breeds sporadically in colonies of up to 200 pairs, often with Rufous-bellied Herons and Dwarf Bitterns (p. 68). Lays 2–4 eggs on a platform of sticks and reeds either in reeds or in a small tree. **Diet:** Small fish, tadpoles and aquatic insects. (Rooikeelreier)

## 3 Rufous-bellied Heron *Ardeola rufiventris*

b b B B B B B B b b b b
J F M A M J J A S O N D

38–40 cm; 300 g  A small heron with a sooty head and breast, and rufous belly, wings and tail. Skulking; normally seen only when flushed. In flight, bright yellow legs and feet contrast strongly with dark underparts. Bill yellowy-green with black tip; pre-br. birds have red lores and legs. Female duller with pale throat. Juv. dull brown with buff streaking on breast and throat. **Voice:** Heron-like 'waaaaak'. **Status and biology:** Fairly common resident in N Botswana; uncommon migrant elsewhere. Occurs in dense marshes and flooded grassland. Breeds singly or in small colonies, often with other small herons. Lays 1–4 eggs in a platform of reeds and sticks built either in reeds or a low tree. **Diet:** Fish, frogs and aquatic invertebrates. (Rooipensreier)

## 4 Squacco Heron *Ardeola ralloides*

B B B B B B b b b b b b
J F M A M J J A S O N D

42–46 cm; 250–350 g  A small, buff and white heron, with a heavy bill with a dark tip. At rest, appears mostly buff and brown, with white underparts. In flight, white wings and tail are prominent; could be confused with Cattle Egret (p. 64), but is smaller and more compact with broad, rounded wings. Br. ad. has blue lores and base to bill, elongate crown feathers and yellow legs (red in pre-br. period). Non-br. ad. has dark brown streaking on body and greenish-yellow legs; bill duller. Juv. has grey-brown body with heavier streaking, but usually not as boldly streaked as non-br. Malagasy Pond-Heron; wings mottled brown; belly pale grey. **Voice:** Low-pitched 'kruuk'; rattling 'kek-kek-kek'. **Status and biology:** Common resident and local nomad along vegetated margins of lakes, pans and slow-moving rivers; skulks in long grass, sitting motionless for long periods. Breeds in small colonies, often with other herons and egrets. Lays 2–4 eggs on a platform of sticks and reeds either in reeds or in a low tree. **Diet:** Fish, tadpoles and aquatic invertebrates. (Ralreier)

## 5 Malagasy Pond-Heron *Ardeola idae*

          ■ ■ ■ ■
J F M A M J J A S O N D

45–48 cm; 280–380 g  Vagrant. Slightly larger than Squacco Heron with a heavier bill. Br. plumage, seldom seen in Africa, is completely white. Non-br. ad. is dark brown (not buffy) above, with much broader and darker streaking on throat and breast than Squacco Heron; tends to show a sharper contrast between streaked breast and white belly. Juv. duller, with brown mottling in wings. **Voice:** Louder 'kruuk' than Squacco Heron. **Status and biology: ENDANGERED.** Rare non-br. visitor to Mozambique and E Zimbabwe from Madagascar. Occurs along vegetated lake shores, often in more open areas than Squacco Heron. **Diet:** Fish, frogs, small reptiles and invertebrates. (Madagaskar-ralreier)

## 6 White-backed Night-Heron *Gorsachius leuconotus*

b b b b b   b B B B B b
J F M A M J J A S O N D

50–56 cm; 400–500 g  A night heron with a large, dark head, conspicuous pale eye-ring, rufous neck and white throat. Generally appears much darker than Black-crowned Night-Heron (p. 68). Dark back and wings contrast with the small white back in flight and during display. Bill black with white base to lower mandible; eyes dark red-brown; lores yellow (blue in pre-br. birds); legs yellow. Juv. paler brown above with a streaked neck and white-spotted wing coverts. Has black (not yellow) bill and larger dark cap than juv. Black-crowned Night-Heron; mantle plain; white back develops with age. **Voice:** Sharp 'kaaark' when disturbed. **Status and biology:** Uncommon resident at slow-moving rivers overhung with dense vegetation. Easily overlooked; roosts during day in dense cover; more nocturnal than Black-crowned Night-Heron. Breeds singly, laying 2–4 eggs on a stick platform built in a low branch overhanging water. **Diet:** Fish, frogs and aquatic invertebrates. (Witrugnagreier)

## 1 Eurasian Bittern  *Botaurus stellaris*

bbb|||||||bbbb
J F M A M J J A S O N D

**65–75 cm; 1–1.3 kg** Rare. Larger than juv. Black-crowned Night-Heron with tawny, heavily streaked plumage, a black crown and broad, conspicuous moustachial stripes. Juv. is less heavily marked above, with reduced black cap. Typically remains in dense cover; more often heard than seen. Flight owl-like, with bowed, rounded wings. **Voice:** Deep, resonant, 3–5-note boom, similar to grunting of a distant lion. **Status and biology:** Rare resident and local nomad in extensive reedbeds, sedges and flooded grassland. Breeds singly, laying 2–4 eggs on a platform of reed stems built low down in dense, marshy vegetation. **Diet:** Fish, frogs and aquatic invertebrates. (Grootrietreier)

## 2 Black-crowned Night-Heron  *Nycticorax nycticorax*

bbbbbbbbBBbb
J F M A M J J A S O N D

**54–60 cm; 500–700 g** A stocky, compact heron with a heavy, blackish bill, reddish eyes and yellow legs. Ad. distinctive: black crown, nape and back contrast with grey wings and tail, and white underparts. Juv. grey-brown with white spotting above; underparts whitish with dark brown streaks; bill yellowish with dark tip. Larger than juv. Green-backed Heron, with shorter, deeper bill. Juv. smaller than Eurasian Bittern; plumage colder grey-brown, lacking black streaking and barring. Yellow bill, spotted (not streaked) back, small cap and paler eyes distinguish it from juv. White-backed Night Heron (p. 68). **Voice:** Harsh 'kwok' in flight. **Status and biology:** Common resident, nomad and migrant at lakes, rivers and rocky shores. A bird ringed in Europe was recovered in Mozambique. Roosts communally in reeds or trees during the day, flying out at dusk to feed. Breeds colonially (up to 1 000 pairs), usually with other herons, egrets, cormorants and ibises. Lays 2–4 eggs on a platform of sticks and reeds, either in reeds or in a tree. **Diet:** Fish, frogs, birds, mammals and invertebrates; often raids nests of other waterbirds, especially Cattle Egrets. (Gewone Nagreier)

## 3 Green-backed Heron  *Butorides striata*

BBBbbbbBBBBB
J F M A M J J A S O N D

**40–44 cm; 200–230 g** A small, dark heron with an erectile black crown. Stands motionless in characteristic hunched posture; bobs and flicks tail when alarmed. Ad. has dark, grey-green back and upperwings and paler grey underparts; black, wispy nape plume is not usually seen. From behind, back is greener and more scaled than Dwarf Bittern; underparts plain grey (not heavily streaked). Bill and legs yellowish, but in pre-br. period bill black and legs orange-red. Juv. is brown above, finely spotted whitish; buff below with dark brown streaks; fledgling has pink-orange legs. **Voice:** Sharp 'baaek' when flushed. **Status and biology:** Fairly common resident and local nomad at sluggish rivers overhung with trees, lake shores (often in rocky areas), mangroves and rocky shores. Breeds singly or in loose colonies, laying 2–5 eggs on a platform of sticks and reeds built among foliage in a small tree, usually over water. **Diet:** Fish, frogs and aquatic invertebrates. Often uses bait to attract fish. (Groenrugreier)

## 4 Dwarf Bittern  *Ixobrychus sturmii*

BBB||||||bB
J F M A M J J A S O N D

**26–30 cm; 130–170 g** A tiny, dark-backed heron with a rather broad neck; appears almost rail-like in flight. Ad. is dark slaty-blue above and buff below, with broad, dark stripes running down throat onto breast and belly. Bill blackish with pale green base to lower mandible. Legs yellowish-green, but orange in pre-br. period. Juv. paler; upperparts scalloped with buff; breast more rufous with finer streaking. **Voice:** Barking 'ra-ra-ra-ra-ra...' in display; otherwise silent. **Status and biology:** Uncommon intra-African migrant, following seasonal rains. Occurs at lakes and ponds surrounded by grass and trees; also mangroves. Breeds singly or in loose colonies, laying 2–5 eggs on a flimsy platform of sticks and grass built in flooded bushes or small trees. **Diet:** Small fish, frogs and aquatic invertebrates. (Dwergrietreier)

## 5 Little Bittern  *Ixobrychus minutus*

bBb|bbbBBBBb
J F M A M J J A S O N D

**30–36 cm; 120–150 g** A tiny, rather pale heron. Pale upperwing coverts contrast with dark flight feathers in flight (lacks uniform dark upperwing of smaller Dwarf Bittern). Male has greenish-black back and crown; female browner above, with striped foreneck. Palearctic *I. m. minutus* is slightly larger and paler than resident *I. m. payesii*, which has more rufous face and neck. Juv. is more heavily streaked below; smaller and more buffy than Green-backed Heron, with greenish (not yellowish) legs. **Voice:** Short bark, 'rao', every few seconds when displaying. **Status and biology:** Uncommon resident and local nomad (*I. m. payesii*) and Palearctic migrant (*I. m. minutus*), mainly in reedbeds. *I. m. payesii* breeds singly or in loose colonies, laying 2–5 eggs on a platform of reed stems among dense reeds. **Diet:** Small fish, frogs and aquatic invertebrates. (Kleinrietreier)

# STORKS

Large wading birds with long legs and necks. Bills usually dagger-like. Most species at least partly aquatic. Sexes alike; juvs distinct. Breed singly or colonially. Monogamous; both sexes incubate and feed the altricial chicks.

### 1 Black Stork  *Ciconia nigra*

J F M A M J J A S O N D

**95–110 cm; 2.5–3.2 kg** A large, glossy black stork with a white belly and undertail. Larger than Abdim's Stork, with black (not white) rump and lower back, red (not greenish) bill, and red face and legs. Juv. browner, with olive-yellow bill and legs. **Voice:** Silent except on nest, when loud whining and bill-clapping are given. **Status and biology:** Uncommon resident and nomad at lakes, rivers, estuaries and lagoons; population 1 000 pairs. Breeds singly, laying 2–5 eggs on a platform of sticks and reeds on a cliff ledge. Often reuses the same nest sites for many years. **Diet:** Mainly fish and frogs. (Grootswartooievaar)

### 2 Abdim's Stork  *Ciconia abdimii*

J F M A M J J A S O N D

**76–81 cm; 1.1–1.6 kg** A rather small, black stork with a white belly and undertail. Smaller than Black Stork, with white (not black) lower back and rump and greenish (not red) bill. Face is blue; legs are grey-green, with pink ankles and feet. In flight, legs do not project as far beyond tail as they do in Black Stork. Juv. duller and browner. **Voice:** Weak, 2-note whistle at nests and roosts; usually silent. **Status and biology:** Common intra-African migrant that breeds in the Sahel. Occurs in grassland and fields, often in large flocks and frequently with White Storks. **Diet:** Insects, especially locusts. (Kleinswartooievaar)

### 3 White Stork  *Ciconia ciconia*

J F M A M J J A S O N D

**100–120 cm; 2.4–4 kg** A large, mostly white stork with black primaries and secondaries. In flight, white tail differentiates it from Yellow-billed Stork. Bill and legs red, but red legs often appear white because birds excrete on them to cool down. Juv. has darker bill and legs; back and wing coverts tinged brown. **Voice:** Silent except on nest, when loud whining and bill-clapping are given. **Status and biology:** Common Palearctic migrant in grassland and fields; occasionally at shallow wetlands. Numbers fluctuate between years depending on rainfall elsewhere in Africa. A few pairs breed in the W Cape, laying 1–6 eggs on a large stick platform built in a tall tree or on a building. Nests often reused, but added to each year, and may reach up to 2 m high. **Diet:** Mainly insects (especially locusts), but also other invertebrates, small mammals, reptiles, chicks, frogs and fish. (Witooievaar)

### 4 Yellow-billed Stork  *Mycteria ibis*

J F M A M J J A S O N D

**95–105 cm; 1.2–2.4 kg** A white stork with black flight feathers and a long, slightly decurved, yellow bill. In flight, differs from White Stork by having black tail. Br. ad. has naked red facial skin and pink-tinged wing coverts and back. Juv. brownish above, washed grey-brown below, becoming whiter with age; head is mostly feathered, and facial skin, bill and legs are duller. **Voice:** Normally silent except during br. season, when it gives loud squeaks and hisses. **Status and biology:** Common resident and partial intra-African migrant at lakes, rivers and estuaries. Breeds colonially (10–50 pairs), often with other storks, herons, egrets, ibises and cormorants. Lays 2–4 eggs on a platform of sticks built in a tree. **Diet:** Fish, frogs and aquatic invertebrates. Feeds by touch with partly open bill, stirring up bottom sediments with its feet. (Nimmersat)

## 1 Marabou Stork  *Leptoptilos crumeniferus*

bBBBBb b
J F M A M J J A S O N D

**130–150 cm; 4.5–8.5 kg**  A huge stork with a grey, blade-like bill, a naked head and a pendulous throat pouch. In flight, head is tucked into shoulders, and dark grey wings contrast with white body. Juv. has head and neck covered with sparse, woolly down. **Voice:** Low, hoarse croak when alarmed; claps bill when displaying. **Status and biology:** Fairly common resident or local nomad in savanna, grassland and at wetlands; often around towns, scavenging at refuse dumps and abattoirs. Up to 30 pairs breed colonially, each laying 2–3 eggs on a stick platform built in a tall tree. **Diet:** Opportunistic; scavenges carrion and refuse; also large insects, fish, reptiles, small mammals and birds up to the size of flamingos. (Maraboe)

## 2 Saddle-billed Stork  *Ephippiorhynchus senegalensis*

bBBBbbbb
J F M A M J J A S O N D

**145–150 cm; 5–7 kg**  A very tall, black-and-white stork with a diagnostic red and black banded bill with a yellow 'saddle' at the base. In flight, wings are striking black and white. Male has brown eyes (female yellow), a small, yellow wattle (absent in female) and more black on wing in flight. Juv. is grey; head and neck brown; lacks yellow 'saddle' on bill; flight feathers greyish; leading edge of wing dark. **Voice:** Normally silent except for bill-clapping during display. **Status and biology:** Uncommon resident and nomad at freshwater dams, lakes and rivers. Usually solitary or in pairs. Breeds singly, laying 2–4 eggs on a large platform of mud, sticks and other vegetation on top of a tree; sometimes on top of an old raptor's nest. **Diet:** Mainly fish; also frogs, reptiles, small mammals, birds and invertebrates. (Saalbekooievaar)

## 3 African Openbill  *Anastomus lamelligerus*

BBBbb bbbbb
J F M A M J J A S O N D

**74–90 cm; 700–1 200 g**  A rather small, all-dark stork with an ivory-horn bill, which has a diagnostic wide, nutcracker-like gap between the mandibles. Ad. has glossy sheen to plumage. Juv. is duller and browner, with pale feather tips; fledges without noticeable bill gap, but this soon develops. **Voice:** Croaking 'honk', seldom uttered. **Status and biology:** Locally common resident and nomad at freshwater lakes and dams. Breeds colonially, occasionally up to 100 pairs, laying 3–5 eggs on a stick platform built in a tree or bush close to water. **Diet:** Mainly snails and mussels. (Oopbekooievaar)

## 4 Woolly-necked Stork  *Ciconia episcopus*

bBBBb
J F M A M J J A S O N D

**80–90 cm; 1.6–1.9 kg**  A glossy black stork with a diagnostic woolly, white neck, white belly and white undertail coverts (which extend to tip of black tail, appearing all-white from below). In flight, has white rump and lower back. Juv. is dull brown; black forehead extends further back on crown. **Voice:** Harsh croak; seldom uttered. **Status and biology:** Uncommon resident and intra-African migrant found at wetlands, often along rivers and streams; also mangroves, coastal mudflats and reefs. Attends grass fires. Solitary or in pairs, seldom in flocks. Breeds singly or in loose, small colonies of up to 5 pairs. Lays 2–4 eggs in a stick platform, well concealed in a large tree, usually overhanging water. **Diet:** Mainly insects; also other invertebrates, fish, frogs and reptiles. (Wolnekooievaar)

# FLAMINGOS

Peculiar waterbirds with long necks and legs, and bent bills adapted for filter feeding. Move between wetlands, mainly at night. Sexes alike, but males larger; juvs distinct. Breed erratically in large, dense colonies when water conditions are favourable. Monogamous; both sexes incubate and feed the semi-precocial chick.

### 1 Greater Flamingo *Phoenicopterus roseus*

B B b b b b b b b b B B
J F M A M J J A S O N D

**125–165 cm; 2.5–3.5 kg** The larger of the 2 African flamingos, with very long legs and neck. Ad. appears mostly white at rest (Lesser Flamingo appears pink); in flight, salmon-pink wing coverts contrast with white body and black flight feathers. Face and bill pale pink with a broad black bill tip; eyes creamy yellow; legs pink. Juv. is dirty grey-brown, becoming paler with age; bill pale grey with a darker tip; eyes brown; legs slate-grey. **Voice:** Noisy; goose-like honking. **Status and biology:** Common resident, intra-African migrant and nomad; 50 000 birds occur at shallow lakes, saltpans, lagoons, estuaries and sandy beaches. Usually in large flocks. Breeds in large colonies, laying 1 egg (rarely 2) in a mound of mud built on an island in a shallow pan. **Diet:** Mainly crustaceans and molluscs; feeds on large prey filtered from bottom sediments. (Grootflamink)

### 2 Lesser Flamingo *Phoenicopterus minor*

B B B B b b b b b b B B
J F M A M J J A S O N D

**90–125 cm; 1.5–2 kg** Smaller and generally brighter pink than Greater Flamingo. At a distance, flocks at rest appear pink, whereas Greater Flamingos appear white. In flight, median coverts are crimson, but appear less contrasting than those of Greater Flamingo. Ad. has a dark red face and bill; bill tip black, but bill appears uniformly dark from a distance. Eyes golden with purple eye-ring; legs pink. Juv. is dirty grey-brown, becoming paler with age; best told from Greater Flamingo by its dark purple-grey bill; legs grey. **Voice:** More muted honking than Greater Flamingo. **Status and biology:** NEAR-THREATENED. Locally common resident, intra-African migrant and nomad at lakes, saltpans and estuaries. Population fluctuates between years. Breeds sporadically in large colonies, laying 1 egg (rarely 2) in a mound of mud built on an island in a shallow pan. **Diet:** Blue-green algae and diatoms, mainly filtered from water surface; often swims in deep water. (Kleinflamink)

# HAMERKOP

A monotypic family confined to Africa and Madagascar. Sexes alike; juv. like ad.

### 3 Hamerkop *Scopus umbretta*

b b b b b b b B B b b b
J F M A M J J A S O N D

**50–58 cm; 400–600 g** A dark brown, heron-like bird with long black legs, a heavy crest and a flattened, boat-shaped, black bill. Hammer-shaped head profile is diagnostic, but often obscured when neck retracted and crest rests on its back. Flight buoyant, often gliding and soaring; could be confused with a raptor. **Voice:** Sharp 'kiep' in flight; jumbled mixture of querulous squawks and frog-like croaks during courtship. **Status and biology:** Fairly common resident at lakes, dams and rivers. Monogamous; breeds singly, laying 3–9 eggs in a huge, domed structure of sticks, with a small side entrance, usually built in a sturdy tree or on a cliff ledge. Both sexes incubate and feed the altricial chicks. **Diet:** Frogs and tadpoles, especially platannas (*Xenopus*); also fish, small mammals and aquatic invertebrates. (Hamerkop)

# SPOONBILLS

Large wading birds related to ibises with straight, spoon-tipped bills. Sexes alike; juvs duller. Breed colonially, often with herons, egrets, ibises and cormorants. Monogamous.

### 4 African Spoonbill *Platalea alba*

b b B B B B B B B b b b
J F M A M J J A S O N D

**86–92 cm; 1.4–1.8 kg** A tall, slender wading bird with diagnostic spoon-shaped bill. Flies with neck outstretched (not tucked in, as in herons and egrets). Ad. has a bare pink-red face, pale eyes, a grey bill with a pinkish border and base, and grey-pink legs. Juv. bill yellow-horn and shorter than ad.; legs dark grey; head streaked grey, and flight feathers tipped blackish. **Voice:** Low 'kaark'; at br. colonies emits various grunts and claps bill. **Status and biology:** Common resident and local nomad at lakes, flood plains and estuaries. Breeds colonially, often with ibises, egrets, herons and cormorants. Lays 2–4 eggs on a platform of sticks and reeds in trees or dense reeds. **Diet:** Small fish and aquatic invertebrates. Feeds with characteristic side-to-side sweeping motion of bill. (Lepelaar)

# IBISES

Fairly large birds with long legs and necks and decurved bills. Most species at least partly aquatic. Sexes alike; juvs distinct. Breed singly or colonially. Monogamous; both sexes incubate and feed the semi-altricial chicks.

## 1 Hadeda Ibis *Bostrychia hagedash*

b b b   b b b b B B B b
J F M A M J J A S O N D

**76–85 cm; 1–1.5 kg** A large, stout, grey-brown ibis with glossy bronze-green wing coverts. Grey face has whitish stripe running from bill to below and behind eye. Shortish, deep bill is dark grey with a red ridge on the upper mandible. Juv. has duller, shorter bill. In flight, wings broad; neck and legs short compared to Glossy Ibis. **Voice:** Noisy; gives a raucous 'ha-da' or 'ha-ha-da-da' call in flight. **Status and biology:** Common resident and nomad in forest clearings, woodland, savanna, grassland, farmland and on lawns. Range has expanded to W Cape in recent years, apparently in response to human habitat modification. Usually in small parties; roosts in trees. Breeds singly, laying 1–5 eggs in a large stick nest in a tree fork. **Diet:** Insects, worms, other invertebrates and small reptiles. (Hadeda)

## 2 Southern Bald Ibis *Geronticus calvus*

b B B b b
J F M A M J J A S O N D

**74–80 cm; 1–1.1 kg** A dark, glossy ibis. Ad. easily recognised by its bald, red head, long red bill, short red legs and glossy green neck ruff. Juv. duller, lacking coppery shoulder patch; head covered in short, light brown feathers; bill red only at base; legs brown. **Voice:** High-pitched, wheezing call. **Status and biology: VULNERABLE.** Endemic. Range has contracted. Locally common resident, with some 8 000 birds (2 000 pairs at about 200 colonies). Occurs in flocks in short grassland, often in burned areas. Breeds colonially, laying 1–3 eggs on a flimsy platform of sticks on a cliff ledge. **Diet:** Mainly insects, worms and other invertebrates. (Kalkoenibis)

## 3 Glossy Ibis *Plegadis falcinellus*

b b b b   b b b B B B
J F M A M J J A S O N D

**50–65 cm; 550–750 g** A rather small, slender ibis with long legs; appears blackish from a distance. In flight, wings, neck and legs are much longer than Hadeda Ibis. Br. ad. has a dark chestnut head, neck and body; wings, back and tail dark, glossy green and purple highlights. There is a narrow bluish-white line around base of bill. Non-br. ad. has a pale-flecked head and neck. Juv. resembles non-br. ad., but body is dull, sooty brown. **Voice:** Normally silent; low, guttural 'kok-kok-kok' when breeding. **Status and biology:** Locally common resident and nomad at lakes, dams, pans, estuaries and flooded grassland. Breeds colonially (up to 200 pairs), often with other ibises and egrets. Lays 2–4 eggs on a platform of reeds and sticks in dense reeds. **Diet:** Frogs, insects and other invertebrates. (Glansibis)

## 4 African Sacred Ibis *Threskiornis aethiopicus*

b b b b b b b b B B B b
J F M A M J J A S O N D

**66–84 cm; 1.2–1.9 kg** A large, white ibis with a heavy, decurved, black bill. Ad. has naked, black head and neck. Elongate, plume-like, black scapulars are fluffed out in display; make it appear black-tailed at rest. Flight feathers are tipped black, giving narrow black edge to wing. Br. ads have dirty yellow flanks and naked, pink skin on underwing (grey in non-br.). Juv. has white-feathered neck and greyish cast to plumage. **Voice:** Loud croaking at br. colonies. **Status and biology:** Common resident in open habitats, from wetlands and fields to grassland and offshore islands. Often in flocks; frequently flies in 'V' formation. Breeds colonially, often with egrets, herons and cormorants. Lays 2–3 (rarely 5) eggs on a platform of sticks or reeds in trees or among reeds. **Diet:** Mainly invertebrates, but also fish, frogs, small mammals, eggs and chicks, carrion and refuse. (Skoorsteenveër)

# DUCKS AND GEESE

Waterbirds with flattened bills that feed by diving, dabbling or grazing ashore. The 3 toes are webbed for swimming. Plumage fully waterproof; flight feathers moulted simultaneously, resulting in 3–4-week flightless period. Males appreciably larger than females (except whistling ducks), and differ in plumage in some species. Mating system varied. Incubation usually by female only; chicks precocial and able to feed themselves.

## 1 Spur-winged Goose  *Plectropterus gambensis*

B B B b b b b b b b B B
J F M A M J J A S O N D

**75–100 cm; 2.5–7 kg** A large, black goose with variable amounts of white on the face, throat, belly and forewings. Bill, face and legs pink-red. In flight, its large size and white forewing separate it from Comb Duck. Sexes alike in plumage, but males are much larger with more extensive facial skin with wattles. Juv. duller and browner; lacks bare facial skin, and white on forewing reduced or absent. **Voice:** A feeble, wheezy whistle in flight. **Status and biology:** Common resident and local nomad at wetlands and nearby grassland and fields. Often in large flocks. Usually monogamous; lays 7–14 eggs in a shallow scrape among dense waterside vegetation; nest lined with grass and down. **Diet:** Grasses, roots and other vegetable matter; often feeds at night. (Wildemakou)

## 2 Egyptian Goose  *Alopochen aegyptiaca*

b b b b b b B B B B B b
J F M A M J J A S O N D

**60–75 cm; 1.5–3.5 kg** A large, goose-like duck; mostly buffy brown with a dark brown face, neck ring and breast patch. Larger and longer-necked than South African Shelduck; stands more erect, and, in flight, the white secondary coverts have a thin, black subterminal bar. Juv. duller; only develops brown mask and breast patch after 3–5 months; forewing greyish. **Voice:** Male utters hoarse hisses, female a grunting honk; both honk repeatedly when alarmed or taking flight. **Status and biology:** Common resident and local nomad at wetlands and adjacent grassland and fields; also suburban areas and sheltered bays on the coast. Often gathers in large flocks when not breeding. Monogamous; lays 5–10 eggs in a shallow scrape on the ground, in a tree hole, an old bird's nest or even on a flat rooftop. **Diet:** Mainly grass and seeds. (Kolgans)

## 3 South African Shelduck  *Tadorna cana*

b b B B b
J F M A M J J A S O N D

**60–65 cm; 900–1 800 g** Smaller, with a shorter neck and legs than Egyptian Goose; stance more horizontal. Plumage warm russet and brown. Male head grey; female has a white face (extent of white varies considerably). In flight, both sexes have white forewings without a black line across the secondary coverts. Juv. is like male but duller, with head suffused brown and dusky brown upperwing coverts. **Voice:** Nasal honk; male voice deeper. **Status and biology:** Endemic. Common resident and local nomad at freshwater lakes and dams in drier areas. Gathers in large flocks at perennial wetlands to moult after breeding. Monogamous; lays 6–14 eggs in a hole in the ground; favours old aardvark burrows. **Diet:** Mainly plant matter, but some aquatic invertebrates. (Kopereend)

## 4 Comb Duck  *Sarkidiornis melanotos*

B B B b b b b B
J F M A M J J A S O N D

**56–76 cm; 1–2.5 kg** A large duck with a speckled head and contrasting blue-black and white plumage. Wings black. Male has a rounded knob on the bill, which enlarges during the br. season. Female is smaller with no bill knob and a paler patch on the lower back. Juv. duller, with dark speckling on the breast, belly and flanks and a pale supercilium and dark eye-line; could be confused with female Garganey (p. 84), but is much larger and lacks scaled breast and flanks. **Voice:** Whistles, but usually silent. **Status and biology:** Locally common nomad and intra-African summer migrant at pans and lakes in woodland and along larger rivers; also forages in old croplands. Polygamous when conditions favourable; otherwise monogamous. Lays 6–14 eggs in a tree hole or old Hamerkop nest. **Diet:** Seeds and other vegetable matter, both on land and in water. (Knobbeleend)

## 1 White-faced Duck   *Dendrocygna viduata*

BBbb bbbbB
J F M A M J J A S O N D

**44–48 cm; 550–900 g** A dark brown duck with a diagnostic white face and throat (sometimes stained brown), chestnut foreneck and blackish belly. Much darker on neck and breast than Fulvous Duck, with finely barred flanks and blackish vent. Appears all-dark in flight apart from the white face. Juv. has a dirty brown face. **Voice:** Distinctive 3-note whispy whistle 'whit we-weeer'. **Status and biology:** Common resident and local nomad at freshwater lakes, lagoons and adjacent grassland, often in large flocks. Monogamous; lays 7–13 eggs in a grass-lined scrape among dense vegetation. **Diet:** Seeds, fresh shoots and invertebrates, taken on land and in water; occasionally dives for up to 10 seconds. (Nonnetjie-eend)

## 2 Fulvous Duck   *Dendrocygna bicolor*

BBBbbbbbbbbb
J F M A M J J A S O N D

**43–50 cm; 600–900 g** Structure similar to White-faced Duck, but with a golden brown head, breast and belly, a dark line down the back of the neck, and conspicuous white flank stripes. In flight, the creamy uppertail coverts contrast with the dark brown wings, rump and tail; vent white. Juv. paler than ad.; lacks buff scaling on mantle. **Voice:** Soft, disyllabic whistle. **Status and biology:** Locally common resident and nomad at freshwater lakes and dams. Monogamous; lays 6–13 eggs in a scrape among dense vegetation; sometimes in a mound of vegetation among flooded reeds or sedges. **Diet:** Aquatic plants, seeds and invertebrates; dives for up to 20 seconds. (Fluiteend)

## 3 White-backed Duck   *Thalassornis leuconotus*

BBBBBbbbbbbB
J F M A M J J A S O N D

**38–42 cm; 560–700 g** A fairly small, compact duck that appears vaguely grebe-like. It is large-headed with a characteristic humped back. Plumage is barred buff and dark brown with a white spot at the base of the bill; the white back is only visible in flight. It is an excellent diver; seldom seen in flight; spends much of the day roosting with its head tucked into its scapulars. **Voice:** A low-pitched whistle, rising on the second syllable. **Status and biology:** Locally common resident and local nomad found at wetlands with water lilies or other floating vegetation. Lays 4–9 eggs on a mound of aquatic vegetation, usually anchored to, and partially concealed by, emergent vegetation. **Diet:** Mainly seeds of aquatic plants. (Witrugeend)

## 4 African Pygmy-Goose   *Nettapus auritus*

BBBbb bbBB
J F M A M J J A S O N D

**30–33 cm; 230–320 g** A tiny duck with distinctive orange breast and flanks, white face and dark greenish upperparts. Male has bright yellow bill and lime green neck patch, neatly edged black. Female and juv. duller with indistinct head markings. In flight has a large white wing patch formed by the inner secondaries and greater coverts; underwing coverts blackish. Often sits motionless among floating vegetation. **Voice:** A soft, repeated 'tsui-tsui'. **Status and biology:** Locally common resident at freshwater lakes with floating vegetation, especially *Nymphaea* lilies. Monogamous; lays 6–13 eggs in a hole in a tree or cliff, usually near water. **Diet:** Mainly seeds and flowers of water lilies; feeds at surface and by diving. (Dwerggans)

## 5 Southern Pochard   *Netta erythrophthalma*

BBBbbbbbBBBB
J F M A M J J A S O N D

**48–51 cm; 550–950 g** A fairly large, dark brown duck. Male glossy with paler, chestnut brown flanks, a pale blue bill and bright red eyes. Female dark brown with pale facial patches: one at the base of the bill, the other a crescent extending behind the eye. Juv. lacks the female's white facial crescent. Both have paler vents. In flight, there is a distinct white wing bar extending onto the primaries. Very different shape from Maccoa Duck, with a slender bill. **Voice:** Male makes a whining sound; female quacks. **Status and biology:** Common resident and local nomad at lakes and dams, preferring areas with deeper water. Monogamous; lays 5–14 eggs in a well-concealed nest on the ground or among aquatic vegetation. **Diet:** Water lily seeds, other plant matter and invertebrates; dives for up to 18 seconds, but also dabbles and grazes. (Bruineend)

## 6 Maccoa Duck   *Oxyura maccoa*

BBBbbbbbBBBB
J F M A M J J A S O N D

**48–51 cm; 550–800 g** A stiff-tailed duck with characteristic dumpy body, short neck and broad, deep-based bill. Br. male has a chestnut body, black head and blue bill. Female and eclipse male are dark brown with a pale stripe under the eye and a paler throat, giving the head a striped appearance (lacks pale crescent behind eye of female Southern Pochard). Sits low in the water, often with its stiff tail cocked at a 45° angle. In flight, the upperwing is uniform dark brown. **Voice:** A peculiar, nasal trill. **Status and biology: NEAR-THREATENED.** Uncommon resident and nomad at freshwater lakes, dams and lagoons. Polygamous; lays 3–9 eggs in a bowl of reeds or sedges built among flooded vegetation. Also dumps eggs in nests of other ducks and coots. **Diet:** Mainly aquatic invertebrates; dives for up to 22 seconds. (Bloubekeend)

## 1 Yellow-billed Duck   *Anas undulata*

B B B b b b B B B B B B
J F M A M J J A S O N D

**52–58 cm; 700–1 150 g**  A dark brown duck with a distinctive bright yellow bill with a black saddle. Sexes alike. Pale feather edges give it a scaled appearance at close range; scaling less distinct in juvs. Structure similar to African Black Duck; told apart in flight by blue-green (not purple-blue) speculum narrowly edged with white, and grey (not white) underwings. **Voice:** Male gives a rasping hiss; female quacks. **Status and biology:** Common resident and local nomad at freshwater lakes, ponds and flooded fields; also lagoons and estuaries. Often in flocks. Monogamous; lays 4–10 eggs in a shallow scrape among dense waterside vegetation; nest lined with grass and down. Occasionally hybridises with Red-billed Teal (p. 84) and Mallard. **Diet:** Aquatic plants and invertebrates, mainly obtained by dabbling or up-ending in shallow water. (Geelbekeend)

## 2 African Black Duck   *Anas sparsa*

b b B B B B B B B b b b
J F M A M J J A S O N D

**48–58 cm; 780–1 200 g**  A dark, sooty-coloured duck with white speckles on the back and orange legs. Darker than Yellow-billed Duck, with a blue-grey bill with a blackish saddle and pinkish base. Sitting on the water, it appears long-bodied. In flight, the purple-blue speculum, bordered white, is bluer than that of Yellow-billed Duck, and the underwing is whitish (not grey). Juv. paler with a whitish belly and less brightly coloured legs. **Voice:** Female quacks in flight; males give high-pitched, peeping whistle. **Status and biology:** Fairly common resident along streams and rivers; less frequent on ponds and dams. Monogamous; lays 4–10 eggs in a deep bowl of vegetation built close to water on the ground or rarely in a tree hole or snag; nest lined with down. Pairs defend territories year-round. **Diet:** Aquatic invertebrates and plants obtained by dabbling or up-ending; forages mainly at dawn and dusk. (Swarteend)

## 3 Mallard   *Anas platyrhynchos*

b b b b b b
J F M A M J J A S O N D

**50–64 cm; 850–1 400 g**  Introduced from Europe. Br. male has a glossy, bottle-green head, white ring around the neck and chestnut breast. Females and eclipse males superficially resemble Yellow-billed Ducks, but are paler brown with a horn-coloured bill and a dark line through the eye. The domesticated form of Mallard is larger with a heavy 'bottom' and has a khaki (not grey) back. **Voice:** Male gives a rasping hiss; female quacks. **Status and biology:** Feral populations derived from escapees occur at some wetlands and are subject to management controls. Hybridises with Yellow-billed Duck, African Black Duck and Cape Shoveler. **Diet:** Aquatic plants and invertebrates; also grass on land. (Groenkopeend)

## 4 Cape Shoveler   *Anas smithii*

b b b b b b B B B B b b
J F M A M J J A S O N D

**48–54 cm; 450–750 g**  An elongate duck with a long, black, spatulate bill. Both sexes have finely speckled grey-brown plumage. Male has a paler, greyer head than female, with a darker bill, paler yellow eyes, brighter orange legs, and more prominent blue-grey upperwing coverts. Female and juv. are darker and less rufous than Northern Shoveler, especially on their head and neck, and have a smaller and darker, slate-grey bill lacking any orange tinge along the margins. **Voice:** Female quacks; male makes a soft, rasping call. Wings make distinctive whirring noise on takeoff. **Status and biology:** Endemic. Common resident and local nomad at freshwater lakes and ponds, often in flocks. Monogamous; lays 6–12 eggs in a scrape on the ground among dense waterside vegetation; nest lined with grass and down. **Diet:** Aquatic invertebrates and plants; feeds mainly in shallow water, filtering water and mud with bill lamellae. (Kaapse Slopeend)

## 5 Northern Shoveler   *Anas clypeata*

**44–52 cm; 350–550 g**  Rare vagrant. Male in br. plumage is unmistakable, with a green head, white breast and chestnut belly and flanks. In flight has a powder-blue forewing. Female and eclipse male are dull rufous brown, paler and warmer than Cape Shoveler, especially on the head and neck; bill heavier, longer and more spatulate. Female has white edges to tail and orange bill margins. **Voice:** Male gives a nasal 'crook, crook'; female quacks. **Status and biology:** Palearctic vagrant to inland water bodies; most records probably are escapees. **Diet:** Aquatic invertebrates and plants. (Europese Slopeend)

## 1 Northern Pintail *Anas acuta*

**50–65 cm; 600–1 200 g** Rare vagrant. Br. plumage male is striking, with a dark, chocolate-brown head, a white stripe running down the side of the neck to the white breast, lanceolate back feathers and long central tail feathers. Female and eclipse male are speckled tan and brown with a blue-grey bill, a long, slender neck, plain buffy face, and a brown speculum with a white trailing edge. Tail pointed in both sexes. **Voice:** Male gives a soft, nasal honk; female quacks. **Status and biology:** Breeds in Palearctic; winters in N Africa; vagrant to freshwater wetlands. **Diet:** Aquatic plants and animals mostly obtained by diving in shallow water. (Pylsterteend)

## 2 Garganey *Anas querquedula*

J F M A M J J A S O N D

**37–41 cm; 300–550 g** Rare vagrant. Br. plumage male has a large white eyebrow and black-and-white, lanceolate back feathers. The brown breast is sharply demarcated by the white belly and pale grey flanks. Female and eclipse male have a pale supercilium and dark eye-stripe. Differ in shape from female Maccoa Duck (p. 80) and juv. Comb Duck (p. 78). In flight, both sexes have pale blue forewings and green speculums superficially similar to Cape and Northern shovelers (p. 82). **Voice:** A nasal 'quack' and some harsh rattles. **Status and biology:** Scarce Palearctic migrant to lakes and marshes. **Diet:** Aquatic plants and animals obtained mainly by dabbling and up-ending. (Somereend)

## 3 Cape Teal *Anas capensis*

b b b b b b B B B B b b
J F M A M J J A S O N D

**44–48 cm; 350–520 g** A pale grey duck with a rather plain, bulbous-looking head, bright red eye and pink bill with black base and bluish tip. In flight it has a dark greenish speculum bordered by white. Easily distinguished from Red-billed Teal by its pale head that lacks a dark cap; wing patterns quite different. Sexes alike; juv. duller with narrower pale feather margins. **Voice:** A thin whistle, usually given in flight. **Status and biology:** Locally common resident and nomad at fresh or saline wetlands, especially saltpans, lagoons and sewage works. Monogamous; lays 4–13 eggs in a shallow scrape among dense waterside vegetation; nest lined with grass and down. **Diet:** Aquatic invertebrates and some plant matter. Mainly feeds in shallow water, dabbling or up-ending, but occasionally dives. (Teeleend)

## 4 Red-billed Teal *Anas erythrorhyncha*

B B B B b b b B B B B B
J F M A M J J A S O N D

**43–48 cm; 400–850 g** Readily identified by its dark cap, pale cheeks and red bill with a dark saddle. Larger than Hottentot Teal, with red (not blue) bill. Told from Cape Teal by its dark cap and darker brown (not grey) plumage. In flight, has warm buff secondaries, lacking an iridescent speculum. Female has a broader black bill saddle than male. **Voice:** Male gives a soft, nasal whistle; female quacks. **Status and biology:** Common resident and local nomad at freshwater wetlands. Monogamous, but male deserts before young can fly. Lays 5–15 eggs in a shallow scrape among dense waterside vegetation; nest lined with grass and down. **Diet:** Mainly seeds and other plant matter obtained in shallow water. (Rooibekeend)

## 5 Hottentot Teal *Anas hottentota*

B B B B b b b b b b b b
J F M A M J J A S O N D

**32–36 cm; 200–280 g** A tiny duck with a dark crown, cream cheeks and distinctive dark smudges extending from the ear coverts down the neck. Much smaller than Red-billed Teal, with a blue (not red) bill. In flight has a green speculum (brighter in male) with a white trailing edge, and a black-and-white underwing. Juv. duller. **Voice:** Generally silent; utters high-pitched quacks on taking wing. **Status and biology:** Locally common resident and nomad at freshwater wetlands, favouring areas with emergent or floating vegetation. Monogamous; lays 5–12 eggs in a deep bowl, close to water, on the ground or among flooded reeds; nest lined with grass, leaves and down. **Diet:** Aquatic invertebrates and plant matter. (Gevlekte Eend)

# VULTURES

Large scavengers with broad wings and deeply slotted primaries adapted for soaring in thermals. Cover vast distances in search of food. Sexes alike in most species; juvs typically duller; take up to 6 years to acquire ad. plumage. Monogamous; breed singly or in colonies. Both sexes incubate and feed the semi-altricial chicks.

## 1 Lappet-faced Vulture *Aegypius tracheliotos*

bBBbbb
J F M A M J J A S O N D

**98–115 cm; 4.5–8.5 kg** A large, blackish vulture with deeply slotted primaries and a short, wedge-shaped tail. Ads have conspicuous white thighs and a white bar across the inner underwing coverts. At close range, horn-coloured bill and wrinkled red face and throat are diagnostic. Juv. is dark brown, with paler head and conspicuous white streaks on mantle; is much larger than Hooded Vulture (p. 88). **Voice:** High-pitched whistling display. **Status and biology: VULNERABLE.** But locally fairly common in savanna, especially in more arid areas. Nests and roosts on trees. Breeds singly or in loose colonies, laying 1 egg (rarely 2) on a large stick platform on the top of a small tree. **Diet:** Dominates other vultures when scavenging from large mammal carcasses; favours skin and tendons over muscle and soft organs. Also takes eggs and kills young antelope and flamingos. (Swartaasvoël)

## 2 White-headed Vulture *Aegypius occipitalis*

bBBbbb
J F M A M J J A S O N D

**92–96 cm; 3.3–5.3 kg** A strikingly coloured vulture; ads have a diagnostic white belly, extending as a white line along the trailing edge of the underwing coverts. Ad. female also has white inner secondaries and tertials. Angular head is white, with naked pink face; bill orange-red, with a pale blue cere. Juv. is dark brown, with a narrow whitish line along the trailing edge of the underwing coverts. **Voice:** High-pitched chittering. **Status and biology: VULNERABLE.** Uncommon to locally common resident and nomad in open savanna; roosts and nests on trees. Territorial; breeds singly, laying 1 egg in a stick nest built on top of a tree. **Diet:** Carrion from large mammal carcasses. (Witkopaasvoël)

## 3 White-backed Vulture *Gyps africanus*

bBbbbb
J F M A M J J A S O N D

**90–100 cm; 4.6–6.6 kg** The most common vulture in savanna areas. Ad's whitish lower back and pale brown mantle and upperwing coverts contrast with dark flight and tail feathers. White underwing coverts contrast with blackish flight feathers and grey-brown body (body and underwing coverts similar colour in Cape Vulture). Body is slightly streaked. Eyes and bill blackish. Juv. is dark brown, with only a thin, pale line on dark grey-brown underwing; underwing coverts darker than juv. Cape Vulture; coverts gradually whiten with age, contrasting with body. **Voice:** Harsh cackles and hisses. **Status and biology: NEAR-THREATENED.** Common in savanna and open woodland, nesting and roosting on trees. Breeds singly or in loose colonies, laying 1 egg (rarely 2–3) on a platform nest built on top of a tree; rarely on a pylon. **Diet:** Carrion from large mammal carcasses; occasionally kills young mammals. (Witrugaasvoël)

## 4 Cape Vulture *Gyps coprotheres*

bBbb
J F M A M J J A S O N D

**100–118 cm; 7.4–10.8 kg** Larger than White-backed Vulture; ad. has much paler, cream body and wing coverts, contrasting with dark tail and flight feathers. At close range, ad's eyes are yellow and it has 2 patches of blue skin at the base of the neck. Greater upperwing coverts have dark centres (more obvious in ads). Juv. has dark eye and neck skin flushed pink; body and wing coverts are darker brown, but shows more contrast with dark flight feathers than White-backed Vulture; little contrast between underwing coverts and body at any age. **Voice:** Cackling and hissing. **Status and biology: VULNERABLE.** Endemic. Range has contracted, but remains locally common in core of range. Roosts and nests on cliffs, ranging out over adjacent grassland and arid savanna in search of food. Scarce in well-wooded savanna; bush encroachment may have contributed to its demise in Namibia. Breeds colonially, laying 1 egg (rarely 2) on a mound of vegetation built on a cliff ledge. **Diet:** Carrion from large mammal carcasses; dominates other vultures, except Lappet-faced. (Kransaasvoël)

## 5 Rüppell's Vulture *Gyps rueppellii*

J F M A M J J A S O N D

**95–107 cm; 6.8–8 kg** Rare vagrant. Intermediate in size between Cape and White-backed vultures (**5 A**: Rüppell's – above, White-backed – below). Ad. has silvery-edged contour feathers that give it a diagnostic scaled or spotted appearance; bill and eyes yellow. Underwing uniform (not 2-tone like Cape Vulture and ad. White-backed Vulture); differs from juv. White-backed Vulture by scaled body and underwing coverts. Juv. has blackish bill and eyes; pale feather edges buffy and much narrower, appearing darker and streaked (not scaled); juv. bill is black; neck reddish-pink. **Voice:** Noisy hissing and cackling. **Status and biology: NEAR-THREATENED.** Vagrant from further N in Africa, occasionally at Cape Vulture colonies. Breeds and roosts on cliffs. (Rüppellaasvoël)

## 1 Bearded Vulture *Gypaetus barbatus*

 J F M A M J J A S O N D

**110 cm; 5.2–6.2 kg** A large vulture with long, pointed wings and a long, wedge-shaped tail. Ad. is mainly dark, with rufous head and underparts. Black facemask has black 'beard', but this is visible only at close range. Juv. is dark brown; underparts gradually lighten with age. **Voice:** Silent except for high-pitched whistling display. **Status and biology:** Uncommon resident in remote, mountainous areas; range has contracted in last century. Breeds singly, laying 1–2 (rarely 3) eggs on a ledge or in a hole on a large cliff face. **Diet:** Mainly bones scavenged from carcasses; swallows smaller bones whole; breaks open large bones by dropping them onto rocks. (Baardaasvoël)

## 2 Palm-nut Vulture *Gypohierax angolensis*

 J F M A M J J A S O N D

**60 cm; 1.4–1.8 kg** A small, black-and-white vulture. Shape resembles that of African Fish-Eagle (p. 90), but is smaller and has very different plumage pattern. Wings are broader than Egyptian Vulture's, with mostly white (not black) primaries; tail is rounded, black, tipped with white (not white and wedge-shaped). Juv. is brown; smaller than Hooded Vulture, and with much heavier bill. **Voice:** Usually silent; 'kok-kok-kok' in flight. **Status and biology:** Local and uncommon in forest, woodland and coastal areas, usually near raphia palms. Occasionally wanders widely. Breeds singly, laying 1 egg in a large nest built high up in the heart of a raphia palm or large tree. **Diet:** Fruit of raphia and oil palms; also fish, crabs and other invertebrates, frogs, small mammals and carrion. (Witaasvoël)

## 3 Egyptian Vulture *Neophron percnopterus*

J F M A M J J A S O N D

**58–71 cm; 1.6–2.1 kg** Vagrant. A small, slender-billed vulture with a bare face and throat and a long tail. Ad. is white, with black flight feathers. In flight, wedge-shaped tail and rather long, narrow wings, bent at wrist, are distinctive. Juv. is dark brown; wedge-shaped tail and long, very slender bill separate it from juv. Palm-nut and Hooded vultures; much smaller than juv. Bearded Vulture with dark body. **Voice:** Soft grunts and hisses when excited. **Status and biology: ENDANGERED.** Formerly bred in grassland and savanna in the region, but local population (which was genetically distinct) is either extinct or close to extinction. Lays 1–2 eggs on a cliff ledge or hole. **Diet:** Scraps and carrion; also Ostrich and other large, ground-nesting birds' eggs. (Egiptiese Aasvoël)

## 4 Hooded Vulture *Necrosyrtes monachus*

J F M A M J J A S O N D

**65–75 cm; 1.8–2.6 kg** A small, brown vulture with a slender bill. Larger than Palm-nut Vulture, with down (not feathers) on head and neck. In flight, wings are broad and tail is rounded (not wedge-shaped, as in Egyptian Vulture). Ad. has mostly bare, pink head. Juv. is darker brown, with blackish-brown head and mostly pale bill. **Voice:** Soft, whistling calls at nest; normally silent. **Status and biology:** Uncommon resident in savanna and woodland. Breeds singly or in loose colonies; lays 1 egg in a fairly small stick nest built in the high fork of a tree, usually concealed in the canopy. **Diet:** Scavenges scraps at carcasses, but displaced by larger vultures. Also insects, including termites, and faeces; rarely kills its own prey. (Monnikaasvoël)

# FISH-EAGLES

Large, broad-winged eagles more closely related to kites than other eagles. Often feed on fish, but take a wide variety of prey, including carrion. Sexes alike; juvs distinct, taking several years to acquire ad. plumage. Monogamous and territorial.

## 1 African Fish-Eagle *Haliaeetus vocifer*

bbBBbb
J F M A M J J A S O N D

**63–73 cm; 2–3.8 kg** A large, broad-winged eagle with a short tail. Ad. has unmistakable black and chestnut plumage with a white head, breast and tail. Female larger with a broader white breast. Juv. is dark brown, with scruffy white patches on head, belly, underwing coverts and primary bases; tail is longer than ad's, white with a brown tip. Head and breast gradually whiten with age, taking 4–5 years to acquire ad. plumage. Could be confused with juv. Palm-nut Vulture, but is larger with longer wings; plumage darker brown and white base of tail is diagnostic. **Voice:** Ringing 'kyow-kow-kow' with head thrown back, from perches or in flight; male's call is higher pitched. **Status and biology:** Common resident at large rivers, lakes, estuaries and lagoons. Lays 1–4 (usually 2) eggs in a huge stick nest built in a tree fork or canopy. Occasionally rears chicks. Pairs remain together in successive years, often re-using the same nest. **Diet:** Fish, birds, small crocodiles, other reptiles, carrion and termites; often steals prey from other raptors. (Visarend)

# OSPREY

A widespread, monotypic family. Legs and feet are adapted for grasping fish, with a reversible outer toe and strongly curved claws. Sexes alike; juv. like ad. Monogamous and territorial.

## 2 Osprey *Pandion haliaetus*

J F M A M J J A S O N D

**52–68 cm; 1.25–1.85 kg** A distinctive hawk with long, narrow wings held with bent wrists, emphasising the black carpal patches on an otherwise pale underwing. Sometimes hovers when hunting. Upperparts are dark brown; underparts and crown white. Much smaller than imm. African Fish-Eagle; easily separated on wing shape. Female has darker partial breast band. Juv. has pale-fringed upperpart feathers and dark-spotted crown. **Voice:** Shrill whistles, but usually silent in Africa. **Status and biology:** Fairly common Palearctic migrant to wetlands, estuaries and sheltered marine areas. May occasionally breed in the region; lays 1–4 eggs on a large stick platform nest. **Diet:** Almost exclusively fish, caught by plunging feet-first from up to 50 m in the air; rarely takes rodents or birds. (Visvalk)

# BATELEUR

A distinctive, short-tailed raptor related to the snake-eagles but with dark eyes at all ages. Highly aerial; soar with characteristic rocking flight action. Sexes distinct; juvs take several years to acquire ad. plumage. Monogamous.

## 3 Bateleur *Terathopius ecaudatus*

bBBBb
J F M A M J J A S O N D

**55–70 cm; 1.9–2.9 kg** Easily identified in flight by its long wings with broad, bulging secondaries and very short tail; toes extend beyond tail tip. At rest, rear crown feathers are elongated, giving a slightly crested appearance. Flight action distinctive: rocks from side to side with wings held in a shallow 'V'; rarely flaps. Ad. has bold black, white and chestnut plumage and bare red face and legs. Male has black secondaries and inner primaries; only tips of flight feathers are black in female, giving a mostly white underwing and a pale grey panel on the upperwing. Back, rump and tail usually russet, but 5–10% have these parts much paler buff (cream morph). Juv. brown with paler feather tips, appearing scaly; tail longer than ad.; legs pale, cere pale blue-green. Imm. dark brown, darker and less scaly than juv.; face dull yellow; legs pinkish. Takes 4 moults and 6–7 years to acquire ad. plumage; older imm. plumages start to show some ad. plumage features, usually in a patchy, incomplete manner. **Voice:** Usually silent; gives a loud bark, 'kow-wah', and makes noisy wing beats in aerial display. **Status and biology:** Common resident in savanna in large protected areas; scarce elsewhere due to poisoning. Often seen on ground at waterholes. Monogamous, often retaining the same mate in successive years. Breeds singly, laying 1 egg in a stick nest built in the main fork of a large tree. Unlike most eagles, both sexes share incubation and brooding duties. **Diet:** Mammals, birds, reptiles and occasional frogs, fish and insects. Mainly a scavenger in some areas, searching for roadkill and attending fires. (Berghaan)

# SNAKE-EAGLES

Fairly small, compact raptors with large, pale eyes set in a fairly large, square head, and bare lower legs (tarsi). Sexes alike, with little size dimorphism; juvs and imms differ. Monogamous and territorial; breed singly. Incubation mainly by female; chick brooded by female only and fed by male.

## 1 Brown Snake-Eagle *Circaetus cinereus*

B B b | | | | b b | | b B
J F M A M J J A S O N D

**70–75 cm; 1.6–2.4 kg** Differs from other brown eagles by its large head (accentuated by elongated rear crown feathers), prominent yellow eyes and pale, bare legs; bill black, cere pale grey. In flight, dark brown underwing coverts contrast with silvery flight feathers; tail uniformly barred. Juv. variable: some all-brown, with a slightly scaled appearance; others have variable white blotches on underparts and white streaking on the crown and nape. Mottled juvs are larger and darker brown than juv. Black-chested Snake-Eagle, with more strongly barred tail. All-brown birds could be confused with juv. Bateleur (p. 90), but have pale eyes; in flight, paler flight feathers and flight silhouette are distinctive. **Voice:** Croaking 'hok-hok-hok-hok' flight call; generally silent. **Status and biology:** Locally common resident and nomad in savanna and woodland. Lays 1 egg in a stick nest built on top of a tree. **Diet:** Mainly snakes; also lizards, small mammals and birds. (Bruinslangarend)

## 2 Black-chested Snake-Eagle *Circaetus pectoralis*

| | | b b b b B B B b |
J F M A M J J A S O N D

**63–68 cm; 1.2–2.2 kg** A small, large-headed eagle with large yellow eyes and pale, bare legs at all ages. Much smaller than Martial Eagle (p. 92). Ad. lacks dark belly spots and has whitish (not dark) underwing coverts; from beneath, flight feathers white with 3–4 black bars across secondaries, inner primaries and tail. Juv. has rufous body and underwing coverts, becoming pale brown below, with pale, lightly barred underwings and undertail. Imm. has brown blotches on the belly and variable pale markings on the head. In flight, wings held angled at the wrist, recalling Osprey (p. 90); sometimes hovers. **Voice:** Rarely calls; melodious, whistled 'kwo-kwo-kwo-kweeu'. **Status and biology:** Uncommon to locally common nomad in savanna, semi-desert and woodland. Lays 1 egg (rarely 2) in a stick nest built at the top of a tree or pylon. **Diet:** Snakes; also lizards, frogs, small mammals, insects and occasional birds and fish. (Swartborsslangarend)

## 3 Southern Banded Snake-Eagle *Circaetus fasciolatus*

| | | | | | | | b b b | |
J F M A M J J A S O N D

**54-58 cm; 920–1 100 g** A small, compact snake-eagle. Grey head and breast, and rufous-barred belly resemble those of African Cuckoo Hawk (p. 114), but it is larger, with a large, rounded head and relatively shorter tail. Strongly barred belly, underwing coverts and tail with 4 dark bars distinguish it from stockier Western Banded Snake-Eagle. Legs and eyes yellowish. Juv. is dark brown above and pale below, with dark streaks on the head and upper breast; tail is barred, like ad's. Imm. may have a whitish head and back. **Voice:** Often calls, especially in early morning: harsh 'crok-crok-crok' and high-pitched 'ko-ko-ko-ko-keear'. **Status and biology: NEAR-THREATENED.** Uncommon resident in forest, woodland and plantations, often near water. Easily overlooked. Lays 1 egg in a large stick nest, usually built in the main fork of a tree. **Diet:** Mainly snakes; also lizards, frogs and insects. (Dubbelbandslangarend)

## 4 Western Banded Snake-Eagle *Circaetus cinerascens*

b b b b | | | | | | | | b
J F M A M J J A S O N D

**56–60 cm; 1–1.2 kg** Larger and more robust than Southern Banded Snake-Eagle, with a darker belly and underwing coverts. Tail is shorter, with a diagnostic broad white central band and dark tip, visible both in flight and at rest. Legs are yellowish. Juv. is pale below, with a dark-streaked head, neck and breast; best told from juv. Southern Banded Snake-Eagle by broad grey tail band. Imm. is dark brown, with a broad grey tail band. **Voice:** High-pitched 'kok-kok-kok-kok-kok'. **Status and biology:** Uncommon resident in woodland, especially along rivers; avoids dense forest. Lays 1 egg in a large stick nest, usually built in the main fork of a tree. **Diet:** Mainly snakes; also other reptiles, small mammals, frogs and insects. Typically hunts from a perch. (Enkelbandslangarend)

# EAGLES

Large, impressive raptors with long, fairly broad wings, deeply slotted primaries and feathered legs. Females are appreciably larger than males in most species; plumage typically the same in males and females, but some species have colour morphs. Juvs distinct, with several imm. plumages. The large, predominantly brown eagles require a combination of structure and plumage details to identify. Monogamous and territorial; breed singly. Females undertake most incubation and brood small chicks; fed at nest by male.

## 1 Tawny Eagle *Aquila rapax*

bBBBbbb
J F M A M J J A S O N D

**65–76 cm; 1.6–2.5 g** A large, brown eagle with a heavy bill and long, broad wings. Slightly smaller than migrant Steppe Eagle with a shorter gape, extending only to below middle of eye (not to back, as in Steppe Eagle). Tail is unbarred or faintly barred (ad. Steppe Eagle's tail is more heavily barred). Colour is variable: most birds are uniformly tawny, but range from streaked dark brown to pale buff. Ad. has pale yellow (not brown) eye; brown in juv. Female is usually darker than male, typically with more marked streaking on the body. Juv. is rufous brown, fading to buff with age; has much less prominent pale wing bars and rump compared to juv. Steppe Eagle. **Voice:** Seldom calls; sharp bark, 'kyow'. **Status and biology:** Fairly common resident and local migrant in savanna and woodland, but range has decreased in S due to persecution. Lays 1–3 eggs in a large stick platform nest built on top of a tree. **Diet:** Mammals, birds, reptiles, frogs, fish, insects and carrion. Competes with vultures at large mammal carcasses and often steals food from other raptors. (Roofarend)

## 2 Steppe Eagle *Aquila nipalensis*

J F M A M J J A S O N D

**70–84 cm; 2–3.8 kg** Larger than Tawny Eagle; bill less massive with a wider gape (extending to back, not middle, of eye). Ad. dark brown with a finely barred tail (visible only at close range); eyes brown (yellow in Tawny Eagle). Most birds in sthn Africa are juvs or imms; these lighter brown, with contrasting dark flight feathers. Juvs have pale windows in base of outer primaries, prominent pale bars along edge of upper- and underwing coverts, pale trailing edge to wing and tail, and pale uppertail coverts forming a distinct U-shaped mark. Paler brown than juv. Lesser Spotted Eagle, with broader white lines on wing coverts; appears larger, with broader wings and a longer tail. At rest, has shaggy leg feathers (not narrow, stove-pipe legs of Lesser Spotted Eagle). **Voice:** Silent in Africa. **Status and biology:** Locally common Palearctic migrant to savanna and open woodland, often in flocks at termite emergences. **Diet:** Mainly termites; also young birds and carrion. (Steppe-arend)

## 3 Lesser Spotted Eagle *Aquila pomarina*

J F M A M J J A S O N D

**58–65 cm; 1.1–2.1 kg** A relatively small, brown eagle with thin, tightly feathered tarsi; could be confused with large buzzards (p. 104); tail rounded and much shorter than in Wahlberg's Eagle (p. 100). Bill is quite small (unlike large, bulky bill of Steppe Eagle); yellow gape extends to middle of eye. In flight has a short, rounded tail, shorter than Steppe Eagle's. Ad. dark brown with blackish flight feathers; from below shows paler undertail coverts in flight; from above has small pale patches in base of primaries and narrow white 'U' across uppertail coverts. Juv. has larger white panel in primaries, extending as a white bar along edge of upper- and underwing coverts, narrower than in paler brown juv. Steppe Eagle. Juv. has broader U-shaped white rump than ad., but it is narrower than juv. Steppe Eagle's. **Voice:** Silent in Africa. **Status and biology:** Locally common Palearctic migrant to savanna and woodland; often in flocks with Steppe Eagles. **Diet:** Mainly termites; also young birds, small mammals and frogs. (Gevlekte Arend)

## 4 Greater Spotted Eagle *Aquila clanga*

**65–72 cm; 1.6–3 kg** Rare vagrant. A large, dark brown eagle with very broad wings and a short, rounded tail. Larger and darker than Lesser Spotted Eagle with broader wings that make the tail appear shorter. Ad. blackish with pale undertail coverts and narrow whitish 'U' on uppertail coverts. Juv. has prominent white spots on upperwing coverts, a narrow white line along the trailing edge of the upperwing coverts and a white 'U' on the uppertail coverts; underwing coverts darker than flight feathers (paler in Lesser Spotted Eagle). Imm. loses white spotting, but retains pale bar across wing and rump. **Voice:** Silent in Africa. **Status and biology: VULNERABLE**. Occurrence in sthn Africa controversial, but 1 sight record from Nylsvlei and 1 bird satellite-tracked to central Zambia. **Diet:** Mainly insects; also small mammals, birds, reptiles and frogs. (Groot Gevlekte Arend)

## 1 Verreaux's (Black) Eagle *Aquila verreauxii*

b B B B
J F M A M J J A S O N D

**80–96 cm; 3–5.6 kg** A large, long-tailed eagle; wings are characteristically narrow at the base, with long secondaries. Ad. is black with a white rump, white 'V' on the back and pale panels in the outer wing. Female larger, with more extensive white back patches. Juv. has mottled brown and rufous plumage, and a diagnostic rufous crown and nape, contrasting with its darker face and throat; best recognised by characteristic flight shape. **Voice:** Rarely calls; melodious 'keee-uup' when breeding. **Status and biology:** Locally common resident, mainly in rocky areas where there are nesting cliffs; occasionally nests on trees or pylons. Lays 1–2 eggs in a large stick nest; the first chick to hatch attacks its smaller sibling, usually killing it. **Diet:** Mainly mammals, especially rock hyrax, although some pairs specialise in birds such as Helmeted Guineafowl. (Witkruisarend)

## 2 Martial Eagle *Polemaetus bellicosus*

b b b B B B b b
J F M A M J J A S O N D

**78–86 cm; 2.4–5.2 kg** A huge eagle with a short crest, dark brown head and upper breast, and a white, lightly spotted belly. Larger than ad. Black-chested Snake-Eagle (p. 92) with much broader wings and shorter tail; underwings mainly dark brown (not whitish) and undertail finely barred (not white with a few dark bands). Juv. has white head and breast; appears cleaner white than juv. African Crowned Eagle with darker, finely barred flight feathers and tail, and unspotted flanks; wings are longer in flight. Imm. gradually attains ad. plumage over 5–7 years; dark brown eyes turn yellow after 3–4 years. **Voice:** Rapid 'klooee-klooee-klooee' in display. **Status and biology:** Locally common in savanna and open woodland, grassland, semi-desert and Karoo. Lays 1 egg (rarely 2) in a large stick nest, built in the main fork of a large tree or on a pylon; rarely on a cliff ledge. **Diet:** Mammals, including hares, mongooses and small antelope, and large birds and reptiles (especially monitor lizards). (Breëkoparend)

## 3 African Crowned Eagle *Stephanoaetus coronatus*

b b b b b B B B b b
J F M A M J J A S O N D

**80–98 cm; 2.6–4.2 kg** A huge, crested eagle with rounded, very broad wings and a long, broad tail. Ad. is dark grey above, with breast and belly heavily mottled black. Underwing coverts, breast and neck are suffused rufous. Flight feathers and tail are heavily barred black; female has fewer wing bars than male. Juv. has creamy white head and underparts; similar to juv. Martial Eagle, but has dark speckling on flanks and legs, and broadly barred tail and underwing. Imm. gradually attains ad. plumage over 4 years. **Voice:** Br. pairs are quite vocal: flight call is ringing 'kewee-kewee-kewee'; male's calls higher-pitched than female's. **Status and biology:** Locally fairly common resident in forest and dense woodland. Lays 1–2 eggs in a large stick nest, usually built in the main fork of a large tree. **Diet:** Mammals such as monkeys, hyraxes, small antelope and mustelids; also occasional large birds. (Kroonarend)

## 1 Long-crested Eagle  *Lophaetus occipitalis*

b b b b b B B B B B B b
J F M A M J J A S O N D

**52–58 cm; 810–1 300 g**  A small, compact eagle with dull black plumage and a long, floppy crest. Ad. has large, yellow eyes and narrow, stove-pipe legs, recalling a snake-eagle (p. 92). In flight, has conspicuous white bases to primaries; told from larger Verreaux's Eagle (p. 96) by its black-and-white barred secondaries and tail, and shorter, broader wings. Flight action is fast and direct on stiffly held wings, with shallow wing beats. Male typically has whiter leggings and a longer crest than female. Juv. has short crest and grey eyes. **Voice:** High-pitched, screamed 'kee-ah' during display or when perched. **Status and biology:** Common resident and local nomad in woodland, plantations and forest edges, especially near water. Lays 1–2 eggs in a stick nest built inside the canopy of a large tree. **Diet:** Small mammals; also reptiles, frogs, invertebrates and occasional birds. (Langkuifarend)

## 2 African Hawk-Eagle  *Aquila spilogaster*

b B B b
J F M A M J J A S O N D

**60–68 cm; 1.2–1.7 kg**  A medium-sized, black-and-white eagle. Larger and longer-winged than Ayres's Hawk-Eagle. In flight, upperwing has distinctive white panels at base of primaries. From below, flight feathers are mainly white and tail has broad terminal bar. Juv. has rufous underparts and underwing coverts, becoming black-streaked with age. Juv. could be confused with juv. Black Sparrowhawk (p. 108), but is smaller with feathered (not bare) legs. **Voice:** Seldom calls; whistled, musical 'klee-klee-klee'. **Status and biology:** Uncommon resident in woodland and savanna; also arid areas with some trees. Lays 1–2 (rarely 3) eggs in the main fork of a large tree; rarely on a pylon or cliff ledge. **Diet:** Game birds, other birds and a variety of mammals. (Grootjagarend)

## 3 Ayres's Hawk-Eagle  *Aquila ayresii*

B B b b b
J F M A M J J A S O N D

**45–58 cm; 620–1 100 g**  A small, compact eagle; appreciably smaller and shorter-winged than African Hawk-Eagle with uniformly barred flight feathers and tail; at rest has uniform dark upperparts and more heavily marked underparts (varying from mostly white with black streaks to almost all-black). Head is usually dark, but is pale in some birds. Has small white 'landing lights' like Booted Eagle, but wings and tail are shorter and more heavily barred. Juv. is rufous below, with more heavily barred underwing than juv. African Hawk-Eagle. **Voice:** Normally silent; shrill 'pueep-pip-pip-pueep' when displaying. **Status and biology:** Scarce br. resident and non-br. intra-African migrant, mainly in woodland and forest. Lays 1 egg in a stick platform built in the canopy of a large tree. **Diet:** Mainly birds, especially doves and pigeons, and occasional mammals. (Kleinjagarend)

## 4 Booted Eagle  *Aquila pennatus*

b b B b b
J F M A M J J A S O N D

**45–55 cm; 520–1 200 g**  A small eagle with a relatively long, rather square-tipped tail and long, slender wings. Most likely confused with Wahlberg's Eagle (p. 100), but tail is shorter, broader and slightly more rounded and wings are broader; also has paler brown upperwing and uppertail coverts as well as diagnostic 'landing lights' on the leading edge of the wing where it meets the body. Commoner pale morph **(4 A)** shows strong contrast between whitish underwing coverts and dark flight feathers. Face is mostly brown, contrasting with white throat (unlike all-pale head of pale Wahlberg's Eagle). Dark morph **(4 B)** appears rather uniformly brown from below, with slightly paler inner primaries. Rare rufous morph **(4 C)** has rich brown underparts. **Voice:** High-pitched 'kee-keeee' or 'pee-pee-pee-pee'. **Status and biology:** Fairly common br. migrant from W Cape to sthn Namibia (Jul–Mar); uncommon Palearctic migrant (Nov–Feb) to open habitats elsewhere; some birds overwinter. Lays 2 eggs in a stick nest usually built on a cliff ledge; occasionally in a tree. **Diet:** Mainly birds; also small mammals, reptiles and termites. (Dwergarend)

## 1 Wahlberg's Eagle *Aquila wahlbergi*

**55–60 cm; 900–1 500 g**  A small, slender eagle with a short, pointed crest on the hind crown. In flight, has diagnostic long, narrow, square-ended tail (longer and more square-tipped than Booted Eagle, p. 98), and slender, straight-edged wings (lacking marked bulge in secondaries). Usually dark brown, but has pale and intermediate colour morphs. Dark morph lacks white 'landing lights' and paler brown upperwing and uppertail coverts of dark morph Booted Eagle. Pale morph **(1 A)** has mostly white head (unlike dark cap and face of pale Booted Eagle). **Voice:** Drawn-out whistle while soaring; yelping 'kop-yop-yip-yip-yip' when perched. **Status and biology:** Common intra-African migrant in woodland and savanna. Lays 1 egg (rarely 2) in a fairly small stick nest built in the main fork of a tall tree. **Diet:** Birds, small mammals, reptiles, frogs and invertebrates. (Bruinarend)

# HARRIER-HAWKS

**Gangly, long-legged raptors with rather small heads and broad, deeply slotted wings. Double-jointed legs are used to extract prey from holes and enclosed nests. Sexes alike; juv. distinctive. Monogamous.**

## 2 African Harrier-Hawk (Gymnogene) *Polyboroides typus*

**60–66 cm; 620–950 g**  A large, broad-winged hawk with a small head, long legs, and loose, floppy flight action. Ad. is grey above and finely barred below, with a bare yellow face (red when agitated) extending around the eye. In flight, broad black tips to flight feathers and black tail with a central white band are distinctive. Juv. and imm. are brown, variably streaked and mottled; at a distance could be confused with brown eagles, but show fewer (4–5) primary 'fingers' in flight, and have long, bare legs. Juv. face greyish. **Voice:** Whistled 'peeer' or 'suuu-eeee-ooo', mainly in the br. season. **Status and biology:** Fairly common resident in woodland, forests and more open, scrubby habitats. Breeds singly, laying 1–3 eggs in a large stick nest built in a high fork of a tree. **Diet:** Birds, reptiles, mammals and frogs; uses its long, double-jointed legs to reach into cavities and nests (e.g. weaver nests). (Kaalwangvalk)

# BUZZARDS

Medium-sized hawks with fairly broad wings and rounded tails. Honey-buzzards are only distantly related to buteonine buzzards, but can be confused in flight. Sexes alike, but most species show considerable variation in plumage coloration; juv. plumage distinctive. Usually monogamous; breed singly. Incubation mainly by female, who also broods the chicks while being fed by the male.

## 1 Steppe Buzzard  *Buteo vulpinus*

J F M A M J J A S O N D

**46–52 cm; 540–920 g**  The most common brown buzzard throughout the region; told from small eagles by its bare yellow legs. Plumage highly variable, from pale brown to almost black. In flight, brown underwing coverts contrast with paler flight feathers. Although many birds have a whitish breast patch, it is generally darker below than Forest Buzzard, with brown or barred flanks; typically occurs in more open habitats; frequently perches on poles. Juv. typically more streaked below with yellow (not brown) eyes and narrower terminal tail bar. Smaller and less aquiline than juv. Jackal and Augur buzzards (p. 104), with narrower wings in flight and less contrast between lesser and other underwing coverts. **Voice:** Gull-like 'pee-ooo'; seldom calls in Africa. **Status and biology:** Abundant Palearctic migrant in open country; generally avoids very arid and forested areas. Some pairs of all-brown buzzards breeding in W Cape may be this species; most breed in trees, but some on cliffs. **Diet:** Small mammals, insects, reptiles, as well as occasional birds and frogs. (Bruinjakkalsvoël)

## 2 Forest Buzzard  *Buteo trizonatus*

J F M A M J J A S O N D

**45–50 cm; 510–700 g**  Slightly smaller and usually paler below than the Steppe Buzzard, with whiter median and greater underwing coverts that don't contrast strongly with the flight feathers. Most birds have white underparts with irregular brown blotches on the thighs and sides of the breast; lack barred flanks, but some are almost entirely brown, making them nearly indistinguishable from Steppe Buzzards. Most juvs are whitish below, with tear-shaped flank streaks. **Voice:** Shrill 'peeoo'. **Status and biology:** Endemic. Locally common resident in forests and plantations, usually foraging along forest edges. Lays 2 eggs in a stick nest built in the fork of a tree. Recently fledged juvs are very vocal, begging for food from their parents. **Diet:** Small mammals, birds, reptiles, amphibians and large insects. (Bosjakkalsvoël)

## 3 Long-legged Buzzard  *Buteo rufinus*

**52–65 cm; 600–1 700 g**  Rare vagrant. A large, bulky buzzard, with long, broad wings. Plumage is variable, but typically has dark belly, pale head and dark carpal patches on underwing. Ad. has plain rufous tail (not finely barred towards tip as in Steppe Buzzard) that appears almost translucent. In flight, has white, unmarked primaries with black tips and trailing edge. Wing beats are slow and deep; hovers more often than Steppe Buzzard. Juv's tail is lightly barred; very hard to separate from other buzzards without direct comparison of size and shape. **Voice:** Silent in Africa. **Status and biology:** Rare Palearctic vagrant, with fewer than 10 records from sthn Africa. Usually recorded in open grassland, arid savanna and semi-desert. **Diet:** Small mammals and reptiles. (Langbeenjakkalsvoël)

## 1 European Honey-Buzzard *Pernis apivorus*

**52–60 cm; 680–810 g** A small-headed, buzzard-like raptor; appears rather kite-like when perched. In flight, tail is long and slightly rounded with a weak central notch; wings are narrower at body; wrists are held slightly bent and wings are bowed when gliding (not horizontal). Pale morph ad. has grey head merging into grey-brown upperparts with paler uppertail coverts; underparts whitish, variably barred and streaked dark brown. Underwings whitish with broad black trailing edge and distinctive blackish carpal mark; remaining underwing coverts variably barred brown; undertail has a broad, dark subterminal tail band and 2 narrow bars (not easily seen) at base of tail. Dark morph has blackish head and body, dark brown underwing coverts and 3 blackish bars across flight feathers. At close range has yellow eyes, scaly face feathers and grey cere. Juv. plumage variable; some all-brown, others paler beneath. Tail barring less distinct; eyes dark brown; cere yellow; best told from Steppe Buzzard (p.102) by shape. Could be confused with juv. African Harrier-Hawk (p. 100), but wings are not as broad or deeply slotted. **Voice:** Generally silent; occasionally gives a high-pitched 'meeuu'. **Status and biology:** Uncommon Palearctic migrant to woodland, forest edge and plantations; attracted to wasp nests. **Diet:** Insects, especially bees and wasps. (Wespedief)

## 2 Jackal Buzzard *Buteo rufofuscus*

**55–62 cm; 900–1 700 g** A large buzzard with a short, rounded tail and broad wings, broader on secondaries. Told from Augur Buzzard by its chestnut (not white) breast and barred black-and-white (not white) belly. Some birds have white breast, but differ from Augur Buzzard by black (not white) underwing coverts. Juv. dark brown above and mottled rufous and brown below, with some dark brown streaking; tail slightly longer than ad.; larger than Steppe Buzzard (p. 102) with broader wings and a more aquiline head; typically shows stronger contrast between dark brown lesser underwing coverts and buffy median and greater underwing coverts. Differs from brown *Aquila* eagles by bare tarsi. Imm. has a mosaic of juv. and ad. plumage. **Voice:** Loud, drawn-out 'weeaah-ka-ka-ka', similar to call of black-backed jackal; male higher-pitched than female. **Status and biology:** Endemic. Locally common resident in karoo scrub, grassland and agricultural land. Monogamous; sometimes polyandrous. Lays 1–3 eggs in a stick nest on a cliff ledge, rarely in a tall tree or on a pylon. **Diet:** Mainly small mammals and reptiles; also birds, frogs and insects. (Rooiborsjakkalsvoël)

## 3 Augur Buzzard *Buteo augur*

**55–60 cm; 900–1 300 g** Similar to Jackal Buzzard, but has white (not chestnut) breast and white (not barred) belly. Underwing is mostly white (lacks dark coverts of Jackal Buzzard), with blackish tips to flight feathers and primary coverts. Ad. is dark grey-black above and white below; female has black throat or partial neck collar. Juv. similar to juv. Jackal Buzard; see that species for separation from Steppe Buzzard (p. 102) and small brown eagles. Dark morph ads have blackish underparts, including underwing coverts; not recorded from sthn Africa. **Voice:** Harsh 'kow-kow-kow-kow' display call. **Status and biology:** Fairly common resident of mountainous and hilly country in woodland, savanna and desert. Monogamous; rarely polyandrous. Lays 1–3 eggs in a stick nest on a cliff ledge or small tree growing on a cliff. **Diet:** Reptiles, small mammals and birds. (Witborsjakkalsvoël)

# HARRIERS

Medium-sized raptors allied to accipiters; characterised by long, angled wings and long, relatively slender tails; flight loose and buoyant; wings usually held in a shallow 'V' above body. Typically hunt by quartering low down, surprising prey on the ground. Sexes differ in Palearctic migrants; similar in locally breeding species. Monogamous; breed singly. Female incubates and broods small chicks; fed at nest by male.

## 1 African Marsh-Harrier *Circus ranivorus*

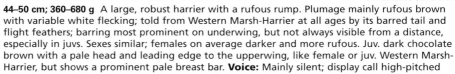

**44–50 cm; 360–680 g** A large, robust harrier with a rufous rump. Plumage mainly rufous brown with variable white flecking; told from Western Marsh-Harrier at all ages by its barred tail and flight feathers; barring most prominent on underwing, but not always visible from a distance, especially in juvs. Sexes similar; females on average darker and more rufous. Juv. dark chocolate brown with a pale head and leading edge to the upperwing, like female or juv. Western Marsh-Harrier, but shows a prominent pale breast bar. **Voice:** Mainly silent; display call high-pitched 'fee-ooo'. **Status and biology:** Locally common at marshes, reedbeds and adjacent grassland. Lays 2–5 (rarely 6) eggs in a shallow bowl of twigs, grass and reeds built among reeds or marsh vegetation. **Diet:** Small mammals and birds, including eggs and chicks; also frogs and fish. (Afrikaanse Vleivalk)

## 2 Western Marsh-Harrier *Circus aeruginosus*

**45–52 cm; 410–780 g** Rare. A large harrier, with longer wings and tail than African Marsh-Harrier. Ad. male has a brown body and wing coverts, variably streaked white on face and breast, pale grey flight feathers with black tips to the outer primaries; tail unbarred. Female is dark brown, with a creamy white cap and throat, and usually has white-edged forewings. Unbarred flight feathers and tail separate it from African Marsh-Harrier, which can show a pale forehead and leading edge to the wings in worn juv. plumage. Juv. resembles female, but can lack the white on the crown and forewings. **Voice:** Silent in Africa. **Status and biology:** Rare Palearctic migrant to marshes and adjoining grassland. **Diet:** Insects, small mammals, birds and reptiles. (Europese Vleivalk)

## 3 Black Harrier *Circus maurus*

**42–50 cm; 350–600 g** Ad. mostly black, with a large white rump, grey-barred tail and silvery wing panels. Differs from very rare dark-morph Montagu's Harrier by white rump and barred tail. Juv. has dark brown upperparts with buff feather edges; underparts buffy, streaked blackish on the breast and flanks; differs from female Pallid and Montagu's harriers by more heavily streaked underparts and by paler ground colour to the barred flight feathers. Imm. similar to ad., but with variable brown mottling on body. **Voice:** Generally silent; 'pee-pee-pee-pee' display call; harsh 'chak-chak-chak' when alarmed. **Status and biology:** **VULNERABLE.** Endemic. Uncommon resident in SW, nomadic elsewhere. Forages over open country. Lays 1–5 eggs in a shallow bowl of twigs and grass built in sedges and scrub, often near water. **Diet:** Small mammals, birds, reptiles, frogs and occasional insects and carrion. (Witkruisvleivalk)

## 4 Pallid Harrier *Circus macrourus*

**40–48 cm; 300–450 g** A small, slender harrier. Male is paler grey than male Montagu's Harrier, especially on the head and breast; underparts plain. In flight, lacks dark bars on wings; black primary patch is smaller; underwings white apart from black tip. Female is brown above, with white uppertail coverts, and buffy below with dark brown streaking on the breast and underwing coverts. Facial mask is slightly more distinct than that of female Montagu's Harrier, with a paler collar around the dark ear coverts. In flight from below, barring on secondaries and base of tail is less distinct, with darker ground colour. Juv. resembles female, but is more rufous and unstreaked below, with a pronounced white collar around the ear coverts and dusky secondaries from below in flight. **Voice:** Silent in Africa. **Status and biology:** **NEAR-THREATENED.** Scarce Palearctic migrant in grassland and open savanna. **Diet:** Small mammals, birds, reptiles, frogs and insects. (Witborsvleivalk)

## 5 Montagu's Harrier *Circus pygargus*

**40–46 cm; 230–440 g** A fairly small, slender harrier. Male is darker grey than male Pallid Harrier; black wing tips are more extensive and has a distinctive black line across the upperwing and 2 lines across the underwing; at close range, shows chestnut-streaked flanks; secondaries are lightly barred below. Female and juv. are plain brown above, apart from paler grey-brown upperwing coverts, white uppertail coverts and a banded tail (so-called ringtails). Female is buff below, streaked dark brown on the breast, flanks and underwing coverts; flight feathers and tail strongly barred. Juv. is rufous-buff below, with little streaking and dusky secondaries. Both female and juv. lack the prominent pale collar behind the ear coverts of Pallid Harrier; female has large white patch behind her eye. **Voice:** Silent in Africa. **Status and biology:** Uncommon Palearctic migrant in grassland and open savanna. **Diet:** Small mammals, birds, reptiles, frogs and insects. (Blouvleivalk)

# ACCIPITERS

Small to medium-sized raptors with short, broad wings and longish tails, adapted for manoeuvring through cluttered habitats. At rest, tail extends well beyond folded wings. Often soar, with wings held level or below body. Identification complicated by age and sex-related plumage differences as well as sex-linked size differences: females are much larger than males, especially in species feeding mainly on birds. Monogamous and territorial; breed singly. Incubation mainly by female, who also broods chicks; fed at nest by male.

### 1 Black Sparrowhawk  *Accipiter melanoleucus*

| b | B | B | B | B | B | B | B | b | b |
|---|---|---|---|---|---|---|---|---|---|
| J | F M A M J J A S O N D | | | | | | | | |

**46–58 cm; 510–1 000 g**  The largest accipiter in the region. Ad. black above; underparts vary from white to black, but most birds have at least a white throat. Pale birds are unmistakable; all-dark birds **(1 B)** are larger than dark morphs of Ovambo Sparrowhawk (p. 110) or Gabar Goshawk (p. 110), with yellow (not orange-red) legs and cere. Juv. polymorphic; most are dark grey-brown above with rufous underparts streaked fine brown (not spotted like juv. African Goshawk); superficially resemble juv. African Hawk-Eagle (p. 98), but are more heavily streaked, with unfeathered tarsi and a different shape and flight action. Other juvs are slate-grey above and white below with brown streaking. Both morphs show pale panels in upperwing. **Voice:** Normally silent except when breeding. Male 'kee-yip'; female loud 'kek-kek-kek-kek'. **Status and biology:** Locally fairly common resident in forest, woodland and plantations; often forages far from cover. Range has expanded recently in W Cape. Lays 1–4 whitish eggs in a stick nest built in a high fork of a tree. **Diet:** Mainly birds, especially doves; also occasional small mammals. (Swartsperwer)

### 2 African Goshawk  *Accipiter tachiro*

| b | b | B | B | B | b |
|---|---|---|---|---|---|
| J F M A M J J A S O N D | | | | | |

**36–44 cm; 180–500 g**  A medium-sized accipiter with yellow legs and eyes and a pale grey cere; rump dark. Ad. male has a plain grey head and upper breast; lower breast and belly finely barred rufous; can appear uniform from a distance, like Rufous-chested Sparrowhawk. Tail dark grey-brown, indistinctly barred, with 2 white spots on central feathers; told from much smaller Little Sparrowhawk (p. 110) by dark rump and grey (not yellow) cere. Female is browner above and barred brown below, with a brown and black barred tail lacking white spots. Juv. dark brown above with an indistinct white supercilium; underparts white with a dark median throat stripe and bold, tear-shaped spots on the breast and belly; flight feathers and tail boldly barred dark brown. **Voice:** Displaying birds give a monotonous 'quick quick quick...' call in flight or from a tree perch, mainly in the early morning. **Status and biology:** Common resident of forest and dense woodland; often forages far from cover. Lays 1–3 eggs in a stick nest built in a high fork of a tree. **Diet:** Small birds, bats, other small mammals and reptiles. (Afrikaanse Sperwer)

### 3 Rufous-chested Sparrowhawk  *Accipiter rufiventris*

| b | B | B | b | b |
|---|---|---|---|---|
| J F M A M J J A S O N D | | | | |

**30–38 cm; 105–210 g**  A fairly small accipiter with uniform upperparts, lacking white in the rump and tail. Ad. male is dark slate-grey above and plain rufous below (including underwing coverts) with a paler throat; rufous lower cheek contrasts with dark crown, giving a capped appearance, unlike the uniform head of African Goshawk. Tail barred grey-brown with a narrow pale tip. Female appreciably larger and browner above. Eyes, cere and legs are yellow. Juv. is brown above, with slight pale eyebrow and mottled rufous underparts, variably streaked white; best told from juv. Ovambo Sparrowhawk (p. 110) by its darker head, more uniform upperparts and yellow (not brown) eyes. **Voice:** Sharp, staccato 'kee-kee-kee' or 'kew-kew-kew' during display. **Status and biology:** Fairly common resident of montane forest and plantations; often forages far from cover. Lays 2–4 eggs in a stick nest in a high fork of a tree. **Diet:** Small birds; also occasional rodents and lizards. (Rooiborssperwer)

## 1 Ovambo Sparrowhawk  *Accipiter ovampensis*

**32–40 cm; 120–300 g** A medium-sized accipiter with yellow-orange legs and a yellow-orange (rarely red) cere. Ad. is uniform grey above (including rump), with darker bars in tail. Larger than Shikra, with dark red-brown (not bright red) eyes, grey (not rufous) barred underparts, and barred central tail feathers with white shaft streaks on pale bars. Rare melanistic form is larger than melanistic Gabar Goshawk, with orange (not red) legs and cere, less distinct barring in wings and tail, and white shaft streaks in its tail. Juv. is brown above with pale feather margins, appearing scaly; head has prominent white supercilium (crown and nape are also pale in some birds); underparts rufous or whitish; cere and legs yellow; best told from juv. Rufous-chested Sparrowhawk (p. 108) by its paler head, scaled upperparts and brown (not yellow) eyes. **Voice:** Soft 'keeep-keeep-keeep' when breeding. **Status and biology:** Uncommon resident in savanna, tall woodland and plantations. Lays 1–5 eggs in a stick nest built in a tall tree. **Diet:** Almost exclusively small birds. (Ovambosperwer)

## 2 Gabar Goshawk  *Melierax gabar*

**28–36 cm; 110–220 g** A fairly small accipiter with a red cere and legs, prominent white rump (not grey as Shikra), and plain grey throat and upper breast (not finely barred as Ovambo Sparrowhawk). Much smaller than Dark Chanting Goshawk (p. 112) with shorter legs. Melanistic form **(2 A)** (5–25% of population) is more common in arid areas; told from melanistic Ovambo Sparrowhawk by more boldly barred wings and tail and red bare parts. Juv. is brown above; breast is rufous-streaked; belly and underwing coverts are barred rufous; eyes yellow; legs orange; only juv. accipiter with a white rump. **Voice:** High-pitched, whistling 'kik-kik-kik-kik-kik'. **Status and biology:** Locally common resident of savanna and semi-arid scrub with at least some trees. Lays 2–4 eggs in a stick nest built in the canopy of a tree; nest usually adorned with social spider webs, possibly for camouflage. **Diet:** Mainly birds, including nestlings; also small mammals, reptiles and insects. (Witkruissperwer)

## 3 Shikra  *Accipiter badius*

**28–30 cm; 80–170 g** A small accipiter; ad. has uniform grey upperparts, lacking the white rump of Gabar Goshawk and Little Sparrowhawk. Differs from larger Ovambo Sparrowhawk by its rufous (not grey) barring below, cherry-red (not dark red-brown) eyes, yellow (not yellow-orange or red) cere, and unbarred central tail feathers. Legs are orange-yellow. Female larger than male, with orange eyes. Juv. is brown above, with streaked breast and barred belly like juv. Gabar Goshawk, but its rump is brown (not white); eyes yellow. **Voice:** Male high-pitched 'keewik-keewik-keewik'; female softer 'kee-uuu'. **Status and biology:** Common resident and local nomad in savanna and tall woodland. Lays 2–3 (rarely 1–4) eggs in a stick nest in the fork of a tree. **Diet:** Lizards, insects and small birds; also occasional small mammals and frogs. (Gebande Sperwer)

## 4 Little Sparrowhawk  *Accipiter minullus*

**23–27 cm; 68–120 g** The smallest accipiter in the region. Ad. is pale grey with breast finely barred rufous or grey and rufous-washed flanks; recalls male African Goshawk (p. 108), but is much smaller with a white rump and yellow (not grey) cere. Told from Shikra by its white rump and the 2 white spots on the uppertail. Juv. is brown above, with dark rump, and white below, with large spots on breast and belly; smaller than juv. African Goshawk; lacks pale supercilium and dark median throat stripe. **Voice:** Male high-pitched 'tu-tu-tu-tu-tu' during br. season; female softer 'kew-kew-kew'. **Status and biology:** Locally common but secretive resident of forest, woodland and plantations. Lays 1–3 eggs in a stick nest built in the main fork of a tall tree; sometimes uses old nests of other accipiters. **Diet:** Mainly small birds; occasional small mammals, reptiles, frogs and insects. (Kleinsperwer)

## 1 Southern Pale Chanting Goshawk *Melierax canorus*

bbbbbBBBbb J F M A M J J A S O N D

**48–62 cm; 620–1 400 g** A large, long-legged goshawk with red legs and cere. Ad. pale grey with a finely barred belly; paler and larger than Dark Chanting Goshawk, with a white rump and very pale grey secondaries contrasting strongly with the dark primaries. Juv. is brown above with buff feather edges; barred and streaked below, with boldly barred flight feathers and tail. Juv. is superficially harrier or buzzard-like, but with long orange legs, pale yellow eyes and pink-orange cere; paler than juv. Dark Chanting Goshawk with a white (not barred) rump. **Voice:** Piping 'kleeu-kleeu-klu-klu-klu', usually uttered at dawn. **Status and biology:** Endemic. Common resident of arid savanna, semi-desert and karoo scrub. Usually monogamous, but sometimes polyandrous (1 female with 2 males, probably brothers); lays 1–2 eggs in a platform of sticks built on top of small tree or pylon. **Diet:** Small mammals, birds, reptiles, invertebrates and carrion. Usually hunts from a perch, taking most prey on the ground, often running after prey. Frequently follows honey badgers and other predators, using them to flush prey. (Bleeksingvalk)

## 2 Dark Chanting Goshawk *Melierax metabates*

bBBBb J F M A M J J A S O N D

**43–50 cm; 480–880 g** Ad. is darker grey than Pale Chanting Goshawk, with a grey (not white) rump and dark grey lesser upperwing coverts contrasting with paler median and greater coverts; secondaries grey (not whitish). Other goshawks are smaller, and most have yellow legs; of those with red legs, Gabar Goshawk (p. 110) is much smaller and has a white rump; Ovambo Sparrowhawk (p. 110) has a barred breast. Lacks black throat stripe of smaller, more compact Lizard Buzzard (p. 114). Juv. best told from juv. Pale Chanting Goshawk by darker, barred rump. **Voice:** Piping 'kleeu-kleeu-klu-klu-klu'. **Status and biology:** Uncommon resident of savanna and open woodland. Monogamous; lays 1–2 (rarely 3) eggs in a platform of sticks, usually festooned with social spider webs, built in a tree. **Diet:** Small mammals, birds, reptiles, invertebrates and carrion. Exploits prey flushed by large mammals. (Donkersingvalk)

# KITES

Kites are a mixed bag of raptors: *Milvus* kites are widespread generalists allied to fish-eagles, whereas *Elanus* kites are rodent specialists that are basal among raptors. Sexes alike in both genera, with little size dimorphism. Breed singly. Incubation mainly by female.

## 3 Yellow-billed Kite *Milvus aegyptius*

bBBbb J F M A M J J A S O N D

**50–58 cm; 570–760 g** A long-winged raptor with a long, shallowly forked tail. Has diagnostic loose flight action, with long tail twisting incessantly. Wings are held level, not canted up as in harriers, and are narrower than buzzards', with bent wrist. Very similar to Black Kite, but ad. has a darker head and bright yellow (not black) bill; eyes dark reddish (not pale yellow); tail more deeply forked. Juv. has buffy feather margins, black bill (cere yellowish), and less deeply forked tail than ad.; separated with difficulty from juv. Black Kite. **Voice:** High-pitched, shrill whinnying; seldom uttered when not breeding. **Status and biology:** Common intra-African migrant found in woodland and open habitats. Monogamous; lays 1–3 eggs in a large stick nest; often re-uses the same nest in successive years. **Diet:** Insects, reptiles, frogs, small mammals, birds as well as carrion and scraps. Feeds on the wing, swooping to take its prey from the ground, or catching it in the air. Attracted to fires and termite emergences. (Geelbekwou)

## 4 Black Kite *Milvus migrans*

J F M A M J J A S O N D

**51–60 cm; 650–920 g** Slightly larger than Yellow-billed Kite; ad. has a paler, grey head, black bill (cere yellow), pale eyes and a less deeply forked tail. Juv. has darker brown face than ad., with a pale-streaked neck and breast, buffy feather margins to back, brownish eyes, and slightly less forked tail. **Voice:** Usually silent. **Status and biology:** Locally common Palearctic migrant in a wide range of habitats from forest edge to semi-desert. Often found in flocks at termite emergences. **Diet:** Diverse range of prey, similar to Yellow-billed Kite. (Swartwou)

## 5 Black-shouldered Kite *Elanus caeruleus*

bBBBbbbBBBbb J F M A M J J A S O N D

**30–33 cm; 210–290 g** A small, grey and white raptor with distinctive black shoulder patches and striking red eyes. White tail often pumped up and down while perched. Juv. is browner above, with a brown crown, grey tail and buff-edged upperpart feathers; eyes yellowish-brown. **Voice:** High-pitched, whistled 'peeeu'; soft 'weep'; rasping 'wee-ah'. **Status and biology:** Common resident and local nomad in savanna, grassland and agricultural areas; moves to exploit rodent outbreaks. Often perches on telephone poles and lines. Monogamous; lays 3–4 (2–6) eggs in a stick platform built at the top of a tree canopy, allowing access from above. Rarely breeds on pylons. **Diet:** Mostly striped mice and other small mammals; occasional birds, lizards and insects. Hunts from perch or by hovering, dropping onto prey with wings in deep 'V'. (Blouvalk)

## 1 African Cuckoo Hawk *Aviceda cuculoides*

b b b ☐ ☐ ☐ ☐ b B B b
J F M A M J J A S O N D

**40 cm; 220–350 g** The long, rather broad wings and slow, relaxed flight separate this species from accipiters. At rest, wings reach almost to tail tip (tail extends well beyond folded wings in accipiters). Plumage recalls African Goshawk (p. 108), but has small crest, short legs and much broader barring on belly and underwing coverts. Male has red-brown eyes; female yellow. Juv. is brown above and white below, with brown-streaked breast and larger spots on belly; best told from juv. African Goshawk by its larger size and shape. Imm. is browner above than ad., with mottled brown (not grey) breast. **Voice:** Loud, far-carrying 'teee-oooo' whistle; shorter 'tittit-eoo'. **Status and biology:** Uncommon resident of dense woodland and forest fringes; unobtrusive. Monogamous; lays 1–2 (rarely 3) eggs on a flimsy platform of twigs and leaves. **Diet:** Mainly chameleons, other reptiles and insects; also crabs, fish and small birds. (Koekoekvalk)

## 2 Lizard Buzzard *Kaupifalco monogrammicus*

b ☐ ☐ ☐ b b b b B B B b
J F M A M J J A S O N D

**35–37 cm; 220–360 g** A small, compact hawk, intermediate in size and shape between buzzards and accipiters. Larger and bulkier than Gabar Goshawk (p. 110); smaller and more compact with shorter legs than chanting goshawks (p. 112). White throat with black central stripe is diagnostic at all ages. Ad. has red cere and legs, and dark red eyes. Juv. has paler cere and legs and pale fringes to upperpart feathers. In flight, shows white rump and 1 (rarely 2) broad white tail bar(s). **Voice:** Noisy in br. season: whistled 'peoo-peoo'; melodious 'klioo-klu-klu-klu-klu'. **Status and biology:** Locally common resident and nomad in more arid areas. Occurs in woodland, well-wooded savanna and forest clearings. Monogamous; lays 1–3 eggs in a stick nest built in a main fork or on a branch below the canopy of a tall tree. **Diet:** Lizards, small snakes, rodents, frogs and invertebrates. (Akkedisvalk)

# FALCONS

**Small to medium-sized raptors, with long, pointed wings. Flight typically is fast and direct; some species often hover. Sexes differ in some species, similar in others; juvs usually distinct. Size dimorphism is marked in bird-eating species, with females larger than males. Typically monogamous and territorial; breed singly. Incubation mainly by female, fed at nest by male.**

## 3 Pygmy Falcon *Polihierax semitorquatus*

b b b ☐ ☐ ☐ b b B B b
J F M A M J J A S O N D

**18–20 cm; 55–66 g** A tiny, shrike-like falcon; male is grey above and white below; female has chestnut back. Juv. has dull brown back and buff-washed underparts. Flight undulating and rapid; white-spotted black flight feathers and tail contrast with white rump. Typically observed sitting upright on exposed perches. Often bobs its head and pumps tail up and down. **Voice:** Noisy; high-pitched 'chip-chip' and 'kik-kik-kik-kik'. **Status and biology:** Locally common in arid savanna. Lays 1–4 eggs in nests of Sociable Weavers and buffalo-weavers, occasionally starling or sparrow-weaver nests. Leaves a distinctive, whitewashed rim around nest entrance. **Diet:** Mainly lizards, small snakes and insects; also rodents and small birds. (Dwergvalk)

## 1 Lanner Falcon  *Falco biarmicus*

J F M A M J J A S O N D

**36–48 cm; 420–800 g**  A large, broad-winged falcon; often soars with rounded wings and fanned tail. Flight silhouette is more slender, with longer and less pointed wings than Peregrine Falcon. Ad. is pale, blue-grey above with rather plain, pinkish-cream underparts. Juv. is dark grey-brown above, with creamy brown crown and nape, and heavy brown streaking on breast and belly (juv. Peregrine Falcon has finer breast streaking). **Voice:** Harsh 'kak-kak-kak-kak-kak', similar to call of Peregrine Falcon; also whining and chopping notes. **Status and biology:** Fairly common resident and local nomad in a wide range of habitats from mountains to deserts and open grassland; avoids forests. Lays 1–5 eggs in a scrape on a cliff ledge, or in an old crow's or other raptor's nest in a tree or on a pylon; 1 record of possible polyandry. **Diet:** Birds up to 1.5 kg; also rodents, bats, reptiles and insects. (Edelvalk)

## 2 Peregrine Falcon  *Falco peregrinus*

J F M A M J J A S O N D

**34–44 cm; *F. p. minor* 500–850 g; *F. p. calidus* 680–1 300 g**  A large, chunky falcon with broad-based, pointed wings and a relatively short tail. Smaller and more compact than Lanner Falcon, with a dark cap and broad moustachial stripes. Flight is dashing and direct. Ad. of resident *F. p. minor* has dark slate-grey upperparts, mostly white breast and finely barred belly. Palearctic *F. p. calidus* **(2 A)** is larger and paler above, with spotted breast and narrower moustachial stripes. Juv. dark brown above with variable paler streaking on crown and pale nape patches; underparts heavily streaked brown. **Voice:** Raucous 'kak-kak-kak-kak-kak' around nesting cliff; also whining and chopping notes. **Status and biology:** Uncommon resident and Palearctic migrant; locally common in W Cape. Br. birds require high cliffs and gorges, or tall buildings, but migrant birds occur in wide range of open habitats; often forage at wetlands. Lays 2–3 eggs on an inaccessible cliff ledge or tall building. **Diet:** Mainly birds, especially pigeons; also occasional bats and insects. Stoops onto prey at up to 300 km/h. (Swerfvalk)

## 3 Taita Falcon  *Falco fasciinucha*

J F M A M J J A S O N D

**25–30 cm; 195–340 g**  A small, compact falcon with a short tail, broad shoulders and large head. Flight silhouette recalls a small Peregrine Falcon with rapid wing beats. Ad. dark slate above, with broad moustachial stripes and rufous-washed breast and belly; rufous underwing coverts contrast with gray and black barred flight feathers. Told from African Hobby (p. 118) by its rufous nape patches, mainly white cheeks and throat, stocky build and shorter tail. Juv. has buff fringes to back feathers, rufous face and throat, and is lightly streaked below; best told from juv. Red-necked Falcon by its stocky build, short tail and preference for cliff habitats. **Voice:** High-pitched 'kree-kree-kree' and 'kek-kek-kek'. **Status and biology: NEAR-THREATENED**. Rare and localised resident closely associated with cliffs and gorges in woodland. Lays 2–4 eggs in a hole or on a ledge on a cliff face. **Diet:** Mainly small birds, especially swallows and other passerines; occasional insects. (Taitavalk)

## 4 Red-necked Falcon  *Falco chicquera*

J F M A M J J A S O N D

**30–36 cm; 150–265 g**  A small, dashing, long-tailed falcon with long, slender wings. Ad. has chestnut crown and nape, uniformly barred, slate-grey upperparts, and a broad subterminal black tail band. Throat and upper breast are creamy buff, sometimes with indistinct rufous breast band; lower breast and belly finely barred. Ad. Lanner Falcon is much larger, lacks barred upperparts and broad tail band, and has plain belly. Head usually appears clean-cut, with narrow, dark brown moustachial stripes on white cheeks. Juv. is duller, with dark brown head, 2 buff patches on nape, and pale rufous underparts, finely barred brown; could be confused with Taita Falcon, but tail and wings are longer. **Voice:** Shrill 'ki-ki-ki-ki-ki' during br. season. **Status and biology:** Locally fairly common resident in arid savanna and woodland, often near *Borassus* palms. Usually perches within tree canopy. Lays 2–4 eggs in the base of a palm frond or the nest of a crow or other raptor in the top of a tree. **Diet:** Mainly small birds; also bats, rodents and insects. (Rooinekvalk)

## 1 Eurasian Hobby *Falco subbuteo*

J F M A M J J A S O N D

**28–36 cm; 135–320 g** A long-winged, relatively short-tailed falcon. In flight, appears almost swift-like. Ad. has creamy (not rusty, as in African Hobby) underparts, with heavy streaking on breast and belly, and rufous leggings and vent. Larger, darker-backed and more heavily streaked below than juv. Amur and Red-footed falcons (p. 122); legs and cere yellow (not reddish-orange). Juv. is washed creamy buff below; lacks rufous vent and leggings; in fresh plumage, has pale fringes to back and crown feathers, appearing scaled at close range. **Voice:** Silent in Africa. **Status and biology:** Fairly common Palearctic migrant mainly in woodland and savanna. **Diet:** Large insects, small birds and bats. Feeds on the wing; often active at dawn and dusk. (Europese Boomvalk)

## 2 African Hobby *Falco cuvierii*

J F M A M J J A S O N D

**28–30 cm; 150–220 g** A rather small, compact falcon, smaller than Eurasian Hobby, with unstreaked, rufous underparts (including throat and face). More slender than Taita Falcon (p. 116), with longer wings and tail and a dark head lacking rufous nape patches. Can appear all-dark in poor light. Juv. has dark-streaked, rufous breast and belly; head and throat colour vary from rufous to white. White-throated juv. resembles a pale-morph Eleonora's Falcon, but is appreciably smaller and much shorter-tailed. Could also be confused with female Red-footed Falcon (p. 122), but is much darker above, with blackish crown and well-developed moustachial stripe; legs yellow (not reddish). **Voice:** High-pitched 'kik-kik-kik-kik' display call. **Status and biology:** Uncommon resident and intra-African migrant in woodland, forest and adjoining open country. Lays 2–4 eggs in an old stick nest of a raptor, crow or other bird built in a tall tree. **Diet:** Small birds, bats and large insects. Often forages at dawn and dusk. (Afrikaanse Boomvalk)

## 3 Eleonora's Falcon *Falco eleonorae*

J F M A M J J A S O N D

**36–42 cm; 340–450 g** Rare vagrant. A large, slender falcon with very long wings and tail and darker underwings than other falcons. Ad. of commoner pale morph **(3 A)** is dark sooty brown above with white cheeks and throat contrasting with dark-streaked rufous breast and belly; larger than hobbies, with longer, darker wings and a longer tail; in good light, rufous extends much further up underparts than Eurasian Hobby. Dark morph **(3 B)** is almost black; much darker and larger than Sooty Falcon (p. 120). Legs are greenish-yellow; male has a yellow cere; female blue. Juv. has buffy fringes to upperpart feathers, appearing scaled at close range; underparts creamy buff to rufous with dark grey-brown chevrons; larger and richer below than juv. Sooty Falcon; rufous underwing coverts contrast with paler flight feathers (coverts uniform or paler in juv. Sooty Falcon). **Voice:** Silent in Africa. **Status and biology:** Palearctic vagrant; most winter in Madagascar. Likely to be found in Mozambique, foraging over savanna, woodland and forest. (Eleonoravalk)

## 4 Bat Hawk *Macheiramphus alcinus*

J F M A M J J A S O N D

**45 cm; 600–650 g** A dark brown raptor, appearing black in the field, with variable amounts of white on the throat and belly. In flight, the pointed, broad-based wings recall a large falcon or even a jaeger. At close quarters, white legs, eyelids and nape patches are distinctive. Juv. has more white on underparts, and pale-spotted underwing and tail. **Voice:** High-pitched whistling, similar to that of thick-knee. **Status and biology:** Uncommon resident in woodland, including plantations, and forest edge. Easily overlooked; crepuscular and nocturnal, roosting in thick foliage during day. Lays 1 egg (rarely 2) in a large stick nest built in a main fork of a tree; favours trees with pale bark to help locate the nest at night. **Diet:** Small, insectivorous bats; also larger bats and small birds, mostly caught at dusk. (Vlermuisvalk)

### 1 Sooty Falcon  *Falco concolor*

J F M A M J J A S O N D

32–36 cm; 200–250 g  A sleek, long-winged falcon, with folded wings extending beyond tail tip (unlike shorter, broader wings of Grey Kestrel). Ad. is plain slate-grey with blackish primaries; lacks chestnut vent of Red-footed and Amur falcons (p. 122), and has yellow (not orange-red) legs and cere. In flight, resembles a long-winged Eurasian Hobby (p. 118) or Eleanora's Falcon (p. 118); has paler body than dark morph Eleanora's Falcon. Juv. is darker grey above, with narrow pale feather margins in fresh plumage; throat is creamy; rest of underparts are buffy, streaked soft grey. Told from juv. Eurasian Hobby by its narrower moustachial streak and paler breast streaking; smaller and paler below than juv. Eleanora's Falcon, with underwing uniform or paler than flight feathers (rufous coverts darker than flight feathers in juv. Eleanora's Falcon). **Voice:** Mostly silent; high-pitched shrieks at nest. **Status and biology: NEAR-THREATENED**. Uncommon non-br. migrant from NE Africa and Arabia; occurs in savanna and woodland. **Diet:** Insects, small birds and bats, mostly caught at dusk. (Roetvalk)

### 2 Grey Kestrel  *Falco ardosiaceus*

J F M A M J J A S O N D

30–35 cm; 190–300 g  A small, compact, uniform grey falcon with barred flight feathers; wings shorter and broader than those of Sooty Falcon; at rest, wings do not reach tip of square tail. Flat crown gives rather square-headed look (rounded in Sooty Falcon), and has more extensive yellow skin around eye. Lacks contrasting pale head and rump and strongly barred tail of Dickinson's Kestrel. Juv. is lightly washed brown; facial skin and cere are greenish. **Voice:** High-pitched, rasping trill. **Status and biology:** Uncommon resident and local nomad in savanna and open woodland, often around palms. Lays 3–5 eggs in a hole in a tree or a Hamerkop nest. **Diet:** Insects and lizards; also small birds, rodents and palm husks. (Donkergrysvalk)

### 3 Dickinson's Kestrel  *Falco dickinsoni*

J F M A M J J A S O N D

28–30 cm; 170–240 g  A grey kestrel with contrasting pale grey head and rump; male slightly paler than female. Tail is strongly barred grey and black, with broader black subterminal bar. From beneath, flight feathers are also conspicuously barred. Head is square, with flat crown; appears large-headed. Ad. has extensive bare yellow skin around eye, joining with cere. Juv. is lightly washed brown, with small, greenish eye-ring and cere; head and rump darker, similar to Grey Kestrel, but is easily separated by its strongly barred tail and wings. **Voice:** High-pitched 'keee-keee-keee'. **Status and biology:** Uncommon resident and local nomad found in palm savanna and open woodland, often near baobab trees. May irrupt out of regular range in some years. Lays 3–4 (rarely 1–5) eggs in a tree cavity (usually in a palm or baobab), old Hamerkop nest or hole in a building. **Diet:** Large insects, crabs, birds, rodents, bats, frogs and reptiles. (Dickinsonvalk)

## 1 Amur Falcon  *Falco amurensis*

J F M A M J J A S O N D

28–30 cm; 100–185 g  A small, kestrel-like falcon. Male is dark slate-grey, with chestnut vent (often not visible at a distance) and diagnostic white underwing coverts. Female is whitish below, with extensive spotting; vent is buffy and unmarked. Superficially resembles Eurasian Hobby (p. 118) but has a white (not dark) forehead, pale grey (not dark) crown, and paler underwing. Juv. resembles female, but is streaked below and has buffy edges to upperpart feathers. **Voice:** Shrill chattering at roosts. **Status and biology:** Common Palearctic migrant in grassland and arid savanna. Roosts communally in tall trees, often with Lesser Kestrels. On southbound migration, probably travels over the Indian Ocean from India to E Africa. **Diet:** Mainly insects (especially termites and grasshoppers); occasional small birds. (Oostelike Rooipootvalk)

## 2 Red-footed Falcon  *Falco vespertinus*

J F M A M J J A S O N D

29–31 cm; 120–200 g  Similar to Amur Falcon, but male is darker with grey (not white) underwing coverts; told from ad. Sooty Falcon (p. 120) by paler flight feathers and rufous vent. Female has rufous head with small, dark mask around eye, and lightly streaked, buffy underparts; in flight, has rufous underwing coverts. From above, superficially resembles Red-necked Falcon (p. 116), but narrower dark subterminal tail bar and different shape and flight action are diagnostic. Juv. has off-white underparts, more heavily streaked than female's. Head is whitish, with dark facemask and indistinct cap; paler than female or juv. Amur Falcon. Underwing is much paler than Eurasian Hobby's (p. 118), with dark trailing edge. **Voice:** Shrill chattering at roosts. **Status and biology: NEAR-THREATENED.** Uncommon Palearctic migrant in grassland and arid savanna. Roosts communally in tall trees, sometimes with Lesser Kestrels and Amur Falcons. **Diet:** Mainly insects and other invertebrates. (Westelike Rooipootvalk)

## 3 Lesser Kestrel  *Falco naumanni*

J F M A M J J A S O N D

26–32 cm; 110–180 g  A small, slender kestrel with a slightly wedge-shaped tail. Male told from other kestrels by its plain chestnut back (lacking spots or barring), grey greater coverts and rather plain, buff (not rufous) underparts. Female is pale rufous above, densely barred; smaller than Greater Kestrel with greater contrast between upper- and underparts and plain (not barred) primaries and primary coverts. Cream underparts have dark spots; face is rather pale, with dark malar stripes. Juv. is slightly more rufous than ad. female, with less well-defined malar stripe and rufous rump. At close range has white claws at all ages. **Voice:** Silent during day, but noisy at roosts: high-pitched 'kiri-ri-ri-ri'. **Status and biology: VULNERABLE.** Locally abundant Palearctic migrant in arid shrubland, grassland and fields. Roosts communally in tall trees, often with Amur and Red-footed falcons. **Diet:** Mainly insects and other invertebrates; occasional small mammals, birds and reptiles. (Kleinrooivalk)

## 4 Rock Kestrel  *Falco rupicolus*

b ▮▮▮▮▮ bbBBBb
J F M A M J J A S O N D

30–34 cm; 185–275 g  A fairly small, slender kestrel with a long, grey tail, chestnut body and grey head. Told from male Lesser Kestrel by its dark spotted back and rufous (not grey) greater upperwing coverts; underparts are darker rufous. Sexes similar, but female is duller and more heavily streaked than male with more barred tail. Juv. similar to ad. female, but more heavily barred above; may show some rufous wash on crown and tail. **Voice:** High-pitched 'kik-ki-ki'.
**Status and biology:** Common resident and local nomad in grassland, scrub and open woodland, usually near rocky areas. Lays 1–5 eggs on a cliff ledge or building; sometimes uses nests of other birds. **Diet:** Reptiles, birds, insects and small mammals. (Kransvalk)

## 5 Greater Kestrel  *Falco rupicoloides*

b ▮ bbbbbbBBbb
J F M A M J J A S O N D

34–38 cm; 200–300 g  A rather large, pale kestrel with dense, uniform barring on the back, and little contrast between the pale rufous upper- and underparts. Plain head lacks malar stripe. In flight, upperwings are predominantly rufous, finely barred dark brown; underwing whitish, contrasting with rufous body. Ad. has grey and black barred tail with white tip and diagnostic whitish eyes. Juv. has rufous, barred tail, dark eyes and streaked (not barred) flanks. **Voice:** Shrill, repeated 'kee-ker-rik'. **Status and biology:** Locally common resident and nomad in arid savanna, grassland and semi-desert. Lays 1–7 eggs in the stick nest of a crow or another raptor in a tree or on a pylon; occasionally breeds in buildings. **Diet:** Insects and other invertebrates; also some small reptiles, mammals and birds. (Grootrooivalk)

# OSTRICHES

The largest bird; adapted for running, with long legs and only 2 toes. Sexes differ; male larger. Polygynous; incubation by alpha female during day and male at night. The precocial chicks lack an egg tooth; they break out of their eggs with muscular spasms.

## 1 Common Ostrich *Struthio camelus*

**1.2–2 m; 60–80 kg** Huge, flightless bird with long, bare legs and neck. Male has blackish plumage with white wings and tail (often stained chestnut). Female is grey-brown. Chicks banded tan and brown, resembling small, downy bustards. **Voice:** Booming, leonine roar, mostly at night. **Status and biology:** Wild populations scarce; restricted to large reserves and wilderness areas. Feral birds derived from farming operations are widespread in parts of S Africa. Occurs in savanna and semi-desert plains. Up to 4 females lay 15–40 eggs in a shallow scrape; alpha female lays 8–14 and keeps her eggs central in nest. Not all peripheral eggs are incubated. **Diet:** All manner of plant material, but favours seeds, fruit and flowers. (Volstruis)

# GUINEAFOWL

An endemic African family of large game birds with mostly naked heads and necks. Often in flocks; roost communally in trees. Sexes alike. Monogamous; chicks precocial, able to fly within a few weeks of hatching.

## 2 Helmeted Guineafowl *Numida meleagris*

**55–60 cm; 1.1–1.8 kg** A large, well-known game bird with blue-grey plumage, uniformly spotted with white. Head pattern varies geographically, but generally naked blue and red with cheek wattles and a pale casque on the crown; birds with white faces are usually hybrids with domesticated strains. Male has a larger casque than female. Juv. plumage browner; head partly feathered with dull blue skin and greatly reduced casque and wattles. **Voice:** Soft 'kek' contact calls given during the day, but noisy at dawn and dusk, making raucous 'kek-ek-ek kaaaaaa' and 'eerrrrk' calls. **Status and biology:** Common resident in grassland, woodland, savanna and fields; may flock in hundreds. Birds pair in spring, following much chasing by males. Females lay 6–12 eggs in a well-concealed scrape. **Diet:** Bulbs, roots, seeds (including fallen grain) and invertebrates. (Gewone Tarentaal)

## 3 Crested Guineafowl *Guttera edouardi*

**46–52 cm; 800–1 500 g** Similar to Helmeted Guineafowl, but with a tuft of curly black feathers on the head, naked blue-grey face, red eyes, black neck and pale blue (not white) spots on the body feathers. The outer secondaries have white outer webs, producing a white wing panel in flight. Juv. duller with short topknot and fine black-and-white barring on its body feathers. **Voice:** A 'chik-chik-chil-urrrrr' and a soft 'keet-keet-keet' contact call. **Status and biology:** Locally common resident of forest edge, thicket and dense woodland. Lays 2–12 eggs in a shallow scrape among dense vegetation. **Diet:** Bulbs, roots, new leaves, seeds, fruit and invertebrates. Sometimes forages on fruit in trees, and often follows troops of monkeys, picking at scraps of fruit and faeces. (Kuifkoptarentaal)

# PEACOCKS

Large, strongly dimorphic game birds with ornate head plumes; ad. males have showy, iridescent plumage. Only one introduced species occurs in the region. Chicks precocial.

## 4 Common Peacock *Pavo cristatus*

**90–120 cm (220 cm incl. train), 2.8–6 kg** Introduced. A large, distinctive game bird. Male readily identified by its crest, long, ocellated train and rufous flight feathers, and iridescent blue head, neck and breast. Female is smaller and duller with greenish neck, black-spotted breast and white belly; lacks long train. **Voice:** Very loud, trumpeting 'kee-ow', mostly heard at dawn and dusk. **Status and biology:** Small feral population on Robben Island; also occurs in some suburban areas. Polygamous; lays 3–12 eggs in a scrape on the ground. **Diet:** Omnivorous. (Makpou)

## SPURFOWL

Medium to large game birds. Sexes alike in most species; females lack leg spurs. Most species occur in small groups when not breeding; often call at dawn. Monogamous and often territorial; breed singly. Precocial chicks can flutter within 2 weeks of hatching, when they are still much smaller than ads.

### 1 Red-billed Spurfowl *Pternistis adspersus*

bbBBBBbbbbbb
J F M A M J J A S O N D

35–38 cm; 350–620 g  A fairly large, dark brown spurfowl with a red bill, dull red legs and a diagnostic yellow eye-ring. Head, neck and underparts are finely barred dark brown and white; lores blackish; back very finely vermiculated, appearing plain brown from a distance. Juv. is browner above than ad., with more prominent dark brown barring; bill and legs brown; yellow around eye reduced. First plumage chick (half size of ad.) has a broad buff supercilium, distinctive whitish stripes on each body feather, a dull horn-coloured bill and pale yellow legs. **Voice:** Loud, harsh 'chaa-chaa-chek-chek' at dawn and dusk. **Status and biology:** Near-endemic. Locally common resident in arid savanna and open, broadleafed woodland, often in thickets along watercourses. Easily observed; less skulking than most other spurfowl. Lays 3–10 eggs in a scrape on the ground; nest poorly concealed compared to other spurfowl. **Diet:** Bulbs, tubers, fruit, seeds and invertebrates. (Rooibekfisant)

### 2 Swainson's Spurfowl *Pternistis swainsonii*

BBBBBbbbbbbB
J F M A M J J A S O N D

33–38 cm; 350–820 g  A large, dark brown spurfowl with black legs and bill and bare red face and throat. Neck and mantle feathers are fringed pale grey, and breast and flank feathers have a prominent blackish central stripe. Juv. is duller and paler, with less extensive red facial skin and yellowish legs; throat patch covered in small, white feathers; belly white, finely barred blackish. In flight, juv. shows barring in flight feathers. Occasionally hybridises with Natal and Red-necked spurfowl. **Voice:** Raucous 'krraae-krraae-krraae' by males at dawn and dusk. **Status and biology:** Common resident in dry savanna and fields, usually in groups of 3–6 birds. Lays 3–12 eggs in a shallow scrape in the ground, well concealed among vegetation. **Diet:** Bulbs, roots, grass leaves, seeds (including fallen grain) and invertebrates. (Bosveldfisant)

### 3 Red-necked Spurfowl *Pternistis afer*

BBBbBBB⬜⬜⬜bB
J F M A M J J A S O N D

35–40 cm; 430–850 g  A large, brown-backed spurfowl with red bill, legs, and bare red face and throat. Plumage varies regionally: in the E of S Africa *P. a. castaneiventer* has a dark brown head and blackish underparts with 2 white stripes on each feather (width of white stripes variable). In Mozambique and E Zimbabwe *P. a. swynnertoni* **(3 A)** has a mostly white head and black belly patch; upperparts paler grey-brown. In NW Namibia *P. a. afer* has a white supercilium and moustache and broad white margins to feathers of lower breast, flanks and belly. Juv. duller with whitish feathers on face and throat; breast and flanks barred buff, white and dark brown; bill and legs dull yellow. Occasionally hybridises with Swainson's Spurfowl. **Voice:** Loud 'kwoor-kwoor-kwoor-kwaaa' at dusk and dawn. **Status and biology:** Fairly common resident of forest edges, thicket, riparian scrub and adjoining grassland. Lays 3–9 eggs in a shallow scrape among vegetation. **Diet:** Bulbs, roots, grass leaves, seeds and invertebrates. (Rooikeelfisant)

### 4 Cape Spurfowl *Pternistis capensis*

bbb⬜⬜⬜bBBBB
J F M A M J J A S O N D

40–43 cm; 650–1 000 g  A large, dark brown spurfowl with a plain, dark brown cap that contrasts with its paler supercilium, sub-loral spot and throat. Bill is dull red with a dark top to upper mandible and yellowish base; legs orange-red; lacks bare red face and throat of Red-necked Spurfowl. At close range, body feathers are finely vermiculated, with bolder buffy-white stripes on the lower breast and flanks, but lower flanks lack broad, creamy feather margins of Natal Spurfowl. Juv. duller with mainly brown bill and dull red-brown legs. **Voice:** Male advertising call, given mostly in the morning, is a series of loud 'ka-ke-KAA' notes, ending in a guttural laugh. **Status and biology:** Endemic. Common resident in lowland fynbos, pastures, fields, large gardens and riparian thickets in the Karoo. Often confiding. Lays 4–8 eggs in a shallow scrape well concealed among vegetation. **Diet:** Bulbs, fruit, seeds and invertebrates. (Kaapse Fisant)

### 5 Natal Spurfowl *Pternistis natalensis*

BBBBBbbbbbbB
J F M A M J J A S O N D

30–38 cm; 330–650 g  A medium-sized, brown spurfowl with orange-red bill and legs and strikingly vermiculated underparts. Smaller than Red-necked Spurfowl, lacking bare red face and throat. Best told from Cape Spurfowl by its much paler lower flanks and belly. Juv. is richly barred above and buff below, with white feather shaft streaks; bill greenish-brown; legs dull red-brown. Occasionally hybridises with Swainson's Spurfowl, and possibly Red-necked and Red-billed spurfowl. **Voice:** Raucous, screeching 'krr kik-ik-ik'. **Status and biology:** Near-endemic. Common resident in woodland, especially riparian thicket. Lays 2–7 eggs in a scrape on the ground among dense vegetation. **Diet:** Bulbs, roots, seeds, fruit and invertebrates. (Natalse Fisant)

## 1 Hartlaub's Spurfowl *Pternistis hartlaubi*

**25–28 cm; 210–290 g** A small, strongly dimorphic spurfowl with a heavy, decurved yellow-horn bill and dull yellow legs. Occurs alongside Orange River Francolin (p. 130), but unlikely to be confused given an adequate view. Upperparts mottled blackish-brown and rufous. Male has a striking black-and-white supercilium and chestnut cheeks; underparts whitish, heavily streaked brown. Female has face and underparts dull orange-brown. Juv. resembles dull, scruffy female; juv. male develops a white supercilium after about 3 months. **Voice:** Distinctive duet, 'ke-rak, keer-a keer-a kew', led by female; calls mostly at dawn. **Status and biology:** Near-endemic. Uncommon and localised resident of boulder-strewn slopes and rocky outcrops. Pairs remain together throughout year. Lays 2–4 eggs in a shallow scrape among boulders. **Diet:** Mainly bulbs and roots dug up with stout bill; also some seeds, fruit and invertebrates. (Klipfisant)

## 2 Chukar Partridge *Alectoris chukar*

**32–34 cm; 380–580 g** Introduced. A handsome partridge with black necklace and black and rufous flank stripes; superficially similar to francolins, but not closely related. In flight, grey rump and central tail contrast with rufous outer tail. Juv. rather drab and plain; lacks bold necklace and flank stripes. **Voice:** A dry 'chuk-chuk-chuk-chukar', hence the common name. **Status and biology:** Small feral population of some 300 birds on Robben Island, W Cape, following release there in 1964. Usually monogamous; lays 6–15 eggs in a shallow scrape on the ground. **Diet:** Mainly roots and seeds; also occasional leaves and invertebrates. (Asiatiese Patrys)

# FRANCOLINS

**Small to medium-sized game birds. Sexes alike in most species. Monogamous and often territorial; breed singly. Precocial chicks can flutter within 2 weeks of hatching, when they are still much smaller than ads.**

## 3 Crested Francolin *Dendroperdix sephaena*

**30–35 cm; 240–460 g** A distinctive francolin with a rather long, black tail that is often cocked at a 45° angle, imparting a bantam-like appearance. Dark cap contrasts with broad white supercilium; neck and breast spotted white; back and wing coverts have distinctive white stripes. Female is duller than male; back finely barred with buff (not white) stripes. Juv. paler above than ad. Kirk's Francolin *D. s. rovuma* of central Mozambique is sometimes considered a separate species; lacks the dark moustache and has dark brown streaks (not fine barring) on belly and flanks. **Voice:** Rattling duet, 'chee-chakla, chee-chakla'. **Status and biology:** Common resident in woodland and well-wooded savanna. Lays 3–7 eggs in a scrape in the ground among dense vegetation. **Diet:** Bulbs, roots, leaves, fruit, seeds and invertebrates. (Bospatrys)

## 4 Coqui Francolin *Peliperdix coqui*

**20–26 cm; 200–300 g** A small francolin with marked sexual dimorphism; bill black with yellow base; legs yellow. Male has a plain, buffy head with darker crown, and heavily barred breast. Female has neatly defined pale throat and supercilium, and plain buffy breast; superficially resembles a female quail, but is appreciably larger. Difficult to flush; shows chestnut wings and outer tail in flight. Juv. like ad. female, but paler above and buffy below with reduced black barring. **Voice:** Distinctive, disyllabic 'ko-ki, ko-ki'; also a fast, trumpeted 'ker-aak, aak, kara-kara-kara' with last notes fading away, given in territorial defence. **Status and biology:** Common to locally common resident of woodland and savanna, especially on sandy soils. Lays 3–6 eggs in a scrape in the ground. **Diet:** Seeds, fruit, leaves, roots and invertebrates. (Swempie)

# RED-WINGED FRANCOLINS

Fairly small francolins with large bills and at least some rufous in their flight feathers; identification based on head, neck and belly patterns. All have similar piping, whistled calls, and occur in pairs or small coveys.

## 1 Grey-winged Francolin *Scleroptila africanus*

`b b b | | | | | | B B B B b`
J F M A M J J A S O N D

30–33 cm; 370–520 g  The most distinctive of the red-winged francolins, identified by its grey-speckled (not white or buff) throat and finely mottled black-and-white belly. Rufous wing patch smaller than other species; largely confined to primary bases. Juv. duller, with whitish throat; acquires grey throat within 2 months of hatching. **Voice:** Whistling, rather variable 'wip wip wip kipeeoo, wip kipeeoo'. **Status and biology:** Endemic. Fairly common resident of strandveld, fynbos, southern Karoo and montane grassland. Usually in coveys of 3–8 birds. Lays 4–8 eggs in a scrape well concealed under a grass tuft. **Diet:** Bulbs, roots and invertebrates. (Bergpatrys)

## 2 Red-winged Francolin *Scleroptila levaillantii*

`b b b b b b b b b b B B`
J F M A M J J A S O N D

33–38 cm; 360–550 g  The largest red-winged francolin; separated from Grey-winged Francolin by its white throat, buffy belly and much more extensive rufous in wing (primaries, outer secondaries and primary coverts). Lacks a moustachial stripe; white throat is bordered by rufous, not a black necklace as in Shelley's and Orange River francolins. Further told from Shelley's Francolin by buffy (not black-and-white) belly, and broad blackish band across upper breast. Juv. duller, with less distinct blackish breast band. **Voice:** Piping 'wip-tilleee', sometimes preceded by several short 'wip' notes. **Status and biology:** Uncommon to locally common resident in grassland and fields, usually on lower slopes and in valleys in mountainous terrain; numbers have decreased in many areas due to unfavourable agricultural practices. Lays 4–10 eggs in a scrape concealed by a grass tuft. **Diet:** Bulbs, roots and invertebrates. (Rooivlerkpatrys)

## 3 Shelley's Francolin *Scleroptila shelleyi*

`b b B B b b b b B B B B`
J F M A M J J A S O N D

30–36 cm; 380–590 g  Superficially resembles Red-winged Francolin, but has a boldly barred black-and-white belly and a moustachial stripe bordering its white throat, forming a narrow black necklace. In flight, primaries and outer secondaries are rufous. Juv. duller with scruffy plumage; chequered belly patch less prominent. **Voice:** Rhythmic, repeated 'til-it, til-leoo' ('I'll drink your beer'); slower and less varied than other red-winged francolins. **Status and biology:** Locally common resident in savanna and open woodland, usually associated with rocky ground. Lays 3–8 eggs in a scrape among dense grass. **Diet:** Bulbs, roots, seeds and invertebrates. (Laeveldpatrys)

## 4 Orange River Francolin *Scleroptila levaillantoides*

`b b b b b b b B B b b b`
J F M A M J J A S O N D

32–35 cm; 360–530 g  Slightly smaller than Red-winged Francolin, with a black moustachial stripe extending as a thin, black necklace around its white throat; lacks a broad, dark breast band. Belly buffy with variable dark streaks; lacks black-and-white belly patch of Shelley's Francolin. Told from Grey-winged Francolin by its white (not grey-freckled) throat. Plumage varies regionally, with paler birds in more arid areas. **Voice:** Rather strident 'kibitele', faster and higher-pitched than that of Shelley's Francolin, mostly at dawn. **Status and biology:** Near-endemic. Locally common resident in grassland and semi-arid savanna. Lays 3–8 eggs in a scrape among dense grass. **Diet:** Bulbs, roots, seeds, flowers, soft leaves and invertebrates. (Kalaharipatrys)

# QUAILS

Small, sexually dimorphic game birds. Run swiftly in a hunched position. Usually seen when flushed; flight action rapid and stronger than buttonquails. Usually monogamous.

## 1 Common Quail · *Coturnix coturnix*

`Bbb` `bBBB`
J F M A M J J A S O N D

16–20 cm; 80–115 g  A small, pale buff game bird, streaked black and white above with a prominent white supercilium; underparts buffy, streaked brown on the breast. Male has a black or russet throat. Slightly larger than Harlequin Quail with paler plumage. Juv. less streaked than ad. **Voice:** A repeated, high-pitched 'whit wit-wit' ('wet my lips'), slower and deeper than Harlequin Quail; also a sharp 'crwee-crwee', given in flight. **Status and biology:** Locally abundant intra-African migrant in grassland, fields and croplands. Lays 2–14 (usually 5–7) eggs in a scrape among dense vegetation. **Diet:** Seeds, bulbs, roots, soft leaves, flowers and invertebrates. (Afrikaanse Kwartel)

## 2 Harlequin Quail · *Coturnix delegorguei*

`BBb` `bbB`
J F M A M J J A S O N D

14–18 cm; 68–90 g  Male is darker than Common Quail, with chestnut and black underparts. Female has buffy underparts, darker than Common Quail, with contrasting white throat; supercilium buff. Juv. paler than female. **Voice:** A high-pitched 'whit, wit-wit', more metallic than Common Quail; squeaky 'kree-kree' in flight. **Status and biology:** Locally common nomad and intra-African migrant in grassland, damp fields and savanna, often in moister areas than Common Quail. Lays 4–8 eggs in a scrape among dense vegetation. **Diet:** Invertebrates, seeds and soft leaves. (Bontkwartel)

## 3 Blue Quail · *Coturnix adansonii*

`bbbb` `b`
J F M A M J J A S O N D

12–14 cm; 40–50 g  Rare. A small quail, similar in size to buttonquails; told from them in flight by its more compact shape and uniform upperwing (lacking paler upperwing coverts). Male told from male Harlequin Quail in flight by its small size and chestnut wing coverts, and blue underparts that typically appear black. On the ground, female and juv. can be distinguished by their barred underparts. In flight they appear small and dark. **Voice:** A high-pitched whistle 'teee-ti-ti'; much less vocal than other quails. **Status and biology:** Rare resident and nomad in damp and flooded grassland. Range has contracted in S in the last century. Lays 3–9 eggs in a scrape among dense vegetation. **Diet:** Seeds, soft leaves and invertebrates. (Bloukwartel)

# BUTTONQUAILS

Small, quail-like game birds that freeze when alarmed; typically only seen when flushed. Flight weaker than quails. Polyandrous; females larger and more brightly coloured; males incubate and care for precocial chicks.

## 4 Kurrichane Buttonquail · *Turnix sylvaticus*

`BBBbbbbbbBBB`
J F M A M J J A S O N D

14–16 cm; 30–70 g  A rather pale buttonquail, appreciably smaller than Common or Harlequin quails; in flight has a longer neck and more rapid wing beats; pale upperwing coverts contrast with darker flight feathers. Paler than Black-rumped Buttonquail; best told in flight by the lack of a dark rump and back. On the ground, told by black spots on the sides of the breast and paler, buffy (not rufous) face. Female is larger and more boldly marked than male. **Voice:** Female advertises with a repeated, low-pitched hoot, 'hmmmm'. **Status and biology:** Locally common resident and nomad in tall grassland, old fields and open savanna. Lays 2–4 eggs in a shallow scrape among grass tufts. **Diet:** Invertebrates and seeds. (Bosveldkwarteltjie)

## 5 Black-rumped Buttonquail · *Turnix nanus*

`Bbb` `bbbB`
J F M A M J J A S O N D

14–15 cm; 40–60 g  Larger and more richly coloured than Kurrichane Buttonquail, with a plain ginger face and throat. In flight shows a diagnostic dark back and rump that contrast with the paler wing coverts. Best separated from female Blue Quail by flight action and contrast between rump and upperwing coverts. Not known to overlap with Hottentot Buttonquail; differs by flesh-white (not yellow) legs and unmarked belly. Female is less barred on breast and flanks. Juv. has a spotted breast. **Voice:** A flufftail-like 'ooooop-ooooop'. **Status and biology:** Scarce to locally common resident and nomad in moist grassland, often around temporary wetlands, but also damp areas in hilly and mountainous terrain. Lays 2–4 eggs in a shallow scrape among grass tufts. **Diet:** Invertebrates and seeds. (Swartrugkwarteltjie)

## 6 Hottentot Buttonquail · *Turnix hottentottus*

`bB` `b`
J F M A M J J A S O N D

14–15 cm; 40–60 g  A richly coloured buttonquail; paler above than Black-rumped Buttonquail, lacking a clearly defined dark back; belly has more extensive black spotting. Legs yellow (bright chrome-yellow in female), not flesh-white. Male is less richly marked. **Voice:** A low, flufftail-like booming. **Status and biology:** Endemic. Locally common resident and nomad in fynbos and strandveld. Usually found in open areas dominated by restios; prefers areas 2–4 years after fires. Lays 2–5 eggs in a shallow scrape among vegetation. **Diet:** Invertebrates and seeds. (Kaapse Kwarteltjie)

# FINFOOTS

Peculiar grebe-like birds with lobed toes and stout, dagger-like bills. Sexes differ in plumage; males appreciably larger than females. Monogamous; females incubate and care for the semi-precocial chicks.

## 1 African Finfoot *Podica senegalensis*

| B | b | b | b | | | | | b | B | B | B | B |
|---|---|---|---|---|---|---|---|---|---|---|---|---|
| J | F | M | A | M | J | J | A | S | O | N | D |

**52–65 cm; 350–650 g** A reclusive waterbird; swims low in the water, snaking head back and forth. Superficially recalls African Darter (p. 56), but with a shorter, thicker neck and a heavy, red bill; seldom dives. Out of the water, the bright red-orange legs and feet are conspicuous. Male is greyer with a plain face; female browner with boldly patterned brown and white face. Juv. has a dark bill and pale belly. **Voice:** Normally silent; occasionally gives a short, frog-like 'krork'. **Status and biology:** Uncommon resident of rivers and streams with well-vegetated banks; usually remains among, or close to, vegetation overhanging water; easily overlooked. Lays 1–3 eggs in an untidy bowl nest close to or over water. **Diet:** Mainly insects; also fish, frogs and invertebrates, taken on land and in water. (Watertrapper)

# COOTS, MOORHENS, SWAMPHENS AND GALLINULES

Large rails that are generally easier to locate and observe than smaller crakes and flufftails. Sexes alike. Usually monogamous and territorial; sometimes helped by young of previous broods.

## 2 Red-knobbed Coot *Fulica cristata*

| b | b | b | b | b | b | b | b | b | b | b | b |
|---|---|---|---|---|---|---|---|---|---|---|---|
| J | F | M | A | M | J | J | A | S | O | N | D |

**36–44 cm; 500–900 g** The most aquatic rail; sometimes mistaken for a duck; long, lobed toes for swimming. Ad. black with a white bill and frontal shield. The dull red knobs on top of the shield are larger in br. birds. Juv. is grey with small frontal shield; lacks whitish flank line and undertail coverts of smaller juv. Common Moorhen. **Voice:** Harsh, metallic 'claak'. **Status and biology:** Common to abundant resident at dams, lakes, slow-flowing rivers and estuaries. Lays 2–6 (rarely up to 11) eggs on a large, floating mound of reeds and sedge leaves. **Diet:** Mainly aquatic plants, but also some invertebrates; rarely carrion. Often feeds by upending or diving. (Bleshoender)

## 3 Common Moorhen *Gallinula chloropus*

| b | b | b | b | b | b | b | b | b | b | b | b |
|---|---|---|---|---|---|---|---|---|---|---|---|
| J | F | M | A | M | J | J | A | S | O | N | D |

**30–36 cm; 180–350 g** A dull, sooty-black gallinule with greenish-yellow legs and red frontal shield. Larger and darker than Lesser Moorhen, with mostly red (not yellow) bill. Juv. is greyer above than juv. Lesser Moorhen, with darker belly and dull brown bill. **Voice:** Sharp 'krrik'. **Status and biology:** Common resident and nomad at wetlands with fringing vegetation. Bolder than other gallinules, often swimming in open water. Lays 4–9 eggs in a cup of reeds and sedges built among dense vegetation near water. **Diet:** Wide range of plants and animals; also carrion. (Grootwaterhoender)

## 4 Lesser Moorhen *Gallinula angulata*

| B | B | B | b | | | | | | | b | b |
|---|---|---|---|---|---|---|---|---|---|---|---|
| J | F | M | A | M | J | J | A | S | O | N | D |

**22–26 cm; 100–160 g** Smaller and more secretive than Common Moorhen, with less conspicuous white flank feathers and mainly yellow (not red) bill. Juv. is sandy-buff (not grey as in juv. Common Moorhen) with a pale belly and dull, yellowish-green bill and legs. **Voice:** A series of hollow notes, 'do do do do do do do'. **Status and biology:** Locally common intra-African migrant in flooded grassland and small, secluded ponds. Lays 4–9 eggs in a shallow cup of grass and sedges built among dense vegetation near water. **Diet:** Plants, seeds and invertebrates. (Kleinwaterhoender)

## 1 African Purple Swamphen  *Porphyrio madagascariensis*

J F M A M J J A S O N D

38–46 cm; 500–700 g  A large gallinule, easily identified by its massive red bill and frontal shield, long red legs, and purplish coloration, with turquoise face and foreneck and greenish back. Juv. is dull brown above and grey below with a large, reddish-brown bill. **Voice:** A variety of harsh shrieks, wails and booming notes. **Status and biology:** Common resident in reedbeds, marshes and flooded grassland. Lays 2–5 eggs in a large cup of reeds among emergent vegetation. **Diet:** Mainly plants; also invertebrates, fish, frogs, birds' eggs and chicks, and carrion. Holds plant stems with foot while eating soft stem pulp. (Grootkoningriethaan)

## 2 Allen's Gallinule  *Porphyrio alleni*

B B B b b ▮▮▮▮▮▮▮ b
J F M A M J J A S O N D

25–28 cm; 110–165 g  Smaller and darker than African Purple Swamphen, with blue (in br. male) or green (in br. female) frontal shield. Non-br. birds have dull brown shield. Ad. differs from ad. American Purple Gallinule by red (not yellow) legs and lack of yellow tip to bill. Juv. is pale buff-brown, often scaly on upperparts, and lacks white flank stripes of juv. Common Moorhen; has pale, fleshy (not greenish as in juv. Common Moorhen, p. 134, or olive as in juv. American Purple Gallinule) legs. **Voice:** 6 or more rapidly uttered, sharp clicks, 'duk duk duk duk duk duk'. **Status and biology:** Locally common resident and br. visitor in flooded grassland. Lays 2–8 eggs in a loose cup of reeds and grass built among dense vegetation near water. **Diet:** Mainly plants, seeds and fruit; also invertebrates and small fish. Holds plant stems and fruit with foot while eating. (Kleinkoningriethaan)

## 3 American Purple Gallinule  *Porphyrio martinicus*

▯▯▯▮▮▮▮▮▮▯▯▯
J F M A M J J A S O N D

27–35 cm; 120–300 g  Smaller than African Purple Swamphen, with bright yellowish-green (not red) legs and yellow tip to bill. Ad.'s frontal shield is pale blue. Most records are juvs, which are similar to juv. Allen's Gallinule but have olive (not flesh-coloured) legs; differ from juv. Common Moorhen (p. 134) by lack of white flank stripes. **Voice:** Harsh, barking calls; usually silent. **Status and biology:** Vagrant from Americas, mostly Apr–Jun, but some remain for many months. Usually in reedbeds, but recent arrivals may occur virtually anywhere; regular vagrant at Tristan da Cunha, and several records from ships at sea. (Amerikaanse Koningriethaan)

## 4 Black Crake  *Amaurornis flavirostra*

B B B b b b b b b b B B
J F M A M J J A S O N D

18–22 cm; 70–115 g  A fairly small, plain black crake with a bright yellow bill and red eyes and legs. Juv. greyer, with a black bill and dark legs. **Voice:** A throaty 'chrrooo' and an hysterical, bubbling, wheezy duet. **Status and biology:** Common resident in marshes with dense cover. Often bold, foraging out in the open. Monogamous, sometimes with helpers at the nest. Lays 2–6 eggs in a deep cup of grass and reeds built in emergent vegetation. **Diet:** Worms, insects, other invertebrates, small frogs and fish, birds' eggs and chicks, seeds and soft parts of plants. (Swartriethaan)

# JACANAS

Rail-like waders with extremely long toes and claws for walking on floating vegetation. Sexes alike in plumage, but females larger than males in most species, linked to polyandry. Male responsible for all parental care in all species except Lesser Jacana.

## 5 African Jacana  *Actophilornis africanus*

B B B b b b b b b b B B
J F M A M J J A S O N D

25–32 cm; 120–250 g  Ad. is rich chestnut with a white neck, yellow upper breast and contrasting black-and-white head that highlights the blue frontal shield. Female appreciably larger than male. Juv. is paler, with white belly, and lacks frontal shield; much larger than Lesser Jacana, lacking white trailing edge to wing in flight. **Voice:** Noisy; sharp, ringing 'krrrek', rasping 'krrrrrrk' and barking 'yowk-yowk'. **Status and biology:** Common resident and nomad at wetlands with floating vegetation, especially water lilies. Polyandrous; female lays 3–5 eggs for up to 7 successive males on flimsy nests of floating vegetation. Male performs all parental duties. **Diet:** Mainly invertebrates; occasional fish and seeds. (Grootlangtoon)

## 6 Lesser Jacana  *Microparra capensis*

▮▮▮▮▮▮▮▮▮ b b b b
J F M A M J J A S O N D

15–17 cm; 40–42 g  Much smaller than African Jacana, with white underparts and eyebrow; upperparts are pale buffy-grey-brown. Much smaller than juv. African Jacana and in flight shows white on trailing edges of secondaries, and pale upperwing coverts that contrast with dark flight feathers; underwing dark. Female only slightly larger than male. Juv. less rufous above than ad. **Voice:** Soft, flufftail-like 'poop-oop-oop-oop'; scolding 'ksh-ksh-ksh'; high-pitched 'titititititi'. **Status and biology:** Uncommon resident and local nomad at flood plains and wetlands with emergent grass and sedge. Monogamous; unique among jacanas in sharing parental duties. Lays 2–5 eggs on a mat of floating vegetation. **Diet:** Insects. (Dwerglangtoon)

# RAILS AND CRAKES

Small to fairly large birds, usually associated with wetlands or damp habitats. Often secretive, best located by calls. Sexes alike in most species (except flufftails and Striped Crake); males generally larger than females. Breeds singly; usually territorial; mating systems varied, although usually monogamous. Chicks semi-precocial, cared for by one or both parents.

## 1 African Rail  *Rallus caerulescens*

27–30 cm; 125–200 g A fairly large rail with a long, decurved, red bill and red legs, grey breast, and black-and-white barred flanks. With a very poor view could be confused with African Crake, but has plain brown (not streaked) back. Juv. has a brown bill and a buff breast. **Voice:** An explosive, high-pitched trill 'trrreee-tee-tee-tee-tee-tee', descending in pitch. **Status and biology:** Common resident of marshes, reedbeds and flooded grassland, usually in areas with standing water. Often ventures into the open, especially in the early morning. Monogamous; lays 2–6 eggs on a platform of flattened grasses, well concealed among dense vegetation. Both sexes incubate and care for young. **Diet:** Worms, insects, frogs, small fish and seeds. (Grootriethaan)

## 2 Corn Crake  *Crex crex*

25–30 cm; 130–200 g A large, pale sandy crake with chestnut-orange wing coverts conspicuous in flight. Paler and larger than African Crake, with a buffy (not grey) breast. Rarely seen except when flushed, when it flies with whirring wings and dangling legs. Juv. more buffy above, with indistinct barring on vent. **Voice:** Scientific name is onomatopoeic, but Corn Crake seldom calls in Africa. **Status and biology: NEAR-THREATENED.** Uncommon Palearctic migrant to rank grassland and open savanna. Occurs around the edges of marshes, but seldom in areas with standing water. Vagrant to the Prince Edward Islands. **Diet:** Insects, grass seeds and leaves. (Kwartelkoning)

## 3 Spotted Crake  *Porzana porzana*

21–24 cm; 70–130 g A medium-sized crake with distinctive white-spotted upperparts and whitish leading edge to wing in flight; bill mostly yellow. Flanks barred, but finer and less boldly marked than African Crake; undertail buff. Told from slightly smaller Striped Crake by spotted (not striped) upperparts, yellowish (not greenish) legs, barred flanks and paler undertail coverts. Often flicks its tail, showing buffy undertail coverts. **Voice:** A short 'kreck' when alarmed; generally silent in Africa. **Status and biology:** Uncommon Palearctic migrant to flooded grassland and wetland. **Diet:** Worms, other invertebrates and seeds. (Gevlekte Riethaan)

## 4 African Crake  *Crecopsis egregia*

19–23 cm; 120–160 g A medium-sized crake; smaller and darker than Corn Crake. Smaller than African Rail with a short, stubby bill and streaked back. Flanks and belly boldly barred black and white. When flushed, it flies a short distance with legs dangling, showing the brown, mottled upperparts and barred flanks. Juv. browner, with less boldly barred flanks. **Voice:** A monotonous, hollow-sounding series of notes, 'krrr-krrr-krrr'. **Status and biology:** Uncommon to locally common intra-African migrant, breeding in damp grassland and at seasonal wetlands. Lays 2–8 eggs on a mat of flattened grass among dense vegetation. Both sexes incubate and care for young. **Diet:** Worms, snails, insects, small frogs and fish, seeds and grass leaves. (Afrikaanse Riethaan)

## 5 Striped Crake  *Aenigmatolimnas marginalis*

18–22 cm; 40–60 g A rather plain, medium-sized crake. Combination of white stripes on its buffy upperparts, plain flanks and russet vent are diagnostic. Female has a blue-grey breast and belly. Male and juv. have buff breast; juv. warmer buff but with reduced stripes. **Voice:** A rapid 'tik-tik-tik-tik-tik', which may continue for a minute or more. **Status and biology:** Uncommon, intra-African migrant to seasonally flooded grassland and marshes. Abundance and range varies in relation to rainfall. Polyandrous; female lays 3–5 eggs in a shallow cup of grass in a dense tussock in standing water. Incubation and care of chicks largely by male. **Diet:** Worms, insects, other invertebrates and tadpoles. (Gestreepte Riethaan)

## 6 Baillon's Crake  *Porzana pusilla*

16–18 cm; 30–45 g Much smaller than African Crake, with white-spotted upperparts and less contrasting black-and-white barring on the flanks and undertail. Barred undertail separates it from larger Spotted and Striped crakes. Juv. paler, mottled and barred below. **Voice:** A soft 'qurrr-qurrr' and various frog-like croaks. **Status and biology:** Uncommon to locally common resident and nomad in wetlands, reedbeds and flooded grassland. Secretive; rarely seen in the open except at dawn or dusk. Monogamous; lays 2–6 eggs in a shallow cup of leaves built among dense vegetation. Both sexes incubate and care for young. **Diet:** Insects, aquatic invertebrates, seeds and grass leaves. (Kleinriethaan)

# FLUFFTAILS

Tiny rails, renowned for their secretive behaviour. Best located by their hooting or rattling calls. Hooting calls could be confused with those of the buttonquails. Many species are crepuscular and call at night. Sexes differ; females hard to identify. Monogamous.

## 1 Red-chested Flufftail *Sarothrura rufa*

**15–17 cm; 30–46 g** Wetland species. Male is distinguished by red of head extending to lower breast and by dark tail. Belly and back are uniformly dark with small white speckles. Darker than Streaky-breasted Flufftail with more extensive red on underparts. Female and juv. are darker than other female flufftails, especially on throat and upper breast. **Voice:** Low hoot, 'woop', repeated 1x per second; more rapid 'gu-duk, gu-duk, gu-duk'; ringing 'tuwi-tuwi-tuwi'. **Status and biology:** Common resident of dense reeds and sedges around marshes and streams. Lays 2–3 eggs in a deep cup of grass and leaves among dense vegetation, often over shallow water. **Diet:** Worms, insects, other invertebrates and seeds. (Rooiborsvleikuiken)

## 2 Striped Flufftail *Sarothrura affinis*

**14–15 cm; 25–30 g** Grassland, fynbos and wetland species. Male has a plain red head and tail; body black, boldly striped white. Female and juv. finely barred buff above and have a chestnut-washed tail. **Voice:** Low 'oooooop' hoot lasting 1 sec and repeated every 2 secs; also high-pitched, chattering trill. **Status and biology:** Locally common resident and local nomad in montane grassland and fynbos; sometimes associated with wetlands. Lays 4–5 eggs in a deep cup of grass and rootlets built among dense vegetation. **Diet:** Insects, worms, other invertebrates and seeds. (Gestreepte Vleikuiken)

## 3 Streaky-breasted Flufftail *Sarothrura boehmi*

**14–16 cm; 25–40 g** Wetland species. Male has less red on breast than male Red-chested Flufftail, with a paler throat and streaked lower breast and belly; when flushed, appears much paler. Female and juv. are paler below than female Red-chested Flufftail. **Voice:** Low hoot, 'gawooo', repeated 20–30 times every 0.5 seconds. **Status and biology:** Uncommon intra-African migrant, breeding in rank, seasonally flooded grassland. Lays 2–5 eggs in a shallow bowl formed in a dense grass tuft at the edge of a wetland. **Diet:** Worms, insects and seeds. (Streepborsvleikuiken)

## 4 White-winged Flufftail *Sarothrura ayresi*

**14 cm; 26–34 g** A wetland flufftail. Both sexes show diagnostic white secondaries in flight and have black and chestnut barred tails and white bellies. Outer web of outer primary white, forming a thin white line on the folded wing. Flight fast and direct, with whirring wing beats. Female differs from female Striped Flufftail by chestnut wash on neck and barred (not plain) tail. **Voice:** Low, deep hoot, repeated every second, often in duet, with differences in pitch between birds. **Status and biology: ENDANGERED.** Rare and localised in upland marshes and vleis, where sedges and aquatic grasses grow in shallow water. Breeds in highlands of Ethiopia; winters in S Africa. **Diet:** Worms, insects and plant material. (Witvlerkvleikuiken)

## 5 Buff-spotted Flufftail *Sarothrura elegans*

**15–17 cm; 40–60 g** Species of forest and thicket. Male's back has large buff spots and black and rufous barred tail. Red on head extends only onto upper breast, not onto lower breast and back as in Red-chested Flufftail. Female and juv. rich brown above, with buff breast and paler, barred belly. **Voice:** Low, foghorn-like 'dooooooooooo' lasting 3–4 seconds, mainly at night and on overcast and rainy days. Calls from elevated perches at night; on or near the ground during the day. **Status and biology:** Locally common resident and nomad in dense forest understorey, adjacent scrub and well-wooded gardens. Lays 3–5 eggs in a domed nest, usually with a short entrance tunnel, built from vegetation on the ground. **Diet:** Worms, insects, other invertebrates and occasional seeds. (Gevlekte Vleikuiken)

# SECRETARYBIRD

A distinctive raptor with long legs and a long neck. Endemic to Africa; placed in its own family. Has long, broad wings and soars strongly, but usually searches for prey by walking through open vegetation; often raises wings when running. Sexes alike; juvs duller. Monogamous and territorial; incubation mainly by female. Chicks altricial.

## 1 Secretarybird *Sagittarius serpentarius*

bbBBBBBBBBbb
J F M A M J J A S O N D

**1.25–1.50 m; 2.8–5 kg** Could possibly be mistaken for a crane, but its long legs, head plumes, long central tail feathers, characteristic long-striding gait and horizontal body posture are diagnostic. In flight, the 2 central tail feathers project well beyond legs, and black flight feathers and thighs contrast with pale grey coverts and body. Juv. has shorter tail and yellow (not red), bare facial skin. **Voice:** Normally silent, but utters deep croak during aerial display. **Status and biology:** Uncommon to locally common resident of savanna and open grassland, usually singly or in pairs. Lays 1–3 (rarely 4) eggs in a huge stick platform on top of a flat-topped tree or bush. **Diet:** Snakes and other reptiles, mammals up to the size of mongooses, birds, frogs and invertebrates, especially grasshoppers. (Sekretarisvoël)

# CRANES

Tall, stately birds of open grassland and wetland. Could possibly be confused with herons (e.g. Black-headed Heron, p. 62). Sexes alike, but males slightly larger. Gather in flocks when not breeding, and roost communally, often at wetlands. Monogamous; both sexes incubate and care for the precocial chicks. Displays include 'dances' with raised wings.

## 2 Grey Crowned Crane *Balearica regulorum*

BBbbbb   bBB
J F M A M J J A S O N D

**100–110 cm; 3–4 kg** A distinctive crane with a large gold crown, white wing coverts, black primaries and chestnut secondaries. Cheek patch is mostly white, with red top. Imm. lacks unfeathered cheek patch, and has smaller crown. **Voice:** Trumpeting flight call, 'may hem'; deep 'huum huum' when breeding. **Status and biology:** Locally common resident and local nomad, moving in response to rainfall. Some 6 000 birds in sthn Africa. Occurs at shallow wetlands, and in grassland and agricultural lands. Commutes to wetlands to roost. Lays 2–4 eggs on a large mound of vegetation in shallow water among dense emergent plants. **Diet:** Wide range of plants and animals. (Mahem)

## 3 Wattled Crane *Bugeranus carunculatus*

bbbbBBBBBbbb
J F M A M J J A S O N D

**120–170 cm; 7–8.5 kg** A very large crane with a white neck and long facial wattles. Can be identified even at long range by white neck and upper breast contrasting with black underparts and grey back. Juv. has pale crown. **Voice:** Loud 'kwaarnk'; seldom calls. **Status and biology: VULNERABLE.** 8 000 birds globally, 2 000 in sthn Africa. Uncommon and localised at shallow wetland and adjoining grassland. Usually in pairs or small groups, but non-br. birds gather in flocks of up to 50. Lays 1–2 eggs on a large mound of vegetation in shallow water among emergent plants. Only raises 1 chick; second egg abandoned after first hatches. Occasionally hybridises with Blue Crane. **Diet:** Mainly plant matter (tubers, seeds); also some animals. (Lelkraanvoël)

## 4 Blue Crane *Anthropoides paradiseus*

bbbb   bbbBB
J F M A M J J A S O N D

**100–120 cm; 4–5.5 kg** A grey crane with a bulbous head and long, trailing 'tail' (actually inner secondaries and tertials). In flight, shows less contrast between flight feathers and coverts than other cranes. Juv. lacks long 'tail' and is paler grey, especially on head. **Voice:** Loud, nasal 'kraaaank'. **Status and biology: VULNERABLE.** Resident and local nomad; some 20 000 birds, most in agricultural lands in W Cape and adjacent Karoo; scarce and decreasing in E grassland; small isolated population in N Namibia. Occurs in pairs or family groups while breeding, but non-br. flocks contain hundreds of birds. Lays 1–2 (rarely 3) eggs in shallow scrape on dry ground or on mound of vegetation in damp areas. Often raises 2 chicks. **Diet:** Wide range of plants and animals. (Bloukraanvoël)

# LARGE BUSTARDS

Large, cursorial birds of open country. Sexes differ; males larger with inflatable throat pouches that create spectacular white balloon displays. Lack a preen gland, but have copious powder down. Polygamous; females select males at dispersed leks. Chicks precocial; cared for by female only.

### 1 Kori Bustard *Ardeotis kori*

B B b b | b b b B B B
J F M A M J J A S O N D

**110–140 cm; 4.5–18 kg**  The largest bustard; flight heavy and laboured. Neck finely barred grey (lacking orange hind neck); crest on rear of crown. Displaying male raises crest, inflates white throat and throws tail forward onto its back, fluffing out its white undertail coverts. Female much smaller. Juv. has paler head, shorter crest and browner back. **Voice:** Deep, resonant 'oom-oom-oom' by displaying male. **Status and biology:** Generally scarce, but locally fairly common resident and nomad in protected areas. Occurs in semi-arid savanna and grassland, usually near cover of trees. Lays 2 eggs in a shallow scrape. **Diet:** Invertebrates, small vertebrates, carrion and a wide range of plant material. (Gompou)

### 2 Denham's Bustard *Neotis denhami*

■■■■■■■ b B B b
J F M A M J J A S O N D

**90–120 cm; 4–14 kg**  Larger than Ludwig's Bustard with a pale grey foreneck, chestnut (not orange) hind neck and black-and-white striped crown. Usually shows more white on folded wing, but this varies considerably. Displaying male inflates throat to form conspicuous white 'balloon'. Female is smaller, with a paler, more mottled back and less white in wings. Juv. has crown mottled brown. **Voice:** Deep booming by displaying male. **Status and biology: NEAR-THREATENED**. *N. d. stanleyi* is a locally common resident and nomad in S Africa; *N. d. jacksoni* is scarce non-br. visitor to N Botswana and Zimbabwe. Occurs in open grassland and agricultural land. Lays 1–2 eggs in a shallow scrape. **Diet:** Invertebrates, small vertebrates and a wide range of plant material. (Veldpou)

### 3 Ludwig's Bustard *Neotis ludwigii*

b b b b b | b B B b b b
J F M A M J J A S O N D

**80–100 cm; 2.2–6 kg**  Smaller than Denham's Bustard with a dark grey-brown (not pale grey) foreneck, more orange (not chestnut) hind neck and largely uniform, dark head. Normally shows less white in folded wing, but amount of white on wings of both species is variable. Male display 'balloon' is grey (not white). Female is markedly smaller. Juv. is paler on head and neck. **Voice:** Displaying male gives explosive, deep 'woodoomp' every 15–30 seconds. **Status and biology:** Near-endemic. Locally common nomad and partial migrant in karoo scrub and arid savanna; frequents drier areas than Denham's Bustard. Lays 2–3 eggs in a shallow scrape. **Diet:** Invertebrates, small vertebrates and a wide range of plant material. (Ludwigpou)

# SMALL BUSTARDS AND KORHAANS

Smaller bustards, regionally known as korhaans. Most genera are polygynous, with marked sexual differences in size and plumage; males give loud, distinctive calls and display flights. Eupodotis korhaans are monogamous, occurring in pairs or family groups year-round; plumage only slightly dimorphic; both sexes call together. Chicks precocial.

## 1 Black-bellied Bustard  *Lissotis melanogaster*

`Bbb` ` ` ` ` ` ` ` `bBBB`
J F M A M J J A S O N D

**58–65 cm; 1.1–2.7 kg** A fairly large bustard with a long, thin neck and a boldly mottled back. Male has a black belly, extending as a thin line up the front of the neck. Male distinctive in flight: underwing black with white panel in outer primaries; upperwing has mainly white primaries, greater and lesser coverts, black secondaries, and brown median coverts. Female is nondescript, off-white below with duller wings (flight feathers mainly dark brown with white spots in outer primaries; coverts brown with white central bar; underwing blackish); best separated from other small bustards by long, thin neck and white belly. **Voice:** In display, male slowly raises head, giving a sharp 'chikk', then pulls head down, giving a loud 'pop'. **Status and biology:** Fairly common resident in woodland and tall, open grassland. Lays 1–2 eggs in a shallow scrape. **Diet:** Invertebrates, seeds, flowers and occasional carrion. (Langbeenkorhaan)

## 2 Red-crested Korhaan  *Lophotis ruficrista*

`Bbb` ` ` ` ` ` ` ` `bBBB`
J F M A M J J A S O N D

**48–50 cm; 400–900 g** A rather nondescript, small bustard with a black belly in both sexes. Male has grey-washed neck; bushy red crest is seen only during display. Female has mottled brown crown and neck; differs from female Northern Black Korhaan by black belly extending onto lower breast, chevrons (not barring) on back and yellow-brown (not reddish) bill. In aerial display, male flies straight up, then suddenly tumbles to ground as though shot, before gliding to land. **Voice:** Song protracted, starting with a long series of accelerating clicks, 'tic-tic-tic...', switching to an extended series of loud, piping whistles, 'pi-pi-pi-pipity-pipity...'. **Status and biology:** Near-endemic. Common resident in dry woodland and semi-desert grassland. Polygynous; males display in traditional areas. Female lays 1–2 eggs in a shallow scrape, usually under a shrub. **Diet:** Invertebrates; also seeds and fruit. (Boskorhaan)

## 3 Northern Black Korhaan  *Afrotis afraoides*

`BbbbbbbbbbbBB`
J F M A M J J A S O N D

**48–52 cm; 520–950 g** Male striking, with black head and neck and white cheek patch. Female and imm. duller with buffy-brown head and neck; differ from female Red-crested Korhaan by black barring (not chevrons) on upperparts and reddish (not yellow-brown) bill. Both sexes differ from Southern Black Korhaan by white inner webs to primaries, forming conspicuous white window on upper- and underwing in flight. **Voice:** Male gives raucous 'kerrrak-kerrrak-kerrrak' in flight and on ground. **Status and biology:** Common resident in karoo grassland and arid savanna. Polygynous; males display by calling in flight or from the ground. Female lays 1–2 (rarely 3) eggs in a shallow scrape. **Diet:** Insects, other invertebrates and seeds. (Witvlerkkorhaan)

## 4 Southern Black Korhaan  *Afrotis afra*

`b` ` ` ` ` ` ` ` `bBBbb`
J F M A M J J A S O N D

**48–52 cm; 600–900 g** Slightly larger than Northern Black Korhaan; best identified in flight when it displays its all-dark flight feathers; lacks white panels in primaries. Female and imm. lack bold black-and-white head and neck. **Voice:** Similar to that of Northern Black Korhaan. **Status and biology:** Common resident in coastal fynbos and karoo scrub. Polygynous. Males have traditional calling sites; also calls in a display flight, dangling its legs as it 'parachutes' to the ground. Female lays 1 egg (rarely 2) in a shallow scrape. **Diet:** Invertebrates; also seeds, other plant material and occasional lizards. (Swartvlerkkorhaan)

## 1 Karoo Korhaan  *Eupodotis vigorsii*

Bb | | | bbbbBBB
J F M A M J J A S O N D

**56–62 cm; 1.1–2 kg**  A drab, grey-brown korhaan with a black throat and nape patch, and contrasting buff and black wings in flight. Female has smaller, less-defined throat and nape patches. Overlaps with Rüppell's Korhaan in S Namibia; has a more subdued face pattern; lacks bluish neck and black line down its throat. Also is darker brown, but northern race *E. v. namaqua* is paler than birds illustrated here. Lacks blue body and wing patch of Blue Korhaan. **Voice:** Deep, frog-like duet, 'wrok-rak' or 'wrok-rak-rak', mostly at dawn and dusk; male utters deeper first syllable, female responds. **Status and biology:** Endemic. Common resident in karoo scrub; locally in open fields in S Cape. Pairs remain together year-round, often accompanied by young from the most recent br. attempt. Lays 1 egg in a shallow scrape, usually among stones and rocks. **Diet:** Invertebrates, small reptiles, seeds, fruit, flowers and leaves. (Vaalkorhaan)

## 2 Rüppell's Korhaan  *Eupodotis rueppellii*

bBBBBBbbbbbb
J F M A M J J A S O N D

**50–58 cm; 1–1.35 kg**  Slightly smaller than Karoo Korhaan with warmer brown upperparts, conspicuous black line down foreneck, blue-tinged neck and contrasting facial pattern, including a black moustache and line behind the eye. Female is less boldly marked than male; lacks black moustache. Juv. duller; lacks black facial markings and has white spots on neck and wing coverts. **Voice:** Similar to Karoo Korhaan's, but slightly higher-pitched. **Status and biology:** Near-endemic. Common resident on gravel plains and arid scrub. Usually in pairs or family groups. Lays 1–3 eggs in a shallow scrape, usually among stones and rocks. **Diet:** Invertebrates, small reptiles, seeds and soft leaves. (Woestynkorhaan)

## 3 Blue Korhaan  *Eupodotis caerulescens*

bb | | b | | | bBBb
J F M A M J J A S O N D

**52–60 cm; 1.2–1.6 kg**  Blue-grey underparts, neck and wing (in flight) contrasting with chestnut back are diagnostic. Male Barrow's Korhaan also has blue-grey foreneck, but has rufous hind neck and white belly. Male has white face with pale grey ear coverts. Female is less brightly coloured, with brown ear coverts; juv. similar with black-streaked ear coverts. Overlaps with closely related Karoo Korhaan in W. **Voice:** Groups utter a hoarse 'krok-kaa-krow', not as deep as Karoo Korhaan; mainly calls at dawn and dusk. **Status and biology:** Endemic. Locally common resident in grassland and eastern Karoo. Usually in groups of 3–5 birds. Lays 1–2 (rarely 3) eggs in a shallow scrape among grass tussocks. **Diet:** Invertebrates, lizards, flowers, seeds and grass leaves. (Bloukorhaan)

## 4 Barrow's Korhaan  *Eupodotis barrowi*

b | | | | | | | | bbBb
J F M A M J J A S O N D

**52–60 cm; 1.2–1.6 kg**  Male's combination of blue foreneck, rufous hind neck and white belly is diagnostic; range does not overlap with that of very similar White-bellied Bustard. Female and juv. are duller, with rufous-brown necks; superficially resemble female Black-bellied Bustard (p. 146), but have shorter necks and legs, and pale underwing coverts. **Voice:** Rhythmic, crowing 'takwarat', higher-pitched and less hoarse than Blue Korhaan; mainly calls at dawn and dusk. **Status and biology:** Endemic. Uncommon resident in open grassland and lightly wooded savanna; prefers taller grass than most other korhaans. Lays 1–2 (rarely 3) eggs in a shallow scrape among tall grass tufts. **Diet:** Invertebrates, lizards, flowers, fruit, seeds, bulbs and soft leaves. (Witpenskorhaan)

## 5 White-bellied Bustard  *Eupodotis senegalensis*

**52–60 cm; 1.2–1.6 kg**  Doubtfully distinct from Barrow's Korhaan. Ad. male of central African race *E. s. mackenziei* (**5 A**) has rufous hind neck extending across breast, separating blue-grey foreneck from white belly; lacks blue-grey spot below eye. Further north, *E. s. senegalensis* has all-blue-grey neck (**5 B**) – not recorded from sthn Africa. Female similar to Barrow's Korhaan, but lacks a brown smudge below eye. **Voice:** Similar to Barrow's Korhaan. **Status and biology:** Status uncertain; vagrant or rare resident in grasslands of N Namibia. **Diet:** Similar to Barrow's Korhaan. (Noordelike Witpenskorhaan)

# CRAB PLOVER, OYSTERCATCHERS, STILTS AND AVOCETS

A diverse group of large, distinctively plumaged waders closely allied to plovers and lapwings. Sexes alike. Usually monogamous, with both sexes incubating and caring for the chicks.

## 1 Crab Plover  *Dromas ardeola*

J F M A M J J A S O N D

**33–38 cm; 250–350 g**  Rare. A large, predominantly white wader with a black back and flight feathers. Large, black bill is dagger-shaped. Long, greyish legs extend well beyond white tail in flight. Imm. has greyer wings and tail, with grey back and streaked hind crown. Juv is mottled brown above. **Voice:** Range of metallic calls: 'kwa-daaa-dak', 'kwa-da-dak' or 'grr-kwo-kwo-kwo'; flight call is 'kwa-da'. **Status and biology:** Uncommon migrant from br. grounds in NE Africa and Arabia; some 200 in Mozambique. Occurs on coastal sandflats, estuaries and mangroves. **Diet:** Mainly small crabs. (Krapvreter)

## 2 African Black Oystercatcher  *Haematopus moquini*

B b b b     b b B B
J F M A M J J A S O N D

**42–45 cm; 600–820 g**  A large, black wader with a bright orange bill and eye-ring, and rather short, dull pink legs. Some ads have small white patches on underparts. Juv. browner, with dark-tipped bill and grey-pink legs. **Voice:** A 'klee-kleeep' call; fast 'peeka-peeka-peeka' alarm call. **Status and biology:** NEAR-THREATENED near-endemic. Common resident along the coast and adjacent wetland from C Namibia to E Cape; scarce further N and E; vagrant to Mozambique. Br. endemic; population some 6 000 birds. Lays 1–2 (rarely 3) eggs in a shallow scrape; occasionally on buildings or even boats. **Diet:** Mussels, limpets, worms and other marine invertebrates; rarely feeds outside intertidal zone. Defends feeding territory year-round. (Swarttobie)

## 3 Eurasian Oystercatcher  *Haematopus ostralegus*

J F M A M J J A S O N D

**40–45 cm; 400–620 g**  Rare. Slightly smaller and more slender than African Black Oystercatcher with white underparts and a bold white wing bar, back and rump. Non-br. ad. and juv. have white throat collar. Juv. has brown-tinged back and duller bill and legs. **Voice:** Sharp, high-pitched 'klee-kleep'. **Status and biology:** Rare Palearctic migrant, mainly wintering N of equator. Occurs at coastal wetland and along the coast, sometimes with African Black Oystercatchers. **Diet:** Invertebrates, especially molluscs and worms. (Bonttobie)

## 4 Black-winged Stilt  *Himantopus himantopus*

b b b b b b b B B B B b
J F M A M J J A S O N D

**35–40 cm; 150–195 g**  A black-and-white wader with extremely long red legs and a very thin, pointed, black bill. In flight, black underwings contrast with white underparts, and long legs trail conspicuously. Head and neck vary from pure white to predominantly dusky; occasionally has black line down nape. Juv. has greyish nape, grey-pink legs and brownish wings with pale trailing edge. **Voice:** Harsh, short 'kik-kik', especially when alarmed; very vocal in defence of nest and young. **Status and biology:** Common resident and nomad at a wide range of wetlands, both fresh and salt water. Regional population some 15 000 birds. Breeds singly or in loose colonies, laying 2–5 eggs in a shallow mound of vegetation and other material. **Diet:** Insects, worms, other invertebrates, tadpoles and small fish. (Rooipootelsie)

## 5 Pied Avocet  *Recurvirostra avosetta*

b b b b b B B B B B b b
J F M A M J J A S O N D

**42–45 cm; 270–380 g**  An unmistakable white-and-black wader with a long, very thin, upturned bill. In flight, pied pattern is striking, and long, bluish-grey legs and toes extend well beyond tail tip. Underwing black only at tip. Juv. has mottled brown back. **Voice:** Clear 'kooit'; 'kik-kik' alarm call. **Status and biology:** Common resident and nomad at wetlands; occasionally on sandy beaches; usually in small flocks. Breeds singly or in loose colonies, mostly at emphemeral wetlands. Lays 1–4 eggs in a shallow scrape, lined with vegetation and other material. Feeds by sweeping bill from side to side. Toes partly webbed; often swims, upending duck-like in deeper water. **Diet:** Crustaceans, insect larvae, other invertebrates and small fish. (Bontelsie)

# PLOVERS AND LAPWINGS

Small to fairly large waders with short bills and necks. Feed mainly visually, picking prey from surface; often stand and scan, then dash forward to grab prey. Most forage singly, not in flocks like tactile-feeding scolopacid waders. Sexes alike, with distinct br. plumages in migratory species. Mating systems varied, but usually monogamous and territorial among species breeding in sthn Africa, with both sexes incubating and caring for the precocial chicks.

## 1 Common Ringed Plover *Charadrius hiaticula*

J F M A M J J A S O N D

**18–20 cm; 45–70 g** A short-legged, brown-backed plover with a white collar above a blackish breast band. Head and breast markings crisply defined in br. plumage, but duller with incomplete breast band in juv. and non-br. plumage. Lacks yellow eye-ring of vagrant Little Ringed Plover and has orange (not pinkish-grey) legs and white wing bar. Bill is usually orange at base. **Voice:** Fluty, rising 'too-li'. **Status and biology:** Common Palearctic migrant at coastal and inland wetlands, preferring patches of soft, fine mud; also on rocky shores. Regional population at least 10 000 birds, mainly along the coast. **Diet:** Worms, small crustaceans, insects and other invertebrates. (Ringnekstrandkiewiet)

## 2 Little Ringed Plover *Charadrius dubius*

**15–17 cm; 30–48 g** Rare vagrant. Smaller than Common Ringed Plover, with a conspicuous yellow eye-ring, slender, all-dark bill, and narrow white line between black forecrown and brown hind crown. Legs pinkish-grey or yellowish (not orange); lacks an obvious white wing bar in flight. Juv. duller with incomplete breast band. **Voice:** Descending 'pee-oo'. **Status and biology:** Palearctic vagrant that usually winters N of equator. Favours dry mud around freshwater wetlands; 1 record: Hwange, Zimbabwe, Jan 2002. **Diet:** Invertebrates. (Kleinringnekstrandkiewiet)

## 3 Three-banded Plover *Charadrius tricollaris*

b b b b b b B B B B B B
J F M A M J J A S O N D

**18 cm; 28–45 g** A small, brown-backed plover with 2 black breast bands, a white ring around the crown, grey cheeks and conspicuous red eye-rings and bill base. Tail fairly long, extending beyond folded wing. Frequently bobs tail when alarmed. In flight, has a narrow white wing bar and white sides to rump, outer tail and tail tip. Juv. duller and slightly scaled above. **Voice:** Penetrating, high-pitched 'weee-weet' whistle. **Status and biology:** Common resident mainly at freshwater wetlands; prefers muddy areas, often close to vegetation. Regional population at least 25 000 birds. Lays 2 (rarely 1 or 3) eggs in a shallow scrape, usually close to water. **Diet:** Insects, worms, crustaceans and other aquatic invertebrates. (Driebandstrandkiewiet)

## 4 Kittlitz's Plover *Charadrius pecuarius*

b b b b b b B B B B B B
J F M A M J J A S O N D

**14–16 cm; 25–45 g** Ad. has distinctively patterned head; banded black and white in br. plumage; dark brown and buff in non-br. plumage. Breast varies from creamy to rich buff. Juv. duller than non-br. ad., with buff frons and broad buff supercilium joining across nape and contrasting with darker brown cheeks. Sometimes confused with non-br. Caspian Plover, but is smaller and has pale band across nape; white wing bar more prominent in flight. **Voice:** Short, clipped trill, 'kittip'. **Status and biology:** Common resident and local nomad around wetlands, fields and short grassland. Regional population at least 55 000 birds. Lays 2 (1–3) eggs in a shallow scrape; typically kicks sand over eggs before leaving nest. **Diet:** Insects, worms, crustaceans and other invertebrates. (Geelborsstrandkiewiet)

## 5 Caspian Plover *Charadrius asiaticus*

J F M A M J J A S O N D

**18–22 cm; 60–78 g** A medium-sized plover of mainly dry-land habitats. Non-br. birds have a complete (or virtually complete) grey-brown wash across breast, and a broad, buffy supercilium. Bill is smaller and thinner than either Greater or Lesser Sand Plover (p. 154). In flight, upperparts are uniform, apart from pale bases to inner primaries. In br. plumage, has a black lower border to broad chestnut neck and breast band, pale eyebrow and throat, and no dark eye patch. Juv. appears buffy-scaled. **Voice:** Clear, whistled 'tooeet'. **Status and biology:** Locally common Palearctic migrant in north; scarce in south. Favours short grassland, bare fields and wetland fringes; usually in flocks. **Diet:** Mainly insects; occasional molluscs and seeds. (Asiatiese Strandkiewiet)

## 1 Chestnut-banded Plover *Charadrius pallidus*

b b b b b b B B B B B B
J F M A M J J A S O N D

**15 cm; 32–45 g** A small, pale plover, with rather narrow habitat requirements. Thin chestnut breast band is diagnostic in ads, but some White-fronted Plovers can show diffuse buff breast band. Ad. male has darker band and neat black forehead and lores. Juv. has incomplete grey breast band; best told from larger White-fronted Plover by lack of white neck collar, paler and greyer upperparts, and short-tailed appearance. **Voice:** Single 'prrp' or 'tooit'. **Status and biology: NEAR-THREATENED.** Locally fairly common resident and nomad at saltpans, estuaries and coastal wetlands. Regional population some 6 000 birds. Lays 2 eggs in a shallow scrape. **Diet:** Insects and small crustaceans. (Rooibandstrandkiewiet)

## 2 Kentish Plover *Charadrius alexandrinus*

**15–17 cm; 32–60 g** Rare vagrant. In br. plumage, differs from White-fronted Plover by having distinctive chestnut crown and nape, and small black patches on sides of breast. Non-br. and imm. birds are very hard to separate from White-fronted Plover, but tend to have longer, darker legs and shorter tail, with wings reaching to tail tip, giving more slender and attenuated appearance. **Voice:** Short, sharp 'wiiit'. **Status and biology:** Palearctic vagrant that usually winters N of equator; 1 specimen claimed from N Namibia; unsubstantiated sight records from Namibia and Mozambique. (Kentse Strandkiewiet)

## 3 White-fronted Plover *Charadrius marginatus*

B b b b b b b B B B B B
J F M A M J J A S O N D

**16–17 cm; 35–60 g** A pale, grey-brown plover with broad white frons, blackish line from base of bill through eye (reduced or almost absent in juv.) and white nuchal collar. Breast varies from white to rich buff. Ad. has black band above white frons (broader in male); absent in juv. Tail is rather long, extending beyond folded wings. Head pattern and paler upperparts distinguish it from Kittlitz's Plover (p. 152). White collar separates it from larger Lesser Sand Plover. Some imm. birds have small, dusky breast patches and could be confused with vagrant Kentish Plover. **Voice:** Clear 'wiiit'; 'tukut' alarm call. **Status and biology:** Common resident along the coast, at estuaries and larger inland rivers and pans. Regional population at least 10 000 birds. Lays 1–3 eggs in a shallow scrape; typically kicks sand over eggs before leaving nest. **Diet:** Insects, small crustaceans, molluscs and worms. (Vaalstrandkiewiet)

## 4 Greater Sand Plover *Charadrius leschenaultii*

J F M A M J J A S O N D

**22–25 cm; 75–130 g** A medium-sized plover, separated with difficulty from Lesser Sand Plover. Slightly larger, with a bigger body, longer legs, a longer, more robust bill and more angular head. In br. plumage, rufous breast band is less extensive. In flight, white sides of rump are more extensive. Leg colour is variable but usually grey-green (rarely black). Caspian Plover (p. 152) has smaller bill and lacks extensive white-sided rump. Juv. has buff-fringed upperparts. **Voice:** Soft, trilled 'tirrrri'. **Status and biology:** Uncommon Palearctic migrant to coastal wetlands; rare vagrant inland. Regional population some 2 000 birds, mainly in Mozambique. **Diet:** Small crabs, other crustaceans, worms and molluscs. (Grootstrandkiewiet)

## 5 Lesser Sand Plover *Charadrius mongolus*

J F M A M J J A S O N D

**19–21 cm; 45–90 g** Very similar to Greater Sand Plover, but slightly smaller, with shorter legs and a shorter, less robust bill; head appears softer and more rounded. Legs almost always very dark grey or black (not grey-green). In br. plumage, rufous breast band is more extensive. Larger than White-fronted Plover with brown nape (lacks pale nape collar). In flight, there is little colour contrast between tail, rump and back. Juv. has buff-fringed upperparts. **Voice:** Hard 'chittick'. **Status and biology:** Uncommon Palearctic migrant to coastal wetlands; vagrant inland. Regional population <1 000 birds, mainly in Mozambique. **Diet:** Worms, small crabs and other small invertebrates. (Mongoolse Strandkiewiet)

### 1 Crowned Lapwing *Vanellus coronatus*

bbbbbbbBBBBB
J F M A M J J A S O N D

**29–31 cm; 150–220 g** A mostly brown lapwing, with a black cap interrupted by a white 'halo'. Legs and base of bill bright pink-red. Sandy brown breast is separated from white belly by black band. In flight, brown back and lesser/median coverts contrast with white greater/primary coverts, and with blackish flight feathers. Juv. has scalloped upperparts, buff-barred crown, and pale yellowish legs and bill base. **Voice:** Noisy; loud, grating 'kreep', day and night. **Status and biology:** Common resident and local nomad in open country, including short grassland, fields and fallow land; seldom associated with water. Often found with Black-winged Lapwing. Regional population some 100 000 birds. Lays 2–3 (rarely 4) eggs in a shallow scrape. **Diet:** Termites, beetles, grasshoppers and other invertebrates. (Kroonkiewiet)

### 2 Black-winged Lapwing *Vanellus melanopterus*

bbbbbbbBBbbb
J F M A M J J A S O N D

**26–28 cm; 150–200 g** Larger and bulkier than Senegal Lapwing, with more extensive white on the forehead (almost reaching to the eye), redder legs and a broader black border separating the breast from the belly. Female has narrower breast band and less white on forehead. Flight pattern similar to Crowned Lapwing, but with black primary coverts, similar to African Wattled Lapwing (p. 158); lacks white secondaries of Senegal Lapwing. Juv. is browner, with buff edges to upperparts. **Voice:** Shrill, piping 'ti-tirree', higher pitched than Senegal Lapwing. **Status and biology:** Fairly common resident and local migrant in grassland habitats, moving to lower elevations in winter in N of range. Regional population some 2 500 birds. Lays 1–4 eggs in a shallow scrape. **Diet:** Termites, beetles, grasshoppers and other invertebrates. (Grootswartvlerkkiewiet)

### 3 Senegal Lapwing *Vanellus lugubris*

b|||||bBBbbb
J F M A M J J A S O N D

**22–26 cm; 100–140 g** Smaller and more slender than Black-winged Lapwing, with a narrow black border to the grey breast, less white on the forehead and a slight greenish tinge to the upperparts. Legs are dull red-brown. In flight, white secondaries and inner primaries are diagnostic. Juv. is paler above, spotted with buff. **Voice:** Clear, double-noted 'tee-yoo, tee-yoo'. **Status and biology:** Uncommon resident and local migrant in open, short-grass savanna; favours recently burnt areas. Lays 3–4 eggs in a shallow scrape. **Diet:** Termites, other invertebrates and occasional seeds. (Kleinswartvlerkkiewiet)

## 1 Long-toed Lapwing *Vanellus crassirostris*

bbbBBBb
J F M A M J J A S O N D

**29–31 cm; 160–220 g** A localised lapwing with distinctive white face, throat and foreneck. Black nape extends down sides of neck to form a broad breast band. Legs and base of bill reddish. Strikingly black and white in flight, with grey-brown back and white wings apart from black outer primaries. Juv. mottled brown on crown, neck and breast. **Voice:** High-pitched 'pink-pink'. **Status and biology:** Locally common resident and nomad in marshes and floodplains. Lays 2–4 eggs on a mound of floating vegetation. **Diet:** Small insects, other invertebrates and occasional seeds; its long toes aid walking on floating vegetation. (Witvlerkkiewiet)

## 2 White-crowned Lapwing *Vanellus albiceps*

b bBBBb
J F M A M J J A S O N D

**28–32 cm; 150–210 g** A striking lapwing with large, pendulous, yellow wattles and yellow legs. White (not brown) breast separates it from African Wattled Lapwing. In flight, wings are mostly white, with only outer primaries and median coverts black. Juv. has brownish crown, smaller wattles and barred upperparts. **Voice:** Repeated, ringing 'peek-peek'. **Status and biology:** Locally common resident and nomad along large rivers, favouring areas with sandbanks. Lays 2–4 eggs in a shallow scrape in sand; cools eggs on hot days by wetting belly feathers. **Diet:** Insects, other invertebrates, and small fish and frogs. (Witkopkiewiet)

## 3 Spur-winged Lapwing *Vanellus spinosus*

**25–28 cm; 135–175 g** Rare vagrant. A small lapwing with a pale brown mantle, white neck, and black breast, crown and throat stripe. In flight, brown back and wing coverts contrast with white greater coverts, and with blackish flight feathers and primary coverts. Juv. has browner crown with fine white spotting, and back feathers edged buff. **Voice:** Loud, screeching, 3–4 note 'ti-ti-tirri-ti'. **Status and biology:** Vagrant to large rivers and floodplains from further north; 5 records from N Namibia, Botswana, Zimbabwe and Mozambique. **Diet:** Insects, other aquatic invertebrates and occasional seeds. (Spoorvlerkkiewiet)

## 4 African Wattled Lapwing *Vanellus senegallus*

bbBBbb
J F M A M J J A S O N D

**34–35 cm; 180–280 g** The largest African lapwing, with a fairly large, yellow face wattle. At rest, appears mostly brown, with black-and-white forehead, streaked head and neck, blackish band across belly and white vent. In flight, has white wing bar between brown inner coverts and blackish flight feathers. Juv. has small wattles and streaked forehead. **Voice:** High-pitched, ringing 'keep-keep'; regularly calls at night. **Status and biology:** Fairly common resident, nomad and local migrant at wetland margins and adjacent grassland. Regional population some 15 000 birds. Lays 2–4 eggs in a shallow scrape. **Diet:** Insects, other invertebrates and some seeds. (Lelkiewiet)

## 5 Blacksmith Lapwing *Vanellus armatus*

bbbbbbBBBBbb
J F M A M J J A S O N D

**28–31 cm; 130–200 g** A boldly marked, black, white and grey lapwing with blackish legs and dark red eyes. In flight, pale grey coverts contrast with black flight feathers. Juv. is duller, with greyish-brown upperparts, and mottled brown head and neck; sometimes confused with Spur-winged Lapwing, but wing pattern quite different (lacks white wing bar). **Voice:** Very vocal; loud, ringing 'tink, tink, tink' alarm call. **Status and biology:** Common resident and nomad at wetland margins and adjoining grassland and fields. Often in flocks when not breeding. Lays 2–4 eggs in a shallow scrape, usually close to water. **Diet:** Small invertebrates; 1 record of killing and eating a Kittlitz's Plover chick. (Bontkiewiet)

## 1 Grey Plover  *Pluvialis squatarola*

J F M A M J J A S O N D

**27–31 cm; 180–300 g** A large, stubby-billed plover. Best told from smaller, vagrant American and Pacific golden plovers by black axillaries, contrasting with the whitish underwings and white rump in flight; at rest it has grey (not gold) speckling on upperparts. In br. plumage, underparts are black and it has white (not golden) speckling on upperparts. Juv. has buffy-yellow markings on upperparts. **Voice:** Clear 'tluuii'. **Status and biology:** Common Palearctic migrant to the coast and adjacent wetlands; rare inland, mainly juvs on migration south. Roosts communally at high tide. Regional population some 25 000 birds. **Diet:** A range of invertebrate prey, especially crabs and worms. (Grysstrandkiewiet)

## 2 American Golden Plover  *Pluvialis dominica*

J F M A M J J A S O N D

**24–26 cm; 120–180 g** Rare vagrant. Slightly smaller and more slender than Grey Plover, with a more upright stance; easily differentiated in flight by plain grey underwing and brown rump. Main challenge is to separate it from slightly smaller Pacific Golden Plover. Appears bulkier and shorter-legged; in flight, toes don't project beyond tail tip. In non-br. plumage, whitish eyebrow is more pronounced and generally appears colder grey, with no buff on breast. In br. plumage, has golden spangling on upperparts, and black underparts extend to undertail; lacks white flank line of Pacific Golden Plover. Juv. has more scalloped and yellow upperparts. **Voice:** Usually single- or double-noted whistle, 'oodle-oo'. **Status and biology**: Nearctic vagrant, mainly wintering in S America. Typically found in short grassland, but also around wetlands; often less coastal than Pacific Golden Plover. **Diet**: Invertebrates. (Amerikaanse Goue Strandkiewiet)

## 3 Pacific Golden Plover  *Pluvialis fulva*

J F M A M J J A S O N D

**23–25 cm; 110–170 g** Rare vagrant. Slightly smaller and more slender than American Golden Plover with less prominent eyebrow in non-br. plumage, when gold-spangled upperparts and buffy breast are typical. In flight, toes project slightly beyond tail tip. In br. plumage, white neck stripe extends down flanks to vent. Juv. has yellower upperparts and breast. **Voice:** Similar to American Golden Plover. **Status and biology:** Palearctic vagrant, wintering from S Asia to Australasia and Oceania. Occurs on coastal mudflats and sandflats; also grassland. **Diet**: Invertebrates. (Asiatiese Goue Strandkiewiet)

# SANDPIPERS, GODWITS, CURLEWS

Shorebirds that mostly breed at high latitudes in the N hemisphere, migrating south for the boreal winter. Juvs of larger species remain in sthn Africa year-round; numbers vary in relation to Arctic lemming cycles (greatest in years with many lemmings, when few shorebird chicks are eaten by predators). Feed by probing or picking. Sexes alike. Most species have distinct br. plumages. Juvs have pale-fringed upperpart feathers. Mating systems vary. Chicks precocial.

## 4 Ruff  *Philomachus pugnax*

J F M A M J J A S O N D

**20–30 cm; male 120–200 g, female 80–140 g** A medium to large wader with conspicuously scaled upperparts and paler feathering at base of bill. Leg colour varies from greenish-yellow to orange-red. Bill may show orange or reddish base, leading to confusion with redshanks, but bill is shorter (0.9–1 x head length) and slightly decurved (not straight). In flight, has dark back (white in redshanks) and distinctive white oval patches on either side of dark rump. Juv. washed buff on neck and breast, but not as extensive as vagrant Buff-breasted Sandpiper. Less than 10% of birds in sthn Africa are male; males much larger than females; some have white head and neck. **Voice:** Generally silent; occasional 'tooi' flight note. **Status and biology:** Common Palearctic migrant, mainly at freshwater wetlands; scarce in coastal habitats; sometimes forages in dry fields. Regional population at least 50 000 birds. **Diet:** Mainly insects and other invertebrates; also some plant material. Often swims in deep water. (Kemphaan)

## 5 Buff-breasted Sandpiper  *Tryngites subruficollis*

**18–20 cm; 45–65 g** Rare vagrant. Smaller than female Ruff, with a short, straight bill (0.6 x head length), spotted sides to breast, buffy underparts extending onto belly and bright yellow legs. In flight, has rather plain upperparts with no white on sides of the rump; dark tips to primary coverts form a dark crescent on mainly white underwing. Juv. has neatly scalloped upperparts; underparts paler buff. **Voice:** Low 'preet'. **Status and biology:** Nearctic vagrant, usually wintering in S America. 9 records from sthn Africa. Occurs in wide range of open habitats, including around wetlands and fields. **Diet:** Invertebrates. (Taanborsstrandloper)

## 6 Pectoral Sandpiper  *Calidris melanotos*

J F M A M J J A S O N D

**19–23 cm; 45–75 g** Uncommon vagrant. A dark-backed wader, similar in size to Curlew Sandpiper (p. 162), with shorter, greenish-yellow (not black) legs and yellowish base to slightly decurved bill. Abrupt division between densely streaked, grey-brown breast and white belly is distinctive. Larger and longer-necked than the stints, with dark-capped appearance. In flight, shows dark-centred rump with white sides. **Voice:** Low trill, 'prrt'. **Status and biology:** Holarctic vagrant that mainly winters in S America, SE Asia and Australia. Occurs at wetlands, mainly freshwater, but also at some coastal sites; prefers muddy areas. **Diet:** Invertebrates. (Geelpootstrandloper)

## 1 Great Knot  *Calidris tenuirostris*

**26–28 cm; 125–220 g** Rare vagrant. Slightly larger than Red Knot with a longer bill (1.1–1.3 x head length) that has a deeper base and more drooped tip; legs darker grey. Wings slightly longer; extend beyond tail tip at rest; wing bar slightly less marked in flight. In non-br. plumage, upperparts are more streaked; in br. plumage, underparts whitish (not chestnut) with dense black spotting on breast and dark grey chevrons on flanks. Juv. darker above with pale fringes to feathers; breast and flanks buffy with brown spots. **Voice:** Soft 'nyut'. **Status and biology:** Breeds in E Siberia; usually winters in Australia and SE Asia. Rare vagrant to Mozambique; one record from Langebaan Lagoon and one from Walvis Bay. **Diet:** Invertebrates. (Grootknoet)

## 2 Red Knot  *Calidris canutus*

J F M A M J J A S O N D

**23–25 cm; 110–200 g** A short-legged, dumpy, rather plain wader. In flight, shows pale wing bar and rump lightly barred grey. Larger than Curlew Sandpiper, with a shorter, straighter bill (1 x head length) and greenish (not blackish) legs. Smaller than Grey Plover (p.160), with a longer bill and uniform grey (not speckled) back in non-br. plumage. Slightly smaller than vagrant Great Knot, with shorter, less deep bill. In br. plumage, underparts deep chestnut-orange; upperparts spangled chestnut and black. Juv. has neatly scalloped upperparts. **Voice:** Soft 'knut', usually given in flight. **Status and biology:** Locally common Palearctic migrant at estuaries and coastal lagoons; vagrant inland. Usually in flocks; roosts communally at high tide. Regional population some 8 000 birds, mainly on the W coast. **Diet:** Mainly small bivalve molluscs; also worms and other invertebrates. (Knoet)

## 3 Curlew Sandpiper  *Calidris ferruginea*

J F M A M J J A S O N D

**18–23 cm; 45–85 g** An abundant, small to medium-sized sandpiper with a long, decurved bill (longer in female) and fairly long, blackish legs. In flight, shows square white rump, which separates it from all other small sandpipers except vagrant White-rumped Sandpiper (p. 164). In br. plumage, underparts and face are chestnut, fringed white and finely barred black; upperparts spangled chestnut and black. Juv. has buffy edgings to upperpart feathers. **Voice:** Short trill, 'chirrup'. **Status and biology:** Abundant Palearctic migrant at coastal and freshwater wetlands, usually in flocks. Many young birds remain year-round. Roosts communally at high tide in coastal locations. Regional population some 300 000 birds. **Diet:** Worms, small snails, crustaceans, other invertebrates and seeds. (Krombekstrandloper)

## 4 Dunlin  *Calidris alpina*

**15–22 cm; 40–70 g** Rare vagrant. Resembles a compact Curlew Sandpiper, usually with shorter legs and shorter, less decurved bill (but beware sex-linked differences in bill size among both species); pale eye-stripe is less marked. Best distinguished in flight by the dark stripe down the centre of its rump. Larger than the stints, with a longer, more decurved bill; lacks striped head of Broad-billed Sandpiper. In br. plumage, has black belly patch and chestnut back and crown. **Voice:** Weak 'treep'. **Status and biology:** Rare Palearctic vagrant that seldom crosses equator; only 2 well-substantiated records: Kruger Park and Langebaan Lagoon. **Diet:** Invertebrates. (Bontstrandloper)

## 5 Sanderling  *Calidris alba*

J F M A M J J A S O N D

**19–21 cm; 45–90 g** Fairly small sandpiper with a short, stubby, black bill and a dark carpal patch. In flight, shows bold white wing bar and darker line through white rump. Pale grey-brown above in non-br. plumage, finely streaked darker brown; white below. Larger than Broad-billed Sandpiper, with shorter bill; lacks head stripes. In br. plumage, upperparts and breast are chestnut and black. Juv. rich brown above and on breast, similar to br. ad. **Voice:** Sharp 'wick' in flight. **Status and biology:** Common Palearctic migrant to coastal habitats: prefers sandy beaches, but also on rocky shores and coastal wetland; rare inland, mainly on migration. Regional population some 85 000 birds. **Diet:** Small crustaceans, insects and molluscs; occasional small fish. Often in flocks; runs up and down the beach following receding waves, searching sand for prey. (Drietoonstrandloper)

## 6 Broad-billed Sandpiper  *Limicola falcinellus*

J F M A M J J A S O N D

**17 cm; 30–45 g** Rare. A small, short-legged wader, slightly larger than the stints, with a diagnostic pale double eyebrow stripe. Bill is relatively long and broad, with drooped, flattened tip. Legs dark greenish-grey. In non-br. plumage is pale grey above, with dark shoulder patch (less pronounced than in Sanderling). In br. plumage, upperparts are blackish with rufous feather margins. Juv. is darker and browner above than non-br. ad. **Voice:** Low-pitched, short trill, 'drrrt'. **Status and biology:** Scarce Palearctic migrant to estuaries and coastal lagoons; favours mangroves and other muddy habitats; vagrant inland. **Diet:** Worms and small crabs. (Breëbekstrandloper)

## 1 White-rumped Sandpiper  *Calidris fuscicollis*

**15–17 cm; 30–45 g** Rare vagrant. The only *Calidris* with a white rump other than Curlew Sandpiper (p. 162), but is smaller with shorter legs and short, rather straight bill; long wings extend well beyond tail tip at rest. Size intermediate between Curlew Sandpiper and Little Stint; similar to Baird's Sandpiper, but paler grey above with dark streaking extending further onto breast and flanks; bill broader-tipped, usually with a paler base. Best told by its white rump (usually only visible in flight), lacking a dark central bar. **Voice:** A high-pitched 'jeet' in flight. **Status and biology:** Nearctic vagrant, usually wintering in S America. Some 10 records, mainly from the W coast. Regular vagrant at Tristan. **Diet:** Invertebrates. (Witrugstrandloper)

## 2 Baird's Sandpiper  *Calidris bairdii*

**15–17 cm; 30–45 g** Rare vagrant. Intermediate in size between Curlew Sandpiper (p. 162) and Little Stint, with long wings extending well beyond tail tip at rest. Structure similar to White-rumped Sandpiper, but has a dark stripe down the centre of the rump. Upperparts rather darker and browner, with buffy wash on upper breast, but little streaking on lower breast and flanks; bill tip rather narrower, and bill usually all-dark. **Voice:** A soft 'treep'. **Status and biology:** Nearctic vagrant, usually wintering in S America. Fewer than 10 confirmed records from W coast, Gauteng and Kruger National Park. Occasional vagrant at Tristan. **Diet:** Invertebrates. (Bairdstrandloper)

# STINTS

The smallest waders; notoriously difficult to identify. Little Stint is the only common species in the region and is quite variable with age, sex and season; jizz varies with posture and behaviour. Identification of vagrant stints requires a sound knowledge of Little Stint variations.

## 3 Little Stint  *Calidris minuta*

J F M A M J J A S O N D

**12–15 cm; 18–35 g** The most abundant stint; plumage and structure rather variable. Non-br. birds have diffuse grey-brown streaks on sides of breast and pale grey-brown upperparts with dark central feather streaks. Br. ad. and juv. rich brown above and on breast; juv. has fine buff margins to feathers. In flight, has narrow white wing bar and white sides to rump. Very similar to Red-necked Stint, but with slightly longer, less stubby bill, longer legs and broader dark centres to upperpart feathers in non-br. plumage. In br. plumage has pale (not rufous) throat with vertical dark streaking. Legs usually black, but occasionally greeny-yellow, causing possible confusion with Temminck's and Long-toed stints. **Voice:** Short, sharp 'schit'. **Status and biology:** Common Palearctic migrant at freshwater wetlands, estuaries and lagoons; rarely on rocky shoreline. Regional population some 100 000 birds. **Diet:** Small invertebrates obtained by picking or shallow probing. (Kleinstrandloper)

## 4 Red-necked Stint  *Calidris ruficollis*

**13–16 cm; 22–35 g** Rare vagrant. Very difficult to separate from Little Stint, except in br. plumage, when throat, neck and cheeks are rufous and lack vertical dark streaking. In non-br. plumage upperparts are pale grey, with narrow dark feather shafts. Bill is shorter and stubbier than Little Stint's, and wings are slightly longer. Often appears more chunky due to crouched posture; black legs typically show little leg above 'knee' joint. **Voice:** Short 'chit' or 'prrp', reputed to be deeper than Little Stint. **Status and biology:** Palearctic vagrant found at muddy fringes of wetlands and saltpans; main wintering areas in S Asia and Australasia. **Diet:** Invertebrates. (Rooinekstrandloper)

## 5 Temminck's Stint  *Calidris temminckii*

**13–15 cm; 18–30 g** Rare vagrant. A plain-backed stint with yellow-green legs and a diagnostic white outer tail. Appears more elongate than Little Stint, and is more plain brown above than Long-toed Stint. Bill has slight droop at tip and dull yellow base. Juv. has upperpart feathers edged buff. **Voice:** Shrill 'prrrrtt'. **Status and biology:** Palearctic vagrant, usually wintering N of equator. Favours muddy edges of freshwater wetlands, often in small openings among vegetation. At least 5 records: Gauteng, KwaZulu-Natal, Namibia and Botswana. **Diet:** Invertebrates. (Temminckstrandloper)

## 6 Long-toed Stint  *Calidris subminuta*

**14 cm; 20–35 g** Rare vagrant. A small, slender stint; legs and neck appear relatively long; bill slender. Yellow legs distinctive (but see Temminck's Stint, and beware aberrant pale-legged juv. Little Stints). Generally darker and browner above than respective plumages of Little Stint; upperpart feathers have broad dark centres in non-br. plumage and are broadly edged rufous in br. plumage. Back more heavily mottled than Temminck's Stint with more strongly defined supercilium and dark (not white) outer tail. **Voice:** Soft 'chirrup'; sharp 'tik-ik-ik'. **Status and biology:** Palearctic vagrant usually wintering in S Asia and Australia. Favours muddy fringes of wetlands; 4 records: Gauteng, E Cape, Botswana and Mozambique. **Diet:** Invertebrates. (Langtoonstrandloper)

**1** non-br. `MD`

**1** br. `TE`

**1** br. `EG`

**2** juv. `TE`

**2** non-br. `PR`

**3** non-br. `JG`

**3** non-br. `TH`

**3** non-br. `IS`

**4** br. `MS/NHPA`

**4** non-br. `MS/NHPA`

**4** non-br. `JL/LOCH`

**5** non-br. `JP`

**5** non-br. `TM`

**5** non-br. `RT`

**6** non-br. `RFP`

## 1 Common Sandpiper *Actitis hypoleucos*

J F M A M J J A S O N D

**19–21 cm; 35–75 g** A fairly small sandpiper with olive-brown upperparts, finely barred dark brown, and an obvious white shoulder in front of the closed wing. Smaller and shorter-legged than Wood and Green sandpipers, with a relatively longer tail and no pale spotting above. In flight, has prominent white wing bar, dark rump and barred sides to dark tail. Regularly bobs tail. Flight comprises rapid bursts of shallow wing beats interspersed by short glides on slightly bowed wings. **Voice:** Shrill 'ti-ti-ti', higher-pitched and thinner than Wood Sandpiper. **Status and biology:** Common Palearctic migrant at wetlands and along the coast. Regional population at least 10 000 birds. **Diet:** Aquatic invertebrates, small fish and frogs, and seeds. (Gewone Ruiter)

## 2 Green Sandpiper *Tringa ochropus*

J F M A M J J A S O N D

**21–24 cm; 75–105 g** Rare. Larger than Wood Sandpiper, with darker greenish upperparts, only finely spotted whitish. Eye has prominent white eye-ring; supercilium does not extend behind the eye. Sides of breast and flanks boldly streaked. In flight, has diagnostic blackish underwing coverts; dark back contrasts with white rump; tail barring broader than in Wood Sandpiper. Juv. is browner above with buff spotting; breast streaking paler. **Voice:** 3-note whistle, 'tew-a-tew'. **Status and biology:** Rare Palearctic migrant, usually at freshwater wetlands. **Diet:** Similar to Wood Sandpiper. (Witgatruiter)

## 3 Wood Sandpiper *Tringa glareola*

J F M A M J J A S O N D

**19–21 cm; 45–80 g** A medium-sized, sandpiper with a grey-brown back and white spotting along margins of tertials, upperwing coverts and back feathers. Paler above than Green Sandpiper, with more obvious pale spotting above; white eye-ring small, but broad pale supercilium extends behind eye. In flight, has dark back, white rump and finely barred tail; underwings pale grey (not blackish). Slightly smaller than vagrant Lesser Yellowlegs (p. 168), with shorter legs, yellowish base to bill and bolder supercilium. Juv. is warmer brown above. **Voice:** High-pitched, slightly descending 'chiff-iff-iff', usually given in flight. **Status and biology:** Common Palearctic migrant at freshwater wetlands; scarce at estuaries and coastal habitats. Regional population perhaps 50 000 birds. **Diet:** Aquatic invertebrates, small fish and frogs, and seeds. (Bosruiter)

## 4 Terek Sandpiper *Xenus cinereus*

J F M A M J J A S O N D

**22–25 cm; 65–100 g** A medium to small wader with short, yellow-orange legs and a long, upturned bill with an orange base. In flight, appears pale grey with white trailing edge to secondaries. Slightly darker and more streaked above in br. plumage. Juv. is buffier above. **Voice:** Series of fluty, uniformly pitched 'weet-weet-weet' notes. **Status and biology:** Uncommon Palearctic migrant at muddy estuaries and lagoons, favouring mangroves and areas with eel-grass (*Zostera*). Regional population some 4 000 birds, mainly in Mozambique. **Diet:** Crabs, insects and other invertebrates. Picks prey from surface and probes deeply with vertical bill. (Terekruiter)

## 5 Common Redshank *Tringa totanus*

J F M A M J J A S O N D

**27–29 cm; 90–150 g** Rare. Smaller and darker than Spotted Redshank (p.168), with a shorter bill (1.1–1.2 x head length), brighter orange-red legs, rather plain face and red at the base of both mandibles. In flight, has white back, finely barred rump and diagnostic white secondaries and outer primaries (broader and more extensive than Terek Sandpiper). Lacks scaled upperparts and plain breast of Ruff (p. 160). Underparts boldly streaked in br. plumage. Juv. is browner, with duller red legs and bill base. **Voice:** 'Teu-hu-hu', first syllable higher-pitched. **Status and biology:** Rare Palearctic migrant at coastal and freshwater wetlands, occasionally in small flocks. **Diet:** Mainly invertebrates. (Rooipootruiter)

## 1 Common Greenshank  *Tringa nebularia*

**30–34 cm; 140–250 g** A fairly large wader with long, greenish legs and toes (rarely yellowish). Larger than Marsh Sandpiper, with heavier, slightly upturned bill with grey-green base. In flight, rather plain upperwing contrasts with white rump and back (back brown in vagrant Greater Yellowlegs); tail mainly white with fine brown bars along outer edge. Br. ad. is more heavily streaked on head and neck. Juv. is browner above with buff feather fringes in fresh plumage. **Voice:** Loud 'chew-chew-chew', usually given in flight. **Status and biology:** Common Palearctic migrant at coastal and freshwater wetlands. Roosts communally at high tide in coastal localities. Regional population perhaps 30 000 birds. **Diet:** Crabs and other crustaceans, worms, aquatic insects, tadpoles and small fish. Feeds mainly visually, often running to catch prey. (Groenpootruiter)

## 2 Asiatic Dowitcher  *Limnodromus semipalmatus*

**34–36 cm, 160–200 g** Rare vagrant. Superficially recalls Bar-tailed Godwit (p. 170), but is slightly smaller and shorter-legged with a heavy, straight black bill that appears almost bulbous-tipped; lacks pinkish base to bill of Bar-tailed Godwit. Lacks wing bar in flight, but outer wing darker. Juv. has buff-fringed back feathers; underparts washed buff. **Voice:** Soft 'chewp' in flight. **Status and biology: NEAR-THREATENED.** Breeds in central Asia and winters in SE Asia and N Australia. Only 1 record: Gauteng, Nov. 2004. **Diet:** Invertebrates. (Asiatiese Snipgriet)

## 3 Lesser Yellowlegs  *Tringa flavipes*

**22–26 cm; 65–95 g** Rare vagrant. Structure recalls Marsh Sandpiper, but is slightly more robust with a heavier, all-dark bill, yellow (not grey-green) legs and white-notched greater coverts and tertials. In flight, back grey-brown (not white). Longer-legged than Wood Sandpiper (p. 166) with a less prominent supercilium and greyer upperparts. Appreciably smaller than vagrant Greater Yellowlegs with shorter (1 x head length), straighter, all-dark bill. **Voice:** High-pitched 'teu', softer and less strident than Greater Yellowlegs. **Status and biology:** Nearctic vagrant, usually wintering in S America. 4 records: Harare, Zimbabwe, Stanger, KwaZulu-Natal and 2 at Berg River estuary, W Cape. **Diet:** Invertebrates. (Kleingeelpootruiter)

## 4 Greater Yellowlegs  *Tringa melanoleuca*

**30–32 cm; 130–180 g** Rare vagrant. Structure recalls Common Greenshank, but bill straighter and has yellow (not grey-green) legs. In flight, back grey-brown (not white). Larger than vagrant Lesser Yellowlegs with longer bill (1.2–1.3 x head length) that has a paler grey-green base (not all-dark). **Voice:** Ringing 'teu teu teu', similar to Common Greenshank. **Status and biology:** Nearctic vagrant, usually wintering in S America. Only 1 record: Cape Peninsula, Dec 1971. **Diet:** Invertebrates. (Grootgeelpootruiter)

## 5 Marsh Sandpiper  *Tringa stagnatilis*

**22–26 cm; 55–95 g** A medium-sized, pale grey wader. Smaller and more slender than Common Greenshank, with a much thinner, straight, black bill, and proportionally longer legs; toes extend further beyond tail tip in flight. Rather plain upperwing contrasts with white rump and back in flight (back grey-brown in vagrant Lesser Yellowlegs and Wilson's Phalarope, p. 174). Wilson's Phalarope also has much shorter, yellow (not grey-green) legs. Br. ad. has blackish mottling on upperparts. Juv. darker and browner above; back feathers edged buff when fresh. **Voice:** High-pitched 'yeup', often repeated; higher-pitched and less strident than Common Greenshank. **Status and biology:** Fairly common Palearctic migrant at freshwater and coastal wetlands. Roosts communally at high tide in coastal localities. Regional population perhaps 10 000 birds. **Diet:** Small insects, crustaceans, worms and other invertebrates. Usually picks prey from surface, often while wading. (Moerasruiter)

## 6 Spotted Redshank  *Tringa erythropus*

**29–32 cm; 125–200 g** Rare vagrant. A large, long-billed wader with long, dark red legs. Larger and paler than Common Redshank, with a longer bill (1.4–1.5 x head length); only the base of the lower mandible red. Head has black line from bill to eye and pale supercilium. In flight, has uniform upperwings, white back and finely barred rump. In br. plumage, body is black, finely spotted and scalloped white; legs black. Juv. is more extensively barred grey below than non-br. ad. **Voice:** Clear, double-noted 'tu wik'. **Status and biology:** Palearctic vagrant that winters further N in Africa. Occurs in freshwater and coastal wetlands; only 5 records from sthn Africa. **Diet:** Invertebrates. (Gevlekte Rooipootruiter)

## 1 Bar-tailed Godwit  *Limosa lapponica*

J F M A M J J A S O N D

**37–40 cm; 200–300 g** A large, pale, long-legged wader with a long, slightly upturned bill. Slightly smaller than Black-tailed Godwit, with a shorter, upturned bill and appreciably shorter legs. Back and wing coverts have distinct pale fringes, making upperparts appear streaked. In flight, shows thin brown tail bars and white rump extending up back; lacks bold white wing bar of Black-tailed and Hudsonian godwits. In br. plumage, head, neck and underparts rich chestnut, finely barred on sides of breast; back black with chestnut feather margins. Female larger with longer bill; br. plumage duller. Juv. darker above and more buffy below. **Voice:** A 'wik-wik' or 'kirrik' call, often given in flight. **Status and biology:** Locally common Palearctic migrant to large, coastal wetlands; vagrant inland. Regional population some 10 000, most in Mozambique. **Diet:** Worms and other marine invertebrates. Feeds by probing deeply, often standing in water. (Bandstertgriet)

## 2 Hudsonian Godwit  *Limosa haemastica*

**40 cm; 200–320 g** Rare vagrant. Structure similar to Bar-tailed Godwit; hard to separate at rest, but in flight has an obvious white wing bar, black tail and diagnostic black underwing coverts. Smaller than Black-tailed Godwit, with shorter legs, slightly upturned bill and dark underwing. **Voice:** High-pitched 'ta-wit' flight call. **Status and biology:** Rare Nearctic vagrant to large coastal wetlands in W and E Cape; usually winters in S America. **Diet:** Invertebrates. (Hudsonbaaigriet)

## 3 Black-tailed Godwit  *Limosa limosa*

J F M A M J J A S O N D

**40–44 cm; 250–400 g** Rare. Larger than Bar-tailed Godwit, with a plain back, longer legs and a long, almost straight bill; pink base to bill larger and more distinct. In flight has conspicuous black (not barred) tail and obvious white wing bar; feet project well beyond tail tip. In br. plumage, neck and upper breast are chestnut; belly barred black and white. Female larger with longer bill. Juv. washed warm brown above, buff below. **Voice:** Repeated 'weeka-weeka', given especially in flight. **Status and biology: NEAR-THREATENED.** Rare Palearctic migrant to freshwater and coastal wetlands. **Diet:** Invertebrates and seeds; regularly forages in deep water. (Swartstertgriet)

## 4 Common Whimbrel  *Numenius phaeopus*

J F M A M J J A S O N D

**40–45 cm; 340–500 g** A large, grey-brown wader with a strongly decurved bill. Smaller and darker than Eurasian Curlew with a shorter bill (2–3 x head length), curved along its full length; head striped (not uniform). In flight, shows white rump and back, and more uniform upperwing than Eurasian Curlew. Female larger with longer bill. Juv. has scalloped upperparts. **Voice:** Bubbling, whistled 'whiri-iri-iri-iri-iri'; highly vocal in non-br. season. **Status and biology:** Common Palearctic migrant at coastal wetlands and, to a lesser extent, open shores; vagrant inland, often in pastures. Roosts communally at high tide. Regional population some 15 000, most in Mozambique. **Diet:** Crabs and other crustaceans, worms and molluscs; occasionally small fish. Feeds both by probing and picking. (Kleinwulp)

## 5 Eurasian Curlew  *Numenius arquata*

J F M A M J J A S O N D

**53–59 cm; 600–800 g** Rare. The largest wader, with a long, decurved bill. Paler than Common Whimbrel, with much longer bill (3–4 x head length) and plain (not striped) head. In flight, shows conspicuous white rump, which extends up back, and pale inner wing contrasting with darker outer wing. Female larger with longer bill. Juv. has buff fringes to back feathers, but these lost by Dec. **Voice:** Loud 'cur-lew'. **Status and biology: NEAR-THREATENED.** Uncommon Palearctic migrant at large estuaries and lagoons; vagrant inland. Roosts communally at high tide. Regional population 1 000, mostly at a few key sites. **Diet:** Marine invertebrates, including worms, crabs and molluscs. (Grootwulp)

## 1 Greater Painted-Snipe *Rostratula benghalensis*

bbBb ⬛ bbBBbb
J F M A M J J A S O N D

**24–26 cm; 90–140 g** Differs from true snipes by having white eye-ring extending onto ear coverts, dark breast band and obvious white breast extending up onto shoulder. Bill shorter than true snipes and slightly decurved; legs longer. Female is dominant sex and is more strikingly marked, with rich chestnut neck and breast and uniform upperparts. Male and juv. are more cryptic, with buff spotting on upperparts and conspicuous golden 'V' on back. Flight is slow, on large, broad wings, with legs often trailing. **Voice:** Silent when flushed; female gives soft 'wuk-oooooo', repeated monotonously, often at night. **Status and biology:** Uncommon resident and local nomad at marshes and flooded grassland. Polyandrous; female lays 2–5 eggs for up to 4 successive males in a shallow cup nest, usually among grasses or sedges. Male performs all parental duties. **Diet:** Worms and other invertebrates. (Goudsnip)

## 2 African Snipe *Gallinago nigripennis*

⬛⬛ bbbbBBBb ⬛
J F M A M J J A S O N D

**28–30 cm; 110–140 g** A long-billed snipe, only likely to be confused with rare Great Snipe. Differs in having a mainly white belly, lacking strongly marked flanks and vent, white central underwing (not barred), and more uniform upperwing, lacking white bars. When flushed, typically calls, jinks from side to side and flies a considerable distance compared to Great Snipe's usually silent takeoff and shorter, more direct flight. Outer tail partly barred (white in ad. Great Snipe). Juv. plainer and duller above. **Voice:** Sucking 'scaap' when flushed; males produce whirring, drumming sound with their stiffened outer tail feathers during aerial display flights **(2 A)**. **Status and biology:** Common resident and local nomad at marshes and flooded grassland, usually in muddy areas with short vegetation. Monogamous; breeds singly, laying 2 (1–3) eggs in a shallow depression formed among marshy vegetation. **Diet:** Worms, insects, other aquatic invertebrates and occasional seeds. (Afrikaanse Snip)

## 3 Great Snipe *Gallinago media*

⬛⬛⬛⬛⬛⬛
J F M A M J J A S O N D

**28–30 cm; 130–220 g** Rare. A large, chunky snipe with a relatively short, heavy bill that is held more level in flight than that of African Snipe. Flight rather heavy; tends to fly directly away when flushed, not jinking like African Snipe. Best distinguished by bold, blackish chevrons on breast, flanks and vent, grey-barred underwing and 2 well-defined white wing bars formed by large white tips to upperwing coverts. Pale 'braces' on scapulars less marked than African Snipe. Juv. more rufous above with brown crescents below; white spots on wing coverts reduced; outer tail barred. **Voice:** Generally silent; occasionally utters 1 or 2 soft croaks when flushed. **Status and biology: NEAR-THREATENED**. Formerly quite common, but now only a scarce Palearctic migrant at marshes and flooded grassland. **Diet:** Invertebrates. (Dubbelsnip)

## 4 Ruddy Turnstone *Arenaria interpres*

⬛⬛⬛⬛⬛⬛⬛⬛
J F M A M J J A S O N D

**21–25 cm; 90–150 g** A stocky, short-billed wader with orange legs. White belly and lower breast contrast with blackish patches on upper breast. In br. plumage has rich chestnut back and striking black-and-white-patterned head and neck. In flight, appears boldly black and white above, with strong white wing bar, white back stripes and rump, and black tail with narrow white tip. Juv. has pale fringes to back feathers. **Voice:** Hard 'kttuck', especially in flight. **Status and biology:** Common Palearctic migrant at rocky shores and estuaries, occasionally on sandy shores and coastal lagoons; rare inland, mainly on migration. Regional population some 40 000 birds. **Diet:** Wide range of invertebrates; also carrion. Often flicks over stones to locate prey, hence common name. Sometimes feeds on land. (Steenloper)

# PHALAROPES

Largely aquatic waders with long, dumpy bodies and lobed toes adapted for swimming. Sexes differ; females larger and more brightly coloured in br. plumage; chicks cared for by male; often polyandrous.

### 1 Red-necked Phalarope *Phalaropus lobatus*

J F M A M J J A S O N D

**17–20 cm; 28–45 g** Rare. Slightly smaller than Red Phalarope, with a darker grey back streaked with white, and a longer, thinner, all-black bill (lacking a yellow base). In flight, appears darker above with a blackish (not grey) rump. Body is dark grey in br. plumage, with rufous neck band; female is more brightly coloured than male. Juv. darker and browner above, with rufous-fringed feathers; breast washed buff. **Voice:** Low 'tchick' in flight. **Status and biology:** Uncommon Palearctic migrant at lakes, saltpans and sewage works; rarely at sea. **Diet:** Small insects and crustaceans, usually obtained by surface picking while swimming. (Rooihalsfraiingpoot)

### 2 Red Phalarope *Phalaropus fulicarius*

J F M A M J J A S O N D

**20–22 cm; 40–65 g** The common phalarope at sea. Larger and paler than Red-necked Phalarope, with a shorter, thicker bill that is broad to the tip and may show a yellow base. Head mainly white with black eye patch. Hind neck, back and rump are rather plain grey, but can look mottled in moulting birds. In br. plumage (rarely recorded in sthn Africa) has chestnut underparts and white face. Juv. browner above; breast tinged buffy. **Voice:** Soft, low 'wiit'. **Status and biology:** Fairly common Palearctic migrant at sea off W coast, becoming rare on S and E coasts; vagrants occur along the coast and on inland lakes. Usually in small flocks at sea. **Diet:** Zooplankton. Forages along drift lines or by spinning in calm weather to pull prey to the surface. (Grysfraiingpoot)

### 3 Wilson's Phalarope *Steganopus tricolor*

**22–24 cm; 40–80 g** Rare vagrant. Larger than other phalaropes, with a longer bill and yellow legs. Swims less than other phalaropes. In non-br. plumage, lacks distinct black eye patch; superficially resembles Marsh Sandpiper (p. 168), but has much shorter, yellow legs. In flight, white rump contrasts with grey-brown tail, back and upperwings. In br. plumage, sides of breast and mantle are washed rufous; female is larger and more brightly coloured than male. Juv. darker above with buff-fringed feathers. **Voice:** Short, grunting 'grrg'. **Status and biology:** Nearctic vagrant, usually wintering in S America. Scattered records from coastal wetlands and saltpans. **Diet:** Invertebrates. (Bontfraiingpoot)

**DF** ① br. ♀

**IS** ① non-br.

**TH** ① non-br.

**EG** ① br. ♂

**WRT** ② non-br.

**EG** ② br. ♀

**HJE/VIREO** ② br. ♀

**JG** ③ br. ♀

**MD** ③ non-br.

**PM** ③ non-br.

# PRATINCOLES

Peculiar waders, closely related to coursers but with long, pointed wings, short legs and short, broad bills adapted for catching aerial prey. Sexes alike, with distinct br. plumages in some species. Breed singly or in loose colonies. Monogamous; both sexes incubate and feed the precocial chicks.

## 1 Collared (Red-winged) Pratincole  *Glareola pratincola*

J F M A M J J A S O N D

24–25 cm; 60–100 g  A large, long-winged pratincole with a pale buff throat. Paler above than Black-winged Pratincole with more distinct white eye-ring and gradual merging of grey breast into whitish belly. Best separated in flight, when pale trailing edge to secondaries and dark rufous (not black) underwing coverts visible (but in poor light, underwing can appear all-dark). In br. plumage, throat patch is edged with thin black collar (incomplete or absent in non-br. birds).  Flight light and graceful, showing conspicuous white rump and deeply forked tail. Juv. lacks clearly defined throat markings and has buff edges to mantle feathers. **Voice:** 'Kik-kik', especially in flight. **Status and biology: NEAR-THREATENED**. Locally common resident and intra-African migrant, usually found at wetland margins and open areas near water. Lays 1–2 eggs in a shallow scrape. **Diet:** Mainly insects caught on the wing, often at dusk and on moonlit nights. (Rooivlerksprinkaanvoël)

## 2 Black-winged Pratincole  *Glareola nordmanni*

J F M A M J J A S O N D

23–25 cm; 90–110 g  Slightly darker and longer-legged than Collared Pratincole, with less distinct eye-ring and sharper divide between grey breast and whitish belly. Buff throat patch often poorly defined. Best distinguished in flight, when it lacks white trailing edge to secondaries and has black (not rufous) underwing coverts. Juv. more drab, with scalloped upperparts, and sometimes has rufous flecking on underwing coverts. **Voice:** Often-repeated, single- or double-noted 'pik'. **Status and biology:** Locally common Palearctic migrant; usually in large, nomadic flocks in grassland, fallow lands and at the edges of wetlands. **Diet:** Insects, especially locusts and termite alates. (Swartvlerksprinkaanvoël)

## 3 Rock Pratincole  *Glareola nuchalis*

J F M A M J J A S O N D

17–20 cm; 42–55 g  A small, dark pratincole with relatively short wings and tail. White stripe behind eye extends to form a nuchal collar. White rump is conspicuous in flight. Juv. is duller; lacks white eye-stripe, and is lightly speckled buff above and on breast. **Voice:** Loud, plover-like 'kik-kik'. **Status and biology:** Uncommon intra-African migrant breeding at rocky areas (occasionally on sandbars) on Zambezi and Kavango rivers; vagrant elsewhere. Regional population <2 000 birds. Lays 1–2 eggs on rocks, usually in a shaded crevice. **Diet:** Insects, mainly caught in flight. Forages at dark around lights. (Withalssprinkaanvoël)

# THICK-KNEES (DIKKOPS)

Large, mainly terrestrial waders with short, stout bills and long, yellow legs. Plumage cryptic at rest, but with bold wing patterns in flight. Active at night; roost during the day. Sexes alike. Nest singly. Monogamous; both sexes incubate (mainly female during the day) and care for the precocial chicks, feeding them for first few days after hatching.

## 1 Spotted Thick-knee *Burhinus capensis*

43 cm; 380–600 g  A large thick-knee with dark brown and buff-spotted upperparts and no grey wing bar at rest. In flight, has small white patches at base of inner and outer primaries; remainder of flight feathers and greater coverts blackish. Underwing white with black trailing edge and median stripe. Juv. similar, but more streaked above. **Voice:** Rising then falling 'whi-whi-whi-WHI-WHI-WHI-whi-whi', usually at night. **Status and biology:** Common resident in virtually any open country, including fields and parks. Often in pairs. Regional population >50 000 birds. Lays 1–3 eggs in a shallow scrape. **Diet:** Mainly termites, locusts, beetles and other invertebrates; occasional reptiles and small mammals. (Gewone Dikkop)

## 2 Water Thick-knee *Burhinus vermiculatus*

38–41 cm; 280–430 g  Smaller than Spotted Thick-knee, with plainer, grey-brown plumage, finely streaked dark brown, and a grey wing panel visible on folded wing at rest and in flight; usually found close to water. Juv. more streaked above. **Voice:** Rather mournful 'ti-ti-ti-tee-teee-tooo', slowing and dropping in pitch at end, usually at night. **Status and biology:** Common resident and local nomad along river and lake shores. Usually in pairs. Regional population some 10 000 birds. Lays 1–3 eggs in a shallow scrape. **Diet:** Aquatic and terrestrial invertebrates. (Waterdikkop)

# SHEATHBILLS

Plump, white, pigeon-like birds with short, stout beaks that develop exaggerated nasal sheaths in ads. Legs thick and scaly. Wings rounded. Sexes alike. Monogamous; both sexes incubate and feed the semi-precocial chicks.

## 3 Lesser Sheathbill *Chionis minor*

36–39 cm; 450–700 g  Told from Greater Sheathbill by its black (not pink) face and blackish (not yellowish) bill; ranges do not overlap. Juv. has smaller facial patch; bill lacks well-developed sheaths. **Voice:** 'Kek-kek-kek'; pairs give soft 'kok' calls during inane mutual bowing display. **Status and biology:** Not recorded from sthn Africa; 8 000 pairs breed in summer at the Prince Edwards (3 000 pairs), Crozets and Kerguelen. Lays 2–3 eggs in a rock crevice in Dec–Jan. **Diet:** Steals food from penguins and shags as they feed their chicks; also carrion, faeces, marine invertebrates and insects. (Kleinskedebek)

## 4 Greater Sheathbill *Chionis albus*

38–40 cm; 500–780 g  Told from Lesser Sheathbill by its pink (not black) face and yellowish (not blackish) bill; ranges do not overlap. Juv. has smaller facial patch; bill lacks well-developed sheaths. **Voice:** Silent in Africa. **Status and biology:** Rare visitor to coastal areas, especially seabird roosts and harbours; most records Apr–Jun. Breeds in summer on Antarctic Peninsula and migrates to sthn S America; all S African records assumed to be ship-assisted with birds landing on ships during their northward migration. **Diet:** Omnivorous. (Grootskedebek)

# COURSERS

Fairly small, long-legged, terrestrial waders, with both diurnal and nocturnal species. Sexes alike. Breed singly. Monogamous; both sexes incubate and feed the precocial chicks.

## 1 Temminck's Courser *Cursorius temminckii*

| b | | | | b | b | b | B | B | B | B | b |
|---|---|---|---|---|---|---|---|---|---|---|---|
| J | F | M | A | M | J | J | A | S | O | N | D |

**19–21 cm; 65–80g** A plain rufous courser with a broad black patch behind the eye. Differs from Burchell's Courser by having rufous (not grey) hind crown; belly has black patch (not bar) between and in front of legs. In flight, underwing black, with narrow white trailing edge to secondaries, but secondaries appear blackish from above. Juv. duller, with lightly speckled breast and scalloped upperparts. **Voice:** Grating 'keerkeer'. **Status and biology:** Locally common resident, nomad and intra-African migrant found in dry, sparsely grassed and recently burned areas. Lays 2 (1–3) eggs on bare ground. **Diet:** Insects (especially termites, grasshoppers and beetles) plus occasional seeds. (Trekdrawwertjie)

## 2 Burchell's Courser *Cursorius rufus*

| b | b | b | b | | | b | B | B | B | B | B |
|---|---|---|---|---|---|---|---|---|---|---|---|
| J | F | M | A | M | J | J | A | S | O | N | D |

**21–23 cm; 70–110 g** A plain rufous courser with a narrow black line behind the eye and a blue-grey hind crown and nape. Paler than Temminck's Courser, with less contrast between upperparts and breast. Black band behind legs separates rufous forebelly from white vent. In flight, has broad white trailing edge to secondaries. Underwing coverts rufous; secondaries mostly white; primaries black. Juv. mottled above, with barred tail tip and poorly defined black belly band. **Voice:** Harsh, repeated 'wark'. **Status and biology:** Near-endemic. Uncommon nomad in dry, sparsely grassed plains and open fields. Small numbers move into W Cape in late winter. Lays 1–2 eggs on bare ground. **Diet:** Insects (termites, beetles, caterpillars, ants) plus occasional seeds. (Bloukopdrawwertjie)

## 3 Double-banded Courser *Rhinoptilus africanus*

| B | B | b | b | b | b | b | b | b | B | B | B |
|---|---|---|---|---|---|---|---|---|---|---|---|
| J | F | M | A | M | J | J | A | S | O | N | D |

**20–24 cm; 70–100 g** A whitsh courser with 2 narrow black breast bands; head plain, with creamy eye-stripe. Upperparts are scaled; dark back and wing coverts have broad creamy-buff edges. In flight, shows white rump and conspicuous chestnut secondaries and inner primaries contrasting with dark outer primaries. Juv. has chestnut breast bands. **Voice:** Thin, falling and rising 'teeu-wee' whistle; repeated 'kee-kee', mostly at night. **Status and biology:** Common resident and local nomad of semi-arid and desert plains, usually in stony areas. Lays 1 egg on bare ground. **Diet:** Insects (termites, beetles and ants). (Dubbelbanddrawwertjie)

## 4 Three-banded Courser *Rhinoptilus cinctus*

| | | | | | b | b | b | b | b | B | B | B | b | b |
|---|---|---|---|---|---|---|---|---|---|---|---|---|---|---|
| J | F | M | A | M | J | J | A | S | O | N | D |

**25–28 cm; 120–150 g** Larger than Double-banded Courser, with rufous, black, and white bands on breast and neck. White eye-stripe forks behind eye and extends into hind collar. In flight has white rump, but upperwings are relatively uniform, with darker brown flight feathers than Double-banded Courser. Juv. like ad., but with barred secondaries and central tail feathers. **Voice:** Repeated 'kika-kika-kika' at night. **Status and biology:** Uncommon to locally common in arid and semi-arid savanna. Largely nocturnal; roosts under bushes during the day. Lays 2 eggs in a deep scrape in bare ground, usually shaded by a bush or tree. **Diet:** Insects. (Driebanddrawwertjie)

## 5 Bronze-winged Courser *Rhinoptilus chalcopterus*

| | | | | | | | | | b | b | B | B | b | b |
|---|---|---|---|---|---|---|---|---|---|---|---|---|---|---|
| J | F | M | A | M | J | J | A | S | O | N | D |

**25–28 cm; 120–165 g** A distinctive courser with a broad, dusky band across the breast and lower neck separated from the pale lower breast and belly by a black line. In flight, white uppertail coverts and wing bars contrast with dark upperparts. Iridescent tips to flight feathers not a field character. Juv. has rufous-tipped feathers on upperparts. **Voice:** Ringing 'ki-kooi' at night. **Status and biology:** Fairly common resident and intra-African migrant in woodland and savanna. Largely nocturnal; roosts under bushes during the day. Lays 2–3 eggs on bare ground, sometimes in a shallow scrape surrounded by twigs and soil fragments. **Diet:** Insects. (Bronsvlerkdrawwertjie)

# SKUAS AND JAEGERS

Medium-sized, gull-like seabirds with mainly brown plumage. Sexes alike, but jaegers have distinct br., non-br. and juv. plumages, as well as pale, intermediate and dark morphs. Plumage highly variable; identification relies largely on size and structure. Females larger than males. Predatory when breeding, feeding on other birds and small mammals; sometimes steal food from other birds. Monogamous; rarely polyandrous trios. Both sexes incubate and feed the semi-precocial chicks.

## 1 Subantarctic Skua *Catharacta antarctica*

J F M A M J J A S O N D

**60–66 cm; 1.3–1.8 kg** A large, heavy-bodied skua with large white wing flashes (reduced in juv.). Short, broad wings, short rump and tail, and heavy build distinguish it from jaegers. Upperparts are variably streaked and blotched buff; plainer in juv. Larger, chunkier and heavier-billed than rare dark-morph South Polar Skua, which has only sparse, fine, pale streaking on upperparts. Race *C. a. lonnbergi* most frequent visitor but at least some *C. a. antarctica/hamiltoni* occur; taxonomy requires revision. **Voice:** Display at colonies is a loud, 'aah aah-aah-ah-ah-ah-ah-ah' with wings raised; generally silent at sea. **Status and biology:** Common in shelf waters. 12 000 pairs breed in summer at sub-Antarctic islands (1 200 *C. a. hamiltoni* at Tristan and Gough, 850 *C. a. lonnbergi* at the Prince Edwards); hybridises with South Polar Skua in area of overlap on Antarctic Peninsula. Lays 1–2 eggs in a shallow cup nest on the ground. **Diet:** Kills burrowing petrels and penguin eggs and chicks at br. islands; scavenges at sea, occasionally stealing food from gannets and shearwaters; regularly attends trawlers. (Bruinroofmeeu)

## 2 South Polar Skua *Catharacta maccormicki*

J F M A M J J A S O N D

**53–60 cm; 1.2–1.5 kg** Rare. Head, neck and breast colour varies from dark brown (dark morph) **(2 A)** to ash (pale morph) **(2 B)**. Pale morph is easily identified by contrast between dark wings and pale head and body. Unfortunately most records from sthn Africa are dark morph, which resembles a small, slender juv. Subantarctic Skua with a small bill; body shape can recall Pomarine Jaeger. Plumage rather plain, with only fine, sparse streaks on neck and back. Often has paler, greyish feathers at base of bill. Intermediate birds usually show a pale hind neck. Juv. plain brown, lacking paler face or nape. Sits more upright on water than other large skuas. **Voice:** Silent at sea. **Status and biology:** Rare passage migrant in sthn Africa. 6 000 pairs breed in summer at ice-free areas in Antarctica. **Diet:** Opportunistic predator; often pugnacious at sea, even tackling Wandering Albatrosses. (Suidpoolroofmeeu)

## 3 Pomarine Jaeger *Stercorarius pomarinus*

J F M A M J J A S O N D

**50 cm (to 75 cm with streamers); 580–800 g** The largest jaeger, characterised by relatively broad wings and large white wing flashes; can also be confused with South Polar Skua. Appears heavily built with a barrel-chest and stout, pale-based bill. Flight direct and powerful. Br. ad. has spoon-shaped (not pointed) central tail feathers. Pale morph predominates; has more extensive dark cap than other pale-morph jaegers. Non-br. ads are barred on vent, flanks and rump. Juv. and imm. boldly barred on belly, vent, rump and underwing. **Voice:** Silent at sea. **Status and biology:** Common Palearctic migrant to coastal waters off W coast; scarce off E coast. Rarely ventures far from land; occasionally roosts ashore. 20 000 pairs breed in Arctic tundra in N summer. **Diet:** Scavenges and steals food from gannets, terns and other seabirds. (Knopstertroofmeeu)

## 4 Parasitic Jaeger *Stercorarius parasiticus*

J F M A M J J A S O N D

**46 cm (to 65 cm with streamers); 380–500 g** A medium-sized jaeger with white wing flashes; usually the most abundant jaeger in the region. Larger and somewhat more heavily built than Long-tailed Jaeger, with broader wings and more prominent white wing flashes; flight more direct and dashing. Plumage generally darker brown (not pale grey-brown). More likely to be confused with Pomarine Jaeger, but is smaller and more slender with relatively longer, narrower wings, smaller bill that appears uniformly dark and a smaller dark hood in pale-phase birds. If present, central tail feathers are relatively short and straight. Pale **(4 A)**, dark **(4 B)** and rare intermediate colour morphs occur. Juv. more rusty brown than other juv. jaegers, with less strongly barred underparts. **Voice:** Silent at sea. **Status and biology:** Common Palearctic migrant to coastal waters. Occasionally roosts ashore; vagrant inland. 100 000 pairs breed in Arctic tundra in N summer. **Diet:** Scavenges and steals food from terns and gulls; rarely kills storm-petrels. (Arktiese Roofmeeu)

## 5 Long-tailed Jaeger *Stercorarius longicaudus*

J F M A M J J A S O N D

**38 cm (to 62 cm with streamers); 250–400 g** The smallest jaeger, with buoyant, tern-like flight on long, slender wings. Almost all birds are pale morphs. Ads are plain, cold greyish above, with only the shafts of outer 2 primaries white; vent and uppertail coverts barred in non-br. plumage. Bill is short; at close range, nail (upper mandible tip) comprises roughly half bill length (less than a third in other jaegers). Very long central tail feathers are diagnostic in br. plumage (beware short streamers when moulting). Juv. colder grey-brown than juv. Parasitic Jaeger with more boldly barred uppertail coverts and underwing. **Voice:** Silent at sea. **Status and biology:** Fairly common Palearctic migrant to oceanic waters off S Africa; scarce close to land; vagrant inland. 50 000 pairs breed in Arctic tundra in N summer. **Diet:** Scavenges at trawlers; seldom harries other seabirds. (Langstertroofmeeu)

# GULLS

Medium-large sea and freshwater birds. Sexes alike in plumage (males larger). Juv. body plumage short-lived in small gulls (and thus unlikely to be observed in sthn Africa for migrant and vagrant species). Some large gulls have 2–3 imm. plumages. Monogamous; both sexes incubate and feed the semi-precocial chicks. Often retain the same mate in successive years.

## 1 Black-legged Kittiwake *Rissa tridactyla*

J F M A M J J A S O N D

**36–40 cm; 320–450 g** Rare vagrant. An oceanic gull, slightly larger than Sabine's Gull, with long wings, a shallow forked tail and short bill. Br. ad. white with pale grey back; upperwing pale grey with narrow white trailing edge and black tips to outer primaries; bill yellow. Non-br. ad. has grey patch on ear coverts and grey smudging on hind neck. Juv. has black 'M' across upperwing, black tail tip (broadest in centre of tail) and black hind collar; bill black. **Voice:** Silent at sea. **Status and biology:** 3 records from W coast; breeds in N Atlantic, seldom crossing equator. **Diet:** Small fish and invertebrates. (Swartpootbrandervoël)

## 2 Grey-headed Gull *Chroicocephalus cirrocephalus*

b b b B B b b b b b
J F M A M J J A S O N D

**40–42 cm; 220–340 g** Medium-sized gull with a pale grey back and upperwings. Br. ad. has diagnostic pale grey head, and bright red bill and legs. Non-br. ad. has largely white head with grey smudges above eye and on cheeks; bill and legs duller. Eyes silver with narrow red outer ring. Imm. has dark smudges on ear coverts and a dark-tipped, pink-orange bill. Juv. is heavily mottled brown on upperwings; secondaries darker grey than ad. Larger than Hartlaub's Gull with a longer bill, slightly drooped at the tip. Easily told from vagrant gulls in flight by grey underwing and mostly black outer primaries. **Voice:** Dry 'karrh'. **Status and biology:** Locally common resident; 10 000 pairs breed in Africa and S America, at least 200 pairs in sthn Africa. Breeds in colonies at wetlands, laying 2–3 eggs in a shallow bowl of vegetation. Occasionally hybridises with Hartlaub's Gull. **Diet:** Opportunistic scavenger and predator, mainly in aquatic habitats, but also around towns and agricultural lands. (Gryskopmeeu)

## 3 Hartlaub's Gull *Chroicocephalus hartlaubii*

b B B B B B b B b b b b
J F M A M J J A S O N D

**38–40 cm; 220–340 g** Endemic to Benguela coast. Slightly smaller than Grey-headed Gull, with a shorter, thinner and darker bill and deeper red legs; eyes dark at all ages. Told from vagrant gulls in flight by grey underwing and mostly black outer primaries. Br. ads have slight lavender shadow line demarcating hood; non-br. birds have plain white head. Imm. has uniform dark bill and dull legs; sometimes shows small dark patches on ear coverts. Juv. is mottled brown on wing coverts, but is less heavily so than juv. Grey-headed Gull. **Voice:** Drawn-out, rattling 'keeerrh'. **Status and biology:** Common resident; 13 000 pairs breed on offshore islands, coastal wetlands and on large buildings at the coast from C Namibia to Port Elizabeth, E Cape. Lays 1–3 eggs in a shallow bowl of vegetation. Occasionally hybridises with Grey-headed Gull. **Diet:** Opportunistic scavenger and predator, mainly in coastal habitats, but also around towns and on flooded fields. Often active at night. (Hartlaubmeeu)

## 4 Slender-billed Gull *Chroicocephalus genei*

J F M A M J J A S O N D

**38–44 cm; 240–320 g** Rare vagrant. A pale grey and white gull with a white head and distinctive head profile: shallow sloping forehead and long bill that droops slightly at the tip. Ad. has pale eye and red bill; underparts washed pink in br. plumage. In flight, wing pattern resembles Common Black-headed Gull's (p. 186), but body appears longer. Imm. has dark smudge behind eye, but this is less prominent than in imm. Grey-headed and Common Black-headed gulls; bill red (not bicolored). **Voice:** 'Ka' or 'kra', deeper than Common Black-headed Gull. **Status and biology:** Breeds in Palearctic, wintering in NE Africa; 1 record: Durban, Sept 1999. **Diet:** Fish and invertebrates. (Dunbekmeeu)

## 1 Sabine's Gull  *Xema sabini*

J F M A M J J A S O N D

**27–32 cm; 160–180 g**  A small, oceanic gull with a shallow-forked tail and buoyant, tern-like flight. In flight, boldly tricoloured upperwing is diagnostic. Ad. bill black with yellow tip; legs black. Non-br. ads have mostly white heads with dark smudges on nape; br. ads have dark grey hood. Juv. upperparts brownish, scaled white; in flight, shows darker upperwing coverts. Bill black; legs grey-pink. **Voice:** Silent in Africa. **Status and biology:** Common Palearctic migrant to coastal waters, including large, sheltered bays; rare ashore or in coastal wetlands. Often in flocks; roosts at sea. **Diet:** Fish, crustaceans and fishery wastes. (Mikstertmeeu)

## 2 Franklin's Gull  *Larus pipixcan*

J F M A M J J A S O N D

**32–36 cm; 240–320 g**  Vagrant. A fairly small, black-headed gull with a rather short, stubby bill and at least partial black hood and white crescents above and below eye at all ages. Darker grey above than other small gulls in the region. In flight, has broad white trailing edge to secondaries; black subterminal band on outer primaries surrounded by a white band. Underwings whitish. Bill dark red in br. plumage; black in non-br. and imm. birds. Imm. has broad subterminal tail band and darker grey wings, but still has broad white trailing edge to secondaries. **Voice:** Silent in Africa. **Status and biology:** Recorded from the coast and adjacent wetlands, but some records from inland waterbodies. Breeds in the Nearctic, wintering in S America. **Diet:** Small fish and invertebrates. (Franklinmeeu)

## 3 Common Black-headed Gull  *Chroicocephalus ridibundus*

J F M A M J J A S O N D

**35–40 cm; 240–360 g**  Vagrant. Paler grey above than Grey-headed, Hartlaub's (p. 184) and Franklin's gulls; in flight, has mostly white outer primaries (but aberrant Hartlaub's and Grey-headed can also show this) and whitish (not grey) underwings. Br. ad. has dark brown hood and partial white eye-ring; bill dark red. Non-br. ads have dark smudges on head and paler red bill with dark tip. Imm. similar but with dark brownish subterminal band across inner primaries, secondaries and tail. Juv. has mottled brown wing coverts; unlikely to occur in this plumage. **Voice:** Typical, small-gull 'kraah'. **Status and biology:** Rare Palearctic migrant, often found with other gulls at coastal or inland wetlands. **Diet:** Omnivorous; mainly invertebrates. (Swartkopmeeu)

1 non-br. — IS
1 non-br. — JG
1 br. — GV
1 non-br. — IS
2 br. — JG
2 br. — JG
2 non-br. — JG
2 non-br. — JG
3 br. — TH
3 non-br. — IS
3 non-br. — PR
3 br. — WRT

## 1 Kelp Gull *Larus dominicanus*

bb||||||||bBBB
J F M A M J J A S O N D

**55–65 cm; 900–1 100 g** The largest gull in the region. Main confusion is with Lesser Black-backed Gull, but is more heavily built with shorter wings and a more robust bill. Ad. has blackish back and upperwings; eyes dark grey-brown (rarely yellow or silver-grey); legs olive-grey (rarely yellowish). Juv. heavily streaked dark brown; bill blackish; legs brownish-pink. Best told from juv. Lesser Black-backed Gull by structure; could potentially be confused with skuas, but bill has typical gull shape. Imm. has white body with diffuse brown smudging; mantle slate-grey with some brown feathers; tail tip blackish; bill pinkish at base and tip. Sub-ad. has mostly ad. plumage but retains some brown in upper- and underwings and dark tail tips; bill sometimes has a dark subterminal mark. Young ads may retain dark tips to outer tail feathers. **Voice:** Display call is long series of 'kee-ah' notes; alarm calls include single 'kee-ah', 'kwok' and 'yap-yap'. **Status and biology:** Common resident in coastal habitats and adjacent wetlands; follows trawlers up to 100 km from shore. Increasingly found on fields up to 50 km inland. Endemic race *L. d. vetula* sometimes considered a separate species (Cape or Khoisan Gull); 20 000 pairs breed in summer; lays 2–3 eggs in a shallow scrape. Nominate *L. d. dominicanus* is regular vagrant from S America to Tristan/Gough and possibly sthn Africa. *L. d. judithae* is resident at sub-Antarctic islands in the Indian Ocean, with 130 pairs at the Prince Edwards. **Diet:** Opportunistic scavenger and predator, taking wide range of prey. (Kelpmeeu)

## 2 Lesser Black-backed Gull *Larus fuscus*

■■■■■■|■|■|■■
J F M A M J J A S O N D

**52–65 cm; 600–1 150 g** Slightly smaller than Kelp Gull with a less robust bill and more attenuated appearance; wings project well beyond the tail at rest. Head less robust with gently sloping forehead. Ads have yellow (not olive-grey) legs and feet. Juvs and imms best differentiated by structure, but legs typically are paler, flesh-coloured (not brownish). Two races occur (sometimes treated as separate species): *L. f. fuscus* (**2 A**) is smaller (600–800 g) with a blackish-grey back in ad. plumage; 'Heuglin's Gull' *L. f. heuglini* (**2 B**) is larger (850–1 150 g) with a longer bill and shallow forehead, giving it a rakish appearance; ad. back dark slate-grey. **Voice:** Typical, large-gull 'kow-kow'; shorter 'kop'. **Status and biology:** Rare Palearctic migrant, mostly Oct–Apr, at coastal and inland wetlands. **Diet:** Omnivorous. (Kleinswartrugmeeu)

# SKIMMERS

Large, tern-like birds with long, broad wings; their elongate lower mandible is trailed through the water in flight to locate small fish and other prey. Sexes alike. Monogamous; often breed in colonies. Both parents incubate and feed the semi-precocial chicks.

## 3 African Skimmer *Rynchops flavirostris*

■■■■■■■■|bBBbb
J F M A M J J A S O N D

**38–42 cm; 120–220 g** Easily identified by its peculiarly shaped long red bill with a yellowish tip; dark upperparts contrast with white underparts, and white trailing edge to wing and outer tail. Upperparts blackish in br. ad.; browner and less crisply defined in non-br. ad. Juv. browner above, with pale feather fringes; bill blackish, gradually turning dull yellow then red from base. **Voice:** Harsh 'rak-rak'. **Status and biology:** NEAR-THREATENED. Locally common resident and local migrant. on large rivers, bays and lakes with sandbanks for roosting and breeding. Total population some 10 000 birds, with 1 000 in sthn Africa. Breeds in small colonies; lays 2–4 eggs in a scrape on a sandbank. Parents wet belly feathers to cool eggs on hot days. **Diet:** Small fish, detected by touch while skimming with lower mandible. (Waterploeër)

# TERNS

Long-winged sea and freshwater birds with loose, buoyant flight; feed by plunge-diving or surface-seizing; also occasionally hawk insects in the air or from ground. Most species roost ashore. Sexes alike, but most species have distinct br., non-br. and juv. plumages. Monogamous; both sexes incubate and feed the semi-precocial chicks.

## 4 Caspian Tern *Sterna caspia*

bbbbbbbbbbbb
J F M A M J J A S O N D

**47–54 cm; 630–740 g** The largest tern, with very heavy red or orange-red bill with black tip. In flight, dark primaries form large blackish tip to underwing. Cap is black in br. plumage, variably streaked white in non-br. plumage. Larger and darker above than Royal Tern, with heavier, redder bill and less deeply forked tail. Juv. has brown fringes to wing coverts, more grey in tail, and more extensive black tip to bill. **Voice:** Deep, harsh 'kraaak'; recently fledged chicks have a whining, begging call. **Status and biology:** Regional br. population some 500 pairs, mainly in S Africa; small numbers in Namibia and Botswana. Usually breeds in small colonies, sometimes with other waterbirds. Lays 2 (1–3) eggs in a shallow scrape. **Diet:** Fish. Locally common resident at large wetlands and sheltered coastal waters. (Reusesterretjie)

## 1 Royal Tern  *Sterna maxima*

J F M A M J J A S O N D

**46–48 cm; 340–420 g** Rare vagrant. A large, pale tern with an orange bill. Smaller than Caspian Tern (p. 188), with a more slender, relatively longer bill that lacks dark tip; in flight, primaries are greyish (not black) on underwing. Most likely confused with Swift Tern, but bill distinctly orange; outer primaries darker grey, contrasting with paler coverts and back. Appreciably larger than Lesser Crested and Elegant terns, with a heavier bill. Br. ads have full black crown with shaggy crest; non-br. ads have extensive white forehead and crown, with often only a small black nuchal patch. Juv. has mottled brown wing coverts. Imm. has dark carpal bar. **Voice:** Loud, harsh 'ree-ack'. **Status and biology:** Breeds W and C Africa; occasionally in small flocks near Cunene River mouth; vagrant further S on Namibian coast. **Diet:** Fish and crustaceans; often crabs. (Koningsterretjie)

## 2 Swift Tern  *Sterna bergii*

b b b b B B b b b | | |
J F M A M J J A S O N D

**46–49 cm; 320–430 g** A large tern with a long, slightly drooped yellow or greenish-yellow bill (not orange, as in Royal, Lesser Crested and Elegant terns). Appreciably larger than Lesser Crested and Elegant terns. Br. ads have black cap and shaggy crest, but black does not extend to bill. Non-br. ads have white forecrown. Back colour pale grey in nominate race; some darker grey *S. b. velox* may occur in Mozambique. Juv. has dull yellow bill; upperparts mottled blackish-brown with blackish margins to flight feathers, appearing dark grey in flight. Imm. retains dark flight feathers. Legs usually black, but some juvs have yellow-orange legs. **Voice:** Harsh 'kree-eck'; juv. has a thin, whistled begging call. **Status and biology:** Common resident and local migrant in coastal waters, rarely out to shelf break; also estuaries and coastal wetlands. Nominate race is endemic to sthn Africa; 6 000 pairs breed colonially at islands and coastal wetlands from C Namibia to Algoa Bay, E Cape. **Diet:** Mainly pelagic fish such as anchovy and sardine. Large numbers follow sardine run along the E coast in winter. (Geelbeksterretjie)

## 3 Lesser Crested Tern  *Sterna bengalensis*

J F M A M J J A S O N D

**35–37 cm; 180–240 g** A medium-sized tern, slightly smaller than Sandwich Tern, with a slender, orange-yellow bill. Smaller, more graceful and generally paler above than Swift Tern; bill lacks drooped tip. Much smaller than Royal Tern; bill more slender. Main identification risk is vagrant Elegant Tern. Juv. has mottled blackish-brown back and wing coverts, and dark grey flight feathers. Imm. retains dark grey flight feathers. **Voice:** Hoarse 'kreck'. **Status and biology:** Fairly common non-br. visitor to E coast, mainly in summer; vagrant to W Cape. Forages in inshore waters, bays and estuaries; roosts along coast and at wetlands. **Diet:** Mainly small fish. (Kuifkopsterretjie)

## 4 Elegant Tern  *Sterna elegans*

**38–41 cm; 200–320 g** Rare vagrant. Slightly larger than Lesser Crested and Sandwich terns; orange bill longer with a drooped tip; underwing tips dark grey. Paler grey above than Lesser Crested Tern with a white (not pale grey) rump and a longer, shaggier crest. Appreciably smaller than Royal Tern with a longer, more slender bill. Br. ad. has full black cap; non-br. ad. has black hind crown (more extensive than Royal Tern, extending in front of eye). Juv. paler grey above and slightly scaled; bill yellow. **Voice:** Grating call similar to Sandwich Tern. **Status and biology:** Vagrant; breeds in Nearctic; 2 records: Cape Town, Jan 2006 and Swakopmund, Jan 2007. **Diet:** Mainly small fish. (Elegante Sterretjie)

## 5 Sandwich Tern  *Sterna sandvicensis*

J F M A M J J A S O N D

**36–40 cm; 200–250 g** A very pale, medium to large tern; bill black with a yellow tip. Bill longer and more slender than Gull-billed Tern; in flight, has white (not grey) rump and more strongly forked tail. Br. ad. has black cap, and breast often has faint pinkish wash; non-br. ads have white forecrown, often with black mottling confined to nuchal collar. Juv. is mottled above with darker flight feathers, but body coverts mostly replaced by the time they arrive in sthn Africa; bill tip dark, turning yellow by Dec. Imm. has some dark outer primaries remaining from juv. plumage. **Voice:** Loud 'kirik'; often noisy prior to migrating N in autumn. **Status and biology:** Common Palearctic migrant to coastal waters, estuaries and bays. At least 10 000 birds visit the region, mainly from W European br. grounds. **Diet:** Mainly small fish. (Grootsterretjie)

## 6 Gull-billed Tern  *Sterna nilotica*

**35–38 cm; 190–260 g** Vagrant. A very pale, relatively long-legged tern with a rather stubby black bill. Similar in size to Sandwich Tern, but is heavier-bodied and broader-winged, with shorter, shallow-forked tail and shorter, more robust black bill that lacks a yellow tip; rump and tail grey (not white). Br. ad. has a full black cap; non-br. birds have black smudge behind eye; crown white. Juv. is mottled brown above; legs greyish (black in ad.). **Voice:** Deep 'kaak' and 'kek-kek'. **Status and biology:** Rare Palearctic vagrant to coastal lagoons and wetlands; sometimes forages over adjacent fields and reedbeds. **Diet:** Fish, frogs and invertebrates. (Oostelike Sterretjie)

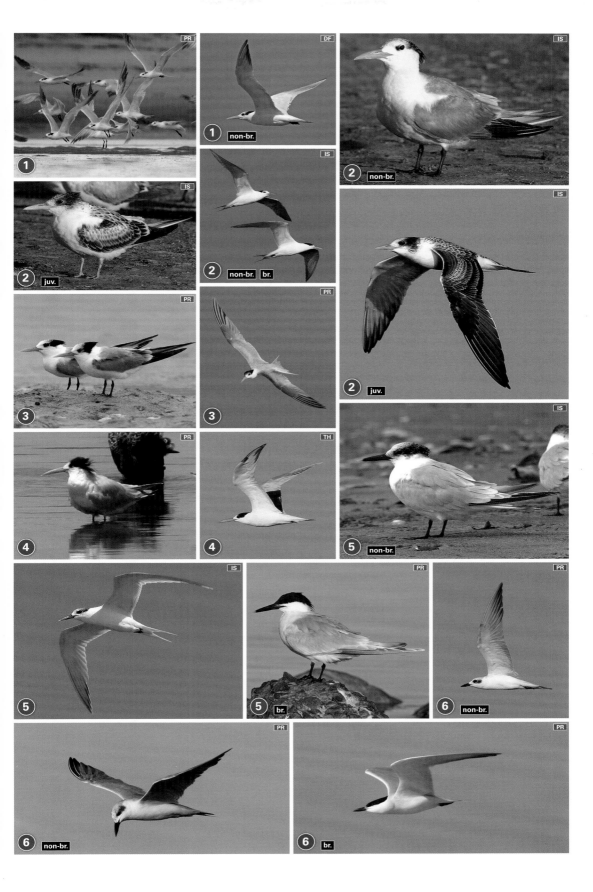

## 1 Common Tern *Sterna hirundo*

J F M A M J J A S O N D

**31–35 cm; 90–150 g** Typically the commonest medium-sized tern, often in large flocks. Differs from Arctic Tern by its longer bill and legs; rump and tail greyish (not white). Less dumpy than Antarctic Tern, with more slender bill and lacks grey wash on underparts. Primaries have broader black webs than in Arctic and Antarctic terns, visible in flight as darker panel on upper- and underwing. Bill shorter and less drooped than Roseate Tern; upperparts darker grey. Rump and tail contrast with darker grey back (uniform grey in vagrant White-cheeked Tern). In br. plumage has black-tipped red bill, light grey wash to breast, and short tail streamers (level with folded wing tips). Juv. mottled brown above. Imm. retains conspicuous dark carpal bars. **Voice:** 'Kik-kik' and 'kee-arh'. **Status and biology:** Abundant Palearctic migrant to coastal waters and adjacent wetlands; vagrant inland. At least 300 000 birds visit the region, mainly from Scandinavia and Baltic Sea br. grounds. Some imms remain year-round. **Diet:** Small fish and crustaceans. (Gewone Sterretjie)

## 2 Arctic Tern *Sterna paradisaea*

**33–35 cm; 80–110 g** Similar to Common Tern, but more compact with a shorter neck, shorter, finer bill and paler outer primaries in flight; rump and tail white (not pale grey). At rest, legs distinctly shorter. Not as dumpy as Antarctic Tern, especially at rest; bill much smaller; bill and legs usually blackish (not red). Br. ad. has full black cap, pale grey wash on breast, dark red bill and legs; tail streamers extend beyond folded wing (but growing feathers are shorter). Non-br. ad. has extensive white frons, and blackish bill and legs. Imm. has a darker carpal bar, but not as strongly developed as imm. Common Tern. **Voice:** 'Kik-kik' given in flight. **Status and biology:** Fairly common Palearctic migrant to coastal and oceanic waters, mainly from W Europe. Most pass offshore en route to and from Antarctic wintering grounds, but some remain over summer. Sometimes roosts ashore; vagrant inland. **Diet:** Small fish and crustaceans. (Arktiese Sterretjie)

## 3 Antarctic Tern *Sterna vittata*

J F M A M J J A S O N D

**34–40 cm; 110–170 g** A rather dumpy, medium-sized tern, with a heavier bill than either Arctic or Common tern. Leg length varies among races from short to fairly long. Br. ad. has full black cap, bright red bill and legs, and grey underparts contrasting with white cheek stripe. Told from vagrant White-cheeked Tern by its white (not grey) rump. Non-br. ad. has paler grey underparts and a white forecrown, but retains red legs and some red in bill (black in non-br. Common and Arctic terns). Imm. has black bill and legs; best told by heavy bill and dumpy body; some retain a few barred juv. tertials. Juv. has chequered brown, grey and white upperparts and diffuse brown wash on sides of breast; differs from juv. Roseate Tern by its shorter, heavier bill and paler cap. **Voice:** High-pitched 'kik-kik' and harsher 'kreaah'. **Status and biology:** Fairly common winter migrant to coastal waters in sthn Africa. 50 000 pairs breed in summer at sub-Antarctic islands and Antarctic Peninsula; 850 pairs at Tristan and Gough; 30 at the Prince Edwards. Breeds singly or in small colonies, often on cliffs, laying 1–2 eggs. **Diet:** Small fish, crustaceans and terrestrial invertebrates at br. islands. (Grysborssterretjie)

## 4 Kerguelen Tern *Sterna virgata*

**32–34 cm; 90–150 g** A darker version of Antarctic Tern with the petite structure of Arctic Tern. Ad. has more strongly contrasting white cheek stripe and grey wash on rump and outer tail. Br. ad. has full black cap and red bill and legs; non-br. ad. has white frons and blackish bill and legs. Juv. sooty grey-brown above, finely spotted whitish; breast mottled grey-brown. Imm. similar to non-br. ad., but retains some juv. wing coverts. **Voice:** High-pitched 'kik-kik'. **Status and biology: NEAR-THREATENED.** Resident in sub-Antarctic; not recorded from sthn Africa. 2 500 pairs breed in summer at the Prince Edwards (50 pairs), Crozet and Kerguelen. Breeds singly or in small, loose colonies, laying 1–2 eggs. **Diet:** Fish, crustaceans and terrestrial invertebrates; often forages over coastal mires. (Kerguelense sterretjie)

## 5 Roseate Tern *Sterna dougallii*

J F M A M J J A S O N D

**33–38 cm; 100–130 g** A sleek, medium-sized tern with very pale grey upperparts and a long, slightly drooped, blackish bill. Legs and wings longer than other medium-sized terns. Underwing appears all-white in flight. Br. ads have full black cap, pink wash to breast, crimson legs, red bill base and long white outer tail feathers that project well beyond wings at rest. Non-br. ads have white forecrown; best identified by long bill and pale colour. Juv. finely barred blackish-brown above; differs from juv. Antarctic Tern by blacker cap, longer bill, greyer wings and more slender body. Imm. retains some juv. tertials and has darker upperwing coverts than non-br. ad. **Voice:** Harsh 'chir-rik' when breeding; also a grating 'aarh'. **Status and biology:** Scarce resident; 250 pairs breed at islands off S coast. Non-br. vagrants may occur along Mozambique coast from populations breeding further N. **Diet:** Small fish. (Rooiborssterretjie)

## 6 White-cheeked Tern *Sterna repressa*

**32–35 cm; 80–100 g** Rare vagrant. A medium-sized tern, resembling a dark Common Tern; differs from this (and Arctic and Antarctic terns) in having a uniform grey back, rump and tail. Br. ads have grey underparts, darkest on belly; could be confused with br. plumage Whiskered Tern (p. 196), but is larger, with a longer bill, forked tail and dusky grey (not white) vent. Imm. white below with mostly black cap and dark carpal bar; best told from imm. Common Tern by grey rump and tail, darker grey upperwings and broad blackish trailing edge to underwing. **Voice:** Ringing 'kee-leck'. **Status and biology:** Vagrant to E coast from tropical Indian Ocean colonies. Roosts with other terns. **Diet:** Small fish and invertebrates. (Witwangsterretjie)

## 1 Bridled Tern *Onychoprion anaethetus*

J F M A M J J A S O N D

**30–32 cm; 110– 170 g** An elegant, dark-backed tern. Smaller than Sooty Tern, with paler, brown-grey upperparts. Narrow white frons extends behind eye, and dark crown contrasts with paler back. Non-br. ads have white spotting on crown. Juv. and imm. have wing coverts finely edged buffy white, and white (not blackish) underparts. **Voice:** 'Wup-wup' and 'kee-arr'. **Status and biology:** Uncommon non-br. visitor to oceanic waters off Mozambique from tropical Indian Ocean colonies; vagrant elsewhere. **Diet:** Small fish, squid and invertebrates. (Brilsterretjie)

## 2 Sooty Tern *Onychoprion fuscatus*

J F M A M J J A S O N D

**40–44 cm; 160–220 g** A fairly large, long-winged, dark-backed tern. Larger and darker above than Bridled Tern, with broader white frons that does not extend behind eye; black crown does not contrast with blackish back. In flight, both species have bold white leading edge to upperwing. Juv. and imm. have blackish throat and breast (juv. and imm. Bridled Tern are white below); could potentially be confused with noddies or imm. jaegers, but neither have largely white underwing coverts. **Voice:** Loud 'wick-a-wick' or 'wide-awake' at colonies; also given when attracted to ships' lights at night. Alarm is harsh 'kraark'. **Status and biology:** Common non-br. visitor to oceanic waters off Mozambique and N KZN from tropical Indian Ocean colonies. Typically remains well offshore, but large numbers may be wrecked ashore or blown inland by tropical cyclones. **Diet:** Squid, fish and invertebrates; picks prey from surface; often forages at night. (Roetsterretjie)

## 3 Black-naped Tern *Sterna sumatrana*

J F M A M J J A S O N D

**30 cm; 90 g** Rare vagrant. A small, very pale tern, superficially resembling a miniature Sandwich Tern (p. 190). Ad. has black band extending behind eye, broadening across nape; crown pure white. Bill and legs black. In flight, only outer primaries are black. Juv. has crown feathers tipped with black, and is mottled brown above. Imm. has dusky carpal bar. **Voice:** Clipped, repeated 'ki-ki'. **Status and biology:** Vagrant to E coast from tropical Indian Ocean colonies; sometimes roosts at estuaries. **Diet:** Mainly small fish. (Swartneksterretjie)

## 4 Little Tern *Sterna albifrons*

J F M A M J J A S O N D

**22–24 cm; 40–60 g** A tiny tern, similar to Damara Tern, but bill is shorter and straighter; rump and tail are paler grey than back, and has greater contrast between dark outer primaries and rest of upperwing. In flight, appears longer-tailed. Br. ad. has a white frons and yellow bill with a small black tip. Non-br. ads have varying amounts of yellow in bill; can appear all-black. Juv. lightly mottled brown above. Juv. and imm. show indistinct darker carpal bars. **Voice:** Slightly rasping 'ket-ket'. **Status and biology:** Fairly common non-br. migrant to shallow coastal waters and estuaries, probably from E Europe or Asian populations. Regular along E coast to W Cape. **Diet:** Mainly small fish. (Kleinsterretjie)

## 5 Damara Tern *Sterna balaenarum*

B b b b b | b B B B
J F M A M J J A S O N D

**21–23 cm; 46–60 g** A very small, rather uniform pale grey tern with narrow wings and rapid wing beats. Differs from Little Tern in having a longer, slightly droop-tipped bill, more uniform upperwing, and uniform grey rump and back; body appears shorter and more dumpy in flight. Br. ad. has diagnostic full black cap and bill. Non-br. ads and imms have mottled grey and white frons. Juv. has buffy-brown barring on mantle, and horn-coloured bill base. **Voice:** Far-carrying, rapid 'chit-ick', higher-pitched than Little Tern. **Status and biology: NEAR-THREATENED.** Near-endemic. Locally common in Namibia (2 000 pairs); rare and local in S Africa (120 pairs). Favours sheltered coastlines, bays and lagoons. Breeds on coastal dunes and saltpans singly or in loose colonies. Lays 1 egg; chick follows ads to sea as soon as it can flutter. Most migrate to W Africa in winter, but some remain year-round. **Diet:** Mainly small fish. (Damarasterretjie)

# NODDIES

Dark brown tropical terns with paler crowns. Flight loose and buoyant; tail long and wedge-shaped with a shallow central notch when fanned. Seldom visit land away from br. colonies. Could be confused with imm. Sooty Tern, but lack white underwing coverts and paler belly. More slender than dark morph jaegers with no white flash in primary bases.

## 1 Brown Noddy *Anous stolidus*

J F M A M J J A S O N D

**36–44 cm; 170–220 g** Rare vagrant. Slightly larger and browner than Lesser Noddy, with a shorter, heavier bill. Pale crown does not extend onto nape and white frons contrasts sharply with brown lores. Shows greater contrast across wings due to paler brown greater upperwing coverts and central underwing. Juv. has pale crown reduced or absent. **Voice:** Hoarse 'kark', seldom heard away from colonies. **Status and biology:** Rare in oceanic waters off Mozambique from tropical Indian Ocean colonies; vagrant elsewhere. Some 600 pairs breed in summer (Sept–Apr) at Tristan and Gough. Breeds singly or in loose colonies in trees or on cliffs; lays 1 egg. **Diet:** Small fish and squid. (Grootbruinsterretjie)

## 2 Lesser Noddy *Anous tenuirostris*

J F M A M J J A S O N D

**30–34 cm; 90–120 g** Rare vagrant. Smaller than Brown Noddy, with a relatively longer, more slender bill. Whitish forehead merges with brown lores and ashy-grey crown extends further back onto nape. Upperwing and underwing are more uniformly dark brown. Juv. has pale crown reduced or absent. **Voice:** Generally silent at sea; short, rattling 'churrr'. **Status and biology:** Vagrant from tropical Indian Ocean colonies. **Diet:** Small fish and invertebrates. (Kleinbruinsterretjie)

# LAKE TERNS

Small, mostly freshwater terns with square tails. Br. plumages distinct, but non-br. birds harder to separate. Often pick prey from the water surface rather than plunge-diving. Sexes alike; juvs distinct. Monogamous; typically breed in loose colonies.

## 3 Black Tern *Chlidonias niger*

J F M A M J J A S O N D

**22–24 cm; 50–75 g** A dark-backed lake tern. In br. plumage, black head, breast and belly merge into dark grey back and wings; lacks contrast of White-winged Tern. Non-br. ad. has diagnostic dark shoulder smudge, more extensive black on head than White-winged Tern, and no contrast between back, rump and tail. Darker than Whiskered Tern, with black cheek spot. Imm. is slightly darker and less uniform above. **Voice:** Usually silent; flight call is quiet 'kik-kik'. **Status and biology:** Common along N Namibian coast and regular in small numbers in KZN; rare elsewhere. Occurs in open ocean, bays and coastal wetlands; usually forages at sea, but many roost ashore; vagrant inland. Breeds in Palearctic; mainly migrates along W coast of Africa. **Diet:** Mainly small crustaceans; also fishing wastes. (Swartsterretjie)

## 4 White-winged Tern *Chlidonias leucopterus*

J F M A M J J A S O N D

**20–22 cm; 45–80 g** The smallest lake tern, with a white rump in all plumages. Striking black and white in br. plumage with pale grey upperwings and black underwing coverts; white rump and tail contrast with black back; legs bright red. Non-br. ad. is much paler above than Black Tern, with black confined to rear of crown, and no black shoulder smudge. Imm. has slight brown tips to upperpart feathers. **Voice:** Short 'kek-kek'. **Status and biology:** Common Palearctic migrant from central Asia, found at lakes, estuaries and marshes; occasionally in sheltered coastal bays and over open country. **Diet:** Small fish, insects and other invertebrates; takes some prey in the air. (Witvlerksterretjie)

## 5 Whiskered Tern *Chlidonias hybrida*

B B B b      B B B
J F M A M J J A S O N D

**24–26 cm; 80–110 g** The largest lake tern with relatively long legs and a heavy bill. Dark grey underparts in br. plumage are diagnostic; superficially resembles White-cheeked Tern (p. 192), but is smaller, with white (not dusky grey) vent and less deeply forked tail. Non-br. birds are larger than other lake terns, lacking dark cheek patch extending below eye. Paler grey above than non-br. Black Tern; rump pale grey (white in White-winged Tern). Juv. is mottled brown on back. **Voice:** Repeated, hard 'zizz'. **Status and biology:** Fairly common resident and intra-African migrant at wetlands and marshes; population estimated to be fewer than 7 500 pairs in sthn Africa. Breeds in small colonies, laying 2–3 eggs on a mound of floating vegetation. **Diet:** Fish, frogs and aquatic invertebrates. (Witbaardsterretjie)

# SANDGROUSE

Terrestrial birds with very short legs; shuffle on the ground. Wings long, slender and pointed; flight swift. Superficially resemble pigeons, but probably distantly related to waders. Sexes differ in plumage; juvs are similar to females. Eat mainly seeds; low water content of diet requires daily flights to drink. Monogamous; both parents incubate. Chicks precocial; feed themselves. Males carry water to chicks in specially adapted belly feathers.

## 1 Double-banded Sandgrouse *Pterocles bicinctus*

b b b B B B B b b
J F M A M J J A S O N D

**25–26 cm; 200–270 g** A small, short-tailed sandgrouse. Male has diagnostic head pattern, black-and-white breast bands and barred belly. Female rather uniformly barred; differs from female Namaqua Sandgrouse by darker, streaked crown, barred (not streaked) upper breast, and short tail. **Voice:** A whistling 'chwee-chee-chee' and a soft 'wee-chee-choo-chip-chip' flight call. **Status and biology:** Near-endemic. Fairly common resident and nomad in woodland (especially mopane), savanna, and locally in arid karoo grassland. Drinks at dusk, often after dark. Lays 2–3 eggs in a shallow scrape. **Diet:** Small seeds, especially of legumes. (Dubbelbandsandpatrys)

## 2 Yellow-throated Sandgrouse *Pterocles gutturalis*

b B B B B b b
J F M A M J J A S O N D

**28–30 cm; 290–400 g** The largest African sandgrouse, identified in flight by its short tail, dark brown belly and blackish underwings. Male has a creamy yellow face and throat, with a broad black neck collar. Female is heavily mottled on the neck, breast and upperparts. **Voice:** Flight call a deep, far-carrying bisyllabic 'aw-aw', the first higher-pitched; sometimes preceded by 'ipi'. **Status and biology:** Locally common resident and nomad in grassland and arid savanna. Drinks during the morning. Lays 2–3 eggs in a shallow scrape. **Diet:** Small seeds, especially of legumes. (Geelkeelsandpatrys)

## 3 Namaqua Sandgrouse *Pterocles namaqua*

b b b B B B B B B b b b
J F M A M J J A S O N D

**24–28 cm; 150–230 g** The only sandgrouse with a long, pointed tail. Male has double breast band, but lacks the black-and-white head bands of male Double-banded Sandgrouse and has a plain (not barred) lower breast and belly. Female has a more buffy yellow throat and breast (streaked, not barred) than female Double-banded Sandgrouse, and has a pointed (not rounded) tail. **Voice:** Distinctive, nasal 'kelkie-vein' call, frequently given in flight. **Status and biology:** Near-endemic. Common nomad and partial migrant in semi-desert and grassland. Moves away immediately after rains when seeds germinate, returning once new growth has set seeds. Drinks 1–4 hours after dawn. Lays 2–3 eggs in a shallow scrape on bare ground. **Diet:** Small seeds, especially of legumes. (Kelkiewyn)

## 4 Burchell's Sandgrouse *Pterocles burchelli*

b B B b b b
J F M A M J J A S O N D

**24–26 cm; 170–230 g** A small, compact sandgrouse with a white-spotted, cinnamon breast and belly. Female resembles a drab male but has a buffy (not blue-grey) face and throat. **Voice:** Flight call is a soft, mellow 'chup-chup, choop-choop'. **Status and biology:** Near-endemic. Scarce to locally common resident and nomad in semi-arid savanna; particularly common on Kalahari sands. Drinks 3–5 hours after dawn, generally later than Namaqua Sandgrouse. Lays 2–3 eggs in a shallow scrape, usually next to a small bush or tussock of grass. **Diet:** Small seeds, especially of legumes. (Gevlekte Sandpatrys)

# PIGEONS AND DOVES

A familiar family of birds with rather short legs, rounded heads and chunky bodies. Bills have soft bases with a waxy cere. Sexes alike in most species. Monogamous; both sexes incubate and feed the altricial chicks. Newly hatched chicks are fed a special secretion, 'crop milk'.

## 1 Speckled Pigeon *Columba guinea*

| B | b | b | b | b | b | b | b | B | B | B | B |
|---|---|---|---|---|---|---|---|---|---|---|---|
| J | F | M | A | M | J | J | A | S | O | N | D |

30–34 cm; 280–400 g  A large, grey pigeon with a dull, brick-red neck, back and inner wing coverts, bare red skin around eyes, red legs and dark grey bill with whitish cere. Derives its name from its white-spotted wing coverts. Tail broadly tipped blackish with a paler grey subterminal band. Occasionally hybridises with Feral Pigeons. Juv. browner with grey-brown facial skin. **Voice:** Deep, booming 'hooo-hooo-hooo'; softer 'coocoo-coocoo'. **Status and biology:** Common resident in rocky areas, coastal cliffs and cities, ranging into fields and grassland to feed. Males clap their wings when taking off on display flights. Lays 2 (1–3) eggs on an untidy platform of twigs built on rock ledges, buildings or in palm trees. **Diet:** Mainly seeds, but also fruit and green plant material. (Kransduif)

## 2 African Olive-Pigeon (Rameron Pigeon) *Columba arquatrix*

| b | b | b | B | B | B | B | b | b | b | b | b |
|---|---|---|---|---|---|---|---|---|---|---|---|
| J | F | M | A | M | J | J | A | S | O | N | D |

38–40 cm; 300–480 g  A large, fairly long-tailed pigeon with dark, purplish plumage, paler grey face and nape, and conspicuous bare yellow face, bill and legs. Wing coverts and belly are finely spotted white. In flight against a pale sky, appears all-dark with pale legs. Juv. paler with whitish fringes to feathers; face, bill and legs duller. **Voice:** Soft, deep 'du-du-du-doo-dooo'; also gives a wailing call, especially on landing. **Status and biology:** Common resident and nomad in forest, thickets and plantations. Movements linked to local fruiting events. Lays 1–2 eggs in a stick nest built in a tree fork. **Diet:** Fruit and seeds. Forages in the canopy and on the ground. (Geelbekbosduif)

## 3 Eastern Bronze-naped Pigeon *Columba delegorguei*

| b | b | b | b |   |   |   |   |   | B | B |   |
|---|---|---|---|---|---|---|---|---|---|---|---|
| J | F | M | A | M | J | J | A | S | O | N | D |

26–28 cm; 140–170 g  A medium-sized forest pigeon, smaller and shorter-tailed than African Olive Pigeon. Male has greyish head and diagnostic pale, crescent-shaped patch on hind neck collar. Iridescent green neck is visible only at close range. Female and juv. lack pale hind collar; dark face and canopy (not understorey) habitat separate it from Lemon Dove. **Voice:** Far-carrying, distinctive 'oo oo oo COO COO COO cu-cu-cu-cu-cu' with a series of fast notes at the end, descending in pitch. **Status and biology:** Uncommon, localised resident of forest canopy. Moves to lower elevations in winter in E Zimbabwe. Lays 2 eggs on a flimsy platform of twigs built among slender branches high in the canopy. **Diet:** Mainly fruit. (Withalsbosduif)

## 4 Lemon (Cinnamon) Dove *Aplopelia larvata*

| b | B | B | b | b | b | b | b | b | B | B |   |
|---|---|---|---|---|---|---|---|---|---|---|---|
| J | F | M | A | M | J | J | A | S | O | N | D |

24–26 cm; 140–190 g  A plump, medium-sized dove of the forest floor. Pale face and habitat separate it from Eastern Bronze-naped Pigeon. Pale forehead and face contrast with darker, iridescent greeny-bronze hind crown, nape and mantle; underparts rich cinnamon. Eye-ring red. In flight, appears all-dark, with slightly paler outer tail tips. Female duller. Juv. has buff barring on mantle. **Voice:** Deep, ooop-ooop, sometimes repeated 6–10 times. May give a series of descending notes similar to Tambourine Dove (p. 204). **Status and biology:** Fairly common resident of forest floor and understorey; rather secretive and easily overlooked. Flushes to a low branch when disturbed. Lays 1–3 eggs in a stick nest built in a small tree. **Diet:** Seeds, fruits and bulbs. (Kaneelduifie)

## 5 Rock Dove *Columba livia*

| b | b | b | b | b | b | b | b | b | b | b | b |
|---|---|---|---|---|---|---|---|---|---|---|---|
| J | F | M | A | M | J | J | A | S | O | N | D |

32–34 cm; 320–450 g  Introduced from Europe. A large, commensal pigeon. Plumage variable; typical form is bluish-grey with black bars on the wings and tail, a white rump patch, and glossy green and purple on the sides of the neck. Other varieties include black, white and reddish forms. Female and juv. duller. **Voice:** Deep, rolling 'coo-roo-coo'. **Status and biology:** Feral populations are common in many urban areas. Lays 2 (rarely 1) eggs on an untidy platform of twigs, usually on a ledge or in a hole on a building. **Diet:** Scraps, seeds, other plant material and occasional invertebrates. (Tuinduif)

## 1 African Mourning Dove  *Streptopelia decipiens*

b b b b b b b b b b B B
J F M A M J J A S O N D

**28–30 cm; 120–200 g** A fairly large, collared dove with a plain grey head and broad, red eye-ring contrasting with the pale yellow eye. Smaller and paler than Red-eyed Dove, but larger than all other collared doves. In flight, has white in outer tail. Juv. browner. **Voice:** Loud 'cuck-ook-oooo'; grating trills, 'currrrrrrow'; throaty 'aaooow' on landing. **Status and biology:** Locally common resident of woodland, riverine forest, thickets and gardens in semi-arid savanna. Males have a high, towering display flight. Lays 1–2 eggs on a platform of twigs built in a fork of a bush or tree. **Diet:** Seeds and occasional insects. (Rooioogtortelduif)

## 2 Red-eyed Dove  *Streptopelia semitorquata*

b b b b b b b b b b b b
J F M A M J J A S O N D

**32–34 cm; 190–300 g** The largest collared dove; overall dark pinkish-grey with a pale face and pinkish head and breast. In flight has diagnostic broad buffy band at tip of tail. Dull red eye-ring is less prominent than that of African Mourning Dove. Juv. is browner, with smaller collar. **Voice:** Typical call, 'coo coo, co-kuk coo coo', is diagnostic; harsh 'chwaa' alarm call. **Status and biology:** Common resident of woodland, forest and gardens. Males fly steeply up in towering display, clapping wings, then glide back to perch in a tree. Lays 1–2 eggs on a flimsy platform of sticks in a tree fork. **Diet:** Seeds and bulblets; occasional insects. (Grootringduif)

## 3 Cape Turtle-Dove  *Streptopelia capicola*

b b b b b b b b b b b b
J F M A M J J A S O N D

**25–27 cm; 100–160 g** A small, pale blue-grey, collared dove with a pinkish wash on the neck. Smaller and paler than Red-eyed and African Mourning doves, with dark eye lacking red eye-ring. In flight, has conspicuous white tips to all but central tail feathers, contrasting with dark grey bases. Juv. duller, with some buff edgings to feathers. **Voice:** 'Kuk-coorrrr-uk', rendered 'How's father?', middle note descending and rolled; harsh 'kurrrr' alarm call. **Status and biology:** Abundant resident and nomad in a wide range of habitats; avoids forest. Males have a high, towering display flight. Lays 1–2 eggs on a platform of twigs in a bush or small tree. **Diet:** Mainly seeds and fruit; occasional nectar and invertebrates. (Gewone Tortelduif)

## 4 Laughing Dove  *Streptopelia senegalensis*

b b b b b b b B B B B B
J F M A M J J A S O N D

**22–24 cm; 80–130 g** A fairly small, pinkish-buff dove with no collar. Black mottling on rich rufous breast and blue-grey greater and median coverts and rump are diagnostic. Smaller than vagrant European Turtle-Dove, with plain wing coverts and no neck patch. In flight, cinnamon-coloured back contrasts with blue-grey forewings; outer tail tips white. Female paler; juv. has pale feather fringes. **Voice:** Rising and falling 'uh hu hu huu hu', rather like a subdued laugh, hence the common name. **Status and biology:** Abundant resident and nomad in a wide range of habitats, including urban areas; avoids forests. Males have a high, towering display flight. Lays 1–3 eggs on a platform of twigs in a small tree. **Diet:** Mainly seeds and fruit; occasional nectar and invertebrates. (Rooiborsduifie)

## 5 European Turtle-Dove  *Streptopelia turtur*

**26–28 cm; 110–180 g** Rare vagrant. A richly coloured dove with diagnostic black-and-white neck patch and strongly patterned wing coverts, with dark feather centres contrasting with broad chestnut margins. Larger than Laughing Dove; lacks rufous breast. In flight, has broad white tips to outer tail, contrasting with blackish subterminal band. Juv. lacks neck patch and has barred and mottled upperparts. **Voice:** Soft, purring 'crrrr roorrrrrrr'. **Status and biology:** Palearctic vagrant, usually wintering N of equator. 5 records from semi-arid savannas in Namibia, Botswana and S Africa. **Diet:** Mainly seeds. (Europese Tortelduif)

## 1 African Green-Pigeon *Treron calvus*

b b b b b b b b b b B b b
J F M A M J J A S O N D

**25–28 cm; 210–250 g** A distinctive, parrot-like pigeon, often seen in small groups clambering around canopy of fruiting trees. Green and grey plumage is unique among local pigeons; bill whitish with red cere; legs red; thighs yellow. In flight, dark flight feathers and greater coverts contrast with paler green forewing; broad grey tip to tail. Ad. has mauve shoulder patches; olive-yellow in juv. **Voice:** Distinctive croaks, wails and whinnying calls. **Status and biology:** Common resident and local nomad in forest, woodland and savanna. Closely associated with fruiting trees, especially figs. Lays 1–2 eggs on a platform of twigs built on a horizontal branch or in the fork of a tree. **Diet:** Fruit; occasional seeds and carrion. (Papegaaiduif)

## 2 Emerald-spotted Wood-Dove *Turtur chalcospilos*

B B b b b b b B B B B B
J F M A M J J A S O N D

**17–20 cm; 55–70 g** A small, compact dove with mainly plain, pinkish-brown plumage, relieved by pale grey crown, 6–8 iridescent green wing coverts, and dark grey bars across the back (2), tail (1). Distinguished from Blue-spotted Wood-Dove by its paler plumage and larger, green (not blue) wing spots. Juv. is browner, barred buff above. **Voice:** A long series of muffled notes, starting hesitantly and descending in pitch at the end: 'hu, hu-hu HOO, hu-hu HOO-oo, hu-HOO, hu, hu, hu-hu-hu-hu-hu-hu-hu-hu'. **Status and biology:** Common resident in woodland and savanna, generally in drier habitats than Blue-spotted Wood-Dove. Lays 1–2 eggs on a platform of twigs built in a bush or tree. **Diet:** Seeds, fruit and some small invertebrates. (Groenvlekduifie)

## 3 Blue-spotted Wood-Dove *Turtur afer*

b b b b b b b B B b b b
J F M A M J J A S O N D

**18–21 cm; 55–75 g** Similar to Green-spotted Wood-Dove, but richer brown, with smaller, blue (not green) wing spots and a yellow-tipped, red bill (only visible at close range). In flight, back and rump appear more rufous. Juv. has a brown bill and reduced wing spots; told from juv. Green-spotted Wood-Dove by its more rufous plumage. **Voice:** Series of muffled coos, shorter and deeper in pitch than Green-spotted Wood-Dove. **Status and biology:** Uncommon to fairly common resident in moist, broadleafed woodland, riparian woodland, forest and thickets. Lays 2 eggs on a flimsy platform of twigs built in a bush or tree; occasionally uses an old thrush nest. **Diet:** Mainly seeds; also termite alates. (Blouvlekduifie)

## 4 Tambourine Dove *Turtur tympanistria*

b b b         b B B b
J F M A M J J A S O N D

**20–22 cm; 60–85 g** Darker above than other wood-doves; at close range has some metallic-green wing coverts, but these are hard to see against dark upperparts. Male has diagnostic white face and underparts. In flight, chestnut underwings contrast strongly with white belly. Female and juv. are greyer below, but still have paler faces and underparts than other wood-doves. **Voice:** Series of 20–40 'du-du-du' notes, deeper than other wood-doves, but not changing intensity or pitch at the end. **Status and biology:** Locally common resident of forest and thickets. Lays 2 eggs on a flimsy platform of twigs built in a bush or tree. **Diet:** Seeds, fruit and some small invertebrates. (Witborsduifie)

## 5 Namaqua Dove *Oena capensis*

b b b b b b b B B b b b
J F M A M J J A S O N D

**28 cm; 30–45 g** A tiny dove with a long, pointed tail, rufous outer wings, 3–5 glossy purple wing coverts and 2 blackish bars on its back. Male has diagnostic black face and throat, and yellow-tipped red bill. Female and juv. lack black face; tails slightly shorter; bills brown. Juv. barred buff and dark brown above. **Voice:** Deep, soft 'hoo huuuu', first note sharp, second longer. **Status and biology:** Common resident and nomad in arid and semi-arid savanna and open woodland. Lays 1–2 eggs in a flimsy saucer of twigs built low down in a bush or small tree. **Diet:** Small seeds. (Namakwaduifie)

# PARROTS AND LOVEBIRDS

A familiar family of cage birds with stout, hooked bills and short legs with zygodactyl toes used for climbing and holding food. Sexes alike in most species. Usually monogamous, with pairs remaining together for successive br. attempts. Incubation by both sexes or female only, in which case she is fed by the male. Chicks altricial.

## 1 Cape Parrot *Poicephalus robustus*

BBbbbbbBBBBB
J F M A M J J A S O N D

**30–35 cm; 270–320 g** A large, green parrot with red wrists and legs. Told from very similar Grey-headed Parrot by its olive-brown (not silvery-grey) head and deeper bill; ranges do not overlap. Female usually has a red forehead. Juv. lacks red shoulders and thighs, but is readily identified by its large size and massive bill. **Voice:** Various loud, harsh screeches and squawks. **Status and biology: ENDANGERED.** Endemic. Uncommon resident in Afromontane forest; commutes to orchards to feed. Usually in pairs or small family groups. Lays 2–5 eggs in a large cavity, usually in a dead tree. Incubation by female only. **Diet:** Fruit, especially of yellowwood trees. (Woudpapegaai)

## 2 Grey-headed Parrot *Poicephalus fuscicollis*

bbbb    bb
J F M A M J J A S O N D

**32–36 cm; 310–340 g** Often considered a subspecies of Cape Parrot, but is slightly larger with a silvery-grey (not brown) head and less massive bill; ranges do not overlap. Larger than Brown-headed Parrot, with a much more massive, pale bill. Some birds have an orange frons; average larger in female, with occasionally the entire crown orange. **Voice:** Similar to Cape Parrot. **Status and biology:** Locally common resident and nomad in riverine forest and broadleafed woodland with large, emergent trees. Usually in pairs or family groups, but flocks gather at fruiting trees. Lays 2–4 eggs in a large cavity, in a baobab or dead tree. Incubation by female only. **Diet:** Fruit and bark. (Savannepapegaai)

## 3 Brown-headed Parrot *Poicephalus cryptoxanthus*

bbb
J F M A M J J A S O N D

**22–25 cm; 125–150 g** A predominantly green parrot with a brown head, diagnostic pale yellow eyes and pale lower mandible. Lacks yellow shoulders and crown of Meyer's Parrot; in flight, rump green (not greeny-blue) and all underwing coverts are yellow; upperwings olive-brown (not brown). Juv. duller, with less vivid yellow underwings and dark eyes. **Voice:** Raucous shrieks. **Status and biology:** Locally common resident and nomad in savanna, riverine forest and open woodland. Lays 2–4 eggs in a tree cavity. Incubation by female only. **Diet:** Mainly fruit and seeds; also flowers, nectar and insects. (Bruinkoppapegaai)

## 4 Meyer's Parrot *Poicephalus meyeri*

bBBbbb
J F M A M J J A S O N D

**21–24 cm; 100–130 g** A medium-sized, mainly brown parrot with conspicuous blue-green rump, yellow shoulders and green belly, with bluish vent. Bill and eyes dark; some birds have a yellow bar across the crown. Distinguished from Brown-headed Parrot by yellow shoulders and crown, dark eyes and dark lower mandible; from Rüppell's Parrot by brown (not grey) head and dark (not red) eyes. Differs from both in flight by having brown (not yellow) inner underwing coverts. Juv. duller and lacks yellow on the crown. **Voice:** A loud, piercing 'chee-chee-chee-chee', and various other screeches and squawks. **Status and biology:** Locally common resident and nomad in broadleafed woodland and savanna. Often in large flocks. Lays 2–4 eggs in a tree cavity. Incubation by female only. **Diet:** Fruit, nuts and seeds; occasional insects. (Bosveldpapegaai)

## 5 Rüppell's Parrot *Poicephalus rueppellii*

BBBbbb
J F M A M J J A S O N D

**21–24 cm; 100–130 g** A grey-brown parrot. Head and throat greyer than Meyer's Parrot, with a grey-brown (not greenish) breast and blue (not green or turquoise) belly; eyes red (not dark). In flight, has blue (not greeny-blue) rump. Female is brighter than male, with more extensive blue on the vent and rump. Juv. duller. **Voice:** Screeches and squawks. **Status and biology:** Near-endemic. Uncommon to locally common resident and nomad in dry woodland, savanna and dry rivercourses. Lays 3–5 eggs in a tree cavity. Incubation mainly by female. **Diet:** Seeds, fruit, buds, bark, nectar and invertebrates. (Bloupenspapegaai)

## 1 Rose-ringed Parakeet *Psittacula krameri*

J F M A M J J A S O N D

**37–43 cm; 115–140 g** Introduced. A long-tailed, green parakeet with yellowish underwing coverts and vent. Confusion only likely with escaped parakeets of other species. Bill dark red. Ad. male has a distinctive black throat extending into a neck collar. Juv. has a shorter tail. **Voice:** Shrieks and screams; particularly vocal at roosts. **Status and biology:** Feral populations occur locally in well-wooded parks and gardens in Gauteng and KwaZulu-Natal (mainly around Durban). Lays 3–4 (rarely 6) eggs in a hole in a tree or building. **Diet:** Fruit, seeds and flowers. (Ringnekparkiet)

## 2 Rosy-faced Lovebird *Agapornis roseicollis*

B B b b
J F M A M J J A S O N D

**15–18 cm; 46–63 g** A small, compact parrot with a pink-washed face and breast, and diagnostic blue rump. Juv. is paler on the face and upper breast. **Voice:** High-pitched screeches and shrieks. **Status and biology:** Near-endemic. Locally common resident and nomad in dry, broadleafed woodland, semi-desert and mountainous terrain. Often in flocks. Lays 4–6 eggs in a deep cup nest built in a rock crevice or in a Sociable Weaver nest. Carries nesting material tucked under rump feathers. Incubation by female only. **Diet:** Seeds, fruit and flowers. (Rooiwangparkiet)

## 3 Black-cheeked Lovebird *Agapornis nigrigenis*

**14–15 cm; 35–46 g** Rare vagrant. Often considered a subspecies of Lilian's Lovebird, but has a dark brown head contrasting with its white eye-ring and reddish bill. **Voice:** High-pitched shrieks. **Status and biology: VULNERABLE.** Locally common in its small range in SW Zambia, but rarely straggles into sthn Africa. Escapees sometimes seen around Victoria Falls. Favours tall mopane woodland, riparian woodland and adjacent fields. **Diet:** Seeds, occasional leaves and fruit. (Swartwangparkiet)

## 4 Lilian's Lovebird *Agapornis lilianae*

J F M A M J J A S O N D

**13–14 cm; 30–40 g** The only lovebird in its range with a reddish face, prominent white eye-ring, pale bill and green (not blue) rump. Female has a paler pink face. Juv. lacks a white eye-ring. **Voice:** A high-pitched, staccato shrieking. **Status and biology: NEAR-THREATENED.** Locally common resident in broadleafed woodland, especially tall mopane woodland. Lays 4–5 eggs in a tree cavity or possibly a buffalo-weaver nest. Female carries nesting material in bill. Incubation by female only. **Diet:** Mainly seeds; occasional fruit and leaves. (Njassaparkiet)

# TURACOS (LOURIES)

Endemic to Africa. Fairly large birds with long tails, short, rounded wings and long legs with strong, semi-zygodactyl toes. Bound up through the canopy, and glide between trees. Many species have bright red flight feathers. Red and green feathers unusual in having copper-based pigments. Sexes alike. Monogamous; both parents incubate and feed the altricial chicks.

## 1 Knysna Turaco  *Tauraco corythaix*

J F M A M J J A S O N D

**40–46 cm; 280–350 g**  A predominantly green turaco with a rounded (not pointed) crest with a narrow white fringe. Occurs at higher elevations where range abuts that of Livingstone's Turaco. Body is much greener than Purple-crested Turaco's, with green (not purple) crest. Juv. has shorter crest that lacks white tips; red in wing confined to outer primaries. **Voice:** Hoarse 'kow-kow-kow-kow'; quieter 'krrr' alarm note. **Status and biology:** Endemic. Common resident in Afromontane forest. Lays 1–2 eggs on a flimsy platform of twigs built in tree canopy. **Diet:** Fruit; some invertebrates, especially when feeding chicks. (Knysnaloerie)

## 2 Schalow's Turaco  *Tauraco schalowi*

J F M A M J J A S O N D

**40–45 cm; 210–270 g**  A green turaco that closely resembles Livingstone's Turaco, but has a longer crest (especially at front of crest), dark blue or purple (not dark green) tail, and slightly paler green underparts; ranges disjunct. Juv. has shorter crest. **Voice:** Similar to Knysna Turaco. **Status and biology:** Uncommon, localised resident and nomad in dense riparian woodland. Lays 1–2 eggs on a platform of twigs in the canopy of a tall tree. **Diet:** Fruit and buds. (Langkuifloerie)

## 3 Livingstone's Turaco  *Tauraco livingstonii*

J F M A M J J A S O N D

**40–45 cm; 260–370 g**  A green turaco that occurs at lower elevations than Knysna Turaco where their ranges abut; differs in having longer, more pointed crest and slightly darker back. The white-tipped crest is more rounded and less pointed in front than that of Schalow's Turaco; also, tail is dark green (not bluish), and is darker on breast; ranges disjunct. **Voice:** Similar to Knysna Turaco. **Status and biology:** Common resident in dense, riparian woodland, extending into montane forest in E Zimbabwe. Lays 2 eggs on a platform of twigs in the canopy of a tall tree. **Diet:** Fruit; also leaves and flower buds. (Mosambiekloerie)

## 4 Purple-crested Turaco  *Gallirex porphyreolophus*

J F M A M J J A S O N D

**41–43 cm; 220–450 g**  A rather dark turaco, separated from 'green' turacos by its purple-blue crown, bluish wing coverts and tail, and green breast washed rose-pink. Juv. duller, with less extensive red in wings. **Voice:** Loud series of hollow 'kok-kok-kok-kok', typically longer and faster than other green turacos. **Status and biology:** Common resident in broadleafed woodland and coastal and riverine forests. Lays 2–4 eggs on a platform of twigs in the canopy of a tree or dense creeper. **Diet:** Fruit; some insects while breeding. (Bloukuifloerie)

## 5 Ross's Turaco  *Musophaga rossae*

**50–52 cm; 300–450 g**  Rare vagrant. A dark purple-blue turaco, with crimson primaries, an erect, fez-like red crest and naked yellow face, bill and frontal shield. Juv. duller, with blackish bill. **Voice:** Loud series of deep, guttural 'caws', often given by several birds at once, producing almost continuous cacophany. **Status and biology:** Vagrant from further north in Africa; only a few records from riverine forest and dense woodland in NE Namibia and N Botswana. Violet Turaco *M. violacea* occurs in small numbers in gardens in N Johannesburg; distinguished by its red (not yellow) bill and face and white cheek stripe. **Diet:** Fruit, flowers, young shoots and occasional invertebrates. (Rooikuifloerie)

## 6 Grey Go-away-bird  *Corythaixoides concolor*

J F M A M J J A S O N D

**48–50 cm; 210–300 g**  An ash-grey turaco with a long tail and loose, pointed crest, similar to that of a mousebird. Juv. paler, more buffy-grey with a shorter crest. **Voice:** Harsh, nasal 'waaaay' or 'kay-waaaay' (rendered 'go-away'). **Status and biology:** Common resident of acacia savanna and dry, open woodland; also gardens. Vocal and conspicuous; small groups often perch on top of acacia trees. Lays 2–3 (rarely 1–4) eggs on a flimsy platform of twigs in the canopy of a tree or bush, especially thorny species such as acacias. **Diet:** Fruit, leaves, buds, nectar and invertebrates. (Kwêvoël)

# CUCKOOS

Small to medium-sized, slender birds, often with fairly long tails. Flight swift and direct; larger species could be confused with falcons or hawks. Sexes alike in some species; differ in others. Most African species are obligate brood parasites. Easily overlooked if not calling. Males call monotonously when breeding. Usually promiscuous, but some species monogamous. Females lay 20–25 eggs each season, usually in batches of 3–6, laying 1 egg per host nest. Eggs typically match host eggs. Chicks altricial, but kill or eject foster siblings to monopolise food from the unwitting foster parents. In some species, chicks mimic begging calls of an entire brood of the adoptive parents' chicks.

## 1 Common Cuckoo  *Cuculus canorus*

**32–34 cm; 105–140 g** A fairly large, grey cuckoo, hard to separate from African Cuckoo, but is slightly larger with spotted (not barred) outer tail, more boldly barred vent and undertail coverts, and generally less yellow at the base of the bill. Female has rare hepatic (rufous) morph, barred black and rufous above **(1 A)**. Juv. may be brown, grey or chestnut; upperparts are usually barred, but with plain rump; underparts heavily barred. **Voice:** 'Cuck-oo'; generally silent in Africa. **Status and biology:** Scarce to locally common non-br. Palearctic migrant in woodland, savanna and riverine forest. **Diet:** Caterpillars and other invertebrates; occasional fruit. (Europese Koekoek)

## 2 African Cuckoo  *Cuculus gularis*

**30–32 cm; 95–112 g** A large, grey cuckoo, similar to Common Cuckoo, but the ad. typically has a more extensive yellow base to its bill, barred (not spotted) outer tail, and vent and undertail coverts more finely barred; call is most distinctive feature. Lacks rufous hepatic morph. Juv. is barred black-and-white, with upperparts blackish, scalloped with white; rump is not plain, as in Common Cuckoo. **Voice:** Similar to African Hoopoe's 'hoop-hoop' call, but slower; female utters fast 'kik-kik-kik'. **Status and biology:** Locally common intra-African migrant in woodland and savanna. Brood parasite of Fork-tailed Drongo. Male assists female to lay by distracting drongos. **Diet:** Caterpillars and other insects. (Afrikaanse Koekoek)

## 3 Red-chested Cuckoo  *Cuculus solitarius*

**28–31 cm; 68–88 g** A long-tailed, dark grey cuckoo. Ad. has a reddish breast and a slate-grey back (darker than African and Common cuckoos). Female has paler rufous breast, often barred grey. Best located by its characteristic 3-note call. Juv. has blackish head, breast and upperparts (not barred, like juv. African and Common cuckoos), with pale feather edges; lower breast and belly are strongly barred black-and-white. **Voice:** Male calls monotonous 'wiet-weet-weeoo' (rendered 'piet my vrou' in Afrikaans); female gives shrill 'pipipipipi'. **Status and biology:** Common intra-African migrant in forest, woodland and gardens. Brood parasite, mainly of robin-chats, but also thrushes, flycatchers and wagtails. **Diet:** Hairy caterpillars and other invertebrates; occasional frogs, lizards and fruit. (Piet-my-vrou)

## 4 Lesser Cuckoo  *Cuculus poliocephalus*

**26 cm; 40–58 g** Rare visitor; possibly overlooked. A grey cuckoo, similar to African and Common cuckoos, but smaller, and with darker upperparts and more heavily barred underparts. In flight, dark tail and rump contrast with paler back, unlike African and Common cuckoos. Very similar to Madagascar Cuckoo, but typically occurs in summer, and has strongly barred, not plain or weakly barred, undertail coverts. Male has grey upper breast; female barred dark grey with buff wash. Has a rare hepatic morph. Juv. is barred above. **Voice:** Staccato, 5–6 note 'chok chok chi chi chu-chu', higher in middle. **Status and biology:** Scarce Palearctic non-br. migrant to savanna and riparian forest. **Diet:** Caterpillars and other insects. (Kleinkoekoek)

## 5 Madagascar Cuckoo  *Cuculus rochii*

**28 cm; 50–65 g** Rare visitor; possibly overlooked. Very similar to Lesser Cuckoo, but typically has plain or weakly barred undertail coverts; best told by call. Winter visitor to E Africa, but sthn Africa records in summer, when calling (possibly overlooked in winter). Plumage worn in late summer, when Lesser Cuckoo in fresh plumage. Lacks a hepatic morph. Juv. is mottled with rufous on upperparts. **Voice:** Similar to Red-chested Cuckoo's, but deeper in tone, and typically has 4 (not 3) notes ('piet-my-vrou-vrou'), last note being lower. **Status and biology:** Rare non-br. visitor from Madagascar to riverine forest, woodland and dense savanna. **Diet:** Caterpillars and other insects. (Madagaskarkoekoek)

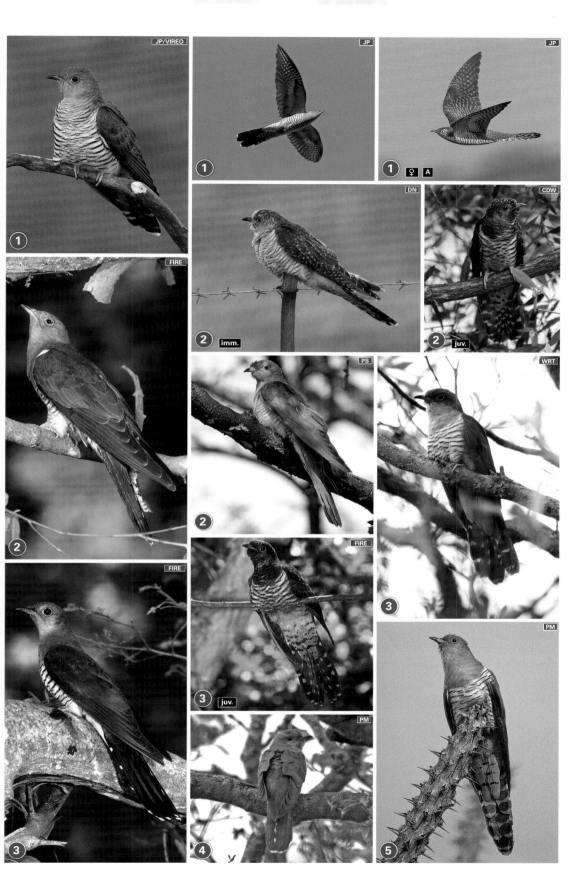

## 1 Black Cuckoo *Cuculus clamosus*

J F M A M J J A S O N D

**28–31 cm; 80–100 g** The only all-black cuckoo. Lacks crest and white wing patches of dark-morph Jacobin and Levaillant's cuckoos. At close range, has indistinct pale tips to tail feathers; female has indistinct paler bars on belly. Juv. duller black, with no white tail tips. **Voice:** Male song is mournful 'hoo hooee' or 'hoo hoo hooeee' (rendered 'I'm so sick'), with last note rising in pitch, repeated monotonously and sometimes ending in excited, rattling 'whurri whurri whurri'; female gives fast 'yow-yow-yow-yow'. **Status and biology:** Common intra-African migrant in woodland, forest and gardens. Brood parasite, mainly of boubous and Crimson-breasted Shrike. **Diet:** Caterpillars and other invertebrates. (Swartkoekoek)

## 2 Levaillant's (African Striped) Cuckoo *Clamator levaillantii*

**38–40 cm; 105–140 g** A large, black-and-white cuckoo with a long crest. Larger than Jacobin Cuckoo, with a distinctive striped throat and breast. Rare black morph has white wing patches and usually has white tail tips; birds with black tails hard to separate from black Jacobin Cuckoo. Sexes alike. Juv. is browner above and buff below, but still shows diagnostic throat stripes; bill black. **Voice:** Loud 'klee-klee-kleeuu', followed by descending 'che-che-che-che'. **Status and biology:** Locally common intra-African migrant in savanna and woodland. Brood parasite of Arrow-marked and other babblers. **Diet:** Caterpillars, other insects and occasional fruit. (Gestreepte Nuwejaarsvoël)

## 3 Jacobin Cuckoo *Clamator jacobinus*

**34 cm; 70–92 g** A medium-sized, black-and-white, crested cuckoo. Smaller than Levaillant's Cuckoo, with no stripes on throat and breast. Dark-morph birds (3 A) are all-black, except for white patch at base of primaries; smaller than dark-morph Levaillant's Cuckoo, with no white in tail. Crest and long, graduated tail separate it from Black Cuckoo. Sexes alike. Juv. is browner above, with creamy grey underparts; dark morph has dull black underparts. Bill yellow. **Voice:** Shrill, repeated 'klee-klee-kleeuu-kleeuu', similar to start of call of Levaillant's Cuckoo. **Status and biology:** Common intra-African br. migrant (*C. j. serratus*) and non-br. migrants from N Africa and S Asia (*C. j. jacobinus* and *C. j. pica*). Occurs in woodland, thicket and acacia savanna. Brood parasite of bulbuls and Common Fiscal, occasionally drongos, mousebirds, flycatchers, wagtails, white-eyes, tit-babblers and bush-shrikes. **Diet:** Caterpillars and other insects. (Bontnuwejaarsvoël)

## 4 Thick-billed Cuckoo *Pachycoccyx audeberti*

**36 cm; 92–120 g** A large, rather hawk-like cuckoo with a noticeably thick, heavy bill. Plain white underparts and lack of a crest are diagnostic. Ad. is dark grey above, with white underparts and broadly barred undertail. Sexes alike. Juv. has striking white head flecked with black, and white-spotted upperparts. **Voice:** Repeated, ringing 'weee we-wick', like a fast, harsh Klaas's Cuckoo. **Status and biology:** Uncommon resident in riparian forest and dense woodland. Brood parasite of Retz's Helmet-Shrike. **Diet:** Caterpillars and other insects. (Dikbekkoekoek)

## 5 Great Spotted Cuckoo *Clamator glandarius*

**38–42 cm; 120–165 g** A large, distinctively patterned cuckoo with a long, wedge-shaped tail and grey crest. Sexes alike. Juv. is also heavily spotted on back, but has small, black crest, buffy underparts and rufous patches on primaries. **Voice:** Loud, far-carrying 'keeow-keeow-keeow'; shorter, crow-like 'kark'. **Status and biology:** Common intra-African migrant in woodland and savanna, including locally br. *C. g. choragium* and non-br. nominate race from African savanna N of equator. Brood parasite of crows and starlings. **Diet:** Caterpillars, other invertebrates and occasional lizards. (Gevlekte Koekoek)

## 1 Barred Long-tailed Cuckoo *Cercococcyx montanus*

**33 cm; 55–70 g** A small, dark cuckoo with a very long tail, brownish, barred upperparts and broadly barred underparts. Sexes alike. Juv. has underparts more dusky, with some streaking. **Voice:** Long series of 'cheee-phweews', increasing in intensity, followed by ringing 'whit whew hew hew', recalling call of Red-chested Cuckoo but with 4–5 notes; shorter 'hwee-hooa' or 'hwee-hooo'; often calls at night. **Status and biology:** Uncommon intra-African migrant in forest, riparian thicket and mature miombo woodland. Seldom seen if not calling. Brood parasite; hosts suspected to be African Broadbill and East Coast Akalat. **Diet:** Caterpillars and other invertebrates. (Langstertkoekoek)

## 2 Diderick Cuckoo *Chrysococcyx caprius*

**17–20 cm; 22–42 g** A small, glossy green cuckoo with diagnostic white wing spots, red eyes and broadly barred green flanks. Ad. has green malar stripe and white supercilium, which extends in front of reddish eye. Female is duller, with barring extending up onto breast; throat is often buffy. Juv. has conspicuous red bill; occurs in green and rufous morphs. **Voice:** Clear, persistent 'dee-dee-deedereek'. **Status and biology:** Common intra-African migrant in woodland, savanna, grassland and suburban gardens. Brood parasite, mainly of weavers, bishops and sparrows, but more than 10 other species recorded. **Diet:** Caterpillars. (Diederikkie)

## 3 Klaas's Cuckoo *Chrysococcyx klaas*

**16–18 cm; 24–34 g** A plain, glossy green cuckoo with a small, white post-ocular eye-stripe; lacks white wing spots of Diderick Cuckoo, but flight feathers boldly barred. Male is white below, with green spurs extending onto sides of breast, and only few green bars on thighs. Female is bronzy brown above and finely barred below. Juv. is barred bronze and green above, similar to female Emerald Cuckoo, but has diagnostic white post-ocular eye-stripe. **Voice:** Far-carrying 'may-i-kie may-i-kie' (rendered in Afrikaans as 'meitjie'), repeated 3–6 times. **Status and biology:** Common resident and intra-African migrant in forest, woodland, savanna and gardens. Brood parasite of batises, sunbirds, warblers and flycatchers. **Diet:** Caterpillars, other insects, fruit and buds. (Meitjie)

## 4 African Emerald Cuckoo *Chrysococcyx cupreus*

**18–20 cm; 33–41 g** A forest cuckoo; larger than other glossy green species. Male has sulphur-yellow lower breast and belly contrasting with brilliant emerald-green throat, upper breast and upperparts; vent is barred green and white. Female and juv. are finely barred green and brown above, and green and white below; lack white eye-stripe of Klaas's Cuckoo. **Voice:** Loud, ringing whistle, 'wit-huu, orr-weee' (rendered 'pretty georg-eee'). **Status and biology:** Common resident and intra-African migrant in evergreen forest. Brood parasite of Green-backed Camaroptera; possibly also White-starred Robin, Black-throated Wattle-eye and Yellow-throated Woodland-Warbler. **Diet:** Caterpillars, butterflies and grasshoppers; rarely fruit. (Mooimeisie)

# COUCALS AND MALKOHAS

Fairly large, heavy-set, cuckoo-like birds with long, broad tails and short, rounded wings. Stout, arched bill adapted for tearing flesh. Legs long and robust; toes zygodactyl. Flight cumbersome. Clamber among dense vegetation, but often perch in the open in the early morning or after rain. Sexes alike, but females larger. Most species monogamous, but sometimes polyandrous, with males doing most parenting. Chicks altricial.

## 1 Coppery-tailed Coucal *Centropus cupreicaudus*

**46–52 cm; 240–340 g** The largest coucal; glossy black crown extends down its mantle (stops at nape in Burchell's and Senegal coucals); tail has a violet gloss. In flight has a distinct brown trailing edge to the wing. Juv. duller; barred above and with white streaks on buffy underparts. **Voice:** A deep, loud, resonant series of 'doo' notes. **Status and biology:** Locally common at marshes, thick reedbeds and adjoining bush. Monogamous; lays 2–4 eggs in an untidy ball nest built low down in reeds or dense grass. **Diet:** Small mammals, birds, reptiles, frogs and invertebrates. (Grootvleiloerie)

## 2 Burchell's Coucal *Centropus burchellii*

**41 cm; 160–210 g** Often considered a subspecies of White-browed Coucal, but ad. has a black cap and mantle (not streaked). Slightly larger than Senegal Coucal, with fine, rufous barring on the rump and the base of the tail (not plain). Juv. has a dark brown cap with a buffy supercilium and barred mantle; white-streaked buffy underparts and barred wings separate it from ad. White-browed Coucal, but similar to juv. **Voice:** Bubbling song like White-browed Coucal. **Status and biology:** Common resident in riverine scrub, reedbeds, thicket and well-wooded gardens. Monogamous, lays 2–5 white eggs in a deep, untidy cup nest in dense vegetation. **Diet:** Small mammals, birds, reptiles, frogs, invertebrates and fruit. (Gewone Vleiloerie)

## 3 White-browed Coucal *Centropus superciliosus*

**40 cm; 145–210 g** A fairly large coucal with a diagnostic white supercilium and heavily streaked nape and mantle. Ad. similar to juv. Burchell's Coucal, but has plain (not barred) wings and generally is whiter below. Juv. is buffier than ad., with less prominent buff supercilium and barred wings; probably not separable from juv. Burchell's Coucal in small area of overlap. **Voice:** A liquid, bubbling 'doo-doo-doo-doo...', falling in pitch, then slowing and rising in pitch at the end. **Status and biology:** Common resident in rank grass, riverine scrub, reedbeds, thicket and well-wooded gardens. Monogamous; lays 3–5 eggs in a deep, untidy cup nest in dense vegetation. **Diet:** Bird chicks, small mammals, reptiles, frogs and invertebrates. (Gestreepte Vleiloerie)

## 4 Senegal Coucal *Centropus senegalensis*

**38–40 cm; 145–180 g** A small, black-headed coucal. Slightly smaller than Burchell's Coucal, with a plain (not barred) rump and uppertail. Much smaller than Coppery-tailed Coucal with rich chestnut mantle and wings; lacks a bluish sheen to head. Juv. is buffy, heavily barred above (not streaked on head and mantle like Black Coucal). Rare rufous morph has rufous underparts. **Voice:** Bubbling call note, similar to that of White-browed Coucal. **Status and biology:** Uncommon to locally common, resident or partial migrant found in tangled vegetation and long grass; less tied to water than most other coucals. Monogamous; lays 2–5 eggs in an untidy ball nest built in tangled vegetation. **Diet:** Mainly grasshoppers and other invertebrates, but some small mammals, birds, reptiles and frogs. (Senegalvleiloerie)

## 5 Black Coucal *Centropus grillii*

**35–38 cm; 95–150 g** A small, dark coucal. Br. ad. has entirely black head, mantle and underparts, contrasting with plain chestnut wings. Non-br. ads and juv. are buff all over, heavily barred blackish on the wings, back and tail; crown and mantle tawny and brown, but lacks a clear supercilium. Darker than juv. Senegal Coucal, with richer chestnut wings and streaked (not barred) head and mantle. **Voice:** Female gives a monotonous, repeated 'pop-op'; also a bubbling call, like White-browed Coucal but faster and higher pitched. **Status and biology:** Uncommon to locally common local migrant in moist grassland. Monogamous or polyandrous; lays 2–6 eggs in a deep cup nest well concealed among rank grass. **Diet:** Grasshoppers and other invertebrates. (Swartvleiloerie)

## 6 Green Malkoha *Ceuthmochares aereus*

**33 cm; 55–75 g** A slender, coucal-like bird with a long tail, large yellow bill, dull green upperparts and grey underparts. Juv. darker above with a duller, greenish bill. **Voice:** A clicking 'kik-kik-kik', winding up to a loud 'cher-cher-cher-cher'. **Status and biology:** Scarce to locally common in forest edge, riparian forest and thicket, often in creepers. Shy; easily overlooked if not calling. Lays 2–4 eggs on a flimsy platform of twigs in a creeper or thicket. **Diet:** Insects, other invertebrates, frogs and occasional fruit. (Groenvleiloerie)

# OWLS

Small to large predatory birds; mostly nocturnal. Flight feathers have soft margins allowing near-silent flight. Eyes fixed in skull; most species have a well-defined facial disc. Sexes alike, although females typically larger. Monogamous and territorial; breed singly; chicks altricial.

## 1 African Wood-Owl *Strix woodfordii*

`b B B b b`
J F M A M J J A S O N D

**30–36 cm; 240–350 g** A medium-sized, chocolate brown owl with a rounded head (lacking ear tufts), dark eyes and yellow bill. Facial disc is finely barred and paler than white-spotted brown head and upper breast; belly is barred brown and white. Plumage varies from very dark brown to russet. **Voice:** Hooting 'hu hu, hu whoo-oo'; also single hoots and a higher-pitched 'who-uuu'. **Status and biology:** Common resident of forest, mature woodland and exotic plantations. Lays 1–3 eggs in a tree hole; rarely on the ground or in an old stick nest. **Diet:** Insects, reptiles, and small birds and mammals. (Bosuil)

## 2 Marsh Owl *Asio capensis*

`b b B B B b b b b b b`
J F M A M J J A S O N D

**35–38 cm; 230–370 g** A plain brown, medium-sized owl with a buff-coloured face, small 'ear' tufts and dark brown eyes. In flight, wings broader than African Grass-Owl (p. 222), with much larger buff 'windows' in primaries, less contrast between coverts and flight feathers, and pale trailing edge to secondaries and outer primaries. Underwing has dark carpal marks; tail barred. **Voice:** Harsh, rasping 'krikkk-krikkk', likened to sound of material being torn. **Status and biology:** Common resident and nomad in marshes and damp grassland; avoids thick reedbeds. Often circles overhead after flushing. Less nocturnal than most other owls. Sometimes roosts in flocks. Lays 2–4 (rarely 6) eggs in a depression among dense vegetation. **Diet:** Small mammals, birds, frogs and invertebrates. (Vlei-uil)

## 3 Southern White-faced Scops-Owl *Ptilopsis granti*

`b b b B B B b`
J F M A M J J A S O N D

**25–28 cm; 150–290 g** A fairly small, grey-backed owl; larger than African Scops-Owl, with bright orange (not yellow) eyes and prominent black-and-white facial disc. Juv. browner, with paler yellow-orange eyes. **Voice:** A fast, hooting, 'doo-doo-doo-doo-hohoo'. **Status and biology:** Common resident and nomad in acacia savanna and dry, broadleafed woodland. Lays 2–4 eggs in the stick nest of another bird (including raptors, crows, doves, sparrows), sometimes evicting small accipiters; also in tree cavities and hollows in tree forks. **Diet:** Small mammals, invertebrates and birds. (Witwanguil)

## 4 African Barred Owlet *Glaucidium capense*

`b b B B b`
J F M A M J J A S O N D

**20–22 cm; 100–138 g** A small, brown-backed owl; slightly larger than Pearl-spotted Owlet, with faintly barred upperparts (lacking white spots), barred breast, and spotted (not streaked) belly; appears larger-headed and shorter-tailed. Large white tips to scapulars form conspicuous line of spots on back. Tail buff with darker brown bars. **Voice:** Series of 6–10 notes, starting softly and increasing in volume, 'kerrr-kerrr-kerrr-kerrr', often followed by series of purring whistles, 'trru-trrre, trru-trrre', second note higher-pitched. **Status and biology:** Locally common in mature woodland, thicket and forest edge. Lays 2–3 eggs in a tree cavity. **Diet:** Large invertebrates, small mammals, birds, reptiles and frogs. (Gebande Uil)

## 5 Pearl-spotted Owlet *Glaucidium perlatum*

`b B B b`
J F M A M J J A S O N D

**17–21 cm; 40–140 g** A small, long-tailed owl. Smaller than African Barred Owlet, with small white spots (not bars) on upperparts and streaked (not barred) breast and flanks; tail dark brown with narrow white bars. Has 2 black 'false eyes' on nape (**5 A**). Told from African Scops-Owl by its rounded head, lack of ear tufts and white spotting on back and tail. Juv. is less spotted on crown and mantle; tail shorter. **Voice:** Series of low hoots, rising in pitch, 'tu tu tu tu tu', then a brief pause following by piercing, down-slurred whistles, 'tseuu tseuu tseuu'; sometimes calls during day. **Status and biology:** Common resident in acacia savanna and woodland. Often active during day. Lays 2–4 eggs in a tree cavity, often an old barbet or woodpecker hole. **Diet:** Large invertebrates, small mammals, birds, reptiles and frogs. (Witkoluil)

## 6 African Scops-Owl *Otus senegalensis*

`b b b B B b`
J F M A M J J A S O N D

**14–18 cm; 45–95 g** The smallest owl in the region. Most individuals are greyish, but some are more rufous. Smaller than Southern White-faced Scops-Owl, with grey (not white) face and yellow (not orange) eyes. Has prominent ear tufts, but these can lie flat on head. **Voice:** Soft, frog-like 'prrrup', repeated every 5–8 seconds. **Status and biology:** Common resident of savanna and dry, open woodland; avoids forests. Typically roosts on branches adjacent to tree trunk. Lays 2–4 eggs in a natural tree cavity, old woodpecker hole or cavity in the base of a large raptor nest. **Diet:** Large invertebrates, small mammals, birds, reptiles and frogs. (Skopsuil)

## 1 Verreaux's (Giant) Eagle-Owl  *Bubo lacteus*

`bBBBb` J F M A M J J A S O N D

**58–66 cm; 1.2–3 kg** The largest owl in the region; easily identified by its large size, rather short ear tufts and finely vermiculated, pale grey plumage. At close range, pink eyelids and dark brown eyes are distinctive. Other eagle-owls are smaller, with more boldly barred or blotched plumage and yellow eyes. Juv. has grey-barred plumage, lacking white tips to greater coverts; black border to facial disc reduced. **Voice:** Grunting, pig-like 'unnh-unnh-unnh'. **Status and biology:** Uncommon to locally common resident in broadleafed woodland, savanna, thornveld and riverine forest. Lays 1–2 eggs in an old crow or raptor nest, or on a Hamerkop, Sociable Weaver or buffalo-weaver nest. **Diet:** Mammals up to 2–3 kg; birds including raptors and other owls. (Reuse-ooruil)

## 2 Pel's Fishing-Owl  *Scotopelia peli*

`bBBBbb` J F M A M J J A S O N D

**60–64 cm; 2–2.4 kg** A large, ginger-coloured owl associated with rivers and other waterbodies. Breast spotted or lightly barred; eyes and bill black. Pale, unfeathered legs and feet are difficult to see in the field. Flight rather noisy; lacks soft fringes to flight feathers. When alarmed, it fluffs up its head feathers, giving it a huge, round-headed appearance. Juv. is paler and more buffy coloured, with an almost white head. **Voice:** Deep, booming 'hoo-huuuum'; juv. makes a jackal-like wailing. **Status and biology:** Uncommon resident that roosts in large trees around lakes and slow-moving rivers. Lays 1–2 eggs in a large tree hole; successful breeders typically only breed every second year. **Diet:** Mainly fish up to 0.3 kg (rarely 2 kg); also small crocodiles and frogs. (Visuil)

## 3 Spotted Eagle-Owl  *Bubo africanus*

`bbbbbbbBBBbb` J F M A M J J A S O N D

**43–50 cm; 500–1 100 g** The commonest large owl. Most birds are greyish; told from Cape Eagle-Owl by their smaller size (especially smaller feet), lack of dark breast patches, finely (not boldly) barred belly and flanks, and yellow (not orange) eyes. Rare rufous morph is more heavily blotched and has orange-yellow eyes; best distinguished from Cape Eagle-Owl by its call and smaller feet. Juv. is browner with shorter ear tufts. Large fledglings out of the nest still retain fluffy white down around the head. **Voice:** Male gives deep 'hoo-huuu', often followed by female's 'huu-ho-huuu', with second note higher-pitched. Hisses and clicks when alarmed. **Status and biology:** Common resident in all habitats except forest; often in gardens. Lays 1–6 (usually 2–3) eggs in a scrape on the ground, in the fork of a tree or in a building. **Diet:** Small mammals and birds; also reptiles, frogs, crabs and insects. Chases bats and insects in flight. (Gevlekte Ooruil)

## 4 Cape Eagle-Owl  *Bubo capensis*

`bBBbbb` J F M A M J J A S O N D

**48–54 cm; 910–1 400 g** A large, heavily marked eagle-owl, typically in mountainous areas. Needs to be separated with caution from smaller Spotted Eagle-Owl; has black and chestnut blotching on breast, and bold (not fine) barring on belly and flanks. Feet are much larger, and has orange (not yellow) eyes (but rare rufous-morph Spotted Eagle-Owl have more orange eyes). Upperparts generally richer and more strongly marked than Spotted Eagle-Owl. Juv. paler with ear tufts absent or shorter. *B. c. mackinderi* in Zimbabwe is appreciably larger; darker above and more heavily marked below. **Voice:** Deep, far-carrying 'hooooo' calls, sometimes 2–3 notes; dog-like bark, 'wak-wak-wak'; seldom duets. **Status and biology:** Generally uncommon resident of rocky and mountainous terrain. Lays 1–3 eggs in a shallow scrape on the ground, often on a cliff ledge, partly concealed by vegetation. **Diet:** Mainly mammals (up to size of hares) and birds. (Kaapse Ooruil)

## 5 Barn Owl  *Tyto alba*

`bBBBBbbbbbbb` J F M A M J J A S O N D

**30–35 cm; 270–500 g** A medium-sized, pale owl with golden buff and grey upperparts, a white, heart-shaped facial disc and off-white underparts. Much paler above than African Grass-Owl, with less contrast between upperparts and underparts. In flight, has distinctive large head and short tail. **Voice:** Typical call is high-pitched 'shreeee'; also hisses and bill-clicks when disturbed. **Status and biology:** Common resident in most open habitats; avoids dense forest. Roosts in old buildings, caves, hollow trees and mine shafts. Lays 2–8 (rarely 19) eggs in a roost site. **Diet:** Mainly small mammals, especially rodents, and birds; also reptiles, frogs and invertebrates. (Nonnetjie-uil)

## 6 African Grass-Owl  *Tyto capensis*

`BBBBB b bbb` J F M A M J J A S O N D

**34–37 cm; 355–520 g** Slightly larger than Barn Owl, with much darker brown upperparts that contrast strongly with pale buff underparts; also habitat differs. Paler beneath than Marsh Owl (p. 220), with pale (not dark) face. In flight has longer, more slender wings than Marsh Owl, with darker coverts contrasting with paler flight feathers and only small buffy bases to primaries; outer tail white. Juv. has rufous facial disc and darker underparts. **Voice:** Soft, cricket-like 'tk-tk-tk-tk' on the wing. **Status and biology:** Uncommon resident and nomad at marshes and tall grassland; roosts on the ground. Lays 2–6 eggs in a depression among dense grass. **Diet:** Mainly small mammals, especially rodents; also frogs and invertebrates. (Grasuil)

# NIGHTJARS

Nocturnal insectivores that roost on the ground or along branches during the day; most prey taken in the air. Identification based largely on wing and tail patterns. Sexes differ. Eggs laid directly on the ground; chicks semi-altricial.

## 1 European Nightjar  *Caprimulgus europaeus*

J F M A M J J A S O N D

26–28 cm; 55–80 g  A large, long-winged nightjar. At rest, appears rather pale grey, similar to Rufous-cheeked Nightjar, but lacks a rufous nuchal collar. Plumage more patterned than Freckled Nightjar, with a buff bar on the folded wing and a pale moustachial streak. In flight, male has white tips to outer tail and white outer primary window. Female has tail and wings all-dark; appears greyer than female Pennant-winged Nightjar; tail more rounded. **Voice:** Has churring song, similar to Rufous-cheeked Nightjar, but rarely sings in Africa; occasionally utters a nasal grunt on flushing. **Status and biology:** Locally common Palearctic migrant in woodland, plantations and savanna. Usually roosts lengthwise on branches; sometimes on the ground. **Diet:** Insects. (Europese Naguil)

## 2 Fiery-necked Nightjar  *Caprimulgus pectoralis*

J F M A M J J A S O N D

23–25 cm; 48–65 g  A dark brown, heavily marked nightjar with a rich rufous collar (not orange-buff, as Rufous-cheeked Nightjar) and a white moustache and throat patch. In flight, male has broad white tips to outer tail and small white primary patches; creamy in female; tail tips smaller. Amount of rufous on face and breast varies considerably. Northern races average paler above with a more prominent collar. **Voice:** Characteristic night sound of Africa: plaintive, whistled 'good lord, deliver us', descending in pitch, first note often repeated. **Status and biology:** Common resident and intra-African migrant in woodland, savanna and plantations. Roosts on the ground under bushes. Lays 1–2 eggs in a shallow hollow on the ground, usually among leaf litter. **Diet:** Insects and occasional spiders. (Afrikaanse Naguil)

## 3 Rufous-cheeked Nightjar  *Caprimulgus rufigena*

J F M A M J J A S O N D

22–24 cm; 45–65 g  A fairly small, variegated nightjar; paler grey than Fiery-necked Nightjar, with narrower, orange-buff (not rufous) collar; male has more prominent white patches in primaries but less white in tail than Fiery-necked Nightjar; female has small buff tail tips and buff primary patches. Smaller than European Nightjar, which lacks a rufous collar. **Voice:** Prolonged churring, usually preceded by choking 'chukoo, chukoo'. **Status and biology:** Locally common intra-African br. migrant in arid savanna, woodland and desert scrub. Roosts on the ground, usually in areas shaded by vegetation. Lays 1–2 eggs in a shallow hollow on the ground. **Diet:** Beetles and other insects. (Rooiwangnaguil)

European Nightjar

Fiery-necked Nightjar

Rufous-cheeked Nightjar

### 1 Freckled Nightjar  *Caprimulgus tristigma*

■■■■■■■■■bBBBb
J F M A M J J A S O N D

**26–28 cm; 70–90 g** A large, dark grey nightjar; differs from European (p. 224) and Pennant-winged nightjars by its plain greyish upperparts, lacking wing bars at rest; blends well with its rocky habitat. In flight, male has white outer tail tips and tiny white spots in primary bases (smaller than European Nightjar). Female and juv. lack white tail patches but have small creamy primary spots (absent in female European and Pennant-winged nightjars). **Voice:** Yapping, double-noted 'kow-kow', sometimes extending to 3–4 syllables. **Status and biology:** Locally common resident and nomad at rocky outcrops in woodland and hilly terrain; roosts in the open on boulders; also on buildings in cities. Lays 2 eggs in a  shallow hollow on a boulder or rooftop. **Diet:** Beetles and other insects. (Donkernaguil)

### 2 Swamp Nightjar  *Caprimulgus natalensis*

■■■■■■■■■bBBbb
J F M A M J J A S O N D

**20–24 cm; 60–70 g** A distinctive nightjar with scaly upperparts due to buff fringes to its mantle feathers; at rest, lacks prominent pale wing bar of most other nightjars, including Square-tailed. In flight, male has white trailing edge to wings, white spots in outer primaries and extensive white tips to 2 outer tail feathers; outer web white. Primary spots and outer tail buff in female. White/buff in outer tail more extensive than in Square-tailed Nightjar. **Voice:** 'Chow-chow-chow' or 'chop-chop-chop'. **Status and biology:** Fairly common, localised resident and local nomad in open grassland and palm savanna, often near damp areas. Roosts on the ground. Lays 2 eggs on the ground or flattened grass, often under a grass tuft. **Diet:** Beetles and other insects. (Natalse Naguil)

### 3 Square-tailed Nightjar  *Caprimulgus fossii*

■■■■■■■■■bBBb
J F M A M J J A S O N D

**22–25 cm; 45–75 g** At rest, recalls Fiery-necked Nightjar (p. 224), but male has white outer tail extending to the base of the tail and more extensive white primary panel. White outer tail narrower than male Swamp Nightjar; differs at rest by having white lines on its wing coverts and back; lacks scaly mantle. Female has buff outer tail and primary patch. **Voice:** Prolonged churring, changing at intervals in pitch ('changing gears'). **Status and biology:** Common resident and local migrant in coastal dune scrub and sandy woodland, often near water. Resident in E lowlands; moves into higher elevations and more arid areas in summer. Roosts on the ground, usually under vegetation. Lays 1–2 eggs on the ground. **Diet:** Beetles and other insects. (Laeveldnaguil)

### 4 Pennant-winged Nightjar  *Macrodipteryx vexillarius*

b■■■■□□□□bBBb
J F M A M J J A S O N D

**23–26 cm (excl. br. male's 'pennants'); 50–95 g** Male has a diagnostic broad white band across primaries, with longer inner primaries giving the wing a peculiar shape. Br. male has long, white inner primaries (especially primary 2), which trail behind the bird. Female lacks any white on wings or tail; more rufous than European Nightjar (p. 224), with boldly barred flight feathers and squarer tail. Juv. like female but duller. **Voice:** Continuous, high-pitched twittering. **Status and biology:** Locally common intra-African migrant in broadleafed woodland. Roosts on ground, but often perches on branches after flushing. Lays 1–2 eggs on the ground, usually among leaf litter. **Diet:** Beetles and other insects. (Wimpelvlerknaguil)

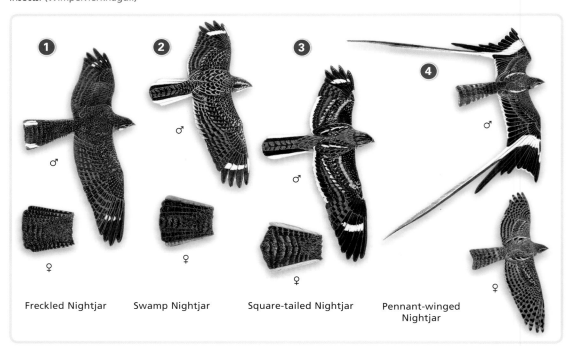

Freckled Nightjar     Swamp Nightjar     Square-tailed Nightjar     Pennant-winged Nightjar

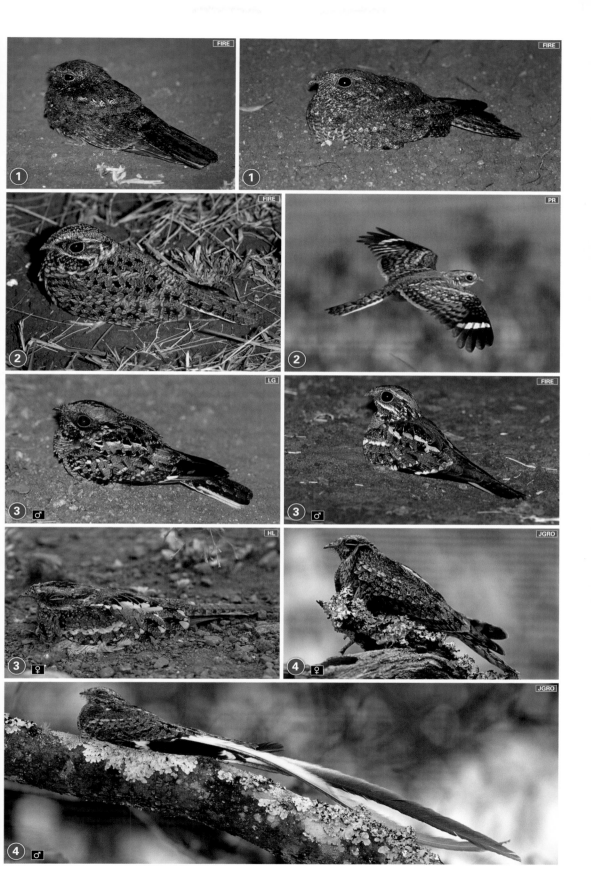

# SWIFTS

The most aerial of birds, feeding and even roosting in flight. Some birds remain on the wing for at least 6–8 months. Legs and toes short, with strong claws. Could be confused with swallows (pp. 274–280), but have scythe-shaped wings and mainly black or brown plumage. Sexes alike. Collect nesting material in the air and glue it to the nest site with saliva. Some species even glue their eggs to the nest. Monogamous; both parents incubate and feed the altricial chicks. Eggs and chicks can survive temporary abandonment, should poor weather force parents to move away.

## 1 Alpine Swift *Tachymarptis melba*

**20–22 cm; 68–90 g** A very large, brown swift with a diagnostic white belly and throat, separated by a dark breast band. Flight swift and direct, with deep beats of long, scythe-like wings. Juv. has pale fringes to brown feathers. **Voice:** Shrill, chittering screams. **Status and biology:** Common resident and intra-African migrant. Often in large, mixed flocks with other swifts. Breeds in small colonies, laying 1–2 eggs in cliff crevices; occasionally on buildings. **Diet:** Aerial insects and spiders. (Witpenswindswael)

## 2 Mottled Swift *Tachymarptis aequatorialis*

**22 cm; 84–92 g** A very large, brown swift. Structure and flight action are similar to Alpine Swift, but has a darker belly and slightly longer, more deeply forked tail. Throat is pale; underparts scaled and mottled. **Voice:** Dry, insect-like trill; usually silent. **Status and biology:** Uncommon resident, usually around rocky areas. Breeds in small colonies, laying 1–3 eggs in cliff crevices. **Diet:** Aerial insects. (Bontwindswael)

## 3 Bradfield's Swift *Apus bradfieldi*

**17 cm; 33–50 g** A grey-brown or warm-brown swift with scaled underparts; usually paler than Common and African Black swifts. Lacks strongly contrasting pale secondaries on the upperwing of African Black Swift; flight feathers tend to be darker than body and wing coverts. Bulkier than Common Swift, appearing similar to vagrant Pallid Swift. **Voice:** High-pitched 'sweer' screams and titters at br. sites. **Status and biology:** Near-endemic. Locally common resident and nomad. Breeds in small colonies, laying 2 eggs in crevices on inland cliffs and on palm fronds. **Diet:** Aerial insects. (Muiskleurwindswael)

## 4 Pallid Swift *Apus pallidus*

**16 cm; 32–48 g** Rare vagrant. Difficult to separate from other all-brown swifts. Paler than African Black and Common swifts, with more extensive white throat patch and paler forehead (but juvs of other species often have paler frons). Tail is less pointed and more shallow-forked than Common Swift, closer to African Swift. Shows some contrast between paler secondaries and back, but less than in African Swift. Probably hardest to separate from Bradfield's Swift, although underparts typically are less scaled. In flight, appears rather robust, with broad wings (especially broad primaries) and slow, leisurely flight action. **Voice:** High-pitched, whistled screams. **Status and biology:** Rare Palearctic vagrant that usually winters N of equator. **Diet:** Aerial insects. (Bruinwindswael)

## 5 Common Swift *Apus apus*

**17 cm; 30–44 g** A fairly large, blackish-brown (*A. a. apus*) or grey-brown (*A. a. pekineensis*) swift with a paler throat patch. Appears more sleek and rakish than African Black and Pallid swifts, thanks to relatively longer wings and tail; tail sharply pointed and rather deeply forked (when not moulting). From above its secondaries are the same colour as its back (not paler). Juv. has a pale forehead. **Voice:** Shrill scream, seldom heard in Africa. **Status and biology:** Common Palearctic migrant, often in large flocks; roosts on the wing. **Diet:** Aerial insects. (Europese Windswael)

## 6 African Black Swift *Apus barbatus*

**18 cm; 35–50 g** A large, robust, blackish-brown swift with a small, paler throat patch; belly often scaled. Slightly larger and bulkier than Common Swift, with a shorter, less deeply forked and less sharply pointed tail and blunter wings. In good light, paler secondaries contrast with the darker back from above. **Voice:** High-pitched 'sweeer' screams in air around br. sites. **Status and biology:** Common resident and partial migrant. Breeds in small colonies, sometimes with Alpine Swifts. Lays 2 (rarely 1) eggs in cliff crevices. **Diet:** Aerial insects. (Swartwindswael)

## 1 Böhm's Spinetail  *Neafrapus boehmi*

BBBbb bbBBB
J F M A M J J A S O N D

**10 cm; 12–16 g** A tiny, very short-tailed swift with a white belly and rump; appears nearly tail-less in flight. Flight is erratic, almost bat-like, with short glides interspersed with rapid bursts of flapping. Wings are short and quite broad, but pinched in against the body. **Voice:** Seldom calls; high-pitched 'tsit-tsit-tsee-tseeuu'. **Status and biology:** Locally common resident and local migrant over savanna and open, broadleafed woodland; often in vicinity of baobab trees. Breeds singly, laying 2–3 eggs inside a hollow tree or a vertical shaft. Nest contains some twigs broken off with feet in flight. **Diet:** Aerial insects. (Witpensstekelstert)

## 2 Mottled Spinetail  *Telacanthura ussheri*

bbbbb J F M A M J J A S O N D bb

**14 cm; 28–36 g** A spinetail with a fairly long, square tail, broad white rump, mottled throat and diagnostic white line across the vent. Larger than Little Swift, with narrow secondaries giving the wings a pinched look near body. **Voice:** Soft twittering. **Status and biology:** Locally common resident over woodland and savanna; often along forested rivers. Breeds singly or in small colonies, laying 1–4 eggs in hollow trees (especially baobabs) or vertical shafts. **Diet:** Aerial insects. (Gevlekte Stekelstert)

## 3 Little Swift  *Apus affinis*

bbb bBBBB
J F M A M J J A S O N D

**12 cm; 20–30 g** A small, square-tailed swift with a broad white rump patch that wraps around the flanks, and a large white throat. In flight, it seems squat and dumpy, with rather short, rounded wings. Smaller than Mottled Spinetail, with no white stripe across belly, plain white throat and different flight action. **Voice:** High-pitched screeching 'tit-trrrrrrrrr', especially while wheeling in tight flocks during display flights. **Status and biology:** Common resident and partial migrant; often in towns. Usually nests in colonies, laying 1–3 eggs in bulky nests under eaves of buildings and rocky overhangs. **Diet:** Aerial insects and spiders. (Kleinwindswael)

## 4 Horus Swift  *Apus horus*

bbbbbbbbbbbb
J F M A M J J A S O N D

**14 cm; 20–34 g** A bulky version of Little Swift with a large white rump and throat, but with a shallow-forked tail, intermediate between Little and White-rumped swifts. Brown-rumped 'Loanda' Swift of Angola apparently is a colour morph of Horus Swift; possible vagrant to NW Namibia. **Voice:** Normally silent; screams 'drreep' and 'whi-whi-whi' at br. sites. **Status and biology:** Uncommon resident and intra-African migrant. Forages over variety of habitats, including grassland, woodland and semi-desert. Breeds in small colonies, laying 2–4 eggs in holes in earth banks, usually made by other birds. **Diet:** Aerial insects. (Horuswindswael)

## 5 White-rumped Swift  *Apus caffer*

Bbbb bBBBB
J F M A M J J A S O N D

**14–16 cm; 18–20 g** A slender, black swift with a fairly long, deeply forked tail and diagnostic narrow white 'U' on the rump. Tail is frequently held closed, appearing long and pointed. Has prominent white throat like Little and Horus swifts. **Voice:** Deeper screams than Little Swift; generally less vocal. **Status and biology:** Common intra-African migrant over open country, often near water. Breeds singly or in small colonies; sometimes has helpers at the nest. Usually breeds and roosts in red-rumped and cliff swallow nests; evicts swallows, often re-using the same nest in successive years; sometimes in holes in buildings. Lays 1–3 eggs (rarely 5, probably by 2 females). **Diet:** Aerial insects and spiders. (Witkruiswindswael)

## 6 Scarce Swift  *Schoutedenapus myoptilus*

b J F M A M J J A S O N D b

**17 cm; 25–30 g** A grey-brown swift with a long, deeply forked tail. Shape intermediate between White-rumped Swift and African Palm-Swift. Flight action rapid and slightly jerky; glides with wings angled down. **Voice:** High-pitched nasal twittering and trills. **Status and biology:** Localised but fairly common br. visitor to E highlands of Zimbabwe, usually over cliffs and rocky bluffs in forested mountain areas. Nest undescribed; probably in cliff crevices. **Diet:** Aerial insects. (Skaarswindswael)

## 7 African Palm-Swift  *Cypsiurus parvus*

BBbbbbbBBBBB
J F M A M J J A S O N D

**16 cm; 12–16 g** A pale grey-brown, very slender, streamlined swift with long, thin, sickle-shaped wings and a very long, deeply forked tail. Has the longest tail of any swift, but beware birds in moult and juvs, which have shorter, less streamer-like tail, and could be confused with Scarce Swift. **Voice:** Soft, high-pitched, twittering screams. **Status and biology:** Common resident and local migrant usually in vicinity of palm trees, including those in towns. Breeds singly or in small colonies. Glues 1–2 eggs into a shallow cup nest attached to a palm frond. **Diet:** Aerial insects. (Palmwindswael)

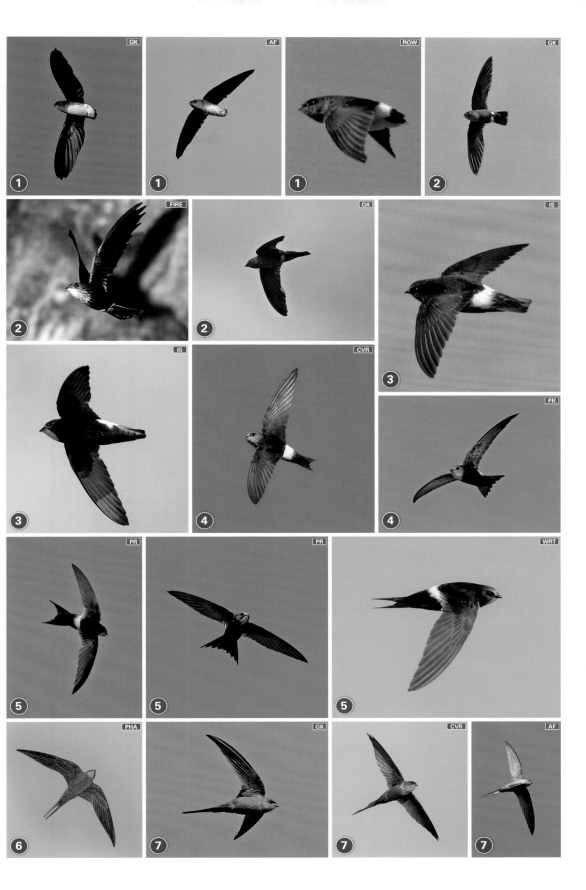

# BROADBILLS

Asian species bright, but most African species drab. Bills broad. Sexes alike; juvs duller. Chicks altricial.

### 1 African Broadbill *Smithornis capensis*

bb | | | | | | | | bbBB
J F M A M J J A S O N D

**12–14 cm; 18–27 g** A dumpy, phlegmatic flycatcher-like bird with heavily streaked underparts. Male has a blackish cap; female is duller with a dark brown cap. Juv. is buffy and less streaked above. **Voice:** Distinctive, frog-like trilling call 'prrrrurrrr', usually dipping in pitch in the middle of the song, only given in display. Male makes short, horizontal, circular flights from a low perch, calling and fluffing out the white 'puffball' on its back. **Status and biology:** Uncommon to locally common resident in forest and thickets. Easily overlooked if not calling. Monogamous; lays 1–3 eggs in an untidy oval nest with a side entrance, usually with a trailing 'tail' of material. Resembles a large sunbird nest; suspended from a small branch of a shrub or small tree, often over a watercourse. **Diet:** Insects and spiders. (Breëbek)

# PITTAS

Brightly coloured birds with long, robust legs and very short tails. Mainly feed on the ground. Sexes alike; juvs duller. Monogamous; both parents incubate and feed the altricial chicks.

### 2 African Pitta *Pitta angolensis*

b | | | | | | | | | BB
J F M A M J J A S O N D

**18–22 cm; 80–95 g** A brilliantly coloured, but unobtrusive forest floor bird. In flight, has white panel in primaries. Juv. duller, with bi-coloured bill. When disturbed, flies into mid-storey and freezes. **Voice:** Displaying birds utter frog-like 'preert', with initial mechanical purr apparently caused by wings as they jump up from a low perch; after calling, they parachute back to perch, then slowly raise their tail, displaying crimson vent. Call is short, ascending croak. **Status and biology:** Uncommon intra-African migrant to riverine thickets and forest. Vagrants occasionally stray well outside usual range. Best located when displaying. Lays 2–4 eggs in a ball-like nest of twigs and leaves with a side entrance, built in the fork of a small tree. **Diet:** Insects and other invertebrates. (Angolapitta)

# MOUSEBIRDS

An endemic African order. Fairly small birds with long, stiff tails, short crests and short legs; toes 1 and 4 reversible. Contour feathers grow over entire body. Flight direct. Clamber in vegetation. Bacteria aid digestion: sun their bellies after feeding to speed fermentation. Occur in small flocks; roost huddled to conserve heat. Sexes alike. Mating systems varied, but both sexes incubate and feed the altricial chicks.

### 3 Red-faced Mousebird *Urocolius indicus*

Bbbbbbbb BBBB
J F M A M J J A S O N D

**34 cm; 40–70 g** A blue-grey mousebird with a buffy face and breast, red facial skin and reddish legs. Tail longer than *Colius* mousebirds; flight faster and more sustained. In flight, pale rump contrasts with darker back, wings and tail. Juv. has greenish facial skin. **Voice:** A whistled 'chi-vu-vu'. **Status and biology:** Common resident and nomad in savanna, woodland and gardens. Monogamous, sometimes with helpers at the nest. Lays 1–4 eggs (rarely up to 7, probably from 2 females) in an untidy cup nest in a shrub or small tree. **Diet:** Fruit, leaves, flowers and nectar. (Rooiwangmuisvoël)

### 4 Speckled Mousebird *Colius striatus*

bbbbbbbb BBBb
J F M A M J J A S O N D

**32 cm; 35–65 g** A warm brown mousebird with a buffy belly and rather broad tail. Face, eyes and upper mandible blackish; lower mandible white. Mantle, rump and breast very finely barred. Legs black in most of region, but dull red or pink in E Zimbabwe and central Mozambique. Darker and browner than *Urocolius*, with weaker flight. Juv. has shorter tail. **Voice:** Dry, harsh 'zhrrik-zhrrik'. **Status and biology:** Common resident and nomad in thicket, riparian woodland and forest edge; also at fruiting trees in gardens. Usually in small flocks. Monogamous or polygamous, often with helpers at the nest. Lays 1–4 eggs (rarely up to 7, probably from 2 females) in an untidy cup nest in a shrub or small tree. **Diet:** Fruit, buds, leaves, flowers, nectar and bark. (Gevlekte Muisvoël)

### 5 White-backed Mousebird *Colius colius*

bbbbbbbb BBBB
J F M A M J J A S O N D

**31 cm; 30–55 g** Paler and greyer than Speckled Mousebird, with bluish-white bill, tipped black, and coral-pink legs. In flight, central back white, bordered by glossy violet stripes (appear black in the field). Juv. has grey rump and blue-green bill with dark lower mandible. **Voice:** Whistling 'zwee we-wit'. **Status and biology:** Common resident of strandveld, coastal fynbos and scrubby areas in semi-desert. Usually in flocks of 3–10. Monogamous, sometimes with helpers at the nest. Lays 1–4 eggs (rarely up to 8, probably from 2 females) in an untidy cup nest in a shrub or small tree. **Diet:** Fruit, leaves, flowers and nectar. (Witrugmuisvoël)

# KINGFISHERS

Birds with long, dagger-like bills, recently split into 3 families. Legs short; toes syndactyl; hunt from perch or while hovering. Some species feed on aquatic prey, plunging into water, but others are terrestrial. Plumage strikingly patterned or coloured; apparently aposematic, because they are foul tasting. Sexes alike in alcenid and dacelonid kingfishers, but differ in cerylid species. Breed in burrows or holes; usually self-excavated. Monogamous or cooperative breeders; both parents incubate and feed the altricial chicks.

## 1 Giant Kingfisher  *Megaceryle maximus*

`b | | | | | | | | b B B B b`
`J F M A M J J A S O N D`

**40–45 cm; 320–440 g** A huge kingfisher with a massive black bill, dark grey, white-spotted upperparts and rufous underparts. Male has chestnut breast, white belly with blackish spots and white underwing coverts. Female has white breast with blackish spots, chestnut belly and chestnut underwing coverts. Juv. male has black-speckled, chestnut breast and white underwings; juv. female has whitish breast and chestnut underwings. **Voice:** Loud, harsh 'kahk-kah-kahk'. **Status and biology:** Common resident at wooded streams and dams, fast-flowing rivers and coastal lagoons. Monogamous and territorial year-round; often with helpers at the nest. Lays 3–5 eggs in a burrow in a bank. **Diet:** Fish, frogs and invertebrates, especially crabs. Usually hunts from exposed perch, but occasionally hovers. (Reusevisvanger)

## 2 Pied Kingfisher  *Ceryle rudis*

`b b b b B B b B B B b`
`J F M A M J J A S O N D`

**23–25 cm; 70–110 g** A large, black-and-white kingfisher, with a long, black bill and short crest. Male has double breast band; female and juv. have a single, incomplete breast band. **Voice:** Rattling twitter; sharp, high-pitched 'chik-chik'. **Status and biology:** Common resident at freshwater wetlands, coastal lagoons and tidal pools. Monogamous, often with helpers at the nest. Lays 4–6 (1–7) eggs in a burrow in a sandbank. **Diet:** Fish and aquatic insects. Frequently feeds by hovering, and forages up to 3 km from land over large lakes. (Bontvisvanger)

## 3 Half-collared Kingfisher  *Alcedo semitorquata*

`b b b | | | b b B B b b`
`J F M A M J J A S O N D`

**18 cm; 35–40 g** A black-billed, aquatic kingfisher with a brilliant blue back and rump. Larger than Malachite Kingfisher, with more subdued crest, blue (not white) cheeks and black (not red) bill (although juv. Malachite Kingfisher also has a dark bill). Juv. duller with black-tipped breast feathers. **Voice:** High-pitched 'chreep' or softer 'peeek-peek'. **Status and biology:** Uncommon resident and nomad at wooded streams, channels in large reedbeds and coastal lagoons. Monogamous; lays 2–5 (rarely 1–6) eggs in a burrow in a bank. **Diet:** Fish, frogs and aquatic invertebrates. (Blouvisvanger)

## 4 Malachite Kingfisher  *Alcedo cristata*

`b b b b b b b b B B B b`
`J F M A M J J A S O N D`

**14 cm; 13–19 g** A small, aquatic kingfisher with a turquoise and black barred crown. Ad. has red bill; slightly larger and in a different habitat from African Pygmy-Kingfisher. Some birds in N have pale bellies. Juv. has black bill and is blackish on back, but is much smaller than Half-collared Kingfisher with rufous (not blue) ear coverts and the diagnostic barred crown. **Voice:** High-pitched 'peep-peep' in flight. **Status and biology:** Common resident and local migrant at lakes and dams, and along streams and lagoons. Monogamous; lays 3–6 eggs in a burrow in a bank. **Diet:** Fish, tadpoles, frogs and aquatic invertebrates. (Kuifkopvisvanger)

## 5 African Pygmy-Kingfisher  *Ispidina picta*

`b b b | | | | | | b B B B`
`J F M A M J J A S O N D`

**12 cm; 12–17 g** A tiny, richly coloured, dry-land kingfisher. Smaller than Malachite Kingfisher, with a mainly rufous face and violet-washed ear coverts. Juv. has blackish bill and diffuse, dark moustachial stripe. **Voice:** High-pitched 'chip-chip' flight note. **Status and biology:** Common intra-African migrant in woodland, savanna and coastal forest. Monogamous; lays 3–6 eggs in a burrow in a bank. **Diet:** Mainly insects and other invertebrates, but occasional lizards and small frogs. (Dwergvisvanger)

## 1 Woodland Kingfisher *Halcyon senegalensis*

B b b | | | | | | b b B
J F M A M J J A S O N D

**22–24 cm; 55–80 g** A striking, blue-backed kingfisher with a red and black bill (rarely all-red). Told from Mangrove Kingfisher by its 2-tone bill, black (not red) legs, black eye-stripe extending behind its eye and paler head with blue wash extending onto the hind crown; underwing all-white. Juv. has dusky reddish-brown bill and is lightly barred grey on sides of breast. **Voice:** Loud, piercing 'chip-cherrrrrrrrrr', latter part a descending trill. Often spreads wings while calling. **Status and biology:** Common intra-African migrant in woodland and savanna with tall trees. Monogamous; lays 2–4 eggs in a hole in a tree, usually an old barbet or woodpecker hole. **Diet:** Large insects, other invertebrates, fish, frogs, lizards, and small snakes, mammals and birds. (Bosveldvisvanger)

## 2 Mangrove Kingfisher *Halcyon senegaloides*

b | | | | | | | | | b b b
J F M A M J J A S O N D

**22–24 cm; 75–90 g** Slightly larger than Woodland Kingfisher with an all-red (not red and black) bill, red (not black) legs, black carpal patch on underwing, and darker grey head. Pale blue back separates it from other *Halcyon* kingfishers. Juv. has brownish bill and dark scaling on its breast. **Voice:** Noisy; loud, ringing 'cheet cheet cheet cheet chroo-choo-chroo-chroo', slower and deeper than Woodland Kingfisher. **Status and biology:** Uncommon local migrant; breeds in coastal forest and riparian thicket; winters in mangrove swamps. Monogamous; lays 2–5 eggs in a burrow in a bank. **Diet:** Similar to Woodland Kingfisher. (Manglietvisvanger)

## 3 Brown-hooded Kingfisher *Halcyon albiventris*

b b b b | | | | b B B b
J F M A M J J A S O N D

**20–22 cm; 50–75 g** Differs from other red-billed *Halcyon* kingfishers by its brownish head streaked with black, rufous patches on sides of breast, and streaked flanks. Larger than Striped Kingfisher, with all-red (not black and red) bill, and lacks white in upper- or underwing. Male has black back; female and juv. have brown back. **Voice:** Whistled 'tyi-tu-tu-tu-tu'; harsher 'klee-klee-klee' alarm note. **Status and biology:** Common resident in woodland, coastal forest, parks and gardens. Monogamous; lays 2–5 eggs in a burrow in a bank. **Diet:** Large insects, other invertebrates, fish, frogs, lizards, and small snakes, mammals and birds. (Bruinkopvisvanger)

## 4 Grey-headed Kingfisher *Halcyon leucocephala*

■ ■ ■ ■ ■ ■ ■ | | | b B B b
J F M A M J J A S O N D

**20–22 cm; 38–48 g** A striking kingfisher with a pale grey head and chestnut belly and underwing coverts. Juv. has a blackish bill and buffy barred head and underparts; lacks streaking on head and flanks of Brown-hooded Kingfisher. **Voice:** High-pitched, rapid 'chee-chi-chi-chi-chi'. **Status and biology:** Locally common intra-African migrant in broadleafed woodland and savanna. Monogamous; lays 3–4 eggs in a burrow in a bank; rarely in a woodpecker hole. **Diet:** Grasshoppers and other insects, arachnids, lizards, mice and occasional fish and frogs. (Gryskopvisvanger)

## 5 Striped Kingfisher *Halcyon chelicuti*

b b | | | | | | | | b B B b
J F M A M J J A S O N D

**16–18 cm; 30–50 g** A small, dry-land kingfisher with a grey-streaked crown, black and red bill and white collar. Smaller than Brown-hooded Kingfisher, with a darker cap and white collar. In flight, shows extensive white on underwing, white flash in upperwing, and blue rump. Male has black band across underwing, which female lacks. Juv. has dusky bill and blackish, scaled breast and flanks. **Voice:** High-pitched, piercing 'cheer-cherrrrrrrrr', rising and falling in pitch and ending in a trill. **Status and biology:** Common resident in acacia woodland, savanna, and edges of riverine forest. Monogamous; lays 2–6 eggs in a hole in a tree (often an old woodpecker or barbet nest), natural cavity or swallow nest. **Diet:** Grasshoppers and other insects; occasional lizards, snakes and mice. (Gestreepte Visvanger)

# BEE-EATERS

Colourful, aerial insectivores with long, decurved bills. Sally from perches or during longer flights. Legs small and weak; shuffle on ground. Sexes alike, but juvs and ads in worn plumage duller. Monogamous or cooperative breeders; both parents incubate and feed the altricial chicks. Breed in burrows or holes; usually self-excavated.

### 1 European Bee-eater *Merops apiaster*

J F M A M J J A S O N D

**25 cm (28 cm incl. streamers); 40–66 g** A large, distinctively coloured bee-eater with a chestnut crown and back, golden mantle, yellow throat and blue breast and belly. Local br. birds are more intensely coloured. Juv. lacks elongate central tail, and has a green back and faded underparts. **Voice:** Far-carrying, frog-like flight call, 'prrrup' or 'krroop-krroop'. **Status and biology:** Common Palearctic migrant Sep–Mar and intra-African migrant breeding in SW South Africa Aug–Feb. Occurs in savanna, broadleafed woodland, fynbos and adjacent grassy areas. Breeds in small colonies, laying 2–6 eggs in a burrow in a low bank. **Diet:** Aerial insects. (Europese Byvreter)

### 2 Blue-cheeked Bee-eater *Merops persicus*

J F M A M J J A S O N D

**25 cm (33 cm incl. streamers); 40–54 g** A large, green bee-eater. Slightly larger than Madagascar Bee-eater, with green (not brown) crown, blue (not white) frons, supercilium and cheek stripe, and yellow (not whitish) chin; rufous throat patch smaller. In worn plumage, blue facial stripes appear white, causing potential confusion with Madagascar Bee-eater; in such birds, green (not brown) crown is key to identification. Juv. duller; lacks tail streamers. **Voice:** Liquid 'prrrup' and 'prrreo', slightly higher-pitched than European Bee-eater. **Status and biology:** Common Palearctic migrant to flood plains and adjacent woodland. **Diet:** Aerial insects. (Blouwangbyvreter)

### 3 Madagascar (Olive) Bee-eater *Merops superciliosus*

J F M A M J J A S O N D

**24 cm (30 cm incl. streamers); 38–48 g** Slightly smaller than Blue-cheeked Bee-eater, with a brown (not green) crown, white (not blue) supercilium and cheek stripe, whitish (not yellow) chin, more extensive rufous throat and paler green underparts. NW Namibia *M. s. alternans* has crown washed green; best told by brownish throat. Juv. duller; lacks tail streamers. **Voice:** High-pitched 'pit-ilup', higher than Blue-cheeked Bee-eater. **Status and biology:** Locally common intra-African migrant in broadleafed woodland near lakes, rivers and swamps. Breeds in small colonies, laying 2–4 eggs in a burrow in a bank. Resident locally in Mozambique. **Diet:** Aerial insects. (Olyfbyvreter)

### 4 White-fronted Bee-eater *Merops bullockoides*

J F M A M J J A S O N D

**22–24 cm; 30–40 g** A mainly green bee-eater with a crimson throat, white cheek stripe and frons, and striking blue rump, thighs and vent; lacks elongated central tail streamers. Juv. duller with a green crown. **Voice:** Querulous 'qerrr' or 'querry', like that of Greater Blue-eared Starling; twittering noises when roosting. **Status and biology:** Common resident in grassland and savanna, usually near rivers and wetlands. Breeds colonially, often with helpers at the nest. Lays 2–5 eggs in a burrow in a bank. **Diet:** Flying insects; takes most prey in air or from foliage; occasionally from the ground. (Rooikeelbyvreter)

## 1 Southern Carmine Bee-eater *Merops nubicoides*

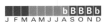
J F M A M J J A S O N D

**26 cm (38 cm incl. streamers); 52–75 g** A bright red bee-eater with a black eye-stripe, blue crown, rump and belly and elongated, blackish central tail feathers. Juv. duller with browner back; lacks an elongated central tail streamer. **Voice:** Rather nasal, deep 'terk, terk'. **Status and biology:** Common intra-African migrant in woodland, savanna and flood plains. Breeds colonially, laying 2–5 eggs in a burrow in a riverbank. **Diet:** Flying insects, rarely small fish. Often attends grass fires. (Rooiborsbyvreter)

## 2 Rosy Bee-eater *Merops malimbicus*

**12–14 cm; 45 g** Rare vagrant. A fairly large bee-eater, with slate-grey upperparts and rosy-pink underparts; told from Southern Carmine Bee-eater by its uniform, slate-grey upperparts and whitish cheek stripe. Ad. has elongate central tail feathers. Juv. is duller. **Voice:** Trilling 'prrp-prrp', higher-pitched than European Bee-eater. **Status and biology:** A tropical forest species that occurs from the Congo Basin to Ghana; only 1 record from sthn Africa: Cape Recife, E Cape, Apr 2003. Possibility of an escapee cannot be excluded. **Diet:** Aerial insects. (Pienkborsbyvreter)

## 3 White-throated Bee-eater *Merops albicollis*

**20 cm (32 cm incl. streamers); 22–30 g** Rare vagrant. A slender bee-eater with a distinctive black-and-white striped head, black breast band and blue-green upperparts. Ad. has very long central tail streamers. Juv. duller green, lightly scalloped above; lacks tail streamers. **Voice:** Mellow 'terruw-uw' or 'tsip-tsip-terruwuw'. **Status and biology:** Vagrant; intra-African migrant in semi-arid and mesic savanna further N in Africa; scattered records throughout sthn Africa. **Diet:** Mainly aerial insects; occasional lizards and fruit. (Witkeelbyvreter)

## 4 Swallow-tailed Bee-eater *Merops hirundineus*

bb  bBBBb
J F M A M J J A S O N D

**20–22 cm; 15–28 g** The only bee-eater with a deeply forked tail. Blue tail and belly are also distinctive among small, green bee-eaters. Juv. duller with buffy throat and green underparts; lacks a blue collar; tail less deeply forked. **Voice:** Soft, twittering 'kwit-kwit-kwit'. **Status and biology:** Common nomad and local migrant in a wide range of habitats from semi-desert scrub to forest margins. Breeds singly or in small colonies, laying 2–4 eggs in a burrow in a low bank. **Diet:** Aerial insects. (Swaelstertbyvreter)

## 5 Böhm's Bee-eater *Merops boehmi*

**18–22 cm; 15–20 g** Rare vagrant. A small, slender bee-eater with brown crown and throat, neat blue cheek stripe and very long central tail streamers. Smaller than Madagascar Bee-eater (p. 238), with dark tail tip and neater head pattern, lacking white stripes. Juv. duller with yellowy green throat; central tail feathers shorter. **Voice:** Soft, high-pitched 'sip'; song a whistled 'swee-deedle-ee-dee jeep'. **Status and biology:** Vagrant from N of Zambezi in Mozambique. **Diet:** Insects; takes some prey on the ground. (Roeskopbyvreter)

## 6 Little Bee-eater *Merops pusillus*

bb  bBBBb
J F M A M J J A S O N D

**15–17 cm; 11–18 g** A tiny, green-backed bee-eater with a yellow throat, black collar and rufous underparts. In flight, shows conspicuous rufous flight feathers with dark trailing edge; underwings are entirely rufous. Central tail green; rest of tail is rufous with black tip. Juv. has paler, buffy throat and lacks a black collar. **Voice:** 'Zeet-zeet' or 'chip-chip'. **Status and biology:** Common resident in savanna, woodland, forest edges and around wetlands. Usually in pairs or small groups. Breeds singly; pairs remain together year-round. Lays 2–6 eggs in a burrow in a bank. **Diet:** Aerial insects. (Kleinbyvreter)

# ROLLERS

**Brightly coloured, medium-sized birds with robust bills. Hunt from perches, dropping to ground or taking prey in the air. Legs short with syndactyl toes. Sexes alike. Monogamous, solitary breeders, sometimes with helpers at the nest. Both parents incubate and feed the altricial chicks.**

## 1 Lilac-breasted Roller *Coracias caudatus*

**29 cm (37 cm incl. streamers); 90–135 g**  Ad. distinctive with pointed tail streamers, turquoise crown and lilac breast. Streamers lost during winter moult, but crown and breast distinctive. Juv. duller; lacks elongated tail feathers; best told from juv. European Roller by smaller head and bill and blue (not black) flight feathers. Told from juv. Racket-tailed Roller by blue (not brown) median wing coverts and uniformly dark blue flight feathers (lacking pale blue bases). **Voice:** Harsh 'chak', often repeated when aroused. **Status and biology:** Common resident in savanna. Perches conspicuously, often along telephone lines. Lays 2–4 eggs in a hole in a tree or termite mound. **Diet:** Insects and occasional small vertebrates. (Gewone Troupant)

## 2 Racket-tailed Roller *Coracias spatulatus*

**29 cm (36 cm incl. streamers); 80–115 g**  Ad. tail is diagnostic, but moulting ad. (winter) and juv. lack diagnostic spatulate tail streamers. At all ages has brown back extending onto median coverts (blue in European and Lilac-breasted rollers) and pale blue wing bar formed by pale bases to flight feathers (uniformly black in European Roller, dark blue in Lilac-breasted Roller). Also lacks sharp demarcation between brownish back and greenish hind neck. **Voice:** 'Chaw' and 'cheer'; less harsh than other rollers. **Status and biology:** Uncommon resident and nomad in tall woodland, especially miombo. Unobtrusive; often perches just below the canopy. Lays 2–3 eggs in a tree hole. **Diet:** Insects and occasional small vertebrates. (Knopsterttroupant)

## 3 European Roller *Coracias garrulus*

**30–32 cm; 105–150 g**  A large, stocky roller with a square tail lacking tail streamers. Larger than Lilac-breasted and Racket-tailed rollers, with a bigger head and bill; flight feathers blackish (not blue) from above. Often in rather scruffy plumage, but ad. has bluish head separated from brown back. Juv. is more olive-green with pinkish wash on throat; told from juv. Lilac-breasted Roller by larger head and black flight feathers. **Voice:** Normally silent in Africa; dry 'krask-kraak' when alarmed. **Status and biology: NEAR-THREATENED.** Common Palearctic migrant to savanna; rare in more open habitats. **Diet:** Large insects and occasional small vertebrates. (Europese Troupant)

## 4 Purple Roller *Coracias naevius*

**35–40 cm; 130–210 g**  A large roller with a broad, whitish supercilium, greenish crown and lilac underparts streaked with white. Juv. duller, more greeny-brown than purple. **Voice:** Harsh, repeated 'karaa-karaa' in display flight, accompanied by exaggerated, side-to-side, rocking motion. **Status and biology:** Fairly common resident and partial migrant in dry thornveld and open, broadleafed woodland. Lays 2–4 eggs in a tree cavity. **Diet:** Large insects and small vertebrates, mainly taken on the ground. (Groottroupant)

## 5 Broad-billed Roller *Eurystomus glaucurus*

**27–29 cm; 85–135 g**  A compact, cinnamon and purple roller with a bright yellow bill. Juv. duller, with browner upperparts and underparts mottled greyish; bill duller yellow. **Voice:** Harsh screams 'garrr' and cackles 'kek-kek-kek'. **Status and biology:** Locally common intra-African migrant to riverine forest and adjacent savanna. Lays 2–4 eggs in a hole in a tall tree. **Diet:** Mainly aerial insects, especially termite alates. (Geelbektroupant)

# GROUND-HORNBILLS

Huge, terrestrial hornbills with mostly black plumage and striking white primaries. Sexes differ in facial ornamentation; males larger than females. Monogamous, often with helpers at the nest. Breed in holes in trees or among rocks. Incubation by female only. Chicks altricial.

### 1 Southern Ground-Hornbill *Bucorvus leadbeateri*

| b | | | | | | | | | b | b | B | B | b |
|---|---|---|---|---|---|---|---|---|---|---|---|---|---|
| J | F | M | A | M | J | J | A | S | O | N | D | | |

**90–130 cm; 2.5–6 kg** A large, turkey-sized black bird with a long, decurved bill and conspicuous red face and throat; white primaries obvious in flight. Ad. female has small blue throat and extensive red neck pouches. Juv. has dull yellowish face and throat. **Voice:** Loud, booming 'ooomph ooomph' early in the morning. **Status and biology:** Scarce resident and nomad in savanna, woodland and grassland with adjoining forest. Now mainly confined to large reserves and national parks. Occurs in family groups. Lays 1–2 (rarely 3) eggs in a cavity in a large tree or among rocks. Usually only 1 chick survives. **Diet:** Large insects, snails, frogs, lizards, snakes, tortoises, birds and mammals up to the size of young hares. (Bromvoël)

# HORNBILLS

Noisy, medium to large long-tailed birds with characteristic long, deep, decurved bills, often with casques. Most species have striking plumage. Sexes usually similar, although females are smaller and have smaller casques. Monogamous; females are cemented into the nest during incubation and part of the nestling period; moult all their feathers in some species. Chicks altricial.

### 2 Silvery-cheeked Hornbill *Bycanistes brevis*

| b | b | b | b | | | | | b | B | B | b |
|---|---|---|---|---|---|---|---|---|---|---|---|
| J | F | M | A | M | J | J | A | S | O | N | D |

**60–80 cm; 1.1–1.4 kg** A large, black-and-white hornbill with predominantly black wings (unlike Trumpeter Hornbill). Lower belly, back and outer tail tips are white, but breast black. Male has huge, creamy casque; female and juv. have much reduced casque. Cheek feathers of ads have silvery tips, giving pale-faced appearance. Flight heavy and noisy compared to Trumpeter Hornbill. **Voice:** Deep wail; harsh 'quark-quark' and nasal 'wheeer-eer' calls. **Status and biology:** Fairly common resident and local nomad in montane and coastal forests. Lays 1–2 eggs in a tree cavity. **Diet:** Figs and other fruit, flowers, and small animals, including bats and bird eggs and chicks. (Kuifkopboskraai)

### 3 Trumpeter Hornbill *Bycanistes bucinator*

| b | | | | | | | | | b | B | B | b |
|---|---|---|---|---|---|---|---|---|---|---|---|---|
| J | F | M | A | M | J | J | A | S | O | N | D |

**50–65 cm; 480–900 g** A medium-large, black-and-white hornbill with a white belly and lower breast. Smaller than Silvery-cheeked Hornbill, with smaller, darker casque and darker bill. In flight, has white trailing edges to its wings and white underwing coverts; uppertail coverts white, but rump and back black. At close range, has pinkish-red (not blue) eye skin. Female has smaller bill and casque. Juv. has almost no casque. **Voice:** Wailing, plaintive 'waaaaa-weeeee-waaaaa'. **Status and biology:** Common resident and local nomad in lowland, coastal and riverine evergreen forests. Lays 2–4 eggs in a tree or rock cavity. **Diet:** Fruits, flowers, invertebrates and bird eggs and chicks. (Gewone Boskraai)

## 1 Bradfield's Hornbill *Tockus bradfieldi*

bb | | | | | | | bbBb
J F M A M J J A S O N D

**50–57 cm; 180–340 g** Paler brown than Crowned Hornbill, with a longer, orange-red bill without a distinct casque; lacks yellow line at base of bill and has a red (not yellow) eye. Differs from Monteiro's Hornbill in having no white in wings and mainly brown (not white) outer tail feathers. Female has a smaller bill, with turquoise (not black) facial skin. Juv. has smaller bill. **Voice:** Rapidly repeated, whistling 'chleeoo' note, with bill raised vertically. **Status and biology:** Near-endemic. Fairly common resident in open mopane woodland and mixed thornveld. Lays 3 eggs in a tree cavity. **Diet:** Mainly insects, other invertebrates, seeds and fruit; occasional small vertebrates. (Bradfieldneushoringvoël)

## 2 Monteiro's Hornbill *Tockus monteiri*

bBBb | | | | | | | bbb
J F M A M J J A S O N D

**50–58 cm; 280–420 g** A brown hornbill with a large red bill. White-spotted (not uniform) wing coverts, and white (not dark) secondaries and outer tail separate it from Bradfield's Hornbill. Female has smaller bill and turquoise (not blackish) facial skin. Juv. has smaller, dull orange bill and pink facial skin. **Voice:** Croaking series of 'tooaak tooaak' notes, uttered with head lowered and wings closed. **Status and biology:** Common resident and local nomad in dry thornveld and broadleafed woodland. Lays 2–6 (rarely 8) eggs in a tree or rock cavity. **Diet:** Insects, other invertebrates, frogs, lizards, bird eggs and chicks, seeds, fruit and bulbs. (Monteironeushoringvoël)

## 3 Crowned Hornbill *Tockus alboterminatus*

b | | | | | | | | bBBb
J F M A M J J A S O N D

**50–54 cm; 180–330 g** A dark brown hornbill with a white belly and a long, red bill. Darker brown than Bradfield's Hornbill, with a yellow (not red) eye, a shorter, deeper red bill with a yellow line at base, and more extensive white tips to outer tail. Male has a large casque and black facial skin; female a smaller casque and a turquoise face. Juv. has an orange bill that lacks a casque. Flight is extremely undulating. **Voice:** Whistling 'chleeoo chleeoo'. **Status and biology:** Common resident and local nomad in dry season. Occurs in coastal and riverine forests, often in flocks. Lays 3–4 (2–5) eggs in a tree cavity. **Diet:** Insects, other invertebrates, frogs, lizards, seeds and fruit. (Gekroonde Neushoringvoël)

## 4 African Grey Hornbill *Tockus nasutus*

bbb | | | | | | bBBB
J F M A M J J A S O N D

**44–50 cm; 130–220 g** A drab, brown hornbill with a creamy supercilium and narrow whitish back, visible in flight. Wings are brown, with narrow pale feather edges; outer tail tips white. Male has dark grey bill with creamy stripe at base of upper mandible. Upper part of female's bill is pale yellow; tip is maroon. Juv's bill lacks a casque. **Voice:** Plaintive, whistling 'pee pee pee pee phee pheeoo phee pheeoo', with bill held vertically and wings flicked open on each note. **Status and biology:** Common resident in acacia savanna and dry, broadleafed woodland. Lays 3–4 eggs in a tree or rock cavity. **Diet:** Insects, other invertebrates, small vertebrates, fruit and seeds. (Grysneushoringvoël)

## 5 Southern Yellow-billed Hornbill *Tockus leucomelas*

BBb | | | | | | bBBB
J F M A M J J A S O N D

**48–60 cm; 145–230 g** Yellow bill, spotted wing coverts and pale underparts are diagnostic. In flight has white inner secondaries and outer tail like Southern Red-billed and Damara hornbills. Female and juv. have smaller bills and shorter casques. **Voice:** Rapid, hollow-sounding 'tok tok tok tok tok tokatokatoka', uttered with head lowered and wings fanned. **Status and biology:** Near-endemic. Common resident in thornveld and dry, broadleafed woodland. Lays 2–6 eggs in a tree cavity. **Diet:** Insects, other invertebrates, small vertebrates, fruit, seeds and leaves. (Geelbekneushoringvoël)

## 6 Southern Red-billed Hornbill *Tockus erythrorhynchus*

bbb | | | | | | bBBB
J F M A M J J A S O N D

**38–45 cm; 100–170 g** A fairly small hornbill with rather short, red bill. White-spotted wing coverts, pale face and white (not brown) throat are diagnostic, apart from very similar Damara Hornbill in N Namibia; differs from that bird by having brown-streaked (not white) facial feathers and pale yellow (not dark) eye. Male has black patch at base of lower mandible; female has smaller, all-red bill. Juv. has grey eyes, a smaller bill with a black patch at the base, and buff (not white) spotting on the back and wing coverts. **Voice:** A long series of 'kuk kuk kuk' calls, becoming faster and louder, ending with double notes 'kuk-we kuk-we'. Does not raise its wings during its display. **Status and biology:** Locally common in savanna and semi-arid woodland. Lays 2–5 (rarely up to 7) eggs in a tree cavity. **Diet:** Insects and other invertebrates; occasional small vertebrates, seeds and fruit. (Rooibekneushoringvoël)

## 7 Damara Hornbill *Tockus damarensis*

BB | | | | | | | | | |
J F M A M J J A S O N D

**40–50 cm; 180–230 g** Slightly larger than Southern Red-billed Hornbill, with a rather plain white head and neck, and typically has brown (not yellow) eyes. Wings are partly opened by male in display. White (not dark) face and breast, more boldly spotted upperwing coverts and relatively small bill separate it from Monteiro's Hornbill. Female and juv. have less black on lower mandible; juv. has grey eyes. **Voice:** Staccato 'kwa kwa kwa kokkok kokkok kokkok'. **Status and biology:** Near-endemic. Locally common in savanna and semi-arid woodland, often in hilly areas. Lays 3–8 eggs in a tree cavity. Hybridises with Red-billed Hornbill. **Diet:** Insects and other invertebrates; occasional small vertebrates. (Damararooibekneushoringvoël)

# TROGONS

Brightly coloured, long-tailed forest birds with short, broad bills and short legs with rather weak, syndactyl toes. Sexes differ. Monogamous; both parents usually incubate and feed the altricial chicks.

## 1 Narina Trogon *Apaloderma narina*

b b | | | | | | | | b B B
J F M A M J J A S O N D

**30–34 cm; 55–70 g** A squat, long-tailed forest bird that often sits quietly in mid-storey and can be hard to locate if not calling. Male bright green with crimson belly and waxy yellow bill. Female duller with rufous-brown face merging into greyer breast and dull crimson belly. Juv. paler than female. **Voice:** Deep, hoarse 'hoo hook', with emphasis on second syllable, repeated 6–10 times; wags tail slightly downwards when calling. **Status and biology:** Fairly common resident and nomad in forest, dense woodland and thickets. Lays 2–4 eggs in a hole in a dead tree stump. **Diet:** Caterpillars, other invertebrates and occasional lizards. Flies from perch to capture prey, mainly among foliage. (Bosloerie)

# HOOPOES, WOOD-HOOPOES AND SCIMITARBILLS

Three families with long, decurved beaks used for probing out invertebrates. Hoopoes strikingly plumaged black, white and buff with an erectile crest; wood-hoopoes and scimitarbills more sombre, although plumage often glossy. All produce foul-smelling secretions from their uropygial glands to deter predators. Breed singly. Monogamous or cooperative breeders; females incubate, fed by males; both parents feed the altricial chicks.

## 2 Green Wood-Hoopoe *Phoeniculus purpureus*

b b B B B b b b B B B b
J F M A M J J A S O N D

**32–36 cm; 60–90 g** A glossy green wood-hoopoe, with a long, decurved, red bill, red legs, white wing bars and long tail with white subterminal bars in outer feathers. In good light, bottle-green head and back distinguish it from Violet Wood-Hoopoe. Male has longer and more decurved bill than female. Juv. lacks glossy plumage and has a black bill; red legs and feet separate it from Common Scimitarbill, but hard to separate from juv. Violet Wood-hoopoe. Juv. male has a brown throat patch; juv. female black. **Voice:** Garrulous chattering and cackling, usually by groups. **Status and biology:** Common resident in woodland, thicket and forest edges. Breeds cooperatively where nest cavities are scarce. Lays 2–4 (rarely 5) eggs in a cavity, normally in a tree. **Diet:** Mainly insects and other invertebrates; also small vertebrates, fruit and nectar. (Rooibekkakelaar)

## 3 Violet Wood-Hoopoe *Phoeniculus damarensis*

b b b | | | | | | | | b
J F M A M J J A S O N D

**34–40 cm; 76–94 g** Larger than Green Wood-Hoopoe with a distinctly longer tail that flops around more in flight; in good light the violet (not bottle-green) head, mantle and back can be seen. Female has a shorter, less decurved bill than male. Juv. lacks gloss on plumage; bill black; male has a brown throat patch; female black. **Voice:** Harsh cackling, slightly slower and deeper than Green Wood-Hoopoe. **Status and biology:** Fairly common resident in dry thornveld and mopane woodland. Lays 4–5 eggs in a tree hole. Hybridises with Green Wood-Hoopoe. **Diet:** Insects and small lizards. (Perskakelaar)

## 4 Common Scimitarbill *Rhinopomastus cyanomelas*

b b | | | | | | b B B B b
J F M A M J J A S O N D

**24–28 cm; 25–40 g** Resembles a small, slender wood-hoopoe with a black, sickle-shaped bill and black (not red) legs and feet. White bars on primaries and white tips to outer tail feathers visible in flight, but lacks white primary coverts of wood-hoopoes. Male glossy black; female and juv. have brownish head and shorter bill. **Voice:** Fairly high-pitched, whistling 'sweep-sweep-sweep'; harsher chattering. **Status and biology:** Common resident of dry savanna and open, broadleafed woodland. Lays 2–4 eggs in a tree cavity, often an old woodpecker or barbet hole. **Diet:** Insects, occasionally nectar. (Swartbekkakelaar)

## 5 African Hoopoe *Upupa africana*

b b | | | | | | b B B B b
J F M A M J J A S O N D

**25–28 cm; 40–60 g** Unmistakable, with its long, decurved bill, cinnamon, black and white plumage and long, black-tipped crest that is raised when the bird is alarmed. Flight buoyant on broad, rounded wings. Female duller with less white in the base of the secondaries. Juv. dull buff below, with a shorter bill and buff tinge to white wing bars. **Voice:** 'Hoop-oop' or 'hoop-oop-oop', typically all notes at same pitch. **Status and biology:** Common resident and local nomad in savanna, broadleafed woodland, parks and gardens. Lays 4–7 eggs in a natural cavity or old woodpecker hole. **Diet:** Insects and insect larvae. Probes in ground for prey. (Hoephoep)

# HONEYGUIDES AND HONEYBIRDS

Rather drab, olive-brown or grey-brown birds. Could be confused with various passerines, but erect stance, undulating flight and prominent white outer tail feathers are distinctive. Sexes alike, except Greater Honeyguide. Honeyguides have stubby bills; feed on bees and wax, and at least one species guides predators to beehives. Honeybirds have slender bills and feed on insects. All are obligate brood parasites. Chicks altricial; cared for by unwitting hosts.

## 1 Greater Honeyguide *Indicator indicator*

b | | b | | | | | b B B B
J F M A M J J A S O N D

**18–20 cm; 40–54 g** A large, grey-brown honeyguide. Ad. has pale edges to wing coverts and olive shoulders. Male is distinctive with a pink bill, black throat and white ear patches. Female lacks a well-marked head and has a dark bill; plain breast and pale edges to wing coverts separate it from Scaly-throated Honeyguide. Juv. is plain brown above, with yellowish throat and breast. **Voice:** Ringing, repeated 'whit-purr' or 'vic-tor' from a regularly used site high in a tree; guiding call when leading to a hive is a harsh, rattling chatter. **Status and biology:** Locally fairly common resident and nomad in woodland, savanna and plantations; avoids forests. Brood parasite of hole-nesting species, incl. African Hoopoe, wood-hoopoes, woodpeckers, barbets, kingfishers, bee-eaters, starlings, tits and swallows. **Diet:** Beeswax, eggs and larvae, termite alates and other insects. (Grootheuningwyser)

## 2 Scaly-throated Honeyguide *Indicator variegatus*

b | | | | | | | | b b b b
J F M A M J J A S O N D

**19 cm; 40–55 g** A large, olive-backed honeyguide with a streaked throat and mottled breast. Base of lower bill pinkish, like Lesser Honeyguide, but is larger and lacks moustachial stripes. Mottled breast and greenish back lacking white feather edgings separate it from female Greater Honeyguide. Juv. has greener throat and breast, mottled with dark spots. **Voice:** Insect-like, ventriloquistic trill, 'trrrrrrrr', rising in pitch and lasting 3–4 seconds, repeated at 1–2-minute intervals; calls from within canopy, often returning to same perch. **Status and biology:** Uncommon to locally common resident of forest and dense woodland. Brood parasite of woodpeckers and barbets. **Diet:** Beeswax, eggs and larvae, other insects and occasional fruit. (Gevlekte Heuningwyser)

## 3 Lesser Honeyguide *Indicator minor*

b b | | | | | | | b B B B
J F M A M J J A S O N D

**15 cm; 25–35 g** Medium-sized honeyguide with short, stubby bill, unlike the thin bills of honey-birds. Resembles grey-headed sparrows, but has white outer tail and streaked, olive wings. Ad. has pale loral stripes and indistinct, dark moustachial stripes. Juv. darker below; lacks moustachial stripes. **Voice:** 'Teuu, frip frip frip...', repeated 12–30 times at short intervals; same call-site is used regularly. **Status and biology:** Common resident in well-wooded habitats from forest to dense savanna; has adapted to suburban gardens. Brood parasite of barbets, and possibly woodpeckers, petronias, wrynecks, starlings and kingfishers. **Diet:** Beeswax, eggs, larvae, and other insects (Kleinheuningwyser)

## 4 Pallid Honeyguide *Indicator meliphilus*

■ ■ ■ ■ ■ ■ ■ ■ ■ b b
J F M A M J J A S O N D

**13 cm; 12–18 g** Resembles a small Lesser Honeyguide, but has a more greenish head and nape, a faintly streaked throat, and a decidedly smaller bill. Lacks moustache of ad. Lesser Honeyguide. Short, thick bill eliminates confusion with honeybirds. **Voice:** Repeated, high-pitched whistled 'whit whit whit...', slower than Lesser Honeyguide. **Status and biology:** Uncommon resident of forest and dense woodland. Brood parasite of White-eared Barbet and probably of tinkerbirds. **Diet:** Beeswax, eggs and larvae, and other insects. (Oostelike Heuningwyser)

## 5 Green-backed Honeybird *Prodotiscus zambesiae*

■ ■ ■ ■ ■ ■ ■ ■ ■ b B B
J F M A M J J A S O N D

**12 cm; 9–11 g** Formerly known as Slender-billed Honeyguide. Slightly smaller and more stocky than Brown-backed Honeybird, with shorter tail and greenish wash on back and rump. Head appears rounded, with large, dark eye. Fluffs out white sides of rump in display. Juv. is paler and greyer, with buffy wash on breast. **Voice:** Repeated 'skeeaa' in display flight; also rapid chattering and 'pee-ee-it' song. **Status and biology:** Uncommon to locally common resident of miombo and other broadleafed woodland. Brood parasite of Yellow White-eyes, flycatchers and sunbirds. **Diet:** Scale insects, other insects and occasional fruit. Active forager, taking insects in air or gleaning from leaves. Regularly joins bird parties. (Dunbekheuningvoël)

## 6 Brown-backed Honeybird *Prodotiscus regulus*

b | | | | | | | | | B b
J F M A M J J A S O N D

**13 cm; 12–17 g** Formerly known as Sharp-billed Honeyguide. A drab, grey-brown honeyguide with a fine bill that superficially resembles Dusky or Spotted flycatchers (p. 340), but has diagnostic extensive white outer tail. Brown back distinguishes it from Green-backed Honeybird, and sharp, slender bill distinguishes it from honeyguides. In display, fluffs out white feathers on sides of rump. Ad. has dark tips to outer tail; completely white in juv. Juv. paler; washed yellow below. **Voice:** Dry, insect-like churring 'chre-e-e-e-e-e-e-e-e-e-e-e' when perched; metallic 'zwick' during dipping display flight. **Status and biology:** Uncommon to locally common resident and nomad in woodland, savanna, forest edge and plantations. Brood parasite of cisticolas and warblers. **Diet:** Scale insects, aphids, other insects and occasional beeswax. (Skerpbekheuningvoël)

# BARBETS AND TINKERBIRDS

Mainly frugivorous birds with large, robust bills used to dig cavities in dead wood for roosting and breeding. Legs robust; toes zygodactyl. Flight direct, often with noisy wing beats. Sexes alike in most species. Monogamous or cooperative breeders. Both parents excavate nests and incubate and feed the altricial chicks.

## 1 Green Barbet *Stactolaema divacea*

| B | | | | | | | | | | b | B |
|---|---|---|---|---|---|---|---|---|---|---|---|
| J | F | M | A | M | J | J | A | S | O | N | D |

**17 cm; 40–60 g** A chunky, olive-green barbet confined to Ngoye Forest, inland from Mtunzini; other races occur in montane forests of East Africa. Slightly paler below, with a darker head and yellow-green ear coverts in sthn Africa. Underwing coverts yellowish-white. In flight, has pale primary bases. Larger, darker and more heavily built than Green Tinkerbird (p. 254). Juv. duller with yellow bare skin on face; lacks yellow ear coverts. **Voice:** Hollow, repetitive 'tjop tjop tjop'; regularly duets. **Status and biology:** Previously considered part of the Green Barbet *S. olivacea* complex, but genetic evidence suggests it is best treated as a separate species. Lays 5 eggs in a cavity excavated in a dead vertical trunk. **Diet:** Figs and other fruit; occasional insects and other invertebrates. (Groenhoutkapper)

## 2 Whyte's Barbet *Stactolaema whytii*

| b | | | | | | | | | B | B | b | b |
|---|---|---|---|---|---|---|---|---|---|---|---|---|
| J | F | M | A | M | J | J | A | S | O | N | D |

**16 cm; 40–55 g** A brown barbet with a prominent white wing panel, pale belly and diagnostic yellowish frons and lores, extending below and behind eye. Bases of outer primaries are white, giving a small, second white panel in folded wing. Juv. has pale base to bill and less extensive yellow on face. **Voice:** Deep hooting call, repeated 1–2 times per second. **Status and biology:** Locally common resident and nomad in miombo woodland and riverine forest, usually near fig trees. Monogamous, but often with helpers at the nest. Lays 3–6 eggs in a cavity excavated in a dead branch. **Diet:** Figs and other fruit; also insects, other invertebrates and nectar. (Geelbleshoutkapper)

## 3 Black-collared Barbet *Lybius torquatus*

| b | b | b | b | | | b | b | B | B | B |
|---|---|---|---|---|---|---|---|---|---|---|
| J | F | M | A | M | J | J | A | S | O | N | D |

**18–20 cm; 48–62 g** A fairly large barbet with a bright red face and throat, broadly bordered with black. Rare yellow morph has yellow face and throat **(3 A)**. Juv. has a dark brown head and throat, streaked with orange and red. **Voice:** Duet that starts with harsh 'krrr krrrr', followed by ringing 'tooo puudly tooo puudly', the 'tooo' being higher-pitched. **Status and biology:** Common resident in forest, woodland, savanna and gardens. Often has helpers at the nest; lays 2–5 eggs in a cavity excavated in a dead branch. **Diet:** Mainly fruits; also insects and nectar. (Rooikophoutkapper)

## 4 White-eared Barbet *Stactolaema leucotis*

| B | b | b | b | | | b | b | B | B |
|---|---|---|---|---|---|---|---|---|---|
| J | F | M | A | M | J | J | A | S | O | N | D |

**18 cm; 48–60 g** A dark brown barbet with a blackish head and prominent white ear-stripes and belly. Juv. has paler base to bill. **Voice:** Loud, twittering 'treee treeetee teeetree'; harsher 'waa waa' notes. **Status and biology:** Common resident in coastal forest and bush, often near wetlands. Moves to lower altitudes in winter in E Zimbabwe. Usually in groups; monogamous, but often with helpers at the nest. Lays 3–6 eggs in a cavity excavated in a dead branch. **Diet:** Figs and other fruit; also insects, especially when feeding chicks, and nectar. (Witoorhoutkapper)

## 5 Crested Barbet *Trachyphonus vaillantii*

| B | B | b | b | b | b | b | b | b | B | B | B |
|---|---|---|---|---|---|---|---|---|---|---|---|---|
| J | F | M | A | M | J | J | A | S | O | N | D |

**24 cm; 60–80 g** The only *Trachyphonus* barbet in sthn Africa, with a distinctive shaggy crest and black, yellow and red plumage. Juv. is browner and duller. **Voice:** Male utters sustained trilling 'trrrrrrrr'; female responds with repeated 'puka-puka'. **Status and biology:** Common resident in woodland, savanna, riverine forest and gardens. Lays 2–5 eggs in a cavity excavated in a dead branch. **Diet:** Insects, snails, fruit and nectar; occasionally bird eggs and chicks. Feeds on the ground more than other barbets. (Kuifkophoutkapper)

### 1 Acacia Pied Barbet *Tricholaema leucomelas*

b b b b | | | | b b B B b
J F M A M J J A S O N D

**16–18 cm; 25–36 g** A chunky barbet with a yellow-spotted black back, red and yellow forehead, and black-and-white striped head; underparts white apart from black throat. Lacks black moustachial stripes of much smaller Red-fronted Tinkerbird; wings less yellow. Juv. lacks red forehead. **Voice:** Soft, low-pitched 'poop-oop-oop-oop' and nasal 'nehh, nehh, nehh' (toy trumpet) call. **Status and biology:** Near-endemic. Common resident in woodland and savanna, especially arid acacia woodland; also gardens. Lays 2–4 eggs in a cavity excavated in a dead branch. **Diet:** Figs, mistletoes and other fruit; also insects, flowers and nectar. (Bonthoutkapper)

### 2 Green Tinkerbird *Pogoniulus simplex*

**10 cm; 8–10 g** Very rare. A dull green tinkerbird with pale yellow wing bars and a yellow rump. Much smaller than Green Barbet (p. 252); ranges do not overlap. **Voice:** Very fast series of 8–10 'pop' notes, accelerating into a trill. **Status and biology:** Poorly known species; recorded from the canopy of coastal forest and dense woodland. Only 1–2 records from S Mozambique. **Diet:** Small fruits, seeds and insects. (Groentinker)

### 3 Yellow-fronted Tinkerbird *Pogoniulus chrysoconus*

b b b | b | b b B B B B
J F M A M J J A S O N D

**11 cm; 11–16 g** A small tinkerbird with white-streaked black upperparts and yellow-washed underparts. Best told from Red-fronted Tinkerbird by yellow (not red) forehead and less extensive yellow feather edges on folded wing. Forehead colour varies from pale yellow to bright orange. Juv. has black (not yellow) forehead. **Voice:** Continuous 'pop-pop-pop ...' or 'tink tink tink ...', similar to Red-fronted Tinkerbird's. **Status and biology:** Common resident in woodland and savanna. Lays 2–4 eggs in a cavity excavated in a dead branch. **Diet:** Mistletoes and other fruit, seeds, nectar and insects. (Geelblestinker)

### 4 Yellow-rumped Tinkerbird *Pogoniulus bilineatus*

B B b b b b b b b b b B
J F M A M J J A S O N D

**12 cm; 12–18 g** A small tinkerbird with a plain, black back and crown, and 2 white stripes on sides of head. Small, yellow rump patch is not easy to see in the field. Juv. has black upperparts narrowly barred and spotted yellow-green; base of bill is paler. **Voice:** 'Pop pop pop pop'; a lower-pitched, more ringing note than that of Red- or Yellow-fronted tinkerbirds, repeated in phrases of 3–9 notes, not continuously; also short trills. Lays 2–5 eggs in a cavity excavated in a dead branch. **Status and biology:** Common resident of forest, forest edge and dense woodland. **Diet:** Mistletoes, figs, other fruit, insects and nectar. (Swartblestinker)

### 5 Red-fronted Tinkerbird *Pogoniulus pusillus*

b | | | | | | | b b B B B
J F M A M J J A S O N D

**13 cm; 13–20 g** Darker above than Yellow-fronted Tinkerbird with a bright red (not yellow) forehead and more extensive yellow feather edges on folded wing. Typically has a neater facial pattern. Juv. has black (not red) forehead. **Voice:** Continuous, monotonous 'pop-pop-pop...', very similar to Yellow-fronted Tinkerbird, but slightly faster and higher pitched. **Status and biology:** Common resident in coastal forest. Lays 2–4 eggs in a cavity excavated in a dead branch. **Diet:** Mistletoes and other fruit, nectar and insects. (Rooiblestinker)

# WRYNECKS

Cryptically patterned birds related to woodpeckers but with soft (not stiffened) tail feathers. Sexes alike. Monogamous; both parents incubate and feed the altricial chicks.

## 1 Red-throated Wryneck  *Jynx ruficollis*

bb | bbbBbb
J F M A M J J A S O N D

**19 cm; 46–58 g** A peculiar thrush or warbler-like bird with a wedge-shaped bill, rufous throat and breast, and mottled, nightjar-like plumage. Sexes alike. Juv. paler, but still shows rufous wash on breast. **Voice:** Series of 2–10 squeaky 'kweek' notes, lower-pitched in male; also repeated, scolding 'peegh'. **Status and biology:** Locally common resident in grassland and open savanna, woodland, forest edge, plantations and gardens. Lays 3–4 (1–6) eggs in a hole, usually an old barbet or woodpecker nest. **Diet:** Mainly ants; occasionally termites. Usually feeds on the ground with jerky, woodpecker-like movements; sometimes on large tree branches. (Draaihals)

# WOODPECKERS

Attractively patterned birds with stiffened tails that mostly feed on tree branches, hammering off bark and probing for prey. Flight undulating. Many species advertise territories by drumming. Sexes usually differ in facial pattern; key identification features include pattern on face, back and underparts. Monogamous or cooperative breeders; both parents incubate and feed the altricial chicks.

## 2 Ground Woodpecker  *Geocolaptes olivaceus*

bBBbbb
J F M A M J J A S O N D

**24–30 cm; 110–130 g** A large, olive-grey woodpecker of open country. Pinkish-red belly and rump, pale eyes and cream-barred wings and tail are diagnostic. Ad. male has red moustachial stripes. Female and juv. have less pink on belly and rump. **Voice:** Far-carrying 'dwerr' or 'tik-werr'; ringing 'ree-chick'. **Status and biology:** Endemic. Common resident on rocky hill slopes in fynbos, karoo and grassland; not associated with trees. Usually in small family parties; often has helpers at the nest. Lays 2–4 eggs in a burrow excavated in a bank or in a rock crevice. **Diet:** Almost exclusively ants collected on the ground; occasional beetles and termites. (Grondspeg)

## 3 Green-backed Woodpecker  *Campethera cailliautii*

bb | bbbbb
J F M A M J J A S O N D

**15–18 cm; 35–46 g** Also known as Little Spotted Woodpecker. A small woodpecker with a rather short bill and plain face, lacking moustachial stripes. Male has a full red crown; female has red nape. Back green, spotted pale yellow; rump and wings finely barred. Underparts creamy, spotted blackish. Juv. resembles female, but red on nape is reduced or absent. **Voice:** High-pitched, whining 'whleeee'; also drums softly. **Status and biology:** Uncommon to locally common resident of forest edge, riparian forest, broadleafed woodland, and thicket near water.  Lays 2–3 eggs in a hole excavated in a dead tree, usually high above ground. **Diet:** Ants and other insects. (Gevlekte Speg)

## 4 Olive Woodpecker  *Dendropicos griseocephalus*

BBBb
J F M A M J J A S O N D

**17–19 cm; 40–50 g** A plain woodpecker with a grey head, olive body and red rump. Male has a red crown; female grey. Isolated population of *D. g. ruwenzori* in eastern Caprivi has red belly patch. **Voice:** Loud 'weet' or 'weet-er', repeated at intervals; seldom drums. **Status and biology:** Common resident in forest and dense woodland; often in small forest patches and near forest edge. Lays 2–3 eggs in a hole usually excavated in a dead, vertical trunk. **Diet:** Insects and other invertebrates. (Gryskopspeg)

## 5 Cardinal Woodpecker  *Dendropicos fuscescens*

bBBBbb
J F M A M J J A S O N D

**14–16 cm; 20–36 g** A tiny woodpecker with a streaked breast and belly, and a boldly barred back (more diffuse in NE). Both sexes have a plain, whitish face with a bold, black moustachial stripe. Forecrown brownish, merging into red hind crown in male; black in female. Juv. duller and greyer with red on crown of both sexes. **Voice:** High-pitched, rather dry, rattling 'krrrek krrrek krrrek' or 'kik-ik-ik krrrek krrrek...'; also drums softly. **Status and biology:** Common resident in most wooded habitats, from forest edge to dry thornveld. Lays 1–3 eggs in a hole excavated in a branch, often quite low down. **Diet:** Insects; occasional fruit. (Kardinaalspeg)

## 1 Golden-tailed Woodpecker *Campethera abingoni*

▮▮▮▮▮▮▮▮▮bBBBb
J F M A M J J A S O N D

**19–22 cm; 62–75 g** Male has full red crown and red moustachial stripes; told from Bennett's Woodpecker by its streaked (not spotted) underparts and ear coverts. Back is greenish, barred pale yellow. Female has white-spotted black crown, red nape, and black-speckled moustachial stripes. Paler than Knysna Woodpecker, with streaked (not spotted) underparts and more prominent barring on the back. *C.a. anderssoni* of semi-arid savanna in the W of its range is more heavily streaked below, sometimes appearing black-throated **(1 A)**. Juv. duller. **Voice:** Loud, nasal shriek, 'wheeeeeaa'. Seldom drums. **Status and biology:** Common resident of woodland, thickets and coastal forest. Lays 2–3 (rarely 4) eggs in a hole excavated in a tree. **Diet:** Ants, termites and other invertebrates. (Goudstertspeg)

## 2 Bennett's Woodpecker *Campethera bennettii*

bb▮▮▮▮▮▮bbBBB
J F M A M J J A S O N D

**22–24 cm; 65–80 g** Male has full red crown and moustachial stripes contrasting with plain face and throat. Best told from male Golden-tailed Woodpecker by white throat and spotted (not streaked) breast. Female has diagnostic brown throat and cheek stripe; forecrown blackish with white spots. Sides of neck, breast and flanks are spotted in nominate race, but *C. b. capricorni* (Namibia and NW Botswana) has little spotting, and is paler, with a yellow wash on underparts and rump. **Voice:** High-pitched, chattering 'wrrrrr, whirrr-itt, whrrr-itt...', often uttered in duet. Does not drum. **Status and biology:** Fairly common resident of broadleafed woodland and savanna; often feeds on ground. Lays 2–4 eggs in a tree hole, either using an old woodpecker hole or excavating its own nest. **Diet:** Ants, termites and other insects. (Bennettspeg)

## 3 Speckle-throated Woodpecker *Campethera scriptoricauda*

bb▮▮▮▮▮▮bbBBB
J F M A M J J A S O N D

**20–20 cm; 60–70 g** Often considered a subspecies of Bennett's Woodpecker, but is slightly smaller with a different facial pattern. Male has fine speckling on throat (not plain white); female has a lightly speckled (not brown) throat, densely speckled (not white) moustachial stripes and white (not brown) cheek stripe. **Voice:** Similar to that of Bennett's Woodpecker. **Status and biology:** Fairly common resident of dense woodland and thickets. Lays 3 eggs in a tree hole. **Diet:** Insects. (Tanzaniese Speg)

## 4 Bearded Woodpecker *Dendropicos namaquus*

▮▮▮▮▮bBBBBbbbb
J F M A M J J A S O N D

**23–25 cm; 70–90 g** The largest arboreal woodpecker with a bold black-and-white face pattern and faintly barred back, wings and tail. Breast and belly diffusely barred lead grey. Male has red hind crown; black in female. Juvs of both sexes have more red in crown than ad. male. **Voice:** Loud, rapid 'wik-wik-wik-wik'; drums very loudly. **Status and biology:** Common resident in woodland, riverine forest and thickets, favouring areas with dead trees; avoids dense forest. Lays 1–2 (rarely 4) eggs in a hole excavated in a dead tree. **Diet:** Insects, spiders and occasional lizards. (Baardspeg)

## 5 Knysna Woodpecker *Campethera notata*

▮▮▮▮▮▮▮▮▮bBBb
J F M A M J J A S O N D

**19–21 cm; 60–70 g** Both sexes are darker than Golden-tailed Woodpecker, with dense, blackish spotting (not streaks) on face and underparts; back darker green, less prominently barred golden. Male's dark red forehead and moustachial stripes are heavily marked with black. Female has indistinct, black moustachial stripes. **Voice:** Nasal shriek similar to that of Golden-tailed Woodpecker. Does not drum. **Status and biology: NEAR-THREATENED.** Endemic. Status due to small range. Locally common resident in forest, riparian woodland, euphorbia scrub, milkwood thickets and alien acacias and eucalypts. Easily overlooked if not calling. Lays 2–4 eggs in a hole, usually excavated in a dead tree. **Diet:** Ants, termites and other insects. (Knysnaspeg)

# CREEPERS

**Distinctive passerines related to wrens that creep along large branches, gleaning invertebrates from crevices with their long, slender bills. Often accompany bird parties. Monogamous; chicks altricial.**

## 6 Spotted Creeper *Salpornis spilonotus*

▮▮▮▮▮▮▮▮bBbb
J F M A M J J A S O N D

**14–15 cm; 14–16 g** A distinctive, small passerine with spotted and barred plumage. Creeps up large tree branches and trunks, probing crevices with its slender, decurved bill. Much smaller than woodpeckers or wrynecks (p. 256). Juv. duller, with whiter underparts. **Voice:** A series of very high-pitched, rather soft notes: 'sweepy-swip-swip-swip'; also a harsher 'keck-keck'. **Status and biology:** Uncommon to locally common resident in miombo woodland; often joins bird parties. Lays 2–3 eggs in a small, neat cup decorated with lichens and plastered onto a slender branch. **Diet:** Insects and spiders. (Boomkruiper)

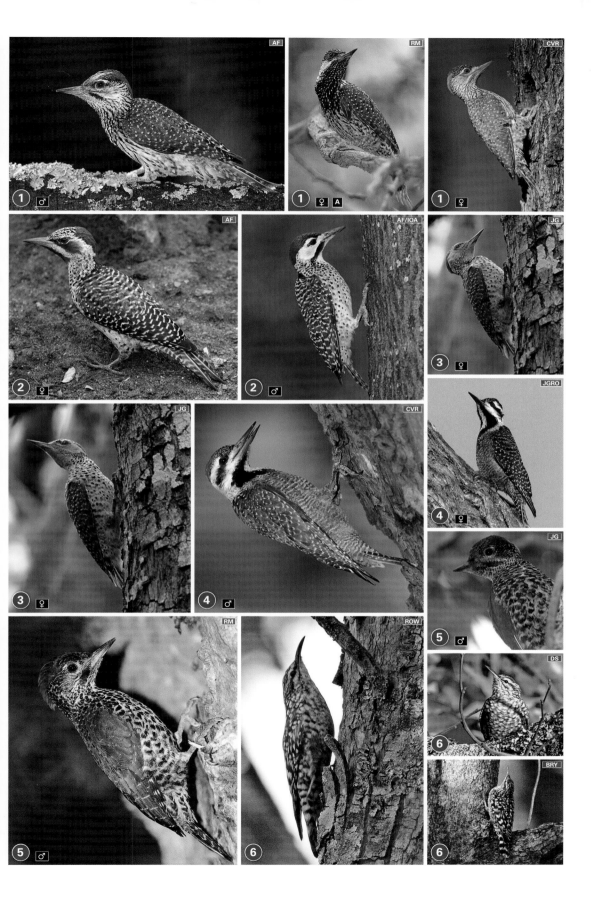

# LARKS

Cryptic, ground-dwelling birds, most likely to be confused with pipits (p. 350). Sexes alike, except in sparrowlarks. Short-lived juv. plumages are typically characterised by pale fringes to upperpart feathers and diffuse breast spots. Many species show marked geographic variation in plumage colour. Monogamous, occasionally with helpers at the nest. Incubation by female in most species. Chicks altricial.

## 1 Red-capped Lark  *Calandrella cinerea*

`b b b b | b b B B B B`
J F M A M J J A S O N D

**14–15 cm; 20–26 g** A long-winged, slender lark with a short, blackish bill and plain white underparts. Ad. has distinctive rufous cap and epaulettes on the sides of the breast; these are larger and more prominent in males. In flight, dark brown wings are more pointed than other larks, with broad bases. Juv. dark brown above, feathers fringed with white; breast heavily spotted. *C. c. spleniata* in NW Namibia is much paler **(1 A)**. **Voice:** Flight call is a sparrow-like 'tchweerp'. Male song is a sustained jumble of melodious phrases, given during high, undulating display flight. **Status and biology:** Common resident, local nomad and intra-African migrant, found in short grassy areas and croplands. Often occurs in flocks. Lays 2–3 (rarely 1–5) eggs in a cup of grass built in a hollow sunk into the ground, usually surrounded by an apron of small stones. **Diet:** Insects, other invertebrates and seeds. Frequently drinks at pools, but can survive without access to water. (Rooikoplewerik)

## 2 Large-billed Lark  *Galerida magnirostris*

`b | b | B B B b`
J F M A M J J A S O N D

**18 cm; 35–48 g** A robust, heavily built lark with a thick-based bill that has a yellow base to the lower mandible. Compared to large-billed forms of Sabota Lark (p. 266), it has a broad buff (not white) supercilium and more heavily streaked underparts. Upperparts sandy grey-brown, streaked dark brown; wings dark brown, lacking rufous panels in flight. It has a small crest that is raised when the bird is alarmed or singing. Juv. has broad buff tips to upperpart feathers; breast streaking more diffuse. **Voice:** A far-carrying, ascending 'troo-lee-liiii', like a rusty gate being opened. Highly vocal; mimics other species. **Status and biology:** Endemic. Common resident in grassland, arid scrubland, and open and fallow fields. Lays 2–4 eggs in an open cup built in a scrape in the ground, often next to a plant, stone or clod of earth. **Diet:** Insects, seeds, fruit and soft leaves. (Dikbeklewerik)

## 3 Dusky Lark  *Pinarocorys nigricans*

`[blocks]`
J F M A M J J A S O N D

**19–20 cm; 30–46 g** A large, thrush-like lark, with a striking facial pattern, heavily streaked breast and strange wing-flicking behaviour. Superficially similar to Groundscraper Thrush (p. 298), but is smaller, with a whitish ring around the eyes (not a vertical dark line through the eyes), no wing bars and shorter, whitish (not brown) legs. Forages on the ground, but often perches on trees or bushes. Male is slightly darker above and whiter below than female, with stronger facial markings. Juv. has broader buff margins to upperpart feathers, appearing scaly in fresh plumage; breast buffy with faint streaking. **Voice:** A soft 'chrrp, chrrp', uttered when flushed. **Status and biology:** Fairly common intra-African migrant that breeds in central African woodlands; occurs in open grassy areas in woodland and savanna, often in recently burnt areas. **Diet:** Insects and seeds. (Donkerlewerik)

## 4 Short-clawed Lark  *Certhilauda chuana*

`B B b | b b B B B`
J F M A M J J A S O N D

**17–19 cm; 28–44 g** A fairly large, slender lark found in semi-arid thornveld and savanna; recalls a long-billed lark, but with distinctive patterned upperparts: feathers dark brown with broad, buff fringes; range barely overlaps that of Eastern Long-billed Lark (p. 262). Lacks the rufous wings and nape of Rufous-naped Lark (p. 264), but has rufous rump visible in flight. The long buff-white supercilium imparts a capped appearance. Juv. has pale tips to upperpart feathers, appearing spotted above. **Voice:** A short 'chreep-chuu-chree', given when perched in a tree. Display flight with descending whistle similar to long-billed larks. **Status and biology:** Endemic. Uncommon to locally common resident in dry acacia savanna. Lays 2–3 eggs in a cup of grass built at the base of a tussock or small shrub. **Diet:** Insects and other invertebrates, especially termites and ants. (Kortkloulewerik)

# THE LONG-BILLED LARK COMPLEX

A group of 5 larks related to Short-clawed Lark (p. 260) that have been variously lumped and split over the years. All are rather large, slender larks with long tails that lack rufous in the wing in flight; bills range from moderate to very long, but are all slender and decurved. Males sing from the ground, low perches, or, in a spectacular aerial display, fly close to the ground then rise vertically 10–15 m, close their wings just before the top of the climb, call, and drop, opening their wings just above the ground. Identification depends on size, plumage colour and extent of streaking; ranges typically don't overlap. Males are appreciably larger and longer-billed than females. Juvs of all species are darker above, with buff tips to upperpart feathers and diffuse brown breast spots.

## 1 Cape Long-billed Lark  *Certhilauda curvirostris*

b b b
J F M A M J J A S O N D

**20–24 cm; 40–60 g** The largest lark in the region; bill long to very long. Upperparts are grey-brown with well-marked dark streaking; underparts white, densely streaked blackish brown, with streaking extending onto flanks and belly. Northern *C. c. falcirostris* **(1 A)** is larger and greyer with truly impressive bill. **Voice:** Song a far-carrying, descending whistle 'seeeooooo' in the N, 2-note 'whit seeeooooo' in the S. Querulous 'whir-irry' contact call. **Status and biology:** Endemic. Fairly common resident in coastal dunes and croplands. Lays 3 eggs in a cup of grass, sometimes domed, built on the ground against a stone, bush or tussock. **Diet:** Insects and seeds. (Weskuslangbeklewerik)

## 2 Agulhas Long-billed Lark  *Certhilauda brevirostris*

b b
J F M A M J J A S O N D

**18–20 cm; 35–48 g** Similar to the sthn nominate race of Cape Long-billed Lark, but its plumage is more buffy and bill and tail shorter; their ranges are not known to overlap. Range abuts that of Karoo Long-billed Lark in the Breede River Valley; differs by being buffy-brown (not rufous-brown) above and by having streaking extending onto the flanks and belly. **Voice:** Display song 2-note 'seeoo seeooo'; first note longer than that of the nominate race of Cape Long-billed Lark. **Status and biology: NEAR-THREATENED.** Endemic. Fairly common resident in fallow fields, croplands, coastal fynbos and semi-arid karoo scrub. Lays 2–3 eggs in a cup of grass built at the base of a small bush. **Diet:** Insects and seeds. (Overberglangbeklewerik)

## 3 Karoo Long-billed Lark  *Certhilauda subcoronata*

b b b b b b b b b
J F M A M J J A S O N D

**18–22 cm; 31–55 g** The most widespread and abundant long-billed lark. Upperpart colour varies from dark chocolate brown in S to reddish in N; hind neck greyer. Streaking reduces S to N, with a marked reduction in Bushmanland, but belly and flanks always largely unstreaked. Overlaps marginally with Cape Long-billed Lark near the Orange River, but easily told by its reddish upperparts and plain belly and flanks. Not known to overlap with Eastern Long-billed Lark, which is less streaked. **Voice:** At close range a soft 'inhalation' can be heard before the long descending whistle 'uh-seeeooooo'. **Status and biology:** Endemic. Common resident in karoo scrub and grasslands W of 25°E; typically in rocky areas. Lays 2–3 eggs in a cup of grass, sometimes domed, built at the base of a small bush or stone. **Diet:** Insects, other invertebrates, seeds, fruit and bulbs. (Karoolangbeklewerik)

## 4 Benguela Long-billed Lark  *Certhilauda benguelensis*

b b
J F M A M J J A S O N D

**18–20 cm; 35–53 g** Replaces Karoo Long-billed Lark in N Namibia, but exact range uncertain because recognition as a distinct species is based on its large genetic difference; identification criteria require clarification. Resembles the N form of Karoo Long-billed Lark, but tends to be slightly more heavily streaked on the crown, back and breast. **Voice:** A slightly quavering, long, descending whistle 'seeoeeooooo'. **Status and biology:** Near-endemic. Common resident on arid hill slopes and plains, apparently N of Brandberg. Lays 2–3 eggs in a cup of grass built in a hollow, often at the base of a small bush. **Diet:** Insects and seeds. (Kaokolangbeklewerik)

## 5 Eastern Long-billed Lark  *Certhilauda semitorquata*

b b B b
J F M A M J J A S O N D

**16–20 cm; 30–48 g** The smallest, least streaked and shortest-billed form of long-billed lark. Upperparts reddish, lightly streaked darker brown in W, virtually unstreaked in E. Buffy below, with light streaking confined to the breast. Elongate shape and relatively short, straight bill (especially females) can result in confusion with pipits (p. 350), but different gait, reddish plumage and lack of pale outer tail feathers diagnostic. **Voice:** A long, descending whistle 'seeeooooo'. **Status and biology:** Endemic. Fairly common resident in grassland, generally on rocky hill slopes. Lays 2–3 eggs in a cup of grass built at the base of a tussock or stone. **Diet:** Insects, other invertebrates, seeds and bulbs. (Grasveldlangbeklewerik)

## 1 Rufous-naped Lark *Mirafra africana*

Bbbb bbbBBB
J F M A M J J A S O N D

**15–18 cm; 34–50 g** The most common large lark of savanna and grassland, characterised by a small, erectile crest, rufous nape and a fairly long, decurved bill. Males sing year-round from the tops of bushes, termite mounds and poles. In flight, has extensive rufous wing panels like Flappet and Eastern Clapper larks, but is larger and longer-billed. Plumage varies regionally; generally paler in more arid areas. Juv. darker above than ad. with pale tips to feathers; breast has diffuse dark spots. **Voice:** Male song a repetitive, 3-syllabled 'tree tree-leeooo', with numerous variations; sometimes preceded by rapid wing vibrating. Fluttering display flight accompanied by a jumbled song often including mimicry of other species' calls. **Status and biology:** Common resident in grassland, savanna and old fields, typically where there are suitable song perches. Lays 2–3 (rarely 4) eggs in a domed or partly domed cup of grass built at the base of a tussock or small shrub. **Diet:** Insects, other invertebrates and seeds. (Rooineklewerik)

## 2 Flappet Lark *Mirafra rufocinnamomea*

BBbb bBB
J F M A M J J A S O N D

**14–15 cm; 21–32 g** A fairly small, compact, dark-backed lark, recalling a small, dark Rufous-naped Lark, but with a shorter bill, no crest and much less rufous in the wing in flight. Smaller than Eastern Clapper Lark, with a slightly longer tail, darker back and different aerial display; at close range, tertials are streaked (not barred); in area of overlap usually occurs in more wooded habitats. Juv. is darker above than ad., with broad buffy fringes to feathers; breast diffusely spotted dark brown. **Voice:** Characteristic display flight includes brief bursts of rapid wing clapping (2–3 phrases, separated by several seconds), but no song. Utters a short 'tuee' when perched. **Status and biology:** Common resident, occurring in pairs in grassland, savanna and woodland with at least some openings. Lays 2–3 eggs in a cup of grass, usually with a domed roof, built at the base of a grass tuft. **Diet:** Insects and grass seeds. (Laeveldklappertjie)

## 3 Eastern Clapper Lark *Mirafra fasciolata*

bbb bBBB
J F M A M J J A S O N D

**15 cm; 26–44 g** A medium-sized, compact lark; larger than Cape Clapper Lark with less heavily barred, more rufous upperparts and paler underparts, more extensive rufous in the wing in flight, a paler, heavier bill, and different display. Southern grassland birds are rufous above and buff below, resembling a small Rufous-naped Lark, but with a shorter bill and no crest; songs distinctive. Northern savanna birds are greyer above, with some races quite pale. Overlaps with Flappet Lark in N Namibia and N Botswana, but occurs in more open habitats and has a slightly shorter tail and barred (not streaked) tertials. **Voice:** Climbs steeply with trailing legs in aerial display, clapping its wings, then parachutes down, calling a long, ascending whistle 'pooooeeee', sometimes followed by other notes. Song has less change in pitch than Cape Clapper Lark and wing-clapping is slow: only 12–14 claps per second. Displays from the ground, from perches or in flight. Often mimics other birds. **Status and biology:** Near-endemic. Common resident in grassland and open savanna. Lays 2–3 eggs in a domed cup of grass, built at the base of a grass tuft. **Diet:** Insects and seeds. (Hoëveldklappertjie)

## 4 Cape Clapper Lark *Mirafra apiata*

bBBb
J F M A M J J A S O N D

**15 cm; 23–38 g** Smaller and darker than Eastern Clapper Lark with richly barred black and rufous upperparts, appearing dark from a distance; underparts buffy-rufous, with darker breast streaks; bill more slender and darker grey-brown (not pale horn). In flight, rufous in the wings is much less prominent. Unobtrusive when not displaying; reluctant to flush. S coast *M. a. marjoriae* is greyer above; sometimes treated as a separate species, Agulhas Clapper Lark. **Voice:** A long, ascending whistle, 'pooooeeee' (*M. a. apiata*) or 2 descending whistles 'tseeoo tseeuuuu' in *M. a. marjoriae*, preceded by fast wing-clapping at 25–28 claps per second. Seldom mimics other birds. **Status and biology:** Endemic. Common resident in karoo scrub, coastal fynbos and rank old fields; favours areas rich in restios. Lays 2–3 eggs in a partly domed cup built at the base of a grass tuft. **Diet:** Insects, seeds and fruit. (Kaapse Klappertjie)

## 1 Melodious Lark *Mirafra cheniana*

J F M A M J J A S O N D

**12 cm; 13–15 g** A small, compact grassland lark with a broad, whitish supercilium. Smaller than Monotonous Lark with a longer tail, well-marked face and buffy (not whitish) belly. Much smaller than Fawn-coloured Lark, with darker centres to upperpart feathers and buffy underparts. Juv. darker above with broad buff margins to feathers; breast diffusely spotted dark brown. **Voice:** Song jumbled and melodious, often mimicking other birds, usually given during high, protracted aerial display. Alarm call 'chuk chuk chucker chuk'. **Status and biology: NEAR-THREATENED**. Endemic. Locally fairly common resident in grassland and pastures. Unobtrusive when not displaying. Lays 2–4 eggs in a domed cup built at the base of a grass tuft. **Diet:** Insects and seeds. (Spotlewerik)

## 2 Monotonous Lark *Mirafra passerina*

**14 cm; 21–28 g** A medium to small, compact, stout-billed lark. Larger than Melodious Lark with a shorter tail, white (not buff) belly and less distinct facial markings, lacking a strong supercilium. White throat contrasts with relatively plain buff breast, and is prominent when singing. In flight, distinguished from paler Stark's Lark (p. 270) by its chestnut wing patches. **Voice:** Usually sings from a bush or tree; a monotonous 'trrp-chup-chip-choop' day and night. Short display flight from a perch, rising 15–20 m, calling all the time. **Status and biology:** Near-endemic. Common resident and nomad in thornveld and mopane woodland with sparse grass cover. Unobtrusive when not calling. Lays 2–4 eggs in a deep cup of grass built in a grass clump, sometimes with surrounding grass bent into a dome over the cup. **Diet:** Invertebrates and grass seeds. (Bosveldlewerik)

## 3 Sabota Lark *Calendulauda sabota*

**15 cm; 21–31 g** A medium-sized lark; more compact and heavily streaked than Fawn-coloured Lark; differs in having malar stripes. The prominent white supercilium extends from frons to nape, giving it a capped appearance. Breast boldly streaked, contrasting with pale throat and belly. Upperpart colour varies regionally, but always lacks rufous in the wing. Bill size varies considerably, with large-billed forms typically in more arid areas; these are sometimes treated as a distinct species 'Bradfield's Lark' *C. s. naevia* (**3 A**). Juv. is darker above with white feather tips, appearing spotted. **Voice:** A jumbled song of rich, melodious 'chips' and twitterings; mimics other birds. Often calls from an elevated perch such as a treetop or telephone wire. **Status and biology:** Near-endemic. Common resident in arid savanna and Nama Karoo. Lays 2–4 eggs in a cup of grass built against vegetation or a rock; nests usually partly or completely domed, in open sites. **Diet:** Insects, other invertebrates, seeds and soft leaves. (Sabotalewerik)

## 4 Fawn-coloured Lark *Calendulauda africanoides*

**14–16 cm; 21–30 g** A medium-sized lark with a fairly long tail usually found on sandy soils. Upperpart feathers dark brown with broad buff margins. Face has a broad white supercilium and white throat; lacks malar stripes of Sabota and Red (p. 268) larks. Underparts mainly white; breast buffy with brown streaks. Smaller than Red Lark, with paler, more streaked upperparts and a plain white throat. Juv. is darker above with white feather tips, appearing spotted. **Voice:** A jumble of harsh 'chips' and twitterings, ending in a buzzy slur, given from a treetop or during the short aerial flight. **Status and biology:** Fairly common resident in Kalahari scrub, broadleafed woodland, savanna and thornveld. Lays 2–3 (rarely 4) eggs in a domed or partly domed cup of grass built at the base of a tussock or small shrub. **Diet:** Insects, other invertebrates and seeds. (Vaalbruinlewerik)

# THE KAROO LARK COMPLEX

A group of 4 larks related to Fawn-coloured and Sabota larks (p. 266) that have been variously lumped and split over the years. All have rather long, heavy tails and lack rufous in the wing in flight; bills range from slender to fairly stout, but are all slightly decurved. Males sing from the ground, low perches, or in a fluttering aerial display, circling 10–30 m over their territories, singing repetitively. Songs are stereo-typed, but with up to 5 song types in any area. All 4 species occur on sandy soils; plumage colour varies in relation to soil colour, independent of species. Identification depends on size, shape and plumage streaking. Ranges typically don't overlap, but there is a hybrid zone between Karoo and Barlow's larks in the N Cape. Sexes alike, but males larger, with longer bills. Juvs of all species have buff tips and darker brown subterminal bars to upperpart feathers, as well as diffuse brown breast spots.

## 1 Dune Lark *Calendulauda erythrochlamys*

b b b b b b b b b b b b
J F M A M J J A S O N D

17–18 cm; 26–33 g  The plainest lark in the Karoo Lark complex; slightly longer-legged than other species. Differs from Barlow's Lark by its unstreaked upperparts and fine, rufous breast streaks (darker, and generally heavier streaking in Barlow's), and longer song. Some Barlow's Larks inland from Lüderitz are virtually indistinguishable from Dune Larks, but ranges not known to overlap. **Voice:** Male song is a series of 10+ 'tip-ip-ip-ip' lead-in notes followed by a whistle and long, uniform trill. Also has strident contact calls and a chittering alarm call. **Status and biology:** Endemic. Fairly common resident in vegetated areas among dunes in the Namib Desert between the Koichab and Kuiseb rivers. Lays 1–2 eggs in a partly domed cup of grass built at the base of a grass tuft or other dune vegetation. **Diet:** Insects, seeds and occasional spiders. (Duinelewerik)

## 2 Barlow's Lark *Calendulauda barlowi*

▮▮▮▮▮▮▮▮ b b b ▮▮
J F M A M J J A S O N D

17–18 cm; 26–36 g  The closest relative of Dune Lark; slightly larger and longer-billed than Dune and Karoo larks. Differs from Karoo Lark in having plain (not streaked) flanks, and often appears 'bull-necked'. Coastal *C. b. patei* (**2 A**) are pale sand-brown above, inland *C. b. cavei* (**2 B**) and *C. b. barlowi* reddish. Nominate *C. b. barlowi* closely resembles Dune Lark in the north, but usually has brown (not rufous) breast streaks and some dark brown streaks in tertials and central tail feathers. **Voice:** Male song is similar to Dune Lark, but with fewer (5–8) lead-in notes and a shorter trill. Also has strident contact calls and a chittering alarm call. **Status and biology:** Endemic. Locally common resident in arid scrubland and vegetated dunes. Hybridises in a narrow contact zone with Karoo Lark between Port Nolloth and the Orange River. Lays 2 eggs in a domed cup of grass built at the base of a tussock or small shrub. **Diet:** Insects and seeds. (Barlowlewerik)

## 3 Karoo Lark *Calendulauda albescens*

▮▮▮▮▮▮ b b b b b ▮
J F M A M J J A S O N D

16–17 cm; 25–33 g  The smallest and most heavily streaked lark in the Karoo Lark complex, and the only species that has streaking extending onto the flanks; bill smaller and finer than other species. White supercilium and throat contrast with its dark ear coverts and boldly streaked breast. Upperparts range from sandy-brown (coastal *C. a. albescens*, **3 A**, and *C. a. codea*), through reddish (W Karoo *C. a. guttata*, **3 B**), to dark brown (E Karoo *C. a. karruensis*). Identification is most problematic around contact zone with Barlow's Lark. **Voice:** Male song 'chleeep-chleeep-trrr-trrrrrrr' shorter and higher-pitched than Barlow's Lark, with only 1–2 lead-in notes; much higher-pitched than Red Lark song. Often located by guttural alarm calls or strident contact calls. **Status and biology:** Endemic. Common resident in Karoo and coastal shrublands. Hybridises with Barlow's Lark in a narrow contact zone between Port Nolloth and the Orange River. Lays 2–3 (rarely 4) eggs in a domed or partly domed cup of grass built at the base of a tussock or small shrub. **Diet:** Insects and seeds; also other invertebrates, fruit, leaves and flowers. (Karoolewerik)

## 4 Red Lark *Calendulauda burra*

b b b b b ▮▮▮ b B b b
J F M A M J J A S O N D

18–19 cm; 32–43 g  The largest lark in the Karoo Lark complex, with a shorter, deeper bill than other species. Upperpart colour varies from unstreaked red on dunes to brown with darker streaks on the plains. Range is not known to overlap with Karoo Lark; Red Lark is appreciably larger with a much heavier bill and plain (not streaked) flanks. Overlaps with Fawn-coloured Lark (p. 266) in north, but is much larger, with a plainer, darker red-brown (not buffy) back. **Voice:** Song similar to Karoo Lark, but slower and much lower-pitched. Also has strident contact calls and a chittering alarm call. **Status and biology:** VULNERABLE. Endemic, threatened by habitat degradation through overgrazing. Locally fairly common in scrub-covered sand-dunes and Nama-Karoo plains. Lays 2–3 eggs in a domed cup of grass built at the base of a tussock. **Diet:** Insects, other invertebrates, seeds and fruit. (Rooilewerik)

## 1 Rudd's Lark  *Heteromirafra ruddi*

B B b b | | | | | | b B B
J F M A M J J A S O N D

**14 cm; 25–28 g** A small, large-headed lark with a short, thin tail. Legs long; gait often more erect than most larks, recalling Spike-heeled Lark (p. 272), but bill is short and broad, underparts are whitish, and has white edges to outer tail (not white tail tips). It has an erectile crest with a buff median stripe, but this can be hard to see in the field. Unobtrusive when not displaying (mainly Oct–Feb). Juv. spotted buff above. **Voice:** Males give a bubbling, whistled song, with 3–4-note phrases repeated several times, switching to a new variation; typically sung in high, protracted display flights that can last up to 30 minutes. **Status and biology: VULNERABLE**. Endemic. Decline due to habitat loss. Uncommon, localised resident in short upland grassland, usually near damp depressions. Lays 2–4 eggs in a domed cup of grass, often with a short entrance tunnel, built at the base of a tussock. **Diet:** Insects, other invertebrates, seeds and bulbs. (Drakensberglewerik)

## 2 Botha's Lark  *Spizocorys fringillaris*

b | | | | | | | | | b b b
J F M A M J J A S O N D

**12–13 cm; 16–21 g** A small lark with a short, fairly stout bill and heavily streaked upperparts. Ad. bill orange-pink; slightly less stout than that of Pink-billed Lark; also differs by its more prominent white supercilium, heavier breast streaking, streaked flanks, white (not rufous) belly and white (not buff) outer tail feathers. Juv. has white spots on crown, buff margins to flight feathers and diffuse brown breast spots; bill dull pinkish-brown. **Voice:** A cheerful, repeated 'chiree'; a 'chuk, chuk', uttered in flight. **Status and biology: ENDANGERED**. Endemic. Threatened by habitat loss. Uncommon resident and local nomad in heavily grazed grassland, often in small flocks of 3–6 birds. Lays 2–3 eggs in a cup of grass built in a hollow in the ground among short grasses. **Diet:** Insects and seeds. Regularly visits water to drink. (Vaalrivierlewerik)

## 3 Pink-billed Lark  *Spizocorys conirostris*

b b b B B B B b b b b b
J F M A M J J A S O N D

**12–13 cm; 12–17 g** A small, compact lark; ad. has a distinctive short, conical, pink bill. Differs from Botha's Lark by its rich rufous-buff underparts, which contrast boldly with the white throat and unstreaked flanks; breast lightly streaked. In flight, outer tail edged buff, not white. W races are paler below, and can be confused with Stark's Lark, but are less grey and lack a crest; bill shorter and more conical. Juv. has a blackish bill; upperparts darker brown with buffy spots; breast with diffuse brown spots. **Voice:** Utters a soft 'si-si-si' when flushed. Male song mixes this call with short, sweet whistles, usually given during a short, jerky display. **Status and biology:** Near-endemic. Common resident and nomad in grassland, pasture and desert scrub. Lays 1–3 eggs in a cup of grass built in a hollow in the ground, often against a tussock or small bush. **Diet:** Seeds and insects. Regularly visits water to drink. (Pienkbeklewerik)

## 4 Sclater's Lark  *Spizocorys sclateri*

| | | | | b b b | B B B B b
J F M A M J J A S O N D

**13–14 cm; 17–21 g** A small, compact lark with a remarkably large bill. Ground colour is buffy-brown, distinctly warmer than grey-brown Stark's Lark. At close range the dark brown 'teardrop' mark below the eye is diagnostic. In flight, has a dark triangle on the tail (broader at the tip), with the white outer tail broadening towards the tail base. Juv. has pale spotted upperparts and diffuse breast spots; teardrop on face less distinct. **Voice:** A repeated 'tchweet-tchweet', given in flight. Displaying males give similar calls in a short aerial display. **Status and biology: NEAR-THREATENED**. Endemic. Uncommon; resident and partial nomad on stony plains in arid Nama-Karoo shrubland. Lays 1 egg in a cup of grass built in a hollow dug in the ground and surrounded by a ring of small stones in the open on a stony plain. **Diet:** Seeds and insects. Regularly visits water to drink. (Namakwalewerik)

## 5 Stark's Lark  *Spizocorys starki*

b b B B B b b b b b b b
J F M A M J J A S O N D

**13–14 cm; 16–22 g** A small, compact lark with an erectile crest and a stubby, pale bill. Much paler above and below than Sclater's and Pink-billed larks. Could possibly be confused with Gray's Lark (p. 272), but has streaked (not plain) upperparts. Juv. spotted white above. **Voice:** A short 'chree-chree' given in flight. Male song is a melodious jumble of notes, given in a high display flight. **Status and biology:** Near-endemic. Common resident and nomad in stony desert scrub, gravel plains and arid grassland. Large flocks follow rain events. Lays 2–4 eggs in a cup of grass built in a hollow in the ground, usually against a tussock, small bush or stone. **Diet:** Seeds, insects and other invertebrates. Regularly visits water to drink, but can survive without drinking. (Woestynlewerik)

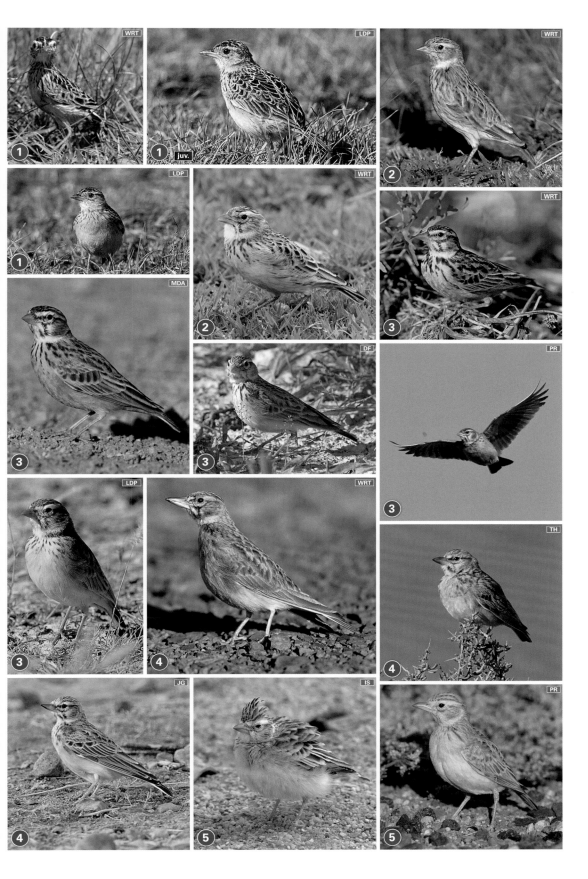

## 1 Gray's Lark *Ammomanopsis grayi*

**13–14 cm; 17–27 g** A small, plain lark of desert gravel plains with a fairly long, stout, pale bill; usually in small groups year-round. Distinguished from Stark's Lark (p. 270) by its unstreaked back, dark tip to the outer tail and rounded head (lacking a crest). Female Grey-backed Sparrowlark also has more mottled upperparts and a shorter, more conical bill. The desert form of Tractrac Chat (p. 272) has longer legs, a dark, slender bill and a white base to its tail. Upperparts darker brown in N Namibia than further S. Juv. lightly mottled above. **Voice:** A short 'tseet' or 'tew-tew', given in flight. Song is a high-pitched mix of descending, metallic-sounding 'tinks' and whistles, normally given before dawn. **Status and biology:** Near-endemic. Fairly common resident and local nomad on gravel plains. Lays 2–3 eggs in a cup of grass built in a hollow in the ground, usually against a tussock, small bush or stone; sometimes breeds cooperatively, with extra birds helping to feed the chicks. **Diet:** Seeds, insects and other invertebrates. (Namiblewerik)

## 2 Spike-heeled Lark *Chersomanes albofasciata*

**13–15 cm; 20–34 g** A fairly small lark with a characteristic upright stance and short, white-tipped tail. Bill long and slightly decurved. Coloration variable, but its white throat contrasts with a rufous or buffy breast and belly; upperparts scaled due to buff fringes to feathers. Almost invariably in small groups; one bird often stands sentry on a low bush. Juv. darker above with whitish feather margins; breast diffusely spotted. **Voice:** A trilling 'trrrep, trrrep, trrrep'. **Status and biology:** Near-endemic. Common resident in a wide range of habitats from moist grassland, through karoo shrubland and semi-desert grassland to gravel plains. Lays 2–3 (rarely up to 5) eggs in a cup of grass built in a hollow in the ground, usually against a tussock or small bush. Some pairs have helpers assisting to feed the chicks. **Diet:** Insects, other invertebrates, seeds and fruit. (Vlaktelewerik)

# SPARROWLARKS

**Small, compact larks with conical bills and marked sexual dimorphism in plumage. Boldly patterned males are easily identified, but females and juvs could be confused with other small larks; differ in having blackish underwing coverts. Some juv. males have a partial moult into ad. plumage, resulting in a transitional imm. plumage. Incubation by both sexes.**

## 3 Chestnut-backed Sparrowlark *Eremopterix leucotis*

**12–13 cm; 12–21 g** Male's rich chestnut back and wings and contrasting black-and-white head are diagnostic; lacks white crown patch of male Grey-backed Sparrowlark; vent white (not black). Female is mottled buff and brown above, darker than female Grey-backed Sparrowlark; told from female Black-eared Sparrowlark by its black lower breast and belly and pale rump. Juv. like female, but with pale spotted upperparts; dark belly patch smaller or absent. **Voice:** A short 'chip-chwep', uttered in flight. **Status and biology:** Common resident and nomad in sparsely grassed savanna and cultivated lands, especially recently burnt areas; usually in flocks. Lays 1–3 eggs in a cup of grass built in a hollow in the ground, often against a tussock or small bush. **Diet:** Seeds and insects. Often visits water to drink. (Rooiruglewerik)

## 4 Grey-backed Sparrowlark *Eremopterix verticalis*

**12–13 cm; 13–21 g** Greyish back and upperwings separate both sexes from Chestnut-backed Sparrowlark. Male also has a white patch on the hind crown and a black (not white) vent. Female's black belly patch and unstreaked flanks separate it from female Black-eared Sparrowlark. Juv. like female but warmer brown with buff spots above. **Voice:** A sharp 'chruk, chruk', given in flight. **Status and biology:** Near-endemic. Common nomad and local migrant in karoo shrubland, semi-desert, grassland, arid savanna and cultivated land. Usually in groups; often congregates in huge flocks following good rains. Lays 1–5 eggs in a cup of grass built in a hollow in the ground, usually against a tussock or small bush. Clutches larger after good rains. **Diet:** Mainly seeds; also insects and soft leaves. Often visits water to drink, but can survive without drinking. (Grysruglewerik)

## 5 Black-eared Sparrowlark *Eremopterix australis*

**12–13 cm; 12–16 g** Male black with broad chestnut margins to back, wing and tail feathers; entirely black underwings are conspicuous in flight. Female is streaked chestnut and dark brown above and heavily streaked with black below; lacks the dark belly patch of other female sparrowlarks and has black secondaries in flight. Juv. like female but spotted buff above. **Voice:** A short 'preep' or 'chip-chip', given in flight; male has a butterfly-like aerial display. **Status and biology:** Endemic. Locally common resident and nomad in karoo shrubland and grassland, Kalahari sandveld, gravel plains and, occasionally, cultivated lands; usually in flocks. Lays 1–4 eggs in a cup of grass built in a hollow at the base of a tussock or small bush; nest rim decorated with sand-encrusted spiderwebs. **Diet:** Seeds and insects. Rarely visits water to drink. (Swartoorlewerik)

# SWALLOWS AND MARTINS

Aerial feeders; told from swifts (p. 216) by angled wings and more flapping flight; also frequently perch. Swallows typically have pale underparts, but some martins are brown below. Sexes alike; juvs duller; in species with tail streamers, those of females and juvs are shorter. Breed singly or colonially; usually monogamous. Incubation mainly by female; chicks altricial.

## 1 Red-breasted Swallow *Hirundo semirufa*

BBbb | bBBBB
J F M A M J J A S O N D

**20–24 cm; 24–38 g**  A large, red-rumped swallow; slightly smaller than Mosque Swallow. Ad. has a red (not white) throat and breast, dark blue (not pale rufous) ear coverts and dull buff (not white) underwing coverts. Larger than vagrant Red-rumped Swallow, with darker rufous underparts and dark (not rufous) nape and cheeks. Juv. has a creamy white throat and breast and short tail streamers; differs from ad. Mosque Swallow by its darker underwing coverts. **Voice:** Soft, warbling song; twittering notes in flight. **Status and biology:** Common intra-African migrant in grassland and savanna. Lays 3–4 (rarely 1–6) eggs in a mud bowl nest with a long entrance tunnel built under an overhang or in a natural cavity. Often raises 2 broods per season. **Diet:** Insects; occasionally forages on the ground. (Rooiborsswael)

## 2 Mosque Swallow *Hirundo senegalensis*

bbbb | BBbbb
J F M A M J J A S O N D

**22–26 cm; 38–50 g**  A large, red-rumped swallow; slightly larger than Red-breasted Swallow, with a white (not red) throat, face and upper breast, pale rufous (not dark blue) ear coverts and white (not buffy) underwing coverts. Juv. duller with short tail streamers and pale buff underwing coverts, but coverts always paler than those of Red-breasted Swallow. **Voice:** Nasal 'harrrrp'; guttural chuckling. **Status and biology:** Locally common resident and partial migrant in open woodland, often near rivers, and especially near baobabs. Lays 2–4 eggs in a mud bowl nest with a long entrance tunnel built under an overhang, or a cup or bowl in a natural cavity. Often raises 2 broods per season. **Diet:** Insects. (Moskeeswael)

## 3 Red-rumped Swallow *Hirundo daurica*

**17–19 cm; 23–30 g**  Rare vagrant. Paler than ad. Red-breasted Swallow with pale rufous (not dark blue) ear coverts and nape. Smaller than Mosque Swallow; paler below with a rufous (not dark blue) nape and blackish (not rufous) undertail coverts. Differs from Greater Striped Swallow (p. 276) by its dark blue (not reddish) cap; underparts plain or only faintly streaked. Juv. duller above; lacks tail streamers. **Voice:** Single-note 'djuit'; also a soft, twittering song. **Status and biology:** Vagrant, presumably from resident E and central African population, although Palearctic migrants may occasionally reach the region; only 5 confirmed records, all from Zimbabwe. (Rooinekswael)

### 1 South African Cliff-Swallow *Hirundo spilodera*

bbbb  bbBBB
J F M A M J J A S O N D

**14–15 cm; 16–24 g** A martin-like swallow with broad wings and an almost square tail, but with a buffy-rufous rump and creamy underparts washed rufous on breast and vent; breast diffusely streaked dark brown. Crown dark brown, slightly glossed in front. Lacks forked tail and well-defined breast streaks of Lesser and Greater striped swallows. Non-br. Barn Swallow (p. 278) often shows similar scruffy breast markings, but lacks a pale rump. Juv. duller, lacking gloss on upperparts. **Voice:** Twittering 'chooerp-chooerp'. **Status and biology:** Br. endemic. Locally common intra-African migrant in upland grassland and karoo scrub. Breeds colonially (20–900 pairs), usually in culverts and under road bridges. Lays 2–3 (rarely 1–4) eggs in a mud bowl nest with a short entrance tunnel; adjacent nests often overlapping. Unusual in having both sexes incubate. Often raises 2 broods per season. **Diet:** Insects. (Familieswael)

### 2 Greater Striped Swallow *Hirundo cucullata*

Bbb  bbbBB
J F M A M J J A S O N D

**16–20 cm; 20–35 g** Larger and paler than Lesser Striped Swallow; striping on the buffy underparts is paler and less well defined; orange crown slightly paler; rump paler rufous; ear coverts whitish (not rufous). Paler overall than vagrant Red-rumped Swallow (p. 274), with more pronounced streaking on underparts; crown rufous-orange (not dark blue). Juv. duller with a reddish-brown crown; tail streamers reduced. **Voice:** Twittering 'chissick' and querulous, nasal notes. **Status and biology:** Common intra-African migrant found in grassland and around wetlands. Lays 2–4 eggs in a mud bowl nest with a long entrance tunnel built under an overhang or in a natural cavity. Raises up to 3 broods per season. Nests often usurped by White-rumped Swifts; also sparrows and chats. **Diet:** Insects; occasional seeds and fruit. (Grootstreepswael)

### 3 Lesser Striped Swallow *Hirundo abyssinica*

Bbbbbbb  BBB
J F M A M J J A S O N D

**15–19 cm; 16–22 g** Smaller and darker than Greater Striped Swallow, with more prominent blackish striping contrasting strongly with whiter underparts; rump darker rufous; ear coverts rufous (not whitish). Female has shorter tail streamers than male. Juv. duller, lacking blue-black gloss above, and has a brown (not rufous) crown; tail streamers reduced. **Voice:** Descending series of squeaky, nasal 'zeh-zeh-zeh-zeh' notes. **Status and biology:** Common resident and intra-African migrant in mesic habitats, often near water. Lays 2–4 eggs in mud bowl nest with a long entrance tunnel built under an overhang or in a natural cavity. Raises up to 3 broods per season. Nests sometimes usurped by White-rumped Swifts, sparrows and chats. **Diet:** Insects; occasional seeds and fruit. (Kleinstreepswael)

## 1 Barn Swallow  *Hirundo rustica*

J F M A M J J A S O N D

**15–20 cm; 16–24 g** An abundant Palearctic migrant. Dark blue or brown above, with white panels in the outer tail; breast and belly varies from off-white to rich buff. Ad. striking in fresh plumage (Mar–May), with long tail streamers and a reddish frons and throat, but streamers often short or missing and throat dull brown when worn. Juv. duller, with browner frons and throat; outer tail feathers short. Slightly larger than rare Angola Swallow; red largely confined to throat (not onto breast), bordered by a complete blackish breast band of relatively uniform thickness; remainder of underparts creamy-buff (not grey). **Voice:** Soft, high-pitched twittering. **Status and biology:** Abundant Palearctic migrant, found in all habitats, often in loose flocks. Roosts communally, usually in reeds. **Diet:** Insects, spiders and occasional seeds. Most prey caught in the air, but some taken on the ground or from vegetation. (Europese Swael)

## 2 Angola Swallow  *Hirundo angolensis*

**14–15 cm; 12–20 g** Rare visitor. Slightly smaller and more compact than Barn Swallow; red throat extends onto breast and is narrowly bordered by an incomplete black band. Upperparts are darker blue and appear more iridescent; underparts grey (not creamy-buff). Outer tail streamers are much shorter than breeding ad. Barn Swallow's, and tail is less deeply forked. Juv. has red of ad. replaced by pale rufous, and is less glossy above. **Voice:** Weak, twittering song; loud 'tsip' call. **Status and biology:** Rare visitor to N grassland. (Angolaswael)

## 3 Wire-tailed Swallow  *Hirundo smithii*

B B B B b b b B B B b b
J F M A M J J A S O N D

**12–14 cm; 10–15 g** A tiny, blue-backed swallow with a chestnut crown and white underparts. Appreciably smaller than White-throated Swallow, with only a partial breast band (but beware juv. White-throated Swallow); entire crown (not just forehead) is rufous, and has longer, narrower tail streamers. Juv. is less glossy blue above with a brown crown. Flight extremely rapid. **Voice:** Call is a sharp, metallic 'tchik'; song is twittering 'chirrik-weet, chirrik-weet'. **Status and biology:** Common resident and intra-African migrant, usually near water. Lays 2–4 eggs in a shallow cup of mud pellets built under an overhang, including bridges, buildings and even inside boats. Raises up to 4 broods per season. **Diet:** Insects. (Draadstertswael)

## 4 White-throated Swallow  *Hirundo albigularis*

b b b b     b B B B b
J F M A M J J A S O N D

**15 cm; 18–28 g** A blue-backed swallow with white underparts and a complete, blue-black breast band. Larger than Wire-tailed Swallow, with rufous confined to the frons (not entire cap), a complete breast band and short, relatively broad tail streamers. Juv. is less glossy above, and has a brownish forehead; breast band dull brown, narrower than ad's. **Voice:** Harsh twittering and nasal notes. **Status and biology:** Common intra-African migrant, closely associated with water. Lays 2–5 (usually 3) eggs in a cup nest of mud pellets built on a vertical rock face, often under bridges and in culverts. Raises 2–3 broods per season. **Diet:** Insects. (Witkeelswael)

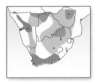

## 5 Pearl-breasted Swallow  *Hirundo dimidiata*

b b b     b B B B B
J F M A M J J A S O N D

**13 cm; 10–15 g** A small, rather plain blue and white swallow, lacking red on its head and white in its tail. Tail has a shallow fork, but lacks tail streamers. Best told from Grey-rumped Swallow (p. 280) and Common House-Martin (p. 280) by its plain blue back and rump (not pale grey or white); from below it differs by its white (not dark) wing linings; has shorter tail than Grey-rumped Swallow, and is more slender than Common House-Martin. Juv. less glossy above and has shorter outer tail feathers. **Voice:** Song is a series of chipping notes. **Status and biology:** Locally common intra-African migrant in grassland, savanna, strandveld and open woodland. Lays 2–4 eggs in a mud cup built inside a large animal burrow, cave or dark building. Raises up to 3 broods per season. **Diet:** Insects and occasional grass seeds. (Pêrelborsswael)

## 1 Blue Swallow  *Hirundo atrocaerulea*

**18–25 cm; 13 g** A dark blue swallow with variably white mottling on the flanks, neck and rump. Most likely to be confused with a saw-wing; flight action is less erratic. In good light, the glossy blue plumage is diagnostic. Ad. male has much longer outer tail feathers than a saw-wing; tail streamers shorter in female, but still more slender than in a saw-wing. Juv. has a dull brown throat and less glossy upperparts. **Voice:** Song is a musical 'bee-bee-bee-bee'. Typical flight call is a soft 'chip'. **Status and biology: VULNERABLE.** Uncommon and localised intra-African migrant in upland grassland, often bordering forests. Lays 2–3 (rarely 4) eggs in a cup of mud and grass built on the vertical wall or overhang of a cave, mineshaft or large animal burrow. Nest lined with white feathers, possibly to aid locating the nest in the dark nest sites. Usually raises 2 broods per season. **Diet:** Insects. (Blouswael)

## 2 Common House-Martin  *Delichon urbicum*

**14 cm; 10–16 g** A rather plump, swallow-like martin with pure white underparts and a diagnostic white rump. In flight, told from Grey-rumped Swallow by its shorter, less deeply forked tail and broader-based, shorter wings. Pearl-breasted Swallow (p. 278) lacks a pale rump. Juv. is less glossy above, with a narrower, pale grey rump band. **Voice:** Hard 'chirrp' or 'prt-prt'. **Status and biology:** Fairly common Palearctic migrant over most open habitats; often feeds higher in the sky than most other swallows. Thought to roost mainly on the wing, but also recorded roosting on cliffs, in reedbeds, trees and buildings; small flocks often gather on wires in the early morning. Occasionally attempts to breed in S Africa and Namibia; lays 3–5 eggs in a mud cup nest built under the eaves of a building. **Diet:** Insects. (Huiswael)

## 3 Grey-rumped Swallow  *Pseudhirundo griseopyga*

**14 cm; 8–12 g** A small, slender swallow with glossy blue upperparts, a long, deeply forked tail, pale grey rump and grey-brown crown; underparts whitish. Juv. Common House-Martin also has a pale grey rump, but is much plumper, with a shorter tail. Pearl-breasted Swallow (p. 278) has a dark blue rump and shorter tail. Juv. is duller above with buffy tips to feathers, appearing scaly in fresh plumage; breast washed grey. **Voice:** Flight call-note recorded as 'chraa'. **Status and biology:** Locally common resident and intra-African migrant, moving out of wet areas in the rainy season. Occurs in open woodland and grassland, often near water. Lays 2–5 eggs on a pad of grass built in a burrow in the ground; usually in an old rodent burrow, but also uses old kingfisher and bee-eater burrows. **Diet:** Insects. (Gryskruisswael)

# SAW-WINGS

**Slender, mainly black swallows of forest and dense woodland. Males have barbs of outer web of outer primary recurved, giving a saw-edged effect. Taxonomy contentious, with Black and Eastern saw-wings sometimes lumped in a widespread *P. pristoptera*. Mainly active at dawn and dusk. Breed in burrows, usually excavated by swallows.**

## 4 Black Saw-wing  *Psalidoprocne holomelas*

**14 cm; 11–13 g** A small, slender, glossy black swallow with a long, forked tail; lacks crisp, white underwing coverts of Eastern Saw-wing. Told from Blue Swallow by its glossy, greenish-black (not dark blue) plumage and shorter tail streamers. Juv. sooty brown; lacks gloss and has shorter tail streamers than ad., but tail longer and more deeply forked than juv. White-headed Saw-wing; throat sooty (not grey). **Voice:** Soft 'chrrp' alarm call. **Status and biology:** Locally common intra-African migrant, mainly wintering on the coastal plain of KZN and Mozambique. Occurs around dense woodland, forests and plantations. Lays 1–3 eggs in a burrow up to 1.2 m long in a bank. **Diet:** Insects. (Swartsaagvlerkswael)

## 5 Eastern Saw-wing  *Psalidoprocne orientalis*

**13 cm; 10–12 g** Sometimes considered a race of Black Saw-wing, but has conspicuous white (not black or greyish) underwing coverts. Juv. very dark brown; lacks gloss of ad. and has grey (not white) underwing coverts. Told from juv. White-headed Saw-wing by its paler underwing coverts and sooty brown throat. **Voice:** Soft twittering; short 'chip'. **Status and biology:** Locally common resident and partial migrant around evergreen forests and dense miombo woodland, often near rivers and streams. Lays 2 eggs in a burrow up to 0.5 m long in a bank. **Diet:** Insects. (Tropiese Saagvlerkswael)

## 6 White-headed Saw-wing  *Psalidoprocne albiceps*

**13 cm; 7–14 g** Rare vagrant. A dark brown saw-wing; ad. male has a distinctive, snowy white head, bisected by a black line running through the eye to the nape; upperparts have a slight greenish sheen. Female has crown grizzled black; throat pale grey. Juv. duller than female, often with brown crown and grey throat. Some juv. females may be entirely brown; told from other juv. saw-wings by shorter, less deeply forked tail. **Voice:** Soft, weak twittering, with harsher chatters. **Status and biology:** Rare vagrant from central Africa; 3 records from Zimbabwe and Kruger NP. **Diet:** Insects. (Witkopsaagvlerkswael)

# MARTINS

Swallows with predominantly brown plumage. Sexes alike. *Riparia* martins nest in burrows, but rock martins are in the large swallow genus *Hirundo*, and build nests from mud pellets.

## 1 Banded Martin *Riparia cincta*

B B b b b · · b B B B B
J F M A M J J A S O N D

**17 cm; 23–29 g** A large, broad-winged martin with mainly white underparts and a brown breast band. Larger than other martins, with white (not dark) underwing coverts, a small white supercilium and a square-ended (not forked) tail. Often has a thin, brown line across vent. Juv. has upperparts scaled with pale buff. **Voice:** Flight call is 'che-che-che'; song is jumble of harsh 'chips', 'choops' and 'chirees'. **Status and biology:** Locally common intra-African migrant to grassland, scrub and other low vegetation. Roosts communally with other swallows. Lays 2–4 eggs in a burrow up to 0.6 m long, dug in the face of a low bank; occasionally in an aardvark burrow or drain pipe. Breeds singly, but often with other bank-nesting birds where suitable sites are scarce. **Diet:** Insects. (Gebande Oewerswael)

## 2 Sand Martin *Riparia riparia*

**12 cm; 11–16 g** A small, slender martin with mainly white underparts and a brown breast band. Much smaller than Banded Martin, with dark underwings (not white underwing coverts), a shallow-forked (not square) tail, and no white supercilium. Differs from Brown-throated Martin by its white (not brown) throat and brown breast band. Juv. has buff margins to upperpart feathers, appearing scaly in fresh plumage. **Voice:** Grating 'chrrr'. **Status and biology:** Locally common Palearctic migrant, usually near fresh water; often feeds in mixed flocks with Brown-throated Martins, but tends to roost with Barn Swallows. **Diet:** Insects. (Europese Oewerswael)

## 3 Brown-throated Martin *Riparia paludicola*

b b b b B B B B B b b b
J F M A M J J A S O N D

**12 cm; 10–16 g** A small, grey-brown martin that lacks the white throat and dark breast band of Sand and Banded martins. Belly usually white, but brown in some individuals (**3 A**). Dark form is smaller than Rock Martin, with colder grey-brown plumage and no creamy tail spots. Juv. is warmer brown than ad. below, with buffy fringes to upperpart feathers, appearing scaly in fresh plumage. **Voice:** Soft twittering. **Status and biology:** Common resident and local migrant in open areas, usually near water. Roosts communally in reeds. Breeds colonially, laying 2–4 eggs in a burrow up to 0.8 m long dug into a sandbank. **Diet:** Insects. (Afrikaanse Oewerswael)

## 4 Mascarene Martin *Phedina borbonica*

J F M A M J J A S O N D

**15 cm; 18–23 g** A fairly large, robust martin, most similar in structure to Banded Martin. Easily identified by its white underparts that are heavily streaked dark brown. Could be confused with juv. Lesser Striped Swallow (p. 276), but lacks chestnut crown and pale rump. Juv. has pale fringes to secondaries and tertials. **Voice:** High-pitched shrieks; usually silent in Africa. **Status and biology:** Uncommon to locally common non-br. visitor from Madagascar, mainly found over miombo woodland and forests, often in flocks with other swallows. **Diet:** Insects. (Gestreepte Kransswael)

## 5 Rock Martin *Hirundo fuligula*

b b b b b b b B B B B B
J F M A M J J A S O N D

**14 cm; 14–16 g** A brown swallow with a warm, buffy wash on the throat and breast. Tail slightly forked, with 8 creamy white spots near the tail tip, visible when the tail is fanned. Larger than sand martins with warmer brown plumage, less of a fork in the tail tip, and distinctive pale tail panels. Juv. has pale edges to upperwing coverts and secondaries. **Voice:** Soft, indistinct twitterings. **Status and biology:** Common resident, usually in rocky areas, although also around farms and old buildings. Some move out of high-altitude areas in winter. Often roosts in small groups on cliff faces or buildings when not breeding. Nests singly, laying 2–3 eggs in a cup nest of mud pellets stuck to the side of a rock wall or building. **Diet:** Insects. (Kransswael)

# DRONGOS

Noisy, conspicuous black birds with erect posture. Aerial-hawk from perches, taking prey in air or from the ground. Could be confused with Southern Black Flycatcher (p. 340), but have red eyes, heavier bills and forked tails. Frequently join bird parties and harass raptors. Sexes alike. Monogamous; both sexes incubate and care for the altricial chicks.

## 1 Fork-tailed Drongo  *Dicrurus adsimilis*

b | | | | | | | | b B B B b
J F M A M J J A S O N D

**23–26 cm; 38–55 g**  A large drongo with a deeply forked tail (but moult can affect tail shape). Ad. is glossy blue-black; in flight, pale primaries contrast with rest of wing. Typically occurs in more open habitats than Square-tailed Drongo. Juv. has buff-tipped wing coverts and underparts; gape yellow. **Voice:** A variety of loud, grating and shrill notes; mimics birds of prey, especially Pearl-spotted Owlet. **Status and biology:** Common resident in woodland, savanna and plantations. Often in pairs. Lays 2–5 eggs in a shallow cup nest suspended in the forked branch of a tree. **Diet:** Insects, especially bees and wasps; also ticks, small birds, chicks and reptiles, fish, nectar and scraps. Steals prey from other birds and mimics alarm call of Suricates to make them drop large prey. (Mikstertbyvanger)

## 2 Square-tailed Drongo  *Dicrurus ludwigii*

b | | | | | | | | | b b B b
J F M A M J J A S O N D

**18–19 cm; 20–40 g**  Smaller than Fork-tailed Drongo, with a shorter and more shallow-forked tail; lacks pale primaries in flight. Heavy bill and red eye separate it from Southern Black Flycatcher (p. 340); vertical posture and habits distinguish it from Black Cuckooshrike. Female is less glossy above; juv. has pale tips to mantle and underpart feathers. **Voice:** Strident 'cheweet-weet-weet' and whistled phrases; often very vocal in bird parties. **Status and biology:** Locally common resident in forests, dense riparian woodland and thickets. Usually found in pairs. Lays 2–3 eggs in a shallow cup nest suspended in the forked branch of a tree. **Diet:** Large insects and nectar. (Kleinbyvanger)

# CUCKOOSHRIKES

Thrush-sized, unobtrusive birds that forage in woodland and forest canopy. Sexes differ in most species; juvs resemble females. Monogamous; both sexes incubate and care for the altricial chicks.

## 3 Black Cuckooshrike  *Campephaga flava*

b | | | | | | | | b B B B
J F M A M J J A S O N D

**18–21 cm; 29–36 g**  Ad. male is all-black, with a prominent yellow gape; some individuals have a yellow shoulder patch. Told from Southern Black Flycatcher (p. 340) by its yellow gape and rounded (not square) tail. Yellow-shouldered male could be confused with a widowbird (p. 390), given a poor view. Ad. female is barred below, with bold yellow edges to wing feathers, superficially recalling Eastern Nicator (p. 296). Juv. resembles female, but is more heavily barred, including on crown. **Voice:** High-pitched, prolonged 'trrrrrrrr'. **Status and biology:** Locally common resident and local migrant in mature woodland and forest margins. Lays 1–3 eggs in a cup of moss and lichens bound onto a large tree branch with cobwebs. **Diet:** Insects and occasional fruit. (Swartkatakoeroe)

## 4 Grey Cuckooshrike  *Coracina caesia*

b | | | | | | | | | b B B
J F M A M J J A S O N D

**25–27 cm; 53–68 g**  The only all-grey cuckooshrike; has a narrow white eye-ring and dark loral patch. Plumage appears smooth, with subtle differences in grey shades from darker upperparts to paler underparts. Female is paler with grey lores. Juv. like female, with buff barring below and white edges to flight feathers and outer tail feathers. **Voice:** Soft, thin 'tseeeeep'. **Status and biology:** Uncommon resident and local altitudinal migrant in forests. Lays 1–2 eggs in a shallow bowl of lichen bound onto a tree branch with cobwebs. **Diet:** Insects, especially caterpillars and spiders. (Bloukatakoeroe)

## 5 White-breasted Cuckooshrike  *Coracina pectoralis*

| | | | | | | | | b B B B b
J F M A M J J A S O N D

**27 cm; 50–58 g**  A grey cuckooshrike with predominantly white underparts, which separate it from Grey Cuckooshrike. Male has grey throat and upper breast, contrasting with white belly; female and juv. are paler, with whitish throats. Juv. has black-and-white barring above and underparts spotted blackish; flight feathers tipped white; tail black. **Voice:** 'Duid-duid' by male; 'tchee-ee-ee-ee' by female. **Status and biology:** Uncommon to locally common resident of tall woodland, especially miombo and riverine forests. Lays 1–2 eggs in a shallow bowl of lichen bound onto a tree branch with cobwebs. **Diet:** Caterpillars and other insects. (Witborskatakoeroe)

# OLD-WORLD ORIOLES

Large, boldly plumaged passerines of woodland and forest canopy; often located by their loud, ringing song. Sexes alike in dark-headed species, differ in golden orioles. Monogamous; both sexes incubate and care for the altricial chicks.

## 1 African Golden Oriole *Oriolus auratus*

**20–24 cm; 70–80 g** Brighter golden-yellow than Eurasian Golden Oriole, with prominent yellow edges to its wing coverts and secondaries at all ages; ads have longer black stripe extending behind their eyes. Female is duller and greener above than male, but is brighter than female Eurasian Golden Oriole, with plain yellowish underparts. Juv. is streaked below and has a dark bill; upperwing coverts and secondaries edged olive-yellow. **Voice:** Liquid whistle, 'fee-yoo-fee-yoo'; also mewling, up-slurred call. **Status and biology:** Locally common resident and intra-African migrant in tall woodland (especially miombo) and riverine forest. Lays 2–3 (rarely up to 5) eggs in a cup nest slung in the forked branch of a tree. **Diet:** Insects and fruit. (Afrikaanse Wielewaal)

## 2 Eurasian Golden Oriole *Oriolus oriolus*

**22–25 cm; 50–80 g** Ad. male is stunning yellow and black; differs from male African Golden Oriole by black wings and black eye-stripe, which extends only marginally behind eye. Female is similar to female African Golden Oriole, but underparts are whitish, finely streaked, with plain wing coverts (lacking yellow edges), and less extensive dark line behind eye. Juv. is whitish below, with dark green streaks; bill is blackish. **Voice:** Song is liquid 'chleeooop', but chattering subsong and grating 'naaah' calls are more typically heard in Africa. **Status and biology:** Fairly common Palearctic migrant to woodland, savanna and exotic plantations. **Diet:** Insects and fruit, especially figs. (Europese Wielewaal)

## 3 Black-headed Oriole *Oriolus larvatus*

**20–24 cm; 60–80 g** The only black-headed oriole in the region. Ad. has plain black head, throat and central breast; mantle and upperwing coverts more olive-green than in golden orioles. Juv. is duller, with dark brown, slightly mottled head and streaked throat and breast; bill darker, dull red. **Voice:** Song is explosive, whistled 'pooodleeoo'; harsher 'kweeer' note. **Status and biology:** Common resident in mature woodland, forest edge and exotic plantations. Some evidence of movement to coastal areas in winter. Lays 2–3 eggs in a deep cup of moss or lichen slung in the fork of a branch. **Diet:** Insects, seeds, fruit and nectar. (Swartkopwielewaal)

## 4 Green-headed Oriole *Oriolus chlorocephalus*

**20–24 cm; 65 g** A highly localised oriole with a moss-green head, yellow collar and green back. From a distance, head appears dark, and might be confused with Black-headed Oriole, but back is darker. Juv. has dull yellow underparts, breast slightly streaked with olive, and pale olive wash on head and throat. **Voice:** Explosive, liquid song, typical of orioles; distinctive nasal mewing, 'waaaarrr'. **Status and biology:** Locally common resident; in sthn Africa, confined to montane forest on Mt Gorongoza, C Mozambique. Clutch size unknown. Nest is a cup of lichen or rootlets slung in the fork of a branch. **Diet:** Insects and fruit. (Groenkopwielewaal)

# RAVENS AND CROWS

Large passerines with mainly black plumage and stout legs and feet. Some species hoard food, demonstrating remarkable memories; others fashion and use tools. Sexes alike. Monogamous; incubation mainly by female; chicks altricial.

### 1 White-necked Raven  *Corvus albicollis*

**bbBBb**
J F M A M J J A S O N D

**50–56 cm; 750–880 g**  A large crow, with a white crescent on the back of the neck and a heavy, white-tipped bill. In flight, has broader wings and a shorter, broader tail than other crows. Juv. is brownish-black; may show some white feathers on its breast. **Voice:** Deep, throaty 'kwaak'. **Status and biology:** Locally common resident in mountainous and hilly areas. Remains in pairs year-round, although sometimes found in small flocks. Lays 2–5 eggs in a stick nest on an inaccessible cliff ledge. **Diet:** Reptiles, insects, small birds and mammals, carrion, fruit and seeds. (Withalskraai)

### 2 Pied Crow  *Corvus albus*

**b        bbBBbb**
J F M A M J J A S O N D

**46–50 cm; 410–610 g**  The only white-breasted crow in the region. From above, has a longer tail, more slender wings and smaller head and bill than White-necked Raven. Juv. is slightly duller, with dusky tips to white feathers, and less crisp margin between black throat and white breast. **Voice:** Croaking, cawing 'krow' or 'kwooork'. **Status and biology:** Common and widespread in virtually all habitats except driest desert areas. Often in flocks. Lays 1–7 eggs in a stick nest (often including some wire) built in a high fork of a tree, telephone pole or windmill; rarely on a building or cliff. **Diet:** Fruit and seeds; also small mammals, birds, reptiles, amphibians, insects and carrion. (Witborskraai)

### 3 Cape Crow  *Corvus capensis*

**b        bbBBbb**
J F M A M J J A S O N D

**45–50 cm; 410–630 g**  A fairly large, slender, glossy black crow with a long, thin, slightly decurved bill. Larger than House Crow, with uniformly black plumage. Juv. is duller, brownish-black. **Voice:** Deep, cawing 'kaah-kaah', as well as an astonishing variety of bubbling calls. **Status and biology:** Common resident in grassland, open country, cultivated fields and dry, desert regions. Usually in pairs, but sometimes in larger flocks. Lays 1–6 eggs in a stick nest built at the top of a tree or telephone pole; rarely on a cliff. **Diet:** Insects and other invertebrates; also small reptiles, frogs, birds, carrion, seeds and fruit. (Swartkraai)

### 4 House Crow  *Corvus splendens*

**b        bBb**
J F M A M J J A S O N D

**38–43 cm; 260–400 g**  Self-introduced from Asia, hitching rides on ships down E coast of Africa. A rather small, slender, long-tailed crow with a diagnostic grey body. Head, wings and tail are glossy blue-black. Bill fairly long; heavier at tip than Cape Crow. Juv. is duller, with a paler, greyish-brown body. **Voice:** Hurried, high-pitched 'kah, kah'. **Status and biology:** Locally common resident, usually found near human habitation. Numbers in Durban and Cape Town are falling due to eradication efforts. Often in small flocks. Breeds singly or in loose colonies. Lays 2–5 eggs in a stick nest built in a tall tree; occasionally on a pole or building. **Diet:** Scavenges food scraps; also small birds, mammals, reptiles, frogs, fish, invertebrates, fruit and seeds. Takes eggs and nestlings from birds' nests, often raiding heronries and weaver colonies. (Huiskraai)

# TITS

Fairly small passerines, usually with some black-and-white plumage. Social and noisy; they occur in small groups and frequently join bird parties. Sexes alike. Monogamous, often with helpers at the nest. Incubation usually by female only; chicks altricial.

## 1 Ashy Tit  *Parus cinerascens*

`b b b | | | | | | | B B B b`
J F M A M J J A S O N D

15 cm; 19–22 g  The arid savanna member of the Grey Tit complex, which are all characterised by a striking black-and-white head and black throat extending as a stripe down the central breast and belly. Differs from Grey Tit by its blue-grey (not brownish-grey) back, grey (not buffy) wash on the flanks and belly, and white (not buffy) nape spot. Told from Miombo Tit by its grey (not whitish) flanks, white (not buffy) cheeks and narrower white edges to its wing coverts. Juv. is duller, with a sooty brown cap and throat; back washed brown. **Voice:** Song is ringing trill 'tlu-tlu-tlu-tlu-tlu', 'tu-tu-tu-tu' or 'tuweee-tuweee-tuweee'; also a harsh alarm call. **Status and biology:** Near-endemic. Common resident in thornveld and arid savanna. Lays 3–6 eggs in a cavity in a tree, bank, pole or old building; sometimes uses old Greater Striped Swallow nests. **Diet:** Insects, spiders, fruit and seeds. (Akasiagrysmees)

## 2 Grey Tit  *Parus afer*

`b b b | | | | b B B b b b`
J F M A M J J A S O N D

15 cm; 18–22 g  Distinguished from Ashy Tit by its brownish-grey (not blue-grey) back, buffy (not grey) belly and flanks, and buff (not white) spot on its nape. Juv. browner above. **Voice:** Song is ringing, whistled 'chiree-wuu-wuu' or 'swit-weeuu-weeuuz'. Alarm call is a series of rasping notes, sometimes preceded by 2–3 high-pitched whistles; typically less harsh than alarm calls of Ashy Tit. **Status and biology:** Endemic. Locally common resident in fynbos and karoo scrub, often near rocky outcrops and old buildings. Lays 2–5 eggs in a cavity in a tree, pole or pipe. **Diet:** Insects, spiders and fruit. (Piet-tjou-tjougrysmees)

## 3 Miombo Tit  *Parus griseiventris*

`| | | | | | | | | b B B b b`
J F M A M J J A S O N D

13 cm; 14–17 g  Paler than Ashy Tit, with whitish (not grey-washed) flanks, creamy-buff (not white) cheek patches and a thinner bill. Also occurs in broadleafed woodland, especially miombo (not acacia savanna). Distinguished from Grey Tit by blue-grey (not brownish-grey) back and pale blue-grey (not buffy) flanks; ranges do not overlap. Juv. duller, with smaller bib reaching only onto its breast; wing feathers edged buff (not white). **Voice:** Scolding 'tjou-tjou-tjou-tjou' and churring notes. **Status and biology:** Common resident in miombo and adjacent broadleafed woodland. Lays 3–5 eggs in a cavity in a tree, pole or termite mound. **Diet:** Insects and spiders. (Miombogrysmees)

## 4 Cinnamon-breasted Tit  *Parus pallidiventris*

`| | | | | | | | | b b b b`
J F M A M J J A S O N D

14 cm; 16–20 g  Sometimes treated as a subspecies of Rufous-bellied Tit, but is slightly smaller and much paler, with a more sharply defined divide between the blackish head and greyish-buff (not rufous) underparts; eyes brown (not yellow); ranges do not overlap in sthn Africa. Juv. duller with pale edges to wing feathers. **Voice:** Whistles and churrs similar to those of Rufous-bellied Tit. **Status and biology:** Local and generally uncommon resident in miombo woodland; sometimes also in climax mopane woodland. Occurs in small groups; often joins bird parties. Lays 3–4 eggs in a tree cavity. **Diet:** Insects. (Swartkopmees)

## 5 Rufous-bellied Tit  *Parus rufiventris*

`| | | | | | | | | b b b b`
J F M A M J J A S O N D

15 cm; 18–22 g  Could be confused with Cinnamon-breasted Tit, but is slightly larger and darker above, with a rich rufous (not greyish-buff) belly. Ad. has bright yellow eyes, conspicuous at close range. Juv. duller, with brown eye and buffy edges to wing feathers. **Voice:** Harsh, tit-like 'chrrr chrrr'; clear 'chick-weeu, chick-weeu' song. **Status and biology:** Locally common resident in broadleafed woodland. Often joins bird parties. Lays 3–4 eggs in a tree cavity. **Diet:** Insects. (Rooipensmees)

## 6 Southern Black Tit  *Parus niger*

`b | | | | | | | | | B B b`
J F M A M J J A S O N D

16 cm; 18–25 g  A mainly black tit, with white edges to wing feathers. Told from Carp's Tit by its barred grey (not black) vent and less white in wings. Male head and body black; female has dark grey head and underparts. Juv. like female, but washed buff below. **Voice:** Lively mix of harsh, chattering 'chrr-chrr-chrr' and musical 'phee-cher-phee-cher' notes. **Status and biology:** Common resident in forest and broadleafed woodland, usually in small groups. Lays 1–6 eggs in a tree cavity. **Diet:** Insects and other invertebrates, fruit and nectar. (Gewone Swartmees)

## 7 Carp's Tit  *Parus carpi*

`b B B B b b | | | | | |`
J F M A M J J A S O N D

14 cm; 14–21 g  Similar to Southern Black Tit, but has a black (not grey-barred) vent and more extensive white in wings. Male has all-black body; female is sooty grey, with a darker belly than female Southern Black Tit. Juv. duller than female, with yellowish fringes to flight feathers. **Voice:** Similar to that of Southern Black Tit. **Status and biology:** Near-endemic. Fairly common resident in semi-arid savanna woodland. Lays 2–5 eggs in a tree cavity or pipe. **Diet:** Insects, fruit and seeds. (Ovamboswartmees)

# BABBLERS

Large, thrush-like passerines that occur in small, noisy groups year-round; birds maintain contact with continuous, raucous babbling calls. Sexes alike; juvs duller. Territorial and monogamous, with helpers at the nest. All group members incubate and care for the altricial chicks. Most species are brood hosts for Levaillant's Cuckoo.

## 1 Arrow-marked Babbler *Turdoides jardineii*

| b | b | b | b | b | b | b | b | b | B | B | b |
|---|---|---|---|---|---|---|---|---|---|---|---|
| J | F | M | A | M | J | J | A | S | O | N | D |

22–25 cm; 60–82 g  The most widespread brown babbler in the region; grey-brown with narrow, white breast streaks (not scalloped like Black-faced and Hartlaub's babblers). Black lores extend around red-rimmed, yellow eyes. Juv. lacks white streaking on breast; underparts buffy with darker streaks; eyes brown. **Voice:** Noisy; raucous 'chow-chow-chow-chow...', with several birds calling together. **Status and biology:** Common resident in woodland and savanna. Occurs in groups of up to 12 birds. Lays 2–3 (rarely up to 5) eggs in a bulky bowl of vegetation built in dense foliage by all members of the group. **Diet:** Mainly insects; also spiders, fruit, seeds and nectar. (Pylvlekkatlagter)

## 2 Black-faced Babbler *Turdoides melanops*

| | | | | | | | | b | b | b | b |
|---|---|---|---|---|---|---|---|---|---|---|---|
| J | F | M | A | M | J | J | A | S | O | N | D |

24–28 cm; 75–80 g  A localised, grey-brown babbler. Differs from Arrow-marked Babbler by its pale scalloping (not streaking) on the breast, pale yellow-green (not red-rimmed yellow or orange) eyes, and larger, more sharply defined black lores. Told from Hartlaub's Babbler by its brown (not whitish) rump and belly and paler eyes. Juv. is paler, with reduced scalloping below; eyes brown. **Voice:** Nasal 'wha-wha-wha'; harsh, fast 'papapapa'. **Status and biology:** Near-endemic. Uncommon resident in broadleafed woodland. Forages in scattered groups; more furtive than other babblers. Lays 2–3 eggs in a bulky bowl of vegetation built in the outer branches of a shrub or small tree. **Diet:** Insects, small reptiles and fruit. (Swartwangkatlagter)

## 3 Hartlaub's Babbler *Turdoides hartlaubii*

| | B | b | b | | | b | b | b | | b | |
|---|---|---|---|---|---|---|---|---|---|---|---|
| J | F | M | A | M | J | J | A | S | O | N | D |

24–26 cm; 70–85 g  The only brown babbler in the region with a white rump. At rest, told from Black-faced and Arrow-marked babblers by its whitish lower belly and vent. Eyes orange-red to crimson. Juv. is paler, especially on the throat and breast. **Voice:** Noisy; loud 'kwek-kwek-kwek' or 'papapapapapa'. **Status and biology:** Common resident, usually close to water, occurring in reedbeds and surrounding woodland. Found in groups of 5–15 (rarely 20) birds. Lays 2–4 eggs in an untidy bowl of vegetation built in dense cover, usually within 3 m of the ground. **Diet:** Insects and fruit. (Witkruiskatlagter)

## 4 Bare-cheeked Babbler *Turdoides gymnogenys*

| | | | | | | | | | | b | b |
|---|---|---|---|---|---|---|---|---|---|---|---|
| J | F | M | A | M | J | J | A | S | O | N | D |

24–26 cm; 70–90 g  A distinctive babbler with a mainly white body. Differs from Southern Pied Babbler by its brown (not white) back, rufous nape, brown (not black) wings, and small patches of bare, black skin below and behind its eyes. Juv. has crown and nape pale grey-brown; edges of wing feathers edged buff; appears darker than juv. Southern Pied Babbler, and is accompanied by ads. **Voice:** Typical babbler 'kerrrakerrra-kek-kek-kek'. **Status and biology:** Locally common resident in arid savanna, favouring taller and denser vegetation along rivers and wooded hills. Occurs in groups of 2–11 birds. Lays 2–3 eggs in a bulky bowl of vegetation built in the fork of a small tree. **Diet:** Mainly insects. (Kaalwangkatlagter)

## 5 Southern Pied Babbler *Turdoides bicolor*

| B | b | b | b | | | | b | b | b | B | B |
|---|---|---|---|---|---|---|---|---|---|---|---|
| J | F | M | A | M | J | J | A | S | O | N | D |

23–26 cm; 70–84g  A striking black-and-white babbler. Ad. told from Bare-cheeked Babbler by its clean white head and back, contrasting with blackish wings. In flight, white wing coverts contrast with blackish flight feathers. Juv. is pale brown, whitening with age; usually paler than juv. Bare-cheeked Babbler, and always accompanied by ads. **Voice:** High-pitched 'kwee kwee kwee kweer' babbling. **Status and biology:** Endemic. Locally common resident in arid savanna, especially thornveld. Occurs in groups of 3–15 birds, although some males fail to attract mates. Lays 2–3 (rarely up to 5) eggs in a large bowl of vegetation built by all group members in a thorn tree. **Diet:** Mainly insects; also ticks, small reptiles, frogs and seeds. Sometimes steals prey from other birds. One member of group scans for predators while others forage. (Witkatlagter)

**BOULDER-CHAT** (see p. 302 for other chats)

## 6 Boulder Chat *Pinarornis plumosus*

| b | | | | | | | | | b | B | b |
|---|---|---|---|---|---|---|---|---|---|---|---|
| J | F | M | A | M | J | J | A | S | O | N | D |

25 cm; 48–72 g  A large, babbler-like chat with blackish-brown plumage and white-tipped tail feathers (central pair often all dark brown). At close range, fine white speckles on chin are visible. Runs and bounds over large boulders, occasionally raising tail well over back when landing. Occurs in the same habitat as Mocking Cliff-Chat (p. 306), but lacks a chestnut rump and belly. In flight shows a row of small white spots on the bases of the primaries and outer secondaries. Juv. is browner, with paler underparts. **Voice:** Clear, sharp whistle; softer 'wink, wink' call, like a squeaky wheel. **Status and biology:** Near-endemic. Locally common resident in well-wooded terrain with large granite boulders. Lays 2–4 eggs in a large cup nest built on the ground next to a large rock or in a rock crevice. **Diet:** Insects and small reptiles. (Swartberglyster)

## 1 Bush Blackcap  *Lioptilus nigricapillus*

J F M A M J J A S O N D

**16–18 cm; 26–33 g** A fairly small, brown-backed babbler whose structure and rich song recall a bulbul. Larger than male Blackcap (p. 314) with red (not greyish) bill, pink legs and black cap extending below eye. Juv. duller with a pink bill. **Voice:** Rich, melodious warbling song 'plik plik toodley-oodley-oodley-ooo'. **Status and biology:** Endemic. Uncommon resident and altitudinal migrant occurring in montane forest and dense scrub; also gardens and coastal forest in winter. Lays 2 eggs in a neat cup nest built in the fork of a leafy shrub or small, sub-canopy tree. **Diet:** Fruit and insects. (Rooibektiptol)

# BULBULS, BROWNBULS AND GREENBULS

Medium-sized passerines, including some of the most abundant species in woodland and forest habitats. Identification of greenbuls can be challenging, but fortunately relatively few species occur in sthn Africa. Sexes alike. Monogamous. Incubation usually by female only; chicks altricial.

## 2 Cape Bulbul  *Pycnonotus capensis*

J F M A M J J A S O N D

**21 cm; 30–46 g** A chocolate brown bulbul with a crest and yellow vent. Told from African Red-eyed and Dark-capped bulbuls by its diagnostic white eye-ring and darker underparts, extending onto lower belly. Juv. has a purplish-grey eye-ring. Hybridises with Dark-capped Bulbul along the Sundays River, and with African Red-eyed Bulbul between Prince Albert and Somerset East. **Voice:** Song is a lively, liquid whistle 'chip chee woodely', higher-pitched and sharper than Dark-capped Bulbul. **Status and biology:** Endemic. Common resident in fynbos, coastal scrub and gardens. Lays 2–4 eggs in a cup nest built in the outer canopy of a shrub or small tree. **Diet:** Fruit, seeds, nectar and insects; sometimes hawks insects. (Kaapse Tiptol)

## 3 African Red-eyed Bulbul  *Pycnonotus nigricans*

J F M A M J J A S O N D

**19 cm; 22–36 g** Told from Dark-capped and Cape bulbuls by its diagnostic red eye-ring. Head is blacker than Dark-capped Bulbul's, contrasting with a greyish neck collar and breast. Juv. has a whitish eye-ring, turning pale pink after 2–3 months. Hybridises with Dark-capped and Cape bulbuls where their ranges meet. **Voice:** Liquid whistles, slightly more fluty than Dark-capped Bulbul's. **Status and biology:** Near-endemic. Common resident and local nomad in arid savanna, riverine bush and gardens. Lays 2–3 eggs in a cup nest built in the fork of a shrub or small tree. **Diet:** Fruit, flowers, nectar and insects; sometimes hawks insects. (Rooioogtiptol)

## 4 Dark-capped Bulbul  *Pycnonotus tricolor*

J F M A M J J A S O N D

**21 cm; 30–48 g** The most common *Pycnonotus* bulbul in the E of the region. Told from African Red-eyed and Cape bulbuls by its black (not red or white) eye-ring. Juv. paler. Hybridises with African Red-eyed and Cape bulbuls where their ranges meet. **Voice:** Harsh 'kwit, kwit, kwit' alarm call; song is a liquid 'sweet sweet sweet-potato'. **Status and biology:** Abundant resident in a wide range of habitats from savanna to forest edge and gardens. Lays 2–3 eggs in a cup nest built in the canopy of a shrub or small tree, sometimes slung between branches with spider webs. **Diet:** Fruit, seeds, flowers, nectar, insects and spiders; sometimes hawks insects, especially termite alates. (Swartoogtiptol)

## 5 Terrestrial Brownbul  *Phyllastrephus terrestris*

J F M A M J J A S O N D

**18–22 cm; 24–44 g** A fairly large, brown-backed understorey greenbul with a whitish throat and pale grey-brown central breast and belly. Juv. is paler with more rufous rump and tail and yellow wash on underparts. **Voice:** Soft, chattering 'trrup cherrup trrup'. **Status and biology:** Common resident in forest understorey and thickets. Occurs in small, noisy groups of 3–6 birds, scuffling around on the forest floor and gleaning among low, tangled vegetation. Lays 2–3 eggs in a shallow, flimsy cup nest built in the fork of a sapling or other low vegetation, usually within 2 m of the ground. **Diet:** Insects, snails, small reptiles, fruit, nectar and seeds. (Boskrapper)

## 1 Sombre Greenbul  *Andropadus importunus*

bbBB
J F M A M J J A S O N D

**18 cm; 30–39 g** A medium-sized, plain olive-green greenbul with a diagnostic pale eye and distinctive song. *A. i. hypoxanthus* (C Mozambique) is greener above and more yellow below; could be confused with Yellow-bellied Greenbul, but has white (not red) eye and lacks narrow white eye crescents. Juv. duller with dark eyes, a narrow pale eye-ring and prominent yellow gape. **Voice:** Song is a piercing 'willie', often followed by a rapid warble, ending in a nasal, querulous note. Alarm call is a loud 'plee plee plee'. **Status and biology:** Common resident in forest and thicket, in canopy and mid-strata. Lays 1–3 eggs in a cup nest built in the fork of a shrub. **Diet:** Fruit; also some flowers, leaves and insects. (Gewone Willie)

## 2 Tiny Greenbul  *Phyllastrephus debilis*

bbbb
J F M A M J J A S O N D

**14 cm; 13–16 g** A small, warbler-like greenbul. Recalls a diminutive Yellow-streaked Greenbul, with a pale grey head, whitish throat and variably yellow-washed underparts. Eyes vary from white to grey-brown; bill slender with a rather pale grey base. Juv. has a greener crown. **Voice:** Nasal, bubbling song 'kwerr kerr ker ker kr-r-rrrr', increasing in pace; shrill 'shriiip' call. **Status and biology:** Uncommon resident in low and mid-elevation forest, forest edge and adjacent thickets. Often occurs in small groups. Lays 2 eggs in a neat cup nest slung in the fork of a sapling usually within 1–2 m of the ground. **Diet:** Insects gleaned from foliage in dense tangles. (Kleinboskruiper)

## 3 Stripe-cheeked Greenbul  *Andropadus milanjensis*

bbb        bBB
J F M A M J J A S O N D

**20 cm; 31–47 g** A localised species in sthn Africa. Slightly larger and stockier than Sombre Bulbul, with a grey (not olive) head, dark eyes and prominent white crescent above its eye. The faint white cheek streaks are only visible at close range. Juv. has a green-washed crown. **Voice:** Throaty 'chrrup-chip-chrup-chrup'. **Status and biology:** Locally common resident in montane forest and forest edge. Sometimes occurs in small groups. Lays 1–2 eggs in a flimsy cup nest built in the canopy of a sapling or creeper. **Diet:** Fruit, seeds, insects and worms. (Streep-wangwillie)

## 4 Yellow-streaked Greenbul  *Phyllastrephus flavostriatus*

bbb        bbBB
J F M A M J J A S O N D

**18–20 cm; 22–38 g** A slender, pale greenbul, best identified by its foraging action: creeps up branches, gleaning insects and continually flicking open one wing at a time. Paler below than other similar-sized greenbuls, with a whitish throat and breast; the faint yellow breast streaks are only visible at close range and in good light. Bill long and slender compared to most other greenbuls. Juv. has breast washed olive. **Voice:** Song is a joyful 'klip, klip-ip-ip, klip-ip-ip, weet-weet-weet-weaat'; also sharp 'kleet kleet kleeat' and dry 'trl-rl-rl-rl' calls. **Status and biology:** Locally common resident in forest mid-stratum and canopy. Usually in small groups of up to 15 birds. Lays 2–3 eggs in a flimsy cup nest decorated with bark flakes, moss and leaves, slung with spider webs in the fork of a small tree, 1–2 m above the ground. **Diet:** Insects, spiders, snails and small fruit. (Geelstreepboskruiper)

## 5 Yellow-bellied Greenbul  *Chlorocichla flaviventris*

bbb        BBBB
J F M A M J J A S O N D

**20–23 cm, 32–50 g** A large, chunky greenbul with olive-brown upperparts, yellow-washed underparts and a diagnostic white crescent above its eye; bill heavy. Larger than Sombre Greenbul, with much brighter yellow underparts and dark reddish (not white) eyes. It has bright yellow underwing coverts that are conspicuous in flight. Juv. duller and paler, with grey eyes and a prominent yellow gape. **Voice:** Nasal 'nehr-nehr-nehr-nehr', often repeated, becoming faster and higher-pitched when alarmed, and interspersed by short, guttural calls. Contact call is a hoarse 'kwoar-tooarr'. **Status and biology:** Common resident of thickets, dense woodland and forest edge; also gardens and mangroves. Often in groups of 2–6 birds. Lays 1–3 eggs in a flimsy cup nest built among dense foliage in a small tree or shrub. **Diet:** Fruit, seeds, insects and flowers. Sometimes hawks insects, and gleans parasites from antelopes. (Geelborswillie)

# NICATORS

An African genus recalling bulbuls or bush-shrikes, but probably best placed in their own family. Sexes alike. Monogamous. Incubation usually by female only; chicks altricial.

## 6 Eastern Nicator  *Nicator gularis*

b          bb
J F M A M J J A S O N D

**20–23 cm; 34–62 g** The only sthn African nicator, a distinctive group of birds that resemble both greenbuls and bush-shrikes. Yellow-tipped wing coverts and tertials are distinctive; shared only with Grey-headed Bush-Shrike (p. 362), but is smaller and much duller with dark (not pale) eyes and more prominent spotting on its coverts. Yellow tips to outer tail are obvious in flight. Often skulking; occurs singly or in pairs. Sexes alike. Juv. duller with yellow-tipped primaries. **Voice:** Distinctive song is a short, rich, explosive, liquid jumble of notes. **Status and biology:** Common resident in dense riverine and coastal forests and scrub, particularly on sandy soil. Easily overlooked if not calling. Lays 2–3 eggs in a shallow depression on top of a platform of twigs, built low down in thick vegetation. **Diet:** Insects; occasionally gleans parasites from antelopes, zebras and warthogs. (Geelvleknikator)

# THRUSHES

Fairly large passerines, often with rufous bellies. Ground-thrushes have distinctive white wing bars. Sexes alike; short-lived juv. plumage has pale spotting on the head and diffuse dark spots on the breast. Flip over leaf litter with their feet and bills to locate prey. Some species use anvils to break open snail shells. Monogamous and territorial. Incubation usually by female only; chicks altricial.

## 1 Olive Thrush *Turdus olivaceus*

b b b b b b b b b B B B B
J F M A M J J A S O N D

**22–24 cm; 55–78 g** An olive-brown thrush, with an orange-washed belly and yellow legs and bill. Has more extensive rufous underparts than Karoo Thrush, with typically stronger black-and-white streaking on the throat, paler vent and less prominent eye-ring. At close range, top of upper mandible and area around nares is blackish (not yellow). Darker than Kurrichane Thrush, with orange (not whitish) central belly, duller bill and less distinct black malar stripes. Juv. has mottled underparts. Probably hybridises with Karoo Thrush where ranges meet; some birds show intermediate characters. **Voice:** Sharp 'chink' or thin 'tseeep' call; song is a rich, melodic whistle 'wheeet-tooo-wheeet', usually given before dawn. **Status and biology:** Common resident and altitudinal migrant in forests, parks, gardens and plantations. Lays 2–3 eggs in a bulky cup nest built in a tree fork. **Diet:** Invertebrates and fruit; occasionally small reptiles. (Olyflyster)

## 2 Karoo Thrush *Turdus smithi*

b b b b      b B B
J F M A M J J A S O N D

**22–24 cm; 60–86 g** A dark, dull version of Olive Thrush, with a more prominent golden eye-ring and an all-yellow bill; rufous underparts are typically restricted to the central belly; flanks and vent greyish. Juv. has mottled underparts. Probably hybridises with Olive Thrush where ranges meet; some birds show intermediate characters. **Voice:** Soft 'tseeeep' contact call; song similar to Olive Thrush's. **Status and biology:** Endemic. Locally common resident in dense vegetation in semi-arid karoo scrub, savanna and grassland; also gardens. Lays 1–4 eggs in a bulky cup nest built in a tree fork. **Diet:** Invertebrates and fruit; occasionally small fish and fledgling birds. (Geelbeklyster)

## 3 Kurrichane Thrush *Turdus libonyanus*

b b b      b B B B b
J F M A M J J A S O N D

**21–22 cm; 50–70 g** A woodland thrush with a white belly and rufous flanks; upperparts are paler and greyer (not olive-brown) than Olive or Karoo thrushes. Black speckling on throat is concentrated into diagnostic broad black malar stripes, and bill is brighter orange than other thrushes. Juv. has mottled underparts and buffy tips to upperwing coverts. **Voice:** Loud, whistling 'peet-peeoo'. **Status and biology:** Common resident and local nomad in woodland; also parks and gardens. Lays 1–4 eggs in a cup nest built from mud and vegetation, usually built in the fork of a tree; occasionally uses nests of other birds. **Diet:** Invertebrates and fruit; sometimes steals food from other birds. (Rooibeklyster)

## 4 Orange Ground-Thrush *Zoothera gurneyi*

b        b B B
J F M A M J J A S O N D

**20–22 cm; 60–74 g** A secretive forest thrush, distinguished from other thrushes with orange underparts by the diagnostic white bars on its upperwing coverts and blackish (not yellow-orange) bill. Habitat overlaps with Olive Thrush; when seen from below, can be told from this species by its white belly. Juv. has pale, spotted upperparts and mottled underparts; throat whitish. **Voice:** Sibilant 'tseeep'; song is a series of rich, melodic whistles. **Status and biology:** Uncommon resident in Afromontane forests; some may winter at lower elevations in E Cape. Lays 1–3 eggs in a bulky cup nest built in a sapling using dead leaves and moss. **Diet:** Worms, snails, insects and fruit. (Oranjelyster)

## 5 Groundscraper Thrush *Psophocichla litsitsirupa*

b b b      b B B B b
J F M A M J J A S O N D

**21–23 cm; 70–85 g** A distinctive, open-country thrush, with a characteristic upright stance and short tail; lacks white wing bars of Spotted Ground-Thrush and is greyer above with bolder, more contrasting face markings; occurs in more open habitats. Larger than Dusky Lark (p. 260), with bolder face markings and plain upperparts (lacks pale edges to wing feathers). In flight, has prominent chestnut bars across its primaries. Juv. paler above, with small white spots on head and mantle and whitish tips to upperwing coverts; streaks on underparts duller brown. **Voice:** Song is less melodic than other thrushes; series of slow notes 'lit-sit-si-rupa'; also clicking call. **Status and biology:** Common resident and local nomad in open woodland, savanna and montane grassland. Lays 2–4 eggs in a cup nest built in a tree fork, often near a Fork-tailed Drongo nest; sometimes has helpers at the nest. **Diet:** Insects and other invertebrates. (Gevlekte Lyster)

## 6 Spotted Ground-Thrush *Zoothera guttata*

b b       B B B b
J F M A M J J A S O N D

**20–22 cm; 62–76 g** A secretive forest thrush, with a spotted breast. Superficially recalls Groundscraper Thrush, but is browner above with bold white wing bars, a longer tail and a more horizontal stance; occurs in forests. Pale pink legs are conspicuous. Juv. has head and mantle spotted buff; underparts buff with darker streaks. **Voice:** Quiet 'tseeeep' call; song is whistled and fluty, with short phrases of 4–5 notes. **Status and biology: ENDANGERED.** Rare resident and partial migrant in forest understorey. Breeds in coastal forests in E Cape and slightly further inland in KZN; both populations winter in coastal forests along the KZN coast. Lays 1–3 eggs in a bulky cup nest built up to 3 m up in a sapling or understorey vegetation. Occasionally re-uses the same nest for successive br. attempts. **Diet:** Worms, snails and other invertebrates. (Natallyster)

# ROCK-THRUSHES

Distinctive, open-country thrushes, typically associated with rocky habitats. Unlike other thrushes, they exhibit marked sexual dimorphism. Juvs distinct. Monogamous and territorial; chicks altricial.

## 1 Cape Rock-Thrush *Monticola rupestris*

`b b | | | | | | | B B B B`
J F M A M J J A S O N D

20–22 cm; 50–65 g  A fairly large rock-thrush, with a longer tail and more horizontal stance than other species. Male distinguished by its brown (not blue-grey) back; blue-grey head restricted to throat. Female generally darker than other female rock-thrushes; rufous underparts extend to top of breast. Juv. is like female, but spotted buff above, scaled blackish below. **Voice:** Song is far-carrying, rather stereotyped 'tsee-tseu-tseet tseu-tseu-tseet chweeeoo' whistle; harsh, grating alarm calls. **Status and biology:** Endemic. Locally common resident in rocky areas in grassland and heaths. Some birds leave high elevations in winter. Lays 2–3 (rarely 4) eggs in a cup nest built in a cavity in a rock face or building. **Diet:** Insects, other invertebrates, fruit, seeds and nectar; also frogs and lizards. (Kaapse Kliplyster)

## 2 Sentinel Rock-Thrush *Monticola explorator*

`b | | | | | | | | b B B b`
J F M A M J J A S O N D

18–20 cm; 44–51 g  A compact, upright rock-thrush, with a shortish tail. Male has a blue-grey back (not brown as Cape Rock-Thrush) and a plain blue-grey head, lacking pale crown of nominate Short-toed Rock-Thrush. Blue-grey throat extends further onto breast than male Cape or Short-toed rock-thrushes. Female duller, usually with a mottled breast that is paler than female Cape or Short-toed rock-thrushes. Juv. has pale-spotted upperparts and brown-scaled underparts. **Voice:** Whistled song is more varied and softer than that of Cape Rock Thrush. **Status and biology:** Endemic. Locally common resident and partial altitudinal migrant in rocky terrain. Lays 2–3 eggs in a cup nest in a rock crevice or on the ground against a rock or grass tuft. **Diet:** Insects, other invertebrates, fruit and seeds. (Langtoonkliplyster)

## 3 Short-toed Rock-Thrush *Monticola brevipes*

`b b b | | | | | | b b B B b`
J F M A M J J A S O N D

16–18 cm; 28–35 g  Male's pale crown contrasts with darker blue-grey face; some have a darker crown, but they usually retain a pale supercilium. Blue-grey throat doesn't extend onto breast as in Sentinel Rock-Thrush. Blue-grey (not brown) back separates it from Cape Rock-Thrush. Female is paler, with whiter throat than female Cape Rock-Thrush; rufous extends to top of breast. Juv. is spotted with buff on upperparts and with black below. Eastern *M. b. pretoriae* is duller, with a browner crown. **Voice:** Thin 'tseeep'; song of whistled phrases is like those of other rock-thrushes; includes some mimicry of other birds' calls. **Status and biology:** Near-endemic. Common resident and local nomad at rocky outcrops, often with some bushes; usually in more arid areas than other rock-thrushes. Lays 2–4 eggs in a bulky cup nest built on the ground or on a rock face. **Diet:** Insects, other invertebrates, fruit and seeds. (Korttoonkliplyster)

## 4 Miombo Rock-Thrush *Monticola angolensis*

`| | | | | | | | | b B B b b`
J F M A M J J A S O N D

16–18 cm; 40–48 g  A woodland rock-thrush, with distinctive black tips to its back feathers and wing coverts in both sexes. Female has blackish malar stripes and whitish belly and vent. Juv. is more heavily mottled below. **Voice:** A 2-note whistle; song is high-pitched variety of melodic phrases. **Status and biology:** Locally common resident and local nomad in miombo woodland, usually in hilly or rocky areas. Often unobtrusive and easily overlooked. Lays 3–4 eggs in a bulky cup nest built in a natural cavity in a tree trunk, usually close to the ground; site often re-used in successive years. **Diet:** Insects, other invertebrates and small reptiles. (Angolakliplyster)

# ROCK-JUMPERS

Babbler-like birds of rocky mountain slopes allied to picathartes from W Africa. Sexes differ; juvs resemble dull females. Monogamous; often with helpers at the nest. Incubation by both sexes; chicks altricial.

## 5 Cape Rock-jumper *Chaetops frenatus*

`b | | | | | | b b B B b b`
J F M A M J J A S O N D

23–25 cm; 50–72 g  Darker and slightly larger than Drakensberg Rock-jumper; ranges do not overlap. Male has a rich rufous (not orange) belly and rump. Female and juv. are rufous below (not buff as Drakensberg Rock-jumper). **Voice:** Series of loud, high-pitched whistles. **Status and biology:** Endemic. Common but localised on rocky mountain slopes. Usually in small groups. Lays 2 eggs in a cup nest built on the ground next to an overhanging rock or tussock. **Diet:** Insects and other invertebrates; occasional small reptiles and frogs. (Kaapse Berglyster)

## 6 Drakensberg Rock-jumper *Chaetops aurantius*

`b b | | | | | | b b B B b`
J F M A M J J A S O N D

21–23 cm; 45–56 g  Paler than Cape Rock-jumper; ranges do not overlap. Male has an orange (not rufous) belly and rump. Female and juv. are pale buff (not rufous) below. **Voice:** Repeated, piping whistles, like Cape Rock-jumper's. **Status and biology:** Endemic. Locally common resident on rocky slopes, typically above 2 000 m. Usually in small groups. Lays 2–3 eggs in a cup nest built on the ground next to a rock or tussock. **Diet:** Insects and other invertebrates. (Oranjeborsberglyster)

# CHATS AND WHEATEARS

A diverse group of medium-sized passerines identified by their distinctive tail and rump patterns. Sexes alike, but differ in a few wheatears and stonechats. Migrant wheatears have distinct br. plumages. Mottled juv. plumages short-lived. Monogamous; incubation usually by female only; chicks altricial.

## 1 Familiar Chat *Cercomela familiaris*

| b | b | b | b | | | | b | B | B | B | B | B |
|---|---|---|---|---|---|---|---|---|---|---|---|---|
| J | F | M | A | M | J | J | A | S | O | N | D | |

**15 cm; 14–26 g** A brown chat that invariably flicks its wings after landing. Rump and basal 3/4 of tail rufous; tail tip and central tail feathers blackish, forming a dark 'T' pattern. Shows less contrast between upper- and underparts than other *Cercomela* chats; stance more horizontal than Tractrac and Sickle-winged chats. At close range it has a narrow pale eye-ring and rufous wash on the ear coverts. Juv. is spotted buff above and mottled on the throat and breast. **Voice:** Harsh, scolding 'shek-shek' alarm call. Male song intersperses whistles among harsh 'chak' notes. **Status and biology:** Common resident and local nomad, usually in rocky and mountainous terrain; often around farm buildings. Lays 2–4 eggs in a cup nest in a rock cavity or building. **Diet:** Insects, other invertebrates and some fruit. (Gewone Spekvreter)

## 2 Sickle-winged Chat *Cercomela sinuata*

| B | b | b | | | | | | b | b | B | B | B |
|---|---|---|---|---|---|---|---|---|---|---|---|---|
| J | F | M | A | M | J | J | A | S | O | N | D | |

**15 cm; 17–24 g** Taller and more 'leggy' than Familiar Chat, with a larger eye-ring and more contrast between the grey-brown upperparts and paler underparts; best identified by its creamy-orange (not rufous) rump and tail base; black in tail forms broad triangle, not reaching base of tail, rather than 'T' as in Familiar Chat. Tail pattern similar to Tractrac Chat, but generally darker with warmer, orange-buff (not white or creamy) rump. Common name derives from its extremely attenuated outer primary, but this is only visible in the hand. Juv. is spotted buff above and mottled on the throat and breast. **Voice:** Soft 'tree-tree' or buzzy 'brrr-brrr' call; male gives a warbled song prior to breeding. **Status and biology:** Endemic. Locally common resident in grassland, taller karoo scrub and fields. Some birds leave high elevations in Lesotho in winter. Lays 2–4 eggs in a cup nest built on the ground next to concealing vegetation; rarely in a cavity in a wall. **Diet:** Insects, other invertebrates and some fruit. (Vlaktespekvreter)

## 3 Karoo Chat *Cercomela schlegelii*

| b | b | b | | | | | | b | b | B | B | b |
|---|---|---|---|---|---|---|---|---|---|---|---|---|
| J | F | M | A | M | J | J | A | S | O | N | D | |

**17 cm; 25–35 g** Larger and longer-tailed than other *Cercomela* chats, with a more horizontal posture. Grey rump and white outer tail feathers framing a dark, triangular central tail easily separate it from Tractrac and Sickle-winged chats. Much paler than female Mountain Wheatear, with pale grey (not white) rump and completely white outer tail feathers. Upperparts vary from pale grey-brown in arid N to medium grey in S. Juv. is spotted buff above and mottled on the throat and breast. **Voice:** Fairly harsh 'chak-chak' or 'trrat-trrat-trrat'. **Status and biology:** Near-endemic. Common resident and local nomad in karoo and semi-desert scrub. Lays 2–4 eggs in a cup nest built on the ground under a shrub. **Diet:** Insects and occasional fruit. (Karoospekvreter)

## 4 Tractrac Chat *Cercomela tractrac*

| b | b | b | b | | | | | B | B | B | b | b |
|---|---|---|---|---|---|---|---|---|---|---|---|---|
| J | F | M | A | M | J | J | A | S | O | N | D | |

**14–15 cm; 20–25 g** A small, pale chat, similar to Sickle-winged Chat, but generally paler, with white or creamy (not orange-buff) rump and tail base. Smaller than Karoo Chat, with different tail pattern (broad black tail tip, not white outer tail) and whitish (not grey) rump. Upperparts vary from very pale grey-brown on gravel plains in the Namib desert to darker sandy-brown in the south. Juv. is spotted buff above and mottled on the throat and breast. **Voice:** Soft, fast 'tactac'; song is quiet, musical bubbling; territorial defence call is loud chattering. **Status and biology:** Near-endemic. Common resident and local nomad in karoo and desert scrub, hummock dunes and gravel plains. Lays 2–3 eggs in a deep cup nest built on the ground next to a stone or under a small shrub. **Diet:** Insects and other invertebrates. (Woestynspekvreter)

## 5 Arnot's Chat *Myrmecocichla arnoti*

| | | | | | | | | b | b | B | B | b |
|---|---|---|---|---|---|---|---|---|---|---|---|---|
| J | F | M | A | M | J | J | A | S | O | N | D | |

**17 cm; 36–44 g** A compact, black-and-white woodland chat allied to Ant-eating Chat (p. 306). Male is distinguished from black morph male Mountain Wheatear by its black rump and tail. Female lacks white cap, but has conspicuous white throat and upper breast, often scaled with black. Juv. is duller, with a mainly black head and throat, but retains white shoulder patches. **Voice:** Song is a varied series of canary-like, warbling whistles; calls are a quiet, whistled 'fick' or 'feee'. **Status and biology:** Locally common resident in miombo and mopane woodland. Lays 2–4 eggs in a shallow cup of vegetation built in a natural tree hole. **Diet:** Insects and other invertebrates. (Bontpiek)

## 6 Mountain Wheatear *Oenanthe monticola*

| b | b | | | | | | | | b | B | B | b |
|---|---|---|---|---|---|---|---|---|---|---|---|---|
| J | F | M | A | M | J | J | A | S | O | N | D | |

**19 cm; 32–45 g** A large, black, grey and white wheatear. Males vary from black to pale grey, but all have a white rump, white outer tail and a white shoulder patch. Some have a white cap, resembling a male Arnot's Chat, but are larger and longer tailed, with white (not black) rump and white outer tail feathers. Female is uniform sooty-brown, except for the white rump and outer tail feathers. Juv. like female; males start to show ad. feathering after 2–3 months. **Voice:** Clear, thrush-like, whistling song, interspersed with harsh chatters. **Status and biology:** Near-endemic. Common resident and local nomad in rocky hillsides and road cuttings. Lays 2–4 eggs in an untidy cup nest on the ground next to a rock, in a rock cavity or in an abandoned building. **Diet:** Insects and other invertebrates; occasional fruit and seeds. (Bergwagter)

## 1 Capped Wheatear  *Oenanthe pileata*

b | | | | | | bb BBBb
J F M A M J J A S O N D

**17 cm; 23–32 g**  A large, striking wheatear with dark brown upperparts, a black crown, face and breast band, and contrasting white throat and supercilium. Sexes alike. Juv. is drab brown and could be confused with non-br. migrant wheatears, but is larger and darker above, with a mostly dark tail and mottled breast band (indistinct in some birds). Juv. could be confused with a female Buff-streaked Chat (p. 306), but has a white (not buff) rump. **Voice:** 'Chik-chik' alarm note; song is loud warbling with slurred chattering. **Status and biology:** Common resident and local nomad in barren areas, short grassland and short croplands. Lays 2–4 (rarely 5) eggs in a cup nest built 0.3–2 m underground in a rodent burrow. **Diet:** Insects and other invertebrates; also some fruit and seeds. (Hoëveldskaapwagter)

## 2 Pied Wheatear  *Oenanthe pleschanka*

**14 cm; 14–20 g**  Rare vagrant. Tail has black T-pattern, with diagnostic broader black tip to outer feathers in all plumages; underwing coverts blackish, darker than other wheatears. Male in fresh plumage (Sept) has buffy crown, brown margins to back and wing feathers and buff wash across its breast. As plumage wears, buff tips to feathers are lost, revealing a silvery crown contrasting with black back, wings and throat; remainder of underparts white. Smaller than male Mountain Wheatear (p. 302), with black (not white) shoulders and more extensive white in its outer tail. Female and juv. are dusky grey-brown above, smaller and darker than female Northern and Isabelline wheatears; lores not appreciably darker than face. Could be confused with female Buff-streaked Chat (p. 306), but has darker throat and different tail pattern. **Voice:** Soft 'zack' call; song incorporates soft whistles and 'zack' notes. **Status and biology:** Palearctic vagrant; only one record of a male from Mtunzini, KZN in Jan 1984. **Diet:** Mainly insects. (Bontskaapwagter)

## 3 Isabelline Wheatear  *Oenanthe isabellina*

**16–17 cm; 21–27 g**  Rare vagrant. A uniform buffy-brown wheatear with no sexual dimorphism. Closely resembles non-br. Northern Wheatear, but is slightly larger and paler, and looks more upright due to its longer legs and shorter, more rounded tail. Black tail tip is generally broader than in Northern Wheatear, which combined with the shorter tail results in a shorter stem to the black T-pattern. At close range, dark alula contrasts with sandy-brown coverts. Underwing coverts white or whitish-buff. Appears larger-headed, and tends to have more direct flight. **Voice:** High-pitched 'wheet-whit' call. **Status and biology:** Rare Palearctic vagrant; occurrence in region based on one record from N Botswana in Dec 1972; subsequent claims not confirmed; at least some involve juv. Capped Wheatear. **Diet:** Mainly insects. (Isabellaskaapwagter)

## 4 Northern Wheatear  *Oenanthe oenanthe*

■■■■| | | | |■■■■
J F M A M J J A S O N D

**14–16 cm; 21–27 g**  Vagrant. Br. male has a diagnostic blue-grey crown and back, and black face; underparts white with buff wash on breast. Other plumages are nondescript buffy-brown with a paler supercilium; easily confused with vagrant Isabelline Wheatear, but has slightly darker wings, shorter legs, a more horizontal stance and narrower black tail tip; dark brown alula shows less contrast with wing coverts. Underwing coverts sooty-grey. Smaller than juv. Capped Wheatear or female Buff-streaked Chat (p. 306), with more white on rump and outer tail, and is usually paler, with a plain (not mottled) breast. **Voice:** Harsh 'chak-chak' or 'wee-chak'; song is jumbled mix of high whistles and squeaks; seldom sings in region. **Status and biology:** Rare Palearctic migrant in open grassland and dry plains. **Diet:** Mainly insects. (Europese Skaapwagter)

## 5 African Stonechat  *Saxicola torquatus*

b | | | | | bBBBbb
J F M A M J J A S O N D

**13 cm; 12–17 g**  Ad. male has a striking black head, chestnut breast and flanks, and white neck patch, belly, rump and wing bar. Female much duller, with a mottled brown head and orange-buff breast; uppertail coverts whitish. Often shows a pale supercilium, but not as broad or prominent as in Whinchat. Juv. is spotted buff above, and is paler below than female, with mottled breast. **Voice:** Song is a fast series of high-pitched warbled whistles; calls 'weet-weet' and harsh 'chak'. **Status and biology:** Common resident in grassland and open areas with short scrub; also around wetlands. In the Drakensberg, some move to lower elevations in winter. Lays 2–5 eggs in a deep cup nest built under vegetation on the ground or a low bank (rarely in a small shrub). **Diet:** Insects and other invertebrates; occasional fruit and seeds. (Gewone Bontrokkie)

## 6 Whinchat  *Saxicola rubetra*

■■■■■| | | | | | |■
J F M A M J J A S O N D

**14 cm; 13–24 g**  Rare vagrant. Most likely confused with female African Stonechat, but has a more prominent supercilium that broadens behind the eye, and extends around the top of the ear coverts. Outer tail feathers have white bases (black in African Stonechat), but rump and uppertail coverts brown (not white). Appears slimmer with longer wings. Br. male has a white supercilium, prominent white wing bar and white patch at base of primaries. Non-br. male, female and juv. are paler than br. male with more buffy plumage and a creamy supercilium; juv. lacks white wing bar. **Voice:** Scolding 'tick-tick'. **Status and biology:** Rare Palearctic vagrant, usually found in open grassland with patches of stunted scrub. European populations declining; only 3 confirmed records from sthn Africa in the last 20 years. **Diet:** Mainly insects. (Europese Bontrokkie)

## 1 Buff-streaked Chat *Oenanthe bifasciata*

bb | bBBb
J F M A M J J A S O N D

**16–17 cm; 31–38 g** A large, compact wheatear, sometimes placed in *Saxicola*; distinguished from other sthn African wheatears by its all-black tail. Male striking, with a distinctive black face, throat and wings, whitish head stripe and wing bar, and buffy underparts. Female is warm rufous-brown with buffy underparts; plumage finely streaked darker brown; darker than juv. Capped Wheatear (p. 304) with a buff (not white) rump and all-black tail. Juv. has buff-spotted upperparts and mottled underparts. **Voice:** A short series of rich warbling notes, given by both sexes. **Status and biology:** Endemic. Common but localised resident, found on rock-strewn, grassy slopes. May move to lower elevations in cold spells. Lays 2–4 eggs in bulky cup nest built on the ground, at the base of a rock or in a crevice in a rock or wall. **Diet:** Insects and other invertebrates; occasional seeds and nectar. (Bergklipwagter)

## 2 Ant-eating Chat *Myrmecocichla formicivora*

bbb | bbBBb
J F M A M J J A S O N D

**17–18 cm; 40–60 g** A medium-sized sooty brown chat with paler feather margins, appearing scaly at close range. In flight, silvery-white primary bases form prominent pale wing panels. Male has a small white carpal patch. Female lacks white carpal patch and is paler brown. Juv. has more prominent pale feather margins; white in primaries reduced. **Voice:** Short, sharp 'pee-ik' or 'piek' call; song is varied mix of whistles and grating notes. **Status and biology:** Endemic. Common resident in grassland, short scrub and open, sandy or stony ground; favours areas dotted with termite mounds. Usually in small groups; sometimes breeds cooperatively. Lays 2–4 (rarely up to 7) eggs in a bowl of vegetation built in a burrow excavated in a bank or the roof of an aardvark den. **Diet:** Insects, other invertebrates and occasional fruit. (Swartpiek)

## 3 Mocking Cliff-Chat *Thamnolaea cinnamomeiventris*

bBBBb
J F M A M J J A S O N D

**22 cm; 46–53 g** A large, distinctive chat that could only be confused with difficulty; see rock-jumpers (p. 300) in S and Boulder Chat (p. 292) in N of range. Male is glossy black, with a bright chestnut belly, vent and rump, and white shoulder patches. Female is dark grey above and chestnut below. Juv. duller with buff tips to contour feathers. **Voice:** Loud, melodious whistled song, often mimicking other birds; also shrill, piercing calls. Both sexes sing. **Status and biology:** Common but localised resident on cliffs and wooded, rocky slopes. Usually in pairs or family parties. Lays 2–4 eggs in a bowl nest built inside a striped swallow nest or a cavity in a cave or culvert; occasionally in a disused building. **Diet:** Insects, other invertebrates, fruit and nectar. (Dassievoël)

## 4 Common Redstart *Phoenicurus phoenicurus*

**13–14 cm; 11–22 g** Rare vagrant. Br. male is striking, with its black face and throat, white forecrown, slate-grey upperparts and red breast. Smaller than male Irania, with black throat and red rump and outer tail. Female and non-br. male are much duller; could be confused with Familiar Chat (p. 302), but have more extensive red rumps and brighter red outer tails, lacking dark tip; tail is continuously 'trembled' up and down. Doesn't wing-flick. Juv. is spotted buff above and barred darker brown below; unlikely to be encountered in sthn Africa. **Voice:** Loud 'hooeeet', similar to that of Willow Warbler, often with harsher notes 'hooeet-tucc-tucc'. **Status and biology:** Rare Palearctic vagrant in semi-arid savanna and woodland; only 2 records from sthn Africa. **Diet:** Insects and fruit. (Europese Rooistert)

## 5 Irania *Irania gutturalis*

**16–17 cm; 16–27 g** Rare vagrant. A skulking robin-chat that frequently cocks its diagnostic black tail; structure and behaviour recall Thrush Nightingale (p. 328). Ad. male is striking; told from male Common Redstart by the narrow white centre to throat (not entirely black), smaller black face (not extending onto frons), clean white vent and black tail; behaviour also differs. Female has plain grey upperparts and head, with only a faint pale stripe in front of its eye and rufous-washed ear coverts. Underparts buffy with faint darker barring and richer rufous flanks; throat paler; vent white. Juv. even duller than female, with buff-spotted upperparts and a more heavily mottled breast. **Voice:** Contact call is grating 'krrrk'; song is mixture of musical whistles and scratchy notes. **Status and biology:** Rare Palearctic vagrant, favouring dry thickets and scrub. Only 1 record, near Williston, N Cape. **Diet:** Insects and fruit. (Irania)

## 6 Herero Chat *Namibornis herero*

bBb
J F M A M J J A S O N D

**17 cm; 23–30 g** A peculiar chat-like bird of uncertain affinities confined to the fore-Namib. Rufous outer tail with dark brown central feathers recalls Familiar Chat (p. 302) or robin-chats (p. 310), but has a distinct face pattern, with a black face and white supercilium. Frequently flicks wings when foraging, possibly to flush prey. Breast streaking is visible only at close range. Juv. is buff-spotted above and has a mottled breast. **Voice:** Mostly silent; melodious, warbling 'twi-tedeelee-doo' song when breeding. **Status and biology:** Near-endemic. Uncommon resident in dry scrub and acacia woodland, often near rocks. Lays 2–3 eggs in a compact cup nest edged into the fork of a small tree. **Diet:** Insects and other invertebrates; occasional fruit and seeds. (Hererospekvreter)

# SCRUB-ROBINS

Rather drab robins with long, white-tipped tails that are often held cocked. Tails lack dark central feathers of robin-chats; most species have white wing bars. All have well-marked heads with a dark eye-stripe and white supercilium. Sexes alike. Juvs spotted buff above, and barred or mottled below. Monogamous and territorial, sometimes with helpers at the nest. Incubation by female only; chicks altricial.

## 1 Brown Scrub-Robin *Cercotrichas signata*

J F M A M J J A S O N D

**16–18 cm; 33–42 g** A dark grey-brown forest scrub-robin; lacks orange-buff flanks and rufous rump and uppertail coverts of Bearded Scrub-Robin, and has a less distinct white supercilium and malar stripe. Juv. is warmer brown above, with black tips to feathers; underparts creamy-buff, with grey mottling or scaling on its breast. **Voice:** Melodious 'twee-choo-sree-sree' introduces varied song; alarm note is sibilant 'zeeeeet'. **Status and biology:** Endemic. Locally common resident in thick tangles of coastal and evergreen forests. Shy and skulking, but is readily observed at dawn and dusk when it often forages in the open. Lays 2–3 eggs in a cup nest built in a tree cavity 1–3 m above ground. **Diet:** Insects and other invertebrates; also some fruit and seeds. (Bruinwipstert)

## 2 Bearded Scrub-Robin *Cercotrichas quadrivirgata*

J F M A M J J A S O N D

**14–16 cm; 22–31 g** Told from Brown Scrub-Robin by rufous (not grey-brown) breast and flanks, and rufous (not brown) rump and uppertail coverts; facial pattern stronger and has more white in the wing. Favours drier habitats than Brown Scrub-Robin. Lacks double white wing bars and rufous base to tail of White-browed Scrub-Robin, most of which have streaked breasts. Juv. has dark tips to mantle and breast feathers, appearing mottled; wing coverts tipped buff. **Voice:** Clear, penetrating song of often-repeated, mixed phrases with short pauses between phrases; alarm call is 1–2 sharp notes followed by 'churr, chek-chek kwezzzzz'. **Status and biology:** Common, but easily overlooked resident of broadleafed woodland and savanna; feeds among leaf litter under thickets and dense tangles. Lays 2–3 eggs in a cup nest built in a tree cavity or fork, usually 1–2 m above ground. **Diet:** Insects and other invertebrates. (Baardwipstert)

## 3 White-browed Scrub-Robin *Cercotrichas leucophrys*

J F M A M J J A S O N D

**14–16 cm; 14–22 g** The most common scrub-robin of savanna and woodland; easily identified by its 2 white wing bars. Rump and base of tail rufous; remainder of tail dark brown, with narrow white tips. Most races have prominent streaking on their breasts and flanks, but *C. l. ovamboensis* (Namibia to NW Zimbabwe) has greatly reduced streaking, mainly on the sides of the rufous-washed breast. Juv. paler above, with buff spots; breast diffusely mottled (not streaked). **Voice:** Harsh 'trrrrrr' alarm note; fluty but repetitive song; characteristic call at dawn and dusk is whistled 'seeep po go'. **Status and biology:** Common resident in woodland and savanna. Lays 2–4 eggs in an untidy cup nest built in a grass tussock or small shrub. **Diet:** Insects and other invertebrates; also some fruit and nectar. (Gestreepte Wipstert)

## 4 Kalahari Scrub-Robin *Cercotrichas paena*

J F M A M J J A S O N D

**14–16 cm; 17–23 g** A pale, sandy brown scrub-robin with no white wing bars. Rump, uppertail coverts and most of tail are pale rufous; tail has a broad black subterminal bar and narrow white tips. Lacks breast streaks and white wing bars of White-browed Scrub-Robin; dark subterminal tail band narrower. Juv. has black tips to head, mantle and breast feathers, appearing mottled. **Voice:** Alarm note is harsh 'zzeee'; contact call is whistled 'seeeup'; musical song of whistles and chirps, more varied than those of Karoo or White-browed scrub-robins; frequently mimics other birds. **Status and biology:** Near-endemic. Common resident in dry acacia savanna, favouring thickets and bushy areas. Lays 2–4 eggs in an untidy cup nest built up to 1.5 m up in a small shrub, grass tuft or on the ground; rarely in a tin or pot. **Diet:** Insects and other invertebrates; also some fruit and small vertebrates. (Kalahariwipstert)

## 5 Karoo Scrub-Robin *Cercotrichas coryphoeus*

J F M A M J J A S O N D

**14–16 cm; 18–23 g** A dark, grey-brown scrub-robin with a blackish tail and contrasting white tail tips; lacks white in wing. Much darker and greyer-brown than Kalahari Scrub-Robin, with no rufous in its tail, rump or wing. Pale throat contrasts with greyish or grey-brown underparts. Juv. is browner above, with buff spots on head and mantle and buffy margins to wing coverts; underparts mottled darker grey. **Voice:** Harsh, chittering 'tchik, tchik, tcheet'; song is mixture of whistles and harsh, grating notes. **Status and biology:** Endemic. Common resident in karoo scrub and strandveld. Usually in pairs or family groups. Male offspring often remain on territory and help with subsequent br. attempts. Lays 2–4 eggs in a cup nest built on the ground at the base of a small bush; occasionally nests up to 1 m up in a bush or on a bank. **Diet:** Insects, other invertebrates and small fruit. (Slangverklikker)

# ROBIN-CHATS, ALETHES, ROBINS AND NIGHTINGALES

Robins with rufous rumps and outer tails. Typically found close to the ground in dense vegetation. Most are accomplished songsters and mimics. Sexes alike. Juv plumage, retained for only a few months, is spotted buff above and mottled buffy-brown below. Monogamous and territorial; chicks altricial.

## 1 Chorister Robin-Chat  *Cossypha dichroa*

**20 cm; 37–56 g** A large, dark-backed robin with orange underparts and a blackish head with no white eye-stripe. Juv. is sooty, mottled tawny-buff above and below. Occasionally hybridises with Red-capped Robin-Chat in E Cape; hybrids have orange supercilium and dusky cheeks. **Voice:** Contact call is plaintive 'toy-toy, toy-toy'; song is loud and bubbly, including much mimicry of other forest birds. **Status and biology:** Endemic. Common resident in forest and coastal thickets. Some local movements from interior to coastal forests in winter. Lays 2–3 eggs in a bowl of material built in a hole or crevice in a tree. **Diet:** Insects, other invertebrates, fruit; occasionally attends driver ant columns and gleans parasites from forest antelope. (Lawaaimakerjanfrederik)

## 2 Red-capped Robin-Chat  *Cossypha natalensis*

**17 cm; 25–36 g** The only robin-chat with a plain rufous face and a slaty-blue back and wings; crown and nape are reddish-brown. When alarmed, frequently flicks up its tail, then slowly lowers it. Juv. dark brown above, with buff spots; underparts duller, mottled on breast. Imm. like ad., but has dusky ear coverts. Occasionally hybridises with Chorister Robin-Chat in E Cape. **Voice:** Call is soft, slightly trilled 'seee-saw', often repeated; song is rambling series of melodious whistles, including much mimicry. **Status and biology:** Common resident and local migrant, found in thickets, forest and dense woodland. Lays 2–4 eggs in a cup nest built in a hole or crevice, low in a tree or on a bank. **Diet:** Insects, other invertebrates and fruit; occasionally hawks insects. (Nataljanfrederik)

## 3 Cape Robin-Chat  *Cossypha caffra*

**17 cm; 23–38 g** A dark-backed robin-chat with a pale orange throat, upper breast, vent and rump; remainder of underparts pale grey; white supercilium is relatively short. Juv. is browner above with buff spotting; underparts dull buffy-brown, mottled darker brown on its breast. Imm. retains some buff-fringed wing coverts. **Voice:** Song is series of melodious phrases, usually starting 'cherooo-weet-weet-weeeet'; often mimics other birds. Alarm call is guttural 'wur-der-durrr'. **Status and biology:** Common resident and altitudinal migrant, found in a wide range of habitats including forest edge, thickets, heath, scrub, gardens and parks; confined to higher elevations in N, but common down to sea level in S Africa. Lays 2–3 eggs in a cup nest built on the ground or in a cavity or shrub. **Diet:** Mainly insects and other invertebrates; also some fruit, kitchen scraps and small vertebrates. (Gewone Janfrederik)

## 4 White-browed Robin-Chat  *Cossypha heuglini*

**19 cm; 29–44 g** A large robin-chat, recalling Chorister Robin-Chat, but with a prominent white supercilium; also occurs at lower elevations and in a different habitat. Juv. is dark brown above, with fine buff spots; underparts buffy mottled blackish. **Voice:** Characteristic, loud, crescendo song of repeated phrases; also is accomplished mimic. Alarm call is a harsh 'tserrrk-tserrrk'. **Status and biology:** Common resident of dense thickets and tangles, gardens and parks. Lays 2–3 eggs in a shallow cup built in a tree cavity, fork or tangle of roots, usually within 2 m of the ground. **Diet:** Insects and other invertebrates; also some fruit and small vertebrates. (Heuglinjanfrederik)

## 5 White-throated Robin-Chat  *Cossypha humeralis*

**16 cm; 19–26 g** The only robin-chat with a white wing bar; orange-rufous tail has a dark tip (outer edges rufous in all other robin-chats). Could possibly be confused with Southern Boubou (p. 360), but easily distinguished by white supercilium and orange rump and outer tail. Juv. lacks white wing bar and supercilium; upperparts brown spotted with buff; underparts buffy mottled black. **Voice:** Alarm call is repeated 'seet-cher, seet-cher'; song is rather short series of rich whistles; often mimics other birds. **Status and biology:** Endemic. Common resident of thickets and riverine scrub in woodland and savanna. Usually feeds on the ground, but sings from elevated perches. Lays 2–3 eggs in a cup nest built on the ground at the base of a small tree or bush; some nests on low banks or in tree cavities or pots. **Diet:** Insects and other invertebrates; also some fruit and small vertebrates. (Witkeeljanfrederik)

## 6 White-chested Alethe  *Pseudalethe fuelleborni*

**18–20 cm; 52 g** Alethes are thrush-like birds found in the understorey of tropical African forests. This species is a large, rather chunky alethe with crisp white underparts contrasting sharply with its dark grey face and crown and rich chestnut upperparts; flanks washed grey. Juv. is blackish-brown above, spotted with buff; underparts creamy-buff, variably mottled and scaled dark grey. **Voice:** Lively, slightly mournful and vibrato 'fweer-her-hee-her-hee-her' series of whistles. **Status and biology:** Uncommon resident of coastal forest in central Mozambique; 1 record from Mt Gorongoza. Monogamous and territorial; lays 3 eggs in a bowl nest built of moss, lichen and dead leaves in a low tree fork or stump. **Diet:** Insects and other invertebrates; also some fruit and small vertebrates. (Witborswoudlyster)

## 1 White-starred Robin  *Pogonocichla stellata*

b▮▮▮▮▮▮▮▮▮bBb
J F M A M J J A S O N D

**16 cm; 18–26 g** A fairly small, compact forest robin. Ad. has slate-grey head and throat, yellow-orange breast and belly, and bright yellow tail windows that are conspicuous in flight. Larger than Swynnerton's Robin, with orange (not white) vent and strongly patterned (not uniform) tail. White 'stars' on lower throat and forehead are usually concealed. Juv. is sooty, streaked yellowish-buff above and below. Imm. dull olive above, yellowish-grey below; tail pattern of both juv. and imm. like ad., but duller yellow. **Voice:** Soft 'chuk' or 'zit' note; whistled 'too-twee' contact call, frequently repeated; quiet, warbling song. **Status and biology:** Common resident of forest understorey, subject to some altitudinal movements in S. Often rather confiding. Lays 2–3 eggs in a domed nest built in dense cover on the ground, usually at the base of a rock or tree trunk. **Diet:** Insects, other invertebrates and fruit; also some small vertebrates. (Witkoljanfrederik)

## 2 Swynnerton's Robin  *Swynnertonia swynnertoni*

b▮▮▮▮▮▮▮▮bBB
J F M A M J J A S O N D

**14 cm; 14–20 g** Smaller than White-starred Robin, with a uniform dark grey tail (lacking yellow windows) and a much larger white patch on upper breast, bordered beneath by a diagnostic black band. Female is duller, with greenish crown and face. Juv. is brown above, spotted with buffy yellow; underparts duller with dark mottling on breast; throat crescent pale grey with brown band below. Imm. like pale female but retains some buff-tipped juv. wing feathers. **Voice:** Song, given by male, is subdued, 3-syllabled 'zitt, zitt, slurr', last syllable lower-pitched; alarm is monotonous, quiet purring. **Status and biology: VULNERABLE.** Endemic. Uncommon resident of montane forest understorey. Lays 2–3 eggs in a bulky cup nest built low down in the fork of a shrub, dragon-tree leaf base or hollow in a tree stump. **Diet:** Insects, other invertebrates and fruit; often attends swarms of driver ants. (Bandkeeljanfrederik)

## 3 East Coast Akalat  *Sheppardia gunningi*

▮▮▮▮▮▮▮▮▮▮bb▮
J F M A M J J A S O N D

**12 cm; 16–19 g** The only akalat in the region. A small, compact robin with brown upperparts, orange throat and breast, olive-washed flanks and a whitish belly. At close range, shows blue-grey upperwing coverts. Head has a faint paler supercilium; white pre-orbital spots only exposed when displaying. Juv. darker above with buff spots; underparts dull yellow-buff, mottled brown. **Voice:** Song is a soft, fast series of high-pitched notes in oft-repeated short phrases. **Status and biology: NEAR-THREATENED.** Uncommon resident in the understorey of lowland forest and thickets in dense woodland. Unobtrusive and easily overlooked. Lays 2–3 eggs in a partly domed nest built on the ground among leaf litter, at the base of a tree. **Diet:** Insects and other invertebrates; also some small vertebrates. (Gunningjanfrederik)

## 4 Thrush Nightingale  *Luscinia luscinia*

▮▮▮▮▮▮▮▮▮▮▮▮▮
J F M A M J J A S O N D

**16 cm; 18–33 g** A skulking, warbler-like bird that is easily overlooked if not calling. Best identified by its warm olive-brown upperparts and rufous-washed rump and tail; underparts whitish with diffuse grey-brown streaking on its breast, flanks and vent. Tail often cocked or waved from side to side. Remains low down in thick tangles, feeding mainly on the ground; could be confused with Terrestrial Brownbul (p. 294). Juv. has buff tips to tertials and greater upperwing coverts. **Voice:** Rich, warbling song interspersed with harsh, grating notes. **Status and biology:** Uncommon to fairly common Palearctic migrant in thickets in savanna and woodland, often along rivers. **Diet:** Insects, other invertebrates and small fruit. (Lysternagtegaal)

# PALM-THRUSHES

**Medium-sized, robin-like birds with plain, rufous-brown tails. Forage on the ground or in thickets; occasionally hawk insects. Sexes alike. Juvs have mottled underparts. Monogamous and territorial; incubation by both sexes.**

## 5 Rufous-tailed Palm-Thrush  *Cichladusa ruficauda*

bbbb▮▮▮▮▮▮bb
J F M A M J J A S O N D

**18 cm; 22–37 g** A richly coloured palm-thrush that lacks the black necklace of Collared Palm-Thrush and has dull red (not pale grey) eyes; ranges do not overlap. Juv. has dark grey mottling on its breast. **Voice:** Loud, melodious whistling, including imitations of other birds' songs. **Status and biology:** Locally common resident in riverine thickets, usually close to *Hyphaene* palms. Lays 2–4 eggs in a deep cup nest built from mud and plant fibres and plastered to a palm frond, wall, rock ledge or tree fork. **Diet:** Insects, other invertebrates and fruit. (Rooistertmôrelyster)

## 6 Collared Palm-Thrush  *Cichladusa arquata*

bbb▮▮▮▮▮bBb
J F M A M J J A S O N D

**20 cm; 29–38 g** Warm brown above, with a grey wash on the face and sides of the neck; throat and breast buffy with a narrow black necklace that is often incomplete. Tail plain rufous-brown, less richly coloured than Rufous-tailed Palm-Thrush; also has pale grey (not red) eyes; ranges do not overlap. Juv. is streaked on the crown and nape and mottled dark brown below; necklace indistinct. **Voice:** Explosive, varied song, often including 'weet-chuk' or 'cur-lee chuk-chuk' phrases. **Status and biology:** Locally common resident in thickets among *Hyphaene* and *Borassus* palm savanna. Lays 2–3 eggs in a cup of mud and roots plastered among the leaf bases of a palm or similar large-leaved plant; sometimes in buildings. **Diet:** Insects, other invertebrates and small frogs. (Palmmôrelyster)

# OLD-WORLD WARBLERS

A group of small passerines that glean insects from foliage. They include several evolutionary lineages. Sexes alike in most groups; juvs often duller. Typically monogamous and territorial; chicks altricial.

## 1 Yellow-throated Woodland-Warbler *Phylloscopus ruficapilla*
J F M A M J J A S O N D | B B b

**11 cm; 6–9 g** A small forest canopy warbler with a distinctive yellow throat, breast and supercilium. Told from Willow Warbler by its brown crown, forest habitat and greater contrast between its greyish belly and bright yellow throat, upper breast and vent. Juv. has a green wash on its breast. **Voice:** Song loud 'seee suuu seee suuu'. **Status and biology:** Locally common resident in evergreen forest, in canopy and mid-strata. Often associates with white-eyes. Lays 2–3 eggs in a domed nest with a side entrance made of moss; usually built on the ground among dense vegetation; sometimes in a small shrub. **Diet:** Insects and spiders. (Geelkeelsanger)

## 2 Willow Warbler *Phylloscopus trochilus*
J F M A M J J A S O N D

**11 cm; 7–12 g** A small, slender warbler with a dark eye-stripe and a pale, yellowish supercilium. Most birds are from W Europe and have olive-washed upperparts and yellow-washed throat and breast, but some are larger, duller birds from Asia (*P. t. yakutensis*) that have yellow-green wash confined to the face. Bill smaller, darker and more slender than Icterine Warbler; yellow usually restricted to throat and breast, but juv. has more extensive yellow underparts. **Voice:** Soft, 2-note contact call 'foo-eet'; short, melodious song, descending in scale. **Status and biology:** Abundant Palearctic migrant in woodland and savanna habitats; usually conspicuous as it forages in the canopy. **Diet:** Small insects obtained mainly by gleaning, but sometimes hawks prey. (Hofsanger)

## 3 Icterine Warbler *Hippolais icterina*
J F M A M J J A S O N D

**13–14 cm; 10–18 g** A more robust warbler than Willow Warbler, with a heavier, yellowish bill and a more angular, sloping forehead, recalling a reed-warbler. Head has a short yellowish supercilium and narrow, pale eye-ring. Ad. has yellow-washed underparts and olive-grey upperparts. Juv. and imm. duller, with yellow wash confined to face and throat; exceptionally drab birds could be confused with Olive-tree Warbler, but are smaller with a much shorter bill; lacks white outer tail. **Voice:** Varied, jumbled notes, including harsh 'tac, tac'. **Status and biology:** Fairly common Palearctic migrant in thickets in savanna and arid woodland, plantations and gardens. **Diet:** Insects, spiders and occasional fruit. (Spotsanger)

## 4 Olive-tree Warbler *Hippolais olivetorum*
J F M A M J J A S O N D

**15–18 cm; 14–22 g** A large, pale grey warbler with a distinctly angled crown. Larger than Icterine Warbler, with a much longer, heavier bill and paler grey upperparts; lacks yellow and green tones in plumage (unlike most Icterine Warblers) and has white edges to outer tail. It has a pale panel in the folded wing; legs are thick with distinctly robust feet. **Voice:** Chattering song is rambling, with harsh, metallic notes, recalling that of Great Reed-Warbler. **Status and biology:** Scarce Palearctic migrant to acacia thickets in arid savanna. Easily overlooked if not singing. **Diet:** Insects. (Olyfboomsanger)

## 5 Garden Warbler *Sylvia borin*
J F M A M J J A S O N D

**15 cm; 16–24 g** A plump, drab grey-brown warbler, paler below, lacking distinctive features. Head is rounded and bill relatively short. Dark eye appears rather large in its otherwise plain face. Other drab warblers all show some eye-stripe or supercilium. Juv. duller with slightly warmer plumage. **Voice:** Subdued, monotonous song, interspersed with soft, grating phrases; call harsh 'tec'. **Status and biology:** Fairly common Palearctic migrant in thick tangles in forest, bush and riverine habitats. Skulks in dense vegetation; easily overlooked. **Diet:** Insects and fruit. (Tuinsanger)

## 6 Common Whitethroat *Sylvia communis*
J F M A M J J A S O N D

**14 cm; 12–20 g** A slender, long-tailed warbler with rufous panels in the folded wing, resulting from broad chestnut fringes to the secondaries and greater coverts. White throat contrasts with pinkish-grey breast and belly. Head often has a slight crest, especially when alarmed. Grey head of male contrasts with silvery-white throat. Female has browner head. Juv. duller with buffy (not white) outer tail feathers. **Voice:** Soft 'whit' and grating 'tchack' and 'tchurr' alarm calls; song harsh, snappy mixture of grating and melodious notes. **Status and biology:** Locally common Palearctic migrant; occurs in shrubs in arid savanna, often near water. **Diet:** Insects, fruit and flowers. (Witkeelsanger)

## 7 Blackcap *Sylvia atricapilla*
J F M A M J J A S O N D

**14 cm; 14–20 g** Vagrant. A compact, grey-brown warbler, distinguished from other warblers by its distinctive crown patch, black in male and reddish-brown in female. Juv. like female but duller. If head not seen, could be confused with Garden Warbler. **Voice:** Call hard 'tac'. Song (Jan–Mar) is a series of varied warbles, initially subdued, but becoming more persistent. **Status and biology:** Palearctic vagrant to woodland, forest edge and gardens; at least 5 records, but may be overlooked, especially in E Zimbabwe. (Swartkroonsanger)

## 1 Victorin's Warbler  *Cryptillas victorini*

J F M A M J J A S O N D  bBBb

**16 cm; 20 g**  A colourful warbler with cinnamon-orange underparts, blue-grey face and striking yellow eyes. Female duller with grey-brown upperparts. Juv. is even greyer above and paler below. Until recently placed in *Bradypterus*, but forms part of an African warbler radiation including Cape Grassbird and crombecs. **Voice:** Male sings a rollicking 'whit-itty-weeo, wit-itty weeo', accelerating towards the end; female gives loud 'weet-weet-weeeo'; both sexes give a harsh, pishing alarm call. When aroused, alarm calls run onto the song. **Status and biology:** Endemic. Common resident in damp, montane fynbos, typically in thick tangles alongside streams and in gullies. Lays 2 eggs in a bulky, deep cup nest built low down in a dense tussock. **Diet:** Insects and other invertebrates. (Rooiborsruigtesanger)

## 2 Broad-tailed Warbler  *Schoenicola brevirostris*

J F M A M J J A S O N D  Bb / bB

**15 cm; 15–17 g**  A small warbler with a long, broad, black tail that is conspicuous in flight. Tail is strongly graduated; feathers tipped buff, visible as scaling on the underside. Flattened head shape is distinctive, with forehead and culmen forming an almost straight line. Skulks among dense vegetation, but often perches in the open after heavy rains to dry its tail and wings. Juv. has warmer brown upperparts and yellowish underparts; tail shorter and narrower. **Voice:** Soft, metallic 'zeenk', repeated at intervals of a few seconds; clear, high-pitched 'peee, peee'. **Status and biology:** Locally common resident and altitudinal migrant in long, rank grass, usually in damp areas. Lays 2–3 eggs in a deep cup nest built in dense grass or sedges within 0.2 m of the ground. **Diet:** Insects. (Breëstertsanger)

# *BRADYPTERUS* WARBLERS

Skulking warblers with broad, heavy tails and fine, slender bills. Typically located and identified by their distinctive songs. Sexes alike. Juvs duller. Monogamous and territorial. Incubation probably by female only; chicks altricial.

## 3 Little Rush-Warbler  *Bradypterus baboecala*

J F M A M J J A S O N D  Bbb / bBBB

**15–17 cm; 12–18 g**  Typically associated with tangled vegetation around wetlands. Differs from reed-warblers by its dark, dusky brown upperparts, dappled throat and breast, and long, rounded tail; dark bill is small and slender. Extent of breast streaking varies from well-defined streaks to diffuse mottling. Juv. has underparts washed pale yellow. **Voice:** Harsh, ratchet-like song, accelerating towards the end 'krrak krrak krrak krrak krk-krk-rk-rk-rk-rk'; often accompanied by a wing rattle; also nasal 'wheeaaa'. **Status and biology:** Locally common resident and nomad in reeds and sedges, usually in denser areas further from water than reed-warblers. Lays 2–3 eggs in a bulky cup nest built in reeds or other rank vegetation close to the ground. **Diet:** Insects. (Kaapse Vleisanger)

## 4 Knysna Warbler  *Bradypterus sylvaticus*

J F M A M J J A S O N D  bBb

**14–15 cm; 15–20 g**  A small, dark olive-brown warbler confined to dense undergrowth in and around Afro-montane forest and coastal thickets. Best told by its distinctive song. Tail is broad and graduated, but is shorter and less graduated than in Barratt's Warbler; breast is plain or finely streaked (less marked than Barratt's Warbler). Smaller and darker below than Little Rush-Warbler. Male has a white loral spot and dark brown eye-stripe. Female has paler throat and less marked face. Juv. has underparts washed pale yellow; breast streaked. **Voice:** Song is an accelerating series of sharp whistles, ending in a dry trill 'wit it it it it-it-it-ititititrrrrrrr'; both sexes make deep 'chack' and dry 'prrt' calls. **Status and biology:** VULNERABLE. Endemic. Uncommon and localised in dense forest understorey; bracken and briar thickets. Lays 2–3 eggs in a cup nest built of dead leaves close to the ground. **Diet:** Insects. (Knysnaruigtesanger)

## 5 Barratt's Warbler  *Bradypterus barratti*

J F M A M J J A S O N D  bBBb

**15 cm; 17–20 g**  Slightly larger and longer-tailed than Knysna Warbler, with paler underparts and a more heavily streaked throat and breast, but best identified by song; ranges overlap in E Cape. Also resembles Little Rush-Warbler, but occurs in forest (not reedbeds) and has a different song. Juv. has slightly warmer coloration than ad., being more olive above and yellowish below. **Voice:** Loud, staccato crescendo 'seee-pllip-pllip' song; also harsh 'chrrrr' alarm calls. **Status and biology:** Endemic. Locally common resident and altitudinal migrant in thick, tangled growth on edges of evergreen forests and plantations. Lays 2 eggs in a bulky cup nest built on the ground or low down in dense vegetation. **Diet:** Insects. (Ruigtesanger)

# REED- AND SWAMP-WARBLERS

A notoriously difficult group to identify; closely related to *Hippolais* warblers, but tails graduated (not square). Individual variation may exceed species differences; identification of some species only possible in the hand. Voice important for identification. Sexes alike, but plumage varies with state of wear. Monogamous and territorial. Both sexes incubate and care for the altricial chicks.

## 1 Lesser Swamp-Warbler *Acrocephalus gracilirostris*

B B B b b  b B B B B B
J F M A M J J A S O N D

**14–16 cm; 12–20 g** A fairly large, slender reed-warbler usually with a fairly distinct, whitish supercilium, long bill, and dark brown legs that appear blackish in the field. Underparts mainly white; rufous wash confined to thighs and lower flanks. Larger than African Reed-Warbler, with a more distinct supercilium, warmer brown upperparts, white breast and darker legs. Wings short and rounded, showing less primary projection than migrant Great and Basra reed-warblers (p. 336); bill more slender. Slightly smaller than Greater Swamp-Warbler (p. 320), with warmer rufous upperparts, whiter underparts and a more prominent supercilium. **Voice:** Rich, fluty 'cheerup-chee-chiree-chiree' song. **Status and biology:** Common resident and local migrant in reedbeds, usually over water. Lays 2–3 eggs in a neat cup nest of plaited reeds attached to 2–3 vertical plant stems (usually reeds). **Diet:** Invertebrates; some small frogs. (Kaapse Rietsanger)

## 2 African Reed-Warbler *Acrocephalus baeticatus*

B              b B B B
J F M A M J J A S O N D

**12–13 cm; 8–14 g** A small, brown reed-warbler with a dull white throat; breast and flanks washed rufous. Told from Marsh Warbler by its slightly longer, more slender bill, warmer brown upperparts, buffy (not greyish) underparts, darker legs and shorter wings (folded wings do not extend beyond rump). Forehead profile is less steep, and is usually found in wetland habitats (at least in E areas, where overlap with Marsh Warbler more likely). Very difficult to differentiate from Eurasian Reed-Warbler, but has a shorter wing (50–65 mm) and is generally warmer brown above and more buffy below. Moults Apr–Jun (not Dec–Mar). Best separated in the hand on wing structure (see next species). Juv. has a rufous rump. **Voice:** Song is harsher, more churring and repetitive than that of Marsh Warbler, typically repeating notes 2–4 times. Sometimes mimics other birds. **Status and biology:** Common resident and intra-African migrant (S of 26°S) in reeds and sedges, rank vegetation and gardens. Lays 2–3 eggs in a deep cup nest bound to vertical plant stems. **Diet:** Insects. (Kleinrietsanger)

## 3 Eurasian Reed-Warbler *Acrocephalus scirpaceus*

J F M A M J J A S O N D

**12–13 cm; 9–18 g** Vagrant or scarce migrant. Very similar to African Reed-Warbler and Marsh Warbler. Differs from Marsh Warbler by its longer, more slender bill, less rounded forehead and typically warmer, olive-brown upperparts, often with a rufous wash on the rump. Distinguishable from African Reed-Warbler with certainty only in the hand, but typically is colder grey-brown above and whiter below, with a more prominent white throat. Moults Dec–Mar (not Apr–Jun). Wing longer (60–76 mm); emargination on P9 less extensive, level with tip of P3 (extends beyond level of secondaries in African Reed-Warbler). **Voice:** Song is probably not distinguishable from that of African Reed-Warbler; call notes include low 'churrr'. **Status and biology:** Rare Palearctic migrant. Generally favours more aquatic habitats than Marsh Warbler, frequenting reedbeds and rank vegetation close to water. (Hermanrietsanger)

## 4 Marsh Warbler *Acrocephalus palustris*

J F M A M J J A S O N D

**12–13 cm; 8–15 g** Very similar to Eurasian and African reed-warblers, but its bill is slightly shorter and stouter; upperparts more olive-grey (less rufous); also has a steeper, more rounded forehead profile. Wings average longer than African Reed-Warbler (primary tips extend beyond rump to uppertail coverts). In the hand, claws are uniform (lack pale undersides). Juv. is warmer brown above, with rufous-washed rump; average paler and more olive than juv. Eurasian Reed-Warbler. **Voice:** Song of clear, melodious phrases is more varied and less scratchy than African and Eurasian reed-warblers, with little repetition; often mimics other birds. Frequently utters a 'chuck' or 'tushr' call note while foraging. **Status and biology:** Common Palearctic migrant in rank vegetation, bracken and briar, forest edge, riverine thickets and dense gardens. **Diet:** Invertebrates; some fruit. (Europese Rietsanger)

## 5 Sedge Warbler *Acrocephalus schoenobaenus*

J F M A M J J A S O N D

**12–13 cm; 9–16 g** The only *Acrocephalus* in the region with a streaked back; head has a striking broad, creamy supercilium and a streaked crown. Tail relatively short, dark brown; contrasts with unstreaked, rufous rump. Larger than cisticolas; tail lacks black-and-white tips. Juv. is yellower and more distinctly marked than ad. **Voice:** Harsh chattering interspersed with sharp, melodious phrases; 'tuk' call. **Status and biology:** Fairly common Palearctic migrant in reedbeds and rank weedy areas bordering wetlands, and thickets sometimes far from water. **Diet:** Invertebrates and some fruit. (Europese Vleisanger)

## 1 Greater Swamp-Warbler Acrocephalus rufescens

J F M A M J J A S O N D

**16–18 cm; 18–28 g** A large, long-billed reed warbler with fairly stout blue-grey legs; virtually confined to papyrus swamps. Slightly smaller than Great Reed-Warbler, with dark grey-brown (not pale rufous-brown) upperparts, greyish-brown flanks, less prominent supercilium and shorter wings. Larger and darker than Lesser Swamp-Warbler (p. 318), with greyish (not rufous) flanks and a much less prominent grey (not white) supercilium. Often raises short crest when singing from top of papyrus; structure bulbul-like; could be confused with Terrestrial Brownbul (p. 294), but habitat and song distinctive. **Voice:** Loud 'churrup, churr-churr', interspersed with harsher notes. **Status and biology:** Locally common resident in papyrus swamps. Lays 2–3 eggs in a deep cup nest bound to papyrus stems. **Diet:** Insects and small frogs. (Rooibruinrietsanger)

## 2 Great Reed-Warbler Acrocephalus arundinaceus

J F M A M J J A S O N D

**18–20 cm; 20–42 g** A very large, robust reed warbler with a fairly prominent buffy supercilium, often located by its harsh, guttural song. Large size readily distinguishes it from most other reed-warblers. Appreciably larger than Lesser Swamp-Warbler (p. 318), with a heavier bill, smaller supercilium, more extensive rufous wash on flanks and longer wings. Paler and warmer brown than Greater Swamp-Warbler. Confusion most likely with rare Basra Reed-Warbler; averages larger and warmer brown above, with a heavier bill and shorter supercilium; at close range has dark shafts to throat feathers. Juv. warmer brown above, underparts have a buffy-orange wash. **Voice:** Prolonged, rambling 'chee-chee-chaak-chaak-chuk-chuk' song comprises harsh elements repeated 2–3 times; delivery slower than smaller reed-warblers. **Status and biology:** Fairly common Palearctic migrant in reedbeds and bush thickets; often near water. **Diet:** Mainly invertebrates; also small frogs and fruit. (Grootrietsanger)

## 3 Basra Reed-Warbler Acrocephalus griseldis

J F M A M J J A S O N D

**15–17 cm; 16–20 g** Vagrant or scarce migrant. A large, slim reed-warbler with a dark tail and a long bill accentuated by the flat forehead. Slightly smaller than Great Reed-Warbler with colder, olive-grey (not rufous-brown) upperparts and whiter underparts (washed pale yellow in fresh plumage, Mar–Apr); lacks dark throat streaks. Narrow, white supercilium extends well behind eye and contrasts with dark lores and eye-stripe. Build is less robust, closer to that of smaller reed-warblers; bill is more slender and appears longer. In the hand, wing 75–88 mm (85–105 mm in Great Reed-Warbler). **Voice:** Nasal, subdued 'chuc-chuc-churruc-churruc-chuc', less harsh and varied than Great Reed-Warbler. **Status and biology:** Status poorly known; apparently a rare Palearctic migrant in reedbeds, thickets and rank vegetation, usually near water. (Basrarietsanger)

## 4 River Warbler Locustella fluviatilis

J F M A M J J A S O N D

**14 cm; 14–20 g** A secretive, dark brown warbler with slightly paler underparts; tail graduated. Best located and identified by its song. At close range shows diffuse streaking on the throat and breast; undertail coverts are brown with broad white tips. Structure recalls a Bradypterus warbler (p. 316), but habitat differs. Could be confused with Thrush Nightingale (p. 328), which also skulks in thickets. Juv. is warmer rufous above and creamy buff below. **Voice:** Buzzy, insect-like 'derr-derr-zerr-zerr' song, heard mainly at dawn during Mar–Apr; contact call is a series of 6–8 'chick' notes lasting 1 second, given before singing. Alarm call is a sharp 'pwit' accompanied by wing- and tail-flicking. **Status and biology:** Scarce Palearctic migrant in dense thickets in woodland and riverine scrub, often close to water. **Diet:** Forages on insects, mainly on the ground. (Sprinkaansanger)

## 5 Dark-capped Yellow Warbler Chloropeta natalensis

J F M A M J J A S O N D

**14–15 cm; 9–14 g** A distinctive, richly coloured warbler, olive-green above and yellow below. Darker above than Icterine Warbler (p. 330), with a dark brownish-olive cap and yellowish rump; tail longer. In flight, underwing coverts yellow. Female duller, with less contrast between back and underparts. Juv. has buff wash above; paler below. **Voice:** Soft 'chip-chip-cheezee-cheezee'. **Status and biology:** Locally common resident and partial migrant in bracken, sedges and tangled vegetation at forest edge and along streams. Often inconspicuous, but sings and may hawk insects from exposed perches. Lays 2–3 eggs in a neat cup nest bound to vertical plant stems or built in the fork of a small shrub. **Diet:** Insects and other invertebrates. (Geelsanger)

## 6 Moustached Grass-Warbler Melocichla mentalis

J F M A M J J A S O N D

**20 cm; 33–38 g** A large, plain grass-warbler with a broad, blackish, rounded tail. Related to Cape Grassbird and Rockrunner (p. 322), but has a plain breast; ranges do not overlap. Much larger than Broad-tailed Warbler (p. 316) with a black malar stripe, pale (not dark) eye, more strongly marked face and plain undertail (lacking buff tips to feathers). Rich, varied song is diagnostic. Juv. duller, lacking chestnut forehead and dark malar stripe; breast mottled brown. **Voice:** Bubbling 'tip-tiptwiddle-iddle-see'. **Status and biology:** Uncommon resident in rank grass adjoining forests and in open glades, often near water. Lays 2–3 eggs in an untidy cup nest built in a dense grass tussock close to the ground. **Diet:** Insects. (Breëstertgrasvoël)

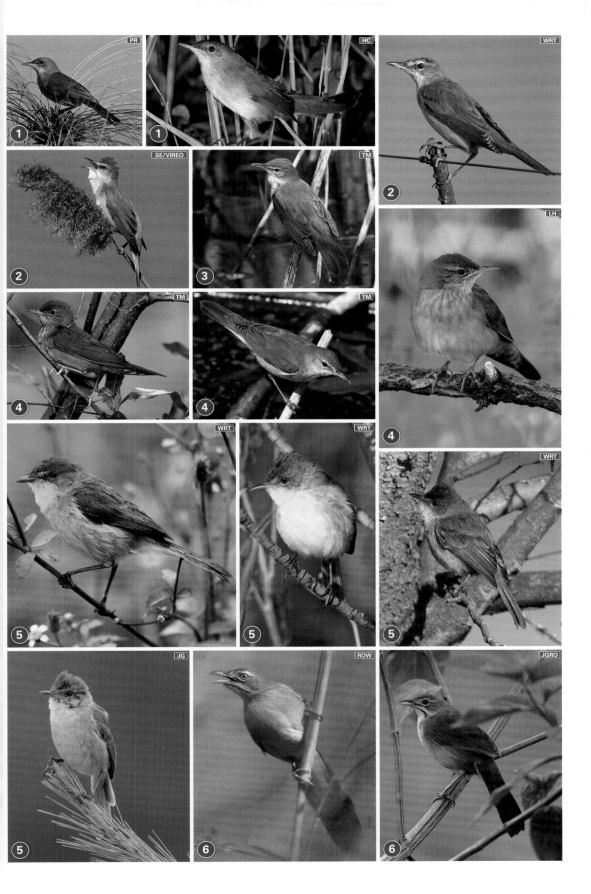

## 1 Rockrunner  *Achaetops pycnopygius*

`B B B` ` ` `b b`
J F M A M J J A S O N D

**20 cm; 26–34 g** A large, striking warbler with a heavily streaked, dark back, white breast spotted with black, and a bright rufous belly and undertail. Bounds across rocks on long legs; sings from exposed perches. Long tail, horizontal stance and distinctive behaviour separate it from chats; could possibly be confused with a scrub-robin (p. 308) or robin-chat (p. 310). Juv. is less distinctly marked and duller. **Voice:** Rich, liquid, melodious song, more varied than Cape Grassbird. **Status and biology:** Near-endemic. Locally common resident on boulder-strewn, grassy hillsides and bases of small hills. Easily overlooked if not calling. Lays 2–3 eggs in a cup nest well concealed inside a dense grass tussock. **Diet:** Insects. (Rotsvoël)

## 2 Cape Grassbird  *Sphenoeacus afer*

`b b b b` ` ` `b B B B B B`
J F M A M J J A S O N D

**17–19 cm; 26–34 g** A large, richly coloured warbler with a long, ratty tail, chestnut cap and black malar stripes. Flight weak. Heavily streaked plumage separates it from Moustached Grass-Warbler (p. 320); much larger than cisticolas. Juv. duller, with a more streaked cap. **Voice:** Song is a stereotyped crescendo, starting as a soft series of warbling notes, builds in volume, pace and pitch, ending in a descending trill; also nasal 'where' call. **Status and biology:** Endemic. Common resident in fynbos and rank grass and ferns on mountain slopes and near water. Mostly remains in dense vegetation, but easily located by its song. Monogamous and territorial; lays 2–3 eggs in a cup nest built within 40 cm of the ground in a restio or other dense vegetation **Diet:** Insects and spiders. (Grasvoël)

## 3 Cinnamon-breasted Warbler  *Euryptila subcinnamomea*

`B B B b b b`
J F M A M J J A S O N D

**12 cm; 10–13 g** A dark brown warbler of rocky hill slopes. At close range the rufous breast band, flanks and rump are diagnostic. Juv. more rufous above. **Voice:** Song is loud, piercing series of whistles: 1–3 long, ascending 'peeeee' notes are often followed by several short, rapid whistles. **Status and biology:** Endemic. Uncommon and localised resident in scrub-covered, rocky hillsides and gorges. Creeps among jumbled boulders, often disappearing into crevices. Lays 2–4 eggs in a thick-walled, oval nest with a side entrance built in a low bush. **Diet:** Insects and other invertebrates. (Kaneelborssanger)

## 4 Stierling's Wren-Warbler  *Calamonastes stierlingi*

`b b b` ` ` `b B B B`
J F M A M J J A S O N D

**13 cm; 12–14 g** A small, wren-like warbler with a fairly long tail, brown upperparts and neatly barred underparts. White spots on tips of upperwing coverts are visible at close range. Differs from Barred Wren-Warbler in having cleaner barred underparts, paler, orange-brown eyes, and flesh-coloured (not brown) legs. Juv. washed yellow below and more rufous above, with dark brown eyes. **Voice:** Song is a fast, repeated 'tlip-tlip-tlip'; also a soft 'preep' and sharp 'tsik' alarm call. **Status and biology:** Fairly common resident in broadleafed woodland, especially miombo. Lays 2–4 eggs in a thick-walled, oval nest with a side entrance built in the mid-canopy of a small tree. Often stitches live leaves to nest. **Diet:** Insects and other invertebrates. (Stierlingsanger)

## 5 Barred Wren-Warbler  *Calamonastes fasciolatus*

`B b b` ` ` `B B`
J F M A M J J A S O N D

**14 cm; 11–14 g** Arid savanna replacement of Stierling's Wren-Warbler; br. male differs by its brown breast, which largely obscures the darker barring. Females and non-br. males have buff underparts with dusky bars, less well defined than those of Stierling's Wren-Warbler; also has darker brown eyes and brown (not flesh-coloured) legs. Juv. is more rufous above, with yellowish wash on breast. **Voice:** Soft, tremulous 'trrrreee trrrreee trrrreee' and rather mechanical 'pleelip-pleelip'; also chattering alarm call. **Status and biology:** Common resident in dry acacia savanna. Lays 2–4 eggs in a thick-walled, oval nest with a side entrance stitched onto live leaves in the canopy of a small tree. **Diet:** Insects. (Gebande Sanger)

## 6 Green-backed Camaroptera  *Camaroptera brachyura*

`b b b b` ` ` `b B B B`
J F M A M J J A S O N D

**12 cm; 9–14 g** A small, wren-like warbler, with plain grey and olive upperparts and whitish underparts; often cocks its short tail. Differs from Grey-backed Camaroptera in having an olive-green (not grey) mantle, back and tail. Lacks distinct br. and non-br. plumages. Intergrades with Grey-backed Camaroptera in Mozambique. Juv. washed yellow below. **Voice:** Song is a loud, snapping 'bidup-bidup-bidup'. Nasal 'neeehhh' alarm call accounts for its common name of Bleating Warbler. **Status and biology:** Common resident in dense undergrowth and tangles in forest and thickets. Usually remains in understorey or mid-strata. Lays 2–4 eggs in a ball-shaped nest stiched into a frame of 4–6 large leaves, usually close to the ground. **Diet:** Insects and other invertebrates. (Groenrugkwêkwêvoël)

## 7 Grey-backed Camaroptera  *Camaroptera brevicaudata*

`b b b b` ` ` `b b B B`
J F M A M J J A S O N D

**12 cm; 8–13 g** Often lumped with Green-backed Camaroptera; the 2 species intergrade in places, but occur in adjacent habitats locally. Has a grey (not olive-green) mantle and tail; wings greenish. Most races have more ashy-brown mantles and backs in non-br. plumage. Juv. washed yellow below. **Voice:** Similar to Green-backed Camaroptera. **Status and biology:** Common resident in dense vegetation in woodland and thickets. In areas of overlap with Green-backed Camaroptera, typically occurs in drier habitats. Lays 2–4 eggs; nest structure similar to Green-backed Camaroptera, but nest is usually less thickly lined. **Diet:** Insects and other invertebrates. (Grysrugkwêkwêvoël)

# EREMOMELAS

Small, short-tailed warblers, of woodland and arid scrub. Usually occur in small groups, and regularly join bird parties. Sexes alike. Juvs duller. Monogamous and territorial. Incubation by both sexes; chicks altricial.

### 1 Burnt-necked Eremomela *Eremomela usticollis*

`b b b b` | | | | `b b B b`
J F M A M J J A S O N D

**10 cm; 7–10 g** Nondescript with pale yellow eyes, rufous cheeks and ear coverts; the small, rusty throat bar often inconspicuous or absent. Larger and darker grey above than Grey Penduline-Tit, with no buff on frons. Juv. lacks rufous patches on face and rusty throat bar; eyes brown. **Voice:** High-pitched 'chii-cheee-cheee-cheee', often followed by a 'trrrrrrrrrr'. Calls include 'tee-up tee-up tee-up'. **Status and biology:** Common resident in acacia woodland; arid broadleafed woodland and dry riverbeds. Usually in small groups; sometimes has helpers at the nest. Lays 1–4 eggs in a small cup nest, tied to twigs in the canopy of an acacia tree. **Diet:** Insects, spiders; also nectar. (Bruinkeelbossanger)

### 2 Green-capped Eremomela *Eremomela scotops*

`b b b b` | | | `b B B B b`
J F M A M J J A S O N D

**11–12 cm; 8–11 g** A handsome eremomela with a greenish crown and grey back; underparts pale yellow, brightest on its breast. Belly paler in Zambezi Valley and N Namibia and Botswana. Most likely to be confused with a white-eye (p. 344), but eyes whitish with a red eye-ring. Juv. paler above; off-white below. **Voice:** Song is a monotonous 'twip-twip-twip-twip'; rasping or chattering 'tweeer' alarm calls. **Status and biology:** Fairly common resident in broadleafed woodland, especially miombo; also in mopane and riverine forests. Usually in small groups; mainly forages in the canopy, and frequently joins bird parties. Often has helpers at the nest. Lays 2–5 eggs in a small cup nest, suspended with cobwebs from the leafy outer branches of a tree. **Diet:** Insects. (Donkerwangbossanger)

### 3 Yellow-bellied Eremomela *Eremomela icteropygialis*

`b b b b b` | | `b B B B b`
J F M A M J J A S O N D

**10 cm; 6–9 g** A pale, grey-backed eremomela with a yellow-washed belly and red-brown (not pale) eyes. The yellow belly tends to be more extensive and brighter in moister areas. Juv. duller. **Voice:** Song is crombec-like: high-pitched, frequently repeated 'tchee-tchee-tchee'. **Status and biology:** Semi-arid savanna, woodland and scrub. Common. Usually solitary or in pairs. Monogamous and territorial; lays 2–3 eggs in a small cup nest, suspended with cobwebs from the outer branches of a shrub or small tree. **Diet:** Insects, spiders; also occasional fruit, seeds and nectar. (Geelpensbossanger)

### 4 Karoo Eremomela *Eremomela gregalis*

`b b b` | `b b b B B B b b`
J F M A M J J A S O N D

**11–12 cm; 7–9 g** A fairly long-tailed eremomela with olive-green upperparts and grey face contrasting sharply with the silvery white underparts. Conspicuous pale eyes, yellow flanks and undertail coverts distinguish it from camaropteras (p. 322); habitat differs. Juv. browner above. **Voice:** Monotonous, frog-like 'swee-er swee-er swee-er' song usually uttered before dawn; also a soft 'pink pink' contact call. **Status and biology:** Endemic. Uncommon to locally common resident in karoo and semi-desert scrub, usually in flat areas with taller than average shrubs; avoids watercourses with trees. Usually in small groups. May have helpers at the nest. Lays 2–4 eggs in a thick-walled cup nest built in the heart of a small bush. **Diet:** Insects and spiders. (Groenbossanger)

# PENDULINE-TITS

Tiny, warbler-like tits with short, pointed, conical bills. Sexes alike. Typically in groups; roost together year-round. Nests oval with a tunnel entrance that is pinched closed and a false entrance to mislead predators such as snakes. Monogamous, sometimes with helpers at the nest. Incubation by both sexes; chicks altricial.

### 5 Grey Penduline-Tit *Anthoscopus caroli*

`b b` | | | | | `b B B B b`
J F M A M J J A S O N D

**8 cm; 6–7 g** A rather nondescript penduline-tit; mostly grey above, with a buffy face, flanks and belly. Lacks distinctive black forehead, eye-stripe and speckled throat of Cape Penduline-Tit. Bill much shorter and tail longer than Long-billed Crombec (p. 328). Juv. paler buff on belly. **Voice:** High-pitched 'tsi-tsi-tsweeee' song, repeated 3–4 times; also buzzy 'chi-zeeee' and 'tsee-wee' calls. **Status and biology:** Common resident and local migrant in broadleafed and miombo woodlands. Usually in small groups. Lays 2–8 eggs in its distinctive ball-like nest suspended from thin branches of a tree. **Diet:** Insects; occasionally nectar. (Gryskapokvoël)

### 6 Cape Penduline-Tit *Anthoscopus minutus*

`B b b b` | `b B B B B B B`
J F M A M J J A S O N D

**8–10 cm; 7–9 g** Differs from Grey Penduline-Tit in having a black forehead extending as eye-stripe, yellowish (not buff) belly and flanks, and speckled throat. Black forehead differentiates it from Yellow-bellied Eremomela. Juv. is paler beneath. **Voice:** High-pitched 'tseeep tseeep tseeep' song; plaintive 'chwee' and bell-like contact calls. **Status and biology:** Near-endemic. Common resident in fynbos, karoo scrub, semi-desert and arid savanna. Lays 4–7 eggs in its distinctive ball-like nest built in a bush or small tree; rarely on a fence. **Diet:** Insects, spiders, small fruits, seeds. (Kaapse Kapokvoël)

# APALISES

Long-tailed warblers of forest, woodland or thicket that feed by gleaning insects. Sexes similar in most species; males slightly larger and more strongly marked. Juvs duller. Monogamous and territorial. Incubation mainly by female; chicks altricial.

## 1 Chirinda Apalis *Apalis chirindensis*

J F M A M J J A S O N D

**11–13 cm; 8–10 g** A drab, pale grey apalis with a white outer tail; confined to E Zimbabwe and adjacent Mozambique. In poor light could be confused with Black-headed Apalis, but pale grey (not blackish) above with orange-brown (not yellow) eyes. Creeps through the canopy; does not fan or flirt its tail like White-tailed Crested-Flycatcher (p. 342). Juv. washed olive above, yellow below, with buffy flanks; eyes grey. **Voice:** Male song is a strident series 'swik swik swik…'; female responds with a lower-pitched 'chip chip chip…'; also a quavering alarm trill. **Status and biology:** Endemic. Locally fairly common resident in montane forest. Nest is oval with a top entrance built high up in a tree; clutch size not known. **Diet:** Insects. (Gryskleinjantjie)

## 2 Black-headed Apalis *Apalis melanocephala*

JFMAMJJASOND

**11–13 cm; 8–10 g** A plain apalis with black or dark grey upperparts and white underparts. Shows more contrast between the yellowish eyes, black face and white throat than Chirinda Apalis. Juv. paler olive-brown above, with yellowish wash on underparts; could be confused with Chirinda Apalis, but occurs at lower elevations. **Voice:** Both sexes give a piercing, repeated 'wiii-tiiit-wiii-tiiit' or 'sweep sweep sweep…'; alarm call a soft 'puit'. **Status and biology:** Locally common resident in the canopy of coastal and riverine forests, especially where there are tangled creepers. Lays 1–3 eggs in an oval nest of lichens, with a side entrance, tied with cobwebs to the outer branches of a tree. **Diet:** Insects; occasional seeds. (Swartkopkleinjantjie)

## 3 Yellow-breasted Apalis *Apalis flavida*

JFMAMJJASOND

**11–13 cm; 7–11 g** The only apalis with a plain yellow breast and no throat collar. Males of some races have a small, black bar beneath the yellow breast. Crown grey, contrasting with olive-green back. Female duller; lacks black breast bar. Juv. has a greenish crown and a paler yellow breast. **Voice:** Male song is a fast, buzzy 'chirip chirip chirip…' or 'kri-krrik kri-krrik, kri-krrik…'; female responds with a series of strident shrieks 'jee jee jee'. Pairs often duet. **Status and biology:** Common resident of woodland, dense savanna and thickets; avoids montane forest. Lays 2–4 eggs in an oval nest with a side entrance, slung from a slender branch in a shrub or small tree. Occasionally uses an old sunbird or weaver nest. **Diet:** Insects and spiders; occasional fruit and nectar. (Geelborskleinjantjie)

## 4 Rudd's Apalis *Apalis ruddi*

JFMAMJJASOND

**11–12 cm; 8–12 g** A dark-eyed apalis with a black breast band. Lacks the white outer tail feathers and pale eye of Bar-throated Apalis, and has a small, white stripe in front of and above the eye. The lime-green back contrasts strongly with the grey head. Female is duller with a narrower breast band. Juv breast band indistinct. **Voice:** Male calls a fast 'trrt trrt trrt…', answered by female with a slower 'prp prp prp…'. **Status and biology:** Near-endemic. Common resident of sandforest and coastal thickets. Lays 1–3 eggs in an oval nest decorated with moss, lichens or dead leaves, and with a side entrance; nest tied to the outer branches of a small tree with cobwebs. **Diet:** Insects; occasional flower buds and nectar. (Ruddkleinjantjie)

## 5 Bar-throated Apalis *Apalis thoracica*

JFMAMJJASOND

**11–12 cm; 9–13 g** A rather variable apalis with a narrow black collar and pale eyes. Upperparts vary from grey to green, underparts from white to greyish and yellow. Pale eyes and white outer tail separate it from Rudd's Apalis. Male has a broader collar. Juv. collar sometimes incomplete. **Voice:** Male utters a harsh 'prrup-prrup-prrup' or 'tilllup-tilllup-tilllup'; female responds with a high-pitched 'ti-ti-ti-ti'. Snaps bill and wings when agitated. **Status and biology:** Common resident of forest, dense woodland and coastal thicket; confined to montane forest in N. Lays 2–4 eggs in an oval nest with a side entrance tied with cobwebs to the outer branches of a shrub or small tree. **Diet:** Insects and spiders; also seeds and fruit. (Bandkeelkleinjantjie)

## FLYCATCHER-LIKE WARBLERS

## 6 Livingstone's Flycatcher *Erythrocercus livingstonei*

JFMAMJJASOND

**11 cm; 5–7 g** A small, olive and yellow flycatcher-like warbler with a blue-grey crown; related to Fairy Flycatcher (p. 328). Easily identified by its long, rufous tail with an indistinct black subterminal band. Constantly in motion, flicking and fanning tail sideways. Juv. has olive back extending onto hind crown; tail lacks dark subterminal band. **Voice:** Melodic, warbled song, often preceded by a series of fast, chittering notes; sharp 'chip-chip' call. **Status and biology:** Locally common resident in riverine and coastal forests. Usually in small groups. Lays 2–3 eggs in an oval nest of dead leaves with a side entrance, built in the canopy of a tree. **Diet:** Insects. (Rooistertvlieëvanger)

## 1 Fairy Flycatcher  *Stenostira scita*

**bBBBbb**
J F M A M J J A S O N D

**10 cm; 4–8 g** A very small, active, flycatcher-like warbler with striking grey, black and white plumage. Ads have a peachy wash on lower breast and belly. Juv. browner above and lacks peach-coloured flanks. **Voice:** Wispy, high-pitched 'tisee-tchee-tchee'; descending 'cher cher cher'. **Status and biology:** Endemic. Common resident and altitudinal migrant in karoo scrub and montane heath in summer, dispersing to acacia savanna in winter. Lays 2–3 eggs in a neat cup nest camouflaged with lichen and bark, built in a dense bush. **Diet:** Insects and spiders. Feeds by gleaning and hawking, often flirting its tail. (Feevlieëvanger)

# TIT-BABBLERS

Compact, babbler-like warblers closely related to migrant *Sylvia* warblers (p. 314). Pale eyes and heavy bills confer a pugnacious appearance. Plumage predominantly grey; tail blackish with prominent white tips and edges. Sexes alike. Juvs duller. Monogamous and territorial. Both sexes incubate; chicks altricial.

## 2 Layard's Tit-Babbler  *Parisoma layardi*

**bbBBBb**
J F M A M J J A S O N D

**14 cm; 14–16 g** Slightly paler than Chestnut-vented Tit-Babbler, with a white (not chestnut) vent; throat streaking often less pronounced. Pale eyes contrast with dark head. Female slightly browner than male; vent tinged buff. Juv. is washed buff; lacks throat streaking. **Voice:** Song is a short, attractive warble; alarm call is a ratchet-like 'tit-trt-trt-trt-trt'. **Status and biology:** Endemic. Common resident in karoo scrub, arid savanna, coastal thicket, and montane scrub in Lesotho; often found in rocky, hilly areas. Lays 2–3 eggs in a cup nest built in a low fork in a bush; nest deeper and thicker-walled than in Chestnut-vented Tit-babbler. **Diet:** Insects, spiders, fruit and occasional seeds. (Grystjeriktik)

## 3 Chestnut-vented Tit-Babbler  *Parisoma subcaeruleum*

**bbbb bbBBBB**
J F M A M J J A S O N D

**15 cm; 12–18 g** Differs from Layard's Tit-babbler by chestnut (not pale grey) vent; throat streaking often bolder and more extensive. Juv. lacks throat streaking; vent paler rufous. **Voice:** Loud, fluty song, similar to Layard's; also imitates other birds. Alarm call is a distinctive 'cher-eeetr tik-tik-tik'. **Status and biology:** Near-endemic. Common resident in savanna, especially acacia thickets, dry watercourses and coastal thicket. Lays 2–3 (rarely 4) eggs in a delicate cup nest in the fork of the outer branches of a tree or bush. **Diet:** Insects, other invertebrates, fruit, seeds, nectar. (Bosveldtjeriktik)

# CROMBECS

Small warblers that appear almost tail-less; bills slender and slightly decurved. Similar to eremomelas (p. 324) but have shorter tails and typically glean from branches rather than foliage. Sexes alike. Juvs duller. Monogamous and territorial. Both sexes incubate and care for the altricial chicks.

## 4 Long-billed Crombec  *Sylvietta rufescens*

**Bbb bBBBB**
J F M A M J J A S O N D

**11 cm; 9–14 g** Longer-billed than other crombecs in the region. Face paler than Red-faced Crombec, with a diagnostic darker grey eye-stripe; upperparts brownish-grey (not ashy grey). Lacks chestnut breast band and ear patches of Red-capped Crombec. Juv. paler below. **Voice:** Song is loud, repeated 'trree-rriit, trree-rriit' or 'trree reee rit' whistle; dry 'prrit' contact call given regularly. **Status and biology:** Common resident and local nomad in woodland, savanna and arid scrublands. In areas with tall trees, seldom ventures into the canopy. Often joins bird parties. Lays 1–3 eggs in a deep, purse-shaped nest with a top-side entrance; slung from twigs or foliage in a bush or the low branches of a small tree. **Diet:** Insects and spiders; also seeds, fruit and nectar. (Bosveldstompstert)

## 5 Red-faced Crombec  *Sylvietta whytii*

**bbbb bBBBB**
J F M A M J J A S O N D

**9 cm; 8–11 g** Slightly smaller than Long-billed Crombec, with plain rufous face and underparts; lacks a dark eye-stripe. Juv. brownish-grey above. **Voice:** Trilling, repeated 'wit-wit-wit-wit'; thin 'si-si-si-see'. **Status and biology:** Locally common in miombo woodland and riparian forests. Typically forages in canopy, but ventures into lower strata in areas without Long-billed Crombecs. Often joins bird parties. Lays 1–3 eggs in a deep, purse-shaped nest with a top-side entrance; slung from the outer branches of a small tree. **Diet:** Insects and other invertebrates. (Rooiwangstompstert)

## 6 Red-capped Crombec  *Sylvietta ruficapilla*

**10 cm; 10–12 g** Rare and localised. Differs from Long-billed and Red-faced crombecs by its chestnut ear patches and breast band; rest of underparts buffy-grey. Back is paler grey than Red-faced Crombec. Juv. more buffy above and paler below. **Voice:** Ringing, repeated 'richi-chichi-chichir'. **Status and biology:** Occurs in tall woodland, especially miombo. Status in sthn Africa uncertain: only 1 record from NW Zimbabwe, but may be resident in small numbers in Tete Province, N Mozambique. **Diet:** Insects. (Rooikroonstompstert)

# CISTICOLAS

A large genus of rufous-crowned warblers that are notoriously difficult to identify. Key features include the extent of back streaking and tail length, but some plain-backed species have streaked non-br. plumage, and tails of non-br. birds are often longer. Song is often the best character. Sexes alike; males much larger in some species. Non-br. and juvs are often yellower beneath, more rufous above. Usually monogamous; some have helpers at the nest. Incubation usually by female only; chicks altricial.

## 1 Zitting Cisticola  *Cisticola juncidis*

B B b b | | | | b b b b B
J F M A M J J A S O N D

**10 cm; 6–13 g** A pale, buffy cisticola with a medium-short tail and strongly marked crown that contrasts with a more finely streaked nape. Darker and more heavily streaked above than Desert Cisticola, with a plain rump; pale brown tail has a prominent dark subterminal band and broad white tip; does not snap wings. Longer-tailed than other short-tailed species. Non-br. ad. is more finely streaked on crown, reducing the contrast between its dark cap and paler nape. Juv. more rufous above, with broad, dull brown streaking, including on its rump. **Voice:** Monotonous 'zit zit zit', repeated 1–2 x per second during its undulating display flight, 5–20 m above territory. **Status and biology:** Common resident in thick grass, rank vegetation and fields, often in damp areas. Often polygamous; male builds distinctive 'soda-bottle' nests with a top entrance among rank grass; female selects a nest, lines it and lays 3–4 (rarely 2–5) eggs. **Diet:** Insects and other invertebrates; also seeds. (Landeryklopkloppie)

## 2 Desert Cisticola  *Cisticola aridulus*

B B b b | | | | | | b B B
J F M A M J J A S O N D

**10 cm; 6–13 g** Structure similar to Zitting Cisticola, but paler and less rufous overall, with a finely streaked rump and darker brown tail lacking an obvious black subterminal bar. Longer-tailed than other short-tailed species. Non-br. ad. is paler above, more buffy below. Juv. easily confused with Zitting Cisticola; best told in hand by lengths of outer primaries: P10 relatively short; P9 long. **Voice:** Song is fast 'zink zink zink', 'sii sii sii' or 'su-ink su-ink su-ink', typically faster than Zitting Cisticola and interspersed with clicking calls and wing-snapping. Display flight low and jerky. **Status and biology:** Common resident in arid grassland and old fields; typically in more arid areas than Zitting Cisticola. Lays 3–4 (rarely 2–5) eggs in a pear-shaped nest, with an entrance near the top, built in a grass tussock. **Diet:** Insects and other invertebrates; also seeds. (Woestynklopkloppie)

## 3 Cloud Cisticola  *Cisticola textrix*

B B b b | | | | b b b B B
J F M A M J J A S O N D

**9–10 cm; 8–13 g** A very short-tailed cisticola, similar to Wing-snapping Cisticola, but more robust with longer legs and typically some streaking on the sides of the breast; best told by distinctive song. Nominate race (W Cape) has extensive breast streaking. Non-br. ad. is paler above; tail longer. Juv. duller with breast washed yellow. **Voice:** Displaying male cruises at great height singing 3–4 whistled notes 'soo-see-see' typically followed by 3 fast wing-snaps; seldom snaps wings before landing, like Wing-snapping Cisticola. **Status and biology:** Near-endemic. Common resident in grassland, fields and lowland fynbos. Lays 2–5 eggs in an oval nest with a side entrance built low down in a grass tussock. **Diet:** Insects and other invertebrates; also seeds. (Gevlekte Klopkloppie)

## 4 Wing-snapping Cisticola  *Cisticola ayresii*

B b b | | | | | | b b B B
J F M A M J J A S O N D

**9 cm; 8–12 g** A very short-tailed cisticola, similar to Cloud Cisticola; appears more slender, with shorter legs and a plain breast; best told by its distinctive aerial display and song. Br. male is shorter-tailed than male Pale-crowned Cisticola, with crown more rufous; dark loral patch smaller, not extending above eye. Non-br. ad. is more rufous and heavily streaked above; underparts richer buff. Juv. duller; breast washed yellow. **Voice:** 3-4 even-pitched notes, slower and deeper than Cloud Cisticola. Sings in high aerial display, interspersed with loud, rapid wing-snapping. On descending, and just before landing, it jinks and loudly snaps its wings. **Status and biology:** Common resident and partial migrant in short grassland; moves to lower elevations in winter, often occurring around marshes. Lays 2–5 eggs in an oval nest with a side entrance, built on the ground between grass tufts. **Diet:** Insects and other invertebrates; also seeds. (Kleinste Klopkloppie)

## 5 Pale-crowned Cisticola  *Cisticola cinnamomeus*

B b b | | | | | | b b B
J F M A M J J A S O N D

**10 cm; 8–11 g** A small cisticola with a short, rounded tail. Male in br. plumage has distinctive black lores contrasting with a pale buffy (not rufous) crown. Non-br. male and female are more buffy below, with a heavily streaked crown and lightly streaked rump; probably not separable from Cloud and Wing-snapping cisticolas in the field. Juv. has throat and breast washed yellow. **Voice:** Song is soft, very high-pitched 'tsee tsee tsee' or 'tsee-tsee-tsee-itititititi'; display flights are at both high and low levels; does not snap wings. Chattering alarm call. **Status and biology:** Uncommon, localised resident and partial migrant in damp or marshy areas in upland grassland, moving to lower elevations in winter. Lays 2–5 eggs in an oval nest with a side entrance, built in a bower of live grass. **Diet:** Insects and other invertebrates. (Bleekkopklopkloppie)

## 1 Grey-backed Cisticola   *Cisticola subruficapilla*

b b ▮ ▮ ▮ ▮ ▮ b B B B B b
J F M A M J J A S O N D

**12–13 cm; 8–15 g** A streak-backed cisticola with a fairly long tail and grey back, contrasting with rufous crown, tail and wing panel. N races are browner above, and more buffy below. Smaller and finer-billed than Wailing Cisticola, with colder greyish-buff underparts. Breast lightly streaked, especially in SW. Lacks a distinct br. plumage. Juv. duller, with yellow-washed underparts. **Voice:** Muffled 'tr-r-rrrrrt' and loud, plaintive 'hu-weeeee', slower and deeper than Wailing Cisticola, given from perch or in air; also harsher 'chee chee' call. **Status and biology:** Near-endemic. Common resident in lowland fynbos, karoo scrub and arid, grassy hillsides, typically in drier habitats than Wailing Cisticola. Lays 2–5 eggs in an oval nest with a side entrance, built low down in dense vegetation. **Diet:** Insects and other invertebrates; also some seeds and fruit. (Grysrugtinktinkie)

## 2 Wailing Cisticola   *Cisticola lais*

B b b ▮ ▮ ▮ ▮ ▮ b b B B
J F M A M J J A S O N D

**13–14 cm; 11–15 g** A long-tailed cisticola with a streaked rufous head, and rufous-brown tail and wing panels contrasting with greyer back. Slightly larger than Grey-backed Cisticola with a heavier bill, heavier back streaking, warmer buff (not cold grey-buff) belly and brighter rufous head. E Cape *C. l. maculatus* has a variably streaked breast. Non-br. ad. has more rufous and heavily streaked upperparts. **Voice:** Rattled 't-trrrrrreee' often followed by 't-pee t-pee t-pee' or a slightly plaintive, drawn-out 'phweeeep', faster and higher-pitched than Grey-backed Cisticola. **Status and biology:** Common resident in rank grass and bracken on rocky hill slopes in moister areas than Grey-backed Cisticola. Lays 2–4 eggs in an oval nest with a side entrance, built low down in dense vegetation. **Diet:** Insects and other invertebrates; also some fruit and other plant material. (Huiltinktinkie)

## 3 Tinkling Cisticola   *Cisticola rufilatus*

B b b ▮ ▮ ▮ ▮ ▮ b b B B
J F M A M J J A S O N D

**12–13 cm; 9–14 g** A streak-backed cisticola with a diagnostic pale supercilium, bright rufous crown and ear coverts, and a long, rufous tail. Smaller and appreciably brighter than Rattling Cisticola, with a prominent supercilium and longer, thinner, rufous tail. Brighter rufous than Grey-backed Cisticola with a more prominent supercilium. Non-br. ad. has a less heavily streaked back and is more rufous above; tail longer. Juv. more buffy above. **Voice:** Tinkling, bell-like notes 'tswee swee swee swee'; alarm call is harsher 'chirrrrr' or 'chit-it-it-rrrrrrrr', often accompanied by wing-snapping. **Status and biology:** Uncommon to locally common resident in dry, broadleafed woodland, savanna and scrub. Shy and easily overlooked. Lays 2–4 eggs in an oval nest with a side entrance, built low down in dense vegetation. **Diet:** Insects. (Rooitinktinkie)

## 4 Croaking Cisticola   *Cisticola natalensis*

B b b ▮ ▮ ▮ ▮ ▮ b b B
J F M A M J J A S O N D

**13–17 cm; male 16–29 g, female 12–18 g** The largest cisticola; robust, decurved bill is black when breeding, yellowish-pink when non-breeding. Female much smaller than male; could be confused with Rattling Cisticola, but has a plain face with a less prominent rufous cap. Juv. has underparts washed yellow. **Voice:** Deep, frog-like 'prrrrp', repeated twice per second and loud 'prrr-CHINK' during bounding display flight or from an exposed perch. **Status and biology:** Common resident in grassland and grassy savanna. Lays 3–4 (rarely 2–5) eggs in an oval nest with a side entrance built low down in dense grass. **Diet:** Insects and other invertebrates; also seeds. (Groottinktinkie)

## 5 Rattling Cisticola   *Cisticola chiniana*

B b b b ▮ ▮ ▮ ▮ b B B
J F M A M J J A S O N D

**12–15 cm; 11–21 g** The most abundant savanna cisticola. A rather large, stout cisticola with a streaked back; female smaller. Has a subdued rufous wash on head, tail and edges of primaries, but duller than Tinkling Cisticola. Non-br. ad. is more rufous above; underparts richer buff. Juv. more buffy above; underparts washed pale yellow. **Voice:** 1–4 loud, scolding notes followed by a trill 'chew chew chew ch-ch-chrrrrrrrrr' or 'chi chi chi chirrreeeee'; alarm call 'chree chree chree'. **Status and biology:** Common resident in woodland, savanna and scrub. Monogamous, sometimes with helpers at the nest. Lays 2–4 (rarely 5) eggs in an oval nest with a side entrance, built low down in dense vegetation. **Diet:** Insects and small invertebrates; also nectar. (Bosveldtinktinkie)

## 1 Rufous-winged Cisticola *Cisticola galactotes*

Bbb | | | | | | | | bbBB
J F M A M J J A S O N D

**12–14 cm; 12–16 g** A wetland cisticola with a boldly striped back, brightly patterned plumage and a fairly long tail. Similar to Luapula Cisticola, but duller with greyer crown and nape and different song; ranges do not overlap. Br. ads told from Levaillant's Cisticola by grey (not brown) tail and plain (not streaked) rump; ranges barely overlap. Non-br. ad. is more rufous above and more buffy below with a browner tail. Juv. has crown streaked dark brown; underparts washed yellow. **Voice:** Single-note, musical, ascending 'phweeep' song; also buzzy 'tzeet' or 'trrrt trrrt'. **Status and biology:** Common resident in reedbeds, long grass and sedges near water. Lays 2–4 eggs in an oval nest of grass leaves with a top-side entrance, built low down in dense vegetation, usually over water. **Diet:** Insects and small invertebrates; also seeds. (Swartrugtinktinkie)

## 2 Luapula Cisticola *Cisticola luapula*

bbbb | | | | | | | | bb
J F M A M J J A S O N D

**12–14 cm; 11–15 g** Recently split from Rufous-winged Cisticola; ranges do not overlap. Slightly smaller and shorter-tailed than Chirping Cisticola with richer crown and wing panel, greyer tail and more boldly marked back; underparts paler. Told from Levaillant's Cisticola by its plain (not streaked) rump and grey-brown (not rufous) tail. Non-br. ad. is more rufous above and more buffy below. Juv. has crown streaked dark brown; underparts washed yellow. **Voice:** Loud 2-note display song 'tid-ick'; also 'tic tic', 'we-we-we' and 'zrrtttt' calls, sometimes in display flight. **Status and biology:** Locally common resident in swamps and marshes; prefers *Phragmites* reeds to dense papyrus. Lays 2–4 eggs in an oval nest of grass leaves with a top-side entrance, built low down in dense vegetation. **Diet:** Small insects. (Luapulatinktinkie)

## 3 Chirping Cisticola *Cisticola pipiens*

bbbb | | | | | | | | bbb
J F M A M J J A S O N D

**14–15 cm; 12–15 g** A wetland cisticola with a boldly striped back and a long, rather broad tail. Slightly larger and longer-tailed than Luapula and Levaillant's cisticolas, with a duller brown crown, wing panel and tail, a less boldly streaked back, and buffy (not whitish) underparts. Best told by its song. Non-br. male is slightly paler above, with buffy margins to mantle and back feathers. Female is paler, less buffy below in fresh plumage. Juv. has crown streaked dark brown; base of tail reddish. **Voice:** Song loud: 2–3 sharp notes followed by a dry, buzzy trill 'chit chit-it trrrrrrrrrrrr'; also plaintive 'chwer-chwer-chwer' and sharp 'chit chit' calls. Sometimes snaps its wings while calling. **Status and biology:** Locally common resident in reedbeds and papyrus swamps. Favours taller vegetation in wetter areas than Luapula and Levaillant's cisticolas. Lays 3–4 eggs in an oval nest of grass leaves with a top-side entrance, built low down in dense grass. **Diet:** Insects. (Piepende Tinktinkie)

## 4 Levaillant's Cisticola *Cisticola tinniens*

bbbb | | | | | bbbbbb
J F M A M J J A S O N D

**13–14 cm; 9–14 g** The brightest wetland cisticola; told from Rufous-winged and Luapula cisticolas by its streaked (not plain) rump and rufous (not grey-brown) tail; song is diagnostic. Slightly smaller than Chirping Cisticola, with paler underparts and much brighter rufous crown, wing panel and tail. Non-br. ad. has buffy-brown (not greyish) margins to the mantle feathers and streaked crown. Juv. is duller above, with less prominent streaking; breast washed pale lemon. **Voice:** Warbling, musical 'chrip-tirrrup-trreee', sharp 'wip wip' and a wailing 'cheee-weee-weee'. **Status and biology:** Common resident in reedbeds, sedges and long grass adjacent to wetlands. Lays 3–4 eggs in an oval nest with a top-side entrance, tied to low vegetation with cobwebs. **Diet:** Insects and spiders. (Vleitinktinkie)

## 5 Red-faced Cisticola *Cisticola erythrops*

Bbb | | | | | | | | bBB
J F M A M J J A S O N D

**13–15 cm; 11–18 g** A plain-faced, warm buff and rufous cisticola found near water. Brown (not rufous) crown and warm rufous face distinguish it from all other plain-backed species. Wings are brown, uniform with the back; lacks Singing Cisticola's rufous edges to primaries. Non-br. ad. has browner crown and richer underparts; tail tipped white. Juv. browner. **Voice:** Piping series of descending notes, increasing in volume 'tee-tee-tee-TAY-TAY-TAY-TOY-TOY-TOY'; also dry 'prrt prrt'. Female usually duets with male, deep 'zidit'. Alarm call is thin, high-pitched 'tseeeep'. **Status and biology:** Common resident of rank vegetation next to pans and streams. Lays 2–4 eggs in a ball nest with a side entrance built in a tailored pouch of living leaves. **Diet:** Insects. (Rooiwangtinktinkie)

## 6 Singing Cisticola *Cisticola cantans*

Bbbb | | | | | | | | bBB
J F M A M J J A S O N D

**12–14 cm; 9–16 g** A plain-backed cisticola similar to Red-faced Cisticola, but has rufous edges to primaries forming a diagnostic rufous wing panel; also rufous (not brown) crown and browner (less rufous) face; underparts often whiter. Non-br. ad. has dark brown streaks on its back coverts; lacks sooty lores; underparts richer buff. Juv. has paler underparts, washed yellow. **Voice:** Loud, disyllabic 'jhu-weee' or 'whee-cho'; chattering alarm call. **Status and biology:** Common resident in rank vegetation, bracken and tall grass with scattered bushes. Lays 2–4 eggs in a ball nest with a side entrance built in a tailored pouch of living leaves. **Diet:** Insects and spiders. (Singende Tinktinkie)

## 1 Neddicky  *Cisticola fulvicapilla*

Bbb||||||bbBB
J F M A M J J A S O N D

**11 cm; 7–12 g** A small, plain-backed cisticola with dark grey (Cape to KZN) or pale buffy-grey underparts, uniform brownish upperparts and a chestnut cap. Longer-tailed than Short-winged Cisticola, with a distinct chestnut cap and different song. Non-br. ad. is brighter above, reducing contrast between crown and back. Juv. more rufous above, whiter below. **Voice:** Ventriloquial song is a high-pitched, frog-like 'tseeep tseeep tseeep'; alarm call is a dry, ratchet-like 'tic-tic-tic-tic'; also 'tuc' notes. **Status and biology:** Common resident in grassy understorey of woodland and savanna; also mountain fynbos and plantations, especially where there are rocks or dead trees. Lays 2–4 eggs in an oval nest with a side entrance tied to low vegetation with cobwebs. **Diet:** Insects and other invertebrates; also nectar, seeds and other plant material. (Neddikie)

## 2 Short-winged Cisticola  *Cisticola brachypterus*

bbb||||||||bb
J F M A M J J A S O N D

**10–11 cm; 6–11 g** A small, fairly short-tailed, nondescript cisticola with a plain, open face. Lacks a rufous crown and is shorter-tailed than Neddicky. Back plain or slightly mottled in br. birds. Non-br. ad. is more heavily streaked above, especially on crown; underparts more buffy. Juv. has underparts washed yellow. **Voice:** Soft, repeated 'see-see-sippi-ippi' or 'tsip tsip seu', falling in pitch; also slurred warble 'tsip tsiddle'; sings from high, exposed perches throughout the day when breeding. **Status and biology:** Locally common resident in rank grass in open woodland and savanna. Lays 2–4 eggs in an oval nest with a side entrance tied to low vegetation with cobwebs. **Diet:** Insects. (Kortvlerktinktinkie)

## 3 Lazy Cisticola  *Cisticola aberrans*

Bbbb|||||bbBB
J F M A M J J A S O N D

**13–14 cm; 10–18 g** Differs from other plain-backed cisticolas within its range by having a pale supercilium, extending well behind eye. Frequently cocks its tail like a prinia; tail lacks dark subterminal bar. Larger than Neddicky, with longer, frequently cocked tail and typically a less well-defined rufous cap. Non-br. ad. has a longer tail; upperparts more rufous, underparts darker buff. Juv. more rufous than non-br. ad. **Voice:** Plaintive 'zweeee-zweeee-zweeee' interspersed by short trills and stutters; sometimes followed by 'peet-peet-peet'. Song is a loud, clear 'twink twink twink' or more plaintive 'tjwert tjwert tjwert'. **Status and biology:** Locally common resident on rocky hill slopes in grassland and woodland. Lays 2–4 eggs in an oval nest with a side entrance built in a grass tussock or rank vegetation. **Diet:** Insects. (Luitinktinkie)

# PRINIA-LIKE WARBLERS

**Four monotypic warbler genera allied to prinias and apalises. Nests not woven like prinia nests. Sexes alike; juvs duller. Monogamous and territorial; chicks altricial.**

## 4 Red-winged Warbler  *Heliolais erythropterus*

b||||||||||bb
J F M A M J J A S O N D

**13 cm; 11–13 g** A long-tailed, prinia-like warbler. Differs from Tawny-flanked Prinia (p. 338) by its bright rufous (not brown) wings, which contrast with dark brown upperparts, and by lack of a prominent white eye-stripe. Non-br. birds are browner above, showing less contrast with the rufous wings. Juv. is paler. **Voice:** Monotonous, rather prinia-like 'pseep-pseep-pseep'; also a chattering alarm call. **Status and biology:** Locally common resident in long grass in woodland clearings and alongside streams. Lays 2–3 eggs in an oval nest with a side entrance built low down in rank vegetation. **Diet:** Insects and spiders. (Rooivlerksanger)

## 5 Rufous-eared Warbler  *Malcorus pectoralis*

bbb|||bbbbbb
J F M A M J J A S O N D

**15 cm; 9–12 g** A prinia-like warbler with a long, slender, graduated tail, diagnostic reddish ear coverts and a narrow black breast band. Female duller than male, with narrower breast band. Juv. lacks breast band and has a brown face; told from cisticolas by its longer tail and lack of a rufous cap; from Karoo Prinia by its plain breast and streaked back. **Voice:** Scolding, high-pitched 'tzee tzee tzee tzee...' repeated 6–20 times; plaintive 'peeee' alarm call. **Status and biology:** Endemic. Common resident and local nomad in arid scrub. Lays 3–5 (rarely up to 7) eggs in an oval nest with a side entrance built in a small bush. **Diet:** Insects, spiders and fruit; often forages on the ground, running swiftly between bushes. (Rooioorlangstertjie)

## 1 Roberts's Warbler  *Oreophilais robertsi*

bb | | | | | | |bBBB
J F M A M J J A S O N D

**13–14 cm; 8–12 g** A rather uniform grey, prinia-like warbler confined to E Zimbabwe highlands and adjacent Mozambique. Darker than Tawny-flanked Prinia, with a grey-washed throat and breast; lacks white supercilium and rufous-edged flight feathers. Pale eye contrasts with dark face. Non-br. birds are paler below. Juv. has dark eye. **Voice:** Raucous chorus of high-pitched, babbler-like chattering, uttered by all members of a group. **Status and biology:** Endemic. Common resident of forest edge, and bracken adjoining forests. Usually in small groups. Lays 2–3 eggs; nest varies from a cup to an enclosed ball with a side entrance; built low down in rank vegetation. **Diet:** Insects and spiders. (Woudlangstertjie)

## 2 Namaqua Warbler  *Phragmacia substriata*

bbb | | | | | | |bBBB
J F M A M J J A S O N D

**13–14 cm; 9–13 g** A slender, long-tailed warbler, recalling a delicate Karoo Prinia, but with a more russet-coloured back, narrow streaking confined to the breast, plain face and thinner, more graduated tail that lacks buff tips. Female has less streaking. Juv. duller. **Voice:** Both sexes give the high-pitched, rattling song 'trip-trip-trrrrrrrrrrrr'; also 'chit' contact call and 'chewy chewy chewy' alarm call. **Status and biology:** Endemic. Common resident in acacia woodland, usually along watercourses with *Phragmites* reedbeds. Pairs defend territories year-round. Lays 2–4 eggs in an untidy, deep cup nest built low down in dense vegetation. **Diet:** Insects, spiders and fruit. (Namakwalangstertjie)

## PRINIAS

**Long-tailed warblers of woodland or scrub, usually in drier habitats than apalises. Lack rufous caps of cisticolas. Sexes alike, or females slightly duller; some species have distinct non-br. plumages. Monogamous and territorial; sometimes with helpers at the nest. Nests neatly woven from strips of grass. Incubation by female only; chicks altricial.**

## 3 Karoo Prinia  *Prinia maculosa*

bbb | | | |bbBBBb
J F M A M J J A S O N D

**12–14 cm; 8–11 g** Sometimes lumped with Drakensberg Prinia, but is more heavily streaked below; streaking usually extends onto its throat and flanks; ranges not known to overlap. Also more heavily streaked than Namaqua Warbler, and is greyer brown above with a broader tail, with buff-tipped (not plain) tail feathers. Female is less heavily spotted. Juv. is yellower below. **Voice:** Wide range of scolding calls, including buzzy 'dzeeep dzeeep dzeeep...', harder 'chip-chip-chip...' and faster 'kli-kli-kli...'. **Status and biology:** Common resident in fynbos, thickets and taller karoo scrub. Territorial year-round. Lays 2–4 eggs in an oval nest with a side entrance tied to branches of a shrub with cobwebs. **Diet:** Insects and spiders. (Karoolangstertjie)

## 4 Drakensberg Prinia  *Prinia hypoxantha*

Bb | | | | | | | |bBB
J F M A M J J A S O N D

**12–14 cm; 9–11 g** Sometimes lumped with Karoo Prinia, but has yellow-washed underparts with streaking usually confined to its breast (not onto throat and flanks); averages warmer brown above. Juv. is paler and less streaked below; upperparts redder above. **Voice:** Similar to Karoo Prinia. **Status and biology:** Endemic. Common resident of forest edges, wooded gullies and bracken tangles, normally at higher elevations than Karoo Prinia. Lays 2–4 eggs in an oval nest with a side entrance built in a small bush. **Diet:** Insects and spiders; occasional nectar. (Drakensberglangstertjie)

## 5 Tawny-flanked Prinia  *Prinia subflava*

BBbb | | | |bbbbBB
J F M A M J J A S O N D

**11–12 cm; 6–12 g** A common, plain-breasted prinia. Differs from non-br. Black-chested Prinia by its white (not yellow) throat and breast, warm buff flanks and belly, and russet edges to wing and tail feathers. Strong white supercilium separates it from larger Red-winged Warbler (p. 336). Br. male has black bill and mouth. Non-br. male and female bill brown. Juv. washed yellow below. **Voice:** Rapidly repeated 'przzt-przzt-przzt...' or 'tsip-tsip-tsip...'; mewing 'zbee' or 'cheeee' alarm call. **Status and biology:** Common resident in woodland and thick, rank vegetation. Lays 2–5 eggs in an oval nest with a side entrance built low down in a bush or rank vegetation; rarely in an old bishop nest. **Diet:** Insects and spiders; occasional nectar. (Bruinsylangstertjie)

## 6 Black-chested Prinia  *Prinia flavicans*

Bbb | | | |bbbBB
J F M A M J J A S O N D

**12–13 cm; 7–12 g** The only prinia with a broad black breast band (narrower in female). In non-br. plumage, when breast band is usually absent, could be mistaken for Tawny-flanked Prinia, but it lacks russet edges to its wing and tail feathers and is usually yellow (not creamy-white) below. Juv. resembles non-br. ad., but is yellower below. Occasionally hybridises with Karoo Prinia. **Voice:** Loud, repetitive 'prrt-prrt-prrt...' or 'dzrrt-dzrrt-dzrrt'; ratchet-like 'zrrrrrrt' alarm call. **Status and biology:** Common resident in arid scrub, savanna, plantations and gardens. Lays 2–4 (rarely up to 6) eggs in an oval nest with a side entrance built in a bush or rank vegetation. **Diet:** Insects and other invertebrates; occasional nectar. (Swartbandlangstertjie)

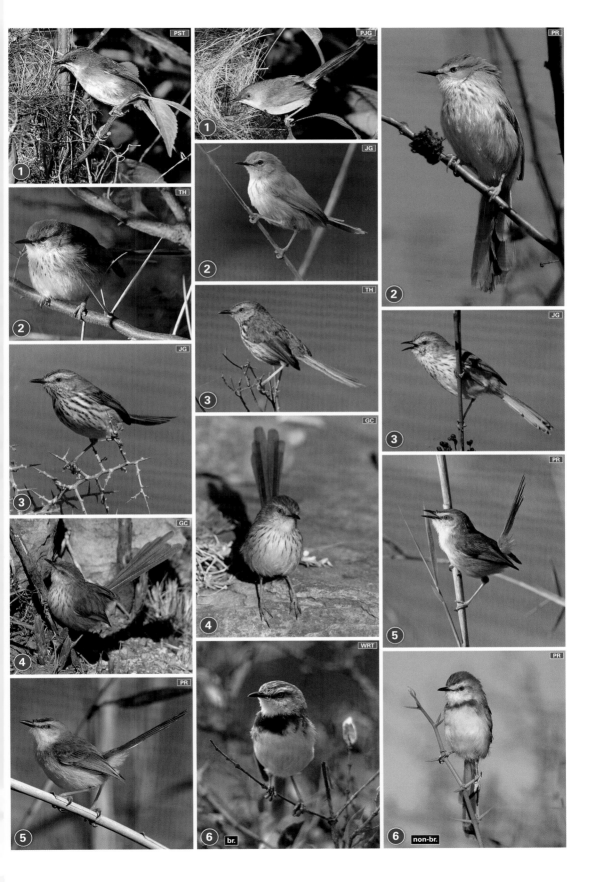

# FLYCATCHERS

Insectivorous passerines that catch at least some prey by hawking. Bills slender, short and broad, often with rictal bristles to aid catching aerial prey. Sexes alike in most species. Juvs spotted buff above and mottled below in muscicapids; like dull females in crested flycatchers. Monogamous and territorial.

## 1 African Dusky Flycatcher *Muscicapa adusta*

J F M A M J J A S O N D

**12 cm; 10–14 g** A small, compact flycatcher. Appears short-winged and dumpy compared with Spotted Flycatcher; crown plain; typically in more forested habitats. Smaller and shorter-tailed than Ashy Flycatcher; upperparts grey-brown (not blue-grey). Breast and flanks have ill-defined streaking. Juv. has buff-spotted upperparts; breast mottled dark brown. **Voice**: High-pitched, descending 'tseeeuu'; also a sharper 'ti-ti-ti-trrrrr' or 'tsirit'; alarm call is a series of sharp clicks. **Status and biology:** Common resident in forest edges and glades, riverine forest and well-wooded gardens. Lays 2–3 eggs in an untidy cup nest built in a cavity or an old starling or weaver nest. **Diet:** Insects; some fruit. (Donkervlieëvanger)

## 2 Spotted Flycatcher *Muscicapa striata*

J F M A M J J A S O N D

**13–14 cm; 15–20 g** A grey-brown flycatcher with a dark-streaked crown and indistinctly streaked breast. Larger and longer-winged than African Dusky Flycatcher, with a more boldly streaked crown; wings extend almost halfway down its tail. Hind crown is slightly peaked. Often flicks its wings on landing. Juv. body plumage moulted before reaching sthn Africa, but may retain some tertials and wing coverts with broad buff margins. **Voice:** Occasionally gives soft 'tzee' and 'zeck, chick-chick' calls. **Status and biology:** Common Palearctic migrant to virtually all wooded habitats, from forest edges to semi-arid savanna. **Diet:** Insects; fruit and seeds. (Europese Vlieëvanger)

## 3 Ashy Flycatcher *Muscicapa caerulescens*

J F M A M J J A S O N D

**14–15 cm; 15–17 g** A blue-grey flycatcher with whitish eye-rings that contrast with its blackish lores. Told from Grey Tit-Flycatcher by its more erect stance, striking facial pattern and plain (not white-edged) tail; hawks prey (doesn't flirt its tail while gleaning). Plumage more blue-grey than grey-brown African Dusky and Spotted flycatchers. Juv. is darker above with buff spotting; breast mottled blackish. **Voice:** Song is a short, descending warble 'sszzit-sszzit-sreee-sreee', lasting 1–2 seconds; alarm call is a piercing hiss. **Status and biology:** Common resident in riverine forest and moist, open broadleafed woodland. Some birds move to lower elevations in winter. Lays 2–4 eggs in a bulky cup nest in a cavity or deep tree fork; occasionally on buildings. **Diet:** Insects; also fruit and small geckos. (Blougrysvlieëvanger)

## 4 Grey Tit-Flycatcher *Myioparus plumbeus*

J F M A M J J A S O N D

**14 cm; 11–13 g** A slender, warbler-like bird that lacks the typical flycatcher's broad bill; usually gleans rather than hawks for insects. Stance horizontal; frequently fans and flirts its tail like a crested flycatcher. Blackish tail has white outer tail and tips; lacks white eye-ring and blackish lores of Ashy Flycatcher. Juv. spotted brown and buff above and below. **Voice:** Soft, tremulous, whistled 'treeoo' or 'treee-trooo'. **Status and biology:** Locally common resident in dense woodland and savanna thickets, riparian woodland and forest edge. Lays 2–3 eggs in a flimsy cup nest in a tree cavity or old woodpecker or barbet hole. **Diet:** Insects. (Waaierstertvlieëvanger)

## 5 Southern Black Flycatcher *Melaenornis pammelaina*

J F M A M J J A S O N D

**18–20 cm; 24–32 g** A large, all-black flycatcher with a long, square tail and erect stance. Thought to mimic a drongo (p. 284), but has a much more slender bill, brown (not red) eyes, and longer legs, standing taller on perch; tail square and relatively shorter; does not flare at tip. Translucent bases to primaries create paler window in flight. Female has sooty brown (not black) body. Juv. sooty brown above with rufous streaks; underparts mottled dark brown and buff. **Voice:** Whistled 2–3-note song, often preceded by a shrill note 'tziiii tsooo-tsoo'. **Status and biology:** Common resident in woodland, savanna and forest edges. Sallies from perches, taking food from ground. Lays 2–4 (rarely 5) eggs in a flimsy cup nest built in a cavity or hollow; sometimes in old weaver, thrush, bulbul or babbler nests. **Diet:** Insects and other invertebrates; some fruit and possibly nectar. (Swartvlieëvanger)

## 6 Fiscal Flycatcher *Sigelus silens*

J F M A M J J A S O N D

**18–20 cm; 22–36 g** A striking pied flycatcher thought to mimic a Common Fiscal (p. 358), but has a much more slender bill, shorter tail and longer legs, standing taller on perch; white in wings is confined to secondaries (not wing coverts). In flight, shows conspicuous white windows in outer tail. Much larger and longer-tailed than Collared Flycatcher (p. 344). Female is browner above and washed darker grey on breast and belly. Juv. is much browner above with buff spots; underparts mottled grey-brown. **Voice:** High-pitched, short, chittering song; 'tssisk' alarm call. **Status and biology:** Endemic. Common resident and partial migrant in woodland and thickets, scrub, gardens and plantations. Moves to lower elevations in winter. Lays 2–4 eggs in a bulky cup nest built in a cavity or tree fork; sometimes in the outer branches of a tree, among aloe leaves or in an old building. **Diet:** Insects, other invertebrates, fruit and nectar. Occasionally kills fledgling birds. (Fiskaalvlieëvanger)

## 1 Chat Flycatcher *Bradornis infuscatus*

b b b b b  b b b B B B
J F M A M J J A S O N D

**20 cm; 39 g** A large, chat-like flycatcher with long wings and tail. Rather nondescript, with paler edges to wing feathers forming slight panel on folded secondaries. Best told from chats by its long, uniform brown tail. Larger than Marico or Pale flycatchers, with darker brown underparts that contrast less with the upperparts. Often lifts its wings and spends more time on ground than other flycatchers. Juv. spotted buff above; flight feathers edged rufous; breast mottled dark brown. **Voice:** Song is deep, warbled 'cher-cher-cherrip', interspersed with hard, grating notes. **Status and biology:** Near-endemic. Common resident and local nomad in semi-arid and arid shrublands. Lays 2–3 eggs in a large, untidy cup nest built in a bush or small tree. **Diet:** Insects and small reptiles, mainly taken on the ground. (Grootvlieëvanger)

## 2 Marico Flycatcher *Bradornis mariquensis*

b b b b b b b b b B B B
J F M A M J J A S O N D

**18 cm; 22–28 g** A fairly large, brown-backed flycatcher; told from Pale and Chat flycatchers by its white (not brownish) underparts; usually occurs in more arid habitats. Juv. spotted buff above, with rufous edges to flight feathers; underparts off-white with dark brown streaking. **Voice:** Song is a series of sparrow-like chirps 'tsii-cheruk-tukk'; soft 'tsee tsee' alarm call. **Status and biology:** Near-endemic. Common resident in semi-arid acacia savanna and sparse woodland. Conspicuous; often perches in the open. Lays 2–3 (rarely 4) eggs in a small cup nest in the outer canopy of a small tree. **Diet:** Insects and occasional fruit. (Maricovlieëvanger)

## 3 Pale Flycatcher *Bradornis pallidus*

b b b        b b B B
J F M A M J J A S O N D

**17 cm; 20–24 g** A fairly large, uniform brownish flycatcher. Told from Marico Flycatcher by its buffy-brown (not white) underparts. Range overlaps slightly with Chat Flycatcher, but is smaller and paler below than that bird; pale panel in folded wing less prominent; tail shorter and narrower. Juv. has fine buff spots above, with broad buff margins to flight feathers; underparts streaked dark brown. **Voice:** Song is melodious warbling interspersed with harsh chitters; alarm call is soft 'churr'. **Status and biology:** Locally common resident in moist, broadleafed woodland. Lays 2–4 eggs in a flimsy cup nest in the outer canopy of a small tree. **Diet:** Insects, occasional fruit and possibly nectar. (Muiskleurvlieëvanger)

## 4 Blue-mantled Crested-Flycatcher *Trochocercus cyanomelas*

b            b b B B
J F M A M J J A S O N D

**13–15 cm; 9–11 g** A black-and-white crested-flycatcher with a prominent white wing bar; tail dark grey, lacking white tip of White-tailed Crested-Flycatcher. Male has glossy black head, crest and throat, contrasting with its white lower breast and belly. Female is paler grey, with fine streaking on throat, and less white in wing. Juv. resembles female, but has shorter crest and buffy wing bar. **Voice:** Frequently calls a harsh 'zweet-zwa', similar to African Paradise-Flycatcher; song is a short series of whistles. **Status and biology:** Common resident in forests; some may move to lower elevations in winter. Lays 2–3 eggs in a neat cup nest bound with cobwebs to a fork in the canopy of a small tree. **Diet:** Insects and spiders. (Bloukuifvlieëvanger)

## 5 African Paradise-Flycatcher *Terpsiphone viridis*

b            b b b B B
J F M A M J J A S O N D

**17–20 cm (plus 18 cm tail in male); 11–17 g** A spectacular crested-flycatcher with rufous upperparts and greyish underparts. Br. male has elongate tail streamers, dark head and breast, and bright blue bill and eye-ring. Female and juv. are duller, with short tails and duller blue soft parts. **Voice:** Harsh 'zway-ter' call; song is loud, whistled 'tswee-tswitty-tswee-tswitty-ter'. **Status and biology:** Common resident and intra-African migrant in forest and dense woodland; also gardens. Departs E and W Cape in winter. Lays 2–3 (rarely 1–4) eggs in a cup nest, decorated with lichens, built in a fork in the canopy of a small tree. **Diet:** Insects. (Paradysvlieëvanger)

## 6 White-tailed Crested-Flycatcher *Elminia albonotata*

b            b B B
J F M A M J J A S O N D

**13 cm; 7–10 g** Resembles a Blue-mantled Crested-Flycatcher, but lacks a white wing bar and has white tail tips. Dusky throat and breast merge into paler belly. Sexes alike. Juv. duller. Actually an aberrant warbler; not closely related to other crested-flycatchers. Darts among foliage with drooped wings and fanned tail. **Voice:** Song is a series of very high-pitched notes 'tsee-tsee-teuu-choo'; rapid 'zitt-zitt-zitt' alarm call. **Status and biology:** Common resident in montane forest. Lays 2–3 eggs in deep cup of moss, decorated with lichens, built in the fork of a small tree. **Diet:** Small insects. (Witstertvlieëvanger)

## 7 Black-and-white Flycatcher *Bias musicus*

b            b b b
J F M A M J J A S O N D

**13–15 cm; 17–22 g** A squat flycatcher related to wattle-eyes and batises (p. 346), but is larger, with an obvious crest. Legs and eyes yellow. Male is black and white with small white patches in the primary bases. Female has bright chestnut back and tail, recalling a female African Paradise-Flycatcher, but is stockier, with a white throat and shorter tail. Juv. resembles female, but is duller and streaked on head. Imm. male has blackish breast and rufous back. **Voice:** Song is whistled 'whitu-whitu-whitu'; alarm note is sharp 'wee-chip'. **Status and biology:** Uncommon and local resident of forest and riparian woodland. Lays 2–3 eggs in a neat cup nest decorated with lichens, built in a fork in the canopy of a tall tree. **Diet:** Insects, spiders and small reptiles. (Witpensvlieëvanger)

### 1 Collared Flycatcher *Ficedula albicollis*

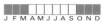
J F M A M J J A S O N D

**12–13 cm; 10–14 g** A compact flycatcher with prominent white wing bars. Told from hyliotas by its longer wings, rounder head and hawking behaviour (not warbler-like gleaning). Br. male blackish above with a complete white collar, large white forecrown and extensive white primary bases. Female and juv. grey-brown with partial collar. Both sexes have a small, pale rump patch and narrow white edges to outer tail bases. **Voice:** Drawn-out 'seep' or soft 'whit-whit-whit'. **Status and biology:** Rare Palearctic migrant to woodland. **Diet:** Small insects. (Withalsvlieëvanger)

## HYLIOTAS

**Small, active gleaners that seldom hawk prey; regularly join bird parties. Molecular evidence suggests they form a distinct family. Males brighter than females; juvs barred buffy above. Monogamous and territorial; chicks altricial.**

### 2 Southern Hyliota *Hyliota australis*

b b b          B B B b
J F M A M J J A S O N D

**11 cm; 10–12 g** Male sooty black above; throat and breast washed pale yellow. Lacks glossy upperparts of male Yellow-breasted Hyliota; white shoulder patch restricted to coverts (not extending onto secondaries and tertials). Female is brown above with a creamy breast; differs from female Yellow-breasted Hyliota by having warmer brown upperparts. Juv. has buff margins to upperpart feathers; underparts washed buff. **Voice:** A soft, high-pitched, rather querulous 'tueet tueet'; also a chittering call. **Status and biology:** Locally common resident in miombo and other broadleafed woodland. Lays 2–4 eggs in a small cup nest, decorated with lichens, built in a fork in the canopy of a tall tree. **Diet:** Insects. (Mashonahyliota)

### 3 Yellow-bellied Hyliota *Hyliota flavigaster*

J F M A M J J A S O N D

**12 cm; 11–14 g** Male differs from male Southern Hyliota by having distinctly glossy blue-black upperparts, richer yellow underparts and white in the wings extending onto the folded secondaries and tertials. Female grey-brown above and duller below; told from female Southern Hyliota by grey-brown (not warm brown) upperparts. Juv. has buff margins to upperpart feathers; underparts creamy. **Voice:** Similar to Southern Hyliota, but deeper and slower. **Status and biology:** Rare resident in broadleafed woodland, including miombo. Not confirmed to breed in sthn Africa. **Diet:** Insects. (Geelborshyliota)

## WHITE-EYES

**Small, greenish-yellow warblers with prominent white eye-rings. Forage in small, noisy flocks; could be confused with eremomelas (p. 324). Sexes alike; juvs duller, eye-ring smaller. Monogamous; both sexes incubate; chicks altricial.**

### 4 African Yellow White-eye *Zosterops senegalensis*

b          b B B B b
J F M A M J J A S O N D

**10–12 cm, 8–11 g** Bright yellow; lacks any green tones in underparts and has yellower upperparts than Cape White-eye. Juv. duller, with greener upperparts. **Voice:** Loud, melodious whistled 'tweee-tuuu-twee-twee'. Groups make continuous, twittering contact calls. **Status and biology:** Common resident in woodland, scrub, forest and gardens. Lays 2–4 eggs in a small cup nest slung from slender branches in the canopy of a tree or bush. **Diet:** Insects, fruit and nectar. (Geelglasogie)

### 5 Cape White-eye *Zosterops virens*

b b b b b b b b b B B B
J F M A M J J A S O N D

**10–12 cm, 8–12 g** A variable white-eye; lower breast and belly vary from grey (*Z. v. capensis* in SW) to green (*Z. v. virens* in N and E), contrasting with yellow throat and vent. Darker green above than African Yellow White-eye and has at least some green wash on flanks. Also darker above than Orange River White-eye; flanks green or grey (not buffy-peach). **Voice:** Loud warbling song uttered mostly at dawn; also constant chittering contact calls. **Status and biology:** Common resident in woodland, forests, thickets, plantations and gardens. Lays 2–4 eggs in a deep cup nest slung between slender branches in the canopy of a tree or bush. **Diet:** Insects, fruit and nectar. (Kaapse Glasogie)

### 6 Orange River White-eye *Zosterops pallidus*

b b b          b b b
J F M A M J J A S O N D

**10–12 cm, 8–11 g** Once lumped with Cape White-eye, but is paler above and has distinctive, peach-coloured flanks. Hybridises with both grey- and green-flanked forms of Cape White-eye in narrow overlap zone in Free State. **Voice:** Higher pitched and more trilling than Cape White-eye. **Status and biology:** Common resident and local nomad in riparian woodland and thickets in the Karoo and semi-arid savanna; regularly wanders outside normal range in W Cape. Lays 3 eggs in a cup nest slung between slender branches in the canopy of a tree or bush. **Diet:** Insects, fruit and nectar. (Gariepglasogie)

# BATISES AND WATTLE-EYES

Small, compact flycatchers, with striking black-and-white plumage. Frequently snap bills and wings. Sexes differ; females often more distinctive than males. Juvs mottled buff above. Monogamous and territorial, sometimes with helpers at the nest. Incubation by female only; chicks altricial.

## 1 Pririt Batis *Batis pririt*

J F M A M J J A S O N D — b B b b

**10 cm; 8–10 g** Female easily recognised by the pale rufous wash over its throat and breast, unlike any other batis. Male is slightly smaller than male Chinspot Batis, with dark mottling on flanks; song differs and ranges overlap only marginally. Juv. like female but buff-spotted above; breast mottled dark brown and buff. **Voice:** A long series of slow 'teuu, teuu, teuu, teuu' notes, descending in scale, often with sharp clicking calls; slower and much longer than Chinspot Batis. **Status and biology:** Common resident in acacia thickets, arid broadleafed woodland and dry riverine bush. Lays 1–4 eggs in a small cup nest on a horizontal branch in a small tree. **Diet:** Small insects. (Priritbosbontrokkie)

## 2 Cape Batis *Batis capensis*

J F M A M J J A S O N D — b b ... b b B B B

**13 cm; 10–14 g** A richly coloured batis with chestnut wing bars and flanks. Male has a broad black breast band and golden eyes; female has a narrower chestnut breast band, discrete chin spot and reddish eyes. Male is the only sthn African batis with rufous wing bars and a black breast. Female is larger and more strongly marked below than female Woodwards' Batis; white supercilium small or absent. Juv. like female, but duller with buff spots above. **Voice:** Song is a series of hooted whistles 'foo-foo-foo'; both sexes give a bubbling alarm call 'kshee kshee kshee ksh ksh ksha'. **Status and biology:** Endemic. Common resident in forests, riparian thickets and well-wooded gardens. May move to lower elevations in winter. Lays 1–3 eggs in a neat cup decorated with lichens or mosses, built on a slender branch or in a tree fork. **Diet:** Small insects. (Kaapse Bosbontrokkie)

## 3 Woodwards' Batis *Batis fratrum*

J F M A M J J A S O N D — b b

**12 cm; 11–14 g** Both sexes have a diffuse, buff-washed breast. Male has white wing bar, resembling female Pririt Batis, but ranges do not overlap. Female has buffy wing bar, paler than female Cape Batis; breast markings paler and more diffuse, lacking a distinct chin spot; has narrow white supercilium (short or absent in Cape Batis). Juv. like female, but duller with buff spots above. **Voice:** Clear, penetrating whistle, 'tch-tch-phoooo', often repeated; also clicks bill. **Status and biology:** Near-endemic. Locally common resident in coastal forests and thickets. Lays 1–3 eggs in a cup nest built among the foliage of a tree or creeper. **Diet:** Small insects. (Woodwardbosbontrokkie)

## 4 Chinspot Batis *Batis molitor*

J F M A M J J A S O N D — b b ... b B B B B

**12–13 cm; 8–14 g** A widespread woodland batis with white wing bars. Female has a neat chestnut breast band and throat spot that are darker and better defined than in female Pale Batis. Male similar to male Pririt Batis, but has white (not dark-mottled) flanks; song differs. Appreciably larger than Pale Batis; male has a broader breast band; female has a darker, better defined throat patch. Juv. like female, but upperparts spotted buff; wing bars buffy. **Voice:** 2–4 clear, descending whistles 'teuu-teuu-teuu' ('three blind mice'); harsh 'chrr-chrr' notes. **Status and biology:** Common resident in broadleafed woodland and acacia savanna. Lays 1–4 eggs in a cup nest decorated with lichens and bark, built in a fork or on a branch of a small tree. **Diet:** Small insects. (Witliesbosbontrokkie)

## 5 Pale Batis *Batis soror*

J F M A M J J A S O N D — b b ... b b B b b

**11 cm; 9–13 g** Resembles a small Chinspot Batis, but male has a narrower black breast band and dappled, grey and white (not uniform grey) back. Female has a narrower and paler breast band (tawny, not chestnut); chin patch is ill defined. Juv. like female, but spotted buff above. **Voice:** Soft, tinkerbird-like whistle 'tcheeo, tcheeo, tcheeo...', repeated monotonously. **Status and biology:** Fairly common resident in miombo woodland and lowland forest. Lays 1–2 eggs in a cup nest decorated with lichens, built in a fork of a tree. **Diet:** Small insects. (Mosambiekbosbontrokkie)

## 6 Black-throated Wattle-eye *Platysteira peltata*

J F M A M J J A S O N D — b B b b

**13 cm; 11–15 g** A small, black-and-white flycatcher with distinctive red eye wattles related to the batises; lacks white wing bars. Male has a narrow black breast band; female has throat and upper breast black. Imm. grey above; throat mottled brown. Juv. has pale brown upperparts with rufous spotting; underparts off-white; eye wattles small and orange. **Voice:** Dry 'wichee-wichee-wichee-wichee...' song; also sings 'ptec ptec ptec' in aerial display. Alarm call is a harsh 'chit chit chit'. **Status and biology:** Locally common resident in thickets, riparian forest and mangroves. Lays 2–3 eggs in a cup nest built in a fork or suspended among the outer branches of a small tree or bush. **Diet:** Insects. (Beloogbosbontrokkie)

# WAGTAILS

Boldly patterned, long-tailed birds that frequently bob their tails up and down. Sexes alike in resident African species; differ in migrant species (also have distinct br. plumages). Juvs duller. Monogamous and territorial; both sexes incubate and care for the altricial chicks.

## 1 Cape Wagtail  *Motacilla capensis*

b b b b b b b B B B B B
J F M A M J J A S O N D

**19 cm; 18–24 g** A greyish-brown wagtail, darker above than Mountain Wagtail with a shorter tail, olive-buff (not whitish) flanks, and less white in wings and outer tail. Juv. browner above, with buffy tips to feathers; belly washed buff-yellow; breast band smaller. *M. c. simplicissima* in N Botswana has breast band reduced to a small spot. **Voice:** Clear, ringing 'tseee-chee-chee' and 'tseep' calls; whistled, trilling song. **Status and biology:** Common resident of open grassland, usually near water, but also in gardens. Lays 2–4 eggs in a bulky cup nest, usually built low down in a shrub or creeper. **Diet:** Insects and other invertebrates; also small fish, reptiles and tadpoles. (Gewone Kwikkie)

## 2 African Pied Wagtail  *Motacilla aguimp*

b B B B b b
J F M A M J J A S O N D

**20 cm; 22–32 g** The only black-and-white wagtail in sthn Africa; white in wing more extensive than other wagtails. Female and non-br. male have duller black upperparts. Juv. is grey-brown above; breast band narrow; wing coverts edged pale buff, but are much broader than in Cape Wagtail. **Voice:** Loud, shrill 'chee-chee-cheeroo'. **Status and biology:** Locally common resident at large rivers, wetlands and coastal lagoons. Lays 3–4 (rarely 2–5) eggs in a bulky cup nest built in a wide range of sites close to water (among vegetation, on the ground, in a rock crevice or even aboard a boat). **Diet:** Insects and other invertebrates; occasional tadpoles, small fish and seeds. (Bontkwikkie)

## 3 Mountain Wagtail  *Motacilla clara*

b b b b b   b B B B B
J F M A M J J A S O N D

**19–20 cm; 16–22 g** Closely related to Grey Wagtail, but has white underparts (lacking any yellow) and more white in its wing and outer tail. Told from Cape Wagtail by its much longer tail, pale grey upperparts, clean white underparts, and more white in wings and outer tail. Juv. is browner. **Voice:** Sharp, high-pitched 'cheeerip' or 'chissik' call. **Status and biology:** Locally common resident along streams in evergreen and coastal forests. Lays 2–3 (rarely 1–4) eggs in a bulky cup nest built in a rock crevice or branch over water. **Diet:** Insects; occasional tadpoles. (Bergkwikkie)

## 4 Grey Wagtail  *Motacilla cinerea*

J F M A M J J A S O N D

**19–20 cm; 14–22 g** Vagrant. A very long-tailed wagtail; structure similar to Mountain Wagtail, but has at least some yellow on its vent, buff (not whitish) flanks and less white in its wing and outer tail. Appreciably longer-tailed than Yellow Wagtail with a blue-grey (not green) back that contrasts with the greenish-yellow rump. Tail-wagging is more exaggerated. Br. male has black throat; speckled in non-br. plumage. Female has white throat; juv. similar but duller. **Voice:** Single, sharp 'tit'. **Status and biology:** Palearctic vagrant at streams and ponds, usually in wooded areas. **Diet:** Mainly insects. (Gryskwikkie)

## 5 Citrine Wagtail  *Motacilla citreola*

**17–18 cm; 17–23 g** Rare vagrant. Slightly larger than Yellow Wagtail with a greyish back (lacking olive tones); appears slimmer due to longer tail and legs. Br. male has a diagnostic all-yellow head and black nape. Non-br. ads easily confused with Yellow Wagtail, but have a paler yellow vent, a more prominent supercilium (extending around the ear coverts) and typically bolder white wing bars. Juv. drab grey with only a buff-yellow wash on its breast. **Voice:** Similar to Yellow Wagtail's, but shorter and shriller 'trsiiip'. **Status and biology:** Rare Palearctic vagrant; only 1 record from Gamtoos Estuary, E Cape in Apr 1998. **Diet:** Mainly insects. (Sitrienkwikkie)

## 6 Yellow Wagtail  *Motacilla flava*

J F M A M J J A S O N D

**17 cm; 14–21 g** A highly variable migrant wagtail. Smaller than Grey Wagtail with a shorter tail and green (not blue-grey) back. Slightly smaller than Citrine Wagtail with typically olive (not greyish) back and a shorter supercilium. Juv. is yellowish-brown above and pale buff below, with a narrow blackish breast band; told from Cape Wagtail by its yellow-washed belly, lacking grey flanks; pale margins to wing coverts are more prominent. Five races occur in the region; br. males vary in head colour: *M. f. lutea* (6 C) (head yellow, sometimes washed olive-green on crown and cheeks), *M. f. beema* (pale grey crown and cheeks; broad white supercilium), *M. f. flava* (6 A) (dark grey crown, black cheeks and narrow white supercilium), *M. f. thunbergi* (dark grey crown, cheeks black with whitish stripe below; breast washed olive-green) and *M. f. feldegg* (6 B) (black crown and cheeks; underparts entirely yellow). **Voice:** Weak, thin 'tseeep'. **Status and biology:** Uncommon to locally common Palearctic migrant to short, grassy areas, sewage ponds and wetlands. Sometimes in flocks. **Diet:** Insects, especially flies; occasional fruit. (Geelkwikkie)

1    FIRE

1    JG    juv.

2    BDP

2    GG

3    ND

4    RT    ♀

4    TM    br. ♂

5    AR    br. ♂

5    AR    ♀

6    BR    ♂ A

6    MP    ♂ B

6    GH    ♂ C

# PIPITS

Cryptic birds of open country or woodland that forage on the ground, but some perch in and call from trees. Superficially recall larks, but are more slender with longer legs and tails; stance more horizontal. Taxonomy contentious in some groups, with geographic variation often exceeding inter-specific differences, especially among larger species. Sexes alike in most species. Juvs more boldly patterned above; feathers darker brown with buff fringes; underparts more heavily mottled or streaked. Monogamous and territorial; incubation mainly by female; chicks altricial.

## 1 African Pipit  *Anthus cinnamomeus*

Bbbbb BBBBB
J F M A M J J A S O N D

**17 cm; 22–28 g** The 'standard' pipit against which others should be compared. Slightly smaller and more slender than other large pipits in the region. Typically has a streaked back, well-marked face, fairly well-streaked breast and plain belly. Underpart coloration varies from whitish to pale buff; base of lower mandible yellowish. Best distinguished from the Long-billed Pipit complex by its smaller size, weaker breast and face markings; outer tail white (not buff). Streaked back separates it from the Plain-backed/Buffy pipit complex (p. 352). Display flight and song distinguish it from all other species except Mountain Pipit – refer to that species for key differences. Juv. darker above, with more heavily streaked underparts. **Voice:** Song a repeated 3–5-note 'trrit-trrit-trrit', usually uttered in undulating display flight. **Status and biology:** Common resident and local nomad in open grassland and fields. Lays 1–4 (rarely 5) eggs in neat cup nest built in a depression in the ground next to a grass tuft, bush or stone. **Diet:** Insects and other invertebrates; some plant material. (Gewone Koester)

## 2 Mountain Pipit  *Anthus hoeschi*

b bb
J F M A M J J A S O N D

**18 cm; 25–28 g** Slightly larger than African Pipit, with more bold breast streaking and pink (not yellow) base to lower mandible; in flight, shows buff (not white) outer tail; song slower and deeper. Distinguished from Long-billed Pipit by its behaviour, display song and heavily marked face and breast. Juv. is blackish-brown above and heavily mottled below. **Voice:** Display song, given in flight, is similar to that of African Pipit, but is deeper in pitch and slower in tempo. **Status and biology:** Br. endemic. Common br. visitor to montane grassland above 2 000 m; non-br. range presumed to be in central Africa, based on specimens collected on passage in Namibia and Botswana. **Diet:** Insects. (Bergkoester)

## 3 Long-billed Pipit  *Anthus similis*

bbbb bbBBB
J F M A M J J A S O N D

**18 cm; 25–35 g** Larger than African Pipit with a heavier build, longer bill, less distinct facial pattern, reduced breast streaking, and different display and song; outer tail white (not white). Upperparts range from pale sandy-brown in the W to darker, grey-brown in the E. Fairly well-marked back differentiates it from Plain-backed/Buffy pipit complex (p. 352). Absent from woodland habitat of Wood Pipit; ranges apparently do not overlap. Reported to be less well marked than Kimberley Pipit, with less prominent supercilium and malar stripe absent or diffuse. Lacks distinct facial pattern and has much less breast streaking than Mountain Pipit, with a different call and display. Juv. scaled buff above and more heavily mottled on breast. **Voice:** High-pitched, 2–3-note song 'tchreep-tritit-churup', usually given from a prominent perch; also sharp 'wheet' call. **Status and biology:** Locally common resident of boulder-strewn hillsides with scant bush cover. Lays 1–4 eggs in a cup nest on the ground next to a rock or grass tuft. **Diet:** Insects and other invertebrates. (Nicholsonkoester)

## 4 Wood Pipit  *Anthus nyassae*

bb bbBBBb
J F M A M J J A S O N D

**17 cm; 22–26 g** Sometimes treated as a race of Long-billed Pipit, but occurs in woodland; ranges apparently do not overlap. Tail and bill shorter than Long-billed Pipit; supercilium whitish (not buffy); tail darker with more extensive pale areas in base of outer tail feathers. Juv. is spotted above, and more heavily streaked below. **Voice:** Song similar to that of Long-billed Pipit, but more variable and slightly higher-pitched. **Status and biology:** Locally common resident of miombo and teak woodland. Forages on the ground, but flushes into trees when disturbed. Lays 1–3 eggs in a cup nest on the ground under a grass tuft. **Diet:** Insects and other invertebrates. (Boskoester)

## 5 Kimberley Pipit  *Anthus pseudosimilis*

bb
J F M A M J J A S O N D

**16–18 cm; 27–35 g** A recently described species, based mainly on genetic evidence; status contentious. Closely resembles Long-billed Pipit, but is claimed to be shorter-billed, with a broader supercilium, blackish malar stripe and rufous ear coverts; upperparts darker, contrasting more with pale underparts. Reputedly appears smaller and longer-legged, and often crouches while feeding. Female duller. **Voice:** Like Long-billed Pipit, but descending in pitch and usually given in fluttering display flight. **Status and biology:** Endemic. Little known; locally fairly common resident of open grassland and sparse savanna. Lays 2–3 eggs in a cup nest on the ground at the base of a grass tuft. **Diet:** Insects. (Kimberleykoester)

## 1 Plain-backed Pipit  *Anthus leucophrys*

bbBBB  J F M A M J J A S O N D

**17 cm; 22–31 g** A rather heavily built pipit, told from African and Long-billed pipits (p. 366) by its uniform (not streaked) back (although streaking is not obvious in some Long-billed Pipits) and indistinct breast markings; outer tail narrowly edged buff. Typically is more compact and less slender than Buffy Pipit with shorter bill, legs and tail; averages colder and darker above with more uniform underparts (lacking buffy flanks); face more strongly marked with yellowish (not pink) lower mandible. Tail-wagging is less pronounced; typically doesn't raise tail above horizontal. Juv. is heavily scaled above and mottled below. **Voice:** Loud, clear 'chrrrup-chereeoo' song similar to Long-billed Pipit, but usually 1–2 notes (not 3). Usually sings from a low perch; sometimes in flight, but does not have a protracted display flight like African and Mountain pipits. Frequently calls 'tsip-tsip' on flushing or when alarmed. **Status and biology:** Locally common resident and nomad, favouring short grass and recently burnt areas; also fields. Some birds move to lower elevations in winter. Lays 2–4 eggs in a cup nest on the ground under a grass tuft. **Diet:** Insects and other invertebrates. (Donkerkoester)

## 2 Buffy Pipit  *Anthus vaalensis*

bb  bbBBBB  J F M A M J J A S O N D

**17–18 cm; 24–36 g** Slightly larger and more slender than Plain-backed Pipit, with longer bill, legs and tail; upperparts often warmer brown and facial pattern less striking; base to lower mandible pinkish (not yellow). Breast markings are often faint, with rich, buffy belly and flanks. Stance typically horizontal, but occasionally stands boldly erect, pushing out its chest. Often bobs its tail up and down in a more exaggerated manner than other pipits, recalling a wagtail; raises tail above horizontal. Juv. is scaled above and mottled below. **Voice:** Repeated, 1–2-note song, 'tchreep-churup', usually given from a low perch; when flushed, gives short 'sshik' or 'ship-ip' call. **Status and biology:** Uncommon to locally common resident, nomad and partial migrant in short grassland and fields. Non-br. birds from central Africa thought to winter in sthn Africa. Lays 1–3 eggs in a cup nest on the ground next to a grass tuft or rock. **Diet:** Insects and other invertebrates; occasional seeds. (Vaalkoester)

## 3 Long-tailed Pipit  *Anthus longicaudatus*

J F M A M J J A S O N D

**19 cm; 30–35 g** A recently described species. A plain-backed pipit, larger and darker than Buffy Pipit, with colder grey-brown upperparts and a long, heavy, square-ended tail. Bill is shorter with a yellowish (not pinkish) base (but beware Plain-backed Pipit, which has a yellowish lower mandible). Stance is even more horizontal than Buffy Pipit; wags tail continually, and seldom stands upright as Buffy Pipit occasionally does. When feeding, head is often held below the horizontal. Juv. undescribed. **Voice:** Single thin, short call note; song unknown. **Status and biology:** Locally fairly common during winter in open grassland and arid savanna; br. range presumed to be in central Africa. **Diet:** Insects. (Langstertkoester)

## 4 African Rock Pipit  *Anthus crenatus*

b  J F M A M J J A S O N D  bBB

**17 cm; 29–32 g** A drab, uniformly coloured pipit of rocky hill slopes; more compact than other large pipits, with shorter legs and tail. Forms a superspecies with Striped Pipit, but is readily distinguished by its rather plain, grey-washed underparts. From a distance, the pale supercilium and throat are the only obvious plumage features; at close range, faint, narrow breast streaking, slightly mottled upperparts and diagnostic yellow-green edges to wing coverts are visible. Usually located by its distinctive song; easily overlooked when not calling. Juv. is mottled above. **Voice:** Far-carrying 'tseeet-tserrroooo', second note descending and usually slightly quavering; sings from a low perch in typical erect stance, bill pointed upwards. **Status and biology:** Endemic. Locally common resident on boulder-strewn, steep, grassy hillsides and Karoo koppies. Lays 2–3 eggs in a cup nest on the ground under a grass tuft. **Diet:** Insects, and spiders; occasional seeds. (Klipkoester)

## 5 Striped Pipit  *Anthus lineiventris*

b  J F M A M J J A S O N D  bBBB

**18 cm; 31–37 g** A compact, heavily built pipit with boldly striped underparts extending over almost the entire belly; upperparts olive-brown, streaked dark brown. At close range has diagnostic yellow-edged wing coverts; tail is very dark brown with conspicuous white outer tail feathers. Larger than Tree Pipit (p. 354) with streaking extending onto belly; lacks white edges to wing coverts. Juv. is paler above and less heavily streaked below. **Voice:** Loud, penetrating, thrush-like song, uttered from a rock or tree perch. **Status and biology:** Locally common resident on boulder-strewn hill slopes in woodland. Flies up into trees when disturbed. Lays 1–3 eggs in a cup nest on the ground next to a rock or grass tuft. **Diet:** Insects and other invertebrates. (Gestreepte Koester)

## 1 Bushveld Pipit  *Anthus caffer*

B B b | | | | | | | b B B
J F M A M J J A S O N D

**13–14 cm; 16–18 g**  A tiny pipit, smaller than Tree Pipit with a shorter tail, indistinct supercilium, paler plumage and finer, more diffuse breast streaking. From a distance, head appears uniform, and lacks Tree Pipit's malar stripe. Slightly larger than Short-tailed Pipit, with a more prominent supercilium, longer, broader tail, paler upperparts and less heavy streaking below; bill more delicate; habitat differs. Typically flies up to an open perch in a tree when flushed. Juv. paler, scaled buff above. **Voice:** Characteristic 'bzeeent' as it flies from ground to tree; song a treble-note 'zrrrt-zrree-chreee' from perch in tree. **Status and biology:** Locally fairly common resident in acacia savanna and open broadleafed woodland. Lays 2–3 eggs in a cup nest on the ground under a grass tuft. **Diet:** Insects. (Bosveldkoester)

## 2 Short-tailed Pipit  *Anthus brachyurus*

b b | | | | | | | | b B B
J F M A M J J A S O N D

**12 cm; 14–17 g**  A tiny, squat pipit with a short tail, plain face and rather heavy bill; darker and more heavily streaked above and on its breast and flanks than Tree or Bushveld pipits; supercilium absent or confined to a small buffy patch in front of the eyes. Underparts white or buffy, possibly differing between the sexes (males washed buff in 2 pairs). In flight, the short, thin tail is distinctive; when flushed, it resembles a female bishop or large cisticola with white outer tail feathers. Juv. has warm rufous-buff margins to upperpart feathers; breast streaking broader and more diffuse. **Voice:** A buzzy, bubbling 'chrrrrt-zhrrrreet-zzeeep', similar to Bushveld Pipit; sings from a perch or during a low, circling display flight. **Status and biology:** Uncommon resident and local migrant on grassy hillsides and glades in miombo woodland; prefers areas of short grass, including recently burnt areas. Does not flush into trees like Bushveld Pipit. Lays 2–3 eggs in a cup nest on the ground under a grass tuft. **Diet:** Insects and occasional seeds. (Kortstertkoester)

## 3 Tree Pipit  *Anthus trivialis*

■ ■ | F M A M J J A S O N D

**15 cm; 18–28 g**  A medium-sized pipit with a heavily streaked breast. Smaller than Striped Pipit (p. 352), with a plain (not streaked) belly and white edges to wing coverts forming 2 indistinct white bars. Longer-tailed and larger than Bushveld or Short-tailed pipits; shows more contrast between pale throat and dark upperparts. Bill rather short and weak. Easily confused with non-br. Red-throated Pipit, but has less clearly streaked underparts and lacks dark brown streaking on rump; at close range has a pale eye-ring. Juv. is buffier. **Voice:** Soft, nasal 'teeez' in flight or when flushed. Melodic, canary-like song is seldom uttered in sthn Africa. **Status and biology:** Fairly common Palearctic migrant to grassy areas in open woodland. Feeds on the ground, but usually flushes into a tree when disturbed, walking along branches like a Wood Pipit. **Diet:** Insects and other invertebrates; also seeds, fruit, buds and new leaves. (Boomkoester)

## 4 Red-throated Pipit  *Anthus cervinus*

**15 cm; 17–25 g**  Rare vagrant. Structure similar to Tree Pipit, but tends to be a little dumpier, with a heavier belly. In br. plumage, easily recognised by its dull red face, throat and breast. Non-br. birds lack the red throat; average darker and richer than Tree Pipit, with no pale eye-ring, less prominent buffy (not whitish) wing bars and bolder streaking: flank streaks broader and rump streaked (not uniform). Mantle often shows 2 creamy stripes on either side. Larger than Short-tailed Pipit, with a longer tail and more strongly marked supercilium. **Voice:** Distinctive, buzzy 'skeeeaz' given in flight or on flushing; also a clear, penetrating 'chup' call. **Status and biology:** Rare Palearctic vagrant to damp grassland and fields, usually near water; only 3 records claimed. **Diet:** Mainly insects; occasional seeds. (Rooikeelkoester)

## 1 Yellow-breasted Pipit *Anthus chloris*

B B B | | | | | | b B B
J F M A M J J A S O N D

**17 cm; 24–26 g** A medium-sized pipit with a rather plain face. Br. birds have diagnostic yellow throat and breast; upperparts grey-brown, heavily streaked blackish-brown. Female duller buffy-yellow below with less distinct breast streaks. In non-br. plumage has boldly scaled, sandy grey-brown upperparts and rather plain, buffy or whitish underparts with fine streaking confined to its upper breast; central belly washed yellow. In flight, yellow underwing coverts and white outer tail contrast with dark upperparts in all plumages. Juv. is more crisply scaled above and buff below. **Voice:** Song is a rapid 'chip, chip, chip' or 'se-chik, se-chik, se-chik', repeated 10–20 times from a perch or low, fluttering display flight; also a subdued 'suwiep'. **Status and biology: VULNERABLE.** Endemic. Uncommon resident and partial migrant in short grassland, moving to lower elevations in winter. Breeds above 1 500 m; lays 2–3 (rarely 1–4) eggs in a cup nest on the ground under a grass tuft. **Diet:** Insects. (Geelborskoester)

## 2 Golden Pipit *Tmetothylacus tenellus*

J F M A M J J A S O N D

**13–15 cm; 18–22 g** Rare vagrant. Male resembles a diminutive, bright golden Yellow-throated Longclaw, but has mainly yellow wings and tail with black tips to the outer primaries and tail feathers; black breast band does not extend up sides of neck. Female is duller, with whitish underparts variably washed yellow; wing and tail feathers edged yellow; lacks a black breast band. Female could be confused with Yellow Wagtail (p. 348), but is smaller with a shorter tail, patterned (not plain) mantle and different gait. Juv. like female but duller, with whitish margins to upperpart feathers and diffuse brown breast spots. **Voice:** Song is a short burst of scratchy, whistled notes with a weaver-like quality; vagrants usually silent. **Status and biology:** Vagrant from E Africa to open, dry woodland and savanna; fewer than 10 records, mainly in summer. May be more common than records indicate, with females and imms overlooked. **Diet:** Insects. (Goudkoester)

# LONGCLAWS

**Fairly large, heavily built birds related to pipits and wagtails. Ads have brightly coloured throats and blackish breast bands. Feed on the ground, but some species regularly perch and call from trees. Flight jerky, with bursts of staccato, stiff-winged flaps interspersed by short glides on downard-angled wings. Females similar to males, but duller. Juvs even duller with reduced breast bands. Monogamous and territorial. Incubation mainly by female; chicks altricial.**

## 3 Yellow-throated Longclaw *Macronyx croceus*

B b b | | | | b b b b B B
J F M A M J J A S O N D

**21 cm; 40–54 g** A large, yellow-breasted longclaw with black streaking below breast band. Slightly larger than Cape Longclaw, with yellow (not orange) throat. Larger than male Golden Pipit with white tips to outer tail and brown (not golden) wings; black breast band extends up side of neck, encircling yellow throat. Female duller, washed buffy below. Juv. lacks black breast band; told from juv. Cape Longclaw by yellow (not buff-orange) belly and less streaked upperparts. **Voice:** Loud, whistled 'phooooeeet' or series of whistles, frequently uttered from the top of bushes or small trees; also calls in flight. Alarm call is a loud 'whip-ip-ip-ip-ip'. **Status and biology:** Common resident in grassy savanna, open woodland and grassland, often near water. Lays 2–3 (rarely 1–4) eggs in a bulky cup nest built on, or close to, the ground in a dense tussock. **Diet:** Insects, other invertebrates and occasional seeds. (Geelkeelkalkoentjie)

## 4 Cape Longclaw *Macronyx capensis*

B b b b | | b B B b B B
J F M A M J J A S O N D

**20 cm; 40–50 g** A compact longclaw with an orange throat; breast and belly richer orange-yellow than Yellow-throated Longclaw. In flight, shows white tail tips, broader towards outer edge, like Yellow-throated Longclaw. Female duller, with narrower black breast band. Juv. has a buffy-orange throat, narrow, brown-streaked breast band and buffy belly; wing feathers edged with buff. **Voice:** Fairly melodious song, 'cheewit-cheewit', often given in flight; nasal 'skeeaaa' alarm call; loud, high-pitched 'tsweet' contact call. **Status and biology:** Endemic. Common resident in coastal and upland grasslands. Lays 2–3 (rarely 1–4) eggs in a bulky cup nest built on, or close to, the ground in a dense tussock. **Diet:** Insects, other invertebrates and occasional seeds. (Oranjekeelkalkoentjie)

## 5 Rosy-throated Longclaw *Macronyx ameliae*

B B b b | | | | | b B B
J F M A M J J A S O N D

**19 cm; 31–39 g** A slender, dark-backed, heavily streaked longclaw. White tips to inner tail feathers are less extensive than other longclaws, but outer tail almost fully white. Male has a pink throat and well-defined breast band; breast washed pink; at close range has pinkish wash to wrist. Female duller, with narrower breast band (sometimes incomplete). Juv. has brown-streaked breast band with a creamy throat and only a faint rosy wash on the belly. **Voice:** Melodious, rather deep 'cheet errr' or 'cheet eeet eet eet eer'; plaintive 'chewit' alarm call. **Status and biology:** Uncommon resident in moist grassland surrounding open areas of fresh water. Lays 2–3 eggs in a bulky cup nest built on, or close to, the ground in a dense tussock. **Diet:** Insects, other invertebrates and occasional small frogs. (Rooskeelkalkoentjie)

# SHRIKES, BUSH-SHRIKES AND HELMET-SHRIKES

A diverse group of shrike-like birds from at least 2 different families. Most are predatory, with stout, hook-tipped bills. Sexes alike in most species. Juvs duller and often finely barred. Usually monogamous and territorial, but some species are group-living and have helpers at the nest. Chicks altricial.

## 1 Common Fiscal  *Lanius collaris*

**21–23 cm; 25–50 g** A distinctive black-and-white shrike with a narrow white scapular bar. Told from boubous (p. 360) by its erect stance, long tail and perch-hunting behaviour; from Fiscal Flycatcher (p. 340) by its heavier bill, longer tail with a narrow white outer tail, and crouched posture when perched; white in wings confined to primaries. Female dark grey above, with dusky wash to breast and chestnut flanks in most races. Juv. is greyish-brown, with fine dark bars on its head, back and flanks. Desert races have a white supercilium **(1 A)**; intergrade with other races. **Voice:** Harsh, grating call 'dwrrr-wrrrr'; song is melodious and jumbled, often with harsher notes and mimicry of other birds. **Status and biology:** Common resident in most open habitats. Often hunts from exposed perches along roadsides. Lays 3–4 (rarely 1–5) eggs in a bulky cup nest built in a dense shrub or tree. **Diet:** Invertebrates, reptiles, birds, frogs, small mammals and fruit. Large prey sometimes cached on thorn 'larders'. (Fiskaallaksman)

## 2 Lesser Grey Shrike  *Lanius minor*

**20–22 cm; 40–65 g** A pale, grey-backed shrike with a bold black face mask; tail shorter than Common Fiscal. Lacks the white scapular bar of Common Fiscal and Souza's Shrike. Male has pinkish wash to underparts in fresh plumage. Female is duller with a slightly smaller black mask. Imm. is like female, but with smaller mask, not extending onto forecrown; often retains some fine barring on crown and flanks; base of bill pink. Juv. plumage (barred above and washed buff below) not recorded in sthn Africa. **Voice:** Soft, warbled chattering song is sometimes heard in autumn before northward migration; alarm call is a harsh, grating 'grrr-grrrr'. **Status and biology:** Common Palearctic migrant in arid savanna and semi-desert scrub. **Diet:** Insects, especially beetles. (Gryslaksman)

## 3 Red-backed Shrike  *Lanius collurio*

**18 cm; 22–44 g** A compact, short-tailed shrike with chestnut back and wings and a fairly short tail (blackish with white base to outer tail). Ad. male has black facemask, grey crown, nape and rump, and plain, pinkish underparts. Male *L. c. kobylini* has grey-washed back. Female is duller, with a dark, grey-brown mask, grey wash on head and rump, and brown chevrons along flanks. Lacks white scapular bar of Souza's Shrike and juv. Common Fiscal (absent in recently fledged Common Fiscal). Imm. is like female, with upperparts finely barred darker brown. Juv. plumage (heavily barred above and below) not recorded in sthn Africa. **Voice:** Soft, warbled song is uttered in autumn before N migration; alarm call is a harsh 'chak, chak'. **Status and biology:** Common Palearctic migrant in savanna and open woodland. **Diet:** Insects; occasional fruit. (Rooiruglaksman)

## 4 Souza's Shrike  *Lanius souzae*

**17 cm; 22–30 g** A slender shrike with a long, thin tail. Recalls female Red-backed Shrike, but with white scapular bars and a longer tail; outer tail feathers completely white (not black-tipped). Female has pale rufous flanks. Juv. is finely barred above and below; could be confused with juv. Common Fiscal, but is smaller and warmer brown above. **Voice:** A long, descending 'beeeeerrrr' song; also grating alarm calls. **Status and biology:** Rare resident of broadleafed woodland. Unobtrusive and easily overlooked; typically in pairs or family parties. Lays 2–3 (rarely 4) eggs in a neat cup nest built in a fork or on a major branch of a tree. **Diet:** Insects and other invertebrates. (Souzaaksman)

## 5 Magpie Shrike  *Corvinella melanoleuca*

**40–50 cm (incl. tail); 60–95 g** A large, very long-tailed black shrike with white scapular bars, white tips to flight feathers and a whitish rump. Female has whitish flanks; tail averages slightly shorter. Juv. is dull sooty-brown, with buff tips to underpart feathers. **Voice:** Liquid, whistled 'pee-leeo' or 'pur-leeoo'; also scolding 'tzeeaa' alarm call. **Status and biology:** Common resident of savanna and open woodland, favouring acacias. Usually in groups of 4–12 birds; sometimes has helpers at the nest. Lays 2–6 eggs in a bulky cup nest built in the canopy of a tree. **Diet:** Insects and other invertebrates; also small reptiles, mice, carrion and fruit. (Langstertlaksman)

## 6 Crimson-breasted Shrike  *Laniarius atrococcineus*

**23 cm; 40–55 g** A striking crimson and black boubou with a white wing bar. Rare yellow morph has yellow underparts. Juv. is finely barred black and buff above and barred greyish-brown below, with crimson initially confined to vent; crimson spreads patchily from 1 month after fledging. **Voice:** Male song is a boubou-like whistled 'qwip-qwip', often followed by female's harsher 'qwee-er, qwee-er'; also various grating alarm calls. **Status and biology:** Common resident of acacia thickets in arid savanna and semi-arid scrub. Lays 2–3 eggs in a neat cup nest built in the fork of a tree. **Diet:** Insects and other invertebrates; also fruit. (Rooiborslaksman)

## 1 Southern Boubou *Laniarius ferrugineus*

**20–25 cm; 44–68 g** A black-and-white bush-shrike with a white wing bar and buff wash on the belly. More richly coloured beneath than Tropical Boubou, with cinnamon (not pinkish) wash concentrated on the belly (not breast). Female is greyer above, with darker, more extensive cinnamon wash on underparts. Juv. is mottled buff-brown above and barred below; wing bar buffy; base of bill paler. **Voice:** Variable duet with basic notes of 'boo-boo' followed by whistled 'whoo-mee'; also harsh, grating alarm calls. **Status and biology:** Common resident of forest edges, thickets and dense coastal scrub. Pairs remain together year-round. Lays 2–3 eggs in an untidy cup nest built in a fork of a bush or small tree. **Diet:** Mainly invertebrates; also reptiles, nestling birds, small mice and fruit. (Suidelike Waterfiskaal)

## 2 Tropical Boubou *Laniarius aethiopicus*

**20–25 cm; 45–65 g** Similar to Southern Boubou, but with pink or cream-washed breast; lacks cinnamon wash on flanks and belly. Underparts are not pure white, as in Swamp Boubou. Juv. is duller, spotted with buff above; underparts whitish with brown wash and darker barring on its breast and flanks. **Voice:** Loud, ringing duet, typically 'haw weerr hooo' or 'haw weerr hooo hooo', usually including some croaking elements; also various harsh, grating alarm calls. **Status and biology:** Common resident in thickets, riverine and evergreen forests, and gardens. Lays 2–3 eggs in an untidy cup nest built in a fork of a bush or small tree. **Diet:** Invertebrates, small reptiles, frogs, nestling birds, small mice and fruit. (Tropiese Waterfiskaal)

## 3 Swamp Boubou *Laniarius bicolor*

**22–25 cm; 44–58 g** Separated from Southern and Tropical boubous by its pure white underparts. Juv. is spotted with buff above and barred grey-brown below. **Voice:** Male's whistled 'hoouu' is usually accompanied by a ratchet-like cackle from the female; also harsh, grating alarm calls. **Status and biology:** Locally common in thickets alongside rivers and papyrus swamps. Lays 2–3 eggs in an untidy cup nest built in a bush or small tree. **Diet:** Insects and other invertebrates; also frogs and fruit. (Moeraswaterfiskaal)

## 4 Black-crowned Tchagra *Tchagra senegalus*

**20–23 cm; 35–60 g** A large tchagra, told from other species by its black forehead and central crown. Larger than female Anchieta's Tchagra, with blackish streaks on its wing coverts and contrast between the brown back and chestnut wings; central tail feathers grey-brown with fine darker bars. Juv. duller with crown mottled brown; bill paler at base. **Voice:** Song, given from perch or in aerial display, is a loud, mournful whistle 'whee-cheree, cherooo, cheree-cherooo', descending in pitch and becoming slurred towards the end. Also various rattling and reeling alarm calls. **Status and biology:** Common resident of savanna, thickets and riverine scrub. Lays 2–3 (rarely 1–4) eggs in a flimsy cup nest built in a fork of a bush or small tree. **Diet:** Insects and other invertebrates; also frogs and small reptiles. (Swartkroontjagra)

## 5 Brown-crowned Tchagra *Tchagra australis*

**17–19 cm; 30–40 g** Smaller than Black-crowned Tchagra with a brown central crown, bordered by black lateral crown stripes (often obscuring the brown crown if viewed from below). Smaller and shorter-billed than Southern Tchagra, which has less prominent lateral crown stripes. Juv. duller, with mottled breast. **Voice:** Male sings in short aerial display, flying up then descending with fanned tail and 'fripping' its wings while giving 8–15 notes, descending in pitch and increasing in duration: 'chi-chi-che-chee-cheeyu-cheeyu-cheeeyuu...'; also nasal and grating alarm calls. **Status and biology:** Common resident of thick tangles and undergrowth in savanna and woodland. Lays 2–4 eggs in a flimsy cup nest built in a fork of a bush or small tree. **Diet:** Insects and other invertebrates; occasional small vertebrates. (Rooivlerktjagra)

## 6 Southern Tchagra *Tchagra tchagra*

**20–22 cm; 42–54 g** A large, long-billed tchagra with a grey-brown crown. Larger and darker than Brown-crowned Tchagra, with a much longer bill; lateral crown stripes dark brown (not black). Juv. duller with buff tail tips. **Voice:** Aerial display and song similar to Brown-crowned Tchagra, but averages deeper and slower. **Status and biology:** Common resident of coastal scrub, forest edges and thickets, but easily overlooked if not calling. Lays 2–3 (rarely 1–4) eggs in a flimsy cup nest built in a low fork of a bush or small tree. **Diet:** Insects and other invertebrates; also fruit. (Grysborstjagra)

## 7 Anchieta's Tchagra *Antichromus anchietae*

**16–19 cm; 30–36 g** A fairly small tchagra identified by its black cap, plain chestnut upperparts and creamy-buff underparts; blackish tail is tipped buff. Female has broad white supercilium. Juv. duller with a buffy supercilium; crown sooty-brown, mottled buff. **Voice:** Song, given in display flight or perched, is a short, melodic 2–3-note whistle 'whit-whee-wheeeu'; also grating contact and alarm calls. **Status and biology:** Uncommon resident in rank bracken and sedges growing in damp hollows, and marshy areas with long grass. Lays 2–3 eggs (rarely 1) in a bulky cup nest built in a fork of a small bush. **Diet:** Insects. (Vleitjagra)

## 1 Grey-headed Bush-Shrike *Malaconotus blanchoti*

bb | b | bbBBBb
J F M A M J J A S O N D

**24–26 cm; 65–95 g** The largest bush-shrike in sthn Africa with a massive bill, rather plain face and yellow eyes. Much larger than Orange-breasted Bush-Shrike with yellow (not dark) eyes, whitish lores (not a yellow supercilium) and less prominent orange wash on breast; yellow tail tips smaller, confined to outer 2 feathers. Wing coverts and tertials are tipped pale yellow-green, but spots much smaller than in Eastern Nicator (p. 296). Juv. has dark eyes and brown mottling on head; pale yellow below. **Voice:** Drawn-out 'oooooop' or 'ooooo-up' (hence colloquial name 'Ghostbird'); also loud clicks and dry 'skeeerrrr'. **Status and biology:** Locally common resident of thickets in acacia savanna and broadleafed woodland. Lays 2–4 eggs in a loose cup nest built in the canopy of a bush or tree. **Diet:** Insects, other invertebrates, reptiles, bats and small birds. (Spookvoël)

## 2 Bokmakierie *Telophorus zeylonus*

bbbbbbBBBbbb
J F M A M J J A S O N D

**22–25 cm; 50–75 g** A striking olive, black and yellow bush-shrike with a grey head, yellow underparts and broad black gorget. In flight, green and black tail with yellow tips is conspicuous. Juv. lacks bold head markings, and is dull olive-green, with smaller yellow tail tips. **Voice:** Varied whistles and harsh calls, including onomatopoeic duet 'bok-bok-kik-ik'. **Status and biology:** Near-endemic. Common resident in shrublands, karoo scrub, strandveld and grassland with scattered bushes. Lays 2–5 eggs in a compact cup nest, well concealed in a dense shrub. **Diet:** Insects and other invertebrates; also reptiles, frogs, small birds and fruit. (Bokmakierie)

## 3 Gorgeous Bush-Shrike *Telophorus viridis*

bb | | | | | BBb
J F M A M J J A S O N D

**18 cm; 30–40 g** A stunning, olive-backed bush-shrike with a red throat and vent, black gorget and yellow central breast and belly. Female is duller, with a narrower breast band. Juv. has yellow throat and lacks black breast band; differs from juv. Orange-breasted and Black-fronted bush-shrikes by olive (not grey) upperparts, but inseparable from juv. olive-morph Olive Bush-Shrike. **Voice:** Often-repeated 'kong-kon-kooit' or 'kong-kooit-koit'; also rasping calls. **Status and biology:** Common resident in dense tangled thickets. More often heard than seen. Lays 2 eggs in a loose cup nest in a bush or creeper. **Diet:** Insects and other invertebrates; also small birds and fruit. (Konkoit)

## 4 Black-fronted Bush-Shrike *Telophorus nigrifrons*

bb | | | | | bBb
J F M A M J J A S O N D

**18–19 cm; 35 g** A richly coloured bush-shrike with a black facemask and dark grey crown; lacks the paler supercilium of Olive Bush-Shrike, and black mask extends onto frons. Only orange morph recorded in sthn Africa; male has rich orange throat and breast, merging into yellower vent. Female is duller, with a smaller black mask; orange wash mainly on sides of breast. Juv. even duller with buffy-yellow underparts barred olive-grey and pale tips to wing feathers. **Voice:** Ringing 'oop-ooop' whistle, often with dry response from female, 'ooop eeerrk'; also harsh 'tic-chrrrrr' calls. **Status and biology:** Uncommon resident of forest canopy and mid-stratum, especially in creepers and lianas. Lays 2 eggs in a flimsy cup nest among dense creepers in a tall tree. **Diet:** Insects and other invertebrates. (Swartoogboslaksman)

## 5 Olive Bush-Shrike *Telophorus olivaceus*

bb | | | | | | bbBb
J F M A M J J A S O N D

**17–19 cm; 25–42 g** A polymorphic bush-shrike. Ruddy or grey morph (5 A) easily identified by its pinkish-buff throat and breast merging into a whitish vent. Male has a grey crown, black mask and an indistinct, whitish supercilium; female has plain grey crown and face. Olive morph is olive-green above, with yellow underparts, washed orange on its breast; male has black mask and yellowish supercilium; told from Black-fronted Bush-Shrike by its olive (not grey) crown and generally duller underparts. Juvs are duller than females, with pale tips to wing feathers and faint barring below. Olive-morph juv. inseparable from juv. Gorgeous Bush-Shrike. **Voice:** Varied series of whistles, such as 'wheee hoo hoo hoo hoo' or descending 'whee-whee-wheoo-wheoo-whoo-whooo'; also harsh, rattling alarm call, 'krrrr krrrr krrrrr', but duets less often than most other bush-shrikes. **Status and biology:** Common resident of evergreen and riverine forests. Lays 1–2 eggs in a flimsy cup nest, well concealed in the canopy of a bush or tree. **Diet:** Insects and other invertebrates; also small birds and fruit. (Olyfboslaksman)

## 6 Orange-breasted Bush-Shrike *Telophorus sulfureopectus*

bbb | | | | bbBBB
J F M A M J J A S O N D

**16–18 cm; 20–30 g** Differs from other bush-shrikes by its yellow forehead and supercilium, yellow throat and orange-washed breast. Smaller than Grey-headed Bush-Shrike, with dark (not yellow) eyes and more extensive yellow tail tips to all but the central pair of feathers. Female is duller, with a paler grey facemask. Juv. has drab grey head, finely barred back and whitish-yellow underparts, variably barred grey-brown. **Voice:** Song is frequently repeated 'poo-poo-poo-pooooo', fading towards the end; deeper 'pu pu pu pu'; harsher 'titit-eeezz'. Seldom duets. **Status and biology:** Common resident in acacia savanna and riverine forests. Lays 1–3 eggs in an untidy cup nest, well concealed in the canopy of a bush or tree. **Diet:** Insects and other invertebrates. (Oranjeborsboslaksman)

## 1 Chestnut-fronted Helmet-Shrike *Prionops scopifrons*

J F M A M J J A S O N D

**18–20 cm; 27–38 g** Smaller and greyer than Retz's Helmet-Shrike with a bristly chestnut (not black) forehead, blue-grey (not red) eye wattles and a small white loral spot. When viewed in canopy, appears paler due to grey (not black) underparts; mantle slate-grey (not dark brown). Juv. is grey-brown with white tips to upperpart feathers; lacks chestnut forehead and eye wattles; eyes brown (not yellow); bill brown (not red). **Voice:** Repeated trilling 'churee', with bill-snapping and other whirring and chattering notes. **Status and biology:** Uncommon resident in dense woodland and lowland forests. Occurs in small groups; sometimes with Retz's Helmet-Shrikes. Breeds cooperatively; lays 3 eggs in a neat cup nest built on a branch or fork in the canopy of a tall tree. **Diet:** Insects and other invertebrates. (Stekelkophelmlaksman)

## 2 Retz's Helmet-Shrike *Prionops retzii*

J F M A M J J A S O N D

**20–24 cm; 38–46 g** A black-bodied helmet-shrike with dark brown back and wing coverts, and red bill and legs. Larger and darker than Chestnut-fronted Helmet-shrike, with black crown and red (not blue-grey) eye wattles. Juv. is paler grey-brown with pale tips to mantle and wing feathers; eyes, bill and legs brown; lacks eye wattles; difficult to separate from juv. Chestnut-fronted Helmet-Shrike. **Voice:** Harsh bubbling and winding call 'tweeerr-r-r-r'. **Status and biology:** Common resident in woodland, including miombo, and riparian forest. In groups of 2–10 birds, often joins bird parties, including with other helmet-shrikes. Breeds co-operatively; lays 3–5 eggs in a neat cup nest built on a branch or fork in the canopy of a tall tree. **Diet:** Insects and other invertebrates; also small lizards. (Swarthelmlaksman)

## 3 White-crested Helmet-Shrike *Prionops plumatus*

J F M A M J J A S O N D

**19–22 cm; 28–40 g** A striking black-and-white helmet-shrike with an erect, whitish forecrown, grey hind crown, broad white collar, yellow eye wattles and orange-pink legs. Juv. is duller, with brown-washed upperparts; feathers tipped buff; eyes brown, lacking yellow eye wattles. **Voice:** Repeated bubbling 'cherow' and various clicks and chattering calls, often chorused by a group. **Status and biology:** Common resident and nomad in mixed woodland and acacia savanna. Occurs in groups of 2–10 birds, often joining bird parties. Breeds co-operatively; lays 2–5 eggs in a neat cup nest built in a fork in the canopy of a tree. **Diet:** Insects and other invertebrates; also small lizards. (Withelmlaksman)

## 4 White-tailed Shrike *Lanioturdus torquatus*

J F M A M J J A S O N D

**15 cm; 24–32 g** A small, shrike-like flycatcher related to batises. The striking black, white and grey plumage, yellow eyes, long legs and short, white tail are diagnostic. Its upright posture contributes to its almost tailless appearance. Juv. has a mottled black-and-white crown and dark eyes. **Voice:** Clear, drawn-out whistles; harsh cackling. **Status and biology:** Common resident of dry savanna and semi-desert scrub; often forages on the ground. Occasionally has helpers at the nest. Lays 2–3 eggs in a deep, compact cup nest built on a branch or fork of a bush or small tree. **Diet:** Insects and spiders. (Kortstertlaksman)

## 5 Southern White-crowned Shrike *Eurocephalus anguitimens*

J F M A M J J A S O N D

**23–25 cm; 56–82 g** A large, heavy-bodied shrike with a distinctive white crown and dark brown eye-stripe. Mantle pale grey-brown, contrasting with dark brown nape, wings and tail. Juv. is paler, with crown mottled brown, smaller dark face patch and yellow bill. **Voice:** Shrill, buzzy 'kree, kree, kree', often chorused by group members; also bleating and harsh chattering calls. **Status and biology:** Common resident of dry woodland and acacia savanna. Usually in groups of 4–6 birds. Breeds cooperatively; lays 2–4 (rarely 5) eggs in a cup nest built in a fork in the canopy of a tree. **Diet:** Insects and other invertebrates; occasional fruit. (Kremetartlaksman)

## 6 Brubru *Nilaus afer*

J F M A M J J A S O N D

**12–15 cm; 22–27 g** A small, black-and-white arboreal bush-shrike with chestnut flanks. Black above, with chequered back and prominent white wing bar and supercilium. Larger than batises (p. 346) with a thicker bill. Female is duller, sooty brown above. Juv. mottled and barred with buff and brown above; wing bar buffy; underparts creamy, barred brown. **Voice:** Trilling 'prrrrr' or 'tip-ip-ip prrrrrrrr' given by male, sometimes answered 'eeeu' by female. **Status and biology:** Common resident of acacia savanna and open broadleafed woodland. Lays 2 (rarely 1–4) eggs in a cup nest, decorated with lichen, built on a branch or fork of a small tree. **Diet:** Insects and spiders. (Bontroklaksman)

## 7 Black-backed Puffback *Dryoscopus cubla*

J F M A M J J A S O N D

**16–18 cm; 20–35 g** A small, compact, black-and-white bush-shrike with white scapular bars and white-edged wing feathers. Male has black crown and red eyes. Female has a prominent white supercilium (shorter than Brubru), slate-grey upperparts and grey-washed underparts; eyes orange-yellow. Juv. like female, but browner above and washed buffy below; eyes brown. **Voice:** Sharp, repeated 'chick, weeo'; in flight, male utters loud 'chok chok chok'. **Status and biology:** Common resident in woodland, thickets and forest canopy. Lays 2–3 eggs in a cup nest built in a fork in the canopy of a tree. **Diet:** Insects and spiders; also fruit and buds. (Sneeubal)

# STARLINGS AND MYNAS

Medium to large omnivorous passerines that usually have some gloss on their plumage. The glossy starlings are difficult to identify, given plumage colour is dependent on lighting and angle. Sexes alike in most species; juvs duller. Only a few species have distinct br. plumages. Usually monogamous and territorial. Females undertake most or all incubation; chicks altricial.

## 1 Greater Blue-eared Starling *Lamprotornis chalybaeus*

b | | | | | | | | b b B B b
J F M A M J J A S O N D

**24 cm; 68–105 g** A fairly large, short-tailed glossy starling that differs from Cape Glossy Starling by its dark blue ear coverts, more prominent black tips to greater coverts, and blue (not green) belly and flanks. Larger than Miombo Blue-eared Starling, with a broader ear patch and longer, heavier bill; belly and flanks are blue (not magenta), but this is often hard to distinguish as it depends on lighting and viewing angle. Juv. is duller and less glossy with dark brown tones to its underparts (not chestnut-brown as in juv. Miombo Blue-eared Starling). **Voice:** Distinctive, nasal 'squee-aar', often incorporated in its warbled song. **Status and biology:** Common resident in savanna and mopane woodland. Lays 2–5 eggs in a tree cavity, including old woodpecker or barbet holes. **Diet:** Insects, fruit and nectar; occasional small vertebrates. (Groot-blouoorglansspreu)

## 2 Cape Glossy Starling *Lamprotornis nitens*

b b | | | | | b B B b
J F M A M J J A S O N D

**25 cm; 65–112 g** A fairly large, short-tailed, glossy starling that differs from the blue-eared starlings by its uniformly glossy green head (lacking darker blue ear coverts), reddish-bronze shoulder patch and glossy green belly and flanks (lacking blue or magenta flanks). Larger than Black-bellied Starling, with much brighter, glossier plumage; belly glossy green (not dull black). Juv. is duller, with straw-yellow (not bright orange-yellow) eyes. **Voice:** Song is slurred warble 'trrr-chree-chrrrr'; flight call 'turreeeu'. **Status and biology:** Common resident in savanna, mixed woodland and gardens; often in quite arid regions. Lays 2–4 eggs in a cavity, usually in a tree (including old woodpecker and barbet holes), but also in poles and banks. Sometimes has helpers at the nest. **Diet:** Insects, fruit and nectar; also scavenges scraps. (Kleinglansspreu)

## 3 Miombo Blue-eared Starling *Lamprotornis elisabeth*

b b | | | | | b B B b b
J F M A M J J A S O N D

**19 cm; 52–66 g** Smaller than Greater Blue-eared Starling, with a more compact head and a finer bill. The blackish-blue ear patch is narrow, appearing as a black line through the eye. Belly and flanks are magenta (not blue), but this is often hard to distinguish as it depends on lighting and viewing angle. Juv. has distinctive chestnut-brown underparts, becoming mottled blue-and-brown in imms. **Voice:** A series of short, staccato notes 'chip chirroo krip kreuup krip', higher-pitched and more musical than Greater Blue-eared Starling; 'wirri-gwirri' flight call. **Status and biology:** Common resident in miombo woodland. Often in large flocks in winter. Lays 2–5 eggs in a tree cavity, including old woodpecker or barbet holes. **Diet:** Insects, fruit and nectar. (Klein-blouoorglansspreu)

## 4 Violet-backed Starling *Cinnyricinclus leucogaster*

B | | | | | | | | | b B B
J F M A M J J A S O N D

**17 cm; 39–56 g** Male unmistakeable with its glossy amethyst head, upperparts and upper breast, and plain white belly. Upperparts may appear bluish or coppery at certain angles. Female and juv. are brown above and white below, both densely streaked dark brown. **Voice:** Song is short series of buzzy whistles 'cheez-i-werrr'; also soft, sharp 'tip, tip' notes. **Status and biology:** Common intra-African migrant in woodland, riverine forests and gardens; a few remain year-round in N of region. Lays 2–4 eggs in a tree cavity or hole in a pole. Occasionally has helpers at the nest. **Diet:** Insects and fruit. (Witborsspreu)

## 5 Black-bellied Starling *Lamprotornis corruscus*

b | | | | | | | | | b B B
J F M A M J J A S O N D

**19 cm; 46–68 g** The smallest and least glossy of the glossy starlings, with a black belly and flanks. Male has bronze gloss on belly that is visible at close range, and has red (not yellow-orange) eyes for a short period during the br. season. Female and juv. are duller than male, often appearing black in the field. **Voice:** Song is a short, rather fast, warble of whistles and chippering notes, sometimes including mimicry of other bird songs. **Status and biology:** Locally common resident in coastal and riverine forests; irregular visitor in extreme S of range. Lays 2–4 eggs in a tree cavity, including old woodpecker or barbet holes. **Diet:** Mainly fruit; also nectar and insects. (Swartpensglansspreu)

## 1 Burchell's Starling *Lamprotornis australis*

b b b | | | | | | b B B b
J F M A M J J A S O N D

**32 cm; 112–128 g**  The largest glossy starling. More heavily built than Meves's Starling, with broader, more rounded wings and a shorter, broader tail. Juv. duller above; matt black below. **Voice:** Querulous, throaty calls 'mreeow' and 'chirow-eeow'; song is a jumble of chortles and chuckles. **Status and biology:** Near-endemic. Common resident in savanna and dry, broadleafed woodland. Lays 2–4 eggs in a tree cavity, including old woodpecker or barbet holes; also holes in cliffs or buildings. **Diet:** Insects and other invertebrates; also fruit, flowers and small vertebrates such as mice. (Grootglansspreeu)

## 2 Meves's Starling *Lamprotornis mevesii*

b b b b | | | | | | b b
J F M A M J J A S O N D

**34 cm; 65–95 g**  A medium-sized glossy starling with a very long, graduated tail. Smaller than Burchell's Starling, with a much longer tail. Juv. duller with brownish head and matt black underparts; tail shorter, but still distinctly long and graduated. **Voice:** Querulous, rather harsh 'keeeaaaa', higher-pitched than Burchell's Starling; also various squawks. **Status and biology:** Locally common resident in tall mopane woodland and riverine forests. Lays 3–5 eggs in a tree hole; also uses holes in poles and pipes. Sometimes breeds in loose groups, with 3 pairs in the same tree. **Diet:** Insects, fruit and flowers. (Langstertglansspreeu)

## 3 Sharp-tailed Starling *Lamprotornis acuticaudus*

| | | | | | | | | b b b b b
J F M A M J J A S O N D

**26 cm; 61–76 g**  Similar to Cape Glossy and Greater Blue-eared starlings (p. 366), but has a distinctive, wedge-shaped tail (not square-tipped). In flight, underside of primaries appears pale (not black as in other glossy starlings). Eyes red (male) or orange (female). Juv. is duller, with a matt grey body, scaled buffy; wings and tail slightly glossy; eyes brown. **Voice:** Reedy 'chwee-chwee-chwee', higher-pitched and less varied than Cape Glossy Starling. **Status and biology:** Rare resident and local nomad in broadleafed woodland and dry riverbeds. Often in small flocks. Lays 3–4 eggs in a tree cavity. **Diet:** Insects and fruit. (Spitsstertglansspreeu)

## 4 Pied Starling *Spreo bicolor*

B b b b b b b B B B B
J F M A M J J A S O N D

**27 cm; 94–112 g**  A large, dark brown starling with a conspicuous white vent. At close range, it has an exaggerated yellow gape, creamy white eyes and glossy wing coverts. Paler primary bases are visible in flight. Juv. is matt black with white vent; gape white; eyes dark. **Voice:** Nasal 'skeer-kerrra-kerrra', often given in flight; also a warbling song. **Status and biology:** Endemic. Common resident in grassland and karoo scrub. Often in flocks, frequently with Wattled Starlings (p. 370). Usually roosts and breeds colonially. Lays 2–6 eggs in holes in banks; may have helpers at the nest; large clutches perhaps laid by 2 females. **Diet:** Seeds, fruit, insects and nectar; takes ectoparasites from livestock. (Witgatspreeu)

## 5 Pale-winged Starling *Onychognathus nabouroup*

b b b b | | | | b B B B
J F M A M J J A S O N D

**26–28 cm; 80–120 g**  Smaller and shorter-tailed than Red-winged Starling with whitish (not reddish) patches in primaries, visible in flight, and bright orange (not dark red) eyes. Sexes alike. Juv. is duller than ad. **Voice:** Ringing 'preeoo' in flight; song is a rambling series of musical whistles; alarm call is a harsh 'garrrr'. **Status and biology:** Near-endemic. Common resident and local nomad in rocky ravines and cliffs in dry and desert regions. Flocks may move long distances to exploit specific food sources. Often breeds in loose colonies, only defending immediate nest site. Lays 2–5 eggs in a deep cup nest built in a rock crevice; rarely on a building. **Diet:** Fruit, insects and nectar. Takes ectoparasites from zebras and antelope. (Bleekvlerkspreeu)

## 6 Red-winged Starling *Onychognathus morio*

b b b b | | | | b B B B
J F M A M J J A S O N D

**27–30 cm; 120–155 g**  A large, black starling with a long, graduated tail and rufous primaries that are conspicuous in flight. Larger and longer-tailed than Pale-winged Starling with dark red (not orange) eyes and striking sexual dimorphism: male all glossy black; ad. female has head and upper breast lead grey. Juv. is dull black. **Voice:** Clear, whistled 'cher-leeeoo' or 'who-tuleooo' call; song is a rambling series of musical whistles; alarm call is a harsh 'garrrr'. **Status and biology:** Common resident in rocky ravines, cliffs and suburbia. Wanders more widely in winter, when often in flocks. Lays 2–4 eggs in an untidy cup nest built on a rock ledge or building. **Diet:** Fruit, invertebrates and nectar; also lizards, small birds, carrion and scraps, and gleans ectoparasites from cattle and game. (Rooivlerkspreeu)

## 1 Common Myna *Acridotheres tristis*

`B b b b b b b b B B B B`
J F M A M J J A S O N D

**25 cm; 65–135 g** Introduced from Asia. Easily identified by its chestnut plumage, white wing patches, white tail tips and yellow facial skin. Moulting ads sometimes lose most of their head feathers; bare head appears all-yellow. Juv. paler with a grey-brown head and narrower buffy tail tips. **Voice:** Varied song comprises jumbled titters and chattering as well as mimicry of other sounds. **Status and biology:** Locally common resident in urban and suburban areas; also around farms. Usually roosts communally. Lays 2–6 eggs in an untidy cup nest built in a building or tree canopy. **Diet:** Omnivorous and opportunistic; takes insects and other invertebrates, fruit, seeds and nectar; also scraps. Sometimes gleans ectoparasites from livestock and game. (Indiese Spreeu)

## 2 Wattled Starling *Creatophora cinerea*

`b b b` ` ` `b b b b`
J F M A M J J A S O N D

**19–21 cm; 52–84 g** A compact, pale grey starling with slender, pale bill and a whitish rump that is conspicuous in flight. Male has black flight feathers; female has a darker grey body and browner flight feathers. Br. male has a bare black and yellow head with variable black wattles on its crown and throat. Some br. females also develop bare heads and small wattles. Juv. resembles a dull, brown female. **Voice:** High-pitched, wheezy hisses and cackles, similar to Common Starling; 'sreeeeo' flight call. **Status and biology:** Common nomad in grassland, farmland, savanna and open woodland. Often in large flocks; regularly join other starlings. Breeds colonially. **Diet:** Insects, fruit and seeds. Gleans ectoparasites from livestock and game. (Lelspreeu)

## 3 Common Starling *Sturnus vulgaris*

`| | | | | | | | | |b B B`
J F M A M J J A S O N D

**20–22 cm; 65–95 g** Introduced from Europe. A compact starling with a pointed bill. Ad. has glossy black plumage with buff-tipped feathers above, white below; pale tips gradually wear off, leaving plain black plumage. Bill yellow during br. season; otherwise blackish. Female paler and less glossy. Juv. drab brown with a paler throat and black bill; lacks pale rump of juv. Wattled Starling. **Voice:** Song is a chattering, high-pitched warble, often including mimicry. **Status and biology:** Common resident in towns and open farmland. Often joins flocks of Wattled and Pied starlings (p. 368). Lays 2–6 eggs in a bulky cup nest, usually in a cavity in a building; rarely in a bush or on the ground. **Diet:** Insects and invertebrates; also fruit, seeds and nectar. (Europese Spreeu)

## 4 Rose-coloured Starling *Sturnus roseus*

**20–22 cm; 62–88 g** Rare vagrant. Structure similar to Common Starling, but ad. has striking pink body, contrasting with black head, wings and tail; bill pink. Juv. has grey-brown head and body, contrasting with darker brown wings and tail; bill yellow-pink (not blackish, as juv. Common Starling); lacks white rump of juv. Wattled Starling. Imm. has blackish head, breast, wings and tail contrasting with grey-brown body, palest on belly. **Voice:** Harsh, chittering calls. **Status and biology:** Rare Palearctic vagrant; only 2 records: Kgalagadi Park, July 2005 and Kasane, N Botswana, Sept 2007. **Diet:** Insects, other invertebrates, fruits and seeds. (Roosspreeu)

# OXPECKERS

**Elongate, slender passerines adapted for grooming ectoparasites from large mammals: tails long and stiffened, legs short with strong feet, and bills flattened for scissoring through fur. Usually in small groups; often breeds cooperatively. Both sexes incubate and care for the altricial chicks.**

## 5 Yellow-billed Oxpecker *Buphagus africanus*

`b b b` ` ` `b B b b`
J F M A M J J A S O N D

**20 cm; 53–71 g** Slightly larger than Red-billed Oxpecker with a pale rump that contrasts with its brown back at all ages. At close range, base of bill is yellow; lacks an eye-ring. Juv. has a pale brown bill (not black tipped) that is deeper than that of juv. Red-billed Oxpecker. **Voice:** Rasping 'kriss' or 'churrr'; also short, high-pitched notes. **Status and biology:** Locally common resident of savanna and broadleafed woodland, often near water. Usually associated with buffalo, rhino, hippo and livestock. Lays 2–3 eggs in a tree cavity. **Diet:** Ectoparasites and blood; also hawks insects. (Geelbekrenostervoël)

## 6 Red-billed Oxpecker *Buphagus erythrorhynchus*

`b b b` ` ` `b b B B`
J F M A M J J A S O N D

**19 cm; 42–59 g** Slightly smaller than Yellow-billed Oxpecker with uniform brown upperparts at all ages; bill more slender. At close range, has prominent yellow eye-rings and all-red bill. Juv. has a black bill with a pale base (not uniform pale brown). **Voice:** Scolding 'churrrr', hissing 'zzzzzzist' and short, high-pitched 'zit' notes. **Status and biology:** Locally common resident in savanna and woodland; associated with game and cattle. Lays 2–5 eggs in a tree cavity; rarely in a rock crevice or wall. **Diet:** Ectoparasites and blood; also hawks insects. (Rooibekrenostervoël)

# SUGARBIRDS

**Large, long-tailed nectarivores closely associated with proteas. They are distantly related to sunbirds, but are placed in their own family. Often located by their raucous, rattling calls. Males make fripping sounds with wings and clatter tails in aerial display. Sexes similar, but females and juvs have shorter tails. Monogamous and territorial. Incubation by female only; chicks altricial.**

## 1 Gurney's Sugarbird *Promerops gurneyi*

Bb b b bBBB
J F M A M J J A S O N D

**23–29 cm; 24–46 g** Slightly smaller than Cape Sugarbird, with a conspicuous rufous breast and crown, greyish (not brown) cheeks and a whitish supercilium; lacks malar stripes. Tails of ad. males are not as long as the longest tails of Cape Sugarbirds. Ranges only rarely overlap in E Cape. Juv. has brown breast and dull yellow vent. **Voice:** Rattling song, higher-pitched and more melodious than Cape Sugarbird's. **Status and biology:** Endemic. Locally common resident and partial migrant in stands of flowering proteas and aloes; some move to lower altitudes in winter. Lays 1–2 eggs in a cup nest built in the fork of a protea bush. **Diet:** Nectar, insects, spiders and pollen. (Rooiborssuikervoël)

## 2 Cape Sugarbird *Promerops cafer*

BBBBBbbbb
J F M A M J J A S O N D

**28–44 cm; 25–50 g** Slightly larger than Gurney's Sugarbird with a brown (not rufous) crown and breast; lacks a supercilium but has distinct malar stripes. Often has yellow, pollen-stained crown. Tail of ad. males varies considerably in length (1.5–3 x body length; female and juv. tail usually 1–1.5 x body length). Juv. duller with a pale brown vent. **Voice:** Rattling song, including starling-like chirps and whistles; harsh, grating noises. **Status and biology:** Endemic. Common resident and local nomad in fynbos; visits gardens and coastal scrub after breeding. Lays 1–2 eggs in a cup nest built in the fork of a protea or other low shrub. **Diet:** Nectar, insects and spiders. (Kaapse Suikervoël)

# SUNBIRDS

**Small, active, warbler-like birds with decurved bills for taking nectar from flowers. Often pugnacious, chasing other birds from flowers. Sexes differ in most species. Males usually have some iridescent plumage and in many species have brightly coloured pectoral tufts that are fluffed out when displaying. Some species have a female-like eclipse plumage. Juvs resemble females. Monogamous and territorial. Nests often decorated with lichen, bark, leaves or other material. Incubation by female only; Chicks altricial.**

## 3 Malachite Sunbird *Nectarinia famosa*

BbbbbbBBBBBB
J F M A M J J A S O N D

**14–25 cm; 11–25 g** A large, long-billed sunbird. Br. male has metallic-green plumage with yellow pectoral tufts (only visible when displaying) and elongated central tail feathers. Female is rather pale, with diffuse mottling on the breast, a small supercilium, pale yellow moustachial stripe and white outer tail. Eclipse male (**3 A**) resembles female, but often retains a few green feathers. **Voice:** Piercing 'tseep-tseep' calls; song is a series of twittering notes, usually including loud 'tseep' notes. **Status and biology:** Common resident, nomad and local migrant in fynbos, grassland and mountain scrub. Lays 1–3 eggs in an oval nest with a side entrance, slung in a low shrub. **Diet:** Nectar, insects and spiders. (Jangroentjie)

## 4 Bronzy Sunbird *Nectarinia kilimensis*

bbb bBBB
J F M A M J J A S O N D

**14–22 cm; 12–17 g** A large sunbird with a strongly decurved bill. Male is metallic bronze-green, much darker than Malachite Sunbird; appears black in poor light. Female is smaller than female Malachite Sunbird with a shorter, more strongly curved bill, paler throat, lacking clear moustachial stripes, and more clearly streaked yellowish breast; tail tip more pointed. Male has no eclipse plumage. **Voice:** Loud, piercing 'chee-wit', repeated every half-second; also high-pitched twittering song. **Status and biology:** Locally common resident and nomad of forest edge, bracken and adjoining grassland. Lays 1–2 eggs in oval nest with a side entrance, slung in a low bush. **Diet:** Nectar, insects and spiders. (Bronssuikerbekkie)

## 5 Orange-breasted Sunbird *Anthobaphes violacea*

bbbBBBBBBbbb
J F M A M J J A S O N D

**12–15 cm; 7–13 g** Male easily identified by its orange belly and purple breast band; central tail feathers elongated; has yellow pectoral tufts (only visible when displaying). Female is olive-green above and yellow-green below (not grey like smaller female Southern Double-collared Sunbird, p. 376); tail slightly pointed. Juv. like female with yellow gape; imm. male (**5 A**) has patchy plumage. **Voice:** Call metallic, nasal twang; rapid 'ticks' given in pursuit flight; song is a soft, high-pitched warble, sometimes mimicking other birds. **Status and biology:** Endemic. Common resident and local nomad in fynbos and adjacent gardens. Lays 1–2 eggs in an oval nest with a side entrance, slung in a low shrub. **Diet:** Nectar, insects and spiders. (Oranjeborssuikerbekkie)

## 1 Collared Sunbird *Hedydipna collaris*

**10 cm; 6–11 g** A small, very short-billed sunbird with metallic-green upperparts. Male has an iridescent green throat and upper breast, separated from the yellow belly by a narrow, iridescent purple band. Pectoral tufts yellow. Smaller and much shorter-billed than Variable Sunbird; throat green (not blue), and extends less far onto breast. Female slightly duller, with yellow underparts; lacks white eye-ring of white-eyes (p. 344). **Voice:** Soft 'tswee' and sharp 'tic' calls; song a series of rather harsh, chirpy notes. **Status and biology:** Common resident in forest, dense woodland and gardens. Lays 1–4 eggs in an untidy oval nest with a side entrance and trailing tail, slung in a small tree, creeper or shrub. **Diet:** Insects, other invertebrates, nectar and fruit. (Kortbeksuikerbekkie)

## 2 Plain-backed Sunbird *Anthreptes reichenowi*

J F M A M J J A S O N D

**10 cm; 7–9 g** A slender, warbler-like sunbird, with olive-brown upperparts and a short bill. Male is pale yellow below with an iridescent blue-black forehead and narrow throat patch, bordered by a yellow moustachial stripe. Imm. male Variable and White-bellied sunbirds can have small blackish throats, but have longer bills, lack iridescent frons and usually have a few iridescent back or wing feathers. Female is duller with a grey-brown throat and breast; told from female Collared Sunbird by its olive-brown (not iridescent green) upperparts; greener above than female Variable Sunbird; lacks white eye-ring of white-eyes (p. 344). **Voice:** A typical, warbler-like 'tsweep tsweep twit tweet tweet' song; soft 'tik-tik' call. **Status and biology: NEAR-THREATENED.** Uncommon resident in moist woodland and coastal forests. Lays 1–3 eggs in an oval nest with a hooded side entrance, slung in a low shrub. **Diet:** Insects, spiders and nectar. (Bloukeelsuikerbekkie)

## 3 Variable Sunbird *Cinnyris venustus*

B BBBBBBBb
J F M A M J J A S O N D

**11 cm; 6–10 g** Male is iridescent blue-green above, with a blue-violet crown and throat, and purple breast band. Told from male White-bellied Sunbird by its yellow belly; has a longer, more decurved bill and more extensive dark breast than Collared Sunbird. Female is grey-olive above and plain yellow-olive below; has blackish tail with more extensive white tail tip than female White-bellied Sunbird. Juv. male has blackish throat; told from Plain-backed Sunbird by its longer bill and some iridescence on wing coverts. **Voice:** Trilling song often starts with a rapid 'tsui-tse-tse...'. **Status and biology:** Common resident in woodland, forest edge, gardens and plantations. Lays 1–2 eggs in an oval nest with a side entrance, slung in a shrub or sapling. **Diet:** Nectar and insects. (Geelpenssuikerbekkie)

## 4 White-bellied Sunbird *Cinnyris talatala*

bbbb bbbBBBb
J F M A M J J A S O N D

**11 cm; 6–9 g** Male has an iridescent green back, head and breast, a purple breast band and a white belly. Female is grey-brown above and off-white (rarely yellowish) below; told from female Dusky Sunbird by its indistinctly streaked (not plain) breast, and only outer tail feathers tipped whitish (not whole tail). Juv male has a blackish throat. **Voice:** Song is a rapid series of trilled notes, often preceded by 'pitchee' call. **Status and biology:** Common resident in dry woodland, savanna and gardens. Lays 1–3 eggs in an oval nest with a hooded side entrance, slung in a thorn tree or near a wasp nest. **Diet:** Nectar, insects and spiders. (Witpenssuikerbekkie)

## 5 Western Violet-backed Sunbird *Anthreptes longuemarei*

BBBBb
J F M A M J J A S O N D

**13 cm; 10–13 g** A small, short-billed sunbird with a glossy purple-black tail. Male has violet head, throat, mantle and rump, appearing blackish in poor light; underparts white. Female is grey-brown above with a conspicuous white eye-stripe; underparts white, washed yellow on belly. **Voice:** Sharp 'chit-chit' or 'skee'; song is a soft, high-pitched warble. **Status and biology:** Uncommon to locally common resident in miombo woodland. Often joins bird parties. Pairs remain together year-round. Lays 1–3 eggs in an oval nest with a side entrance, built among dead leaves and seed pods in a bare tree. **Diet:** Insects, spiders and nectar. (Blousuikerbekkie)

## 6 Dusky Sunbird *Cinnyris fuscus*

bBBBbbbbbbbb
J F M A M J J A S O N D

**11 cm; 6–11 g** Male has a glossy black head, throat and back, merging into a white belly; pectoral tufts orange. Female is light grey-brown above and off-white below; paler below than female Southern Double-collared Sunbird (p. 376); breast plain (not lightly streaked as female White-bellied Sunbird). Juv. male has a blackish throat. **Voice:** Short, canary-like song usually ends in a trill; sharp 'tsik' and 'ji-dit' calls. **Status and biology:** Near-endemic. Common resident and nomad in arid savanna, acacia thickets and karoo scrub; irrupts into more mesic areas in some years. Lays 2–3 eggs in an oval nest with a side entrance built in a small tree or shrub. **Diet:** Nectar, insects and spiders. (Namakwasuikerbekkie)

## 1 Greater Double-collared Sunbird *Cinnyris afer*

b b b b b b B B B B B b
J F M A M J J A S O N D

**14 cm; 10–18 g** Appreciably larger than Southern Double-collared Sunbird with a longer, heavier bill. Male has a broader red breast band bordered above by a more violet-blue band. Pectoral tufts yellow. Female grey-brown above, paler below; best separated from female Southern Double-collared Sunbird by its larger size and longer, heavier bill. Imm. male has only a few red breast feathers (**1 A**) or sometimes a narrow breast band. **Voice:** Harsh, 'tchut-tchut-tchut' calls; song is fast and twittering, but deeper and slower than Southern Double-collared Sunbird. **Status and biology:** Endemic. Common resident in tall shrubs, forest fringes, clearings and gardens. Lays 1–2 eggs in an oval nest with a hooded side entrance, slung among the outer branches of a small tree. **Diet:** Nectar, insects and spiders. (Groot-rooibandsuikerbekkie)

## 2 Southern Double-collared Sunbird *Cinnyris chalybeus*

b b b b b B B B B B B b
J F M A M J J A S O N D

**12 cm; 6–10 g** Smaller than Greater Double-collared Sunbird, with a shorter, more slender bill; male has a narrower red breast band. Pectoral tufts yellow. Female is grey-brown (not olive, as female Orange-breasted Sunbird, p. 372), darker above than below, but not as pale below as female Dusky Sunbird (p. 374). Juv. like female with yellow gape. Imm male has patchy plumage. **Voice:** Harsh 'chee-chee' call; song is a very rapid, high-pitched twitter, rising and falling in pitch. **Status and biology:** Endemic. Common resident in coastal and karoo scrub, fynbos and forests (in NE and extreme W). Lays 1–3 eggs in an oval nest with a side entrance, slung among slender branches in a low shrub. **Diet:** Nectar, insects and spiders. (Klein-rooibandsuikerbekkie)

## 3 Miombo Double-collared Sunbird *Cinnyris manoensis*

b b b b b b b B B B B b
J F M A M J J A S O N D

**13 cm; 8–11 g** Similar to Southern Double-collared Sunbird, but male has dull olive-grey rump (not iridescent green); ranges don't overlap. Told from Shelley's Sunbird (p. 378) by its pale olive (not blackish) belly and violet-blue (not green) uppertail coverts. Female is grey-brown above and pale grey below, often with a yellowish wash on the central belly. Mt Gorongoza, Mozambique *C. m. amicorum* is larger, recalling Greater Double-collared Sunbird. **Voice:** Song is a rapid warble, similar to Southern Double-collared Sunbird. **Status and biology:** Common resident in miombo woodland, gardens and edges of montane forest. Lays 1–3 eggs in an oval nest with a hooded side entrance, slung from a slender branch in a tree. **Diet:** Nectar, insects and spiders. (Miombo-rooibandsuikerbekkie)

## 4 Neergaard's Sunbird *Cinnyris neergaardi*

b               b B B b
J F M A M J J A S O N D

**10 cm; 5–7 g** A tiny, compact sunbird with a short, thin bill. Male has a red breast band and sooty black belly; smaller and shorter-billed than rare Shelley's Sunbird (p. 378); ranges do not overlap. Pectoral tufts yellow. Female is grey-brown above and pale yellow below, not streaked like female Purple-banded Sunbird. **Voice:** Thin, wispy 'weesi-weesi-weesi'; short, chippy song. **Status and biology:** NEAR-THREATENED. Endemic. Common, localised resident in acacia savanna and sand forest. Lays 2 eggs in an oval nest with a hooded side entrance, built in a tree among epiphytic lichens or orchid roots. **Diet:** Nectar, mistletoe fruit, insects and spiders. (Bloukruissuikerbekkie)

## 5 Marico Sunbird *Cinnyris mariquensis*

b b               b B B B b
J F M A M J J A S O N D

**12 cm; 8–14 g** Larger than Purple-banded Sunbird with a longer, thicker and more decurved bill. Male has a black or sooty-grey belly and a narrow violet-blue breast band above a broader purple-maroon band. Purple breast band is broader than that of male Purple-banded Sunbird; uppertail coverts green (not blue). Female has grey-brown upperparts and pale yellow, dusky-streaked underparts; tail dark grey with white outer edges. **Voice:** Long series of rapid 'tsip-tsip-tsip' phrases; fast, warbling song. **Status and biology:** Common resident in woodland and savanna, often in fairly arid areas. Lays 1–3 eggs in an oval nest with a hooded side entrance, slung from a branch in a tree. **Diet:** Nectar, insects and spiders. (Maricosuikerbekkie)

## 6 Purple-banded Sunbird *Cinnyris bifasciatus*

b b b               b B B b
J F M A M J J A S O N D

**10 cm; 6–9 g** Smaller than Marico Sunbird, with a thinner, shorter and less decurved bill. Male has a narrower purple breast band and blue (not green) uppertail coverts. Female is pale yellow below with less streaking than female Marico Sunbird; tail lacks white outer edge. Eclipse and juv. male resemble female, but have a dark throat. **Voice:** High-pitched 'teeet-teeet-tit-tit' song, accelerating at end, not sustained as call of Marico Sunbird. **Status and biology:** Common resident in woodland, moist savanna and coastal scrub. Lays 1–2 (rarely 3) eggs in an oval nest with a side entrance and a trailing tail, slung from a slender branch in a tree. **Diet:** Nectar, insects and spiders. (Purperbandsuikerbekkie)

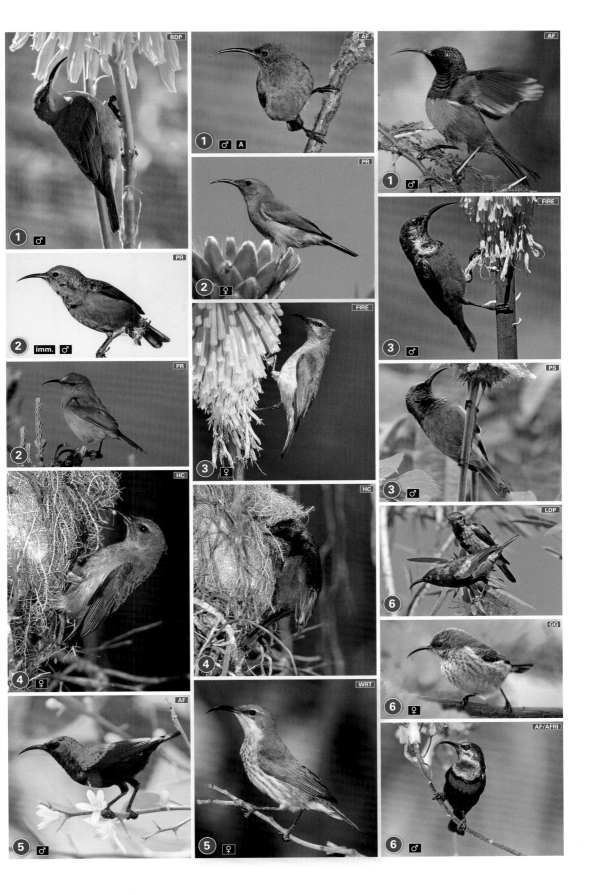

## 1 Scarlet-chested Sunbird *Chalcomitra senegalensis*

B b b b b b b b B B B B
J F M A M J J A S O N D

**14 cm; 10–17 g** Male easily identified by its mainly black body and scarlet breast; iridescent green crown and throat visible in good light; lacks pectoral tufts. No eclipse plumage. Female is dark greyish-olive above; throat and breast darker and more heavily mottled than female Amethyst Sunbird; pale supercilium starts above eye (not at base of bill). At close range, has whitish edges to wrist feathers (lacking in Amethyst Sunbird). **Voice:** Loud, whistled 'cheeup, chup, toop, toop, toop' song; 'chak chak' alarm call. **Status and biology:** Common resident, nomad and local migrant in woodland, savanna and suburban gardens; some birds move out of arid areas in winter. Lays 1–3 eggs in an oval nest with a hooded side entrance, slung in the canopy of a tree or shrub, often near wasp nests. **Diet:** Nectar, insects and spiders. (Rooiborssuikerbekkie)

## 2 Amethyst Sunbird *Chalcomitra amethystina*

B B b b b b b b B B B B
J F M A M J J A S O N D

**15 cm; 11–19 g** Male appears all-black, but in good light shows an iridescent green forecrown and violet-purple throat, shoulders and rump; lacks pectoral tufts. No eclipse plumage. Female similar to female Scarlet-chested Sunbird, but throat and breast paler and less heavily streaked; supercilium starts at base of bill (not above eye). **Voice:** Quite deep, fast, twittering song; loud 'chip chip' calls. **Status and biology:** Common resident, nomad and local migrant in woodland, forest edge and gardens; some birds move out of arid areas in winter. Lays 1–3 eggs in an oval nest with a hooded side entrance, slung in a tree or creeper. **Diet:** Nectar, insects and spiders. (Swartsuikerbekkie)

## 3 Copper Sunbird *Cinnyris cupreus*

b b b b
J F M A M J J A S O N D

**13 cm; 8–12 g** A slender, short-billed sunbird with a fairly long tail. Male is blackish with coppery iridescence; smaller than Bronzy Sunbird (p.372) and lacks elongated central tail feathers. Female grey-brown above, creamy below with a pale supercilium contrasting with dark face; tail blue-black with narrow white tips and outer edges. Eclipse male retains coppery wing coverts and rump; flight feathers black. **Voice:** Harsh 'chit-chat' call; high-pitched warbling song. **Status and biology:** Uncommon to locally common resident and local nomad in woodland and forest edge. Lays 1–2 eggs in an oval nest with a hooded side entrance and trailing tail, slung in a tree or shrub. **Diet:** Nectar, insects and spiders. (Kopersuikerbekkie)

## 4 Shelley's Sunbird *Cinnyris shelleyi*

b B b
J F M A M J J A S O N D

**11 cm; 9–11 g** Rare. Male has a broad red breast band and sooty black belly; larger and longer-billed than male Neergaard's Sunbird (p. 376) with a broader red breast band; ranges do not overlap. Eclipse male has a paler belly; could be confused with Miombo Double-collared Sunbird (p. 376), but rump iridescence green (not blue). Female has lightly streaked underparts (not plain as female Miombo Double-collared Sunbird); shorter-billed, greyer above and less yellow beneath than female Marico Sunbird (p. 376). **Voice:** A 'didi-didi'; a nasal 'chibbee-cheeu-cheeu' song. **Status and biology:** Rare resident and nomad in broadleafed woodland. Lays 1–3 eggs in an oval nest with a side entrance, slung in a tree or creeper. **Diet:** Nectar, insects and spiders. (Swartpenssuikerbekkie)

## 5 Grey Sunbird *Cyanomitra veroxii*

B b b b B B B
J F M A M J J A S O N D

**14 cm; 11–15 g** A nondescript sunbird; sexes alike. Dark grey face and upperparts contrast with paler grey underparts (unlike Olive Sunbird and female Greater Double-collared Sunbird, p. 376); pectoral tufts red. At close range, crown, back and wing coverts are faintly washed blue-green. Juv. is more yellow-olive below; more similar to Olive Sunbird. **Voice:** Song loud series of well-spaced 'chreep chreep choop' phrases; call harsh, grating 'tzzik, tzzik'. **Status and biology:** Locally common resident in coastal and riverine forests. Lays 2–3 (rarely 1–4) eggs in an oval nest with a hooded side entrance and a long, trailing tail, slung from a shrub. **Diet:** Nectar, insects and spiders. (Gryssuikerbekkie)

## 6 Olive Sunbird *Cyanomitra olivacea*

B b b B B B B
J F M A M J J A S O N D

**15 cm; 8–15 g** A dull olive sunbird. Much greener than Grey Sunbird, with less contrast between the dark upperparts and paler underparts. Juv. has a rust-coloured throat. Both sexes have yellow pectoral tufts in lowland populations; males only in E Zimbabwe highlands. **Voice:** Call sharp 'tuk, tuk, tuk'; song is a series of descending, piping notes, accelerating in pace, and sometimes increasing in pitch at the end. **Status and biology:** Common resident in coastal, riverine and montane forests; usually the most abundant forest sunbird in its range. Lays 1–3 eggs in an untidy oval nest with a hooded side entrance and trailing tail, slung in a tree or shrub. **Diet:** Nectar, insects, spiders and occasional fruit. (Olyfsuikerbekkie)

# SPARROWS

Familiar, finch-like passerines with stout, conical bills. Most species have rufous or chestnut backs. Sexes differ in most species; juvs like dull females. Bill often black when breeding. Usually monogamous. Both sexes incubate and care for the altricial chicks.

## 1 Great Sparrow  *Passer motitensis*

B B B b | | | | | | b B B B
J F M A M J J A S O N D

**15 cm; 26–35 g**  Larger than House Sparrow with a heavier bill. Male has paler chestnut nape and back, and chestnut (not grey) rump. Female has chestnut back and shoulders (not sandy-brown as female House Sparrow); crown pale grey (not brown). Told from female Cape Sparrow by its dark eye-stripe, chestnut supercilium and dark-streaked (not plain) chestnut mantle. **Voice:** Slow, measured 'cheereep, cheereeu', slower and slightly deeper than House Sparrow. **Status and biology:** Near-endemic. Locally common resident in semi-arid acacia woodland. Lays 2–4 eggs in an untidy ball nest with a side entrance built in a thorn tree or bush. **Diet:** Seeds and insects. (Grootmossie)

## 2 House Sparrow  *Passer domesticus*

b b b b b b b b B B B B
J F M A M J J A S O N D

**14 cm; 22–30 g**  Introduced from Europe and India. Smaller than Great Sparrow with darker, reddish-brown upperparts and grey (not chestnut) rump. Black bib more prominent in br. season, when exposed by wear of buff feather tips; size signals social status. Female is sandy grey-brown with a pale buff supercilium that is much smaller than that of Yellow-throated Petronia; also smaller with a shorter, stouter bill. **Voice:** Song is a medley of chirps, chips and 'chissick' notes. **Status and biology:** Locally common resident in and around human habitation. Small flocks may occur away from buildings. Nests singly or in loose groups. Lays 1–6 eggs in an untidy ball or deep cup nest usually built in a cavity in a building; occasionally in a tree. **Diet:** Seeds, fruit, insects, nectar and scraps. (Huismossie)

## 3 Cape Sparrow  *Passer melanurus*

B B b b b b b b B B B B
J F M A M J J A S O N D

**15 cm; 22–36 g**  Male has a striking black-and white head. Female duller, with pale grey head, white supercilium that almost links with whitish throat; mantle unstreaked (unlike female House and Great sparrows). **Voice:** Series of musical cheeps 'chirp chroop, chirp chroop'; also a short, rattled alarm call. **Status and biology:** Near-endemic. Common resident in grassland, fields and large gardens; also in some urban areas. Lays 2–6 eggs in a bulky, untidy ball nest built in a bush or small tree (often a thorn tree), or in a wall or roof cavity. **Diet:** Seeds, fruit, buds, nectar and insects. (Gewone Mossie)

## 4 Yellow-throated Petronia  *Petronia superciliaris*

b b b | | | | | b B B B b
J F M A M J J A S O N D

**15 cm; 21–29 g**  A grey-brown sparrow with a broad creamy-white supercilium. Sexes alike. The small yellow spot at the base of the white throat is seldom visible; absent in juv. Smaller and much duller than White-browed Sparrow-weaver (p. 382); rump grey-brown (not white). **Voice:** 3–4 fast, chipping notes, either all the same, or first or last differing. **Status and biology:** Locally common resident in dry woodland, savanna and riverine bush. Forages on the ground and along larger branches of trees. Lays 3–4 (rarely 2–5) eggs in a tree cavity or old woodpecker or barbet hole. **Diet:** Insects, spiders, seeds and nectar. (Geelvlekmossie)

## 5 Southern Grey-headed Sparrow  *Passer diffusus*

b b b b | | | b b b | | |
J F M A M J J A S O N D

**15 cm; 20–30 g**  A plain sparrow with a warm brown back and soft grey head; sexes alike. Told from all other species except localised Northern Grey-headed Sparrow by its plain grey head. **Voice:** Rather slow series of chirping notes 'tchep tchierp tchep'; also an alarm rattle. **Status and biology:** Common resident in woodland and other areas with trees; occurs in gardens but generally avoids urban areas. Lays 2–6 eggs in a hole in a tree, pole or building; also old nests of other birds. **Diet:** Seeds, fruit, nectar and insects. (Gryskopmossie)

## 6 Northern Grey-headed Sparrow  *Passer griseus*

B B b b | | | | | | | | |
J F M A M J J A S O N D

**16 cm; 34–43 g**  Slightly larger and darker than Southern Grey-headed Sparrow. Dark grey head contrasts more with rufous mantle and whitish throat; white shoulder stripe reduced or sometimes absent. Bill is heavier and is black year-round (lacks pale non-br. bill of Southern Grey-headed Sparrow). **Voice:** More variable with some higher-pitched notes than Southern Grey-headed Sparrow. **Status and biology:** Locally common, mainly around settlements. Lays 2–7 eggs in a cavity nest; occasionally in a ball nest built in a tree. **Diet:** Seeds, fruit, insects and scraps. (Witkeelmossie)

# WEAVERS

A diverse group of sparrow-like finches renowned for weaving complex, ball-like nests. Sexes usually differ. Males of open country species have an eclipse plumage and are often hard to identify outside the br. season, whereas forest and woodland species lack an eclipse plumage and have more distinctive females. Juvs like dull females. Mating systems range from polygynous through monogamous to cooperative. Female only incubates in polygynous species, but both sexes in monogamous species; chicks altricial.

## 1 Red-billed Buffalo-Weaver *Bubalornis niger*

B B B b b b | b B B B
J F M A M J J A S O N D

**21–24 cm; 64–92 g** A large, heavy-billed weaver. Male black with white wing panel and an orange-red bill. Female is browner and slightly scaled. Juv. is paler beneath with more prominent scaling. **Voice:** Chattering medley of slightly scratchy, nasal notes; also harsh calls. **Status and biology:** Common resident and local migrant in dry woodland and savanna. Lays 2–4 eggs in a large, untidy nest of dead sticks built in a large tree or electricity pylon. Each nest contains 1–10 br. chambers. Some males polygynous, building multiple nests to attract females; other males form coalitions and assist with raising chicks. **Diet:** Insects, seeds and fruit. (Buffelwewer)

## 2 White-browed Sparrow-Weaver *Plocepasser mahali*

b b b b b b b b b B B B
J F M A M J J A S O N D

**17 cm; 41–54 g** A chunky, sparrow-like weaver with blackish, brown and white plumage. Larger and much more boldly plumaged than Yellow-throated Petronia (p. 380). Bill black (male), horn-coloured (female) or pinkish-brown (juv.). In NE, *P. m. pectoralis* has brown breast spots. **Voice:** Loud, liquid 'cheeoop-preeoo-chop' song; also harsh 'chik-chik' call. **Status and biology:** Common resident in acacia savanna and dry woodland. Usually in small groups; breeds cooperatively. Nests are untidy bundles of grass built in the edge of the canopy of a thorn tree. Most nests for roosting; only the dominant pair breeds, laying 1–3 eggs. **Diet:** Insects, seeds, fruit and leaves. (Koringvoël)

## 3 Thick-billed Weaver *Amblyospiza albifrons*

B B b | b B B
J F M A M J J A S O N D

**18 cm; 35–56 g** A large, dark brown weaver with a massive bill and large head; appears long-tailed in flight. Male warm brown with a white frons and wing patches; bill blackish. Female is whitish below, heavily streaked brown, with a paler bill. **Voice:** High-pitched, chattering song; high-pitched 'tweek tweek' or 'pink pink' flight call. **Status and biology:** Common resident and local nomad of forest edge and rank vegetation, usually near water. Polygynous; usually in small colonies. Lays 2–4 eggs in a neat, finely woven nest with a side entrance attached to reeds. Roosting nests have larger entrances than br. nests. **Diet:** Fruit, seeds and insects. (Dikbekwewer)

## 4 Dark-backed Weaver *Ploceus bicolor*

b b | b B B B
J F M A M J J A S O N D

**15 cm; 28–43 g** A forest weaver with blackish-brown upperparts that contrast with golden-yellow breast and belly. Sexes alike with no eclipse plumage; throat variably grizzled grey. See also localised Olive-headed Weaver (p. 386). **Voice:** Song is a squeaky, musical duet, interspersed with shrill, buzzing notes; also a soft, high-pitched 'tseep' call. **Status and biology:** Common resident in forest and dense woodland; often joins bird parties. Monogamous and territorial; pairs remain together year-round. Breeds singly; lays 2–4 eggs in a nest, finely woven from vines and creepers, with a long entrance tube, suspended from a slender branch stripped of leaves. **Diet:** Insects, spiders, fruit, nectar and flowers. (Bosmusikant)

## 5 Sociable Weaver *Philetairus socius*

b b B B b b b b b b b
J F M A M J J A S O N D

**14 cm; 24–32 g** A sparrow-like weaver with a pale bill, black facemask and scaly back; see Scaly-feathered and Red-headed finches (p. 404). Sexes alike. Ads have scaly black flanks. Juv. duller; lacks black chin and has a finely streaked crown. **Voice:** Metallic, chattering 'chicker-chicker' song; 'chip' contact call. **Status and biology:** Endemic. Common resident and local nomad in semi-arid savanna and karoo scrub. Gregarious, cooperative breeder. Lays 3–4 (rarely 2–6) eggs in a chamber in a communal thatched nest, built in a tree or on a pole or windmill. Some nests huge, with up to 500 chambers. **Diet:** Seeds and insects. (Versamelvoël)

## 1 Village Weaver *Ploceus cucullatus*

BBbb · · · bBBBB
J F M A M J J A S O N D

**16 cm; 30–46 g** A large, heavy-billed masked-weaver with a mottled black and yellow back; eyes dark red. Extent of black on br. male's head varies: crown mostly yellow in *P. c. spilonotus* (S Africa and adjacent Mozambique); entire head and nape black in *P. c. nigriceps* further N. Female and non-br. male have prominent yellow supercilium, throat and breast; belly whitish; back dull, mottled, greyish; eyes red-brown. **Voice:** Buzzy, swizzling song; throaty 'chuck-chuck' call. **Status and biology:** Common resident in savanna, fields and gardens; often in large flocks. Polygynous. Breeds colonially in trees, palms and reedbeds. Lays 2–5 eggs in a rather untidy nest with a short entrance tube. **Diet:** Seeds, insects, nectar, flowers and scraps. (Bontrugwewer)

## 2 Southern Masked-Weaver *Ploceus velatus*

BBbb · · · bbBBBB
J F M A M J J A S O N D

**16 cm; 30–44 g** Br. male told from Village Weaver by its mostly plain, greenish back (not mottled black and yellow). Larger than Lesser Masked-Weaver, with a heavier bill and red (not whitish) eyes; legs pinkish (not blue-grey). Female and non-br. male much duller with buffy yellow breast and white belly; bill paler and eyes duller red-brown. **Voice:** Typical swizzling weaver song; sharp 'zik, zik' call. **Status and biology:** Common resident in savanna, grassland, watercourses in arid areas, fields and gardens. Polygynous. Breeds singly or in small colonies in trees or reeds. Lays 1–4 eggs in a neat ball nest with short entrance tube. **Diet:** Seeds, fruit, insects, nectar and scraps. (Swartkeelgeelvink)

## 3 Lesser Masked-Weaver *Ploceus intermedius*

Bbb · · · bbBBB
J F M A M J J A S O N D

**13 cm; 15–32 g** A small masked-weaver with a slender bill and whitish eyes. Br. male has a black mask extending onto its forecrown and a notch above its eye. Female and non-br. male washed yellow below; told by pale eyes and blue-grey legs. Juv. eye brown. **Voice:** Typical swizzling weaver song. **Status and biology:** Locally common resident in savanna and woodland. Polygynous. Breeds colonially in trees and reeds near water. Lays 2–4 eggs in a rather untidy nest with a short to medium entrance tube. **Diet:** Insects, fruit, seeds, nectar and flowers. (Kleingeelvink)

## 4 Spectacled Weaver *Ploceus ocularis*

Bbb · · · bBBB
J F M A M J J A S O N D

**15 cm; 27–32 g** A bright yellow weaver with a plain, olive-green back, slender bill and black eye-stripe; eyes whitish. Male has black throat and chestnut-brown wash on face and breast. Lacks an eclipse plumage. Juv. lacks eye-stripe. **Voice:** Descending 'dee-dee-dee-dee-dee' call given by both sexes; male has short swizzling song. **Status and biology:** Common resident of forest edge, moist woodland, thickets and gardens; usually in pairs. Monogamous. Breeds singly; lays 1–4 eggs in a finely woven nest with long entrance tube. **Diet:** Insects, other invertebrates, fruit, nectar and small geckos. (Brilwewer)

## 5 Red-headed Weaver *Anaplectes melanotis*

bb · · · bbBBBB
J F M A M J J A S O N D

**14 cm; 17–26 g** A grey-backed weaver with yellow-edged wing feathers and a long, slender orange-red bill; belly white. Br. male has a scarlet head and breast; lemon yellow in female and non-br. male. **Voice:** High-pitched swizzling song; squeaky 'cherra-cherra' calls. **Status and biology:** Locally common resident in woodland, savanna and gardens. Usually monogamous. Lays 2–3 (rarely 1–4) eggs in a thin-walled nest with a very long entrance tube, suspended from branches or wires. **Diet:** Insects, spiders, seeds and fruit. (Rooikopwewer)

## 6 Chestnut Weaver *Ploceus rubiginosus*

BBBb · · · b
J F M A M J J A S O N D

**15 cm; 25–37 g** Br. male has distinctive chestnut body and black head. Female and non-br. male sandy brown, heavily streaked dark brown above, with whitish-buff edges to wing feathers; lack yellow-green in plumage of other female and non-br. weavers. Recall non-br. widowbirds; best told by reddish eyes and heavy bills. Juv. has streaked breast. **Voice:** Swizzling weaver song at colonies. Typical call is a melodic 'whut whut'; also harsh 'chuk'. **Status and biology:** Locally common resident and partial migrant in arid savanna and grassy woodland. Polygynous. Breeds in large colonies in trees. Lays 1–6 eggs in an untidy nest with a short entrance tube. **Diet:** Seeds, insects and nectar. (Bruinwewer)

## 1 Cape Weaver *Ploceus capensis*

b b | | | | | b b B B B B B
J F M A M J J A S O N D

**17 cm; 28–54 g** A large weaver with a long, pointed bill. Br. male is less yellow above than 'golden' weavers, with chestnut wash on face and throat; lacks well-defined bib of Southern Brown-throated Weaver; eyes whitish (not red-brown). Female and non-br. male are olive above and dull yellow below; lack pale belly of female Southern Masked-Weaver (p. 384). Female has brown eyes. **Voice:** Harsh, hysterical swizzling song; 'chack' contact call. **Status and biology:** Endemic. Common resident in grassland and scrub. Polygynous. Usually breeds colonially in reeds or tall trees. Lays 2–5 eggs in a large nest with a short entrance tube. **Diet:** Seeds, fruit, buds, nectar, insects and scraps. (Kaapse Wewer)

## 2 Southern Brown-throated Weaver *Ploceus xanthopterus*

b | | | | | | | | b B B
J F M A M J J A S O N D

**14 cm; 18–30 g** Br. male is bright yellow, with a distinctive chestnut (not black) bib confined to the face and throat, not extending onto the forecrown as in Cape Weaver; eyes red-brown (not whitish). Br. female has yellow underparts and brown eyes. Non-br. birds duller, with horn-coloured bills, buff breasts and flanks, and white bellies; rump and back washed rufous. **Voice:** Swizzling song often ends with 2 buzzy notes, 'zweek, zweek'. **Status and biology:** Locally common resident in forest and scrub close to marshy br. sites. Polygynous. Breeds singly or in small colonies, often with other weavers, in reedbeds, frequently over water. Lays 2–3 eggs in a rather scraggly nest with no entrance tube. **Diet:** Seeds, fruit, flowers and insects. (Bruinkeelwewer)

## 3 Golden Weaver *Ploceus xanthops*

B B b b | | | b b B B B
J F M A M J J A S O N D

**17 cm; 35–50 g** A large golden weaver with pale yellow eyes and a heavy bill; lacks an eclipse plumage. Male's bright yellow head and breast lack richer tones of male Yellow Weaver. Female duller, with an olive wash on the head and underparts; lacks whitish belly of most other female weavers. Juv. has brown eyes. **Voice:** Typical swizzling weaver song, deeper than Yellow Weaver; also 'chuk' call. **Status and biology:** Locally common resident in woodland and savanna. Usually monogamous. Breeds singly or in small colonies, usually over water. Lays 1–3 eggs in a compact nest with a short entrance tube. **Diet:** Fruit, insects and nectar. (Goudwewer)

## 4 Olive-headed Weaver *Ploceus olivaceiceps*

b b | | | | | b b b b
J F M A M J J A S O N D

**14 cm; 18–24 g** A woodland weaver that differs from Dark-backed Weaver (p. 382) by its olive (not blackish-brown) upperparts and pale (not dark) eyes. Male has an olive-yellow crown and chestnut breast. Female has olive head and small chestnut breast patch. Juv. paler. **Voice:** Soft whistled contact calls and short song. **Status and biology: NEAR-THREATENED.** Uncommon resident in miombo woodland with abundant epiphytic lichens; only some 100 pairs around Panda in sthn Mozambique. Often joins bird parties, gleaning along branches. Monogamous; breeds singly. Lays 2–3 eggs in a well-camouflaged nest of lichens with a longish entrance tube slung under a branch in the canopy of a tall tree. **Diet:** Insects and spiders. (Olyfkopwewer)

## 5 Yellow Weaver *Ploceus subaureus*

b b | | | | | | B B B B
J F M A M J J A S O N D

**15 cm; 22–39 g** Br. male is smaller than Golden Weaver with a smaller, shorter bill and orange wash to head and breast; eyes red (not yellow). Non-br. male duller with olive crown and cheeks contrasting with yellow supercilium. Female has heavily streaked back and wings, olive-yellow head and breast and a whitish belly; bill pale pink; eyes brown. **Voice:** Typical swizzling weaver song, higher-pitched than Golden Weaver; soft 'chuk' contact call. **Status and biology:** Locally common resident in woodland, savanna and gardens. Polygynous. Usually breeds colonially in reedbeds and trees near water. Lays 2–4 eggs in a compact nest with no entrance tube. **Diet:** Seeds, insects and nectar. (Geelwewer)

BROSE

1 ♂

IS

1 ♂

IS

1 ♀

CVR

2 br. ♂

BDP

2 ♀

CVR

2 br. ♂

LDP

3 ♀

GK

4 ♂

GK

4 ♀

LDP

3 ♂

GU

5 ♀

PR

5 br. ♂

# QUELEAS

Small, compact weavers, often in large flocks. Males have striking br. plumages; females, non-br. males and juvs nondescript; typically more slender than bishops, with plain (not streaked) breasts.

## 1 Red-billed Quelea  *Quelea quelea*

B B B b | | | | | | b B
J F M A M J J A S O N D

**11–13 cm; 15–26 g** An abundant quelea; bill red (male) or yellow (female). Most br. males have a black face and a buff or pinkish crown and breast **(1 A)**; some have creamy or pinkish-purple faces **(1 B)**. Non-br. male and female have a strong whitish supercilium and paler underparts than other queleas. Juv. has a pale brown bill. **Voice:** Song is jumble of harsh, weaver-like calls, interspersed with more melodious notes; chittering contact calls. **Status and biology:** Abundant nomad in savanna and cereal fields, often in drier areas than other queleas. Feeds, roosts and breeds in large flocks, sometimes of millions of birds. Monogamous. Lays 1–5 eggs in a woven oval nest with a side entrance built in a thorn tree, with hundreds or thousands of nests per tree. **Diet:** Seeds, insects and other invertebrates. (Rooibekkwelea)

## 2 Red-headed Quelea  *Quelea erythrops*

B b b | | | | | | b B
J F M A M J J A S O N D

**11–12 cm; 15–25 g** Br. male has a neat red head and a blackish (not red) bill; most likely confused with rare Cardinal Quelea, but see also Red-headed Finch (p. 404). Br. female has a pale orange wash on its face and throat. Non-br. birds have brown bills (not red or yellow as Red-billed Quelea); supercilium and throat yellowish; breast buff. Juv. more buffy on head, with broad buff margins to back feathers. **Voice:** Sizzling chatter; also a sharp 'chip' call. **Status and biology:** Uncommon intra-African migrant in damp grassland and adjoining woodland. Polygynous. Breeds in colonies, usually in reedbeds; lays 1–3 eggs in a woven oval nest with a side entrance. **Diet:** Seeds and insects. (Rooikopkwelea)

## 3 Cardinal Quelea  *Quelea cardinalis*

**10–11 cm; 11–15 g** Rare vagrant. Slightly smaller than other queleas. Br. male has a red head that extends further onto its nape and breast than in male Red-headed Quelea; throat plain red (not finely barred blackish). Non-br. male and female have a streaked crown and face and a strong buff supercilium; throat and breast yellowish; bill horn-coloured. Juv. is buff below with dusky breast streaking. **Voice:** Sizzling chatter; also a soft 'zeet' call. **Status and biology:** Rare vagrant to wooded grassland and cultivated areas. Only 1 confirmed record: Mana Pools, Zimbabwe, in March 1999. **Diet:** Seeds and insects. (Kardinaalkwelea)

# BISHOPS AND WIDOWBIRDS

Strongly dimorphic birds related to weavers. Br. males are black with red or yellow patches; females, non-br. males and juvs nondescript; more compact than queleas with streaked breasts. Often in flocks when not breeding. Polygynous; incubation by females only; chicks altricial.

## 4 Yellow-crowned Bishop  *Euplectes afer*

B B b b | | | | | b b b
J F M A M J J A S O N D

**10 cm; 13–19 g** A tiny bishop. Br. male has a diagnostic yellow crown. Displaying birds appear almost spherical, fluffing out their golden back and rump feathers. Non-br. male and female are smaller than other bishops with whiter (less buffy) underparts and a prominent buffy-yellow supercilium contrasting with darker ear coverts. **Voice:** High-pitched buzzing and chirping notes. **Status and biology:** Locally common resident and local nomad in grassland. Breeds in small colonies in marshes, laying 2–4 eggs in an oval nest with a side entrance built low down in grass or reeds. **Diet:** Seeds and insects. (Goudgeelvink)

## 5 Southern Red Bishop  *Euplectes orix*

B B b b b b b b b B B B
J F M A M J J A S O N D

**12 cm; 18–29 g** Br. male is black and red; told from male Black-winged Bishop by its black (not red) forecrown and brown (not black) flight feathers; latter difference retained year-round. Non-br. male and female have a broad, buffy supercilum, finely streaked breast and brownish bill. **Voice:** Advertising males give buzzing, chirping song; also 'cheet-cheet' flight call and nasal 'wheet' contact call. **Status and biology:** Common resident and local nomad in grassland, savanna and fields. Feeds, roosts and breeds in flocks. Lays 1–5 eggs in an oval nest with a side entrance, usually in a reedbed. **Diet:** Seeds, insects and other invertebrates. (Rooivink)

## 6 Black-winged Bishop  *Euplectes hordeaceus*

b B B b | | | | | | | |
J F M A M J J A S O N D

**12 cm; 18–28 g** Br. male told from Southern Red Bishop by its full red crown and blackish (not brown) flight feathers (retained in non-br. plumage). Female similar to non-br. Southern Red Bishop, but has a heavier bill. **Voice:** Buzzing chatter, faster and higher-pitched than Southern Red Bishop. **Status and biology:** Locally common resident in damp grassy areas and fields. Lays 2–4 eggs in an oval nest with a side entrance in rank vegetation. **Diet:** Seeds and insects. (Vuurkopvink)

**1** br. ♂ A · LDP

**1** br. ♂ B · LDP

**1** ♀ · WRT

**2** br. ♂ · NB

**2** ♀ ♂ · JG

**2** ♂ · JG

**3** ♂ · JD/VIREO

**4** br. ♂ · PHILP

**4** br. ♂ · HPHP/PA

**4** ♀ · DCHP

**5** trans. ♂ · PR

**5** ♀ · PR

**5** br. ♂ · CVR

**5** ♀ · JG

**6** br. ♂ · PS

## 1 Yellow Bishop *Euplectes capensis*

BBbb | bBBBbB
J F M A M J J A S O N D

**15–18 cm; 25–50 g** Br. male is black and yellow; much larger than Yellow-crowned Bishop (p. 388) with a black crown; shorter-tailed than Yellow-mantled Widowbird, with a yellow rump and lower back (not a yellow mantle). Non-br. male is heavily streaked buffy-brown, but retains the bright yellow rump and shoulder. Female is more heavily streaked below than female Yellow-mantled Widowbird, with an olive-yellow rump; appreciably larger and more streaked than other female bishops. Juv. has buff back and less streaking below. Bill much bigger in SW.
**Voice:** Displaying males give high-pitched 'zeet, zeet, zeet' or buzzy 'zzzzzzzzt' calls. **Status and biology:** Common resident in damp grassy areas and heathlands. Males territorial; attract up to 4 females. Lays 2–4 eggs in an oval nest with a side entrance built in dense vegetation. **Diet:** Seeds and insects. (Kaapse Flap)

## 2 Yellow-mantled Widowbird *Euplectes macrourus*

Bbb | b
J F M A M J J A S O N D

**14–20 cm; 15–28 g** Br. male is black and yellow with a longer tail than Yellow Bishop; yellow on mantle (not lower back and rump). Non-br. male retains yellow shoulders and blackish wings; tail longer and is less heavily streaked than male Yellow Bishop. Female is less heavily streaked on breast; lacks olive-yellow rump of female Yellow Bishop. **Voice:** Buzzing song typically varies in pitch 'buzz-itty buzz-itty...'; also dry 'tseep' call. **Status and biology:** Locally common resident in damp grassland and marshy areas. Males territorial; attract up to 5 females. Lays 2–3 eggs in a bulky oval nest with a side entrance built in dense grass. **Diet:** Seeds and insects. (Geelrugflap)

## 3 White-winged Widowbird *Euplectes albonotatus*

BBBbb | b
J F M A M J J A S O N D

**16 cm; 16–26 g** Male has a diagnostic white wing bar formed by white bases to its black flight feathers; coverts also edged white. Br. male black with yellow shoulders; lacks yellow on back or rump. Non-br. male buffy brown, but retains white wing bars and yellow shoulders. Female has brown wings; lesser coverts edged yellow; underparts whiter and usually less streaked than other female widowbirds. **Voice:** Dry, high-pitched rattle 'zeh-zeh-zeh', sometimes with squeaky or buzzy notes. **Status and biology:** Common resident in tall grass in savanna, marsh edges and rank vegetation. Males territorial; attract up to 4 females. Lays 2–4 eggs in an oval nest with a side entrance built in dense grass. **Diet:** Seeds and insects. (Witvlerkflap)

## 4 Fan-tailed Widowbird *Euplectes axillaris*

Bbb | bbB
J F M A M J J A S O N D

**15 cm; 20–32 g** Br. male has red shoulders and buff-orange greater coverts. Tail much shorter than Long-tailed Widowbird, but could be confused with males moulting into br. plumage. Broad, rounded tail is fanned in display. Non-br. male retains black primaries and red shoulders. Female is heavily streaked above with reddish-brown shoulders and a large, buffy supercilium; underparts buffy-white, lightly streaked on its breast and flanks. **Voice:** High-pitched trilling and hissing calls given in display. **Status and biology:** Common resident in reedbeds, rank grassland and sugarcane fields. Males territorial; attract up to 4 females. Lays 2–4 eggs in an oval nest with a side entrance built in dense vegetation. **Diet:** Seeds and insects. (Kortstertflap)

## 5 Long-tailed Widowbird *Euplectes progne*

BBbbbb | bBB
J F M A M J J A S O N D

**16–20 cm (br. male 60 cm); 25–46 g** A large widowbird. Br. male has very long tail and broad blackish wings with red shoulders bordered by whitish-buff. In display, male flies slowly with trailing tail laterally compressed. Non-br. male retains black flight feathers and red shoulders; larger than Fan-tailed Widowbird, and wings appear disproportionately broad. Female is larger than other female widowbirds; underparts buffy-white, lightly streaked on its breast and flanks. **Voice:** Male calls a buzzy 'chi-chi-cheet, cheet' and harsher 'zzit, zzit' in display. **Status and biology:** Common resident in open grassland, especially in valleys and damp areas. Males territorial; attract up to 5 females. Lays 1–4 eggs in an oval nest with a side entrance built in dense grass. **Diet:** Seeds and insects. (Langstertflap)

## 6 Red-collared Widowbird *Euplectes ardens*

BBbb | bBB
J F M A M J J A S O N D

**12 cm (br. male 25 cm); 14–25 g** Br. male black with a red breast band and a long, slender tail; much smaller than Long-tailed Widowbird, with uniform black wings. Female and non-br. male have boldly streaked upperparts with a large, buffy supercilium and unstreaked underparts with a chestnut-brown wash on their breasts; male retains black flight feathers. **Voice:** Fast, high-pitched 'tzee-tzee-tzee' or 'tee-tee-tee' by displaying male. **Status and biology:** Locally common resident in rank grassland and fields. Males territorial; attract up to 3 females. Lays 2–4 eggs in an oval nest with a side entrance built in dense grass. **Diet:** Seeds and insects. (Rooikeelflap)

# WHYDAHS AND INDIGOBIRDS

Brood-parasitic finches that typically parasitise estrildid finches. Br. male whydahs are distinctive, but indigobirds are difficult to identify; song and host range are important. Males have a scratchy, territorial song, irrespective of species. Sexes differ, and males have a female-like non-br. plumage. Juvs are plain brown with a paler supercilium and belly. Polygamous brood parasites. Males territorial, with favoured display arenas. Often lay >1 egg per host nest; unlike cuckoos, the altricial chicks do not eject host eggs or chicks, and both species are reared together.

## 1 Pin-tailed Whydah *Vidua macroura*

B B B B b | b B B B B
J F M A M J J A S O N D

**12 cm (br. m 34 cm); 13–17 g** Br. male is easily identified by its black-and-white plumage and long, wispy tail. Non-br. ads have boldly striped, black and buff heads with diagnostic moustachial stripes and red bills; underparts typically less buffy than other non-br. whydahs and indigobirds. Br. female has a blackish bill. Juv. is plain brown with a buffy supercilium; throat whitish, remainder of underparts pale buff; bill black with a red base. May hybridise with Dusky Indigobird (p. 394), resulting in all-black males with shorter tails. **Voice:** Sharp 'chip-chip-chip', often while jerkily hovering. **Status and biology:** Common resident and local nomad in savanna, grassland, scrub, parks and gardens. Br. males are very aggressive, chasing other species. Females lay about 20 eggs per season in sets of 2–4, mainly in Common Waxbill nests; also Orange-breasted and Swee waxbill. **Diet:** Seeds; some insects. (Koningrooibekkie)

## 2 Shaft-tailed Whydah *Vidua regia*

B B B B b | | | | | | | b
J F M A M J J A S O N D

**12 cm (br. male 34 cm); 12–17 g** Br. male easily told from male Pin-tailed Whydah by its buff and black plumage, all-dark wing, black rump and diagnostic tail. At a distance, the shaft-like central tail is almost invisible, leaving the spatulate tips suspended behind the bird. Female and non-br. male have less boldly streaked heads, lacking moustachial stripes; bill orange-pink or brownish. Juv. dull brown, with faint darker streaking on its back; throat and breast buffy-brown, merging into a white belly; bill black. **Voice:** High-pitched, squeaky and slurred whistles; mimics Violet-eared Waxbill. **Status and biology:** Near-endemic. Common resident and local nomad in grassy areas in acacia savanna. Parasitises Violet-eared Waxbill nests; females lay 3–4 eggs on successive days; total number of eggs per season unknown. **Diet:** Seeds. (Pylstertrooibekkie)

## 3 Long-tailed Paradise-Whydah *Vidua paradisaea*

b B B B B b | | | | | |
J F M A M J J A S O N D

**15 cm (br. male 36 cm); 15–28 g** Br. male has a long, 'humped-backed' tail; told from Broad-tailed Paradise-Whydah by its more slender tail with long, pointed tips, as well as its golden-yellow (not orange-chestnut) nape patch and paler chestnut breast. Female and non-br. male have black and whitish-buff striped heads; remainder of upperparts streaked grey-brown; breast pale buffy-grey, lightly streaked; bill dark grey, typically darker than Broad-tailed Paradise Whydah. Juv. is plain brown with a paler belly. **Voice:** Male has a high-pitched song including mimicry of the chittering calls and high-pitched whistles of Green-winged Pytilia; also sharp 'chip-chip' call. **Status and biology:** Common resident and local nomad in woodland and acacia savanna. Parasitises Green-winged Pytilia nests; females lay about 22 eggs per season in sets of 3–4. **Diet:** Seeds; some insects. (Gewone Paradysvink)

## 4 Broad-tailed Paradise-Whydah *Vidua obtusa*

b b b | | | | | | | | |
J F M A M J J A S O N D

**15 cm (br. male 27 cm); 18–26 g** Br. male has a shorter, much broader tail than male Long-tailed Paradise-Whydah, with a darker orange-chestnut (not golden-yellow) nape patch and breast. Female and non-br. male typically are less heavily streaked above and have a paler pinkish-grey bill than Long-tailed Paradise-Whydah; face less strongly marked (blackish eye-stripe doesn't wrap around the ear coverts to the same extent). Juv. is plain brown with a paler belly. **Voice:** Mimics piping whistles and sharp 'chip' calls of Orange-winged Pytilia. **Status and biology:** Uncommon to locally common resident and nomad in miombo and other broadleafed woodland; abundance varies between years. Parasitises Orange-winged Pytilia nests; females lay 3 eggs on successive days; total number of eggs per season unknown. **Diet:** Seeds. (Breëstertparadysvink)

IS

IS

IS

TCA

**1** ♀

**1** non-br. ♂

**2** br. ♂

A&ST

LDP

**1** br. ♂

**2** ♀

**2** ♀

AF

AF

WRT

**3** ♀

**3** trans. ♂

**3** ♀

AF

NB

PS

**3** br. ♂

**4** br. ♂

**4** br. ♂

## 1 Dusky Indigobird  *Vidua funerea*

J F M A M J J A S O N D

**12 cm; 12–18 g**  Br. male black with a slight bluish gloss (typically less marked than in Purple Indigobird); wings dark brown. In S African *V. f. funerea*, combination of whitish bill and red or orange-red legs is diagnostic, but northern *V. f. nigerrima* has pinkish-white legs, similar to Purple Indigobird. Female and non-br. male resemble a female whydah, but have whitish bills and red (S) or whitish (N) legs. Juv. plainer than female, with more buffy underparts; bill and legs grey. **Voice:** Short, canary-like jingle and scolding 'chit-chit-chit' mimicry of African Firefinch's alarm call. **Status and biology:** Common resident of forest edge, woodland and moist savanna. Parasitises African Firefinch nests; females lay 3 eggs on successive days; total number of eggs per season unknown. **Diet:** Seeds. (Gewone Blouvinkie)

## 2 Purple Indigobird  *Vidua purpurascens*

J F M A M J J A S O N D

**11 cm; 12–15 g**  The combination of white or pinkish-white bill, legs and feet distinguish both male and female from other indigobirds in S Africa. In Zimbabwe and central Mozambique, could be confused with northern race of Dusky Indigobird, which also has pinkish-white legs; in good light, male typically shows more purple gloss on plumage. Female and non-br. male resemble Dusky Indigobird; only separable in S Africa, where leg colour differs. **Voice:** Mimics purring calls, whistles and trills of Jameson's Firefinch. **Status and biology:** Common resident and local nomad in savanna, especially acacias. Parasitises Jameson's Firefinch nests; females lay 3–4 eggs on successive days; total number of eggs per season unknown. **Diet:** Seeds. (Witpootblouvinkie)

## 3 Village Indigobird  *Vidua chalybeata*

J F M A M J J A S O N D

**11 cm; 11–15 g**  In most of its range, the red bill, legs and feet differentiate both male and female from other indigobirds. West of Victoria Falls, *V. c. okavangensis* has a whitish bill, but is the only indigobird in the area with red legs. Br. male has blackish plumage, darker than most other male indigobirds, with narrow white edges; body plumage has a bluish sheen. Female and non-br. male are told from non-br. Pin-tailed Whydah (p. 392) by pink (not dark) legs and less boldly striped head; from non-br. Shaft-tailed Whydah (p. 392) by its smaller bill and paler head. Juv. as juv. Dusky Indigobird. **Voice:** Mimics dry rattling calls and clear, whistled 'wheeetoo-wheeetoo-wheet' song of Red-billed Firefinch. **Status and biology:** Common resident and local nomad in woodland and savanna. Parasitises Red-billed and Brown firefinch nests; females lay 22–26 eggs per season in sets of 1–4. **Diet:** Seeds. (Staalblouvinkie)

## 4 Twinspot Indigobird  *Vidua codringtoni*

J F M A M J J A S O N D

**11 cm; 12–14 g**  Br. male is glossy greenish (rarely bluish) with black (not dark brown) wings; lacks pale primary edges of other male indigobirds and in good light shows a matt, dark grey breast. Bill whitish; told from N race of Dusky Indigobird by its orange-red (not pinkish-white) legs and feet. Female and non-br. male have greyer breasts than other indigobirds; leg colour distinctive. Juv. as juv. Dusky Indigobird. **Voice:** Mimics trill call and song of Red-throated Twinspot. **Status and biology:** Little known; apparently scarce resident in moist woodland and forest edge. Parasitises Red-throated Twinspot nests; females lay 3 eggs on successive days; total number of eggs per season unknown. **Diet:** Seeds. **Note:** Birds mimicking Pink-throated Twinspot may represent an undescribed species of indigobird. (Groenblouvinkie)

## 5 Cuckoo Finch  *Anomalospiza imberbis*

J F M A M J J A S O N D

**13 cm; 20–23 g**  A weaver-like finch related to the indigobirds that resembles a plump, short-tailed weaver with a stubby bill. Male could be confused with a weaver, but is smaller, brighter yellow (especially below) and has a heavy, black bill. Female and juv. are buffy with heavy dark brown streaks above; told from female bishops or queleas by relatively plain buffy face and short, heavy bill. Juv. is like female but more buffy on face and underparts. **Voice:** Swizzling song and soft, chipping flight calls. **Status and biology:** Uncommon resident (Zimbabwe) or summer migrant in open grassland, especially near damp areas. Parasitises cisticola and prinia nests. Females lay 30 eggs per season in sets of 1–4. **Diet:** Seeds; occasional insects. (Koekoekvink)

# WAXBILLS AND RELATED FINCHES

A diverse group of small, colourful, seed-eating finches. Most species are found in flocks, but some forest species occur singly or in pairs. Feed mainly on grass seeds, coming into the open to feed and retiring to adjacent cover when disturbed. Sexes alike or differ; juvs typically much duller. Monogamous; most species breed singly and are territorial. Both sexes incubate and care for the altricial chicks.

## 1 Violet-eared Waxbill  *Granatina granatina*

BBBBB bb bbB
J F M A M J J A S O N D

**13 cm; 8–14 g** A large waxbill with violet cheeks, a warm brown body, electric blue rump and frons, and a long, black, graduated tail; bill red. Male deeper chestnut with a black throat; female paler with buffy underparts. Juv. has a black bill and pale tan face. **Voice:** Dry, buzzy 'tziit' contact call; song is a whistled 'tu-weoowee'. **Status and biology:** Near-endemic. Common resident and local nomad in acacia woodland, savanna and dry thickets. Pairs remain together year-round; lays 2–7 eggs in a bulky oval nest with a short entrance tube built in a shrub or small tree. Brood host for Shaft-tailed Whydah. **Diet:** Seeds; also insects and small fruit. (Koningblousysie)

## 2 Black-faced Waxbill  *Estrilda erythronotos*

BBB bbbb
J F M A M J J A S O N D

**12 cm; 7–11 g** A large grey and crimson waxbill with barred wings, a prominent black face and fairly long, black tail; bill black with a blue-grey base. Female duller with grey vent. Juv. mostly grey; barring more diffuse; bill black. **Voice:** High-pitched 'chuloweee' contact call; song is a short warble. **Status and biology:** Common resident and local nomad in arid savanna and riverine thickets; requires water to drink. Often in small flocks. Lays 2–6 eggs in a bulky oval nest with a long entrance tube built in a thorn tree. **Diet:** Seeds; also insects, small fruit, flowers and nectar. (Swartwangsysie)

## 3 Common Waxbill  *Estrilda astrild*

BBbbbbbbBBBB
J F M A M J J A S O N D

**11 cm; 7–10 g** A grey-brown waxbill with a red eye-stripe and bill and a pinkish-red belly. At close range shows finely barred upperparts and flanks. Juv. duller with less barred plumage and a black bill. **Voice:** Harsh, nasal 'di-di-CHEERRR' song, descending slightly on last note; distinctive, high-pitched 'pink, pink' flight note. **Status and biology:** Common resident in long grass, rank vegetation, reeds and scrub, often near water. Usually in small groups. Lays 3–6 (rarely up to ) eggs in a pear-shaped nest with a short entrance tunnel; lining often contains fur from mongoose scats, giving the nest a distinctive scent thought to deter predators. Nests usually built close to the ground in dense vegetation; many have a cock's nest on top, where the male roosts. Main brood host for Pin-tailed Whydah. **Diet:** Seeds; also insects and small fruit. (Rooibeksysie)

## 4 Grey Waxbill  *Estrilda perreini*

bbb bbb
J F M A M J J A S O N D

**11 cm; 7–9 g** A slate-grey waxbill with a black eye-stripe and deep crimson rump. Told from Cinderella Waxbill by its black and grey (not reddish) bill and grey (not red) thighs; ranges do not overlap. Longer-tailed than Yellow-bellied and Swee waxbills (p. 402), with a grey (not olive) back. Juv. duller; lacks black eye-stripe. **Voice:** Soft, whistled 'pseeu, pseeu' contact call; song is a mournful 'fweeeeeee'. **Status and biology:** Locally common resident along forest margins, and thick coastal and riverine thickets. Lays 2–5 eggs in an oval nest with a short side entrance tube, built in a small tree; occasionally uses an old weaver nest. **Diet:** Seeds; also insects, small fruit, flowers and nectar. (Gryssysie)

## 5 Cinderella Waxbill  *Estrilda thomensis*

BBB bb
J F M A M J J A S O N D

**11 cm; 7–9 g** Shorter-tailed and slightly paler than Grey Waxbill, with a red-based bill and red (not grey) thighs. Male has pinkish wash to breast and blackish vent; female duller with grey vent. Juv. duller grey-brown; lacks red on rump and flanks; bill pink and brown. **Voice:** Thin but penetrating, reedy 'sweee-sweee-sweee-woooo'; short, repeated 'trrt-tsoo' or 'trrt-trrt' contact call. **Status and biology:** Locally common resident and local nomad in semi-arid savanna and scrub. Lays 3–4 eggs in a bulky oval nest with a long entrance tube; sometimes has a cock's nest on top. **Diet:** Seeds; also insects, flowers and nectar. (Angolasysie)

## 6 Blue Waxbill  *Uraeginthus angolensis*

BBBbbb bbbbb
J F M A M J J A S O N D

**12 cm; 8–13 g** Easily identified by its powder blue face, rump and underparts. Female usually slightly paler blue, often with buffy flanks and vent. Juv. paler, with blue restricted to its face and throat. **Voice:** Piercing 'sree-seee-seee', sometimes with melodic warbles; also dry 'krrt' notes. **Status and biology:** Common resident and local nomad in dry woodland, savanna and gardens. Breeds singly or in loose colonies. Lays 2–7 eggs in an oval nest with a short side entrance tube, built in a small tree; occasionally uses an old weaver nest. **Diet:** Seeds; also insects and small fruit. (Gewone Blousysie)

## 1 Green-winged Pytilia  *Pytilia melba*

**13 cm; 9–19 g** A fairly large finch with a grey head, green back and red rump; bill red with dark top to upper mandible. Told from Orange-winged Pytilia by its uniform olive-green wings (lacks golden feather edges) and more boldly barred underparts. Male has scarlet frons and throat; female head all-grey. Juv. browner above, plain buff below with a pinkish bill. Rare yellow morph has yellow (not red) face and rump. In central Mozambique *P. m. grotei*, male breast washed pink (not olive-green). **Voice:** Stuttering song with trilling whistles, often rising and falling in pitch; also short 'wick-ick-ick' call. **Status and biology:** Common resident in acacia savanna and dry woodland. Lays 2–5 eggs in an untidy, ball-shaped nest with a side entrance, built in a small bush. Brood host for Long-tailed Paradise-Whydah. **Diet:** Seeds, insects and spiders. (Gewone Melba)

## 2 Orange-winged Pytilia  *Pytilia afra*

**13 cm; 15–18 g** Darker and shorter-tailed than Green-winged Pytilia with golden-yellow edges to its wing feathers, forming a golden panel on the folded wing; belly and flanks are mottled olive (not barred grey). Male has less crisply defined red face patch, and green back extends onto the nape. Juv. browner above with only a faint yellowish wing panel; bill brown with a pink base. **Voice:** 'Seee, seee' piping whistle; also sharp 'tsik' call. **Status and biology:** Fairly common resident and local nomad in thick, tangled scrub and understorey of miombo woodland. Lays 2–5 eggs in an untidy, ball-shaped nest with a side entrance, built in a small tree. Brood host for Broad-tailed Paradise-Whydah. **Diet:** Seeds and insects. (Oranjevlerkmelba)

## 3 Locustfinch  *Paludipasser locustella*

**9 cm; 8–12 g** A compact finch, smaller and darker than African Quailfinch, with reddish wings. Male appears black and red, with a bright red face, throat and breast; at close range shows fine white bars on thighs and white spots on back. Female whitish beneath, with barred flanks; told from female Quailfinch by its rufous wings and plain face (lacking white 'spectacles'). Juv. is browner than female; wing feathers edged brown (not rufous); bill black. **Voice:** Fast 'tinka-tinka-tinka', higher-pitched than Quailfinch. **Status and biology:** Uncommon resident and local nomad in moist grassland and vleis; often in small groups. Lays 4–8 eggs in a neat, ball-shaped nest with a side entrance, built in a grass tussock. **Diet:** Seeds. (Rooivlerkkwartelvinkie)

## 4 African Quailfinch  *Ortygospiza atricollis*

**10 cm; 9–14 g** A small, compact finch with dark grey upperparts, barred breast and flanks, and an orange-buff central belly and vent; bill entirely red (br. male) or upper mandible brown (female and non-br. male). At close range, has a narrow white 'spectacle' around its eye and a white chin. Female paler with less distinct barring; lacks black on face and throat. Juv. paler than female with only faint barring on thighs; bill dark brown. **Voice:** Distinctive, tinny 'chink-chink' in flight. **Status and biology:** Common resident and nomad in short grass and bare areas in grassland and fields, often near water. Lays 3–6 eggs in a coarsely made, ball-shaped nest with a side entrance, built on the ground next to or in a grass tussock. **Diet:** Seeds; also insects and spiders. (Gewone Kwartelvinkie)

## 5 Orange-breasted Waxbill  *Sporaeginthus subflavus*

**9 cm; 6–10 g** A tiny, short-tailed waxbill with a prominent orange-red rump, which separates it from African Quailfinch; lacks grey head and olive back of Yellow-bellied and Swee waxbills (p. 402). At close range the orange-yellow underparts with olive-barred flanks are diagnostic. Male has orange-red supercilium; female duller with paler yellow underparts. Juv. duller, with dark bill and plain flanks; browner than juv. Yellow-bellied Waxbill. **Voice:** Soft, clinking 'zink zink zink' flight call; rapid 'trip-trip' on take-off. **Status and biology:** Common resident in grassland and weedy areas, especially near water; sometimes in large flocks. Lays 3–7 eggs in an old bishop or weaver nest; occasionally builds its own untidy, ball-shaped nest with a side entrance. Regular brood host for Pin-tailed Whydah. **Diet:** Seeds; also insects and soft leaves. (Rooiassie)

## 1 Pink-throated Twinspot *Hypargos margaritatus*

J F M A M J J A S O N D

**12 cm; 12–14 g** Male is paler than male Red-throated Twinspot with a pinkish face, throat and breast and a brown (not grey) crown. Female has a pale grey-brown throat, breast and belly; lacks orange or pink wash on throat and breast of female Red-throated Twinspot; belly much paler. Juv. brown above, pale grey-buff below, lacking spots; paler than juv. Red-throated Twinspot. **Voice:** Soft, high-pitched, insect-like trill. **Status and biology:** Endemic. Locally common resident in thornveld thickets and coastal scrub. Lays 3–4 eggs in an untidy, ball-shaped nest with a side entrance, built low down in dense vegetation. **Diet:** Seeds and insects. (Rooskeelkolpensie)

## 2 Red-throated Twinspot *Hypargos niveoguttatus*

J F M A M J J A S O N D

**13 cm; 13–17 g** Male is darker than male Pink-throated Twinspot, with a deep red face, throat and breast and a grey (not brown) crown. Female has pinkish-orange wash across breast and sooty-grey central belly. Juv. dull brown, lacking flank spots; darker than juv. Pink-throated Twinspot with a blackish (not grey-buff) belly. **Voice:** Insect-like trill, longer and deeper than Pink-throated Twinspot; song includes mournful, slurred whistles and 'chink' notes. **Status and biology:** Locally common resident of dense thickets, rank growth and forest edge; prefers moister habitats than Pink-throated Twinspot. Lays 3–4 (rarely 6) eggs in a bulky oval nest with a side entrance, built low down in dense vegetation. Nest unusual among finches in seldom containing grasses. Brood host for Twinspot Indigobird. **Diet:** Seeds, insects and spiders. (Rooikeelkolpensie)

## 3 Green Twinspot *Mandingoa nitidula*

J F M A M J J A S O N D

**10 cm; 8–11 g** A tiny twinspot with green (not brown) upperparts. Boldly spotted flanks and green (not rufous) back separate it from Red-faced Crimsonwing. Male has a red face and black belly, boldly spotted white. Female has a buff face and olive-grey belly, spotted white. Juv. duller with unspotted, pale olive-grey underparts. **Voice:** Soft, rolling, insect-like 'zrrreet' and whistled notes; contact call is a very high-pitched 'zeet'. **Status and biology:** Locally common resident and altitudinal migrant in forest, usually near clearings or areas with dense undergrowth; also woodland and coastal scrub in winter. Secretive and easily overlooked. Lays 4–6 eggs in a bulky oval nest with a short, side entrance tube, built in a tree canopy. **Diet:** Seeds and insects. (Groenkolpensie)

## 4 Red-faced Crimsonwing *Cryptospiza reichenovii*

J F M A M J J A S O N D

**12 cm; 12–17 g** A forest finch with a dull red back, rump and wings. Male has red face; female yellow-buff. Larger than Green Twinspot with plain (not spotted) olive flanks and belly; smaller than Lesser Seedcracker with a black (not red) tail and dull red (not olive-brown) back and wings. Juv. has browner upperparts; face dull olive. **Voice:** Soft, very high-pitched trills or 'zeet' calls. **Status and biology:** Locally common resident of forest understorey, but easily overlooked. Lays 3–5 eggs in an oval nest with a short, side entrance tube, built in the fork of a small tree or fern. **Diet:** Insects and seeds. (Rooiwangwoudsysie)

## 5 Lesser Seedcracker *Pyrenestes minor*

J F M A M J J A S O N D

**14 cm; 18 g** A large, chunky finch that appears all-dark in poor light. Larger than Red-faced Crimsonwing, with red head, olive-brown (not reddish) back and wings, and red (not black) tail. Male has more extensive red on its head that extends onto its breast. Juv. dull brown with reddish wash on rump and tail. **Voice:** A soft, chittering trill; also a deep 'chat-chat chat' and 'tseet' calls. **Status and biology:** Uncommon resident in tangled growth in moist miombo woodland, thickets and forest edge; also in tea plantations. Lays 3 eggs in an untidy oval nest with a short entrance tube at one side, built in the fork of a bush or small tree. **Diet:** Seeds and insects. Bill size polymorphic, with larger-billed birds taking larger seeds. (Oostelike Saadbrekertjie)

## 1 African (Blue-billed) Firefinch  *Lagonosticta rubricata*

B B B B b b | | | | | b b
J F M A M J J A S O N D

**11 cm; 8–13 g**  A dark, richly coloured firefinch with blue-grey bill and legs and blackish vent and tail. Male is redder (less pink) than male Jameson's Firefinch, with brown back and wings lacking any pink wash. S African *L. r. rubricata* has a distinctive grey (not pink) crown and nape, but *L. r. haematocephala* (Zimbabwe and central Mozambique) has a red wash to its crown and reddish cheeks. Female is pinkish-brown below, darker than female Jameson's Firefinch. Juv. brown above, buffy yellow below; only rump red. **Voice:** Dry 'trrt-trrt-trrt-trrt' and high-pitched alarm trills; whistled song includes clear 'wink-wink-wink' and fast trills. **Status and biology:** Common resident of thickets in woodland, savanna and riverine scrub. Lays 2–5 eggs in a ball-shaped nest with a side entrance, built in dense vegetation. Brood host for Dusky Indigobird. **Diet:** Seeds and insects. (Kaapse Vuurvinkie)

## 2 Jameson's Firefinch  *Lagonosticta rhodopareia*

B B B B b b b b b b b B
J F M A M J J A S O N D

**11 cm; 8–13 g**  Paler pink than African Firefinch, with the crown, nape, back and wing coverts suffused pink. Dark bill, legs, vent and tail separate it from Red-billed Firefinch. Male is pink below; female pinkish-buff with red lores. Juv. duller; lacks red lores. **Voice:** Long trills, interspersed with sharp 'vit-vit-vit' and 'sweet sweet sweet' whistles. **Status and biology:** Common resident and local nomad in thickets and grassy tangles in savanna and dry woodland. Lays 2–4 (rarely up to 7) eggs in an untidy oval nest with a side entrance, built low down in dense vegetation. Brood host for Purple Indigobird. **Diet:** Seeds and insects. (Jamesonvuurvinkie)

## 3 Red-billed Firefinch  *Lagonosticta senegala*

B B B B b b b b b b b B
J F M A M J J A S O N D

**10 cm; 7–10 g**  Ads are identified by their mostly red bills, pinkish legs, narrow yellow eye-rings and brown (not blackish) vent and tail; rump red (not grey-brown as Brown Firefinch). Male has head and underparts pink. Female is pale brown, with only lores, rump and uppertail pink. Juv. bill dark; lacks yellow eye-ring and white breast spots. **Voice:** Fairly melodic, slurred 'sweet er-urrrrrr' song; also sharp, fast 'vut-vut chit-it-errrr' and dry rattling 'trrrt' call. **Status and biology:** Common resident and local nomad in semi-arid woodland, especially near water; also gardens. Lays 2–6 eggs in a ball-shaped nest with a side entrance, built low down in a bush (rarely in a thatched roof or wall cavity). Brood host for Village Indigobird. **Diet:** Seeds and insects. (Rooibekvuurvinkie)

## 4 Brown Firefinch  *Lagonosticta nitidula*

B B B b | | | | | b b b
J F M A M J J A S O N D

**10 cm; 9–12 g**  A rather drab, red-billed firefinch with a diagnostic grey-brown (not red) vent; vent pale grey; legs pinkish. Male has pinkish-red face, throat and upper breast, with small white spots on the sides of its breast. Female duller, with only a faint pink wash on its face and throat. Juv. all-brown with a dark bill. **Voice:** High-pitched, chittering song; also 'tsiep, tsiep' flight call. **Status and biology:** Locally common resident of thick scrub and reeds close to water. Lays 3–6 eggs in a bulky oval nest with a side entrance built low down in dense vegetation; also uses old weaver and sunbird nests. Brood host for Village Indigobird. **Diet:** Seeds and insects. (Bruinvuurvinkie)

## 5 Yellow-bellied Waxbill  *Coccopygia quartinia*

B b b b | | | | | | | B
J F M A M J J A S O N D

**9 cm; 5–9 g**  A tiny, olive-backed waxbill with a bright red rump, black tail, greyish head and breast and yellow-washed belly. Sexes alike; male lacks black face of Swee Waxbill; ranges do not overlap. Ads have a black upper mandible and red lower mandible. Juv. duller with a black bill; told from other juv. waxbills by its olive-tinged back. 1 recent record in NW Namibia of *C. m. bocagei*, which has a finely barred back; male has a black face like Swee Waxbill. **Voice:** 'Swee-swee' contact call, usually given in flight; song is a soft, high-pitched warble. **Status and biology:** Locally common resident of forest edge and plantations with rank vegetation. Lays 4–5 eggs in an oval nest with a side entrance in a small tree. **Diet:** Seeds and occasional insects. (Tropiese Swie)

## 6 Swee Waxbill  *Coccopygia melanotis*

B b b b | | | | | b B B
J F M A M J J A S O N D

**9 cm; 5–9 g**  Often treated as a race of Yellow-bellied Waxbill, but male has a distinctive black face. Female resembles Yellow-bellied Waxbill, but typically has paler underparts; ranges do not overlap. Juv. duller, with an all-black bill. **Voice:** Soft, high-pitched 'swie swie sweeeeeuu' song; also 'swee-swee' contact call. **Status and biology:** Endemic. Locally common resident of forest edge and wooded areas with rank vegetation; also gardens. Lays 3–6 eggs in an oval nest with a side entrance, built in a tree or creeper. **Diet:** Seeds and occasional insects. (Suidelike Swie)

## 1 Bronze Mannikin *Spermestes cucullatus*

**9 cm; 7–12 g** A small, brownish mannikin, lacking the chestnut back and barred wings of Red-backed Mannikin. Smaller than Magpie Mannikin with a much shorter bill, finely barred (not heavily blotched) flanks and barred (not blackish) rump. Juv. is uniformly dun brown with barred undertail coverts; lacks contrast between a darker face and pale throat and plain undertail coverts of other juv. mannikins. **Voice:** Soft, buzzy 'chizza, chizza'; also a dry 'krrr krrr'. **Status and biology:** Abundant resident in grassy areas in woodland, forest edges and gardens. Often in small flocks. Breeds singly or in loose colonies. Lays 2–8 eggs in an untidy ball-shaped nest with a side entrance in a bush, tree or building cavity; also uses old weaver and waxbill nests. **Diet:** Seeds; also insects, nectar and fruit. (Gewone Fret)

## 2 Red-backed Mannikin *Spermestes bicolor*

**10 cm; 8–11 g** A striking mannikin with a black head and breast, chestnut back and wing coverts, and white spots on the outer webs of its flight feathers, forming a finely barred black-and-white wing panel. Bill pale blue-grey, lacking darker upper mandible of other mannikins. Juv. much duller, but differs from other juv. mannikins by its reddish-brown back. **Voice:** Sharp, high-pitched 'whit weet weet'; soft 'seeet-seeet' when flushed. **Status and biology:** Locally common resident of moist woodland and forest edge; often in small flocks. Lays 2–7 eggs in an untidy oval nest with a side entrance in a bush or tree. **Diet:** Seeds and insects. (Rooirugfret)

## 3 Magpie Mannikin *Spermestes fringilloides*

**13 cm; 16–19 g** The largest mannikin with a much longer bill than Bronze Mannikin. Has black pectoral patches and broad blotches (not fine barring) on its chestnut-washed flanks; rump blackish (not barred). Juv. is grey-brown above, larger than other juv. mannikins, with plain undertail coverts. **Voice:** Chirruping 'peeoo-peeoo', deeper than other mannikins. **Status and biology:** Uncommon resident and local nomad in moist, tall-grass savanna and bamboo at forest edge; locally in gardens. **Diet:** Seeds, other plant material and insects. (Dikbekfret)

## 4 Cut-throat Finch *Amadina fasciata*

**12 cm; 17–18 g** A heavily barred brown finch with a whitish bill. Male easily identified by its pinkish-red throat band. Female is smaller than female Red-headed Finch, with a barred crown and nape, mottled back, buffy wash on breast and more widely spaced, irregular barring on its flanks. Juv. like female; imm. male has a narrow pink throat band. **Voice:** Melodic, buzzy song; also 'eee-eee-eee' flight call. **Status and biology:** Locally common resident and nomad in dry, broadleafed woodland. Often in flocks, frequently with other seedeaters. Lays 4–6 (rarely 2–7) eggs in a ball-shaped nest with a short entrance tunnel, built inside an old weaver nest, woodpecker hole or natural cavity. **Diet:** Seeds and insects. (Bandkeelvink)

## 5 Red-headed Finch *Amadina erythrocephala*

**14 cm; 18–27 g** Male has a distinctive red head; its barred or scalloped underparts and whitish bill distinguish it from male queleas (p. 388). Female is larger than female Cut-throat Finch with a plain grey-brown crown and mantle (not barred and mottled), and more uniformly barred underparts, lacking a warm buffy breast wash. Juv. duller. **Voice:** Dry, buzzy 'chuk-chuk' song; 'zree, zree' flight call. **Status and biology:** Near-endemic. Common resident and nomad in dry grassland, acacia and broadleafed woodland; occasionally irrupts outside its normal range. Often in large flocks, frequently with other seedeaters. Breeds singly or in small groups. Lays 4–6 (rarely 2–11 eggs) in an old weaver nest or in a hole in a tree or building. **Diet:** Seeds and insects. (Rooikopvink)

## 6 Scaly-feathered Finch *Sporopipes squamifrons*

**10 cm; 9–13 g** A small, finch-like bird related to sparrows and weavers. Ads are easily identified by their petite pink bill, broad black malar stripes, finely speckled forecrown and white-edged wing feathers; tail black with white edges. Juv. lacks black malar stripes and freckled forecrown. **Voice:** Song is a rather shrill, sparrow-like, monotonous 'creep-creep' or 'creep-crop'; also a soft 'chizz, chizz, chizz' flight call. **Status and biology:** Near-endemic. Common resident and nomad in dry savanna, bushy desert watercourses and fields. Often in small groups frequently with other seedeaters. Lays 2–7 eggs in a ball-shaped nest with a short entrance tunnel at one side, built in a thorn tree; sometimes in old weaver nests; builds on top of other bird nests. **Diet:** Seeds and insects. (Baardmannetjie)

# CANARIES

A diverse group of seed-eating birds. Occur singly or in flocks. Sexes similar in most species; differences greatest in species that flock when not breeding. Juvs duller and more streaked. Monogamous; most species territorial. Incubation by females only; chicks altricial.

## 1 Yellow Canary *Crithagra flaviventris*

| B | B | B | b | b | b | b | B | B | B | B | B |
|---|---|---|---|---|---|---|---|---|---|---|---|
| J | F | M | A | M | J | J | A | S | O | N | D |

**13 cm; 13–20 g** A strongly dimorphic canary. Male is bright yellow below and olive green above, finely streaked darker. S and E races are darker green above with strongly contrasting face patterns; *C. f. damarensis* in N has a yellower head. Smaller than Brimstone Canary with a much smaller bill; has brighter yellow underparts in area of overlap, and is usually found in drier or more open habitats. Larger than Yellow-fronted Canary; lacking a grey-washed crown, bright yellow rump and white tail tips. Female is much duller olive-grey above and pale grey or lemon below, streaked brown. Juv. is more heavily streaked than female. **Voice:** A typical canary warbling medley, faster and typically more varied than Yellow-fronted Canary. **Status and biology:** Near-endemic. Common resident and local nomad in Karoo, coastal scrub and semi-desert. Often in large flocks with other seedeaters. Lays 2–5 eggs in a cup nest built in a shrub or small tree. **Diet:** Seeds, fruit, insects and nectar. (Geelkanarie)

## 2 Brimstone Canary *Crithagra sulphuratus*

| b | b | b |  | b | b | b | B | B | B | b | b |
|---|---|---|---|---|---|---|---|---|---|---|---|
| J | F | M | A | M | J | J | A | S | O | N | D |

**14 cm; 15–23 g** A large, greenish-yellow canary with a yellow supercilium and stout bill. Larger than Yellow Canary with a much heavier bill; in area of overlap, *C. s. sulphuratus* (S South Africa) has a yellow throat contrasting with its olive-washed breast and flanks. Other races smaller with yellower face and underparts. Larger than Yellow-fronted Canary with a much heavier bill; lacks grey-washed crown, bright yellow rump and white tail tips. Female duller. Juv. duller and greyer than female; lightly streaked on flanks. **Voice:** Rich 'zwee zwee duid duid duid tweer weerr' song; is deeper and slower than other yellow canaries. **Status and biology:** Common resident in woodland, mesic thickets and gardens. Usually feeds in the canopy. Seldom occurs in flocks. Lays 2–4 eggs in a bulky cup nest in a  bush or small tree. **Diet:** Fruit and seeds; also leaves, nectar and insects. (Dikbekkanarie)

## 3 Yellow-fronted Canary *Crithagra mozambicus*

| B | B | B |  |  |  |  |  |  | b | b | B |
|---|---|---|---|---|---|---|---|---|---|---|---|
| J | F | M | A | M | J | J | A | S | O | N | D |

**11–12 cm; 9–16 g** A small canary with a blackish malar stripe and bright yellow frons and supercilium that contrast with the grey-green crown. Smaller than Brimstone and Yellow canaries, with a more strongly marked face, bright yellow rump and white tail tips. In flight, the conspicuous yellow rump and white tail tips recall Black-throated and Lemon-breasted canaries, but it is much yellower. Female is duller, with paler yellow underparts. Juv. has buffy yellow, lightly streaked underparts. **Voice:** Sweet, rather monotonous 'zeee-zereee, zeee-zereee chereeo', with occasional trills and flourishes; occasionally mimics other birds. **Status and biology:** Common to abundant resident in open woodland, savanna and gardens. Gregarious; often in flocks with other seedeaters. Lays 2–5 eggs in a small cup nest built in the fork of a small tree, bush or creeper. **Diet:** Seeds, insects and nectar. (Geeloogkanarie)

## 4 Black-throated Canary *Crithagra atrogularis*

| B | B | b | b | b | b | b | b | b | b | B | B |
|---|---|---|---|---|---|---|---|---|---|---|---|
| J | F | M | A | M | J | J | A | S | O | N | D |

**11 cm; 9–16 g** A small, pale grey-brown canary, streaked dark brown above, with a bright lemon-yellow rump and white tail tips. Underparts pale grey-brown, variably streaked darker brown. Blackish throat is often hard to see; most obvious when breeding. Lacks white face patches and dark malar stripe of Lemon-breasted Canary. Female duller, sometimes with no black throat. Juv. has a buffy-grey throat. **Voice:** A prolonged series of wheezy whistles and chirrups. **Status and biology:** Common resident and local nomad in acacia savanna, dry woodland and fields. Usually in flocks. Lays 2–4 eggs in a cup nest built in a bush or tree. **Diet:** Seeds, flowers, nectar and insects. (Bergkanarie)

## 5 Lemon-breasted Canary *Crithagra citrinipectus*

| B | b |  |  |  |  |  |  |  |  |  | B |
|---|---|---|---|---|---|---|---|---|---|---|---|
| J | F | M | A | M | J | J | A | S | O | N | D |

**11 cm; 10–13 g** Appears intermediate between Yellow-fronted and Black-throated canaries. Male has a pale lemon throat and upper breast, peachy-buff flanks and a white belly. Has bold head markings of Yellow-fronted Canary, but with white (not yellow) wing bars and face patches; upperparts grey-brown (not greenish). Female duller, lacking lemon throat and breast; told from Black-throated Canary by its dark malar stripe and peachy-buff wash below. **Voice:** A rather short, warbled song, higher-pitched and less melodious than Black-throated Canary with shorter phrases. **Status and biology:** Near-endemic. Locally common resident in palm savanna and adjacent acacia woodland and grassland. Lays 3 eggs in a deep cup nest wedged into the leaf base of a Lala Palm. **Diet:** Insects and seeds. (Geelborskanarie)

## 1 Cape Canary  *Serinus canicollis*

b b b b b | B B B B B
J F M A M J J A S O N D

**11–13 cm; 12–22 g** A slender canary with a smooth blue-grey hind crown, nape and mantle. Male has mustard yellow frons, face and throat; female is duller, lightly streaked above and on the flanks, with a grey wash on the face and breast. Juv. browner above and greenish-yellow below with heavy brown streaking; lacks yellow supercilium of Forest Canary or juv. Yellow Canary (p. 406). **Voice:** Male gives protracted, warbling song from a prominent perch or in 'butterfly' display flight; flight call is distinctive 'peeet' or 'pee-weee'. **Status and biology:** Endemic. Common resident in fynbos, grassland, coastal dunes and gardens; often in small flocks. Lays 3–4 (rarely 1–5) eggs in a cup nest built in a bush or tree. **Diet:** Mainly seeds; also fruit, flowers and insects. (Kaapse Kanarie)

## 2 Forest Canary  *Crithagra scotops*

b b b | | | | | | b B B
J F M A M J J A S O N D

**13 cm; 12–20 g** A dark canary, streaked above and below, with a black chin and greyish cheeks that contrast with the yellow supercilium and pale bill. Female and juv. have little or no black bib and are more heavily streaked below. **Voice:** High-pitched warbling song, often with querulous notes; also a very high-pitched 'tseeek' contact call. **Status and biology:** Endemic. Locally common resident in forest, forest edge and clearings. Lays 2–4 eggs in a bulky cup nest built in the fork of a bush or small tree. **Diet:** Seeds, fruit, flowers, leaves and insects. (Gestreepte Kanarie)

## 3 White-throated Canary  *Crithagra albogularis*

b b b b b b b B B B B b
J F M A M J J A S O N D

**16 cm; 18–38 g** A large, pale grey-brown canary with a heavy bill, white throat, small white supercilium and diagnostic greenish-yellow rump. Lacks black face of Protea Seedeater. Paler than Streaky-headed Seedeater, with a paler face, less prominent supercilium and shorter, heavier bill. Larger than female Yellow Canary (p. 406) with a much larger bill and an unstreaked breast. Juv. is lightly streaked above and on breast. **Voice:** Song is a rich jumbled mix of melodious notes; contact call is a querulous 'tsuu-eeeee'. **Status and biology:** Near-endemic. Common resident and local nomad in coastal thicket, karoo scrub and semi-desert. Lays 2–5 eggs in a cup nest built in the fork of a bush or small tree. **Diet:** Seeds, fruit, flowers, leaves and insects. (Witkeelkanarie)

## 4 Protea Seedeater  *Crithagra leucopterus*

| | | | | | | | | b b B b
J F M A M J J A S O N D

**15 cm; 18–25 g** A drab brown canary with a diagnostic blackish face and chin that contrast with its pale bill and whitish throat. In flight, lacks the greenish-yellow rump of White-throated Canary. Narrow white edgings to secondary coverts result in two diagnostic white wing bars, but these are only visible at close range. **Voice:** Contact call is 'tree-dili-eeee'; song intersperses the contact call with harsh, repetitive elements. **Status and biology:** Endemic. Uncommon to locally common resident in thick, tangled scrub and dense fynbos, not especially near proteas. More abundant in drier areas. Lays 2–4 eggs in a cup nest built in the fork of a bush or small tree. **Diet:** Seeds, fruit, flowers and buds. (Witvlerkkanarie)

## 5 Streaky-headed Seedeater  *Crithagra gularis*

B b b | | | | | b B B B
J F M A M J J A S O N D

**14–15 cm; 12–25 g** A fairly large, grey-brown canary with a broad creamy or buff supercilium and relatively long, slender bill. Grey or dark grey (not black) face, plain (or very lightly streaked) breast and warmer brown upperparts separate it from Black-eared Seedeater. Juv. is more heavily streaked above and below. **Voice:** Short, rather deep, melodious song; soft 'trrreet' contact call. **Status and biology:** Common resident in woodland, thickets and dense scrub, often in hilly areas. Frequently associated with aloes. Lays 2–4 eggs in a cup nest built in the fork of a bush or tree. **Diet:** Seeds, fruit, flowers, buds, nectar and insects. (Streepkopkanarie)

## 6 Black-eared Seedeater  *Crithagra mennelli*

B b b b | | | | b B B b
J F M A M J J A S O N D

**14 cm; 13–18 g** Slightly paler and colder grey above than Streaky-headed Seedeater with a white (not buff-tinged) supercilium and more heavily streaked breast; bill heavier. Male has distinct black cheeks and a more crisply streaked black-and-white breast. Female and juv. have dark grey cheeks. **Voice:** Long, rambling song 'teeu-twee-teeu, twiddy-twee-twee'; soft 'see-see-see' contact call. **Status and biology:** Uncommon to locally common resident in miombo and mopane woodland. Often associated with bird parties. Lays 2–3 eggs in a cup nest usually made from old man's beard lichens built in a fork in the canopy of a tree. **Diet:** Seeds, flowers, buds, nectar and insects. (Swartoorkanarie)

## 1 Black-headed Canary  *Serinus alario*

b b b b b B B B B B B b
J F M A M J J A S O N D

**12 cm; 11–13 g** A small, slender canary. Male superficially recalls male Cape Sparrow (p. 380), but is much smaller with plain black head, no white wing bar and much brighter rump and tail; lacks white face markings of male Damara Canary. Female much duller, with a streaky grey-brown head and back but still has the distinctive chestnut wing coverts, rump and tail. Told from female Damara Canary by its plain grey-brown head and throat, lacking whitish patches. Juv. is like female, but more heavily streaked. **Voice:** Soft 'sweea' or 'tweet' contact call; song is a rambling warble incorporating call notes. **Status and biology:** Endemic. Locally common resident and local nomad in karoo scrub, usually in better vegetated areas, and fields. Regularly visits water to drink. Lays 2–5 eggs in a small cup nest built in a small bush. **Diet:** Seeds, fruit, flowers and insects. (Swartkopkanarie)

## 2 Damara Canary  *Serinus leucolaema*

b b b b b B B B B B B b
J F M A M J J A S O N D

**12 cm; 11–13 g** Often treated as a race of Black-headed Canary, but they are not known to hybridise despite broadly overlapping ranges and occurrence in mixed flocks. Male has a pied (not black) head. Female resembles a female Black-headed Canary, but with a whitish throat and cheek patches. **Voice:** Similar to Black-headed Canary. **Status and biology:** Endemic. Fairly common resident and local nomad in arid plains, mountain scrub and fields. Occasionally irrupts south of its normal range. Lays 2–5 eggs in a small cup nest built in a small bush. **Diet:** Seeds, fruit, flowers and insects. (Bontkopkanarie)

## 3 Cape Siskin  *Crithagra totta*

b b B B b
J F M A M J J A S O N D

**12 cm; 10–16 g** A brown-backed canary with rather dull yellow underparts and a blackish tail with white tips. Differs from Drakensberg Siskin by having white tips to its primaries and tail feathers (not white outer tail feathers); ranges do not overlap. Female duller, with streaked throat and less extensive white tips to primaries and tail. Juv. is heavily streaked on head and breast; lacks white in wing and tail. **Voice:** Diagnostic, querulous 'voyp-veeyr' contact call, often given in flight; wispy, canary-like song often incorporates its contact call. **Status and biology:** Endemic. Locally common resident in mountain fynbos, forest margins, and sometimes along coast; also exotic pine plantations. Favours rocky areas and recently burnt fynbos. Lays 3–4 (rarely 5) eggs in a cup nest built in a rock crevice or among vegetation. **Diet:** Seeds, buds, flowers, nectar and insects. (Kaapse Pietjiekanarie)

## 4 Drakensberg Siskin  *Crithagra symonsi*

b b B
J F M A M J J A S O N D

**13 cm; 12–18 g** Sometimes considered a race of Cape Siskin, but has white outer tail feathers (not white tail tips) and lacks white tips to primaries; ranges do not overlap. Female duller, lacking yellow in plumage. Juv. is drab brown, heavily streaked on head, mantle and breast. **Voice:** Similar to Cape Siskin's, but more strident; contact call is sharper 'voyp-wvip'. **Status and biology:** Endemic. Locally common resident in mountain scrub and grassland. Lays 2–4 eggs in a cup nest built in a grass tuft, small bush or rock ledge. **Diet:** Seeds, buds and insects. (Bergpietjiekanarie)

## 5 Common Chaffinch  *Fringilla coelebs*

b B b
J F M A M J J A S O N D

**14–16 cm; 16–21 g** Introduced from Europe. A sparrow-sized finch with 2 distinctive white wing bars. Male striking, with a pinkish face and breast, blue-grey head and nape, and a vinous back. Female duller, olive-brown above and pale grey-brown below. **Voice:** Short, hurried song, descending in pitch, is delivered monotonously from high in a tree; also a sharp 'pink, pink, pink' call. **Status and biology:** Fairly common resident on Cape Peninsula in pine plantations and well-wooded gardens. Lays 3–4 eggs in a cup nest built in a tree. **Diet:** Seeds, fruit, buds, insects and other invertebrates. (Gryskoppie)

# BUNTINGS

Sparrow-like birds with boldly marked head patterns in most species. Occur singly, in pairs or in small flocks when not breeding. Sexes alike or similar. Juvs duller. Monogamous; incubation by female only in some species; by both sexes in others. Chicks altricial.

## 1 Golden-breasted Bunting *Emberiza flaviventris*

Bbbb | | | | | bBB
J F M A M J J A S O N D

**15 cm; 15–22 g** Differs from Cabanis's Bunting in having a white stripe below the eye, entirely yellow throat, chestnut (not greyish) mantle and a warmer, orange-yellow breast. Female duller with a sooty-brown head. Juv. is like female but duller with a slightly streaked breast. **Voice:** Song is a loud, whistled 'weechee, weechee, weechee' or 'sweet-cher, sweet-cher, sweet-cher'; also a nasal, buzzy 'zzhrrrr'. **Status and biology:** Common resident in woodland and moist savanna. Lays 2–3 (rarely up to 5) eggs in a loosely made cup nest built in a small tree or bush. **Diet:** Seeds, buds and insects. (Rooirugstreepkoppie)

## 2 Cabanis's Bunting *Emberiza cabanisi*

bbbbb | | | bBBb
J F M A M J J A S O N D

**16 cm; 15–25 g** Differs from Golden-breasted Bunting by its solid black cheeks, lacking a white stripe below the eye, white sides to its throat, greyish (not chestnut) mantle and plain yellow breast. Female duller with a mottled crown and sooty-brown cheeks; upperparts browner. Juv. resembles a drab female. **Voice:** Song is a high-pitched 'swee-swee-swee' or 'swi-swee-er, swe-er, swee-er'; also a clear 'tsseeoo' contact note. **Status and biology:** Uncommon to locally common resident in woodland and moist savanna. Lays 2–3 eggs in a cup nest built among dense foliage in a small tree or bush. **Diet:** Seeds and insects. (Geelstreepkoppie)

## 3 Cinnamon-breasted Bunting *Emberiza tahapisi*

BBBBbb | | | bBB
J F M A M J J A S O N D

**14 cm; 12–20 g** A dark, richly coloured bunting. Male has rich chestnut upperparts and warm cinnamon-brown underparts; female paler with grey wash to nape and mantle. Both sexes differ from Cape Bunting by their black or greyish (not whitish) throat, cinnamon (not pale grey) underparts and presence of a pale median crown stripe. Juv. like female but with a mottled breast. **Voice:** Short, dry rattling song 'cher-ippity-prrreee'; also a querulous 'where-wheer' call. **Status and biology:** Common resident and partial migrant on rocky slopes in grassland and open woodland. Lays 2–4 eggs in a cup nest built on the ground, often against grass tuft, rock or in a hollow on a rocky outcrop. **Diet:** Seeds and insects. (Klipstreepkoppie)

## 4 Cape Bunting *Emberiza capensis*

bbbbbbbBBBb
J F M A M J J A S O N D

**16 cm; 17–27 g** Paler than Cinnamon-breasted Bunting with a whitish throat and pale grey breast; crown lacks a pale median stripe. Chestnut wing coverts contrast with greyish nape and mantle. Female has face stripes washed buff. Juv. duller with mottled breast. Intensity of grey wash on underparts varies geographically, and is slightly buffy in some races. **Voice:** Song is a cheerful 'chrip chip chup chip tur-twee', accelerating and fading away at the end; typical call is a nasal, ascending 'wer we-wer' call. **Status and biology:** Near-endemic. Common resident in S, becoming local and uncommon in N. Occurs on rocky hill slopes, usually with bushes or shrubs. Lays 2–3 (rarely up to 5) eggs in a cup nest built in a low shrub or creeper, often against a rock outcrop. **Diet:** Seeds, fruit, buds and insects. (Rooivlerkstreepkoppie)

## 5 Lark-like Bunting *Emberiza impetuani*

bBBBbbbbBBbb
J F M A M J J A S O N D

**14 cm; 13–20 g** A rather nondescript, superficially lark-like bunting, but with a short, stout bill, long tail, short legs and hopping (not walking) gait. Main features are a broad buffy supercilium, pale cinnamon wash on breast and rufous-edged wing feathers. Sexes alike; juv. paler with mottled breast. **Voice:** Song is a short, rapid series of buzzy notes, accelerating and ending in a dry trill; also a soft 'tuc-tuc' call. **Status and biology:** Near-endemic. Common to abundant nomad in semi-desert plains, karoo scrub and arid savanna. Regularly visits waterholes to drink. Gathers in huge numbers to breed following good rains. Lays 2–4 eggs in a loosely made cup nest built on the ground, often at the base of a grass tuft, small bush, or rock. **Diet:** Seeds and insects. (Vaalstreepkoppie)

## 1 Gough Bunting  *Rowettia goughensis*

**23–26 cm; 50–56 g** Endemic to Gough Island, where it is the only small land bird. A large bunting with a long, slender bill. As olive green with black bib and mask (blacker in male). Juv. is buff, heavily streaked dark brown. Imm. buffy-olive with faint darker streaks. **Voice:** Male has high-pitched 'tseeep' whistle; female responds with deeper chattering call. **Status and biology: CRITICAL**. Predation by introduced mice; 500 pairs and decreasing. Most birds now confined to highlands and coastal cliffs where mice are less abundant. Lays 2 (rarely 1 or 3) eggs in a cup nest, on or close to the ground. **Diet:** Insects and other invertebrates, seeds, fruit and carrion. (Goughstreepkoppie)

## 2 Nightingale Bunting  *Nesospiza questi*

**16–18 cm; 24–28 g** Endemic to Nightingale and offshore islets. Much smaller than Wilkins' Bunting with a much smaller bill. Ad. male is yellow-olive green with lemon yellow throat; female slightly duller and more streaky above. Juv. much duller and more streaky. **Voice:** Song is rapid, high-pitched 'whit-wheeu'; female gives querulous whistle. **Status and biology: VULNERABLE**. Common resident with some 4 000 pairs, threatened by the risk of accidental introductions of predators. Lays 1–2 eggs in a cup nest in dense vegetation close to the ground. **Diet:** Seeds and invertebrates. (Nightingalestreepkoppie)

## 3 Wilkins' Bunting  *Nesospiza wilkinsi*

**20–22 cm; 46–54 g** Endemic to Nightingale Island. A large, chunky bunting with a massive bill adapted to crack open fruits of the Island Tree. Much larger than Nightingale Bunting with a bill almost twice as deep; ad. male typically has pale base to lower mandible. **Voice:** Male song is a repeated 'whut-preeu', deeper and slower than Nightingale Bunting. **Status and biology: ENDANGERED**. Only 50 pairs associated with groves of Island Trees. Lays 1–2 eggs in a cup nest. **Diet:** Fruit of Island Tree, plus other seeds, and invertebrates. (Dikbekstreepkoppie)

## 4 Inaccessible Bunting  *Nesospiza acunhae*

**17–21 cm; 24–49 g** Endemic to Inaccessible Island. Highly variable with 3 ecomorphs: 2 small-billed forms, drab olive-grey *N. a. acunhae* in lowlands and brighter yellow-olive *N. a. fraseri* in highlands, and large-billed *N. a. dunnei* mainly associated with stands of fruiting Island Trees. Formerly considered 2 species, but there is extensive hybridisation on the eastern plateau. **Voice:** Male song repeated series of 3–4 notes, more varied than Nightingale Bunting. Dunn's Bunting song slower and deeper than the 2 small-billed forms. **Status and biology: VULNERABLE**. Common resident with some 12 000 pairs, but threatened by the risk of accidental introductions of predators. Lays 1–2 eggs in a cup nest in dense vegetation usually on or close to the ground. **Diet:** Seeds and insects; Dunn's Bunting takes large numbers of Island Tree fruit. (Inaccessiblestreepkoppie)

## 5 Tristan Thrush  *Nesocichla eremita*

**23–25 cm; 80–120 g** Endemic to the Tristan archipelago. A compact, streaky brown thrush with a long, stout bill, short, rounded wings and long, robust legs and feet. Juv. has buff margins to feathers. **Voice:** Usually calls are shrill, high-pitched whistles; song is a soft warble. **Status and biology: NEAR-THREATENED**. 1 200 pairs, but only 50 survive at Tristan due to introduced rats. Lays 2–3 eggs in a deep cup nest up to 1 m up in dense vegetation or on a bank or cliff. **Diet:** Supreme opportunist; eats invertebrates, eggs, fruit and even kills ad. storm-petrels. (Tristanlyster)

## 6 Inaccessible Island Rail  *Atlantisia rogersi*

**13–15 cm; 34–52 g** Endemic to Inaccessible Island. A tiny flightless rail that creeps mouse-like on the ground; wings greatly reduced. Seldom ventures far from cover. Dark, sooty grey with chestnut-barred back and fine white spots on wing coverts and vent. Female and juv. duller; juv. with brown eyes. **Voice:** 'Chik' or 'chik-ik' contact call; territorial call is a strident trill. **Status and biology: VULNERABLE** due to the risk of accidental introduction of predators, but still common; 5 000 pairs throughout the island. Monogamous; lays 2 eggs in a domed nest in dense vegetation, usually accessed through a short tunnel. **Diet:** Mainly invertebrates. (Inaccessibleriethaan)

## 7 Gough Moorhen  *Gallinula comeri*

**34–38 cm; 400–530 g** A large, flightless form of Common Moorhen, endemic to Gough Island, but with a feral population in natural vegetation on the main island of Tristan. Gallinules around the village on Tristan are more likely to be vagrant American Purple Gallinules or Common Moorhens. Ad's legs mostly red (not yellow) and wings reduced. Juv. brown, paler than ad., with a dull, blackish bill and small frontal shield. **Voice:** Loud 'chuk chik-chuk' advertising call; soft 'kek' contact call. **Status and biology: VULNERABLE**. Accidental introduction of predators poses a risk. Fairly common in fernbush and tussock grass; 3 500 pairs on Gough, 2 000 on Tristan. Lays 2–5 eggs in a cup nest built in dense vegetation. **Diet:** Invertebrates, plant matter and carrion. (Goughwaterhoender)

# LIST OF PHOTOGRAPHERS

A&ST Ann & Steve Toon
ADT André du Toit
AF Albert Froneman
AFRI Afripics
AJ Andrew Jenkins
ALW Alan Weaving
AM Arthur Morris
AN André Nel
AQJ Arnoud Quanjer
AR Adam Riley
ARS Aaron Russ
AT Alan Tate
AW Alan Wilson
AWM Arthur McKellar
AZ Ariadne Van Zandbergen

BC Burger Cillié
BDP Barry du Plessis
BF Bruce Finocchio
BIOS Biosphoto
BO Bernie Olbrich
BR Brian Rode
BROSE Barrie Rose
BRY Brendan Ryan
BSM Bill Schmoker

CC Christopher Courteau
CD Cliff & Suretha Dorse
CDW Clifford de Wit
CK Clive Kaplan
CLH Clem Haagner
CT Chris Townend
CVR Chris van Rooyen

DB Daryl Balfour
DCHP DCH Plowes
DE Derek Engelbrecht
DF Dick Forsman
DFR David Fisher
DH Dominique Halleaux
DN Doug Newman
DO Deirdre Outram
DR Dave Richards
DS David Shackelford
DV Daniel Voges
DVN DJ van Niekerk
DW Dave Watts

EAJ EA Janes
EB Emile Barbelette
ED Eckart Demasius
EDA Ed Aylmer
EG Eirik Gronningsæter

FIRE Geoff McIlleron: Firefly
  Images
FO Frank Opsomer
FVW Fred von Winckelmann

GA G Armistead

GC Gerald Cubitt
GE Göran Eskröm
GG Gerhard Geldenhuys
GH Gordon Holtshausen
GJCW Gina JC Wilgenbus
GK Graham Kearney
GL Geoff Lockwood
GO Georges Olioso
GU Guy Upfold
GV Gerrit Vyn

HA Henk Alting
HC Hugh Chittenden
HDK Hannelie de Klerk
HERB Herman van den Berg
HJE Hanne & Jens Eriksen
HL Hanno Langenhoven
HN Hennie Niemand
HPHP HPH Photography
HS Hadoram Shirihai 'Photos con-
  tributed from the on-going and
  forthcoming project, Shirihai, H.
  & Bretagnolle, V.
  In prep. *Albatrosses, Petrels and
  Shearwaters of the World: a
  handbook to their taxonomy,
  identification, ecology and con-
  servation.* (Illustrated by John
  Cox.) A & C Black, London.'
HVDB Heinrich van den Berg

IM Ian Merrill
IOA Images of Africa
IS Ian Sinclair
IST Index Stock
IVDB Ingrid van den Berg

JAK JA Kruger
JBP J&B Photographers
JC J Culbertson
JCPJ JC Paterson-Jones
JD Jackie During
JFH Jean-Francois Hellio &
  Nicolas van Ingen
JG John Graham
JGRO Johann Grobbelaar
JGS JG Swanepoel
JH Josef Hlásek
JJ J Jantunen
JJB JJ Brooks
JL Jiri Lochman
JLM Jean-Louis Le Moigne
JMA José Manuel Arcos
JMS Jean-Marc Strydom/Souwest
  Photography
JMY Jean Mayet
JP Jari Peltomaki
JW Jack Weinberg
KB Keith Begg
KBF Kobus Fourie

KDN Kim de Necker
KJG Klaus J Gesell
KK Kobus Kruger
KR Kevin Ravno
KW Kerry Wright

LDP LNJ du Plessis
LG Lizet Grobbelaar
LH Lubomir Hlásek
LOCH Lochman Transparencies
LX Lex Hes

MB Mike Buckham
MBO Maans Booysen
MD Mike Danzenbaker
MDA Mark D Anderson
MH Martin Harvey
MHL Martin Hale
MHV MH Veldman
ML Mike Lane
MM Mariluo Manning
MP Mike Pope
MPAX Mark Paxton
MPI Minden Pictures
MS Morton Strange
MY Mike Yudaken

NB Neville Brickell
NBW Nik Borrow
ND Nigel Dennis
NG Neil Gray
NGR Nick Greaves
NHPA Natural History Picture
  Agency/Photoshot
NM Nico Myburgh
NP Niall Perrins
NS Neil Smith
NW Neil Whyte

PA Photo Access/Digital Source
PATH Patricia Humphrey
PCC Peter Craig-Cooper
PCHAD Peter Chadwick
PGT Pierre Goutet
PH Pete Hancock
PHILP Phil Penlington
PJG Peter Ginn
PL Penn Lloyd
PLT P La Tourrette
PM Pete Morris
PR Peter Ryan
PRG Patricia Robles Gil
PS Philip Stapelberg
PST Peter Steyn
PVDB Philip van den Berg
PW Peter Webb
RB Richard Booth
RC Richard Crossley
RCS Rod Cassidy
RCX Régis Cavignaux

## REFERENCES AND FURTHER READING

The essential reference for southern African birds is *Roberts' Birds of Southern Africa* (7th edition, edited by Phil Hockey, Richard Dean & Peter Ryan, Trustees of the John Voelcker Bird Book Fund, Cape Town, 2005). This fully referenced handbook to the region's birds is augmented by *The atlas of southern African birds* (2 volumes, edited by James Harrison, David Allan, Les Underhill, Mark Herremans, Tony Tree, Vincent Parker & Chris Brown, BirdLife South Africa, Johannesburg, 1997; out of print).

For additional assistance with identification, consult *SASOL Birds of Southern Africa* (Ian Sinclair, Phil Hockey & Warwick Tarboton, Struik Publishers, Cape Town, 2002) or *The Larger Illustrated Guide to Birds of Southern Africa* (Ian Sinclair & Phil Hockey, Struik Publishers, Cape Town, 2005).

# INDEX TO SCIENTIFIC NAMES

# INDEX TO AFRIKAANS COMMON NAMES

# INDEX TO ENGLISH COMMON NAMES